de Gruyter Studies in Organization 42

Reworking the World

de Gruyter Studies in Organization

International Management, Organization and Policy Analysis

A new international and interdisciplinary book series from de Gruyter presenting comprehensive research on aspects of international management, organization studies and comparative public policy.
It will cover cross-cultural and cross-national studies of topics such as:
— management; organizations; public policy, and/or their inter-relation
— industry and regulatory policies
— business-government relations
— international organizations
— comparative institutional frameworks.

While each book in the series ideally will have a comparative empirical focus, specific national studies of a general theoretical, substantive or regional interest which relate to the development of cross-cultural and comparative theory will also be encouraged. The series is designed to stimulate and enourage the exchange of ideas across linguistic, national and cultural traditions of analysis, between academic researchers, practitioners and policy makers, and between disciplinary specialisms.
The volumes will present theoretical work, empirical studies, translations and 'state-of-the-art' surveys. The *international* aspects of the series will be uppermost: there will be a strong commitment to work which crosses and opens boundaries.

Editor:

Prof. Stewart R. Clegg, University of St. Andrews, Dept. of Management, St. Andrews, Scotland, U.K.

Advisory Board:

Prof. Nancy J. Adler, McGill University, Dept. of Management, Montreal, Quebec, Canada
Prof. Richard Hall, State University of New York at Albany, Dept. of Sociology, Albany, New York, USA
Prof. Gary Hamilton, University of California, Dept. of Sociology, Davis, California, USA
Prof. Geert Hofstede, University of Limburg, Maastricht, The Netherlands
Prof. Pradip N. Khandwalla, Indian Institute of Management, Vastrupur, Ahmedabad, India
Prof. Surendra Munshi, Sociology Group, Indian Institute of Management, Calcutta, India
Prof. Gordon Redding, University of Hong Kong. Dept. of Management Studies, Hong Kong

Reworking the World

Organisations, Technologies, and Cultures in Comparative Perspective

Editor: Jane Marceau

Walter de Gruyter · Berlin · New York 1992

Editor:

Professor Jane Marceau
Urban Research Program, Research School of Social Sciences,
The Australian National University, Canberra, Australia

With 8 tables and 9 figures

Library of Congress Cataloging-in-Publication Data

Reworking the world : organisations, technologies, and cultures
in comparative perspective / editor, Jane Marceau.
      (De Gruyter studies in organization ; 42)
      Includes bibliographical references.
      ISBN 3-11-013158-7. — ISBN 0-89925-903-0 (U.S.)
      1. Industrial organization—Cross-cultural studies. 2.
Organizational change—Cross-cultural studies. 3. Technological innovations—Economic aspects—Cross-cultural
studies. 4. Corporate culture—Cross-cultural studies. I.
Marceau, Jane. II. Series.
HD31.R469 1992
302.3'5—dc20   92-32150
                                                      CIP

HD
31
R49
1992

Die Deutsche Bibliothek — Cataloging-in-Publication Data

Reworking the world : organisations, technologies, and cultures
in comparative perspective / ed.: Jane Marceau. — Berlin ;
New York : de Gruyter, 1992
      (De Gruyter studies in organization ; 42)
      ISBN 3-11-013158-7
NE: Marceau, Jane [Hrsg.]; GT

Typesetting: Arthur Collignon GmbH, Berlin. — Printing: Ratzlow-Druck, Berlin. —
Binding: Dieter Mikolai, Berlin. — Cover Design: Johannes Rother, Berlin. —
Printed in Germany.

To my mother and Rob who have always adapted so well to the reworking of their world.

To the memory of my father who tried hard to change the world.

Preface

This book, like the reworking of the world it describes, has been some time in the making. Each chapter in the volume has been extensively reworked since being presented as a paper at the Third International Colloquium of Asian and Pacific Researchers in Organisation Studies (APROS) held in Canberra, at the Australian National University, in December 1989. The period of the making of the book has seen both extensive change in the society and politics of the geographical regions discussed and the accelerated reworking of the world of economic production and distribution. Europe as a social, economic and political entity is closer to the date set for the Single Market and in that sense more firmly integrated. In contrast, events in the European Communist world have provided yet another dimension to the convergence of industrial societies thesis and now mean that 'Europe' will be diluted, somewhat delayed and different. Seen from the vantage point of Australasia, further changes to the Pacific area of the world are clear — much greater economic integration of Asia and Australasia, changed relationships with the USA and Canada, more rapid 'Japanisation' at the same time as new frameworks for interaction emerge through the Asia Pacific Economic Cooperation Agreement, for example, and as Malaysia and Thailand arrive close to 'take off' point. We know more now perhaps about the close linkages between Japan's internal productive structures and domestic development policy and the country's external relationships in constituting that country as an important motor of growth in the Asian region and as a major component of the Japanese business system. The reworking of the papers takes account of these trends.

The chapters in the book which follows map the changes underway at different levels — national, macro- and micro-economic — tracing out the contours of the emerging systems, relating them to what happened before and reminding us of the ubiquity of power struggles and the role of local rationalities in determining the outcomes of movements underway. They focus particularly on the transformation of the productive world, presenting new ways of analysing events as well as detailing changes to the operation of factory and office. They indicate the complexities of the relationships between organisations, technologies and cultures, reminding us that technological change itself flows in many directions and through varied channels. APROS is itself a transfer, a clone of EGOS, its European parent, transplanted to a new environment, a new set of organisations and cultures. The participants in the Canberra APROS Colloquium were from Australasia,

Asia, Europe and North America, representing many emerging links, many cultures and many organisations. Their shared research is a promise of things to come, reminding us of the importance of local variants in a globalising world but also highlighting the rewards of common purpose and multinational collaboration in reworking not only the world itself but also our understanding of it.

In the making of the book, many people played a part. Rosemarie Gill and Margot Martin of the Public Policy Program at ANU helped organise the conference. Xiao Hua Yang both rescued me from my own technological frailties – her Apple LC ran hot for many months – and created the index. Bianka Ralle has been a sympathetic and encouraging publisher. My co-authors were cooperative in allowing me to make repeated changes to integrate their work into the book. May they all be thanked here. My intellectual debts are too numerous to list but I am sure will be obvious to discerning readers, both in Australia and beyond. My thanks are also due to Kluwer Academic Publishers for permission to print an amended version of the chapter by Nicole Biggart (1991) which first appeared as 'Explaining Asian Economic Organisation' in *Theory and Society*, volume 20, pp. 199 – 232 and to Elsevier for permission to print the chapter by Elizabeth Garnsey and John Roberts, parts of which were first published as 'Growth through acquisition for small high technology firms' in S. Birley (ed.) *Building European Ventures*, pp. 15 – 32, published by Elsevier (Amsterdam) in 1990.

August 1992   *Jane Marceau*

Contents

Introduction. Reworking the World: Organisations, Technologies and Cultures in Comparative Perspective

Jane Marceau

Organisations, technologies and cultures are increasingly recognised by sociologists and other observers as inextricably linked. The new ethnography of business enterprises and public sector structures which has emerged over the last decade or so has pointed inexorably to the diverse business 'recipes' which have been produced in different areas of the world as non-western countries have rushed to industrialise. With the recognition of the effectiveness of many of the recipes put into practice, especially in the highly successful East Asian countries led by Japan, has come the further realisation that there is nothing sacred or necessary about the particular rationalities which have dominated the organisation of economic and administrative enterprise in the West over the last century or so. Far from accepting Kerr's (and others') classic view that as societies industrialise they necessarily came to resemble each other in organisational terms, a view which had the corollary that all eventually would converge, adopting the then dominant American form, analysts now recognise that a great many 'rationalities' and 'logics of action' (Clegg 1990b; Whitley 1990) shape the organisational forms empirically found in industrialised countries across the world.

In accounting for these differences both in intra-firm and inter-firm organisation, increasing reference is made to the cultures surrounding and permeating enterprises. These cultures inform and shape decisions about internal and external relationships between the individuals and groups who both form the enterprise as a legal entity and constitute the 'environment' in which the enterprise acts and to which it necessarily relates in all its productive activities. The 'cultures' considered generally are formed of institutions which have developed historically as a result of the rules governing relationships between individuals and social groups and of the values incorporated within these rules. The major institutions concerned are the systems of kinship and authority relations, dominant local economic production and distribution practices and the arms of the state used in its role of regulating and developing both the systems and the individuals, groups and intermediate organisations which comprise them in any society.

It is thus now widely recognised that one cannot understand the organisational forms adopted in a society without understanding the influence of the cultures concerned and understood in this way (Redding 1990; Whitley 1990).

Into this picture has also come increasing recognition of the importance of the technologies adopted in the production enterprise. First thought by some observers to determine organisational designs, technologies are now understood to be but one ingredient, if a major one, in the final designs chosen. The term 'technologies' has also increasingly been understood to cover not only the physical equipment and technical productive processes used but also the ways in which an enterprise, whether public or private, is structured and effectively operates. The technologies adopted are thus to be understood as much as the rules of the game used and the practices derived from those rules as they are the machines which stamp out or assemble automotive parts, cut the material and sew the seams on dresses or mix the dough and bake the French bread, as described by Clegg below. It is the interaction of people, rules (formal and informal) and machines which constitute the technologies considered in most current analyses.

In some respects, of course, this conception is not new and 'work methods' were clearly considered part of the technology at an organisation's disposal by the founders and disciples of 'Scientific Management' in the early decades of the twentieth century. It is new, however, in that the focus on technology in present analyses understands technology as a strategic tool to be used by the enterprise as a whole rather than a set of practices related only to the execution of specific tasks. Moreover, the advent of new computer-related physical technologies has opened a whole range of organisational possibilities and may have ushered in a world so different that it can only be understood as constituting a new techno-economic paradigm (Perez 1983; Freeman and Perez 1988).

It is clear from this discussion that organisations, technologies and cultures are indeed the inextricably interlinked elements that make up any particular productive system. The present book focusses on their interactions in a variety of countries around the world, ranging from East Asia and Australia to Europe, and examines them at both macro- and micro-economic and societal levels. More particularly, the book focusses on these three elements in the context of rapid economic, technological, cultural and social transformations in all countries and in both private sector and public organisations. Together the chapters explore the enormous changes currently occurring and which are effectively 'reworking the world'.

The changes which form the subject of the book may be discerned at many levels. First, they can be seen in the observable, and sometimes radical, reorganisations occurring in factory and office, trade union and governmental institutions, in both markets and hierarchies, in products made and the processes used to make them. These transformations are the central subject of the body of the book.

The changes are so important that they may also be seen in the analytical approaches used to understand the transformations of the world around us. At the most general level, the approach to the analysis of organisations pioneered by Max Weber and popularised even while criticised and modified by sociologists everywhere over half a century has recently been called into question. In particular, the view that modern productive organisations would become an 'iron cage', imprisoning both chiefs and workers alike, has been turned upside down (Clegg 1990b). Instead the diverse approaches developed in different disciplines (and, like technologies, transferred as their utility was revealed) which have become collectively known as 'postmodernism' have finally taught us rather about the likelihood of retention of organisational diversity across cultures, across industries and over time and the absence in organisational terms of any 'one best way' to achieve a given end. Indeed, even the certainty which so long prevailed in the West among both analysts and practitioners that a particular division of labour was the 'most efficient' now seems as outmoded as the belief that the earth is flat. Our expectations about the determinants of social, economic and organisational forms have been fundamentally shaken — as much perhaps by the speed and flood of events in Eastern Europe as by intellectual and theoretical insights. We are in the process of re-learning not only what makes up the world but also how the world works and is likely to be re-worked.

Analytical diversity has thus now become the norm and we are more than ever learning that little that is socially constructed can be taken for granted. There is as little consensus about the emerging directions of change as there is great consciousness of the changes actually occurring. This book, as is appropriate, contains a diversity of approaches at the same time as it signals new directions in the world it examines.

This diversity of approach, however, contains many common threads. Important to most chapters is awareness of the importance of comparisons and, in making these, of comparing like with like. Each recognises the socially embedded nature of the institutions and organisations discussed while also conceding that 'culture' is too broad a term to be useful in sociological analysis until unpacked into its constituent elements. Each recognises the linkages between cultures, organisations and technologies as discussed at the beginning of this chapter. In particular, each recognises the links between the specific organisation forms and changes discerned and particular elements of the 'environment'. These elements are seen in social forms and values and in public policies, particularly in the infrastructure and regulations which shape the market and polity in which the organisations are operating. Finally, each recognises as a fundamental tenet that markets themselves are socially shaped, that markets vary between countries and in turn vary the shapes which productive organisations adopt. Whether the shapers of the market are families, states, or other enterprises and administrative units the analyses examine the same variables, though these are sometimes described in different terms. All, for example, analyse power relations within and between enterprises, interaction between social groups and organisations, the values and ideologies which colour reactions to and acceptance of change as well as the direction of change, and the social forces pushing the transformations as well as the transformations themselves. In addition, some use local socio-economic history to explain present-day organisational patterns while others focus on both the actors and the politics concerned in the changes, or proposals for change, observed.

All the analyses, then, however diverse, focus on the *social* as an explanatory device in analysing organisational forms found and the cultures in which they operate. In a period of few theoretical certainties it is this focus, learned long ago from Durkheim, that distinguishes the sociological from other approaches.

The World Transformed

The analytical approaches used in understanding the world are both changing and separate; even more fast-moving and diverse are the transformations being observed in the world. Everywhere one looks, it seems that the last decades of the twentieth century are a period of great movement and diversification. Our established assumptions are all being called into question by events which appear every day on our television screens as well as by the ways in which people are carrying on their daily social and productive activities. Our long-held belief that the direction of change was towards centralisation, hierarchy and large scale in the organisations dominating societies increasingly, despite more or less frequent and effective challenges by local communities, regions, workers or branches, has been challenged. Used to the tension, in democracies as well as more totalitarian regimes, in factories and in educational institutions, between central control and 'workers' rights', we became accustomed to assuming that the large, best organised and thus apparently stronger would win. We now know that we must question this — whether talking of companies or states there is much room for new arrangements. Accustomed equally to differentiation of function and an ever-increasing division of labour, again our analyses have been challenged by several discoveries: of alternative organisational designs, of a strong trend to collaboration rather than competition between companies facing new competitive challenges or responding to new tasks, and of a move towards broadbanding work tasks rather than ever greater specialisation. In short, as Clegg (1990b) says, our ideas have been challenged by 'de-differentiation'.

Indeed the present decade is one *par excellence* in which Western social and economic analysts have been obliged by the force of the success of forms of industrial organisation developed in non-western societies both to revise their opinions of dominant social and organisational trends and to re-analyse their own societies' development. In this re-thinking they have had both to re-examine the organisations concerned and the cultures within which they have been created to re-view their own paths of development.

Into this process of re-discovery have come technological changes so important that they have come to be seen as heralding a new organisational, and with it socio-economic, age. These technological changes were related first to the emergence and rapid spread of micro-electronic devices into almost every leading area of the production process, including both office and factory. More recently, we have seen the emergence of other core technologies, such as biotechnology and new materials. These new technologies together, combined with the organisational alterations which have become associated with them, have led some observers to talk of a paradigm shift since the present situation can no longer be explained in terms of the old categories. Thus, Freeman and Perez (e. g. Perez 1983; Freeman and Perez 1988) have been led to speak of the emergence of a new techno-economic paradigm.

Macro-level Changes

The productive world then is being radically reworked. First, this can be seen in global change. The hugely successful industrialisation of Japan in the 1970s and 1980s and its challenge to American world economic supremacy, only beaten off by a mixture of American protective measures and Japanese reluctance to generate open economic confrontation, caught most western observers by surprise. Used to thinking of Japanese managerial practices, production technologies and products as essentially derived from the West or else as 'hangovers' from an earlier form of social organisation (e. g. Abegglen 1958), few analysts had understood the strength of the 'Japanese system' of factory organisation, long investment timeframes and close inter-relations between government and business. Blinded by their analytical lenses which viewed American industrial forms as the most efficient, perhaps to be tempered for social reasons by such initiatives as 'job enrichment' schemes, many failed to notice the giant steps being taken by the Japanese politico-industrial regime until confronted by a flood of cheap, good quality and well-designed cars which, left to itself, would have overwhelmed European and North American markets. Highly protective of its own industries, fledgling or developed, Japan subsequently also took the lead in many areas of micro-electronics, notably in the consumer goods sector, including video recorders, TVs and other electronic household equipment.

The business recipes used so successfully by Japan are now the mainstay of the recipes peddled to enterprises elsewhere in the world by management consultants and others interested in what has become the new 'modernisation' orthodoxy. The transfer of the technologies used has taken place both through the relocation of some Japanese enterprises overseas and through foreign observers' favourable appraisal of Japanese efficiency. Japanese 'transplant' enterprises, notably in the automotive industry in the USA and the UK, have ensured that Japanese producers have been able to acquire markets for their products in countries which have protective tariffs against the import of the finished goods. Where the Japanese set up manufacturing or assembly operations overseas they transplant at least the obvious parts of their 'system' to the new location, taking on local workers and training them in Japanese work practices and reorganising relationships with component and service suppliers (see e. g. Mair, Florida and Kenney 1988). These transplants are as productive overseas as at home, suggesting the crucial role of technologies and organisation rather than culture in their success.

The other mechanism for transfer of ideas is the adoption of Japanese management technologies by firms in other countries. What is understood, and frequently misunderstood, as the Japanese system is increasingly seen, in a quite extraordinary *volte face*, by most managers and many observers as the new panacea for the industrial ills of many developed countries. By the late 1980s and the early 1990s the Japanese system, far from being relegated to 'archaism', came to be recognised as a leading world system of industrial production: the way forward for other countries, therefore, often seems to be in adopting as fast as possible the techniques seen as central to the system. The 'Japanisation of the world", to quote the title of a chapter in this book, is well-advanced, at least in the realm of acceptance of Japanese management ideas, and raises questions about the international convergence of business recipes world-wide in a new version of the 'one best way'. The *practice* of such ideas by non-Japanese companies, however, may not have gone so far and several papers in the book explore the extent of adoption and the mechanisms used for the transfer of the technologies in non-Japanese environments as diverse as the UK (Wilkinson, Morris and Oliver), France (Gorgeu and Mathieu) and Australia (Marceau and Jureidini). The trend, however, seems clear.

A new globalisation of both ideas and management practices, at least in some forms, is thus apparent. Just as the organisational forms which developed in the nineteenth and twentieth centuries in Europe and were perfected in the United States were long thought of by many observers and practitioners as the ultimate stage of the industrial organisational evolutionary tree but have been superceded so current beliefs in the power and invincibility of Japanese forms are certain eventually to be overtaken. Following ideas put forward by Lamming (1989), Sabel, Kern and Herrigel (1989) have already suggested that a 'post-Japanese' system is developing, a system in which large firms collaborate with a few other large firms. They suggest that, for example, in the automotive sector, the industry currently most associated with the success of the Japanese system, BMW and General Motors already show two possible 'post-Japanese' models. BMW, for instance, has moved towards becoming a 'hollow corporation', to use Lambooy's (1986) phrase, a systems-integrator in which almost all functions are contracted out to a collaborating network of companies. General Motors has moved towards a different kind of collaborative manufacturing, operating though specialised consortia in which in-house suppliers form collaborative links with similar units outside the firm to provide the specialist parts or services required. In both systems the order-givers are the driving force but are essentially dealing with a collaborative network of large (mostly) and a few small firms. In Lamming's (1989) view, soon the automotive industry will be organised worldwide in such a way that only 150 or so prime or first tier suppliers will serve all the world's assemblers.

At present, however, despite these suggestions, it is hard to discern either which systems will supercede the Japanese model or which forces, systems or countries will become the new leaders whose ideas are hailed as the panacea for twenty-first century industrial and economic problems. Perhaps new physical technologies allied to more strident public demands for environmental health and conservation as well as for material well-being will shift the focus of the search for new models to countries quite different, such as Denmark or other currently small industrial nations. The search will clearly be worldwide.

Despite a search for new organisational forms, however, it is also likely that the policy options available to and organisational hybrids developed in most countries will become even more limited. This scenario has been put forward by Rob van Tulder, an author of a paper on a different subject in this book, and colleagues in the Netherlands who see that the increasing concentration of development in the core technologies (micro-electronics, biotechnology and new materials) in large companies in large nations. They believe that the growth of the Asian Newly Industrialising Countries (NICs) will destroy the niche markets long the mainstay of small industrial nations and squeeze the latter out from the global manufacturing race because of the NICs' advantage of cheap labour (van Tulder, ed. 1990).

This scenario takes account of two major new factors. The first is the globalisation of industry around the world as seen in the strategies developed by large companies. At present the automotive, pharmaceutical and electronics industries have the most comprehensive and far-reaching global strategies (although with some world 'regionalising' in auto production) but others are already following suit. Already, too, financial markets are global, with many stock markets and financial institutions open for business around the clock using funds transferred instantly by electronic means. No longer, to use Porter's (1985) words, will multinational companies operate 'multi-domestic' portfolio strategies, treating each national market separately: rather they will become 'true' multinationals, dividing their operating procedures and productive facilities on a truly global basis.

Globalisation and financial deregulation thus seem here to stay. It is interesting that in the industrial nations most affected by these trends a political debate is raging among both observers and those with direct leadership responsibility about appropriate public policy responses and directions to take in attempting to ensure continued economic development for their populations. Should public authorities deregulate their economic institutions and open their frontiers to world economic players, creating, in a phrase beloved by Australian politicians and economists, a 'level playing field'? or, given the uneven strengths of the players, should countries affected act defensively, relying on governments to structure the market in ways which protect local industries, even though, in the short term at least, this may lead to dearer goods? And how seriously can one take — and how easily can a policy-maker respond to — Porter's now influential view that manufacturing advantage is indeed manufactured rather than developing from what is more usually considered to be a country's international 'natural' comparative advantage? Porter's important work also implicitly raises the question of how far one can extrapolate from the past in predicting and advocating a particular path of future action: while 'clusters' may be the secret of manufacturing strength in many countries historically, how dependent is this strategy on particular historical world conditions? Is it indeed, destined, like the standard American production system, to disappear as surrounding social and organisation factors are themselves transformed?

A major factor in these debates and an equally important aspect of recent global changes is, of course, the rise to prominence in the world economy of the Asian NICs. The rapid industrialisation of these countries and their success in competing with older, western, industrial nations have seconded the rise of Japan in focussing attention on Asia as a node of economic growth and development. In cars, textiles and electronics, these countries have rapidly acquired a significant market position as yet another variant of the development modes of what has become known collectively as 'Asian capitalism' (Biggart 1990; Redding 1990; Whitley 1990). Analyses of these countries have increasingly focussed on the institutional, rather than pure 'market' factors, which have produced this economic success. The roads to current positions have indeed been diverse. Reworking the world in these countries has depended on the leadership role of the state allied, for example, to enormous family-controlled conglomerates (*chaebol*) in Korea (Hamilton, Zeile and Kim 1990; Orrú, Biggart and Hamilton 1991; Whitley 1990). In Taiwan and Hong Kong, in contrast, the model organisation derives from the traditional Chinese family whose networks and mutual obligations structure productive organisation, both within and between firms as they do in non-economic spheres of life (Redding 1990). In Singapore the organisational ingredients of the model are different again. The form of organisation adopted, however, may also owe much to the transfer of ideas from elsewhere and their use in a different socio-economic context which lacks crucial elements or involves an interventionist state. In this book, Nishida presents a fascinating account of technological transfer, not from West to East or vice versa but between Eastern countries, in her account of the adoption and modification of practices developed by Japanese cotton spinners in Shanghai and then by Chinese spinners first in Shanghai and then in Hong Kong.

The rise of the NICs has thus brought observers' attention to focus on a new area of the world. As different aspects of global change come to the fore, so the countries in focus change too, reworking our picture of trends, transformations and organisational options and our image of world organisation systems.

Middle Level New Organisational Forms

The globalisation of company operations and strategies and the rise of the NICs bring the observer to focus on macro-level changes. It is important to remember, too, however, that at other levels of organisation the world is also being reworked. Globalisation strategies bring changes both for the organisation of the firm as a whole and that of the firm's individual branches. They bring new tasks, new rewards and new understandings to managers and workers alike, just as they bring altered strategic options and priorities. They are increasingly leading to the creation of new organisational forms.

Globalisation means that multinational companies make production, marketing and distribution decisions on the basis of considering the position of each aspect of their operations worldwide. Globalisation does not mean, however, that all multinational enterprises organise all aspects of their production decisions in the same way or with the same outcome. Much continues to depend on the national context. Writers using the business strategy approach are helpful in understanding both how the decisions are made and the outcomes which can be expected.

The activities carried out in different parts of the production value chain of any industry are linked together in diverse ways. The manner in which one activity is performed often affects the cost or effectiveness of other activities. The linkages not only connect different elements of the value chain but spread outwards to suppliers, distributors and buyers. Each of these three elements also has its own value chain, called by Porter (1987) a *value system*, of which the organisation of the value chain of the core firm forms a frequently central part. The connections between these activities are said by Porter to become also essential to competitive advantage (1987: 33 and 1990 passim) and hence to affect future development. According to Porter again, the analysis of business forms chosen must also include the notion of *competitive scope*. This is composed of four elements — segment scope, industry scope, vertical scope and geographic scope. These elements together inform enterprise strategies, both nationally and internationally (Porter 1987: 33), and hence organisation shape.

Decisions about organisation form include decisions about distinctions to make between upstream and downstream activities. In Porter's view, downstream activities, such as a firm's reputation, brand name and service network, grow out of a company's activities in each country and are largely country-specific, suggesting a multi-domestic strategy and continuing differences in national industry structures and presumably in the organisation forms observed which must take account of these variations. In contrast, gaining comparative advantage in upstream (and support) activities, such as technology development and production, suggests that firms may best gain advantage from a global division of labour and a different organisation form.

Industries operating truly global strategies at present are relatively few but, as was indicated above, include the leading players in the realm of new core technologies — automobiles, aerospace, semi-conductors, consumer electronics, pharmaceuticals and, increasingly, telecommunications. These industries are reworking the world in several ways: first through their products which often soon become included in the process technologies or products of others, thus creating dependencies and particular lines of power across the world; second through their own reorganising activities which change the environment of other industries; and, third, through their creation of international coalitions which mean the development of new organisational forms to cope with these unstable but critical relationships spanning such a large area.

It has become clear, moreover, that not only these connections but also interlinkages of all kinds have become central to many firms' competitive success. The growth of such interlinkages increasingly suggests the permeability of firms' boundaries and that in many cases the effective economic actors are new entities, hard to describe and delineate using the traditional categories of either economists or organisational analysis. Thus, for example, John Child (1987) has pointed to the importance of relationships developed between organisations which engage in regular mutual service or supply within the same sector to the design of the organisations in question.

Similarly, in some industries new competitive challenges, particularly the need for huge investments in R & D or specialised production equipment and the long lead times inevitable in the production of highly complex products or the design of new technologies, have also encouraged much interfirm cooperation. In another paper (1987), Child points, for example, to the new forms of inter-organisation links represented by coordinated contracting, coordinated revenue links, joint ventures, co-making and spot networking. Some of these, of course, extend across national boundaries, notably in aerospace and automotive production. In others, they increasingly form the central core of the industrial system.

The importance of 'horizontal' inter-linkages has also become clear through the recent rediscovery of 'networking' among small firms, in particular in Italy, Denmark, Germany and Japan. The pioneering work of Piore and Sabel (1984) who re-analysed the industrial structures of Italy, notably in Emilia Romagna, and found a series of strong network and collaborative arrangements, including 'spot sub-contracting' according to the flow of business, indicated that there was nothing 'necessary' about the rise to prominence and dominance of the large-scale, corporate firm. The existence of such Italian 'industrial districts' showed that the TINA — There Is No Alternative — Tendency as it has been dubbed by Clegg (1990b) needed to be replaced in the analysis of modern organisational forms by a set of much more diverse approaches. Indeed, it has become clear once again that particular corporate configurations can only be understood by including major 'external' influences, such as the role of the state in encouraging particular business organisation 'designs', as the chapter by Weiss in the present volume shows.

Inside Organisations: Re-working the World at Microlevel

Just as we have gained a sense of historical relativity in analysing the overall organisational recipes which appear in western industrial nations in particular so we have had to rework our ideas about the 'natural' configuration of relationships between different groups of workers *within* enterprises. We have discovered, for example, that the apparently 'necessary' division of labour between management and execution of production work which has long characterised American, British and Australian enterprise is merely a consequence of particular power struggles in the early days of industrialisation which were transferred from country to country and between companies within countries. Both through increased curiosity about the Japanese system and through comparative work on European countries it has become clear that production can be organised with very different divisions of labour and responsibility; this is true even within the same sector, within companies which make the same products, which use similar physical technologies, and which are of the same size and physical location. A famous study by Maurice and his colleagues of engineering companies in France and Germany in the 1970s showed, for instance, that there were four major areas of difference (see e. g. Maurice, Sorge and Warner 1980).

First, they showed that the company hierarchy in France almost always includes more management positions and levels than in Germany. Secondly, technical departments and offices in France always have a larger staff, are organised more hierarchically and are more separated from the production process. Third, the commercial function management of all French companies employs significantly more personnel than its German counterpart and again is organised more hierarchically. Fourth, white collar employees and managers are not only more numerous in France than in Germany but they also earn more in relation to blue-collar workers. In brief, the French companies emphasised the *control* functions of the production process, employing many managers to supervise largely unskilled workers, while in Germany the factories had few managers but employed highly skilled workers, lowering the amount of necessary supervision. Thus, companies identical in size, product and technology defined 'jobs' in different ways and saw quite different skills as essential to the productive process in each country.

It is clear, too, that in Japan at least core workers have a great deal more responsibility for their production organisation decisions and especially for quality assurance than is common in the West. As was suggested earlier, acceptance in the West of these different forms of division of labour has introduced new ideas about 'the end of the division of labour' (Kern and Schumann 1984), and the growth of flexible specialisation, heralding the end of 'Fordism' and the advent of 'post-Fordism' (Dohse, Jurgens and Malsch 1985) or even of 'Fujitsuism' (Kenney and Florida 1988). Although there is considerable disagreement among commentators about whether what is emerging is 'neo' or 'post-Fordism' (see e. g. Hirst and Zeitlin 1989; Greig 1990) and the exact ways in which the new system manifests itself, there seem to be a few key distinctions. 'Fordist' mass production techniques include a complex division of labour and many levels of control associated primarily with emphasis on capturing economies of scale and competition on the basis of price. In contrast, 'post-Fordism' is typified by the adoption of organisations shaped by greater concern for competitiveness through superior quality and the elimination of waste and through decentralisation and fewer layers of control.

The 'post' or 'neo-Fordist' or 'flexible specialisation' approach to the organisation of production has gradually been transferred to the world of work in the West in certain leading sectors such as automotives, electronics and aerospace. It has included the introduction of new physical technologies which in another era might have been associated with an emphasis on shedding labour or retaining greater control of workers. This was the assumption of theorists about the labour process who were writing in the early 1970s in the early stages of the 'computerisation' of work, notably in offices (see e. g. Braverman 1974). More recently writers such as Shaiken (1985) have indicated that the technology can be used to deskill or to upskill and has variable effects according to the management framework and ideologies which shape the organisation chosen. Shaiken shows, for instance, that in metal manufacturing the computer-controlled machines can be programmed either by skilled workers on the shop floor, giving them greater power over production decisions, or by specialist programmers working in offices away from the floor. In many industries, skill levels needed, or at least demanded, may also change and with them pre-existing relationships between different groups of workers and between workers and managers. These changes are explored in the present volume in a second paper by Gorgeu and Mathieu on the automotive and aerospace industries in France.

In addition, the skill-level and organisational choices made when leading companies in a *filière* or production chain adopt Just-in-Time production methods, and strongly encourage their suppliers to do the same, have considerable implications for trade unionism. In the reworking of the world of the factory, therefore, workers' organisations have had to rethink their role.

The reasons why specific choices in the area of the introduction of new technologies are made are many and vary significantly with the surrounding economy and culture. As Theresa Poon shows in her discussion of the introduction of new technology to Hong Kong in a chapter in Section Two of this book the outcome will depend on the culture of the enterprise and its controllers, on the products or services offered and on the surrounding economic climate, itself shaped by government action. The reworking which occurs cannot be read off from a single principle and may have different consequences over time.

Changes in work practices and organisation can occur as a result of many factors. Some may take place through changing the bargains struck between employers and workers, some through the introduction of new technologies and some through changes in the business environment which stem from government action while most are a combination of all three. In addition, some may occur through a gradual re-working of managers' ideas about how to manage which they learn as part of a package extolling the virtues of a particular organisation form and justifying a particular design. Thus in the early years of systematised mass production in the West the managerial movement known as 'Scientific Management' developed by F. W. Taylor 'perfected' the work organisation associated with the Fordist system. The modern 'post-Fordist' or 'Japanese' variant of factory organisation also comes complete with its managerial movement, in this case that of Quality Assurance, as Palmer and Allan show in their chapter in this book. This movement has spread the gospel of Total Quality Control, publicised the message of quality assurance and promoted the creation of new professional managers to oversee its introduction. While it is clear that the implementation of its message in any economy outside Japan is still patchy in the extreme, once this movement takes root, one may consider that the techno-economic paradigm is well and truly in the process of shifting.

That paradigm shift may manifest itself indeed not only in the creation of particular changes in individual factories or offices but also in the widespread push by interested parties to create a whole new model of organisation. In this case the innovative practices concerned are taken up and pushed forward by an alliance of some of the major social partners. In the Australian case, for example, as John Mathews shows in this book, the Trade Union movement, in conjunction with the federal Labor governments of the 1980s and certain key employer groups, has pushed to rework the whole of the working world in Australia through the creation of a complete new model. Following a blueprint created from a mix of Swedish ideas and established Australian bargaining practices (the centralised wage fixing system operating through a body now called the Industrial Relations Commission), the Australian Council of Trade Unions (ACTU) has pushed forward the reform of the organisation of the national productive system. In the process, the movement has been seeking to greatly reduce the number of unions recognised in such industries as the metal trades, to create superannuation schemes for all workers and to encourage government to adopt industry policies which favour manufacturing and particularly the production of high value-added goods.

Within factories, the Australian model seeks to encourage broadbanding of tasks — now reduced to fourteen categories in the metal trades, for instance — with new qualifications to cover new technologically created skills such as mechatronics and to create new career paths with promotion on the basis of skills and qualifications, whether acquired on the job or through separate formal educational channels.

The objective, then, is a new productive ethos and a way forward to greater industrial development and economic welfare for all through a new and distinctive Australian model. The changes involve not only the private but also the public sector, with classification changes being used in the federal public service to create new organisational forms and to foster new skills, as Selby-Smith's paper here shows. Australia is thus contributing to the reworking of the world through the provision both of a new set of social goals and of a new model of how to achieve the goals set. It will be very interesting to see how far this model succeeds or how far it reaches the stalemate which Higgins, in his chapter later in the book, suggests has been reached in Sweden.

Reworking the World: Conflict, Struggle and Partial Resolution

The changes thus being made in the world are sweeping. Every aspect of industrial societies and the traditional organisational forms of these societies seems to be in turmoil and to be subject to reworking. Whether the focus of analysis is technological change, the relationships between groups at work, between enterprises in a sector or national industrial system or between states and their constituent groups, the ways in which the world seems to have gone about its business for a long time are being revamped. Over the last two decades new countries have emerged as world economic leaders while yet others are beginning to appear on the horizon. Innovation is the buzz word and the order of the day, even if its translation into practice is still far from perfect.

The changes, affecting every section of society in its work roles, every productive service and administrative organisation, necessarily create conflicts and proceed through struggles of various kinds. The papers in this volume show how innovation in practice is patchy and is mediated through local cultural practices and powerful groups or coalitions. It is these struggles and counter-movements which seek to mould the new order according to particular tenets and interests and which create the different national configurations concerned. To discussion of organisations, technologies and cultures as explanatory agents must clearly be added that of conflict and partial resolutions. Everywhere in industry and the service sector the move to a new order means struggles between firms, between large and large,

large and small, and small and small companies whose collaboration is not always as smooth as the Piore and Sabel model might suggest. There are conflicts between both companies and countries for resources, for skills and for competitive advantage. Firms collaborating at one level may have to compete at others. Within enterprises and administrations, too, we see struggles between groups of employees, between workers and managers, between divisions and between managers and managers, at both senior and junior levels. Some of these produce the motor for new spin-off enterprises and ultimately for new competitive alliances. New technologies and organisational forms as they emerge create new arenas for playing out old tensions as well as reshuffling the cards with which each group plays its game.

Facing their competitive challenges, firms struggle against each other, the strong seeking to seize the advantages held by weaker but more innovative colleagues, leading to mergers and take-overs, which may in turn destroy their advantage as Garnsey and Roberts show in this volume. The interests and appropriate organisational forms of large and small firms may differ radically, again as Garnsey and Roberts show, a factor seldom discussed in the literature on either innovation or mergers. In turn, the search for innovation may spawn new organisational forms, such as the multi-cell form of the biotechnology company discussed by Dodgson in this book, where structure clearly follows strategy, and contain conflicts by distributing equitably internally the resources generated by growth.

Where firms must collaborate for a new technology to succeed they nonetheless fight for advantage through a series of formal bodies created, apparently at least, to seek consensus. Thus, while in the past a single telephone system prevailed in most countries, it is now much harder to create the common technological standard for communications which has become appropriate and the outcome depends on the relative power of the participants; in the case of equal or countervailing power the outcome is stalemate, as van Tulder and Dankbaar show when analysing the failure of European nations to create a common standard for electronic networking across companies, sectors and countries despite the 'obvious' advantages in the long term to all. Van Tulder and Dankbaar indicate that the outcome of these struggles is a likely win by the most powerful vendors who ultimately may take little account of the interests of other players whether these are users of their products or the unions whose members will work in the Computer Integrated Manufacturing system of the factory of the future. Reworking our world does not always prove to be easy.

Re-working the world also poses important questions about the directions of industrial development to be taken in the twenty-first century and particularly the forms and focuses of the economic development ahead. Much depends, as it always has done, on the configurations of the social forces in each country and culture concerned. Thus, Higgins, in his chapter in the book analysing the reasons for the failure in Sweden of the move to allow workers' funds full rein in the Swedish capital system — and through it the social and political system — indicates the choices which are to be made and the likely hurdles to the realisation of particular directions, especially those which change the existing distribution of power and rewards in any significant manner. While we are re-working the world, especially the world's productive systems, we should not assume any particular social outcome. Re-working the world of work in the twenty-first century seems likely to revolve around the same struggles as in earlier periods.

The present book as a whole thus emphasises the transience of particular organisational forms but also their continued power through the transfer process. It indicates the changing physiognomy of the industrial nations of the world and re-focusses the observer's image to look at Asian captialism, French bread, Italian fashion and production of the world's cars as examples both of the diversity of organisational structures and their points of convergence as elements of each form 'escape' from the social structures in which they were originally embedded and are adopted by others. Indeed, it is clear that certain managerial strategies, along with the emerging physical technologies associated with micro-electronics, are more likely to emerge predominant from the current turmoil than are others. Convergence, however, is never complete and adoption of the particular technologies and organisational forms is mediated by cultures and strong social forces. Besides, new business recipes are constantly being manufactured and put into action.

Finally, this book, through the examples each chapter presents of the different aspects of the change to a new techno-economic paradigm, indicates how complex are the factors concerned, how unpredictable the outcomes and how inextricably linked are organisations, technologies and cultures in determining the patterns not only familiar now but likely to emerge in the future.

Section One
Re-Analysing the World

Introduction

Jane Marceau

This section of the book invites readers to redirect their analysis of the organisation of economic activities worldwide and to rework their approaches to the organisation forms emerging. Inspired by examples from both the West and the East the chapters point particularly to the importance of an *institutional* analysis.

The first paper, by Nicole Woolsey Biggart, emphasises the need, in a world whose regions are increasingly economically interlinked, to develop theories to explain organisation structure and strategies for managing economic activity which allow for comparison and do not have an inherently regional bias. The need arises because of the multiplicity of international interlinkages developing through the creation of a single market in Europe, the globalisation of giant firms' activities and the increasing transfer of both technologies and managerial strategies. With these goes increasing recognition that no structures in the world can be explained simply in terms of national or regional specificities or by using a single principle such as 'efficiency' which assumes the determining influence of market pressures. Of course, there is already a long tradition in sociology which recognises the importance of external policies and practices on the creation of particular forms of economic development and, with it, of the organisational forms which dominate an economy. In the late 1960s and early 1970s, for instance, a great deal of work, such as that of Gunder Frank (1969), pointed out how much more the so-called 'underdeveloped' nations of the world owed their particular plight to international power relations and the creation of economies where both capital-formation and public policies were dominated by a comprador bourgeoisie than to their 'backward' internal economic structures. The economic elite in such countries essentially looked outside the country's boundaries for its economic ventures or to the development of primary resources and did not use its capital to create an industrial base. We can only understand what were often presented as problems resulting from 'pre-modern' economic forms, which would disappear once 'modernisation' was achieved, by understanding that the motors for action were less internal than external and by accepting that the resulting structures were created by groups made strong by their links with outside forces at least as much as by their 'traditional' position. We can only understand the problems of Latin America and Africa, for example, by referring first to their colonial past and second to their weak international position as a quarry of raw materials used by the industrial nations.

The countries dealt with in this book are not 'underdeveloped' nations: on the contrary, they are mostly strong developed economies or the Newly Industrial Countries (NICs), the four tigers or five dragons, depending on which countries are counted, of Asia. Increasingly, however, we need to understand how the structures in each emerged and are linked with others. Equally important, we need to account both for the similarities and differences between them and the social and political forces which have led to the development of distinctive economic structures. Some of these forces are national, some international. All are *institutional*, as Woolsey Biggart emphasises.

Emphasising that the driving motors of the emerging structures are institutional does not mean that factors such as market efficiency, power or cultural values are ignored. Rather, it means that to understand a society it is important to focus on the ways in which the dominant groups use 'local rationalities' *in conjunction* with other factors to create distinctive forms of economic organisation. The factors to consider include the history of the area and, more specifically, the roles played in economic, cultural and political life by the dominant types of family structure, by rural economic activities, by particular cultural practices, by the form of state organisation and activity and, in many cases, by the relationship between the country concerned and others. The chapters presented here by Biggart and Clegg both specifically argue for an approach which is neither 'under-socialised', taking no account of the social context of and constraints on economic actors, nor 'oversocialised', allowing no room for economic factors other than those traditionally subsumed in the local 'cultures' concerned. Both thus argue for accounts which are socially *embedded*, following Granovetter's (1985) terminology, but which allow sufficient room for the play of values, power relations, considerations of market efficiency and other elements of local 'cultures'.

Both papers indicate that the only form of analysis which has sufficient explanatory power takes account of internal and external factors, of existing and new technologies and organisational forms and of the power of *particular* cultural practices (as opposed to an overarching 'culture' seen as a total value system). In addition, the approach chosen must explain how the principal actors concerned are able to draw on the cultural, political and economic framework available to them both to develop existing practices and to create new organisational forms. Clegg, in particular, focusses on the creation and play of local modes of rationality and the way in which these are created through the 'principles of dominance' which act as the conduits of ideas and actions through the network of relationships which form the basis of any social structure. These modes of rationality explain the ways in which economic actors 'make sense' of the world and justify the way in which they act to change it and create organisational forms which are a mix of both old and new, of local, national and, increasingly, international elements.

In her chapter, Nicole Biggart takes the reader through the four main existing approaches to the study of economic organisations. These she characterises as those of: political economy, which focusses on the relationship between the state and the economy, seeing the economy as a product of society; the market approach (in its several variants) which explains industrial structure as a response to economic conditions such as the growth of markets made possible by new technologies of production and transformation and which sees society as a result of economic factors; the cultural approach which sees economies as the subjectivist product of social action rather than as the result of highly structured social action. The fourth approach is an institutional explanation, which again has several variants. There are held together by the rejection of technical causation of economic forms and the belief that organisations are socially constructed and a product of actors' social realities. They do not deny the importance of the material impulses behind economic gain: rather, they investigate structural and institutional factors in seeking to explain the particular patterns resulting.

Each of the first three approaches discussed has major limitations, failing to explain the activities of particular firms (political economy), focussing only on the macro level, failing to recognise the essentially social basis of economic action (market theories), and failing to explain differences between societies with a similar overarching 'culture' such as Confucianism (or 'post-Confucianism') and changes in these societies over time (the cultural approach). In the 'institutional' theory which she puts forward to remedy such limitations, Biggart emphasises instead four elements: the need to recognise economic action as social action; the embeddedness of economic activity in institutional settings; the non-variable (universal) character of institutional explanation and the necessarily multi-level nature of an institutional argument.

The institutional theory recognises the routinised character of social relations, including economic relations and views the economy as interpenetrated by other societal sectors. She thus recognises that the state may influence the economy through regulation, the education system and the family, through socialisation for work and religion and through an orientation to material goods. All are affected by the supra-organisational logic (culture) of the system as a whole.

Both Clegg and Woolsey Biggart examine the ways in which individuals are connected to the 'system'. Values, networks of relations and socially constructed rules shape organisations by limiting possibilities, making some forms of action more likely because more 'reasonable' than others. In understanding the outcomes in a particular society, history is a crucial element because it indicates important events. Institutional logics provide the framework for understanding the outcomes of these events while also themselves being the product of social action in what Giddens (1979) refers to as the dialectical process of structuration.

In his chapter in this section, Clegg takes the argument further. He bases himself on fascinating case studies from Europe — the organisational forms in which French bread is made and in which Italian fashions are both fabricated in Italy and marketed worldwide — and from Asia, notably discussing the overseas Chinese family system and the state structures of Japan and the little dragons of South Korea, Taiwan and Hong Kong. Using this material as illustration for his theoretical discussion, Clegg focusses his analysis on the need for a socially embedded explanation which gives due but not excessive weight to social action, to culture and to the effects of historical events in the interpretation of current socio-economic action. These factors are particularly important to understanding the creation of what are mostly highly efficient economic organisational forms as judged on the usual economic criteria. He especially emphasises local *modes of rationality*.

As Clegg says, the appropriate object of analysis in discussing economic organisations from a comparative perspective is not the organisation *per se*. At the centre of analytical focus should be the cultural and institutional frameworks which facilitate the diverse forms of calculation and modes of rationality used and which specify the forms of organisation taken up. Historically, in the West as elsewhere, the fabricators of organisations naturally drew on the material culture of their immediate environment.

In explaining both outcomes and their diversity it is important, Clegg insists, to remember that the institutional frameworks in which organisations are embedded frequently contain quite divergent and contradictory pressures. These contradictions are resources which actors can use to their own advantage in obtaining particular organisational outcomes. Moreover, organisations usually contain multiple centres of power and within organisational arenas actors struggle using the resources at hand (internal or external) to impose their own ideas on the direction and functioning of the organisation as a whole. In this struggle, the actors convert organisational and cultural 'resources' into different modes of rationality, built out of the locally available social materials in which economic action in embedded.

In understanding how these conversions work, Clegg suggests, it is important to consider the notions of 'trust' or 'contract' which are built up and form the framework within which economic action works, is developed and ultimately transformed. They help determine stable patterns of action but also shape and then reproduce innovatory activities. As a result of earlier innovations, organisations must be considered as 'sedimented', containing elements which were introduced and mandated by earlier internal actors or external authoritative regulation, as when governments decree particular aims and operating procedures, such as equal employment opportunity.

Change occurs, suggests Clegg, when the rules of the game as played in particular organisations change through a change in the critical issues faced and resulting changes in practice. These alterations in turn may come from modifications in the organisation's institutional framework. Most important among these in many societies in East Asia, as elsewhere, are changes in the role of the state, in the actors controlling it and the conceptions which they impose. These in turn may be forced to change by external threat such as war, by external influence through international political or economic power relations seen, for instance, in the push into the societies by multinational companies. In many cases, local organisational responses stem not from weak but from strong cultural practices which enable resistance by the local population. In the process of resistance, however, new modes of rationality may be developed, or older ones be resurrected and repolished, and new organisational and institutional structures emerge.

This analysis is useful in understanding organisational forms found both in Europe and in East Asia. The third paper in this section focusses on the particular organisational forms developed in a European country and the 'local rationalities' behind their growth to the prominence both in the economy of Italy and in the attention of analysts which they currently enjoy internationally. In this third chapter Linda Weiss discusses the unusual strength and economic success of the small business enterprise, often in manufacturing, sector in Italy and in Japan. Weiss rejects dualist theories which explain the 'survival' of small firms in these, and other countries, on the basis of their utility to the much larger ones. Weiss indeed rejects the focus on the 'survival' of small enterprises at all, suggesting instead that the question is not about the survival of the sector but rather the means, mechanisms and reasons for its marginalisation in so many industrial societies. The answer, Weiss suggests, lies in political processes and particularly in the role of the state. In Italy and Japan, the state has enacted policies designed to strengthen small, owner-operated, enterprises in both manufacturing and services. These policies provide support for a range of business activities. This support is financial (facilitating access to cheap training facilities and capital) and institutional, as in labour laws, or taxation regimes. Together these enable small enterprises to cooperate and collaborate, creating a division of task and labour that is 'flexibly specialised' between whole firms rather than between the divisions or subsidiaries of a large firm. In this way the risks associated with entrepreneurship are minimised, the problems of marketing by small firms are overcome and innovation is encouraged. The famous Italian and Japanese post-war 'miracles', Weiss suggests, cannot be understood except in this way. It is to such public (state) policies that the equally famous 'networking' structures of economic enterprise found in the Third Italy, from the Veneto to Emilia Romagna, are largely due. The Italian state, it is important, of course, to underline, did not *create* these structures — they pre-existed current state activity and derived from an earlier economic and social order — but it did support and encourage them to grow in a period when the strength of giant firms, often based outside Italy, could have eliminated or marginalised them as happened elsewhere. To use Clegg's phraseology, certain local modes of rationality in economic organisation received state sanction and, with this support, were able not only to resist the onslaught of otherwise more powerful forces but also to grow considerably, especially over the last two decades.

Similarly, Weiss suggests that there is no economic 'necessity' for the dominance of the large corporate form in other modern western societies. Just as the strength of the small firm sector is owed in good part to the state, so the form and power of the large corporations owe much to specific public policies. This is particularly clear in France, West Germany, Britain and the USA.

The reasons which led different states to adopt particular policies and to give primacy to supporting and/or developing economic organisations of a particular kind and size seem to be similar in both Europe and Asia. They seem to lie in a particular combination of internal power structures and external power or threats. Thus, in both East Asia and Europe, the states were shaped by the history of each country, by external threats (leading in many cases, such as Japan and Italy, to defeat), by internal power struggles at home (Japan, Italy, Korea, Taiwan) and by the 'explanations' accepted in each countries to account for their particular difficulties. Thus, in post-war Italy, for example, explanations for the problems which had led to war and defeat were cast in terms of weaknesses and divisions at home such that the development of a 'property-owning' democracy seemed a way to political security.

Following Clegg and Biggart, it could also be said that much depended on the local rationalities and socio-economic and cultural resources available to the actors who were in powerful positions at the crucial moment. In South Korea, these resources included a group of extremely strong families who accepted the need to reorganise and industrialise to keep power but who needed the state's support to realize their ambitions. In Taiwan, Chinese family traditions limited the growth of this option and encouraged a different kind of economic organisation with different state participation and support. Similarly, in Japan, the importance of the American presence initially constrained the development of obvious economic power within the large firm sector while the earlier *zaibatsu* structure provided the local resources for the basis of economic growth. The result, it could be argued, was state support for both large and small business sectors.

In summary, then, the papers in this section are all designed to encourage a comparative perspective on the understanding of the growth in given historical periods of particular economic organisational forms. They all, directly (Clegg and Biggart) or indirectly (Weiss), give support to the institutional approach to such understanding. All, again directly or implicitly, emphasise the importance of a socially embedded interpretation of the forms of economic activity observed in the widely differing economies, societies and cultures found worldwide. The chapters indicate both a set of approaches and a guide to the selection of important variables so as to compare the comparable.

Institutional Logic and Economic Explanation

Nicole Woolsey Biggart

Introduction

Accounting for organisational structure and managerial strategy is the ambition of several theoretical traditions in the social sciences including anthropology, psychology, economics, and sociology. These disciplines explain industrial arrangements and practices in diverse ways, from the ego-centered leadership studies of organisational psychology to the logically opposite personless models of population ecology (see Biggart and Hamilton 1987). Four perspectives, however, have research traditions that are both sophisticated and suited to the analysis of industrial arrangements in advanced societies: a political economy approach, a market approach, a cultural approach and, my own chosen framework, an institutional approach.

World economic trends such as the anticipated development of a Single Market in Europe and the rapid growth of the Pacific economic region, increasingly demand theories of economic organisation that allow for comparison and, most importantly, do not have an inherently regional bias. My purpose here is to take an accounting of current theories of economic organisation by discussing their underlying assumptions and suggesting their strengths and limitations in explaining international industrial patterns and organisational processes. Although the political economy, market, and cultural approaches are each useful in important ways, I argue for the particular utility of an institutional perspective rooted in Weberian sociology. Unlike any one of the other three perspectives, I argue that institutional theory accounts well for both ideal and material factors, may be used to explain both micro and macro level patterns of organisation, may allow for the agency of actors, readily allows comparison, and has no inherent Western bias.

In this chapter I characterize in turn the political economy, market, and culture approaches to economic organisation. Although there are variations within these theoretical traditions, I focus on the assumptions that are broadly associated with each perspective. I then assess the strengths and weaknesses of the theories in accounting for organisational patterns and

arrangements. Finally, I argue for a form of institutional theory, suggesting
how it builds on the other perspectives while avoiding their limitations.
Throughout the discussion I utilize recent analyses of Asian economies to
provide an illustration of the ways in which each perspective tries to account
for organised economic action and arrangements.

The Political Economy Approach

Political economists do not usually discuss firms or markets per se but
rather focus on the relationship between the state and the economy. Political
economists are concerned with macrostructural political institutions and
their consequences for such social outcomes as the particular routes to
modern state formation taken in different countries, the role of bureaucratic
state arrangements in political and economic affairs, the influence of democratic institutions on state functioning, and the fiscal crises of capitalist
regimes forced to satisfy competing claims on state resources.

There are different theories of the state — (Alford and Friedland (1985),
for example, identify three basic types) — but political economy theories
generally assume that the character and policies of the state are determined
by the character of the economy and that other institutions (e. g. educational, ideological, family) are shaped by their role in sustaining political-
economic relations. To oversimplify for the purpose of argument, socialist
states, mercantilist states, corporatist states, and fascist states are seen as
necessarily maintaining different social institutions to support their different
characteristic economies.

Political economy theories support structural analyses. Capitalist societies, they argue, structure relations between owners and workers and
between officials and citizens in predictable ways. To understand the dynamics of a given capitalist society one must understand the way in which
power is structured between major social groupings since individuals act in
terms of their structural, often described as 'class', location. Thus, for
instance, managers are said to act as they do because of the interests and
powers inherent in their class position. Likewise, workers and officials act
as they do because of their different interests and locations in the structure
of power. Moreover, states themselves have relatively more or less powerful
positions in the world economic structure. A state's structural location, for
example as a developed core state or as a clientelist dependent state, is seen
to shape its policies and behaviour.

Structural theories of this sort rarely examine the activities of individual firms or economic decision makers because these are assumed to act in ways that express their social position within the market structure. Nonetheless, theories of the state have been employed frequently to explain, at a general level, economic patterns and outcomes. Several theorists, for example, account for Asian development through largely structural analyses. The main arguments focus on one or more of three basic components: the state, multinational corporations (MNCs), and the local bourgeoisie. Political economists typically emphasize the similarities between, for example, Taiwan and South Korea. Both countries are thought to occupy a position of political and economic dependence in relation to developed nations (especially the U.S. and Japan) and their success is equally attributed to a dependent relationship. One observer (Cummings 1984), for instance, argues that Taiwan and South Korea are economic military protectorates of the United States, and economic vassals of Japan. He suggests (1984: 3) that the path of development for both countries has been drawn by the larger industrial powers so that, for instance, declining sectors in Japanese industry are cyclically passed on to Korean and Taiwanese industries. Both countries, Cummings asserts, share the common features of 'bureaucratic-authoritarian-industrializing regimes' (state autonomy, central coordination, bureaucratic planning, private concentration in big conglomerates, military strength, and authoritarian repression). Although he acknowledges that 'what could be done with economic incentives in Taiwan required coercion in Korea,' (1984: 11) and that 'Taiwan produced a weak nationalist impulse, Korea an extraordinarily strong one' (1984: 12), he still equates the two, contending that 'by the 1960s both Taiwan and South Korea possessed strong states that bear much comparison to the bureaucratic-authoritarian states in Latin America' (1984: 28).

Focusing directly on the state, Gold (1986) proposes a less deterministic version of Taiwan's dependent development, resorting to Cardoso and Faletto's 'historical-structural methodology.' In Gold's words, this approach allows one to appreciate how 'economic relationships and the social structure that underlies them arise as a result of human activity, and how they can be transformed through social action' (1986: 126). While Gold offers good insights into the changing posture of the Taiwan state over the decades, his final analysis remains the view that 'the KMT state controlled the way Taiwan incorporated into the world system in a way few other countries have' (1986: 10). Similarly, Amsden argues that 'the balance of power between the state and both labour and capital was weighted far more to the state's advantage,' while she concludes that the state 'can be said both to have transformed Taiwan's economic structure and to have been transformed by it' (1985: 101). In his analysis, Myers places importance on a partnership between the Taiwan state and MNCs, particularly in the development of new economic sectors such as electronics (1984: 516).

Japan, no less than Taiwan and South Korea, has been subject to analysis by political economists. In addition to scholarly treatments of the sort described above, popularized treatments embracing a political economy logic have explained Japanese economic success as a product of the organising skill of the Japanese state. These arguments often describe Japan's government as 'Japan, Inc.,' portraying officials as managers of the economy. Some Western writers have suggested that state officials and industrial managers, more than orchestrating the economy, have conspired to protect Japanese firms from international competitors (cf. Brandon 1983; Taylor 1983; Wolf 1983).

Political economists, for the most part, do not have a theory of social action. Actors are unimportant factors, they merely play the roles assigned them by their place in society. Structural factors, especially the state in its role as guardian of economic interests, are causal. The economy is a political arena whose operation reflects the relative power of domestic and multinational economic actors and the nation's position in the world economy. The economy thus produces *and* reflects structures of power.

The Market Approach

The market approach, which has several variants, explains industrial structure as a response to economic conditions. Its most famous expression lies in the work of economic historian Alfred Chandler. In *The Visible Hand* (1977), Chandler chronicles the replacement of traditional forms of enterprise in the United States by the modern 'multiunit business enterprise' or divisionalized firm. His explanation for the development of new organisational forms centres on market factors, the growth of markets made possible by new technologies of production and transportation and the development of professional managers to coordinate within the enterprise activities such as financing and distribution previously conducted in the marketplace. New enterprise forms replaced the old because of lower costs and improved coordination. Chandler argues that firms developed and took the forms they did because they were economically and technologically superior.

Related, but more abstract and ahistorical, economic explanations are found in the work of industrial organisation (IO) economists. One important variant comprises elaborations of the work of Oliver Williamson and his 'markets and hierarchy' thesis (1975). According to Williamson, every economic transaction — production, purchasing, hiring, distribution — contains costs, including those that ensure that each party to an exchange lives up to the terms of the agreement. Entrepreneurs will go to the marketplace to conduct business as long as their transaction costs are low but when costs associated with maintaining contracts, searching for skilled labour and guarding against cheating, and other diseconomies become too great, entrepreneurs will organise these activities within a firm or 'hierarchy' where they have managerial control. Hierarchies, Williamson maintains, have their own maintenance costs but also countervailing economies, notably economies of scale and ease of monitoring. Whether economic activity takes place in a market or in a hierarchy depends on which mechanisms for doing business have the lowest transaction costs. Moreover, decisions about the structure of an organisation, about whether a company vertically integrates or merges with another, depends on a calculus of the most efficient (least expensive) way to conduct business. The organising strategies of business people, according to both Williamson and Chandler, can be traced to the rational weighing of economic costs and benefits. A given organisation, whether large, small, vertically integrated or divisionalized is the efficient product of entrepreneurs' rational response to market conditions.

Despite depending on a Western theoretical perspective (and in the case of Chandler that derived from the American experience) the Chandler-Williamson form of market explanation has been used to explain Asia's business structures. For example, Cochran (1982) explains the changing form of Chinese business enterprise involved in interregional trade from 1850 to 1980 using a transaction-cost model. According to Cochran, first traditional native-place associations, later proto-modern sales organisations, and, finally, bureaucratic state commercial companies successively dominated trade in tobacco and textiles. He explains the development of each subsequent form of organisation as a solution to transaction-cost problems imposed by the changing requirements of Chinese governments. In another work, Cochran echoes Chandler's argument about the growth of firms as a response to the geographically larger markets made possible by new transportation technology: 'The large enterprises that introduced vertical integration into China in the early twentieth century responded to technological opportunities for controlling space not available to their predecessors' (1982).

A complementary market explanation is found in the work of strategy theorists such as Porter (1985) and the related 'structure-conduct-performance' school of industrial organisation that derives from the work of Bain (1968) and Mason (1960). These theorists explain organisational form and functioning as a consequence of industry structure. Industrial organisation (IO) economics assumes a structure of homogeneous firms whose behaviour is dictated by market structure, for example by whether a market is concentrated or has barriers to entry. Porter and other economists interested in strategy take IO economics from the point of view of a local firm to argue that a firm should foster structural 'imperfections' in a market to its own competitive advantage. Chamberlinian economics, on the other hand, assumes a structure composed of heterogeneous firms and argues that firms behave in ways that exploit their competitive advantages such as patents and technical know-how. The *structure* of the industry — concentration rates, barriers to entry, product diversity and demand — influences a firm's conduct on quality, price and capacity, which in turn influences performance, allocative efficiency (profitability) and technical efficiency (cost minimization). The form and functioning of firms, then, is explained by firms' rational responses to an industry's structure of opportunity and constraint.

Several theorists use variants of the structure-conduct-performance model to explain Asian business organisation and strategy. One of the most prominent analysts, for example, attributes Taiwan's spectacular success to market conditions that approximate economists' hypothesized 'perfect market,' one characterized by many small autonomous firms facing few barriers to entry (Little 1979). Little argues that a laissez-faire state did not saddle the economy with inefficient regulations and state agencies, instead stimulating the economy through low taxes and high interest rates. Market structure favored the entrepreneurial response of many individuals who formed small competitive firms with resulting strong economic performance for the economy as a whole. Lee analyzes South Korean economic performance in a similar way. He argues that the Korean state, unlike the Taiwanese, 'distorted' the marketplace by sheltering firms from international competition and interfering with financial markets. The result was low levels of technical efficiency caused by reduced competitive pressures.

Economists have also proposed other theories to explain organisation and management practice. For example, agency theory posits that firms are legal fictions, suggesting that a firm is 'really' the sum of contracts between owners, employees, managers and suppliers. The structure and performance of a firm are thought to be predictable from the nature of its contracts and the monitoring (control) devices used to maintain adherence to contractual terms (Jensen and Meckling 1976).

Use of this market approach, as I define it, as a method of explanation, however, is not limited to economists. Others, including anthropologists and sociological exchange theorists, have embraced logically similar models and see social organisation emerging from a utilitarian calculus (Hamilton and Biggart 1989). Sociologist Harrison White, for example, qualifies Williamson's market failures thesis with a social constructionist twist but his revisionism remains 'a special case of "rational expectations"' (1981: 518).

A market approach, in all its disciplinary variants, however, is commonly characterized by assumptions of economic rationality and sees the atomized individual, whether a firm or a person, as the crucial economic actor. Market theories further assume that the economic system is an aggregated outcome of the production, exchange, and consumption of goods and services and that it is through the self-interested and rationally calculated pecuniary activity of individuals that social order, including organisation form, emerges. In this view, economy produces society.

The Culture Approach

The cultural approach reverses the market theory's hypothesized causal relation, viewing, as do political economists, the economic system as a product of the social order. In this view, society produces economy rather than the reverse. The culturalists, however, reject the structuralism and materialism of political economy and market theory. Instead, they see economies as the subjectivist product of social action. Structure, if it is acknowledged at all, is seen merely as the aggregation of meaningful interactions.

In the culturalists' vision, economic exchange materially sustains society to be sure but, more importantly, the patterned circulation and use of goods is an idealist accomplishment, a celebration of common beliefs and social solidarity. Economic institutions emerge from, are possible only because of, society. Anthropologist, Mary Douglas, for example, expresses a cultural view of economic activity in her discussion of consumption:

'Consumption has to be recognized as an integral part of the same social system that accounts for the drive to work, itself part of the need to relate to other people, and to have mediating materials for relating to them. Mediating materials are food, drink, and hospitality of home to offer, flowers and clothes to signal shared rejoicing, or mourning dress to share sorrow. Goods, work, and consumption have been artificially abstracted out of the whole social scheme.' (Douglas and Isherwood 1988: 4).

The number and variety of culture theories of economic organisation is large and includes conceptualisations of culture as a regulatory mechanism, a system of shared cognitions, a symbolic system, and a universal infrastructure of the mind's unconscious. What the theories have in common as a cultural approach is the explanation of organisational structure and practice as a collective enactment of beliefs and values or of shared cognitive structures (Smircich 1983). Although this approach does not deny the material constraints or benefits of organising, it explains organisational patterns as driven by shared ideas and understandings.

This 'cultural' approach has also often been used to explain the structures of Asian business. For example, Japanese organising practices, such as the subordination of individuals to the group, seniority (*nenko*) systems, collective exercises and singing and consensual decision making, are explained as an expression of the widely held Japanese belief in *wa* or harmony (see e. g. Abegglen 1958). Similarly, Chinese business practices and structure are explained as a derivation of Confucianism (see e. g. Silin 1976). The self-discipline of workers, the loyalty to superiors, the preference for patrilineal relations as business partners, all these and more are explained as organisational outcomes of a Confucian belief system.

Western organisations have also been examined by culture theorists. Among the most scholarly work is Foucault's sophisticated analysis of asylums and prisons in France which he described as representations of European beliefs about the nature of madness and crime and, further, about what is socially deviant and normal (1965 and 1979). The objective purposes of these organisations — isolation and incarceration — are secondary factors in his explanation of why they were structured and operated as they were. According to Foucault, forms and practices say more about society than about the institutions or their tasks. Other scholars have looked at contemporary organisations in Sweden, Yugoslavia, England, and France, seeing factories and offices in each nation as shaped by cultural traditions (e. g. Crozier 1964; Blumberg 1973; Dore 1973; Tannenbaum et al. 1974).

Until recently the cultural perspective was the province of scholars who were ethnographers and comparative culture theorists but in the 1980s management consultants and applied researchers also embraced this approach to understanding corporate organisation. The phenomenal success of *In Search of Excellence* by Peters and Waterman (1982) demonstrated how attractive and sensible a cultural explanation is to people who work in modern American enterprise. Similarly, Ouchi's popular book on Japanese management, *Theory Z* (1982), explained consensual decision making and the promotion of cohorts rather than individuals as expressions of Japanese 'groupness'. These widely-read books repudiated rational approaches to organising (management by numbers) and focused instead on organisations as cultural systems. According to these authors, promoting shared beliefs and meaningful interaction outweighs financial analysis as the crucial management task. Their works, and the work of other corporate culture writers, have established the cultural perspective as an alternative to the economic rationality paradigm in popular management literature.

Assessing the Political Economy, Market, and Culture Perspectives

The political economy, market, and culture perspectives have each proven useful in explaining economic arrangements. Although I have emphasized their often logically oppositional assumptions, in fact they have rarely been pitted one against the other as alternative forms of explanation. For the most part, political economy, market and culture models have been used for different purposes: political economy to explain patterns and rates of development, market models to understand regulatory prescription and economic prediction and cultural models for ethnographic description. Each has largely been suited to its respective scholarly tasks. Each, however, has distinctive abilities and limitations for the *comparative* analysis of economic patterns and organisation. The institutional approach which I describe in the pages ahead employs the strengths of each in contributing to international comparative analysis of economic action, while avoiding some of their limitations for this purpose.

Political economy models have several advantages for performing the kind of comparative analysis necessary to understanding economic action in a multinational environment. First, political economists, unlike market and cultural theorists, focus our attention on the *state* as a crucial force in advanced capitalist societies. It is difficult to imagine an explanation for patterns of Asian (or other) capitalism that did not account for the state's roles in development policies, the regulation of markets and the maintenance of political stability necessary for foreign and domestic investment. Second, political economy models recognize the importance of both material and ideal factors in explanation. Market models are concerned with materialist explanation while cultural models focus largely on such ideal factors as values and beliefs but neither accounts well for the other factor. Political economists take seriously material factors, usually expressed as group interests or class location, as well as ideal factors such as democratic values, class consciousness and capitalist ideologies. Third, political economy theories are sensitive to the connections between social institutions (however, although the state is usually seen as the most important institution in economic maintenance, the connections existing between the polity, culture and economy are usually assumed and not examined). Finally, political economy explanations are sophisticated about the role of power in social outcomes. While one might argue with political economists' conceptualization of power as merely structural, neither the market nor the culture approach conceptualizes power as well as does political economy (see Hamilton and Biggart 1985).

There are limitations to the political economy perspective, however. First, the structure of the economy is assumed to be the determining factor in all societies. While this may be true of any given case, such an assumption prejudges the character of social relations in a society, relations which should be the object of investigation. Second, political economy arguments are open to the charge of functionalist teleology: state theories categorize a type of state, for example capitalism, and then conceptualize the structures essential to a capitalist society, for example, a bourgeoisie and a proletariat. To have a capitalist society one must, by definition, have private ownership of the means of production and working classes because it is in the nature of capitalism to have them. This creates a circular, undisprovable logic, a functional necessity which 'causes' workers and owners to act as they do. If they did not, then there would be no capitalism.

Third, and related to the above, political economy theories have 'over-socialized' conceptions of social action. Individuals are seen to act only as agents of their class or interest group; industrialists act like industrialists and state officials act according to the functional needs of their position in running a capitalist state. Social action, in this conceptualization, becomes depersonalized and stylized, with individuals portrayed as unknowledgeable automatons. Finally, the state is usually conceptualized in terms of the Western state. Recent scholarship, in contrast, suggests that although Japan, for example, has a Parliamentary democratic state form, power in fact is diffused through an array of institutions quite different from those of its Western counterparts (van Wolferen 1989).

The macro-logical orientation of political economy is excellent at bringing attention to the effects of structure on social relations but conceptualizes only crudely the link between structure and action. It fails to see how organisational structures, including the state, institutionalize and appropriate social relationships, including economic relationships. They may suffer Western biases.

Market models make very strong assumptions about economic action and market structure. Typically, they assume that atomized individuals are economic decision makers and have complete information of offers to buy and sell in the marketplace. They assume that commodities are homogeneous, that firms act independently and that no firm is sufficiently large or powerful to dominate a market. These presuppositions, which have the status of disciplinary dogma among economists, produce clear and elegant models which allow the contrasting of real-world economies with an assumed perfect market. Deviations are explained by discovering 'imperfections' in the real world. Social relations, for example, are seen as 'friction' that interrupts the smooth relations of the impersonal, hypothesized ideal.

Strong, widely-shared assumptions about economic action and structure have produced this tradition of clear, elegant models which are ideally suited to comparison since the same assumptions underlie economic research wherever conducted and 'imperfections' may be compared readily. Moreover, at the macro-structural levels at which economic models have been most often applied, the relatively crude characterisations of people and social processes — a common criticism of a market approach — is probably adequate. At least it would seem that the hypothesized economic calculus of atomized individuals has some validity in Western economies: in the West the social ideal of individualism is widespread and educational and legal institutions sustain individual rights and responsibilities in, for example, contract law.

Importantly, it seems, the market approach correctly draws our attention to economic factors, including market concentration, labor costs, technology and competitive advantages, which factors that obviously have effects on the development of an economy and are all too often overlooked by psychological, sociological, and anthropological theories. Poor resources, outdated industrial processes and barriers to market entry clearly make an economic difference. Economically rational social action is widespread in a capitalist economy; it would be amazing if it were not. However, I believe, and have argued before, that economic factors better explain patterns of *growth* than patterns of *organisation* (Hamilton and Biggart 1989). An abundance or scarcity of resources speaks to whether an economy expands or stagnates rather than to the precise structure of organisation which it utilizes to transform and distribute the resources available.

The success of a market model, and of the discipline of economics generally, has in recent years stimulated criticisms (some by economists) as rationalistic models have been applied to more micro-level settings, including organisations. Four critiques are worth noting. First, the evolutionary model proposed by Chandler and the related markets and hierarchies thesis of Williamson posit that firms develop because they are more efficient or effective than other forms of enterprise. Perrow (1981) has charged that efficiency is a possible but not necessary explanation of firm development: firms better control labour and may be 'economic' insofar as they provide effective means of extracting productivity form workers. Where Chandler and Williamson see effectiveness and efficiency, however, Perrow sees control and power. Second, and relatedly, Roy, while applauding Chandler's historical scholarship, has attacked his logic. Roy charges that 'Chandler's narrow technological focus ignores important empirical factors, especially political factors. This omission is not merely myopic but derives from the logical error of equating causes and consequences' (1987: 5). Chandler's functionalist logic, akin to that of political economy explanations, explains firm development as a necessary consequence of technological advance, necessity having been the mother of invention. His causality is teleological and does not leave open either the possibility of an alternative outcome or an explanation of why an economically superior firm was socially and politically possible. Roy deals only with Chandler's work but a similar critique can be made of Williamson's argument: how can we know that all existing structures are the most efficient (have the lowest transaction costs) if only the fittest survive? A functional logic does not leave open the possibility of refutation.

Third, market models have been criticized, most persuasively by Granovetter (1985), as providing an *undersocialized* conception of human agents who everywhere act alike, rationally pursuing unspecified interests. Market models cannot account for the impact of social networks, gender, class, culture or religion — the entire panoply of social life that so apparently influences what people want and how they go about getting it. Despite recent attempts by market theorists to incorporate a more sensitive model of individual decision making the result has been too often the joining of a naive psychology with a reified methodological individualism (see e. g. Tversky and Kahneman 1974). Concrete social relations, the economic networks that characterize most real-life market activity, are absent from market models, even those with a psychologized component.

Finally, it is crucial to question the applicability of a model based on the primacy of individual actors to explain Asian economies where individualism is unimportant ideologically and institutionally and does not capture the experience of social life. Organisations and markets in Asia are built on groups and networks of people and firms, not on the individual actors hypothesized by Western models although this has sometimes been recognised by economists (e. g. Caves and Williamson 1976).

This fact causes economic theory to face difficulty in characterizing Asian business networks, the single most important market structure in Asia, and leads market theorists to see Asian economies as distorted despite their obvious success. The neoclassical paradigm can only conceptualize two efficient economic structures, markets of autonomous actors, and hierarchies or autonomous firms which may arise under certain conditions, for example to achieve economies fo scale. Networks of social relations between economic actors can only be conceptualized as aberrations that arise due to imperfections of the hypothesized perfect market. For example, Chandler characterizes the Japanese *zaibatsu*, the pre-World War II business networks that are precursors to modern business groups, as 'an organisation comparable to the M-form' or multidivisional firm that originated in the U. S. Chandler characterizes a network of socially-interdependent Japanese companies as a single firm, although each constituent company has its own management, employees, and stockholders. He explains the rise of Japanese business groups as a technical response to 'undeveloped' capital markets in Japan. 'Undeveloped' as used here is a comparative term using the West as benchmark. Chandler and other market theorists look at the East through the lens of the West when they employ the neoclassical paradigm to explain Asia and in so doing find it 'imperfect' and 'distorted'.

Cultural models, in contrast to those of political economy and market approaches (see Hamilton and Cheng-Shu Kao 1990), are filled with the stuff of social life. They are often detailed, close-up examinations of people going about their business and working together in organisations. Cultural models put society back into an organisational explanation: society is not just an epiphenomenon and organisations are not just instrumental by-products of the pursuit of economic utilities. Rather, society provides the very means by which organised economic activity can be sustained — common understandings, social values and rewards, ideologies of work and management. As Mary Douglas put it, 'For discourse to be possible at all, the basic categories have to be agreed on. Nothing else but institutions can define sameness. Similarity is an institution' (1986: 55). Beliefs, categories of sameness, what political economists describe uncritically as 'interests' and the market model either assumes without question or dismisses as 'friction' and 'imperfection', the culture model sees as central problems for explanation. Moreover, social actors are taken seriously by the cultural perspective and are the central figures in any research program.

Despite, and perhaps because of, the richness of many culture studies of organisations this perspective also has limitations. Often the studies are so particularistic that generalisation of features, and hence comparison, is problematic. Even explicitly comparative culture studies when conducted in the same cultural arena, such as Japan and Taiwan, cannot explain differences. Cultural continuities such as the influence of a Confucian ethic throughout East Asia cannot explain why Japanese and Taiwanese businesses are organised so differently. It can only explain why there are similarities such as, for example, obedience to superiors and a disciplined orientation to work.

The culture approach also has difficulty explaining changes over time, even within the same society. Culture is relatively constant, transforming only slowly. How then can a culture theory explain Japanese labour practices before World War II, when seniority systems and lifetime employment in core industries were not widespread, as well as the postwar practices we now associate with Japanese management (Jacoby 1979)? If *nenko* and other management policies are expressions of group-oriented Japanese culture, as they surely are, how can we explain their emergence at a particular historic moment? Moreover, how can a culture model explain differences in a society in a given period, that is, account today for Japan's large organisations as well as its small ones, those privately held as well as those publicly-traded? Culture is too much a background factor, important to be sure but by itself insufficiently specific to explain differences in organisational structure and functioning. And, finally, where market theories suffer from an undersocialized conception of actors, culture theorists, like political economists, often err in the opposite way, seeing actors as unwittingly propelled by values and social pressures.

This characterisation of the political economy, market, and culture perspectives is just that, a characterisation which captures neither the variety of viewpoints within each perspective nor the substantive merits of the research produced by each which are admittedly considerable. Rather, my purpose has been to sketch the theoretical underpinnings of these alternative explanations in an attempt to create an approach to industrial patterns that avoids some of their shortcomings.

I am not alone in this endeavour. Indeed, the development of economic theories that account better for political, and especially social and cultural factors, is something of a boom industry at the moment, not least among economists. In addition to the psychologizing of economic models, some economists have embraced social structural and cultural concepts in recent years. Two examples suggest the direction of these efforts.

First, industrial organisation economists have attempted to introduce an explicitly cultural variable into their models. Ouchi (1980) has joined with Williamson in arguing that the most efficient forms of organisation may be those in which solidarity norms are strong. Mission-oriented firms, 'clans' in their terminology, will arise in situations where markets 'fail' and hierarchies have high costs, perhaps because of the complexity of work and the difficulty of monitoring or enforcing contract compliance. 'Culture' becomes the grease that reduces the costly friction of social relations.

Another observer, Jones, pursuing this logic, has asked how different cultures arise. He argues that 'the norms and values that govern organisational action emerge from the way in which property rights are distributed, enforced, and guaranteed in the organisation' (Jones 1983: 455). Jones distinguishes between property rights that are 'strong', which are vested in persons and are precise, inclusive and enduring, and 'weak' property rights which are vested in positions and are imprecise, limited, and transitory. Organisational cultures of different types emerge from the structure of property rights along these dimensions 'as norms and values emerge to actualize rights and enact obligations' (1983: 458). Where do property rights come from? According to Jones, property rights develop as an efficient response to transaction-cost problems and culture develops out of the structure of property rights. 'Culture' here is similar to that of the culturalists' view, as a lubricant, not an impediment, to economic relations.

Another important attempt by economists to lead towards integrating social structural variables is represented in institutional economic history (to be distinguished from the institutional school of organisational analysis described below) best developed in the writings of North (1981). North takes seriously analysis of the historically developed institutions of a society, including the state, and social ideology. For example, he writes that 'strong moral and ethical codes of a society is (sic) the cement of social stability which makes an economic system viable' (1981: 47). More importantly, North's project is concerned with how institutions are constraints upon the hypothesized neoclassical model, asking how economic rationality, an unquestioned assumption, can proceed given social and political formations. North and his colleagues examine historical market settings and 'fit' the neoclassical model within them.

Institutional economists have come far from the formal neoclassical models of mainstream economics in an attempt to account for the social and cultural factors that so obviously influence economic organisations. They do so in a way, however, that preserves the primacy of the economic over the social. Williamson and Ouchi, Jones, and North all see social variables as outcomes of, or constraints upon, the economic. Jones, for example, never asks why a given set of property rights − a social and political institution − is made possible by the institution of the state or why it comes to comes to be understood as efficient.

I do not intend to argue with the culturalists that economic activity presupposes shared meanings, with the economists who see culture emerging from exchange or with political economists who see the economy as a consequence of state structure. Rather, I develop an institutional theory that regards political, market, and culture factors as crucial variables in any explanation of economic organisation. I believe economic rationality is indeed widespread in market societies as economists assume but not that it is a state of human nature from which all else, including organisation, follows. Rather, I suggest that economic rationality is socially produced and culturally maintained. For economic rationality to exist social and cultural underpinnings of the sort that capitalist societies maintain − legal, educational, political, and ideological institutions − are necessary. Moreover, economic rationality is not everywhere the same, an undifferentiated force of social nature: it varies substantially with the history, culture, and institutions of a society and may have variable expression. While a merchant in Imperial China may have been just as profit-seeking as a contemporary Wall Street investment banker and just as 'economically rational', his reasons for pecuniary pursuit, his norms of exchange, his networks of financial relations, his conceivable strategies of accumulation, indeed, his entire orientation to gain, were strikingly different. In explaining such differences in economic behaviour, a sociological 'institutional theory' draws on state, market, and culture factors but in a way that makes none logically prior.

What is an Institutional Explanation?

The institutional school of organisational analysis is a loose agglomeration of theoretical approaches which vary considerably but largely reject explanations for organisational structure and functioning that rest solely on technical causes such as task requirements, size or market factors. Institutionalists tend to view organisations as socially constructed, as a product of actors' subjective realities, rather than as objective, material artifacts: they do not deny the material impulse behind organising, such as an orientation to profit, but seek beyond economic rationality for explanations of the structures which people manufacture in their pursuit of gain. It is not my purpose here to review the variation or detail in the institutional perspective, which has been ably described by others (e. g. Zucker 1987). Nor do I want to suggest that this is the first attempt to employ an institutionalist argument in regard to understanding economic organisation; indeed there are several institutional explanations, broadly conceived, of Asian economies (see Johnson 1982 and Westney 1987). Rather, because of the diversity in this perspective and the debates between practitioners, I want to suggest what I intend as an 'institutional theory' and to make explicit the assumptions on which it rests. There are four elements to the institutional theory of economic organisations that I propose: economic action as social action, the embeddedness of economic activity in institutional settings, the non-variable character of institutional explanation, and the necessarily multi-level nature of an institutional argument.

Economic Action is Social Action

The economic man of market models is an odd creature. He enters the marketplace alone and is influenced not at all by the people he meets there. He is motivated by greed only: other human passions have no place in his heart. His purchases are based on one criterion — price. Quality, fashion, features, none of these enter his calculus. He is troubled not at all by the requirements of enormous memory nor daunted by complex calculations in seeking the best buy. Economic man is an avaricious hermit, a super smart, selfish individual without history or tradition, without friends or enemies.

This character is the useful fiction employed by economists to depict decision making in market settings. Few, if any, economists would argue that real people acted like the miserly loner of their models. The advantage of the fiction is not to mirror reality but to simplify it, to reduce to essentials the general orientation of people as they buy and sell goods and services in a market.

This simple fiction yields the virtue of elegance in micro-economic model marking but it is not without critics. David Teece, an industrial organisation economist, for example, acknowledges that real markets are not peopled with 'faceless economic agents'. Instead,

'Reputation effects, experience ratings, and the like are the very stuff which permits markets to operate efficiently. To strip such considerations out of the theory renders it impotent before many strategic management problems ... The abstraction [of hyperrational decision makers] may be appropriate for framing certain problems, but it is generally an approach which managers find quite unhelpful. It is not a characterisation of individual behaviour and, even more so, of organisational behaviour.' (1984: 91—92)

Market theorists such as Teece recognize that economic actors indeed have histories, suffer forgetfulness, and are propelled by desires. While acknowledging that economic man is a useful caricature for modelling the behaviour of populations of actors, they understand the limits of the caricature for describing the activities of real people close-up.

At the heart of these limits, I believe, is the presumption that economic action is *asocial*, that it is conducted without consideration of others. While it is possible to conceive of asocial economic activity, it is so evidently rare in enduring conditions of exchange, as Teece suggests, that it can only be a weak basis for theory building. Rather, I propose constructing theories of economic action based on observed reality: economic action is social action.

What is social action? According to Weber, it is action oriented to others and includes both failure to act and passive acquiescence. It may be oriented to the past or the future, as well as the present. Social action may be motivated by revenge, peer pressure, desire for power or gain, the memory of one's ancestors, any motivation that considers or expects the response, intentions, feelings, beliefs, or attitudes of others.

'The "others" may be individual persons, and may be known to the actor as such, or may constitute an indefinite plurality and may be entirely unknown as individuals. (Thus, money is a means of exchange which the actor accepts in payment because he orients his action to the expectation that a large but unknown number of individuals he is personally unacquainted with will be ready to accept it in exchange on some future occasion.).' (1978: 22)

Not all human action is social: 'Social action does not occur when two cyclists, for example, collide unintentionally; however, it does occur when they try to avoid the collision or sock one another afterwards or negotiate to settle the matter peacefully.' (Weber 1978: 1375) Moreover, autonomous individuals reacting to a common factor, as in a crowd of persons all putting on coats against the cold, does not constitute social action. Human contact that is not meaningfully oriented toward others is not social.

It is clear, however, that much of what we consider to be economic action is indeed social action. Haggling over price, forming partnerships, purchasing a gift, negotiating a contract, hiring a worker, attempting to outwit a competitor, regulating a market, all of these activities anticipate the actions or feeling states of others and imply some judgement of how those others will react in given circumstances. Much business activity, and all organised enterprise, is social action.

Weber described four forms of social action: instrumentally-rational, value-rational, affectual, and traditional. Instrumentally-rational action involves an individual's calculation of a course of action in the pursuit of a rationally determined end, for example, profit or market share. This, of course, is the economic rationality of market models but in Weber's conceptualization it includes a calculus of more than price: it considers as well the likely actions of others as an individual pursues profit or other rational goals.

Instrumentally-rational social action predominates in market societies but it is not the only form of social action involved in the economy. Value-rationality is action that is oriented toward beliefs or values. Ethically-constrained economic behaviour or economic activity that is entwined with religious beliefs, such as titheing, provides examples of value-rational economic activity. Affectual social action is oriented toward feeling states, particularly emotions. Economic activity that is motivated by revenge or the anticipation of pleasure constitutes an affectually-driven form of social action. Finally, traditional social action is prompted by custom or habit, often the habits of generations. For example, the economic patterns of craft guilds in the Middle Ages, were oriented more toward custom than the maximization of profit.

Each of these four types of social action is an ideal type, a model of human orientations to activity, and each is always combined with others in some way. It is clear that real economic action is not merely 'economically rational' in an abstract, impersonal way. The economy is filled with more than greedy hermits and includes people moved by ethics, regulation, hate, status aspirations and custom. Economic action — not all of it, but most of it — is social action. An institutional explanation of the sort that I describe begins with the assumption that people consider others when they do business and are not the isolated individuals of market models. My argument for an institutional theory premised on social action differs from that of theorists who describe institutions as taken-for-granted ways of acting in the world. In the latter conceptualization institutions obscure the interests of actors by promoting uncritical modes of behaviour. It is far more useful to see *the extent to which* actors are active agents, channelled (but not necessarily determined) by the institutional environment in which they are embedded.

The Embeddedness of Economic Activity in Institutions

If economic action is rarely contained in the autonomous activities of atomized individuals, then it is in the relations of mutually-aware persons. Where does such 'awareness' come from, and what consequences does it have for the development of firms and other organised economic structures?

It is evident that individuals do not reconstruct norms of exchange each time they meet rather than develop mutually agreeable means for the repetitive conduct of business. With time, these patterns become routinized, taken-for-granted understandings of 'the way things are done'. Indeed, social order of any form, not just the economy, cannot proceed without common understandings.

'Social order comes into being as individuals take action, interpret that action, and share with others their interpretations. These interpretations, or 'typifica- tions' are attempts to classify the behaviour into categories that will enable the actors to respond to it in a similar fashion. The process by which actions become repeated over time and are assigned similar meanings by self and others is defined as institutionalization.' (Scott 1987: 495)

It becomes difficult, if not impossible, for individuals to pursue economic action in disregard of the institutionalized behaviour patterns of others, particularly if the efforts or goods of others are necessary to any actor's project.

Persons who have had a part in the formation of institutionalized eco- nomic norms or who become knowledgeable about them develop a stake in their maintenance: established norms make continuous exchange predict- able and simpler than constant negotiation of the terms of exchange. In this sense of making action 'simpler' institutionalized norms are 'efficient' since they provide previously negotiated, ready-made means for taking care of business. Clearly, efficiency in this sense is not measured against a 'most efficient' abstract standard but actors who disregard institutionalized patterns will certainly meet with social friction of the type hypothesized by market theorists. The most efficient form of economic action from the

point of view of an actor is institutionalized action, that is, action knowledgeable in the ways of insiders (Meyer and Rowan 1983).

It is clear, moreover, that patterns and structures which develop over
time for purely instrumental purposes may become infused with value, as
Selznick has noted: 'They are products of interaction and adaptation; they
become the receptacles of group idealism; they are less readily expendable'
(1957: 22). Institutionalized patterns and structures then have both instrumental and value components, both technical and ideal qualities. Failure
to act in ways that accord with institutionalized norms, even if more
abstractly efficient, may signal that the actor is outside the system morally
as well as instrumentally and is thus not to be trusted (Biggart and Hamilton
1984).

Organisational and ideological arrangements develop to sustain the patterns that have been worked out by actors. Economic organisations such
as banks and equity markets, for example, are routinized means for raising
capital. Negotiable instruments such as letters of credit and stock certificates
routinely allow the transfer of funds to those who accept the terms that
are implied by their use. Even money, that most basic of economic instruments, is useful only insofar as it is socially accepted, as Weber wrote.
Confidence in the economic system is crucial to its working and may have
only a tenuous relation to the technical health of an economy, as students
of market crashes can testify. Ideologies, too, support economic norms.
Ethics of 'fair business practice' and 'usual and customary' terns of exchange
may be merely understood or may be enforced legally.

Indeed, legal and other non-economic institutions are also vital to sustaining the economy in any developed market society. This view of the economy
as inter-connected with other social spheres is a crucial element in any
institutional explanation and distinguishes it most clearly from market
theories. As Granovetter put it, market theorists see 'the economy as an
increasingly separate, differentiated sphere in modern society, with economic transactions defined no longer by the social or kinship obligations of
those transacting but by rational calculations of individual gain.' (1985: 482)
Institutionalists, in contrast, see the economy as more or less interpenetrated
with other societal sectors. For example, the state may influence the economy through regulation, the educational system and family through social-
ization for work, and religion through and orientation toward material
goods. Typical of an institutionalist perspective is Zelizer's (1985) study of
the historically contingent social value of children which shows the impact
of changing norms and family structure for such economic practices as
insurance, trust funds, and child labour. One of my own studies (1989)
shows how the patriarchal structure of many modern families is a useful
vehicle for the organisational control of women direct selling workers.
Hamilton (1978) likewise shows in a study of gold rush adventurers that

the orientation to economic risk varied systematically with the character of the actor's social structure of origin. An institutional perspective looks at economic and organisational activity not as apart from but as embedded in society. The particular character of that embeddedness — networks of relations, social beliefs, gender and family structure, and other institutionalized forms of social order — influences how economic activity will be organised and conducted.

Organisational Logics

In what ways are societal sectors connected to each other and, in particular, to the economy? There is no easy answer to this question, and indeed the answer will vary across societies. The extent to which, for example, the polity and the economy are mutually supportive, relatively autonomous or overtly antagonistic is a subject of institutional explanation and not an *a priori* assumption. For the most part, however, institutionalists expect that societal sectors have connections of some sort and, in particular, that intra-sector social relations will frequently share similar organising logics.

Supra-organisational forms and patterns that express those norms serve as common resources for the structuring of social relations in a sector. In their article, 'The Iron Cage Revisited', DiMaggio and Powell (1983) have highlighted the phenomenon of organisational isomorphism — the tendency of organisations within an institutional environment to resemble each other because of similar constraints and resources (e. g. state regulation, professional group norms). Isomorphism also results from the application of a similar organisational logic across a societal sector. Organisations and individuals communicate effectively with each other by adopting similar organisational logics, or to put it in C. Mills' words, by adopting a similar 'vocabulary of motives'. We extend DiMaggio and Powell's important insight to argue that organisational logics often extend *across* institutional sectors within a society. Different spheres — the family, the polity, the economy may use the same or related logics to organise members and to pattern interaction. By 'organisational logic' I mean a legitimating principle that is elaborated in an array of derivative social practices. In other words, organisational logics are the ideational bases for institutionalised authority relations.

For example, in my study with Gary Hamilton and Marco Orrú, we have noted the differing logics that organise business groups in Asia (1991). Japanese firms enact a communitarian logic, Korean firms a patrimonial logic, and Taiwanese firms a patrilineal logic (see also Whitley 1990).

Although all are network logics they differ qualitatively from each other
and each has important implications for how workers are organised, for
the character of subcontracting relations between firms, for investment
patterns and for a host of other economic relations. Each of these logics
informs not only business relations but also social relations in other institutions in each society. The patrimonial logic of Korean business groups for
example, is reproduced both in the relations between the state and business
and within Korean families. Patrimonialism has deep historic roots in Korea
and provides a readily understood basis on which to organise social relations
of various types (Biggart 1990). Different spheres — the family, the polity,
the economy — may use the same or related logics to organise members
and to pattern interaction.

Institutional logics may at times be challenged and the tenacity of a
dominant logic in the face of changing environments is variable, according
to recent studies. Westney, for example, has found that industrialising Japan
in the late 19th century adapted organisational forms from Europe and the
US, but not in a wholesale manner. She reports that 'In the early Meiji
period, Western models provided both inspiration and legitimation; later
they continued to supply inspiration, but the grounds for legitimation were
increasingly sought in the Japanese tradition and environment.' (1987: 220)
The research of Richard Florida and Martin Kenney suggests that organisational logics may be deeply rooted in legitimation and practice and survive
transplant to an alien institutional arena: Japanese auto companies in the
US reproduce the communitarian relationship they have with subcontractors in Japan.

Crucial to any institutional explanation of the economy is an identification of the supra-organisational logics that are widespread in the society
and that influence both market and firm structure and the social relations
of business people.

Institutional Explanations are Non-Variable Explanations

If actors construct social order, including the economy, by interacting and
assigning meaning to their interactions, then it is clear that those meanings
exist only for those within the bounds of a social order. This basic premise
of an institutional argument has important consequences for research
methods and causal explanation used.

Explanations for institutional structure and practice must be adequate
at the level of meaning, that is, understandable from the points of view of
participating actors. Organisations, seen from an institutional perspective
(and similarly from a cultural perspective), are the consequences of people
working out routine means for handling repetitive economic functions.

Arrangements are not the 'best-adapted', or 'most efficient' in an instrum-entally-abstract way. Nor are they 'necessary' outcomes of a stage of economic development, as Chandler's theory of the firm suggests. Institutional arguments reject the above forms of explanation as limited by functionalism, that is, confusing consequences with causes.

Rather, I argue that institutional factors such as values, networks of relations, and socially-constructed rules, shape organisations by limiting possibilities, making some forms of action likely or more 'reasonable' because they have the force of understanding and acceptance in the community. Institutional factors do not 'cause' organisations in the sense implied by variable analysis. Variable analysis, such as that favored by market models and other forms of explanation that rely on statistical methods, seeks explanation in the correlation of variables such as size, industry characteristics and product diversity (see Ragin and Zaret 1983). These variables are conceived transhistorically and assume that anywhere that the same variables are aggregated in similar ways the same or like outcome(s) will occur. Any method which relies on such high levels of abstraction and seeks to find universal laws to explain social phenomena will have difficulty uncovering institutional logics where the context is crucial.

Because it assumes the primacy of context in the meaningful construction of organisation, institutional explanation rejects variable-based forms of explanation. Instead, institutional factors are seen as interlinked elements that contribute to social forms in a historically-contingent way. Elements of organisation can only be examined in terms of concrete cases, not as abstractions that would everywhere yield the same result. Avoiding universalistic propositions avoids the problem of misinterpreting like actions or forms in different societies: because a practice looks the same to an outsider does not mean it has the same status or function within all societies.

This is not to suggest that generalisation is impossible in an institutional explanation but the generalisations generated are of a limited form and resemble the ideal types of Weberian analysis. Ideal types summarize common elements of a limited number of real instances of a phenomenon, such as bureaucratic organisation or rational capitalism. Generalization exists at an intermediate level between the hypothesized universal laws of market theories and the unique explanations of some forms of cultural and historical analysis.

History, though, is crucial to an institutional argument because it is through the historical process that events occur and meanings are assigned to events. Institutional logics provide a framework for the interpretation of an historical moment and for the patterned response to historical opportunity. The institutional framework is both the structure within which activity takes place and is itself the product of social action, developing in what Giddens (1979) refers to as the dialectical process of structuration. This means understanding that history is not just the recorded working out of economic laws as implied by institutional economics: rather, is the handing down of previously-constructed patterns as a context for ongoing interaction. In an institutional explanation, for example, there is no necessary law of marginal utility or other impersonal system of laws that works to produce a particular economy: individuals may *enact* a 'law' of marginal utility by assuming the individualistic, calculating orientation that such a law implies but this does not mean that the 'law' has status independent of the actors who produce and reproduce it through social interaction. Actors make social and economic systems and through their knowledgeable reproduction of its patterns maintain it or change it incrementally through the coursing of history.

Because institutional factors represent both the structural outcome of past interactions as well as the medium through which ongoing interaction is possible, institutional analysis requires a method that gets at both the past and the present, that indeed unearths the *past in the present*. An institutional method, therefore, must strive toward a research strategy that is at once synchronous, comparing different institutional expressions at a given historic moment and diachronic, showing developmental changes over time.

One must caution against seeing an institutional argument as a deterministic one. While a particular institutional logic may be overwhelming in a society and may greatly constrain the responses of actors, there is always room for the creative adaptation of patterns of interaction. Within any society, institutional logics may be contested, there may be oppositional forms and individuals and groups may push the bounds of accepted practice. Among the most fascinating social phenomena are those in which dominant logics are being called into question, as for example in the present day contesting of unlimited merger and acquisition activity in the United States, and where the institutional logic and rhetoric of 'free market' economic activity is under debate by important economic actors who are reinterpreting the bounds of accepted practice.

This suggests that an institutional analysis is a political analysis in the sense that it is ultimately about power and control or, in Williamson's (1975) terminology, 'governance'. Institutional logics have political consequences insofar as they are constellations of interests and through material and symbolic means maintain the ordering of the world in a way that favours some over others. As Alford and Friedland put it, 'The limits, the instruments, the structure of power vary institutionally. It is those limits, and how they change, that are at issue. It is the institutional origins and consequences of uncertainty and power that are theoretically problematic' (1985: 20–21).

Institutional Analysis is Multi-Level Analysis

Market theories and some forms of political economy explanation locate crucial explanatory factors in supra-organisational phenomena — for example, the state, industry structure, or economic resources. Cultural analysis often locates the crucial factors at the *intra*-organisational level, in the minds of actors or in patterns of interpersonal relations. An institutional analysis, because of its concern with both structure and action, is necessarily a *multi-level* analysis. It must examine both micro- and macro-level phenomena and also do so in a way that shows their simultaneity: the structure that shapes action, the actions that reproduce structure.

Although institutional research is concerned with both micro- and macro-levels of analysis, the focus is primarily on the middle-range of social life. Institutionalists are concerned mostly with the organised relations and practices that are common to the economy — the structures of business ethics, the networks of ownership and production, the concrete arrangements that direct investment and trade in particular ways. It is in the intermediate range that we are best able to see the impact of both large-scale influences, such as state regulation, and the acts of individuals, such as investment decisions.

Conclusion

Social theorists everywhere are currently being challenged to explain an increasingly complex economic order. It is clear that old theories which posited a developmental sequence from 'undeveloped' to 'industrialized' cannot explain the diversity or patterns of industrialization that are evident. Japan is clearly as developed as Western nations but its patterns of development, its economic norms, and its industrial practices are substantially different from these of the U. S. and even from those of its Asian neighbours in Taiwan and South Korea. We need theories which can account for such differences without reducing cases to unique instances, which do not assume the individualistic character of Western social orders, and which are sensitive to an array of ideal as well as material factors operating in different locations. Although political economy, market, and culture theories each have contributions to make, an institutional perspective of the type I outline may be especially suited to the comparative analysis of emerging world economic organisation.

French Bread, Italian Fashions and Asian Enterprises: Modern Passions and Postmodern Prognoses

Stewart Clegg

Introduction

Organization studies in the past have drawn on a range of both materials and of theoretical approaches which has been too restricted. Consequently, they have failed to reflect the complexity of the organizational world outside the limited range of empirical examples considered. Upon such a small slice of available reality some fairly large assumptions have been spread. One of these has been a tacit reliance on the categories and concepts of modernist thought. Conceiving the present simply in terms of modernity, however, hardly does justice to a world in which the 'postmodern' is such an avid topic for cultural discussion of all kinds. Yet it is by no means clear that 'modernity' has in actual fact been superceded. Some writers talk of the present as an era of 'high modernism': others prefer the rubric of 'postmodernism'. Of course, we do not know what the outcomes of present practices and debates may be so these matters of interpretation cannot easily be settled, yet they are of considerable significance for the study of organizations. The terms of the debate are complex and have been subject to considerable discussion. Rather than reflect all of the nuances of this complexity, it is more productive to steer a simple and direct path through the debates linking modernity with postmodernity by focusing on a common core component, that of the direction and the degree of 'differentiation' or division which characterizes a period. Postmodernity may be distinguished from modernity principally by its reversal of earlier tendencies to increasing differentiation.

The importance of the debate around modernity for organization studies is very simply proposed: organization theory is a creation of modernity, in particular in the debt it owes to Max Weber. Current empirical tendencies in some international contexts, however, may be such that organization practice may well have transgressed the limits to understanding which are framed by this modernist theory or indeed never approximated them in the first place. The crucial hallmark of 'modernity' is taken to be the centrality of an increasing 'division of labour'. This will be referred to for economy as a process of 'differentiation'. Recently it has been suggested that modernity may not be an endless process. Debate has focused increasingly on what happens 'after' modernity, on what is 'postmodernity'. It has been proposed by contrast to the stress on increasing differentiation as the motif of modernity that the crucial hallmark of 'postmodernity' is a decrease in differentiation. Within the world of organizations and work this might be economically translated as a process of 'de-differentiation'.

Processes such as those of differentiation/de-differentiation assume an earlier evolution from the pre-modern to the modern, in which industrialization is usually seen as the mechanism promoting change. It is assumed by several influential theories that industry structure characteristics will follow a logic which shapes the organization structures of those firms comprising it. Certain products are seen as quintessentially 'industrial' and the logic of their industrialization to impose a logic upon their organizational form. Part of the intention of this chapter is to suggest that such perspectives are too 'economistic' in orientation. They fail to recognize adequately the authentic variety of an organizational world which does not conform to an implicit evolutionary schema in which product form determines neither industry nor organization structure.

According to Williamson's (1975) widely influential views, one would anticipate that a product like French bread ought to be made in large, oligopolistic, vertically integrated and bureaucratically organized factories. It is not. The reason for thinking so is that it is invariably made that way in the United States and this case is taken as the paradigmatic framework for interpreting the modern organizational world. It is not only the artisanal mode of production of French bread which appears problematic for such chauvinism. The making of Italian fashions, in particular those of Benetton, seems also to contradict a great deal of the conceptual thrust of contemporary organization studies. Much of this activity is premised on the study of organizations as mechanisms that have been designed to handle a level of environmental uncertainty, the totality of which they can never succeed in containing. Benetton, however, appears to come close to this containment. It offers a new conception of the management of organizations and markets. In the process it serves to pose a challenge to many of our ideas about the system boundaries of the organization.

It is, moreover, not only French bread and Italian fashion which pose fascinating puzzles for organization theory. In Japan, in South Korea and in overseas Chinese family businesses in countries like Taiwan and Hong Kong, there are Asian enterprises which Western analysts may feel do not seem to be developed by people with a good grasp of the contingency design features of rational organizations. Despite this handicap, they appear to be rational and efficient in their functioning. Indeed, the organization of production in Japan has increasingly become the case that is taken to prefigure what modern, perhaps even postmodern, management might be.

Can the distinctiveness of these cases be due simply to culture? It would be tempting to think so, particularly in the East Asian cases. Moreover, bearing in mind Crozier (1964), there are precedents for thinking similarly of the French case as well: vive la difference! Nor would this be merely an impulse of an earlier and now superceded social theory. In some recent and influential contributions, such as that of Berger (1987), there has been a tendency to see the success of East Asian enterprise, at least in part, as a function of a unique cultural configuration of values termed 'post-Confucianism'. These values are alleged to function as a source of entre-preneurial excellence, managerial acumen and organizational efficiency in much the same way that Weber (1976) saw the 'Protestant ethic' operating for nineteenth century European capitalism. Some critical distance is taken from such views here since the deficiency of universalizing theory premised on markets and efficiency is not easily rectified through a conception of culture which is equally essentialist in its reduction of explanation to one all-encroaching variable. I argue instead, following Granovetter (1985), that such reductionism makes too easy recourse to an 'over-socialized' view of economic action. Such a view is the direct antithesis of 'under-socialized' views, evident in universalizing, generalizing 'market' theories. Against these perspectives, Granovetter suggests, one must develop an 'embedded' view of the social organization of economic action.

Embeddedness refers to the configuration of those relations of 'relative autonomy' and 'relative dependence' which exist between forms of economic and social organization and the respective national frameworks of cultural and institutional value within which they are constituted. These configur-ations are an 'achieved' phenomenon. They are socially constructed, emer-gent, produced and reproduced. Forms of agency therefore stand at the centre of the analysis.

Agents are not necessarily people. Provided there are mechanisms in place for achieving effective subordination and control of individually effective agents then agency may take either an organizational or sub-organizational form. Agency wreaks its action on the world through the attempted accomplishment of projects which make sense in terms of the forms of calculation which agents have available to them. One of the important ways in which these vary is in the institutional frameworks within which action is lodged; these in turn vary nationally. The forms of economic calculation which agents have available to them are in part constituted by and always profoundly affected by nationally variable institutional phenomena such as tax regimes, accounting conventions, religious beliefs, formally constituted public policies in respect of matters of gender, equal opportunity, industry and regional policy and so on. The term 'modes of rationality' refers to attempts by agents to make sense of the potentially ambiguous, contradictory and uncertain nature of these available frameworks. Analytically, they are the patterned interpretations which can be made of the sense which agents appear to be making.

We will see that it cannot be assumed that the sense that they are making is necessarily best interpreted from modernist auspices. An embedded perspective on organizations does not assume the necessity of focussing on organizations as a central object of analysis or on the necessity of seeing them through any of the pervasive meta-narratives of modernity: contingency theory; population ecology; transaction cost analysis, strategy/ structure perspectives, etc. Each of these sees organizations as necessarily constituted by some source of determinism, be it environment, size or whatever. There is another way in which the embedded perspective differs from most others: it has no recourse to either an 'over-socialized' or an 'under-socialized' conception of the actor.

Unlike 'under-socialized' market views an embedded perspective does not operate with a pre-social or asocial version of agency. It makes not *a priori* assumptions about the nature or existence of specific forms of rationality privileged by the terms of neo-classical economic orthodoxy. In other words, an embedded perspective recognizes that there are likely to be a great many salient identities available for assembly and use and not merely that of the 'rational economic person'. On the other hand, it does not propose that the range of these identities will be given by the 'central value system' or core culture of a society. It seeks to avoid the reduction of analysis to one identity, that of the market actor. This is the common economistic error. There is a sociologistic error which it is also as well to avoid. Identities are not transmitted or read-off from some over-arching culture. There is not some necessary relationship between culture and practice, although there may be contingent ones.

It is important to resist any analytic impulse to reduce identities to one functionally efficient core culture. Many things which might appear to be superficially similar in cultural terms, such as the organization of Asian enterprise in the common cultural space of 'post-Confucianism', are on closer inspection far more variegated: even within the common cultural frame there are significant variations variations which are not explicable in purely cultural terms. Moreover, they are so in ways which do not appear to be readily amenable to many of the concerns of contemporary organization studies. There appears to be something in each case which is over and above markets and culture. What is additional is not simply specifiable in terms of a common set of organizational properties which can be termed 'hierarchy' but is dependent upon the practical exigencies of agency and situated action.

Agents are practical experimentalists confronted by a potentially far more uncertain, ambivalent, contradictory and ambiguous world than any natural scientist might anticipate finding in the laboratory. Upon this chaotic canvass they seek to impose their own 'circuits of power', configuring the field of action in such a way as to realize the conditions under which their conceptions of their own interests, and the enrolment and translation of other agencies to these conceptions, may eventuate. A major mechanism for stabilizing the fields of force which they traverse will be the construction of relatively stable networks with only a limited number of ways or conduits through them, under the control of the agencies in question. Culture has often been regarded as such a conduit, particularly in its form as religious knowledges, beliefs and practices which apply to a whole population. Weber's (1976) analysis of *The Protestant Ethic and the Spirit of Capitalism* remains the classic text of this genre, with its conception of the formation of Protestantism as a conduit for meaning having the unanticipated consequence of producing a life-line through which capitalism might also flourish.

Three 'Counter Intuitive' Examples

French Bread

Odds are that most readers of this chapter, at least if they are resident outside the 'Latin' European countries, often eat what Daniel Bertaux and Isabelle Bertaux-Wiame (1981: 155) term 'industrial bread', 'industrial food' wrapped in a shroud of cellophane which is sold in the supermarkets of the Western world under the somewhat euphemistic label of 'bread'. This industrial bread accounts for almost all the bread sold in the United States, Canada, Australia, New Zealand and much of Europe. The reasons for the supremacy of 'industrial bread' are evident from what we have learned from Chandler (1962). It is usually one product-line, often produced from within a division, of a giant food conglomerate formed by merger and based around vertical integration from flour milling to bread and related food retailing. It is a classic case of an industry in which, as organizations merged and became conglomerates, divisionalization occurred and products diversified, a diversification typical of the industrialized foods industry.

One of the characteristics of Chandler's (1962) account is that it is specifically about the United States. If the thesis that he advances were to be the basis for a scientific generalizing account of how and why organizations have the structures they do, as Donaldson (1987) suggests, then a single appropriate counter-factual would serve if not to disconfirm it at least to demarcate some of its limits. According to Donaldson's view of the Chandlerian thesis, efficient, successful organizations in similar industries should adopt the same type of strategy and structure, irrespective of their geographical or cultural location. Another way of thinking of this would be to say that the organizational characteristics of an industry which has divisionalized in the United States ought to be the same for the organizations in the same industry making the same product in an economically similar advanced capitalist country.

So, how is French bread possible? How has the market dominance of conglomerate oligopoly manufactured bread been avoided? Why should it be that in France the equivalent of these manufacturers control only about 10 percent of the market whereas in other countries, such as Britain and the United States, it is far closer to 100 percent? This question has generated one of the more entertaining studies in social research, whose entertainment value is particularly marked in contrast to a great deal of organization theory. Perhaps for this reason, or because of the bibliographic habitat of many organization theorists, one has rarely seen it cited in the annals of those interested in the study of organizations (Marceau 1989 is an exception). The article is called 'Artisanal Bakery in France: How it Lives and Why it Survives', by Daniel Bertaux and and Isabelle Bertaux-Wiame (1981).

What is French bread? Visitors to and residents of France know it as a crusty baguette or half pound loaf. It looks good and it tastes good. However, to describe it does not tell us what French bread is. It is clearer, perhaps, if we determine what it is not. First, it is not a standardized, easily transportable, mass-produced product, one whose quality is, as Bertaux and Bertaux-Wiame (1981: 159) say, 'invariable (or invariably poor)'. It is not a heavily marketed, brand-identified, size-invariant, shrink-wrapped and sliced product sold identically in virtually similar supermarket chains throughout the country and amenable to being mass-marketed and distributed. It is neither an industrial product nor the product of a capitalist mode of production but an artisanal success story.

Why is it that the huge bread factory, a division of an even more huge merged conglomerate food producer based on flour, distributing its standardized, industrialized product across the nation has not exploited the efficiencies of the divisional form to colonize the French market for bread and, in so doing, make the science of organizations truly generalizable, truly universal, truly a positive science? Do the French not know their contingency theory?

It is not just a matter of the culture of France, as one might think. After all, as Bertaux and Bertaux-Wiame (1981: 158) note, despite the famed *gastronomie* of the French and their penchant for long lunches, this has not stopped other areas of the national culture being undermined: 'No doubt, the French used to like good wines, good poultry, good cheese but that did not prevent all these foods from becoming food products, industrialized, standardized, homogenized; dead things. Still the French eat them, albeit with a grimace'. What is so special about bread?

It is not as if the normal forces of the market, from which theorists such as Chandler and Donaldson would make a theory, have not operated in France. They have, but the outcomes have been different. In the 1950s a broad front campaign was waged against traditional (artisanal) bread by the industrial foodstuffs manufacturers. It was fattening, it was claimed, in comparison to dietarily desirable rusks (a charge which research commissioned by Le Syndicat de la Boulangerie did not support). During the 1950s, perhaps in part in response to this campaign, the staple product of *les boulangers* changed from a one pound loaf to the crustier half pound baguette. 'More crust, less crumb' as the researchers put it. The baguette was a major success. It possessed an inherent quality of 'freshness'. It was not a stable industrial product which could be easily transported through space and time. It was a perishable product, one whose intrinsic, positional value was that it was fresh, that it did perish, and that it could not be bought other than on a daily basis. It incorporated everything that industrial bread could not be.

In 1966 the largest flour milling group in France, which had a virtual monopoly of the supply of flour to the Paris market, was rumoured to be preparing a huge bread factory close to the Seine in order to supply industrial bread to the French market. Given the support that *les boulangers* enjoyed for their baguettes it would first be necessary to batter down the bakers with whatever artillery (or 'resource dependency') came to hand. The monopoly was the evident answer. One day, without warning, the flour-milling company changed the terms of trade: henceforth, only full truckloads would be delivered, a crippling blow to bakers who had neither the market nor the storage capacity to warrant such an amount. However, after a week of panic the small bakers discovered:

'that some small mills were still functioning in the rural regions surrounding the Paris area. These mills were on the verge of closing down, as they were only working at 20 per cent of their capacity. They were, of course, extremely happy to accept the orders of the small bakers, and thus to reach full capacity. After one month of groping about, it appeared that the new network could quite possibly function smoothly. The big flour-milling company understood it had lost the fight; it went back to its previous policy of retail delivery, lowered its prices to get back its former customers, and put the plans for the factory back in the safe where they are waiting for the next opportunity.' (Bertaux and Bertaux-Wiame 1981: 161).

Hence, the survival of the small bakers has not been not achieved without struggle. The struggle is occasionally dramatic, fought against those forces which would rationalize the world of French bread, scenting a profit, and an opportunity to internalize a potentially profitable transaction. The work-day life of the small baker is also a daily struggle and it is in this struggle, in particular, that the organizational form of French bread is reproduced and *les boulangeries* survive all efforts to achieve their structural adjustment to a more efficient form.

It is not a rational life, baking bread. It has always been hard work for small returns. Before the war the working day would often start as early as midnight, or earlier, with the preparation of the first batch of dough. The oven had to be warmed next so wood had to be cut, the fire lit and so on. At around two in the morning the first batch had to be cooked and so on in successive batches through to noon. Lunch and sleep followed till four, when the baker and the young apprentice would load up the cart and attend to their rural rounds delivering bread to the farms. Returning home form this later that evening they would have time for a few hours sleep until midnight rolled round again and the quotidean round recommenced.

Well, things have improved a little. In 1936 the state decreed that all bakers shops had to shut for one day a week which meant that on the previous day the baker worked twice as hard to make double the bread for loyal customers to take them through the day off. This batch was known as *le doublage*. Nowadays wood no longer has to be cut and dried; much of the actual process of production has been mechanized and the baker has 'only' to start the working day at three or four in the morning and work 'only' nine or ten hours, albeit more intensively than in the olden days as there are now machines to be kept up with. *Le doublage* still remains. Despite laws against it, these hours are usually the hours of the apprentice as well: how else would they learn the trade?

What of the bakers' wives? Their day is also long and their role important. The shop opens from eight in the morning, or seven in working class districts; it may shut from one till four, and then re-open, closing finally at eight. This is a long day's work 'which by the way gives no salary, no social rights whatsoever, and no property rights either' and to which 'they must add the work of any housewife and mother. The closing day is used not for rest or leisure, but in making up the for the accumulated backlog of cleaning, washing, shopping ...' (Bertaux and Bertaux-Wiame 1981: 163). Yet, in the whole process whereby the artisanal bakeries have been repro-duced in France while in most other places they have been rationalized out of existence, it is the wives who are the most important actors. They are the street-level workers, the front-line marketers. Good bakers bake good bread but it is good wives who sell it, who create a regular custom attracted to a particular bread and a particular shop. Additionally, they are not only the marketers and sales-persons: they are also the accountants, cashiers and trusted confidantes. A good wife will not cheat a good husband, one who is also a good baker. While wives who become widows can hire bakery workers to continue the business, husbands who have become widowers or whose wives have left them find it difficult to continue in the business without an unpaid and trustworthy partner. Anyone else cannot be trusted not to cheat; besides, they have to be paid. Good wives are good investments in more ways than one. It is on the wives' judgement that the reproduction of this whole enterprise depends. It is the wives' judgement which preserves for the French their bread and provides this fascinating counterfactual to the efficiency ethic of some colleagues in organization theory.

Once upon a time bakers were born into the trade. The professional organization of bakers saw to it that in almost every case the only way to become a baker was to be born the son of a baker. The role of the wife was literally to reproduce the next generation to mind, manage and eventually take over the business. These days, with enhanced possibilities of occupational and social mobility, few parents who are bakers would want to see their children destined for the same end and few children who have seen what is entailed at close quarters would want to end up like their parents. 'Today's bakers are not born bakers; this is the key discovery' (Bertaux and Bertaux-Wiame 1981: 164). Given the nature of the trade, only someone who had been apprenticed in it could possibly run the business. Most present day bakers are former bakery workers who became self-employed at an early age. Initially, this was puzzling for where would a lowly paid worker in a low-status trade, in all probability with no collateral, raise the 100,000 Francs necessary to buy even one of the smallest going concerns? Certainly not from a bank.

There are two sides to any transaction. Consider an old couple whose life has been their bakery and who want to retire. They have no children to hand the business on to: perhaps they are childless or their children have gained other skills and followed other opportunities. How can they retire? Only if they can sell the business as a 'going-concern' complete with 'goodwill' to someone who will continue to use the premises as a bakery. Only if the bakery is to be continued as a bakery can that 'goodwill' (a set of stable customer relationships with a specific local population) return an appropriate monetary value which the machinery, frequently worn-out, will not. Premises are invariably rented. The only people who can take over the trade are the young men who have been apprenticed in it. They the only ones who 'know' the trade and its skills. Usually these young men (and their brides) are from a rural background and for them the prospect of arduous work for low rewards but also the 'freedom' of being their own *patron* is an inducement few others would accept.

For those young men who stay in the trade after military service has broadened the possibilities of their occupational horizons (many quit as the demographics show) becoming a self-employed baker consummates the hard union of their apprenticeship, long hours and low pay. It is this ever-present project which makes *existing* as a lowly worker not equivalent to *being exploited* as a miserable proletarian. It is a temporary state of affairs en route to the *petite bourgeoisie*.

Still, two aspects of this puzzle remain to be completed. First, how are these bakery workers able to afford to become honourable proprietors in Le Syndicat de la Boulangerie? Second, what is distinctive about France which allows this to happen, which saves the French from the dubious delights of industrial bread and disconfirms those contingency theorists who, on the basis of an industry, a technology, a product, a market, would predict a certain scale and mode of productive organization?

The wife is the key to the whole enterprise it has been said but first, how do bakery workers become proprietors and old couples retire from the trade? The retiring couple *lend* the money which is necessary to the bakery worker. For the incoming baker and his wife it means eight years of relative hardship and privation as they save to repay the value of the goodwill (based on the value of an average month's sale of bread). For the retiring couple it means placing tremendous trust in the new couple, for the turnover may be a risky business: if they do not succeed in the trade then they cannot repay the loan. Actually, the trust is placed not so much in the couple, for the bakery worker is expected to 'know' the trade on the basis of his ten years or so service; rather trust has to be placed in the young wife who is entering the trade: She is the secret of the future success of the *boulangerie*; has she got what it takes to be a good shopkeeper? Can she tolerate the long hours of work during the day and the emptiness of the nights as her husband toils in the bakery? Does she know what being a baker's wife means and entails? Will she resent the customers who, arriving after hours, will nonetheless disturb her because they want, expect, fresh bread? As the researchers note 'it is extremely interesting to observe the practices of the two couples during the crucial period of passage. Pretending to show the young lady how to behave as *boulangère*, the experienced woman will also check her spontaneous reaction and try to uncover her fundamental values' (1981: 167). A good baker needs a good wife as well as money to succeed. If he does not have the former it is unlikely he will make the latter. A baker's marriage is not just a transaction between marital partners: it is also a transaction between an artisan and a shopkeeper who are bonded together.

The second and remaining piece of the puzzle is why should it be that these social relations and this bread have survived in France (and some other Latin countries such as Spain and Italy)? The clue to the answer is the largely rural background of new entrants to the trade. The bakeries as an artisanal pursuit have for most of their history (the past ten centuries) been an urban phenomenon. Peasant women typically baked their own bread until the early years of this century, although this is no longer the case (Beck and Child 1978: 84). Only in the late nineteenth century did rural bakers appear, sometimes by diffusion from urban areas, sometimes through local millers using newer technologies to extend their trade to capture what had previously been done as domestic labour (in rural-industrial areas where they emerged with the flour mills). During the early twentieth century a dense ecology of bakeries developed, each one serving about 500 to 1,500 people and with it a new pool of labour was tapped from the ranks of the independent peasantry, a peasantry embodying a fierce individualism and a commitment to good husbandry, to a job well-done. These people were the vital part in the continuity of the *boulangerie*.

The baker's sons disappeared as recruits for reproduction of the artisanal form. In France, with its peculiar peasant structure located in the post-Napoleonic settlement and reproduced even today, potential bakery workers embodying peasant values were available to take over the enterprises that the owning families vacated. The peasant values embodied over the course of the apprenticeship become overlain, interpenetrated and nurtured by a new set of rhythms acquired as a constitutive part of the job:

'the trade penetrates the body ... you have to transform your body completely. Its natural rhythm has to be reversed, the body must learn to sleep during the day and be awake in the dark hours of the night. The speed of movements has to be augmented ... It means a trained body, which lives on its nerves; and the training, the restructuring of the body is what apprenticeship is all about: So it may be said that while bakers make the bread, the bread also makes the bakers; if the population needs bread to live, the artisanal form needs the bakers' bodies in order to to survive. The relations of production produce the people who will reproduce them ... through competition between bakers, this rhythm becomes the rhythm of the whole trade, and if one considers not only one bakery but fifty thousand with their long opening hours and the hard work which takes place around the ovens, all this for relatively low economic rewards; if one considers the amount of work invested, then one understands better why it is so difficult for industry to take over the market for bread'. (Bertaux and Bertaux-Wiame 1981: 175 – 176).

The space in which industrial bread could be made, the space, that is, in which it could be consumed, because the alternative had disappeared, never occurred in France. The reason the form was able to survive because that it was able to reproduce due to the survival of the French peasantry into the twentieth century, a survival contingent on a complex of state actions and public policies from the post-revolutionary settlement to the present day.

This case teaches us some profoundly important things about organizations. First, organizations are composed around a core of value imperatives. At every stage where the *boulangerie* might have been annihilated at the hands of industrial bread and its organizational form, the resources of deeply embedded cultural values were there to enable resistance. Resistance is grounded in the cultural resources which people have available to them in any specific institutional context. For the *boulangeries* of France these resources were a supply of potential *petits bourgeois* drawn from the ranks of an independent peasantry which the transition to modernity had either almost eliminated elsewhere or which had never been fabricated in anything like the same form (Moore 1968).

Second, organizations are embedded within a complex field of force laced together by the capillary power of culturally embedded ways of doing, ways of being and ways of becoming (Clegg 1989b). Sure, there are contingencies and there are transaction costs and there are pressures of efficiency. We saw how the industrial flour-millers sought to exercise power and dispense with the regrettable contingency that French consumers would not and will not willingly purchase the kind of industrial bread that they could make. Sure, the transaction costs are expensive and inefficient for all concerned. The customers have to shop for bread almost every day whereas with industrial bread the transaction costs could have been minimized to just one weekly supermarket trip. For the bakers the costs are even higher. They have to endure a long, arduous and unremunerative apprenticeship; they have to borrow heavily at the beginning to become proprietors and to lend heavily at the end to become retirees; they have to take the extraordinary risk that at the end of their lives the transaction costs associated with retirement may never be recouped; they leave themselves open at the most vulnerable stage in their lives to the transacting party operating both opportunistically with considerable guile or foolishly with insufficient acumen. They place their fate in the hands of a transacting party that they could never be sure to trust in a transaction which has no guarantees. Yet they still do all these things. They choose to be bakers. In addition, their customers choose to eat baker's bread rather than its industrial counterpart.

Perhaps it would be more efficient if the French government simply invited some major United States organization theorists to conduct a consultancy into the efficiency and effectiveness of the system for the production and distribution of bread. It is certain that such persons would be appalled at what they saw (though they might be surprised by what they ate). One could anticipate that they would recommend dismantling the inefficient supply system that exists (50,000 bakeries!) in order to achieve proper economies of scale, reasonable transaction costs and an appropriate contingency-designed organization form to deliver it. They might, indeed probably would, recommend inviting Goodman Fielder Wattie or Rank Hovis McDougal in for a slice of the action. But would a government that did this ever dare face the electors again?

Reductionism: A Modern Passion

The preceding analysis of 'French bread' is a testament to what Granovetter (1985: 481−482) has termed the 'embeddedness' of economic action: 'the argument that the behaviour and institutions to be analyzed are so constrained by ongoing social relations that to construe them as independent is a grievous misunderstanding'. Granovetter attempts to correct this 'misunderstanding' by focusing on the central role of networks of social relations in producing trust in economic life. Seen from this perspective, the reproduction of the *boulangerie* is not only a mode of organization but also a complex of cultural and economic practices. In its exclusion of forms which are, from certain influential perspectives, transactionally more efficient, contingently more appropriate and organizationally more rational, not to mention more rationalized, it is a classic case of embeddedness.

One consequence of an embedded analysis is a perceptible transformation in the object studied. The focus of interest is shifted from concrete empirical objects, such as the 50,000 small bakeries, to the network of social relations in which these organizations are constituted, embedded and reproduced. It enables one to appreciate that 'small firms in a market setting may persist because a dense network of social relations is overlaid on the business relations connecting such firms' (Granovetter 1985: 507). Granovetter's emphasis on 'embeddedness' is quite at odds with the conventional conceptions of most proponents of an 'efficiency' perspective on organizations. In the terms which he proposes such theorists operate with an 'under-socialized' conception of action in their models and analysis, one modelled on the abstractions of 'economic rationality'. Together with its antinomy of an 'over-socialized' conception (a term which he adopts from Wrong's (1961) famous critique of Parsonian functionalism), these provide the framework for a modern passion of social analysis to 'explain' by reduction.

The concern with the cultural embeddedness of French bread should not lead one to think that a straightforward transfer from an 'under-socialized' and 'economistic' an 'over-socialized' and 'culturalist' account is being proposed. Such culturalist accounts are available and it is worthwhile considering them in order to show the ways in which the account proffered here differs. Probably the most sophisticated of recent defences of a culturalist account is that of Peter Berger. It is Berger who has has recently coined the concept of 'economic culture': 'the social, political, and cultural matrix

or context within which particular economic processes operate' (1987: 7).
At base what Berger (1987) argues is that some cultures, which are
nationally specific, may be more 'efficient' economically than are other
cultures. The outcomes which are valued by 'efficiency' theorists, it is
argued, can be achieved through the means which are ordinarily the focus
of more 'institutional' theory. The culture and the means turn out to be
those of a relatively unbridled captialism. (Clegg, Higgins and Spybey
[1990] and Clegg [1990b] contain critical considerations of the concept of
'economic culture'.)

Berger (1987) is not alone in seeing this concern with culture as having
a particular efficacy in explaining how and why successful enterprises have
in the recent past developed in both form and location outside the patterns
of an earlier history. At the beginning of the twentieth century Weber (1976)
also charted the role of culture in the explanation of economic organization.
The more recent specification by Berger (1987) of the contemporary existence of culture and meaning institutionally fused in the economic code of
modern capitalism would have been an agreeable paradox for Weber.
Agreeable, because his basic conception of economics was not one which
stressed it as a natural science, concerned purely with criteria of efficiency.
Instead, he regarded it as a cultural science. The paradox would arise
because it was Weber's view that although modern industrial capitalism
had been forged in the heat of religious values and culture it would
henceforth be firmly set in a mould from which these sources of meaning
had drained away. His nightmare was that the pan-cultural value of rational
action would transform the contours of modern capitalism to a uniformity
in which cultural value was absent.

Ideas such as these were at the crux of the Weberian (1976) hypothesis
concerning the 'Protestant Ethic' which sees the specific cultural embeddedness of Protestantism as a major causal agency in the genesis of modern
capitalism, an analysis elaborated and extended rather than undercut in his
later work (Weber 1923; see Collins 1980). *The Protestant Ethic and the
Spirit of Capitalism* is the original locus of that metaphysical pathos which
has so frequently characterized thinking about organizations. It was one
which posited a gloomy view of his future and our present. Weber anticipated an horizon of meaninglessness, an 'iron cage' of bureaucracy entrap-
ping us as 'little cogs' in a vast machinery of effort expended to no higher
purpose and to no other cultural ideals than those of dull compulsion,
necessity and relentless striving.

An additional legacy from Weber to contemporary organization analysis
has been the assumption that the organization is both the object of analysis
and that, as such, its 'essence' is constituted by simple contracts of employment. As an employee of a firm one belongs to it, one is 'inside' it, one is
a member and one can be counted as a statistic in determining the firm's
size. Indeed, when we consider the importance which has been attached to

'size' as a determining force in structure, in the research programs of both the Aston school as well as the transaction cost analysis approach, we can see how decisive has been this simple assumption that organizations are an envelope which one enters by being an employee. Simply by being hired by an employer, or being fired, one may be contributing to the structuring of modernity!

Consider a model in which organizations grow or decline in size simply by taking on or shedding labour and in which size is a determinate and independent variable related to a number of dependent variables, such as formalization, standardization etc. It is assumed that organizations are unitary centres of calculation to which a number of other relationships, including the employment contract, are subordinate. An organization has a boundary defined by the sum of its contracts of employment. If it grows it opens more contracts with additional people; if it shrinks it terminates present contracts with existing employees, or simply does not replace people when they leave its employment. Thus, if one named a firm like 'Ford' one could have a nationally specific picture of it as an enterprise composed of a number of sites, containing a number of people, people who were defined as employees by their contracts of employment. If it grew it hired more people and this had effects for the administrative carrying capacity of the firm. Of course, there were always complex inter-dependencies with sub-contractors, but these did not effect the size variable. These were separate entities with separate employees and were subject to separate analysis, even where the firm in question might be effictively 'captured' by Ford, produc-ing a component entirely for it. The latter would then become an issue for inter-organizational analysis.

Employment relations do not need to be enveloped within the corporate form of a singular organization. It has merely been conventional that this should be the case. One of the strengths of the transaction costs approach is that it enables one to see clearly that economic activity might be organized by the envelope of a formal, recurrent hierarchical structure, or it might be left to a series of transactions on the market. In considering economic activity which is not contained within the envelope of the formal organiza-tion it is useful to have a concrete example to hand. The one I have in mind is derived from the world of Italian fashion.

Italian Fashion: The Colours of Benetton

'The colours of Benetton' is a captivating slogan for a firm which now has an upmarket presence in many cities around the world, selling brightly coloured and coordinated casual clothing in highly fashionable designs, for both men and women as well as boys and girls. Benetton fashions are oriented primarily to an affluent and style-conscious market. Many readers have probably seen Benetton shops; some may even have bought things there but how many people know the organizational story behind the brightly coloured retail facade?

'Benetton, an Italian family firm described as 'one of the most successful clothing companies in Europe', is organized in a flexible network of production and distribution. At the market end it has 2,500 national and international outlets, furnished with specially designed electronic cash registers that transmit on-line full data about which items are being sold, their sizes and their colour. This information is centrally received and processed for decision-making at the design and production end. There, the output mix flexibility of the main production facilities is complemented by a network of 200 small firms in a sort of 'putting out system' that provides additional flexibility regarding volume, although possibly at the expense of these indirect workers. Allegedly the re-sponse time to market change is reduced to 10 days'. (Perez 1985: 454).

What is the organization 'Benetton' in this system? Does it include the 2,500 retail outlets, for instance? Not really, because these are retail franchises, although they sell only Benetton products. Employees of these franchises are not Benetton employees but they are nonetheless utterly dependent on Benetton. Is Benetton the design and production facilities located in the North of Italy? Well, certainly it is this but is it just this? On a 'contract of employment' basis it would certainly be just this but would not this be isolating only a part of a network? What about the 200 small firms involved in something approximating a 'putting out system', are these part of Benetton? Are they really a 'putting out system', some kind of primitive anticipation of a modern organizational form in which the work will once more be brought under the surveillance of an internal contractor and eventually, perhaps, the hierarchy of complex organization? Or, with Benet-ton, are we dealing with something completely different from a traditional organization? Is Benetton perhaps better thought of as less an organization per se and rather more as an organized network of market relations premised on complex forms of contracting made possible by advances in microelectronics technology? What sense does it make to write of an organization coping with uncertain contingencies when it appears to nest in a system whose major virtue appears to be that it has just about minimized whatever uncertainty there was in what was once a highly uncertain environment? The combination that is Benetton is indeed complex but is it a singular complex organization? Consider the following elements: instantaneous market signals from the point of purchase are electronically transmitted to Benetton headquarters; a precise knowledge of what lines to ship to which retail outlets is provided; flexible manufacturing can rapidly respond to product design changes determined by the precise market knowledge of 'what lines are selling where' which this instantaneous market signaling allows; extensive sub-contracting allows for smaller production runs and the rapid shifting of production schedules as demand varies. All these advantages, plus the fact that one has no direct competition at the point of sale, seem to signify a very different type of organization in the fashion industry to the large corporation such as Levi Strauss in the late 1970s, with its different product lines organized divisionally: over here 501s, over there shoes, here shirts, and so on. Benetton appear to have subverted the basis for those conventional assumptions which have been implicit in organization theory about the employment relations involved in manufacturing and marketing a commodity. In so doing are they perhaps heralding the limits of a scientific enterprise defined by an empirical object which may well be in the process of relative extinction? By posing the question this way one raises the possibility that the conventional organizational form, which grows by taking more people on to its payroll, in which its size (measured in terms of numbers of employees) will always correlate positively with its bureaucracy (measured in terms of formalization, standardization etc), may be a historical moment rather than an eternal verity. Indeed, the fate of some times, perhaps, but not necessarily our times. If this were the case then the analytical strategy of focusing on 'transactions', irrespective of the particulars of how it is done, may be a sounder strategy.

What makes Benetton distinctive is the combination of several things. First, at the core of Benetton is a highly modern information technology. Second, Benetton operates a retailing system based entirely on franchising. It is not a system of franchising which is based on either highly formal regulation (as is McDonalds for instance) nor is it one in which the retailers have to pay royalties to the Benetton organization. However, a Benetton shop is entirely a Benetton shop, it is not allowed to sell any other make of product. Nor does Benetton retail its products other than through these outlets. 'In essence it exports the entire selling strategy: not only its products but also the Benetton style, shop organizattion and marketing strategy' (Belussi 1989: 119). Third, the strategy is based on a well-established putting-out strategy, which, rather than being an innovation, built upon the basis of local practice in the Veneto region of North-East Italy, where Benetton began in 1965. In this region the extensive use of sub-contracting had never been wholly superseded by the factory organization of production.

Subcontractors are involved in all the labour intensive phases of Benetton production — assembly, ironing and finishing. Four categories of subcontactor have been identified by Belussi (1989: 119): financially subordinated firms who are effectively controlled by a Benetton holding company; 'affiliate' firms; independent firms and homeworkers. Affiliate firms belong either to former Benetton employees or to present managers and clerks. Such firms have been 'grown' by Benetton through guaranteeing orders in the start-up phase. Extensive subcontracting has two major benefits. First, it uses external managerial resources in whom the managerial and financial controls are located, rather as in the internal contract system. As in this system it is the ability of the subcontracted management to tightly control the pace and intensity of work which delivers the benefits for Benetton. Second, it significantly reduces the unit labour costs that Benetton would otherwise experience by about 40 per cent (Belussi 1989: 120). Subcontractors are exclusive to Benetton. The agreement to subcontact is attractive because it guarantees both demand and profit margins (the latter at about 19 per cent for work undertaken).

The Benetton information system has a crucial nodal point in its circuits of power. These are the 'sales agents'. Their function is to present the Benetton collection to shop operators in their own territory and to collect orders for the initial stock and subsequent re-orders, as well as to coordinate extensive advertising for 'The colours of Benetton'. These agents, of whom Belussi (1989: 120) advises that there were 35 in late 1982, will frequently supervise and hold an interest in a number of stores, each one of which is recognizably Benetton by its colours, design, displays and open shelves. The latter are very important. There is nothing to a Benetton shop that the customer does not see. All the stock is on the shelves. The use of information technology enables the retailers to use a retailing philosophy of 'just-enough'. Benetton's production, warehousing and retailing form a tightly coupled system with rapid feedback responses built in to minimize error. The rapidity of the feedback depends upon the combination of new forms of organization, premised on the subcontracting system, with new forms of information technology.

It is the use of information technology which links together production and distribution. Almost the whole of Benetton's production is made in response to retailers' orders. These are collected initially by agents and updated by shops feeding back through the computer link information on what sizes, colours and models are selling where and when. No production is for stock. Inventory and warehousing costs are slashed to a minimum. Re-orders can be supplied within about ten days. It may be said, with Belussi (1989: 128) that we have in this case 'the domination of the market by the firm'. However, it is a domination premised on an entirely new set of strategies to those which in the past consisted of domination through size. (On the strategies in more detail see Belussi [1989: 128–129].)

It is important to emphasize that Benetton is not some exotic and rare example of the impact of new technology on enterprises. For instance, Lorenz's (1988) study of small and medium size French firms in the engineering industry revealed that substantial 'downsizing' of these organizations had occurred at the same time as a sharp increase in sales during the early 1980s. In part this was contingent upon improvements in productivity wrought by the adoption of new forms of computer controlled machine tools but largely it was due to 'a substantial increase in their use of subcontracting for intermediate component production'. Subcontracting was not novel: few firms 'were of sufficient scale in their operations to warrant investing in plant for such specialized tasks as gear grinding or heat treatment' (Lorenz 1988: 195). Moreover, because of French redundancy laws, subcontracting was an attractive strategy for dealing with temporary fluctuations in demand requiring extra capacity. More than this was involved, however.

'It was a shift to subcontracting on a permanent basis for such standard operations as turning, milling, and drilling. It allowed the firms to avoid making investments in up-to-date machine tools and was frequently the occasion for a reduction in capacity, with some existing plant being sold off. While the general type of operation subcontracted was not specialised or specific to the particular firm in question, the design and specifications of the components were. Thus it was not a case of substituting in-house production for standardized components available in the market: rather, components were being machined (turned, milled, etc.) by subcontractors according to firm-specific plan produced in the design offices of the client firm'. (Lorenz 1988: 195).

Microelectronics appear to be not only contributing to the transformation of design, production and distribution and the way these are linked together but also to be raising questions about the appropriate objects of analysis for economic sociologists interested in organizations. The questions are normative, the subject-matter of the specialism. Rather than the organization per se, perhaps the focus should be the network in which organizations are embedded? Organizations similar to Benetton may be witness to the decline of a model of organization based on a number of sharp distinctions. The distinctions in question would include being 'in' and 'of' the organization as opposed to being 'out' of it, as well as between conception and execution. A complex functionally differentiated internal hierarchy, the classic Weberian bureaucracy in the superstructure, based upon an equally classic 'Fordist' substructure, may be being subject to replacement with what Perez (1985: 453) terms 'systemation', 'the new trend towards merging all activities — managerial and productive, white and blue collar, design and marketing, economic and technical — into one single interactive system'. We shall return to the implications of this 'new flexibility' later in the chapter. Let us note just one thing for the present: under conditions of a new flexibility then organization design may well allow of more variation than has hitherto been anticipated in contingency theory.

The Benetton model presents a clear example of one type of embeddedness of an organization form whose size and complexity would be somewhat
obscured by application of criteria which were premised only on a 'focal'
model of the organization. The Benetton we see is quite different if we look
only at the focal firm or if we look more broadly at the social relations in
which it is embedded. What makes Benetton possible, in part, is a sophisticated application of 'telematics' to enable a far more flexible manufacturing
system than an older, labour intensive organization could have achieved.

Benetton differs markedly from both an older 'sweat-shop' model of
'putting-out' in the garment industry by design-houses or from the divisionalized structure of other well-known 'brandname' manufacturers in the
fashion industry. Its most distinctive feature, from the perspective of an
interest in organization analysis, is the way in which it confounds assumptions about what the appropriate unit of this analysis should be.
Without entering into this in detail, it is clear that some aspects of the
Benetton story are specific to the fabric of social relations in the 'Third
Italy' of Emilia. Lest it be thought that with embeddedness one is dealing
with a purely local datum, specific only to Emilia or to the fashion industry,
or, mindful of Lorenz's (1988) analysis, only to 'high-tech' French engineering, we shall consider the case of East Asian enterprise. It will be seen that
similar characteristics of embeddedness structure the complex diversity of
organizational relationships which characterize economic action in the
Newly Industrialized Countries (NICs) of East Asia.

The protagonists of the 'culture' literature, such as in Peters and Waterman (1982), were responding to an economic threat which they perceived
as emanating from Japan. In their response what we find is a quest for
patterns of transformational leadership which would enable managers to
walk tall and be authentically American. It was the perceived difficulties
of American business in the face of the Japanese challenge which spurred
the renaissance in studies of 'organization culture' during the 1980s. To
many observers it seemed as if 'corporate culture' might be what gave the
Japanese their competitive edge and that was good reason enough for its
study. It was the 'threat' from Japan which captured 'culture' as a market-
able item. During the 1970s and into the 1980s, as conventional economic
criteria failed to capture the reasons for the economic success of Japanese
firms, this success increasingly became understood in terms of specifically
'cultural' phenomena.

These 'culturalist' accounts proved to be theoretically somewhat deficient,
precisely in terms of their 'over-socialized' conceptions. In fact, the proposed singularity and coherence of 'post-Confucian' culture cannot be
sustained upon detailed investigation (Hamilton and Biggart 1988; Clegg
1990b). Culturalist explanations in Confucian terms are too general, too
unspecific. Consider the vast canvass of 'East Asia'. While culture can

explain some common patterns across the East Asian societies, such as familism, it cannot explain the variations within and between these societies which are of considerable importance at the enterprise level (Hamilton and Biggart 1988). Moreover, if the cultural factors are deep rooted in the historical 'collective consciousness', why did they only become effective in the postwar era and under certain, diverse institutional conditions? It is an irony of contemporary sociology that factors which an earlier generation of scholars, such as Weber, saw as inimical to rational, efficient capitalism, should now be seen as central to its very essence!

While 'culture' does have a role to play in explanation it is not the role that adherents of the 'post-Confucian' ethic have proposed. 'Culture' requires re-specification in terms of institutional phenomena which both gain their specificity from and vary within and between national frameworks. While not denying the existence of 'efficiency' as an imperative, it is doubtful whether any single 'efficiency' oriented theory of organizations can be endorsed as the counter-factual example of French bread indicates. In contrast, arguments from culture which rely too readily on an overly functionalist, unitary conception of culture conceived as some kind of nationally homogeneous central value system from which all else flows are quite simply wrong, as the critics of the 'dominant ideology thesis' have established both empirically and theoretically (Abercrombie, Hill and Turner 1980).

Understanding is not enhanced by focussing on any univariate or single factor model which can be assumed to be appropriate for all countries, whether it is 'efficiency' or 'culture'. Social reality is too complex for any single factor model to adequately represent its processes. While 'efficiency' is not unimportant, as Weber knew only too well, its importance resided precisely in its symbolic value, as one of the highest cultural values of modernity. Few people want to be seen to be endorsing inefficiency. To not be for efficiency is tantamount to being against modernity! To be efficient is to be modern, it is to bask secure in one of the self-images of the age.

Countering the construction of explanations based on efficiency arguments involves constructing an account in such a way that it is clear that one is not placing a normative value on inefficiency (or conversely efficiency) so the best line of critique is empirical and counter-factual. If the arguments from efficiency predict a certain state of affairs, such as the triumph of divisional organization structures in certain product markets or industries, then the provision of just one counter-factual case destroys the generality of the theory. Thus, one way of under-cutting efficiency arguments as explanations of organisation form is through furnishing counter-factual cases. The analysis of French bread above provided such a case. Here is a product, bread, and an industry which throughout most of the advanced capitalist world confirms the outcomes predicted from efficiency theory, but France is different. The production of a staple product of advanced industrial capitalist societies, it seems, is capable of interpretation through diverse modes of rationality.

Building Embedded Theory through Modes of Rationality

The major thrust of 'efficiency' as explanation of organization forms has been towards predicting convergence in the range, found in modernity, suggesting the pressure of efficiency leads on a global basis to more and more organizations becoming less and less different from each other. Diversity, is thus an indication of 'underdevelopment'. Clearly, if one were to establish a significant number of organization forms which were unquestionably 'of' and 'in' modernity, and which were at the same time distinctly different from the form that one might predict from an efficiency perspective, then this would represent a further undercutting of the argument from efficiency to modernity as something which gives rise to only a rather limited range of organizational experience. Consideration of material from East Asia provides such an argument (e. g. Clegg, Higgins and Spybey 1990; Hamilton and Biggart 1988).

Organizations are embedded in ways which the conventional distinction between organizations as focal objects of analysis and their environments does not sufficiently capture. Had one studied French bread through an analysis purely of its 'small business' organization form, in a cross-sectional framework, it is doubtful whether one would have arrived at the insights which Bertaux and Bertaux-Wiame (1981) were able to generate from their deeply embedded account. One would have looked to a whole range of other phenomena 'outside' the organizations in question. Where organizations find their expression in institutionally framed and culturally embedded terms of relationships which structure the field of force in which they are constituted, then the appropriate object of analysis is composed of the diverse rationalities of these relationships, rather than the structural features of a central but limited element of them. Again, this aspect comes out clearly in reference to the East Asian materials, particularly those from Taiwan (Hamilton and Biggart 1988).

From a perspective of cultural embeddedness the appropriate object of analysis is less likely to be 'the organization' per se. At the centre of analytical focus one is more likely to find the cultural and institutional frameworks which facilitate the diverse forms of calculation and modes of rationalities within which are constituted networks of organizational relations. The actual form that organizations take occurs within the specification of these features. Organizations are human fabrications. They are made out of whatever materials come to hand, can be modified or adopted. Organizations are concocted out of whatever recipe-knowledge is locally available. Thus, a contingency framework certainly appears to be appropriate for organization analysis, but it would be one where 'context-free' contingencies vary not only organizationally but also in terms of national institutional patterns. The variation in the latter, it will be proposed, may be such as to 'over-determine' the former.

In the early stages of modernity it was quite natural that the fabricators of organizations would draw from the material culture of their immediate institutional environment. Such environments are frequently constituted in national terms and instilled with value in cultural terms (Anderson 1983). For instance, the values of the peasantry in France, their peasant culture, were essential to the reproduction of the *boulangerie* into the late twentieth century in not only an urban but also a rural location. It was the characteristic values, forming the strategies and modes of rationality of *les boulangers*, derived from this peasant background, a background which is indubitably nationally framed, which enable the French to have their baguette and eat it.

We have seen clearly that if *les boulangers* were unable to trust their loans to the potential next-generation of breadmakers then the baguette could hardly be taken for granted. This premise of trust is actually not at all unusual in organizational action: as Lorenz (1988: 198) puts it, 'If transaction costs are thought of as friction in the economy, then trust can be seen as an extremely effective lubricant'. Organizations operate in uncertain environments deploying the calculations of agents whose rationality can never be unbounded or unlimited. These problems of boundedness and uncertainty are compounded when organizations externalize their recurrent routines and relations to agencies which are outside their control or authority. Under such conditions trust .becomes more than usually expedient. It is what makes forms of action calculable as elements in modes of rationality constructed as responses to uncertain environments and limited knowledge.

Recently, these concerns have been framed as a central issue for the substantive concerns of the sociology of organizations in terms of a choice between adopting a culture-free perspective as against one which stresses cultural specificity (Child and Kieser 1979). Within organization studies the strongest proponents of the former are contingency theorists such as the Aston school (e. g. Donaldson 1985) who provide an organization-level specification of the thesis of convergence (see Clegg and Dunkerley 1980: ch. 6, for a general discussion). The latter position has been associated with writers with more of an anthropological than a managerial or sociological orientation, perhaps because they are more disciplinarily attuned to difference. Crozier (1964) is probably the best known example in mainstream organization analysis.

One study which sought to test the extent to which cultural specificity enters into organizational contingencies was the comparison of German and British organizations conducted by Child and Kieser (1979). Briefly, they found that on standardized Aston data a sample of German organizations was consistently more centralized than the British one, something which they put down to specific cultural effects. It was suggested that these effects over-determined more generalized institutional effects such as the impact of models of 'good' and efficient' practice retailed by international consulting agencies. Models derived from this provenance should tend to produce more of a convergence as they erode the value-basis of cultural specificity, in this case a German predisposition towards more centralized control.

The institutional frameworks within which organizations are embedded may frequently contain quite divergent and contradictory pressures, as Child and Kieser's (1979) research suggests. It will be a matter of local detail, the embeddedness of cultural resistance and the prescriptive power of external regulative agencies as to the resolution of these institutional pressures in specific settings. One might anticipate that convergence on the context-free contingencies of organizational design will be lower where the embeddedness of cultural resistance is high, where agents are able to draw on cultural reserves of great specificity. Alternatively, where institutional frameworks and pressures of regulation (in particular, by professions such as law and accounting, and by government and the state) have a highly developed specificity, then context-free contingencies may well be shaped in nationally specific ways.

Within the perspective employed here organizations are conceptualized as a multiplicity of centres of power (also see Clegg 1989b). Within the organizational arena agents with varying strategies are seen to struggle to constitute the capacities of the organization in policy terms which represent their conceptions of their interests. In so doing, they will bargain with whatever resources can be constituted as strategic. Such resources may be located either within or without the organizational arena. It is not just that there are resources waiting to be activated: rather, these are constituted in struggles which may be represented discursively as diverse ways of being 'rational' in Weber's sense of substantive rationality. Hence they may be termed 'modes of rationality'.

Structures of dominance articulate around more or less abstract cultural values and achieve their expression through organizationally situated actions and vocabularies of motive (Mills 1940). These are the normal ways of accounting for action. It is through such 'accounting' that one may make reference to the socially available and publically accountable complexes of reasons with which one might seek to justify organizational actions. Such 'rationalities' when considered collectively may be seen as 'modes' of rationality. No assumption of 'unity' or 'coherence' should be read into this designation. It is quite conceivable that organizations, and the agents located in and around them, may construct diverse and simultaneous rationalities which cohere neither across space nor through time.

Modes of rationality are built out of locally available conceptions which embed economic action. These may be derived either from local custom or practice, as these have been shaped either by culture or by the institutional framing of available vocabularies of motive. Consider an example taken from the construction industry in Britain. There is a dominant mode of rationality of the key agents involved in the contractual relations which constitute the construction-site. The contract is central to any understanding of what occurs on site. It stands as the reason for the site-organization's existence, because if there were no contract there would be no site. The contract also determines the categories of occupational action one will encounter on the site, as well as the nature and types of activity, working to what plans and what schedule, using what material, and so on.

The contract provides for just about everything other than its own interpretation. Its meaning is never exactly clear. It is rare indeed that a contract can be read without the need for interpretation of what ethnomethodologists call the 'indexical particulars'. These are aspects of the interpretation of the documents which cannot depend upon their interpretation by 'disinterested' agents. Agents such as the contractor, sub-contractor, consultants, architect's office and client will routinely seek to interpret the inherent 'indexicality'of the contract to their advantage. The fact is that understanding the contract is never a self-evident process. The contract does not smooth out the transaction and eliminate costs; in fact, it generates costs and conflicts. Contracts always have to be interpreted, they never provide for their own interpretation. Consequently, conflict is endemic to the construction industry and much of it arises from the contractual relations rather than in spite of the contractual relations. The major resources for seeking to fix diverse interpretations, which always involve different conceptions of interest, are the relations of power/knowledge which are present in the division of labour, particularly the professional division of labour. Occupational identities, knowledges and practices are resources for striving to secure interpretation fixed on one's own terms, rather than those of some other parties to the contract. Consequently, the modes of rationality which are characteristic of the construction industry are deployed around diverse modes of accomplishing the calculations appropriate to 'professional' interpretations. From the contractor's point of view this all occurs within the dominance of the 'profit principle' as a form of life. Indeed, where the reproduction of this principle seems unlikely, for whatever reason, on any particular project, the indexicality of the contractual documents offers an opportunity for attempts at renegotiation of the contract in order to better secure the profit principle. (All this is discussed at length in Clegg [1975]).

The modes of rationality of French bakers are a contrary case. Here everything hinges on negotiating and securing interpretations of common interest which bind formally non-contractual parties such that at the end of their careers and prior to their retirement they find it quite rational to lend a great deal of their savings in order that some post-apprentice in the trade may be able to buy their business as a going concern. The key mechanism securing reproducibility of this organization form is the trust which they extend to these others, people tied to them only by the experience of working in a bakery, being married and wanting to be their own *boulanger*.

Both trust and contracts are defined by the cultures of local knowledge and local practice. These may be composed out of a complex pot-pourri of ingredients. One may be dealing with aspects of a traditional local culture, an occupational or organizational culture, or the clashes between them. One may be dealing with the way in which frames of meaning are subject to regulation by legislation, the norms of professional practice, or rationalized bureaucracy. Even contracts, seemingly the most rational and transcendent of forms, when studied empirically in local practice, require large elements of trust which may not be forthcoming for all sorts of good economic reasons which have nothing to do with the 'trustworthiness' of the parties but everything to do with substantively rational action.

Elements of trust are frequently at the centre of the embeddedness of economic action (see Gambetta 1988; Fox 1974). Trust, along with a limited range of other devices such as the structuring of members' (and clients', customers' etc.) conceptions of their self-interests in ways which are compatible with organizationally approved actions, serves to produce 'rationalities' conducive to organizational understanding: that is, stable patterns of action extending beyond immediate co-presence and through space and time. The rationalities which can be called upon tend, in the first instance, to derive from whatever seems to work best in a particular environment. They are culturally available in a particular place and time. Here, elements of the population ecology argument are useful. Innovation may occur for all sorts of contingent reasons and when it does some forms will tend to survive and be reproduced with a greater frequency than will others. Thus, organizations may well persist in displaying the characteristics which attended their formation, as Stinchcombe (1965) suggests. The structure of organizations is 'sedimented' as different concerns and issues are laid down in it. Sedimentation will occur particularly as organizations have to take on functions to deal with aspects of their institutional environment which are externally mandated by authoritative regulation, by government, for instance, which seeks to see that organizations comply with some statutory objectives, such as being equal opportunity employers or ecologically acceptable manufacturers or disposers of waste. Frequently, the criteria of regulation are developed in the context of professional practice, as DiMaggio and Powell (1983) have suggested. What survives organizationally may not be most 'efficient' but survives because at some time in the past of the organization it came to be instilled with value in that specific institutional context. It is this which is the essential insight of the institutional school. Things, forms and practices may well be valued for and in themselves, irrespective of their contribution to the efficiency of the organization. Historically one might think of the place that the latin mass once had in the Roman Catholic church or the role that the confessional still plays. Such practices do not necessarily make priests more efficient but they are valued as legitimate icons in their own right. They are constitutive parts of a ceremonial fabric with an explicable past cultural context.

At the centre of analysis will be organizational agencies. Such agencies may be individuals or they may be collective agencies of some sort which have developed mechanisms for both the calculation and the representation of interests. They are able to make these calculations through the various discursive forms available to them. In particular, one thinks of the articulation of the various scientific, technical and other knowledges which constitute the primary occupational identities and resources of organizational agencies. Other sources of discursive availability will be drawn from whatever regulative (i. g.: political, legal, economic, accounting etc.) and local frameworks of meaning present themselves, as well as from the many competing sources of value representation which surround any agency.

'Local' refers to specific sites of organizations, sites which empirically offer a plenitude of possible meanings and memberships with which to organize or to resist. Consequently, what are constituted as local frameworks of meaning may be embedded in an infinite variety of contexts. In Hong Kong, for instance, it would be an imprudent Chinese organization which did not consult the *feng-shui* specialist in designing its buildings, moving into new offices, choosing a chief executives office or determining the layout of the furniture, the location of doors and windows. It should be clear from the colourful example of *feng-shui* that in considering local context one is thinking of the discourse of various substantive rationalities which are capable of being regarded as 'ultimate values' of some kind: discourses pertaining to represent the interest of efficiency, of equality, of the market, of the ecology, of *feng-shui*, of a specific ethnicity or place. Indeed, almost any abstractions can be expressed as icons of modernity.

Practices in and around organizations will be constructed on the contested terrain of these various knowledges. It is by no means clear that the outcome of these struggles will always be decided in terms of the technically rational, as the success of 'green' values should serve to demonstrate. Whichever values achieve stable articulation as necessary nodal points through which organizational discourse must pass become what Weber referred to as 'principles of dominance (see Clegg 1989b for a discussion of 'necessary nodal points'). The triumph of efficiency has no necessity attached to it.

What is constituted as efficiency is itself subject to the processes which have been described. As Weber was well aware, efficiency is a term derived from the discourse of accounting conventions which vary widely with national frameworks. Principles of domination are derived from the complex fabric of the surrounding material culture of members' knowledges and the practices which these knowledges can be claimed to license, to authorize, to enable or to approve. Where these practices can be represented as the principal conduits serving decisive ultimate values, such as efficiency, in the context in question they are that much more secure against the strategic play of alternate discursive forms. An empirical specification of these views is presented in Fligstein's (1985) findings that organizational power, expressed in terms of occupational identities and knowledges, was a major factor in organization structuring, a finding supported by data which showed that in different historical periods, different departments were likely to control large firms and to do so for different reasons. Thus, as the rules of the game shifted different issues became the critical issues for considerations of organization strategy. Each set of critical issues stood in determinate relationships privileging specific forms of occupational knowledge in the organizational division of labour, giving different personnel the advantage in terms of the rules of the game. The rules were nationally specific and shaped by the institutional framework structured by that specific nation state. Since theoretically, 'power' and 'institutional' perspectives are interpenetrated what facilitates power is rules and rules are institutionally structured. Discursive forms of knowledge and the practices which are coterminous with them are not random, happenstance or merely contingent. They are actions produced and reproduced according to rules which are constructed, reconstructed, transformed and innovated through practice. In the same way that an evidently material structure such as a building is an application (and sometimes and extension or innovation) of design, engineering and other construction rules, so an organization form is only a marginally less material structure composed through available rules. Taken together, where these achieve dominance in and as an organization form they display a 'mode of rationality'.

As suggested earlier, the specificities of local practice should be seen as a reservoir of potential resistance to the contingent pressures of organizations. We can view instances of French artisanal bakery and project manager's strategies on construction sites in this light, as well as the struggles which took place over wages and enterprise unions in the immediate postwar era in Japan. There are also pressures which are institutionally derived which may go either with or against the grain of some local practices. Even within a single overarching framework, such as post-Confucianism, the institutional fabric may be cut quite differently. In one place it is subsumed to the local warp and weft of the cultural context; elsewhere it derives less from local cultural practices and more from the regulative aspects of the national institutional framework. In either case, the outcomes tend rather more to organizational diversities than they do to a rationalized convergence on a collective fate inside a common iron-cage. These issues are explored in the next section.

Asian Business: Ethnicity and Family as Resources for Rationality in East Asia

East Asia has been a test bed for much cultural theory as well as a death bed for a great deal of economic theory. Of interest here is the way in which it offers relevant examples of diverse forms of 'embeddedness'. In the many countries in the region which have an ethnically dominant Chinese business elite, familialism is the basic building-block of modes of rationality. Organization structures are embedded in family values. In other places the state has a far more important role in embedding economic action.

In East Asian countries where economic action is constructed from institutional values defined in terms of a particular aspect of Chinese familial lineage rules, which are based on patrilineage and equal rights of inheritance between sons, assets are distributed equally but authority is highly age-stratified. The eldest son inherits the mantle of elder from the father. Authority is due to the elder as the first-born. As Hamilton and Biggart note:

'Because all males remain in the line of descent, the patrilineage quickly expands within just a few generations ... Equally privileged sons connected to networks of relatives create a situation of bifurcated loyalties, with wealth itself becoming a measure of one's standing in the community of relatives. Accordingly, conflict between sons is ubiquitous, intralineage rivalries are common, and linage segmentation is the rule.' (1988: S84)

It is from these that much of the characteristic mode of rationality of Chinese family business organizations is derived. Historically, as Redding (1990) observes, within the Chinese business community there have been good reasons for keeping business within the family and as far away from rapacious outside interests as possible, particularly those associated with the imperial state and its bureaucracy. Contemporary experience, both on the mainland and in many of the overseas contexts in which Chinese business activity flourishes, would have done little to change this view on the part of many for whom it is now almost instinctive.

Chinese businesses have typically developed as small family-ran firms in which there is strong patrimonial and personalistic direct control, rather than relying on the more impersonal, formalized and standardized control of the rational-legal bureaucratic model which we are familiar with from the West (for example, see Wong 1985; 1988; Redding 1990). Control is equally personalistic when it covers inter-organizational linkages which are premised on individuals one can 'trust' and who are 'face-worthy' (Redding 1990). These personalistic relations connect both backwards to sources of supply and forwards to markets for the company's product or service, employing a complex web of putting-out and contracting systems, satellite factory systems and distributional systems based on particularistic and personalistic ties (Hamilton and Biggart 1988: S85).

Redding (1990) has referred to the Chinese family business form as 'a family fortress'. Consequently, Chinese family businesses rarely grow in the way that one would credit from a knowledge of either strategy and structure or markets and hierarchies. They are clearly not irrational but their mode of rationality is derived from a quite different agenda than that which is apparent from reading the disembedded accounts of undersocialized agents which dominate a great deal of organization theory.

The Chinese family business is organized with the contingency, or ultimate value, of inheritance as uppermost. The head of the household heads the firm. The central tasks of managerial surveillance and control are kept, wherever possible, within the family. There is a substantial motive for continuous bifurcation or innovation of new enterprises given the combination of familism and patrilineally equal inheritance. As a company prospers, the profits can be used to start other enterprises which sons or, less frequently, other family members will run. When the founder-father dies sons inherit the assets for which they were stewards during their father's life. In turn, they follow the same pattern in running their business in relation to their own sons. Principles of divisibility, familial control and strategic management of the asset-base in the long-term interests of the family are the structures of dominance within which Chinese business modes of rationality are constructed.

In many respects such characteristics are those of a small family business anywhere but close observers of the form such as Redding (1990) see the Chinese business specificity in the fact that characteristics of small scale, such as paternalism, personalism, opportunism and flexibility are retained, even where organizations grow to a larger scale. What the form of company management does not have is as important as what it does have. It is rare to find the same degree of professionalization, specialization, credentialization, 'careerization', formalization, standardization, legitimation, impersonalization and 'disciplinization' in these organizations as in comparable organizations in the West. It is not just that the companies are located at different points on scales of these variables, Redding suggests, but that the variables themselves are simply not foremost in the way in which Chinese organizations operate. Familism as the central principle of the operating core militates against any wider sharing of trust as a basis upon which decentralization might operate and structure develop. Legitimate authority springs only from ownership and ownership is a strictly family business. Such an inviolable fortress is particularly dependent upon both the quality of the family's genetic pool and the wisdom of its example as a means of organizational reproduction. In practice this means a strong cultural commitment to an autocratic, didactic and patrimonial style as the modus operandi of choice for if assets are to remain safe for the family, preserving family honour and standing there is a moral obligation of responsible stewardship on the leader. This responsibility cannot be taken lightly and its burden is expressed in terms of an ethic of direct control of relationships. Thus, direct business control is not simply some primitive form of managerial skill which will eventually be overtaken by technical bureaucratic control: it is intentionally striven for and replicated as sons set up their own businesses. No guarantees exist that elder sons will inherit if they 'shame-face' or show themselves unworthy in some other way.

The tensions which patrimonial control can give rise to, between members of the same family jockeying for influence over the control of the assets in the succession process are a source of fission and schism which cannot easily be contained within the fabric of an autocrat's control where that person is convinced that he (it is usually a he but not always) knows best. It is far easier to establish one's own sphere for autonomy/autocracy rather than to battle for that of an elder. Chinese business organizations thus remain relatively small and relatively unstructured but far more centralized than is usual in the West.

Not only are Chinese family businesses a different type of organization in their internal characteristics: they are also different in their external linkages. Intra-organizational linkages are based less on the family and more on clan and regional networks, as well as personal ties, and the maintenance of face within these. It is from these networks and ties that most capital is raised, normally in an informal manner, untouched by legal agreements or contracts. Where the networks are successful they seem to function in a similar fashion to the 'inner circles' of Western business that Useem (1979) has studied as far as the exchange of information is concerned. Transaction costs are trimmed greatly if the overheads of eternal vigilance of those others with whom one does business can be avoided. Where trust operates effectively, then legally institutionalized surveillance, arbitration and conciliation costs can be avoided. The core organizational activities of producing particular goods or services can be focused upon and budgeted for to a much greater extent while there is less development of highly specialized and expensive technical knowledge-applications in the organization, both in terms of capital resources and skill resources. Since firms tend to be small, are unlikely to be capital-intensive and seldom involve multiple discrete knowledge-based skills, the coordinative overhead costs associated with large types of organization are avoided.

One consequence of this reliance on trust, however, is to greatly restrict the circles from whom a businessman may draw resources, particularly those of capital and non-recourse to institutionally regulated sources of capital, together with the particularism of managerial practices, leads to considerable overhead costs even as transaction costs are economized. The complexities of managing networks of trust tend to limit their number and thus 'contribute to keeping businesses fairly small and investment patterns directed towards conglomerate accumulations rather than vertical integration' (Hamilton and Biggart 1988: S85).

The overseas Chinese business organizations of places such as Taiwan and Hong Kong are examples of firms whose modes of rationality derive very clearly from the culturally embedded local resources of familism and clannism. This produces organizations which do not behave at all as they should if they were rationally efficient in terms of the precepts of efficiency theory, which is not to say that they are either inefficient or irrational. The usual kinds of economic indicators demonstrate that they are indeed efficient and rational. This is one mode of rationality, one which has its drawbacks as other operating modes do too. Modes of rationality always display some strengths and weaknesses. The weaknesses of the Chinese family business, with its mode of rationality constructed around an ultimate value of family, surrounded by loyalties derived from clan and locale, and a structure of dominance which is heavily personalistic and autocratic, are evident. The degree of particularism makes it difficult for those outside the charmed circles ever to gain admittance.

Differences of perspective indicate strengths or weaknesses, however, and when seen from an 'inside' perspective some aspects of organisational practice that to an outsider might seem to be weaknesses may, in fact, be seen as strengths. For instance, the fact that the majority of organizations constructed according to this mode of rationality produce relatively small organizations which find it difficult to grow and to expand is hardly a weakness if personal direct control is taken as an ultimate value. However, it does mean one is constantly running up against the limits of personal surveillance from which even a modicum of organizational systematicity, in terms of formalization or standardization might deliver one and hence may be seen as a weakness.

Another instance of a weakness which may have some strengths is factionalism, something which has been observed to be particularly rife. Conflict, as sociologists have long known, has its functions (Coser 1956). Familial factionalism, if not too poisonous and if well-managed, may serve as a competitive framework within which rival ideas may flourish, existing practices be improved and innovation arise. Where the cultural grain and the organizational form together conspire against upwards initiative this may be especially valuable.

Other aspects of Chinese business organisation, however, do create persistent problems, such as that of how to arrange managerial succession where the pool of possible talent is unduly restricted by mechanisms which extend trust only to those who are family. As well as limiting innovation, complexity and size this often shows up in problems in the third generation, the generation which has never known the hardships and commitments which their fathers and their fathers' fathers went through in building the assets whose fruits have, perhaps, become taken for granted, and who choose other, more intrinsically interesting and often, in the context, counter-cultural interests. This, however, is also a problem in Western family businesses, as many studies have shown.

As already emphasised, overseas Chinese organizations in Taiwan and Hong Kong remain small. Little external regulation is applied to them either directly by the state or indirectly through professional practice which might serve to encourage or promote growth. Both the Taiwanese and Hong Kong states are markedly laissez-faire in their regulation of the business environment, even though they are highly regulatory elsewhere (for instance, in the housing market in Hong Kong and in military, defence and foreign affairs matters in Taiwan). Chinese family business in Hong Kong and Taiwan clearly have developed specific forms of organization which capitalize on the cultural capital of familism, clan and locale, in order to produce a form which has flourished in the niche of ethnicity in ways which, on a more market or contingency based set of expectations, one would not have predicted. As a form, these organizations typically do not develop great complexity or size even though some of them dominate industries, like bicycle transport in Taiwan. In overseas Chinese organizations the local resources of a specifically 'Chinese' culture dominate in modes of organisational rationality and the institutional framework is experienced primarily in terms of cultural reserves, rather than as a regulatory environment.

Institutional Frameworks and Resources for Rationality in East Asia

When we consider the other major NICs in the East Asian context it is clear that in South Korea, Japan and Singapore the state is a far more pervasive actor and institutional regulator than is familism. It is the institutional framework of the state which is decisive in the constitution of modes of rationality. In Japan and South Korea state intervention takes an explicitly economic cast, while in Singapore, as well as being involved in major housing subvention, the state is an extremely active practitioner of a moral regulation in which attempts at cultural manipulation are explicit (Wilkinson 1986). In the cases of Japan and South Korea the building-blocks of rationality are located in practices which have a far greater institutional framing in the regulatory context than they do in local reserves of culture.

In some respects the conclusion of the last paragraph may strike one as surprising if one is familiar with some of the Western views of Japanese organizational success which frequently attribute the success to culturally specific factors. What might appear as quite naturally a cultural matter to an outside observer, dazzled by the charms of difference, may in fact be the result of institutional arrangements which have very few roots in a specific culture. One may identify as 'cultural', and thus relatively unchangeable, something which is in fact far more of an institutional fabrication cut from cloth which displays little specific cultural influence in its design. For instance, in each of Taiwan, South Korea, Japan and Singapore industrialization has been actively promoted by the state. Initially this was in terms of a product life cycle pattern in which the initial post-war era of import substitution switched to an era of primarily low-wage labour assembly zones. More recently the transition has been into contemporary export-led growth premised on high technology development (Cummings 1984; Ting 1986). (The city state of Hong Kong, with the PRC cheap labour zone in its backyard, where during the 1980s two and a half million low-level jobs were generated in neighbouring Guandong province, is rather different in this respect). The state policies under which these transformations occurred were in each case somewhat different. As a result, the impact of state regulation on the availability of vocabularies of motive for constituting modes of rationality has differed.

In South Korea the process of industrial transformation is very much top-down. Organizations are expected to work within frameworks which government makes available. Planning is centralized, implementation forced, control is direct and bureaucratic for public enterprises and routed through financial controls on banks and the supply of credit for the private sector (Hamilton and Biggart 1988: S77; sourced from Bunge 1982: 115; Mason et al. 1980: 257; Westphal et al. 1984: 510)). There is no ideology of a liberal, neutral or laissez faire state. Instead, South Korea has a strongly interventionist, proactive and coercive state actively pushing a very definite policy line on the benefits of 'bigness': state policies encourage economic concentration for large enterprises and government regulation for many medium-sized ones. It is therefore clear that the major reason why organizations are so much bigger in South Korea than elsewhere in East Asia is that the state makes them bigger. The chief contingency in organization growth and size is political will, its effective implementation and regulation. At the organization level modes of rationality have to be geared towards the all-pervasive facts of state regulation. The strategies which sustain familism in Hong Kong or Taiwan have little play here.

The state in South Korea has a peculiar pervasiveness, born in part out of the fragile legitimacy it has had throughout its existence. South Korea is clearly the least stable of the East Asian NICs and has had the highest levels of labour and political mobilization. The factors which contribute to both state dominance and instability seem to be tied up with aspects both of the country's route to modern industrialization and state development. The route to 'modernity' has been founded on the creation of very large, centralized urban enterprises, in which an independent unionism has flourished, despite official sanction against it and this labour organization has become a major actor in the struggles for democracy which characterize South Korea. Koo (1987: 11) has noted, 'Frequent state intervention in labour conflicts [has] led to the politicization of labour relations and to the development of an alliance between the labor movement and other political movements'. Thus, of the East Asian economies, South Korea has the industrial structure which is closest to that which Marx in the 'Communist Manifesto' thought most conducive to proletarian class formation. It is also a nation which has long had a vociferous and highly political student body. Workers and students together confront a state regime which differs significantly from those of the other East Asian countries under consideration.

South Korea was founded in the immediate post war era in close concert with the leading industrial enterprises and in alliance with a landlord class whose legitimacy was tarnished by war-time collaboration with the Japanese colonialists. Consequently, the South Korean state, suggests Koo (1987), has never enjoyed civil hegemony. It continues to use 'systematic torture' in order 'to intimidate and suppress political opposition ... carried out with the tacit approval of senior officials' (International Commission of Jurists Report on South Korea; Sydney Morning Herald, January 14, 1988: 10). (Not that the other East Asian NICs are immune to charges of considerable official neglect of what are the norms and procedures of their own constitutions with respect to the use of forced confessions, torture and due process, as McCormack (1986) and Igarashi (1986) discuss with respect to Japan.) The state and economic action have been closely interlinked in South Korea from the outset.

While the South Korean state has not enjoyed civil hegemony, nor have the post-war Taiwanese, Japanese, and Singaporean states: Hong Kong's legitimacy was premised less on its state form and more on its being an industrially and capitalistically dynamic haven for refugees fleeing from Chinese Communism. Civil hegemony does not just happen and state and organizational relations are not necessarily imbued with legitimate authority. Hegemony has to be produced and re-produced and where it does not have a strong root a strong state may indeed be a necessity. The East Asian NICs have expended considerable effort on 'manufacturing consent' (Burawoy 1979. See also Sugimoto (1986) for Japan and Wilkinson (1986) for Singapore, in particular). With the partial exception of South Korea, which has strong civil movements for democratization, NIC states have had considerable success in quelling opposition. They have done so on the basis of continuous and strong economic growth and prosperity. The role of the state must enter into specific explanations for the economic success of the East Asian NICs. It is essential to shaping the fabric within which institutional frameworks serve to structure modes of rationality through regulation.

Although it was once the colonial power whose hegemonic sway extended over South Korea, Japan state formation is quite different. The popular outside perception of Japanese public organisation is as 'Japan Inc.'. In this the focus is invariably on the Ministry of International Trade and Industry (MITI) and sometimes the Ministry of Finance and the Economic Planning Board and the 'Japanese Industrial System' is indeed characterised by 'constant and quite detailed levels of interaction between executives in the corporate sector and the government ministries, even among low level officials, in an attempt to reach overall consensus on a coherent and long range vision of the forward direction of the economy' (McMillan 1984: 44). In this development, interaction is not between atomistic enterprises and a coercive government: organizations in the private sector are generally formed into intermarket groups which are as cohesive as government organizations. The latter, particularly MITI, administratively guide economic calculation and aid the formulation of specifically Japanese modes of economic rationality. MITI's role with respect to administrative guidance is not simply confined to the better known aspects of 'industry planning' which writers like Johnson (1982) have focused on with respect to industrial decline and renewal, (see the discussion in Ewer, Higgins and Stevens [1987] for instance), but reaches down to guide the important small business and sub-contracting sector:

'MITI has developed a number of programs to assist the small business sector, including the establishment of the Small Business Promotion Corporation, provision of technical guidance and subsidies for R & D, policies for accelerated depreciation for certain machinery and facilities, programs for management consulting and management education, encouragement of cooperatives formed through prefectual federations of small business associations, regulation of sub-contracting relations, and funding of the Small Business Investment Company. In all there are sixteen major laws on small business in Japan (ten passed since 1961) which both individually and in combination with Japan's Fundamental Law of Small-Medium Enterprises, passed in 1963, form an integrated framework for small business development. Not only is the tenor of this legislation interventionist in flavour and biased towards "eliminating the barriers associated with smallness", it is aimed at making the small sector modern and efficient within the context of the total economy.' (McMillan 1984: 59–60).

What eventuates is a complex set of stable relations governing 'horizontal' access by firms to financial resources and the vertical integration of satellite sub-contractors into the orbit of the big-name firms. It is the stability of these relations which appears to be crucial.

A key component of the vocabularies of motive from which modes of rationality may be constructed is the forms of financial calculation which frame managerial action, the centre of Weber's (1976) classic analysis. In Korea, organisational networks are highly structured from the state downwards, while in Taiwan and Hong Kong they are far more horizontal, working through kin, clan and locale. In Japan, straightforward state regulation of banks, channelling semi-public funds directly into manufacturing, and strong institutional links, including a system of 'stable shareholders' who take up new share issues in manufacturing firms and undertake not to trade in them, help to produce a highly stable framework in which planning can occur. In recent years, however, the relationship with banks has become somewhat weaker. Many firms have begun to rely more on the stock market and on internally generated funds (Kosai and Ogino 1984). Both bank and internal sourcing ensure that stable frameworks for calculation can be constituted at the enterprise level. Within the *keiretsu* and the inter-market groups stable sources of finance and share holding have been organized as well as more general matters of strategic policy. Those firms which are members of 'independent groups', groups that are vertically rather than horizontally organized, typically cluster around a big name firm. Such firms organize satellite subcontractors and are interlinked through stable mutual shareholdings with other enterprise groups. At least part of the Japanese answer to the need for integrated financing, manufacturing and market structures thus emerges.

A similar integration is achieved in South Korea with different mechanisms. Here the enterprise groups (*chaebol*) are usually owned and controlled by a single person or family and generally operate in a single industrial sector. They do not rely on stable sub-contracting relations but vertically incorporate most component producers. While control is associationally negotiated in Japanese firms, in the South Korean enterprise it is familially unified. Consequently while the negotiation of trust and financial stability is achieved in Japan by highly organized joint stockholding, in Korea it is achieved by family control and financing, together with board links to government controlled financial institutions, the major source of externally generated capital. Family control ensures continuity of purpose and ownership.

Family control also characterizes overseas Chinese organizations, such as are found in Taiwan, but there family sources of finance are of most importance (Orrù, Biggart and Hamilton (1988: 22) report that over 60 per cent of capital is derived from family and friends). Consequently, business groups here are familially inter-linked through individual family members holding positions in multiple firms. In Taiwan this linkage occurs within the context of a state which, in respect of the export sector, offers effective support through mechanisms such as special tax breaks and export zones (Gold 1986; Amsden 1985) as well as strong regulation of one part of the savings area of the financial sector. In Taiwan state planning of a strong regulatory or indicative type with social concerns appears to be absent, with the consequence that Taiwan has had one of the most polluting and polluted of post-war industrial developments.

Conclusion

The discussion above clearly indicates that the state form varies widely in these East Asian economies, as does the extent which local cultural resources are drawn on and it is thus not surprising to find there is a great diversity of organization forms, ranging from the primarily market co-ordinated multiplicity of small, family controlled, sub-contracting Taiwanese firms, characteristic of overseas Chinese business, to the large hierarchically, impersonally controlled Japanese enterprise groups, the even larger South Korean state financed enterprises or the major sector of Singaporean foreign owned multinationals. All such evidence suggests that efficient performance cannot be adduced solely to the level of organization variables (Orrù, Biggart and Hamilton 1988). Measures of typical organization size characteristic of the states in question do not strongly or easily correlate in terms of national growth rates, as a measure of the overall effectiveness of the economy and typical enterprise size depends very much on the state's role in developing the economy, in shaping the capital market, in regulating inter-organizational relations, and so on. Moreover, while the market may be important in explanation of Taiwan and Hong Kong, it is of less importance in Japan than an appreciation of the role of the Japanese Industrial System (McMillan, 1984) or, for instance, that of the state corporations in the financing of enterprises in South Korea. Singapore also represents a singular case. Neither the state nor families are the major loci of capital formation due to the preponderance of foreign investment in Singapore. The multi- national penetration of Singapore, much of it Japanese as well as British and American, is not mirrored as extensively elsewhere.

It would thus seem that major contingencies derived from culture, markets, the state and organizational characteristics carry differential explanatory weight in each case, as a different balance of factors comes into play. The picture is of organizations constructed under contingent pressure, where local practices are the ultimate contingency. These practices may be sources of resistance to rationalizing pressures from markets, efficiency, ecology and institutions or they may be facilitative. Everything will hinge on the modes of rationality which agencies in and around organizations construct, on the material that is stressed in its fabrication. In one place it may be familism 'overdetermining' economic rationalism and pressures towards greater efficiency and goodness of fit of contingencies and structure in the Chinese form; in another it may the economic rationalism which deploys a local peasant culture to reproduce businesses, retirements, and baguettes; in another it may be the power and strategic control of capital resources by the state which exerts pressures towards the reproduction of extremely large organizations.

Are Chinese family businesses any less 'rational' than South Korean *chaebol*? Is French bread an 'irrational' product in the same way that a Taiwanese bicycle is? Only from a perspective which is ignorant of the rationalities which the agents themselves construct, of the local practices which enter into its fabrication and reproduction.

At the heart of rationalization stands material culture, sometimes resisting, sometimes bending, but never discountable, together with the enveloping frame of the state and national institutions, within which organizational forms are fabricated. The material reviewed shows that across countries there are clear diversities between contemporary forms of organization. The contrasts can be attributed to the different modes of rationality available for organizational fabrication in diverse settings. These differences result from the interplay of local cultures with processes of institutional framing and regulation which derive both from the state and from other agencies of rationalization. It is from this matrix of possibilities that resources are drawn for power-play within organizations.

Certain universalistic contingency theories of organization which seek to use 'effectiveness' to explain the ascendancy of only a limited number of organization forms are not quite as universalistic in scope as they might appear to be. Not only can one distinguish significant counterfactuals, particularly in the economically successful East Asian cases but these counterfactuals themselves conform to no one precise structural form. Rather than universal convergence on a dominant organization form, there appears to be a considerable range of what Cole (1973) once referred to, in the context of Japan, as 'functional alternatives'. Organizations per se are not necessarily the sole most appropriate theoretical object with which to construct a sociology of the organization of economic action. Conceptions of 'embedded' economic systems are equally important for analysis.

These conclusions are profoundly disturbing for some orthodox conceptions of the sociology of organizations since the discourse is no longer necessarily tied to the employment contract as an implicit fundamental of analysis and a constitutive element of key variables such as 'size'. Indeed, in a move frequently foreshadowed by Western analyses of Japan (although it could equally be informed by Benetton, for instance), it may be said that a possible object of postmodern organization analyis is presaged. Such an object will be one not contained in the simple legal fictions of the employment contract but constituted through a range of other social relations, notably extensive subcontracting and networking, and characterized above all by an extensive de-differentiation of aspects of organizational life. Interestingly and initriguingly one can note that in the cases of French bread, Italian fashions and Asian enterprise which have been discussed here, the precursors of 'postmodern' organization have in each case drawn from culturally 'premodern' contexts. It is from the analysis of similar tendencies and contexts, untrammelled by the reductionisms of modernist theory, that an adequate organization analysis must develop. However, a fuller elaboration of the 'postmodern' prognosis is another story (Clegg 1990a; 1990b).

In conclusion, let it suffice for now that some ground has been cleared somewhat. Certain reductionist outcrops, which have littered the landscape upon which theory may be constructed, have been levelled. On a clear site one can design far more easily.

The Politics of Industrial Organisation: A Comparative View

Linda Weiss

Introduction

The study of comparative political economy has enjoyed a revival in the last two decades when world-wide economic dislocations revealed that industrial expansion could not be taken for granted. In an era in which many economies seemed moribund, observers sought for the institutional preconditions of sustained growth. From this undertaking emerged two discoveries that defied common expectations: first, that industrial concentration was not the universal experience of the major OECD nations; and, second, that countries which had preserved their small-scale manufacturing systems — most notably Italy and Japan — were able to respond more flexibly to the costs of economic adjustment, as can be seen in the ability of Japanese and Italian industry, for example, to maintain relatively high rates of growth.

Yet, despite the predominance and vitality of small firms in these two economies, students of political economy have been remarkably slow to readjust their visions. With one or two noteworthy exceptions (e. g. Friedman 1988), social scientists still produce books on Japan as if it were entirely a big business success story, whilst the significance of the Italian case is only now being appreciated outside a narrow circle of experts. To the extent that the small firm economies have attracted commentary, the result has usually been to encourage observers to reinstate the functionalist presuppositions of dualist analysis, not least the notion that small firms persist to the extent that they have certain uses for large companies.

Taking issue with that conception, this paper addresses two questions: Why, in particular, and in contrast to the prevailing pattern of development, have small manufacturing firms become such a weighty economic force in some advanced industrial settings, such as Italy and Japan? And why, more generally, have the ascendancy of big business and the decline of small industry become the dominant trend of twentieth century capitalist development? The dominant sociological theories of industrialism and capitalism, whether derived from Marx or Weber (see Berger and Piore 1980; Bottomore 1985), are of little use to us here. Far from equipping us to deal with these sorts of questions, they exclude altogether the possibility of asking them.

Nowadays, of course, there is little need to belabour the point that such theories have overstated the degree of homogeneity within and between societies. This applies equally to Marxist and liberal-functionalist traditions, each of which has posited some law-like tendency to produce similar economic and social structures. Common to both perspectives is the assumption that big business is the superior economic form destined to dominate economic space, whilst small capital is at best an anachronism destined for the dustbin of economic inefficiency.

The defects of these 'convergence' theories have already been amply and lucidly exposed elsewhere (see Berger and Piore 1980, especially chapter 5; Abrams 1982, chapter 1; Goldthorpe 1984). Nevertheless, whilst clearly aware of the inadequacies of the conventional models, even the most theoretically explicit critiques succumb to the classical habit of invoking a logic of capitalism. There is, in short, a strong tendency to accept the necessitarian premise that the ascendancy of big business capitalism, symbolised in mass production, the large factory and the giant corporation, is somehow 'natural', the inevitable outcome of market forces.

In taking on board that premise, much of the critical literature became obsessed with the question of small firm survival. Thus, social scientists today no longer chorus its demise. On the contrary, they tend to worry over the conditions of its persistence (even its 'success'), precisely because the preponderance of big business is taken for granted. Yet therein lies the problem. For rather than rejecting wholesale the classical rule, they have (unwittingly it would seem) reinstated it with a theory of dualism which suggests that small independent production is possible because it is functional, even necessary, for large-scale industry (Berger and Piore 1980; Goldthorpe 1984). The main point of this literature can be simply stated: the classical position misled because it underestimated the functional value of the small firm for large industrial enterprise.

But there are now at least three grounds for rejecting this concentration orthodoxy. First, whilst the economic and sociological literature is pervaded by the notion that bigness is more efficient, it is clear from rigorous investigation that the economic case for economies of scale is not at all established (Prais 1976, chapters 2 and 3). Second, the reinterpretation of the history of industrialisation now under way in Europe gives grounds for concluding that the mass-production model of manufacturing won and maintained pre-eminence over its rivals for political reasons that have little to do with its intrinsic technical efficiency (Sabel and Zeitlin 1985). One general set of reasons for this conclusion has to do with the varied ways in which state power was mobilised against artisanal forms of manufacturing and in support of the hegemonic ones (Weiss 1988, chapter 8). Third, the concentration orthodoxy has been steadily eroded, if not exploded, by the rise of Japan and Italy to the status of second and fifth industrial power respectively. As the two countries where the challenge of small firms has been most vigorous, above all in Italy, they exemplify the success of conglomerations of small flexible producers in their capacity to conquer world markets.

These observations pave the way for an entirely different set of questions. What they imply is that the survival of small producers is not especially problematic. If anything, what is really puzzling is not that they persist, but that they became so marginalised in most advanced industrial settings. One way to approach that issue is to take seriously the proposition that capitalist development is inherently neutral and to consider the various ways in which states have historically shaped the character of a nation's industrial organisation (see Weiss 1988). Such an approach has much in common with the work of Hamilton and Biggart (1988) whose illuminating comparison of industrial organisation in Taiwan, Japan, and South Korea leaves little doubt as to the political basis of enterprise structure, although in the case of Taiwan they link the small business structure to a laissez-faire approach.

Taking a similar tack, this paper suggests that if our theories of organisational development are inadequate, this is not because they overplayed the dominance of big business or the decline of the workshop economy. It is because they underestimated the role of the state in that process. The argument to be advanced here develops two main points. First, the dynamics of industrial organisation are not independent of national politics, nor indeed of the international role of nation-states. Whether in pushing concentration generally or promoting dispersion in particular, we will see that states have helped to generalise distinctive patterns of ownership and organisation that market and other 'society-centred' forces alone would very likely not have produced. In short, the argument is that states do not simply support economic accumulation in an undifferentiated way. They actively channel and mould economic activity into particular forms.

The second, related point bears on the potentially autonomous character of state activity. Whether states typically sponsor concentration or foster dispersion, we cannot intelligibly read off distinctive strategies for industrial order from the 'needs of capitalism' or the 'interests of class'. 'What gets done' in the policy arena is not readily explained in terms of society-centred demands, needs or interests. As much recent research emphasises, states — as organisations controlling socio-spatial units which exist within a multi-state system — are potentially independent sites of policy-making activities. Whether to maintain domestic order, to establish international position or to defend national sovereignty, states attempt to meet such challenges in ways that highlight their powers as society-shaping forces (see Skocpol

1985 for a review). In short, to explain the general bias towards bigness or the particular predisposition towards small enterprise, the geo-political and domestic objectives of states must be central to our analysis.

I develop these points in two parts. The first focuses on two cases, Italy and Japan, which depart significantly from the concentration norm, and considers why, in these two countries, small manufacturing firms have continued to occupy a very large and expanding space in the post-war economy, whereas in most other national settings, at least until recently, the trend since 1945 has been one of decline. The main argument developed here — which covers the period since 1945 — is that the small firm economy expanded and prospered because it had something its European counterparts did not: a highly supportive state. While governments else-where celebrated its contraction or encouraged its elimination, the Italians and Japanese created a distinctive category of small enterprise and, in the case of Italy at least, for ideological and political reasons, set about populating and replenishing it.

To leave the analysis at this point though would seem to imply that only the small firm economy is a political creation. Historical comparative analysis buries that possibility by demonstrating that if Japan and Italy were distinctive at all, this was not because the state intervened to shape industrial organisation, but because it did so in a highly particular way. In short, the concentration of manufacturing in large enterprise, so characteris-tic of industry in Europe and America, is itself a state creation. This is discussed in the second part of the paper. If there is a 'logic' to the concentration process, its main motor, the discussion concludes, has not been economic, but military and geo-political.

Organisational Structure and Industrial Performance

The distinctive features of industrial production in Italy and Japan can be highlighted by noting that in the 1980s, each country remains unusually blessed with small firms and that nowhere in the industrialised West has the economic vitality of small industry been more pronounced. Whilst industrial concentration has been the norm in Europe and the United States for the post-war period as a whole, in Italy and Japan, manufacturing increasingly took place in small firms.

By the 1970s, firms with fewer than 100 employees already employed well over half of their country's manufacturing workforce, a share at least two to three times greater than that of other major industrial powers, and accounted for most of the nation's manufacturing output (Friedman 1988: 10; Schiattarella 1984: 93 – 96).

Thus, the prominence of the small manufacturer is not a phenomenon of the 1980s. At the height of its economic expansion, between 1954 and 1977, Japan doubled the number of its manufacturing firms from 429,000 to 720,000. By way of contrast, American firms registered only a tiny increase, from 288,000 to 350,000. By 1977, although its population was only half that of the United States, Japanese manufacturing took place in twice as many enterprises (Friedman 1988: 10).

The Italian picture is even more striking. There, the small firm economy has developed to a degree unprecedented within the advanced industrial nations. By 1971, firms employing fewer than 100 persons engaged 54 per cent of the industrial workforce. By the 1980s, the number of manufacturing firms had risen by 40 per cent and the average number of employees had fallen from 10 to 7.9. Today, in manufacturing industry alone, around five in every 10 employees work in firms with fewer than 50 employees (*Annuario di statistico Italiano* 1986: 347 – 377).

Attempts to dismiss such figures with the claim that many or most small enterprises in these settings are simply either big businesses in disguise (subsidiaries), or else their expedient creations, have not been substantiated. Even if the official statistics do not always exactly represent the realities of ownership, this is perhaps much less a problem in Japan and Italy than in most other advanced economies. One reason is that the large majority of smaller firms are too small (fewer than 100 employees) to attract or involve equity links with larger concerns. Even in Japan where the corporate sector has extensive ownership links with its suppliers (the largest concerns owning at least 10 per cent of the capital in other firms whose number ranges from 11 to 200), such suppliers are generally rather larger (the so-called medium-sized firms with 100 – 300 employees) than the firms discussed here. (See Pempel 1978: 150; Friedman 1988). Another, even more powerful reason is that certain small-firm legislation actually excludes ownership links with large enterprise. In Japan and Italy, the typical small manufacturing unit is independently owned and operated and employs a maximum of 15 – 20 persons, the nature and size of the firm being designated by law for the purpose of targetting the beneficiaries of special small business measures (Vepa 1971; Weiss 1988). In Italy, for example, such firms are classified as 'artisan enterprise' and this status is denied to all shareholder companies and limited partnerships. On the other hand, partnerships and cooperatives are permitted artisanal status if a majority of the owners are directly engaged in production.

Clearly, then, small firms in Italy and Japan, regardless of the manufacturing sector in which they operate, are not typically large-firm 'satellites'.

Nor do small firms simply 'survive' in these settings — they contribute massively to economic dynamism and employment. Japan's experience of record growth rates and consistently low unemployment is by now a well-told story. Although less well known, Italy, too, has established itself as a strong industrial performer. Despite its recent agricultural beginnings and the perennial Southern question, Italy has more than doubled its share of manufacturing exports since 1945 and maintained higher rates of growth and lower rates of unemployment than the rest of the EEC as a group. Italian industry has also sustained a higher than average job-creation record. According to OECD figures (1986), whereas industrial employment between 1973 and 1985 remained virtually flat in the rest of Europe, in Italy it rose by 6.5 per cent. Moreover, this was the result of vigorous job creation in the small firm districts of the Third Italy (to be discussed below).

In view of the regnant assumptions about economic development, how can this spectacular growth of small firms throughout the long boom be explained? And how can one reconcile this picture of decentralised production with vigorous industrial performance? It is time to address these issues.

Explaining the Small Firm Economy

Industrial Dualism: A Concept Whose Time has Passed?

We have moved a long way from the type of account which first dismissed these developments as a product of industrial immaturity or delayed development — or have we? Consider the view of Japan's small firm sector that emerges from one of the most sophisticated accounts of Japanese industrial arrangements. Under the heading of 'the dual economy', the authors write:

'The army of peripheral workers employed by smaller organizations enjoy relatively poor pay and conditions in comparison to their counterparts in the large corporations. [They] serve the functions of bearing the brunt of economic misfortune ... Hence these workers could be construed as supporting the lifetime employment policies, generous benefits and so on enjoyed in the large corporations by [enabling management to export] potential problems outside these organizations' (Oliver and Wilkinson 1988: 168; cf. also Johnson 1982: 13).

Shock absorbers of the business cycle, outlets for the displacement of risk, a vast sponge for the unemployed labour of large enterprise, a form of exploitation practised by larger firms, such are the prevailing images projected of small firms in Japan.

In Italy, explanations of the origins and characteristics of this form of development have been shaped by similar conceptions, even while these have been steadily refined over time. In a highly influential interpretation originating among trade unionists within the Marxist left, dualist assumptions figure heavily in the notion that the growth of small manufacturing was induced principally by large firms in their endeavour to circumvent trade union restrictions by devolving parts of the production process to small workshops (for a representative statement of this position see Berger and Piore 1980: Chapter 4). Remarkably little evidence for this view, however, has been forthcoming. Indeed, recent research suggests that small firm ties with large manufacturing enterprise are either insignificant or non-existent in a wide variety of industries (Goglio 1982). Nevertheless, whilst Italian researchers are now engaged in serious reappraisals of the whole question, contemporary understanding of organisational development in Italy is still very much in the grip of dualist theory, in particular the assumption that the fate of the small firm sector is ineluctably determined by the needs and interests of the corporate sector.

As an example of the way scholars have absorbed the dual structure argument for Italy, consider Goldthorpe's juxtaposition of Sweden and Italy as two contrasting forms of political economy, to which he assigns the labels 'corporatism' and 'dualism'. As the main alternative paths to economic and social flexibility, Sweden and Italy are held to represent two extreme solutions to the problem of reconciling social citizenship (in the form of interest representation of workers) with international competitiveness. It takes no great leap of the imagination to anticipate where he locates Italy! Thus, whereas corporatism represents a political and collectivist solution eliciting maximal participation of workers as citizens, Italian-style 'dualism' supposedly entails a retreat to individualism and market discipline, thus reviving a classical capitalist order of compulsive co-operation (Goldthorpe 1984).

This conception shares much in common with the more traditional variant of dualist theory, in particular the notion that small firms persist because they perform a variety of functions essential to the changing political economy of capitalism. Some of these functions stem from the very nature of modern (mass production) technology. For one thing, the specialised equipment that mass producers require to turn out their standardised goods cannot itself be mass produced. For another, a mass production economy generates an organised labour force that cannot be readily dismissed in times of slack demand. Above all, Fordism must avoid markets for products where demand is fluctuating and uncertain. The subsequent displacement of risk thus produces a segmentation of the market: on the one hand, a core of large and powerful firms with well-protected workers; on the other, a periphery of small subordinate units whose labour force is highly 'disposable'. As Goldthorpe puts it, 'the logic of capitalism has required, as the counterpart to the evolving mainstream or primary labour force, the creation of a further body of labour that is still capable of being treated as a commodity' (1984: 335). The main point of the dualist argument, then, is that there is an economic logic to organisational development but it is one which sets limits to the large firm's capacity to fill economic space. In so far as small firms meet that problem by populating the periphery of economic uncertainty, their survival is therefore crucial to the modern economy. In this way, by construing the small firm sector as the subordinate periphery necessary to the mass production core, dualist theory merely saves the classical rule of concentration by providing it with a 'functionalist' exception (Sabel and Zeitlin 1985: 138).

Some of this reasoning is perfectly sensible. Aspects of 'dualism' in the senses indicated exist in all economies and should not be ignored. Yet to explain away the small firm economies of Italy and Japan as forms of dualism is to disregard a great deal of evidence to the contrary. Dualist theory predicts that on a range of criteria such as wage levels, job security, trade union representation and technological sophistication, small firms are significantly inferior to their larger counterparts. Let us therefore confront these expectations with a brief review of the available evidence.

In reviewing the evidence about the Italian setting, we must focus on the 'Third Italy', so-called to distinguish it from the traditional industrial centres of Genoa, Milan, and Turin and the chronically underdeveloped South. The Third Italy is the prosperous heartland of the nation's industrial districts stretching from the Venetian provinces in the North through Bologna and Florence to Ancona in the Centre-East. Dotted right across these regions are centres of sophisticated manufacturing industry based on complex systems of small firms producing everything from knitted goods (Carpi), to textiles (Prato), special machines (Parma, Bologna), agricultural equipment (Reggio Emilia), hydraulic devices (Modena), shoes and electronic musical instruments (Ancona).

To what extent do the characteristics of this economy vindicate dualist assumptions? Do small firms depend on a low-wage regime for their existence? Are they subservient to large companies, cushioning the latter from the ups and downs of the business cycle? Are they unable to offer job security or the acquisition of technical skills? Is their existence inimical to the organisation of trade unions? On all these issues, there is now sufficient evidence to undermine the dualist model. Let us review some of it, beginning with wages.

In the 1970s, the labour costs of industrial enterprises increased substantially and, in virtually all of the small-firm industrial districts, wage levels approached the national average or exceeded those in the traditionally advanced industrial triangle (Bagnasco and Pini 1981). Moreover, since 1979, even the tiniest workshops (classified as artisanal enterprise) guarantee employees the same wage increases as those in large industrial firms. Far from depending on cheap labour, small employers in the Third Italy increasingly negotiate and police local and national wage scales with trade unions. Nor is it difficult to see why artisan employers associations like the National Confederation of Artisans (CNA) take a strong interest in wage regulation. For these districts, price competition with low-wage mass producers would be ruinous. Instead, they match broadly skilled workers to flexible machines to make a wide variety of semi-custom goods. Their success rests on the ability to continuously change, rather than cheapen, products and processes, on innovation rather than cost-cutting. Little wonder, then, that along with fiscal evasion, violation of the wage contract is viewed as a form of unfair competition among member firms.

This is not to deny the existence of low wages in some areas of the small firm economy but low pay tends to be associated with the gendering of certain industries. The low-wage clothing and textile industry, for example, traditionally colonised by women, can be neatly contrasted with the male-dominated mechanical-engineering sector which pays higher than average wages. Thus, in so far as dualism is evident in wage differentials, these would appear to be structured by gender, rather than size of firm, and this is traditional (cf. Blackburn and Mann 1979: 301).

Equally damaging for the dualist model is the well-documented capacity of the industrial districts to consistently create, rather than shed, jobs and to do so while continuously updating technology. Between 1971 and 1981, for example, while companies employing more than 1,000 persons in the 'advanced' technology sector shed more than 5 per cent of their work force, firms with fewer than 100 employees expanded theirs by more than 50 per cent. Most spectacular of all, the tiniest high-technology, artisan firms (engaging fewer than 10 employees) increased their workforce by just under 96 per cent, partly as a result of the new firm formation documented earlier and partly as a result of internal expansion (Centro Studi Confindustria 1984). Moreover, the fact that workers in craft enterprise must acquire a broad range of skills on the job increases job stability since employers are loathe to lose those trained in-house. Indeed, in some small firm districts, employers have begun to espouse the Japanese management philosophy that 'employment should be seen as permanent' (Lazerson 1988: 337).

On these indicators, there is little to support the image of subservience to large enterprise so central to dualist theory. The nature and extent of subcontracting in this regard is especially illuminating. For, despite a widespread tendency in the literature to link the importance of small firms to the decentralising strategies of big business via the process of subcontracting, there are at least two reasons why the extent of that practice should not be exaggerated. First, even in Italy's most mature industrial regions centred on the corporate empires of Fiat, Pirelli, Olivetti and the like, the bulk of small firms produce directly for the market. Despite sweeping generalisations that the growth of small enterprise is the result of big industry's 'decentralisation' strategies, very little evidence has been forthcoming. In Lombardy, centre of large-scale industry, surveys showed that more than 70 per cent of small industrial firms produce directly for the market. Furthermore, the proportion had increased by 4 points between 1969 and 1974, precisely in the period when larger firms were supposedly contracting out more work (Gasparini 1977). Another survey of the arti-sanat in the same area for 1974 produced similar results: 87 per cent of the region's artisan production consisted of finished products, of which only 13.6 per cent was destined to industry (Giunta Regionale della Lombardia 1974: 64; see also Piore and Sabel 1984: 227 on regional trade).

Second, the small firm's role in subcontracting is not generally that of recipient of orders from the large. More frequently, it is the initiator of such commissions. Indeed, all the research shows that is the artisan or mini enterprise, not the large industrial firm, that typically acts as the major independent source of subcontracting. An inquiry into the metallurgy industry in Bologna province in 1977 showed that the smallest firms (20–49 employees) subcontracted out a much larger proportion of their total production (30 per cent) than those with over 1,000 employees (17 per cent) (Capecchi and Pugliese 1978: 9). In the metallurgy sector, Brusco (1982) found that many already tiny factories contracted out all or most of their production, such as dishwashers, and machinery for the textile and paper industries, to other small firms, confining their operations to the construction of prototypes and final assembly. Similar subcontracting networks have been reported for the knitwear industry (see Solinas 1982). The important point to emphasise is that subcontracting is a time-honoured practice among small businesses, almost a structural characteristic of the Italian economy, by which dependent labour is kept to a minimum, the scale of operations contained and family control ensured. One must not underestimate here the impact of government legislation (see below). Since firm size is highly regulated, these subcontracting networks also enable the small firm to remain small and thus continue to be eligible for the dedicated small firm benefits.

This is not to suggest that independence, dynamism and sophistication infuse every corner of the small firm sector. Readers of *Time* magazine will be familiar with the vast back-street apparel industry of Naples whose (Communist) mayor once boasted that 'Naples exports five million pairs of gloves a year, yet we do not have a single factory'. But the important point to stress is that the sweatshop image which the Neapolitan system evokes is a far cry from the modern industrial districts of the Third Italy. Here, flexibility is achieved not via 'sweating', which is 'the generic response of embattled firms — whether mass or small producers', but through a loose division of labour and a broadly skilled workforce able to switch rapidly to new products and processes (Piore and Sabel 1984: 265, 269).

What needs to be stressed, then, is that the classic secondary labour market characteristics of low pay, poor conditions and traditional technology apply only to certain corners of the dispersed economy. For the core of this domain, notably the 'flexible specialists' of the third Italy, shares with the corporate sector not only its competitiveness on the world market but also its advanced technology, its innovative capacity, and its ability to pay high wages (Brusco 1982: 183; Solinas 1982). This may even be an understatement. For on a wide variety of dimensions, from job creation to profit margins, investment per capita, technological change, productivity and value added, data covering the 1970s and early '80s show that small firms in all sectors have outperformed the big companies (Schiattarella 1984: 93 ff.).

Thanks to a number of excellent studies we now know much more about the sources of this extraordinary vitality. One source, highlighted by Piore and Sabel (1983; 1984), can be traced to the technical virtuosity of the craft principles typically deployed by small Italian firms (for which Sabel has coined the term 'flexible specialisation'). By matching multi-purpose machinery to skilled workers to turn out a wide range of specialist goods, flexible producers gain the edge over their mass-production counterparts in the ability to continuously reshape the production process. Another, alluded to earlier, rests on distinctive organisational strategies facilitated by the dense clustering of small producers in specialised industrial districts. Here, the close physical proximity of specialist workshops, co-ordinated and sustained by a public infrastructure, has generated an economics of co-operation, a point which anticipates my discussion of state support below.

A full-bodied account of small firm vitality might also hasten to point out that the relatively stronger performance of small firm districts has been boosted by the advent of numerically controlled technologies, as well as by shifts in demand for non-standardised goods. But in seeking to account for 'vitality' we are now racing ahead too fast. For the more important point, surely, is that changes in markets and technology would count for naught without the organisational structures already in place to sustain them. Why were these structures so much more developed in the two countries under discussion? This is the question that we must continue to address. Thus far, dualism has been of little use in explaining the Italian pattern. Can it do better for Japan?

For Japan, there is much illumination to be gained from the extensive research of Derek Friedman whose monograph, *The Misunderstood Miracle* (1988), offers a novel and, in many respects, convincing explanation of Japan's industrial success. In his account, it is not the corporate giants which occupy the centre stage but the nimble dwarves which sometimes (but not always) cluster around them. Friedman takes issue with both market and state regulation approaches, arguing instead that Japanese dynamism rests upon the organisational flexibility afforded by a highly innovative small firm sector whose development was 'politically' stimulated. Friedman extends the concept 'political' to include everything from workers' career expectations to inter-firm relations. Ironically, although he labels his approach 'political', he is less happy about including state support under this heading. Perhaps this is because he tends to see state action reductively, as nothing but the embodiment of market and efficiency imperatives. Nonetheless, much of Friedman's own evidence, as we shall see, points consistently in the direction of government initiatives to extend and consolidate the small sector.

Friedman shows that small Japanese firms, like their Italian counterparts, compete as much through product differentiation as through price; that conventional approaches have 'profoundly misrepresented the economic role of Japanese small manufacturers' and significantly overplayed the 'industrial planning' power of the government; and that regional economies of small-scale firms in remote mountain areas 'have played a large, if unexpected, role in the high-tech resurgence of Japanese manufacturing'. This is a brave and stimulating thesis for it not only takes on the whole field, it also gives explanatory primacy to organisational forms widely dismissed by Western and Japanese analysts as inferior.

To develop his argument, Friedman rigorously tests and rejects a range of hypotheses drawn from dualist theory. One key premise of dualist theory is that small firms are dependent upon subcontracting and from this dependency, it is claimed, flow certain consequences which make them subservient to larger companies for capital and technical assistance, and force them to cut costs by depressing wages. The following statement from Nakamura, cited and endorsed by Hamilton and Biggart (1988: S58–59), expresses the orthodox view that

'This system of subcontracting allows large firms to increase their use of small firms during times of expansion and to decrease their use during times of business decline ... the 'subcontractorization' of small firms by the large has been seen as the "greatest problem" confronting the Japanese economy because of the inequality and dual-wage system that it spawns.'

Several notions are at work here. The first is that small firms act as a 'shock absorber' for large firms. If correct, then, this should be reflected in changes in employment figures for both sectors. We should expect to find that as the economy contracts, large-firm employment would remain stable, while small firms reduce their workforce. Friedman tests that proposition with reference to the four severe economic recessions since 1920 to determine which classes of firms suffered the most. In some instances, the adjustment patterns were precisely the opposite of what the 'dual structure' hypothesis would predict, with large firms shedding personnel as small firms increased theirs. Only one period, 1952—1954, conformed to the 'dual structure' predictions, and it was from this point onwards that small firms began, in many sectors, to break away from 'dualist' tendencies (Friedman 1988: 132). This was made possible, as we will see in the section to follow, by the state's creation of an extensive infrastructure for small manufacturing enterprise.

A further assumption of the dualist argument contained in the above statement is that wage differentials are very marked and, thirdly, that these are generated as a result of small firms being forced to reduce pay scales to become attractive subcontracting sources. Let us take wages first. Examining wage profiles and patterns of career formation of workers in small firms, Friedman (1988: 138—144) makes a number of observations damaging for dualist theory. First, wage differentials have been much exaggerated: initially about the same as in the United States, they declined steadily from the 1960s onwards, narrowing by close to 20 points for all small size classes. Second, wages for both white and blue collar groups are about the same until workers reach their mid-thirties. It is only at this point that 'small-firm, blue-collar workers begin to experience a wage gap relative to blue-collar workers in large firms'. For small-firm (10—99 employees) white collar workers, however, wages are virtually identical to those of blue collar workers in firms of a thousand or more employees (see Friedman 1988: Figure 4.13). The final observation that weakens the dualist claim relates to the career paths of small-firm workers. Along with Kazuo Koike (1983), Friedman notes that self-employment is 'an important career option' for blue-collar workers and a significant number of them — between 50 and 70 per cent according to different estimates — become owners of small workshops after a period of training in small firms. Indeed, Friedman comments, 'the startups for new manufacturing firms are so high in Japan that in any given year the number of new, small-scale, startup factories is equal to more than half the total number of manufacturing factories' (1988: 144). One important consequence of this career pattern, which undercuts the dualist argument, is that the gap between high-wage large firms and low-wage small firms in some sectors is substantially reduced once the career paths and lifetime earnings of workers in each organisational setting are compared. As Friedman (1988: 145) concludes from a review of the data: 'Workers who obtain training for five to ten years and then become self-employed can make much more money than is possible in large firms' (see also Koike 1983).

An examination of the processes which created wage differentials in the first place provides even more damaging evidence against dualism. The conventional view suggests that the wage gap emerged as large industrialists sought to secure internal harmony with attractive incentives while forcing small companies to squeeze their workers by cutting costs. A more historically sensitive picture shows, on the contrary, that the prewar wage gap developed because 'workers forced industrialists to pay a premium for work in large factories'. As more and more giant factories were created in the interwar period, the new recruits began to agitate for higher wages and job security. But those demands were not shaped in a cultural vacuum. Workers brought to the large factories certain preconceptions, expectations about job rights, whose immediate source was none other than the dominant organisational form — the small firm (Friedman 1988: 135–136).

Throughout the inter-war period, as Japan's industrialisation intensified, small firms preserved the *deishi* system, a form of close personal training resembling the apprenticeship system of the European guilds (on this system in a modern guise, see Pelzel 1979). This gave workers the chance to acquire manufacturing skills that would subsequently enable them to set up independently. Lower wages were thus accepted as 'the price for training that might lead them to become independent factory operators' (Friedman 1988: 135). But as large factories mushroomed, the possibility of intensely personal training and the promise of independence were increasingly denied. Consequently, as Yasukichi argues, workers forced the large companies to make organisational changes and thus deliver certain payoffs as compensation for the loss of particular small-firm advantages.

'Traditional human relations continued into the modern period in small businesses where, with the system of apprenticeship, paternalistic care of the workers and hope for future independence could compensate for low wages. In larger businesses, however, it was becoming increasingly difficult for employers to keep close informal contact with workers. The hope for future independence was also diminishing. As a result, the old *deishi* (apprenticeship) system was becoming unpopular in larger businesses even in the Meiji period, as exemplified in a most dramatic way by the strike of workers at Harimaya ([later] Sogo Department Store) demanding the modern salary wage system. Thus, it was natural that larger firms should institutionalize paternalism into seniority-oriented, higher wages and richer fringe benefits.' (Cited in Friedman 1988: 136).

The general historical pattern, then, does not support the dual economy argument. Rather than enabling large firms to cushion the costs of union representation, the small firm system entered into the very creation of those costs. This casts an interesting light on 'culturalist' explanations of Japanese management practices for it suggests that the 'cultural' itself can be more fruitfully understood in 'organisational-materialist' terms (in this instance, the way in which the system of small-firm social relations framed both workers' expectations and demands and, subsequently, the organisational response of big business. The term was coined by Anderson to describe Mann's (1986) approach).

At this point, proponents of the dual economy thesis would want to counter that, regardless of the data on wages, there is no mistaking the extensive nature of subcontracting in the Japanese economy and this in itself must reduce substantially the degree of autonomy, technical and otherwise, enjoyed by the small manufacturing enterprise. Is this the case?

In general, in contrast to the situation in Italy, the degree of corporate 'dependence' on smaller suppliers is unusually extensive. In 1976, for example, the proportion of smaller manufacturing firms (up to 300 persons employed) which acted as subcontractors exceeded 60 per cent. Of these, the proportion of the tiniest industrial firms (1 – 19 employees) relying on subcontracting orders for at least 80 per cent of their production was 81 per cent (JETRO 1981: 24).

These figures tell us that subcontracting (used here in the broadest sense to mean production of finished or semi-finished products for other firms) is by no means the universal experience of small Japanese firms. Around 40 per cent of all small firms produce directly for the market, primarily in sectors such as furniture, food, and clothing. Yet the JETRO figures also obscure important aspects of small-firm 'dependence', which serve to undermine the notion of a dual structure. First, they hide the fact that, as in Italy, small firms subcontract on their own as much as they accept orders. Thus, there exists 'a horizontally organized network of subcontracting work [which] reduces the cost pressures assumed to exist in the vertical system' (Friedman 1988: 149). Furthermore, the vast majority of small firms which do operate in the vertical system reduce their dependency on large firms by accepting orders from multiple clients. In the general machinery sector, for example, the official Small Business Survey of 1983 revealed that firms with 10 – 19 employees averaged five clients each, whilst firms in the 50 – 99 size category could count on at least double that number (see Friedman 1988: 149). Finally, of those who do produce to order, over 60 per cent do not have any other links to their clients, and thus do not rely on large firms for technical, capital or other assistance. Indeed, the percentage of suppliers receiving capital or personnel assistance from clients increased significantly with firm size. In general machinery, the percentages ranged from 2.9 to 14.6 for firms with 1 – 50 employees but in firms in the size categories of 101 – 300 and more than 300 employees the share of vendors receiving such assistance rises dramatically to a range of 37.8 to 58.4 percentage points (Friedman 1988: 151).

In testing and rejecting dualist assumptions about small firm dependency (and thus, by implication, dualist explanations for the development of a small firm sector), one does not wish to imply that there is no darker underbelly to the small firm economy, whether in Japan or anywhere else. Nor is there any intention to deny the claims of those who would insist on the relatively precarious position of many small firms in other national settings such as Britain and America. But such observations fail to address the main issue, namely: Can dualist theory account for the preponderance of small manufacturing firms in the postwar economies of Japan and Italy? On the strength of the evidence examined thus far, it is hard to escape the conclusion that it cannot. As Friedman (1988: 34) observes, the 'dual structure' argument 'explains away' the extensive role small firms play in the Japanese and Italian economies 'by treating small producers as less modern than, or [in the up-dated versions of dualist theory] as exploited by, the large ones'. Whether in traditional or modern guise, the traditional stereotype of the small firm promulgated by dualist theory now seems seriously out of touch with the vitality of small firm districts.

As a symbol of that vitality, consider, for instance, Sakaki, a high-tech manufacturing village in Nagano Prefecture, which produces general-purpose machine tools (typically lathes, boring machines and mills), which are used by other manufacturers to make their own products. Sakaki's small family-owned workshops account for one of the world's highest concentrations of advanced production machinery: the area has 0.02 per cent of the national population but 0.2 per cent of the nation's stock of numerically-controlled (NC) machine-tools (Sabel 1989: 23). Nor is there only one Sakaki. After all, by the 1970s, Japan's smaller factories were purchasing 70 per cent of the nation's entire NC output! The significance of this figure can be easily appreciated by way of comparison with the situation in the United States where it was the large mass-production firms which accounted for 75 – 80 per cent of U.S. demand (Friedman 1988: 253). Moreover, there is some evidence of pre-war vitality among small firms, which suggests that it is not simply a consequence of recent technology, but of much more long-standing craft principles (Lockwood 1954).

The use of the most up-to-date equipment is of course not the only ingredient in the vitality of Sakaki (and other Japanese regions). Like the flexible specialists of Italy's industrial districts, Sakaki's small independent producers form regional associations which defend them from wage and price pressures, whether from other producers or from larger customers. Indeed, as already indicated for Italy, regional cooperation is vital to the health of the small firm population. In Sakaki, cooperation is one way that small firms 'enforce what they regard as legitimate dealings upon larger companies', while at the same time enabling them to develop new product markets (Friedman 1988: Capther 5).

Friedman's re-interpretation of the Japanese enigma, based on a radical reappraisal of the small firm economy, is likely to spawn a whole new debate whose outcome, already evident in Italy, will be the rejection of the (mass-production) orthodoxy that big equals 'more efficient'. Only the bare bones of that analysis have been possible here. What can be confidently stated at this point, though, is that for our purposes, dualist theory lacks explanatory power. To explain why this alternative form of production flourished and expanded in Japan and Italy in the period after 1945, yet was crowded out in most other advanced industrial settings, we must rely on a comparative-historical analysis of state activity.

In the following section, I sketch an argument that the greater diffusion of flexible manufacturing concerns in these two countries can be explained primarily as the result of an extensive system of small-firm support which, for broadly political reasons, governments have created and extended throughout the postwar years. The theoretical position informing this analysis is drawn from the work of the 'new state theorists', including Skocpol (1985), Mann (1986; 1988), and Hall (1986), who analyse state action non-reductively.

Why States Matter

As dramatically different as manufacturing and industrial structures in Japan and Italy may seem at first glance, there are some important common features. These range from the preservation of craft principles in the organisation of work around broadly defined responsibilities to inter-firm arrangements which permit co-operative action. An even more remarkable feature common to each case is the fact that the vast majority of Italian and Japanese firms are born small and are destined to remain small. As we saw earlier, Italian and Japanese firms tend to share economic space rather than to vertically integrate, expand or amalgamate. One striking manifestation of that tendency is the proliferation of subcontracting arrangements within the small firm population, not just when orders are booming, but as a matter of routine practice. Why is this the case?

The main piece in that puzzle centres on the postwar activities of the state. By remaining small, firms retain the special benefits that they would otherwise lose by expanding. As a special category in Italian and Japanese law, the small manufacturing firm is thus the target of numerous benefits, qualifications for which are crucially dependent upon firm size, size being defined by number of workers employed.

The crucial point to be stressed here, however, is not simply that the state recognises small industry as a special and separate category of economic activity but that it backs up that recognition with a precise targetting of provisions and, crucially, that it has done so consistently over a long period. It is on these three closely related indicators that Italy and Japan stand apart from other major industrial powers. In Germany and France, for example, artisan industry is a professional category rather than simply a legal regime. It is defined on the basis of professional 'lists' of activities, rather than in law on the basis of an employment ceiling (see Barberis 1980). Indeed, in West Germany, the form of the enterprise is entirely at the discretion of its promoter. There, artisan industry can even be a joint-stock company! In fact, so concentrated has the sector become since the end of the war that by the late '70s, the German artisanat had lost some 50 per cent of its enterprises and averaged 141 employees per establishment (Barberis 1980: 9; Sauer 1984: 82). In France, as in Britain, the public promotion of small manufacturing is a relatively recent phenomenon, the aim of French policymakers since 1945 being to remake France's artisanal economy in the Fordist image of American mass production (Piore and Sabel 1984: 141). It is surely highly significant that Japan, the only other major industrial country which matches Italy in all three respects — legally specifying size limits for the purpose of providing extensive small firm assistance over many decades — is also abundantly endowed with small manufacturing enterprise. It is of course quite possible that other lesser or smaller industrial powers with substantial small firm sectors, like Belgium and Spain, have instituted similar programmes to promote small industry. If so, this would clearly reinforce my argument.

As the preceding observations imply, Italy and Japan's distinct approaches to production were not mere 'accidents' of history. In each national context, they have been made possible by the existence of a vast infrastructure established by postwar governments to foster the creation and modernisation of small manufacturing firms. In other words, small-scale manufacturing was able to triumph in these two countries primarily because governments set about promoting it in two main ways: first, by creating special financial institutions dedicated to the investment needs of small manufacturing enterprises; and, second, by encouraging co-operation among small producers in everything from the construction of industrial estates to the marketing of products abroad. The importance of these measures warrants a closer look.

Turning first to Italy, a survey of all the major laws on incentives to industry (predominantly manufacturing industry) since 1945 reveals a copious legislation of support, all privileging firms of small dimensions. Many of the most important schemes were initiated in the 1950s, extended throughout the '60s and early '70s, and since then, enhanced and developed in important ways with the advent of regional governments. Although too numerous to detail, one can mention here some of the more important schemes iniated before the advent of regional governments which have extended these in important ways. Among the numerous measures provided, the Artisan Act alluded to above deserves special mention. In 1956, the Italian state constructed a special category of small business designated as 'artisan enterprise'. In Italian law, as we have seen, the latter is distinguished and defined not by the owner's qualifications or the nature of the product, but by the size of a firm's workforce. Generally speaking, most small manufacturing firms thus defined are restricted to 22 employees, a limit which may be exceeded by 20 per cent for a period of up to three months per year. The law is clear that the artisan 'must commit a substantial portion of his own labour to the productive process', and in addition to limited partnerships, and shareholder companies, firms that rely entirely on mass production are denied artisan status. Firms classified as 'artisan' are entitled to a rich array of benefits, ranging from generous health and pension schemes to cheap loans for new workshops and equipment.

Of especial importance is the financial infrastructure dedicated to supplying the investment needs of smaller enterprises. Artisans, for instance, have their own permanent loan fund, financed, subsidised and guaranteed by the state, yet run independently of the central bureaucracy. In the first 20 years of the Artisan Fund's existence, some 300,000 firms obtained cheap investment credit. Even more significant, these loans covered a full 64 per cent of artisanal investment requirements and the number of beneficiaries involved were equivalent to 75 per cent of new artisan firms established between 1953 and 1971.

Another way of highlighting the impact of government programmes is to ask which regions fared best as a result of the various loan schemes for small industry. The data covering the period 1956 – 1976 show that, on virtually every indicator (such as number and amount of loans per firm), the regions of the Third Italy obtained the lion's share (Weiss 1984: 239).

To these observations, we can add another feature of government programmes, which highlights the collective nature of the small producer regime. The key feature here is the way the programmes privilege collaboration and joint ventures in virtually everything from industrial estates to export consortia, which achieve for small firms economies of scale in administration, purchasing and marketing. As in Japan, these consortia, cooperatives and other associations of small producers organise marketing, bulk buy raw materials, prepare the pay slips, accounts and taxes and negotiate cheap loans for their members. The building of industrial estates or 'parks' to house small workshops operating common facilities is one further development along these lines. And again, as in Japan, many of these ventures have been initiated with the backing of national and local governments, including, in the Italian case, a very considerable input since the 1960s from the Communist administration at municipal and regional levels (see Weiss 1989). More generally, whether to bulk buy raw materials, to handle marketing and administration, to secure guaranteed loans or to share common facilities, small firms participating in these ventures are offered loan and export subsidies, infrastructure and preferential tax treatment. Little wonder then that today artisan enterprise is the most favoured organisational form in Italian manufacturing.

By encouraging small firms to group together to share facilities and to provide each other with orders, the co-operative form of industrial estate combines the advantages of decentralised flexible production with economies of centralised service provision. Similarly, by sponsoring industrial parks and export consortia, the regions (which increasingly administer and extend the national schemes) enable small producers to reap the advantages of collective arrangements and, by running retraining and vocational schemes with the assistance of local employers and trade unions, they ensure a constant supply of skilled labour and entrepreneurial experience. Whether seen in the mobilisation of business organisations and trade unions to participate in the planning and administration of public services or in the encouragement of small producers to pool their efforts, it is clear that government initiatives embody important, if unexpected, 'collectivist' elements, an anathema to the free market thinking that so frequently underpins small business programmes in other nations (for a discussion of British and American programmes, see Weiss 1988: Chapter 9).

How do we explain this sustained and intensive public promotion of the small firm? Excluding Japan, it is certainly without parallel in the major industrial powers. The answer lies in the way Italy's dominant party, the Christian Democrats (CD), sought to consolidate their rule at the end of the war by creating a 'property-owning democracy'. This project, whose chief objective was to strengthen and extend the small-scale productive structure, was shaped ideologically and reinforced politically. It was ideologically shaped in that the CD invested small enterprise and its owner-promoters with high moral significance, as a place where the 'dignity' of labour could be restored, where the capital-labour split could be transcended; and as a positive social force whose task it was to mobilise others to similar pursuits. In short, the CD positively valued the *ceti medi* (independent middle class) and sought to create more of them and thereby to generalise for all society the ideals of economic independence symbolised in the small firm and the skilled craftsman. Although these cultural preferences have long historico-political roots, they were reinvigorated, made more resonant, by the resurgence of a highly politicised labour movement whose support for the Communists worried the CD. Thus, the project for a property-owning democracy was also a project to 'deproletarianise the workers'. It offered an alternative to the assembly-line system, thus sustaining the 'demobilising dream' of quitting the factory and setting up independently. In this sense, the governing party's social project was carried forward politically.

As we have seen, the main impact of central policies has been to consolidate a decentralised productive system in which particular combinations of firms are preferred. Contrary to what one might expect, then, Italy's flourishing small firm economy owes nothing to neoclassical political economy. On the contrary, it owes a great deal to an economic and social infrastructure which allows the constant innovation, investment and upgrading of skills on which the industrial districts depend. The foundations of that infrastructure were laid by national governments pursuing their own social and political objectives. It is now being extended and managed in innovative ways by regional and local authorities.

So much for Italy. Can the argument be extended to Japan? Indeed it can, at least as far as the 'infrastructural' dimension is concerned. There are striking similarities in the small business programmes of each nation. As in the case of Italy, 'dedicated' lending institutions and organisational strategies for inter-firm co-operation form the backbone of the numerous schemes for smaller enterprise. These include financial laws — People's Finance Corporation Law (1949), Mutual Finance Bank Law (1951), Credit Bank Law (1953), Small Business Credit Insurance Law (1950), Credit Guarantee Association Law (1953), Small Business Investment Company Law (1963); modernization laws — Small Business Structural Modernisation Subsidisation Law (1956), Medium and Small Enterprise Guidance Law (1963), Small Business Modernisation Promotion Law (1963), Provisional Machinery Industry Promotion Measures (1956), Small Business Modernisation Subsidisation Law (1956); organisation laws; Smaller Enterprise Organisation Law (1957); Smaller Enterprise Cooperative Law (1949) and the Organisation of Commercial and Industrial Associations (1960) (Vepa 1971: Appendix; JETRO 1981). This is but a fraction of a veritable mountain of legislation.

These initiatives have played a significant part in the diffusion of flexible manufacturing in Japan. By encouraging small manufacturers to invest in new equipment throughout the high growth period, the Small Enterprise Development Programme prevented the consolidation of a 'dualistic' structure. Throughout the '60s, as smaller firms sought more and more skilled personnel, these units registered wage rises three to four times higher than in large firms, and the starting wage of a high school graduate — barely 75 per cent of the large-firm wage in 1955, was by the late '60s actually higher (Vepa 1971: 56).

A more direct measure of policy 'impact' can be obtained by asking how important for small firms was loan capital from public or government-funded sources. The answer is that it was exceptionally important. By the 1970s such financial organs accounted for almost 80 per cent of all investment capital in small firms. Dedicated financial support almost doubled for the smallest classes of firm (1−9, 10−19, 20−29), and 'the smaller the company, the larger was the role of the state in funding entry into the market' (Friedman 1988: 174). As Friedman (1988: 171−174) concludes from a review of the available data, 'The importance of government and government-supported private institutions to the spectacular emergence of high-tech manufacturers in Japan is clear in the extent to which small enterprises made use of them.'

The research enabling us to account for the state's small firm support in Japan remains to be done. But it seems likely that when the tale is unravelled it will be somewhat more complex than the Italian story. The state's role in Japan is a contradictory one. Friedman, for instance, is adamant that the state should have little credit for Japan's nimble dwarves. As far as he is concerned, though effective in their consequences, the policies themselves were a result of 'bureaucratic failure', not success: 'If the MCI, [the prewar industrial bureaucracy] and later MITI, had realized their objectives, small producers would have been consolidated and flexible production attenuated in postwar Japan.' (1988: 162).

There is something to this. The industrial bureaucracy, first MCI (Ministry of Trade and Industry) then MITI (Ministry of International Trade and Industry) has long vaunted the merits of giantism, particularly in conjunction with its military and geopolitical ambitions, a point that can be generalised to most nations, as the final section here shows. In various 'spurts' of rationalising fervour − initially, after the first world war, then again in the early '60s amid fears of foreign takeovers − the bureaucracy tried to merge small producers (most notably in the notoriously 'strategic' machine tools sector), promoting cartels and joint arrangements as a means of hastening the event. Paradoxically, these state-sponsored organisational resources − by encouraging coordinated and collective action − strengthened firms in their 'smallness', thus enabling them to resist what the state wanted.

Pushing Friedman's line of reasoning to its logical conclusion implies that if the industrial bureaucracy had had its way, most of Japan's nimble dwarves would never have seen the light of day. This view seems exaggerated. It is certainly hard to reconcile with the mountain of legislation, much of it encouraging new firm formation. One wonders how it is possible to put so much organisational energy into something if the aim is to destroy it! The more likely story is that Japan's bureaucrats did not 'succeed' in pushing giantism too far because they did not try too hard. Why? For three reasons. First, in a community steeped in the social relations of family enterprise (as in Italy, almost everyone has an entrepreneur somewhere in the family), there is strong popular sentiment for support of small firms. Thus, in the 1950s, a public outcry ensued over the abuse by large firms of their subcontractors. The state stepped in with protective legislation. Second, whatever its own preferences, the bureaucracy must deal with another 'state elite': the governing Liberal Democratic Party which has long championed the cause of the small producer, its key constituent. Finally, the unusual degree of corporate dependence on small suppliers in key sectors in Japan must place very obvious political, not to mention market, limits on the bureaucracy's penchant for giants.

Thus, an account of small firm support in Japan would need to take account of these seemingly 'contradictory' domestic and international objectives of the state. On one hand, the new postwar government had to rebuild its legitimacy and its seems doubtful that the main contender for power, the LDP, could establish a moral basis for its rule that was divorced from the workshop economy. On the other hand, Japan's traditional state elite sought to reconstitute the power of the nation-state by creating large-scale industrial organisations that could both fend off external challenges and defend Japan's interests abroad. But perhaps, unusually, the contradictions in pursuing both objectives, in fostering both large and small firms, were minimised in this instance for in Japan, to a far greater degree than anywhere else in the industrialised world, these organisations are inextricably interconnected.

What About Culture?

In aiming my explanatory arrows at the question of small firm proliferation I have not dealt at length with the question of the 'success' of small-scale production. Can the political explanation developed here be of use? Let us first reconsider the key features of small firm success.

The popular image of small manufacturing as deeply 'disorganised', in the sense of being predicated on 'competitive individualistic atomised markets', does not square well with either the Italian or Japanese regime of flexible production. For one thing, the 'territoriality' of the craft economy — concentration in dense regional conglomerations of firms specialising in one industrial sector — pulls the whole structure together in important ways. So too does the extensive collaboration that has come to characterise the relations both among and within small enterprise. Two close observers of the Italian regime, Piore and Sabel (1983: 404), describe the defining characteristics of the small Italian firm as 'close collaboration between manufacturer and client; close collaboration between different groups within the firm, between the firm and its neighbours; and, as a corollary to these, general-purpose machines and a broadly skilled work-force'.

It appears, then, that the success of these small flexible specialists depends on a degree of 'collectivism' inconceivable in the orthodox understanding of the small firm. This takes a variety of forms, from consultation on technical matters, to sharing the costs of new innovations, to guaranteeing each other orders to disperse the risks of investment in sophisticated technologies.

The ability to co-operate with competitors has been documented also by Friedman (1988) for Japan and may therefore be considered as one important ingredient in the success story of small-scale manufacturing. Some commentators have sought to account for this unusual ability by invoking a 'culture of community' (Trigilia 1986). Piore and Sabel (1984: 266, 278), for instance, have argued very generally that the collaborative regime of flexible production depends on prior socialisation into some form of community, whether ethnic, political or religious. If such communities do exist in the settings in question, this has yet to be convincingly demonstrated. Even if they do exist, it may well be that forms of social co-operation and 'communitarianism' generally are consequences rather than causes of small firm organisation (see Bonacich and Modell 1980).

It is possible to explain the collaborative character of craft production, however, without recourse to prior conceptions of community. Basically, two elements are involved. First, a public infrastructure of industrial estates, training institutions, etc., promotes co-operative behaviour (a function of politics) and, second, the organisation of specialist production (a function of market strategy) which encourages the pooling of ideas and information in the interests of problem-solving. The first point has already been discussed. For the second, it is important to recall that the core of craft production is continuous innovation. Here, firms must permanently anticipate and accommodate change by continuous product differentiation. It is this strategic commitment to the ceaseless transformation of 'new product ideas into actual market offerings' that pushes the flexible producer to maximise co-operation both within the firm and with its specialist neighbours (Friedman 1983: 354–355).

We have then an explanation for social co-operation that does not depend solely on the fertility of Italian or Japanese soil; the strategy of flexible production provides the driving force while public infrastructure furnishes the material means. To this one might add that settlement patterns (regional conglomerations) supply the opportunity. But there is a more important point that deserves emphasising. For, regardless of the ingredients of small manufacturing success in Italy and Japan — its flexibility and co-operation — it is a fair bet that they would have little import today without the productive structures and public infrastructures to sustain them, in other words, if the Italian or Japanese had pursued the policies of their European and American counterparts since the end of the last war. It is to the development of that theme that we now turn for it bears directly on the issue of why states matter to industrial organisation.

Big Structures, Huge Companies, Large Factories: The Geo-Politics of Giantism

The previous analysis opens up another puzzle. If economic success need not come in a big business package and industrial development does not preclude the extensive presence of small-scale production, why then is the latter so comparatively rare? My main argument has been that the key to that puzzle lies with the state. Flexible production has flourished in those settings where it has had an unusually 'sympathetic' state, one whose project-oriented managers remained (in Italy most clearly) more attentive to the internal rumblings of class politics than to the external pressures of international rivalry. But it is possible and necessary to extend this point and to show that a similar 'state-centred' perspective applies to the formation of big business economies. This time, however, geo-politics, which was of minor importance to the Italian case and significantly qualified in the Japanese case, must be central to that analysis (for the European and American evidence, see Weiss 1988: Chapter 8).

The implication of this analysis is that the Italian and Japanese experiences cannot be explained away as a special instance of politics triumphant over market. To accept that interpretation would merely reinstate the classical rule of concentration, with the one qualification that, provided states do not interfere with market forces, large-scale organisation will prevail. This rule will not stand, for the simple reason that states in other European settings have not been neutral bystanders. On the contrary, just as the Italian and Japanese have promoted economic dispersion, so other national authorities have more typically sponsored concentration. Giants no less than dwarves are in significant part a political creation. From this perspective, politics does not so much 'triumph over' market forces as enter into their overall configuration.

As outlined at the beginning of this paper, the argument develops two general points about the state's relation to industrial capitalist development. The first is that states, not markets *per se*, have generalised the impulse to scale and concentration. Whilst clearly not all instances of concentration are state induced, even the most 'mature' of industrialism's creations owes considerably more to the rationalising activities of states than existing theories allow (see Skocpol 1985; Hall 1986). The second point, which relates to the issue of autonomous state action, is that the the substitution of large-scale organisation for small has typically gone hand in hand with the state's response to crises generated by external challenges. The attempt to mediate and manage pressures of interstate competition, both military and economic, has at critical moments during this century spurred states to centralise facilities, foster Fordist arrangements and eliminate small undertakings. Whether in seeking to protect, enhance or recuperate their own powers within the international political system, national authorities have thus pushed into prominence a set of concentration policies, extending the tracks that capitalist activity would follow, blocking or shortening others which traced out alternative paths. The argument therefore introduces a hitherto neglected geo-political dimension into the analysis of comparative industrial organisational structure.

These points can be substantiated by analysing the links between international relations, state intervention, and the substitution of large-scale for small industry in Europe (Britain, France, West Germany) and the USA. The period after 1914 marks the ascendancy of corporate capitalism with its big structures, huge companies and large factories. Three observations are relevant in this regard. Before 1914, national economies were highly decentralised. The overall pre-war picture (drawn from statistics on the distribution of industrial employment by size of enterprise) is one of economic dispersion, not concentration (on the military origins of large-scale industry in the nineteenth century see Mann 1990, Vol. 2). Second, on the eve of World War 1, the presence of mass production methods was very limited. Outside America, the mass manufacturers of standardised goods had made little headway before the sudden emergency of the First World War. Even the manufacture of automobiles, that giant symbol of the modern Fordist economy, remained more a matter of craft methods than mass assembly. But when European states entered into battle, 'thereupon jigs and dyes and automated assembly lines came rapidly into their own' (McNeill 1983: 330–331).

Assessing the material changes wrought by the war economies (including that of the Second World War) on patterns of ownership is clearly a hazardous exercise. Nevertheless, wherever appropriate time series data are available, a strong pattern emerges. In virtually every case, including Germany, France, Japan, the USA and Britain, one can glimpse in the relative share of employment major shifts from small- to large-scale production and these shifts tend to be most strikingly concentrated within the time span of the two major wars. By contrast, the inter-war pattern is one of overall stability, marked occasionally by the resurgence of small firms, as in Germany and Japan (for the relevant national data see Hardach 1980: 219; Lévy-Leboyer 1976: table 10; Granovetter 1984: 326, 330; Bolton 1971).

Finally, these transformations were not simply incidental by-products of the war effort but were very closely related to the concentration policies adopted by national governments. Where small manufacturing was mo-bilised not via direct incorporation into larger units but via co-operative mechanisms (as in Germany, for example, in the First World War), the small sector held its own. By contrast, in Britain, where smaller units were either excluded or (in some industries) encouraged to consolidate facilities, the purgative effects of war tended to be more marked.

For these three reasons the period after 1914 is critical to an understand-ing of the dynamics of the 'replacement process' whereby large-scale indus-try replaces small. The significance of mass mobilisation warfare is that it issues in a clash not just of national armies but of state-managed and state-organised economies. As a consequence, differences in state capacities, structures and traditions rapidly dissolved as each national authority set about organising the nation as one giant commercial and industrial enter-prise (McNeill 1983: 320–326).

It is difficult to systematise analytically the structural-economic effects of international struggle for these impinged in varied ways in different national settings. What can be generally stated is that critical events like the two world wars are crucial for explaining the so-called 'logic' of organisational development. On each occasion, states became central man-agers of their economies, sponsoring mass-production methods, centralising industrial facilities and in some cases (as in Nazi Germany under Hitler's rearmament policy) deliberately and systematically combing out small pro-ducers.

The forms of co-operation that twentieth century war established between industry and the state, the concentration of resources required to conduct it, the manufacturing responses it invited, even the national defeat and humiliation it brought about (especially for France), all generated a momen-tum for change that could not be halted with the peace. In many instances, the wars fuelled government-backed movements for national regeneration, seeking rationalisation, efficiency and growth. With varying success and encountering more or less resistance, state elites thus set about extending to the industrial economy as a whole the giant structures associated with state power.

Interstate competition in the form of total war is thus one key chapter in the replacement process. But it is not the closing chapter. Another phase of that process spans the period since 1945. Whereas phase one is characterised by the effects of total war, the second phase is marked by the transition from militarism to industrialism. In this period, the rationalising activities of states can be related to changes which helped displace traditional power rivalry from primarily military to primarily economic competition.

There are two such changes of special importance. First, there has been a change in the nature of militarism (the emergence of the nuclear age). This has rendered warfare ineffective as a tool of state competition. Second, there has been a change in the nature of the international economy which has made national capital, the material base of sovereignty, more vulnerable to external forces. Together, these changes imply that industrialism is now the most important base of state power, breaking finally the traditional equation of prosperity with military strength.

The combined effect of these changes has been twofold. The first has been to make the state increasingly important as an economic actor in its own right, compelled to act in the international arena in order to maximise the world surplus in its own favour and at home to increase the competitiveness of its national capital. As a result, states increasingly look to big business, not Big Berthas, as the crucial vehicles of competitive strength, both to defend markets at home and to win them abroad. The transition to modern militarism has therefore meant that industrialism (ever increasing economic growth) has become the *sine qua non* of international position and domestic legitimacy and that states in order to achieve this have, for the most part, chosen the 'big business' route.

This argument can be demonstrated by examining the big business push in three countries, France, Britain, and West Germany. In each case, it can be shown how this push occurred in response to crises precipitated by external-international pressures that were not directly 'economic'. For example, in Germany, the period after occupation is critical for explaining the dynamics of industrial concentration. Territorially divided, physically devastated and defunct as an independent military power, the last remaining sinew and symbol of national might for Germany was industrial giantism, yet this too was under threat. Thus, against the efforts of the Allied powers to break up its giant combines, Germany's political leadership reacted by strengthening and extending the organisational and structural features of German capitalism.

In France, too, the experience of occupation and defeat provided a spur to industrial giantism that saw the decimation of its workshop economy. Weakness before German aggression in both world wars and, above all, wholesale defeat and occupation in 1940 led to a reversal of French political economy after 1945 that bureaucrats had attempted without success after 1918. In 1919 as in 1945, military relations had dramatised for France the links between industrial strength and national security but in 1945 state elites were able to exploit a much more thoroughgoing sense of crisis and national decline. Equally important, the state was now able to outflank capital which stood condemned for collaboration and was associated with defeat. Consequently, when the politicians and planning elites looked to the industrial landscape they did not see, as in Italy, a model suited to the national way of life. Nor did they see a potential or necessary bulwark against the threat of Communism and 'proletarianisation'. They saw only a threat to the nation's resurgence, an artisanal economy and society destined to remain the 'prey' of industrial nations (Kuisel 1981: 154). Industrial organisation thus became a means of furthering the political power of France as a nation and to that end the French technocrats and politicians set about emulating the giant structures and Fordist techniques of the American economy.

In Britain, the new 'rationalisation restlessness' which gathered pace from the late '50s had its roots in the Suez crisis. The political events of 1956 dramatised the superior economic (and military) power of the United States and forced Britain's retreat, thus precipitating its decline as a world poweer. Thus began a period of intense scrutiny of the nation's economic problems at a time when Britain's growth rates and trading performance constituted dramatic improvements upon its pre-war position. As was the case for France and Germany, international pressures and geo-political interests served to focus state attention on reorganising the nation's productive base.

The Italian experience offers a contrasting case in support of the argument. Italy suffered no similar externally induced crisis. Somewhat ironically, it was the only belligerent nation to emerge as it had entered the war, as 'the least of the Great Powers'. True Italy had suffered defeat, but it was not their country's international weaknesses that the Italians held up for political scrutiny. It was the age-old internal divisions which the collapse of Fascism had unleashed and revealed. Thus, whereas the French, for example, twice the victim of a stronger industrial power, defined their failures in primarily economic-external terms, the Italians perceived their weaknesses as predominantly political and domestic. For them, this meant a focussing of political energies not on external weakness, but on the more pressing problem of internal social cohesion.

Conclusion

Overall, my analysis suggests a primary and dynamic role for interstate relations in shaping the industrial giantism typical of contemporary Western economies. This has obvious implications for theories of the state's relation to the economy for it ties one of the most formative experiences in the

making of twentieth-century capitalism to a sphere of power and activity —
interstate competition — quite distinct from (i. e. irreducible to) the organisational power and interests of capital. As the evolving literature on states
makes clear (see Hall 1986: 1 – 21), it is precisely this international system
which constitutes an autonomous arena of social action. To the extent that
the rationalising activity of states flows from that arena it is irreducible to
market forces. Consequently, it may well be that the logic of conventional
theories needs to be reversed. For, as is well known, in these accounts the
compulsive logic of economic relations creates a world dominated by big
business which in turn dominates the state. In getting behind the present,
however, we have seen how national political agencies have themselves
contributed independently to the development of that world. In the process
it was not states undertaking functions for capital that seemed paramount
but the way in which capital has been called on to undertake tasks for the
state.

   If there is a single conclusion to the discussion as a whole, it is that
industrial development is by and large neutral about organisational forms.
Politics is not. Decentralised production is therefore no mere exception to
the classical rule of concentration, for no such rule exists. Just as there was
nothing necessary about the general decline of small-scale manufacturing,
so conversely, no capitalist law of motion, no industrial logic makes the
spread and triumph of giantism irresistible. It does indeed depend significantly on what states do.

   It is not only our theories or our comprehension of small-scale production
in Italy and Japan that are affected by these findings. They also have a
very direct bearing on how we interpret our own industrial options. Does
this mean that the successful small-firm models of other countries can be
replicated elsewhere? If so, do their advantages outweigh possible disadvantages? These, I believe, are some of the more interesting questions for future
analysis.

Section Two
Learning from the East

Introduction

Jane Marceau

Reworking the productive world, at both micro-(intra-organisational) and macro-levels is being led by a few major industries. Large companies and certain countries, especially Japan and Germany and, to a much lesser extent, the USA and the Asian NICs, are leading the way both in the development of the crucial computer-related physical technologies and in the managerial strategies which are now seen as a central part of competitive success. In particular, the automotive industry is at the forefront of the changes now considered typical of the emerging techno-industrial paradigm. As the papers in this section of the book show, the lead of the automotive assembly 'core' firms is being followed by firms in the other sectors, although the paradigm organisational form for the new system remains that of the auto industry.

Changes to the organisation of production in the motor vehicle sector are rebuilding or 'de-maturing' a long-established industry, one only quite recently (into the 1980s) believed by many analysts to be on the decline. The industry, which developed in the West using the form of factory work and organisation which gave its name to the 'Fordist' system of production, after one of the sector's leading protagonists, is now rapidly adopting quite different methods of organisation. Arguments abound about whether the emerging internal work organisational system is 'post-Fordist' or 'neo-Fordist' (for a summary, see Greig 1990) and we return to this question below in the last section of this book on 'reworking work'. There is no doubt, however, that the new managerial strategies and their correlates in worker practices have been essentially developed in Japan. In this area, the West is quite clearly learning from the East. The elements of the system are summarised in such well-known initials as JIT (Just-in-Time) and TQC (Total Quality Control) and terms such as *kaizen* (cooperative problem-solving), *kanban* (order 'card' or 'tickets') or *jidoka* (line stop). All refer to concepts and practices central to the system which are now in common use by managers in the automotive industry in all vehicle-producing nations. Other established industries are now following suit, especially at the hi-tech end of manufacturing where quality is all important. Aerospace, electronics and indeed all defence-related industries have introduced or are now introducing similar production organisation systems. At the low-tech end of the industrial spectrum as well there is increasing interest; in the clothing industry, for example, the introduction of bar-coding and a 'pull system' of production driven by information from retail sales have been part of the creation of a quasi-JIT system known as Quick Response.

Japan and Japanese production practices in both automotive and other industries are thus at the forefront of a new industrial system and the system is clearly being applied to central industries in the West where Japanese performance is setting the new overall standard of excellence.

The emergence of the system in Japan and its apparent wholesale adoption by key industries in the West raises the question again of the convergence of organisational patterns in the industrialised world. If the Japanese system is so powerful and if it is so widely applauded in the West, will East and West begin to look much more similar in their productive systems? Will the reworking of the industrial world at the level of the organisation of material production mean the end of 'culture' as an element of the local rationalities used to design the business recipes adopted? Will, indeed, 'technologies', broadly defined, come to be the determinants of organisation in a way currently dismissed by observers?

The answer, of course, is a complex one and no definitive response can even be attempted as yet. The factors in the equation, however, are becoming clearer. They continue to relate to the traditional factors of diversities in social, cultural and political contexts as well as to more particular, nationally specific, elements such as government policies and broader institutional contexts. This is made clear in papers in the section of the book which follows. In particular, the importance of inter-organisational power relations is made evident.

As I have said, the elements of the 'Japanese' system are well-known. The consequences of the adoption of these elements by major 'core' companies, however, are much less frequently considered. The adoption of Just-in-Time production, in particular, has very serious implications not only for internal organisation but also for external relations, notably between client companies and their suppliers. In many ways, indeed, the JIT system breaks down the boundaries between companies, especially where a network is built using Electronic Data Interchange directly between clients and their suppliers. An advanced example of this is provided by a BMW plant in Germany where BMW computers command a textile supplier's computers to provide car-seat cloth of a specified type and colour for delivery direct to the production line with split second timing. In this system, suppliers may be seen as a kind of external labour force, to be managed in much the same way as employees working for the core firm. JIT as a *production*, rather than simply an inventory control system, involves a complex bargaining system between core firms and first tier suppliers, who must negotiate allocation of responsibility not only for perfect quality but also for design, R & D and the production of the modules attached to basic car platforms.

The core firms in the automotive industry, therefore, followed by their colleagues in the aerospace industry, as seen in the first chapter on France by Gorgeu and Mathieu presented below, are engaged not only in reworking their internal production structures but also in reworking their external relations. As they do this, they similarly rework both internal production structures and the external relations of their suppliers. These in turn rework the structures and activities of their own suppliers. JIT as a complete system of production thus has a major impact on the whole chain of production and is a very important tool for changing the practices, technologies and corporate cultures of a much broader range of firms than at first sight appears. Not only are firms in one chain affected but the cumulative effects of JIT ultimately spread across several chains because the advanced engineering areas involving complex assembly work draw, further down the chain, on companies which supply several chains. These companies are broader in range in terms of products, sectors and size of firm. Even small firms are affected, especially where they supply simple products for a variety of end-users. Indeed, even first tier suppliers outside Asia are seldom engaged solely in supplying the automotive industry. In Australia, for instance, Pacific Dunlop is a major supplier to car firms, to the textile and clothing sector and to the electronics industry, providing similar products (e. g. fabrics) to each but also having to cope with quite different specific demands.

The importance of the push from core firms, notably vehicle assemblers and their prime suppliers, for physical technological change but also for altered management strategies is thus very considerable. The 'management' by core firms of the network of companies who are and wish to remain their key suppliers and by chosen first tier suppliers of their own suppliers is by no means a smooth process but one essentially entailing competition, struggle and conflict, both internal and external. The speed but also the direction of the changes ocurring is much determined by the power relations established between key players, including not only the companies themselves but also other actors in the institutional structure, notably governments (of all levels) and trade unions. These processes are illustrated in this section in papers by Wilkinson, Morris and Oliver and by Marceau and Jureidini who show, for instance, how small companies protest new impositions by clients, how public authorities affect outcomes through competition for local location decisions, and how different interests may clash in the construction of the new order. These clashes may be especially evident in a country such as Australia, where all key players are multinationals, long protected by high tariff walls only now being dismantled, but they are also apparent in the UK. The situation in the car industry indicates the struggles and problems to be resolved in other industries as new manufacturing methods learned from the East push further and further into Western industrial structures. There is, for example, conflict over the speed and direction of change, over the relative importance of price, delivery and quality in the new competitive field, over control of crucial design and purchasing policies. In many cases, the 'stress' model of client-supplier relationships in the car industry described by Lamming in the UK (1987) is far from being resolved. Satisfactory outcomes to such conflicts are especially complex to obtain when major decisions about investment and production strategies are taken outside the country which is the immediate arena of conflict, important decisions being the prerogative of overseas HQs with broader strategic aims, especially where switching from a multidomestic to a global strategic approach (Porter 1987). In addition, much geographic and 'political' refocussing is needed — in Australia on the recognition of the need to develop close ties with Asia, for instance, and in Europe because of the creation of the European single market, a new factor which also exercises the minds of boards of directors in Japan and the USA.

Nor are decisions about what and how to produce in any one country the only elements of the new system which transform the productive structure. The world is being rapidly reworked by the strategic location decisions made by both core firms and their major suppliers. In the 1960s and 1970s the move of 'Fordist' producers of cars and also of many other complex manufactured commodities to low-cost less-developed nations became familiar. Now car firms, notably Japanese car firms, are relocating into the original heartlands of the car producers — the USA, Canada and the UK (as a first step into Europe) — and, from an earlier date, into Australia as part of their worldwide production and marketing strategies. When these firms have 'transplanted' themselves to Western nations they rework the existing industrial geography of their host countries. In the UK and the USA they have selected greenfields sites, usually away from established industrial areas, as Wilkinson and his colleagues show in this book. In North America, for instance, they have established an 'auto alley', a corridor leading south from Ontario to Kentucky. Because of the importance of all aspects of the JIT system, the assemblers have been followed by their key suppliers, also moving to greenfields sites, using previously non-industrial labour and spreading the new industrial message to rural areas (Mair, Florida and Kenney 1988). In France, too, there is some evidence of a change in locational patterns (Gorgeu and Mathieu, below) and also in Holland as Penner (1990) indicates. If the 'tail' of smaller suppliers drops off in each auto-producing country, as seems inevitable, further reworking of the geographical picture seems likely.

Reworking the world through the adoption of JIT and other central elements of the Japanese productive system also, of course, involves reworking the world of work. This is apparent everywhere and is taken up in a later section of the book. Reworking relationships also involves management's search for *control*, both of the processes of change and their outcomes, and new strategies for control and the conflicts which arise in the strategies' implementation, too, are the subject of a later section of the present volume.

The three papers on the automotive industry in this section are essentially concerned with the transfer of technologies, embodied both in machines and in management strategies, from East to West. It is important to recall, however, that historically technology transfers have proceded in many directions. In thinking of Japan, observers now frequently forget both how long was the period of Japanese borrowing technology from the West and how far Japan has been instrumental in transferring technology within the East, among her Asian neighbours. In this section, Judith Nishida's chapter reminds us how Japan in the late nineteenth and early twentieth centuries borrowed cotton-spinning techniques from the West and set up factories both in Japan and China, thus transferring the technology again. Nishida, in examining this and a subsequent transfer to Hong Kong, demonstrates how crucial was the institutional structure surrounding and supporting the cotton-spinners to the successful use of the physical technology and factory organisation selected. The business recipes devised owe much to structures generated by local rationalities, as Clegg describes them above, and relied much on factors outside the individual productive organisations themselves and the institutional structure whose importance is made clear by Biggart in her chapter in this book. In the case described by Nishida, the relations *between* organisations, notably between producers, marketing groups and financial institutions were particularly close. When the technology was transferred to the *Chinese* within China, as opposed to the *Japanese* in China, to a society which did not supply such broader institutional support, an identical factory organisation did not flourish. Only when a further transfer took place to Hong Kong, where an appropiate institutional structure could be built, did the technology succeed again.

The Japanese-Chinese cotton-spinners example is one instance of technology transfer between different cultural, geographical and institutional settings within the East. The next chapter in this section of the book also examines a less-often discussed technology transfer, that of computer-related technologies and altered managerial strategies developed in the West and adopted in Hong Kong by a range of business and public organisations, both Chinese and British owned or managed.

Using a framework developed from Western writings on worker-oriented managerial strategies, Teresa Poon illustrates different reactions to the technological changes introduced. As an additional complication to the 'culture' explanation for diverse reactions, Poon shows that there is no clear correlation between the 'culture' of the organisation (whether Chinese or Western-owned/managed) and particular outcomes of change and instead points to the importance in assessing both organisational changes and worker reactions to them of factors outside the organisations themselves. In the Hong Kong example, labour supply seems to be a crucial issue as well as diverse government policies on technology transfer. But most important of all in determining reactions during the period discussed by Poon was labour security, the expansion rather than contraction of the organisations concerned so that no one was immediately threatened with loss of livelihood by the changes introduced. While 'Chinese' attitudes are recognised in the chapter to contribute to some 'docile' reactions to technological change, Poon poses the question of how long such 'cultural' attitudes may be expected to last as the changes concerned increase in scope and intensity or as economic downturn leads to insecurity.

In short, then, in this section of the book the chapters raise questions about many aspects of technology transfer which concern organisational changes. All emphasise the extent to which transfer of physical technologies involves organisations outside the particular innovating enterprises, whether private or public. Neither the process nor the outcomes of such changes can be understood without analysis of the social organisation and the industrial, financial and political factors which make up the environment of the enterprises introducing new technologies. These factors, whatever the 'cultures' concerned, seem ultimately to determine the outcomes. On the other hand, they are themselves in part the result of particular cultural configurations, as shown notably here in both Nishida's and Poon's papers. While the production world is being reworked by international borrowings both of managerial strategies and physical technologies the organisational processes of change and the outcomes are much affected by vastly broader cultural and institutional factors. Conflicts and tensions vitally affect both technological and organisational outcomes. This is evident in the automotive industry where the West is learning from the East in the construction of the new techno-economic paradigm but it is also clear in transfers within the East itself and from West to East.

Japanizing the World: The Case of Toyota

Barry Wilkinson, Jonathan Morris, Nick Oliver

Introduction

The term 'Japanization' is used here as shorthand for the diffusion of Japanese management systems and practices, whether this be via Japanese direct investment overseas or the emulation of such systems and practices in non-Japanese organizations. Based on the philosophies of Total Quality Control (TQC) and Just-In-Time (JIT) production, the Japanese organizational form has been held up as a new 'paradigm' which challenges the logic of traditional Western production regimes (Aoki 1987; Oliver and Wilkinson 1988) and has crucial implications for both intra- and inter-organizational structures and relations of power and control (Wilkinson and Oliver 1989).

The overseas productive capacity of Japanese industry has grown enormously during the 1980s and is set to grow even more markedly over the next few years. Table 1 summarizes the published intentions of the Machinery Exporters Association.

Table 1   Overseas Productive Capacity of Japanese Industry (% of total)

	1988	1992
Office Machinery	12,1	39,0
Cars	11,5	30,0
Machine Tools	5.2	27,0
Computer	5.7	25,0
Semi-Conductors	2,5	12,0

Source: James (1988)

Toyota is an important case study because it is the largest Japanese company in an industrial sector (automobiles) which is rapidly shifting production overseas. Toyota is also widely credited with the invention and refinement of the Just-In-Time (JIT) system of production, which companies across the world are now attempting to emulate; indeed the term 'Toyotism' has been coined to distinguish such a system from 'Fordism' (Dohse, Jürgens and Malsch 1985).

The question addressed in this paper is whether it is possible that Toyota could re-create overseas the special conditions necessary for the successful operation of a JIT production regime. The first section examines Toyota's production system as developed and refined in Japan and indicates the political and social supports which appear necessary to maintain such a system of production. We then describe the recent spread of Toyota's manufacturing capacity across the world and the reasons for overseas expansion. Using Toyota transplants as examples, analysis of the social, political and organizational aspects of the systems of production being established is provided.

The Toyota Production System

Toyota opened its first assembly plant in 1938, but most rapidly expanded its production during the 1960s and 1970s (Table 2). Today Toyota is the largest of the Japanese automotive manufacturers by a large margin — in 1988 the company produced almost four million vehicles compared with less than 2.2 million by its nearest rival, Nissan. It is currently the third largest auto maker in the world, following General Motors and Ford. Toyota is also considered widely to be the most efficient vehicle producer, the efficiency being indicated in Table 3. A recent international study into productivity in the world vehicle industry claimed that the average Japanese plant in Japan can produce a car of comparable complexity and specification with half the human effort needed in European-owned plants in Europe (Jones and Womack 1988).

The efficiency of Toyota, and other Japanese manufacturers, is accounted for in large part by its JIT production system and associated Total Quality Control (TQC) practices. Led by Ono Taiichi, Toyota began experimenting with JIT production in 1948, the system being transferred from shop to shop and plant to plant over the next fifteen years or so (Cusumano 1985). Later other Japanese companies adopted JIT techniques and in recent years they have spread to the West. Schonberger (1982: 16) captures the essence of JIT production as follows:

'The JIT idea is simple: produce and deliver finished goods just-in-time to be sold, sub-assemblies just-in-time to be assembled into finished goods ... and purchased materials just-in-time to be transformed into fabricated parts.'

The philosophies and practices of JIT and TQC have been described in detail elsewhere (Wilkinson and Oliver 1989). To put it very simply, JIT is

Table 2   Toyota Factories in Japan, 1984

Factory Name	Opened	Employees	Functions (Manufacturing and Assembly)
Honsha (Main)	1938	2,326	Truck and bus assembly, prefabricated housing
Motomachi	1959	5,095	Car assembly
Kamigo	1965	3,346	Engines, transmissions
Takaoka	1966	5,727	Car assembly
Miyoshi	1968	2,081	Suspension subassemblies
Tsutsumi	1970	5,570	Car assembly
Myochi	1973	1,679	Engines, suspension cast parts
Shimoyama	1975	1,679	Engines, emission control equipment
Kinuura	1978	1,969	Transmissions, drive trains
Tahara	1979	3,429	Car and truck assembly
		32,901	

Source: Cusumano (1985)

Table 3   Vehicles per Employee 1960 – 83

	1960	1970	1982
General Motors	8	8	10
Ford	14	12	12
Nissan	12	30	41
Toyota	15	38	56

Source: Cusomano (1985)

a philosophy which aims at reducing material and human slack in an organization by attacking waste, which is defined as anything which adds cost but not value to a product. Ideally, production occurs 'just-in-time' to meet customer demand ('customers' may be internal or external to the organization) so that inventories, work-in-progress and stocks of finished goods (all of which carry costs) are eliminated. This philosophy contrasts with the so-called 'just-in-case' system typical outside Japan, where human and material slack is carried in order to cope with the vagaries of the market place and uncertainties of the labour process. Uncertainty is attacked by the practices associated with the complementary philosophy (arguably a necessary adjunct of JIT) of total quality production. This means what it says: just-in-time deliveries, inside or outside the factory, must be defect-free in a context where the 'slack' of inspectors, progress chasers, and even supervisors, is reduced to its bare minimum. Similarly, JIT creates the imperative of total management control over the labour process. A strike, a work-to-rule, or even a mere refusal to work flexibly or work overtime or lunch-breaks as demand from 'customers' dictates, could pose severe problems to JIT production. This is because JIT means a highly inter-dependent production system, such that any stoppage anywhere in the system has an immediate and pervasive impact.

Hence the achievement of JIT and TQC ideals — whether in Japan or overseas — is dependent on the implementation of a whole set of organiza-tional and work practices. Typically, workflows are simplified and machines based around product groups rather than functions or processes. This means that complexity is reduced and that visibility (and hence controllabil-ity) is heightened. Work is organized into teams or 'cells', each team having responsibility for an identifiable 'product'. Specialists in quality control, maintenance, materials handling, etc. are dispersed into the cells, and each team becomes answerable to the next cell downstream in the system. A 'customer ethos' is deliberately developed whereby each team has an identifiable 'customer', and produces to each customer's demands (which might be transmitted via *kanban* cards) rather than production being 'pushed' by a grand production master plan (Aoki 1987; Sayer 1986). Tight in-process controls such as Statistical Process Control (SPC) are needed for such an interdependent system — there is no room for defects. Any 'participatory institutions', such as *kaizen* groups or quality circles, nor-mally based on work team, give everyone a responsibility for continuous improvement as JIT and total quality ideals are pursued (Oliver and Wilkinson 1988; Schonberger 1982; Parnaby 1987); indeed, any lack of contribution to the system's efficiency from the worker's mental rather than merely physical capabilities could be considered 'wasteful'.

Toyota extended JIT to its suppliers during 1954–55, with daily as opposed to monthly (or longer) deliveries, and around the same time extended JIT forward by allowing Sales to take the lead in production planning. This depended on Sales producing accurate forecasts of demand. With these developments, inventories, work-in-progress and stocks of fin-ished goods were minimized throughout the entire production system.

Such a production regime places considerable demands on workers. Domingo (1985: 22) argues that the Toyota system 'requires an almost military discipline' and that it 'indefinitely simulates a crisis so that manage-ment and workers are always on their toes'. Similarly, Slaughter (1987) refers to 'management-by-stress'. This is because of the obsession with eliminating 'waste', which includes the 'idle time' of workers as well as machines. Work cycle times are systematically minimized and workers typically operate more than one machine so that the 'idle time' of waiting for machines to finish is eliminated; in the case of demand fluctuations, output can be raised quickly (within limits) by adding overtime or (often part-time or temporary) workers. Slaughter (1987) is critical of the system, as is Kamata (1983) who described a Toyota 'factory of despair' which led to accidents, high turnover and even suicides. Domingo (1985: 22), on the other hand, argues that

'the tension generated ... is a positive tension and seldom results in any counter-productive fear or undue anxiety ... every working day (is) a challenge, a victory to achieve rather than merely a boring expanse of time.'

Domingo argues that the culture and values of the Japanese people pre-dispose them to enjoying work under such a regime. However, Toyota workers attempted to resist the imposition of the 'positive tension' because of the request to operate several machines and the elimination of 'idle time'. But the Toyota union was by the mid-1950s relatively weak, and Ono himself had spent a year in 1947 as a union official and had a degree of influence over the leadership; by the end of 1955 Ono claimed he had overcome most of the opposition to the new production techniques (Cusumano 1985). This was in the context of a nation-wide purge of radicals in all sorts of Japanese institutions during the early 1950s and the establishment and spread of enterprise unions across Japanese industry (Littler 1982).

The expectations which Toyota and other JIT manufacturers place on suppliers are also relatively high. Toyota expects many of its primary suppliers to deliver small lots several times a day. This, together with the fact that Toyota, like other Japanese auto makers, out-sources far more components than is typical in the West, poses logistical problems. However, unlike Western companies which share suppliers in common, Toyota (and other Japanese manufacturers) sit at the top of their own 'pyramid' of sub-contractors. Toyota has 176 primary auto parts suppliers, many of them more or less dedicated and often located very close to Toyota's factories. These in turn rely on an estimated 4,000 secondary and tertiary sub-contractors which pay relatively low wages and take on more labour intensive jobs (Dodwell 1986). Toyota's suppliers are hence treated more like extensions of Toyota's own factories than as independent organizations. Clearly spatial concentration makes JIT supply easier and Toyota was aided in developing its JIT supplies by enjoying a relatively rural location in 'Toyota City'. In return for long-term contracts and the participation of Toyota in developing supplier competences, the supplier is expected to deliver defect-free goods just-in-time at minimum cost.

With regard to both supplier and employee relations just-in-time production heightens the dependency between company and constituents. At

Toyota, as in many Japanese companies, life-time employment (for core workers), seniority-based pay systems, and company-oriented enterprise unions mean employees are as dependent on the company as the company is on its workforce. The inherent vulnerability of the JIT regime is hence less likely to be a pawn in industrial action. Similarly, with regard to suppliers, the dependence of the company on sole suppliers rather than multiple competing suppliers who are easily substitutable is tempered by suppliers' dependence on Toyota as the main customer. And Toyota often has a financial stakeholding in the supplier which increases further its ability to exert leverage.

Hence Toyota's JIT regime in Japan is supported by particular economic, social and political relationships constructed between the company and its major constituent elements. These relationships were in part engineered by the Toyota Motor Corporation itself and in part reflect wider trends and developments in the twentieth century Japanese political economy. After describing the economics of Toyota's recent acceleration of overseas production, we will address the question of how the Toyota production system works on foreign soil.

Toyota's Overseas Production

In the 1970s and 1980s Toyota lagged behind Nissan and Honda in offshore production, concentrating on exports. In 1986 Toyota depended on exports for around 47 per cent of its sales (Dodwell 1986). Although in 1987 Toyota had interests in 29 assembly and auto parts plants around the world, many of these employed small numbers of people. In Asia, Africa and Latin America Toyota's presence has often been in the form of joint ventures or licensing agreements in response to host governments' import substitution policies. The Toyota presence in these countries has existed since the 1960s but has increased steadily since then, often in response to gradual increases in local content requirements. In the 1980s, however, political pressures and a strong yen have forced manufacturers to locate production in their major market places − the USA and Europe (Steven 1988). The most important investments announced by Toyota in the 1980s have been: NUMMI in California, a joint-venture with GM which employs around 2,500 people; a plant in Cambridge, Ontario in Canada, which is expected to employ 1,000 in the near future (presently 600); a large plant in Georgetown, Kentucky in the USA, which will employ 3,500 at full capacity (1,700 in 1989); and an assembly plant at Burnaston, Derby in the UK, which is expected to employ around 3,000 by the mid 1990s. There have also been important developments in Australia, where Toyota is merging operations with GM Holden to become one of three local producers in line with government policy (Robertson 1988).

There is strong political and economic pressure from Noth America and Europe on Japanese companies not only to assemble within the market place but also to ensure the quality of investment commitment is high — for instance, by bringing high value added or R & D operations — and to source locally. This means that full, integrated production is in the process of development in America and Europe, however reluctant Toyota may have been, and makes the study of the transferability of JIT regimes all the more feasible.

Laying out the Welcome Mat

In North America and the UK Toyota has been given a warm welcome by the media and local power holders, often in the context of the company's proposed location in pockets of high unemployment and inter-regional competition for investments. Areas without vehicle assembly traditions appear to have been preferred by most of the Japanese assemblers including Toyota. Toyota and GM announced their decision to open a joint-venture (exceptionally, at an old site) in Fremont, California in February 1983, one year after the closure of GM's Fremont operation. In 1983, unemployment nationally in the US auto industry was 15–20 per cent and four out of the five auto plants in the West (including Fremont) had closed since the late 1970s (Brown and Reich 1989). Toyota's announcements of investments in Ontario, Kentucky and Derby (in 1985, 1985 and 1989 respectively) were also widely welcomed for the jobs which they would provide both directly and through the attraction of auto supply companies to the locality (Morris 1988; Center for Business and Economic Research 1988). In the cases of Ontario and Kentucky, government financial assistance was provided as an incentive to Toyota. A breakdown of the Toyota Georgetown investments costs is provided in Table 4.

In Cambridge, Ontario, a more modest investment creating 1,000 jobs attracted financial support from both local and national governments. Financial incentives were not available for Toyota's production facility in Burnaston, Derbyshire, but Derbyshire County Council provided every assistance it could in making Toyota feel welcome in the face of fierce competition from other local authorities across Britain. The effort was clearly considered worth it. Derbyshire County Council

Table 4   Breakdown of Toyota Georgetown Investment Costs

Item	Cost to Kentucky	Cost to Toyota
Land Purchase	$ 12.5 m	
Site Preparation	$ 20.0 m	$ 23.9 m
Highway Improvements	$ 47.0 m	
Toyota Employee Training	$ 65.0 m	
Toyota Families Education	$ 5.2 m	
Miscellaneous	$ 9.0 m	
Bond Interest	$ 166.7 m	
Plant Construction		$ 340. m
Machinery		$ 460.0 m
Total Cost	$ 325.4 m	$ 823.9 m

Source: Center of Business and Economic Research (1988)

leader David Bookbinder, on hearing the announcement that Burnaston had been chosen, declared.

'On behalf of all the people of Derbyshire I am deeply honoured to welcome Toyota to our beautiful county. I feel greatly privileged that you have chosen Derbyshire for this exciting project and I am confident that your decision represents the beginning of a fruitful and rewarding partnership. This development is an inspiration to all of us and I look forward to mutual understanding and a deep friendship between our peoples.'

The Labour controlled County Council is to invest ú20 million of its pension fund (the maximal permitted) in the new Toyota plant (an investment of around ú700 million) and Bookbinder recently announced an intention to introduce Japanese studies as a compulsory part of the curriculum in all Derbyshire's secondary schools, including the Japanese language and Japanese modern history (*Financial Times* 4 September 1989). The latter intention may be difficult to implement if the Japanese Language Asssociation's estimation that there is only one person in Britain with a degree in Japanese and a teaching certificate is correct (*Financial Times* 25 November 1989) but the attempt to offer a welcoming enviroment is probably appreciated by the Japanese.

   Opposition to the plant was largely limited to a small number of people directly affected by the Compulsory Purchase Order for 620 acres of land for the site. (620 acres is more than twice the amount of land necessary for immediate production requirements. At the CPO hearing Toyota stated that it needed the land as an assurance for the future, when it might expand capacity and/or invite suppliers to locate on site.) Dillow (1989) lists a political welcome together with low wages and reduced trade union power as a major factor in the concentration of Japanese companies within Europe in the UK and contrasts this welcome with the hostility expressed by France and other EC countries.

In Georgetown, Kentucky, in contrast, although the local media generally orchestrated the celebrations of the Kentucky State authorities in winning the investment, there were loud voices of criticism, particularly about hiring practices, the impact on the community and State provision of financial assistance. Some complained of the fact that Toyota took 12 months to evaluate applications for jobs and stressed attitudes and teamwork ability in selection decisions. A study by Kentucky University registered fears among Georgetown's 12,000 population that crime, low moral values and an influx of people who 'weren't like them' could result (*Industry Week* 5 June 1989). And questions were raised, including by the Attorney General, about the morality and legality of Kentucky State giving cash handouts for private use (Kane 1989). The criticism were equally loudly countered by both Toyota and the State authorities. Toyota handed out several million dollars to local educational institutions and a community centre and set up a liaison committee in Georgetown to improve communications. These activities meant that Toyota could be held up by its media supporters as a model of the 'good corporate citizen'.

The most embarrassing event faced by Toyota was probably in June 1986 when a dispute over union recognition broke out between construction workers and the Japanese company building the plant, Ohbayashi. Labour leaders televised their dispute with Ohbayashi and Toyota (though some stations refused to broadcast the advertisement because they thought it too controversial) and by November labour leaders were announcing an anti-Toyota rally on the 7th, Pearl Harbour Day (Kane 1989). The dispute was settled on the 25th November when Ohbayashi agreed that the AFL-CIO could play the role in labour assignments it wanted. Although the law suits against Toyota and Ohbayashi continued to be pursued, calmer relations between Toyota and its community have prevailed since then.

Supplier Relations

It appears that where posible Toyota, in common with other Japanese auto assemblers in North America, has sought to move towards the sorts of relationship with suppliers which it enjoys in Japan and there are reasons to suspect that the same will hold true in the UK. At Georgetown, local content in 1989 was 60 per cent, expected to rise to 75 per cent when the on-site powertrain plant became fully operational, and even to go higher as Toyota improves its local sourcing base. All potential local suppliers are put through an extensive selection process which can last up to three years. So far approval has been given to 200. Suppliers are put on one year contracts, although long term relationship are expected. A Toyota spokesman in Georgetown commented:

'We're partners, and we expect them to work in that Kaizen way ... We ask them what they have in their structure to improve their costs, and how they encourage their employees to participate in improving the process.' (Economist Intelligence Unit 1989).

Only parts from Japan are kept in any quantity (four weeks stock), most deliveries being on a JIT basis by both road and rail. Suppliers have not yet set up on Toyota's own site (Toyota has excess land) but since the Georgetown site was announced 37 out of 44 auto parts suppliers newly-locating in Kentucky State have been Japanese, mostly joint-ventures.

Sixteen of the 44 new supplier organizations supply Toyota, the rest serving the growing number of car and truck assembly plants in the newly emerged 'auto alley' of which Kentucky (and Ontario, where the closely linked Toyota Cambridge plant is located) is a part. The Kentucky State government is proud that these plants together represent an investment of over US$1 billion and 8,800 new jobs. Similar numbers of autorelated Japanese investments have sprung up in the other auto alley States of Ohio, Illinois, Michigan, Tennessee and Indiana, which suggests that already most of Toyota's suppliers are Japanese rather than American-owned. Between 1985 and 1987 42 of Toyota's suppliers from Japan set up facilities in the USA, and the number has increased since then (Fujita and Child-Hill 1988).

California-based NUMMI, in contrast, has been reported as having JIT delivery problems because many components have to be sourced several days away, increasingly from auto alley. Only a small number of Japanese suppliers have located close to the NUMMI plant, most suppliers preferring to be in a position to meet the demands of more than one assembler. Most Japanese assemblers in the USA have reported problems in the quality of supply using American firms and this may be an important reason why Japanese suppliers have rapidly and apparently easily won contracts not only with Japanese assemblers but also with Ford, Chrysler and General Motors. Despite firms' problems in initially establishing an adequate supplier base, both productivity and quality at Japanese assemblers in North America are reported to be similar to levels found in Japanese plants in Japan, and higher than the American 'big three' (Mair, Florida and Kenney 1988).

In the UK Toyota will face a 'local content' ruling which specifies that 60 per cent of the value of parts should be sourced within the European Community, rising to 80 per cent two to three years after production start-up (*Financial Times* 19 April 1989). Nissan, which started production in North East England in 1986, currently claims a local content of 70 per cent, to rise to 80 per cent in 1990 (*Financial Times* 18 April 1989). Ninety per cent of its local content is sourced within the UK, the other 10 per cent coming largely from West Germany (Trade and Industry Committee 1987). Non-auto Japanese manufacturers in the UK have frequently expressed problems with regard to the quality, delivery and cost of local supplies (Dunning 1986; *Financial Times* 5 April 1988) and it is predicted that Japanese component suppliers will take advantage of these shortcomings and displace indigenous suppliers in non-auto industries as well (Trevor and Christie 1988).

In the UK auto industry, Ford, Rover and others, in attempting to adopt their own JIT regimes, have faced difficulty in securing quality assured supplies delivered just-in-time. How much this is the fault of the supplier, however, is unclear. On the one hand, some suppliers interviewed by the authors have cried foul play and argued that JIT is being used as an excuse to pass on stock-holding costs to companies located elsewhere in the supply chain (Oliver and Wilkinson 1988). On the other hand, a recent extensive survey of the West Midlands auto parts industry concluded that

'Many suppliers are not equipped for the responsibilities of 'partnership' sourcing or JIT supply, and many others are not financially sound enough to make the necessary investments (Turnbull 1989).'

This, together with Toyota's experience in America, would suggest that Toyota is likely to attract large numbers of its suppliers from Japan to England. Derbyshire County Council leader, David Bookbinder, has claimed that over 20 Japanese auto suppliers will arrive in Derbyshire in the near future.

The 'dispersal' of Toyota City, which was the ultimate in spatially concentrated production and ideal for a JIT supply regime, is apparently inevitable as Toyota is forced to venture abroad. It is arguable just how far Toyota could go in reproducing such a system in different countries. One possible reason for Toyota's reluctance to venture overseas, as compared with the attitude of other Japanese companies, could indeed have been its fear of losing the advantages afforded its home base arrangements. With dispersal, Japanese suppliers often have to look to other auto-makers, Japanese or non-Japanese, in order to keep their order books full, with the threat to 'obligational contracting' which that entails. Nonetheless, all the evidence suggests that at least in its major plants overseas JIT supply systems are being established, spatial concentration is developing, and familiar demands on new suppliers are being maintained. And as in other aspects of industrial organization, Toyota is providing the lead to the rest of the world's automobile industry in its supplier relations.

Manufacturing and Working Practices

The Toyota factory regime, with its emphasis on quality, teamwork and attention to detail and its obsessional concern with eliminating waste, is similarly being transplanted abroad. The Georgetown plant has been described as a copy of the Tsusumi plant in Japan, with Japanese management and production methods being rigorously applied. Much of the production machinery was actually used on a pilot production line in Japan before being dismantled and shipped to Kentucky. Production is organized on a just-in-time basis with *kanban* controls and *kanban* are transferred between work stations by workers on bicycles (Economist Intelligence Unit 1989). All work is assigned to teams at work stations, typically of between five and eight people, which have responsibility for their own production, quality, cost and safety. The team leader makes individual assignments and reports to a group leader who has responsibility for promoting good communications and morale. Morale boosting includes a 10 minute voluntary exercise period before shift starts. Teamwork extends beyond working hours, members being encouraged to participate in organizational events such as golf tournaments, baseball and outings (Economist Intelligence Unit 1989). Ono's elimination of waste principles are also applied through rigorous time and motion study, as are the celebrated principles of *kaizen* (continuous improvement) and *jidoka* (line stop).

Toyota-style teamwork and waste elimination programmes had in fact already been implemented in the NUMMI plant earlier in the decade (Slaughter 1987; Brown and Reich 1989). Drastic changes had been made, including a flattened management hierarchy (with a completely new management), the reduction of job classification from over 80 to one for production workers (and from 200 to four overall), and the establishment of flexible working. Quality and productivity are claimed to have soared above the GM-Fremont level to levels comparable with Japan (Brown and Reich 1989; Kenney and Florida 1988).

In the UK, Japanese companies, including Nissan, appear to have been similarly successful in gaining acceptance of JIT regimes on the part of employees. Western companies attempting to change well-established work practices, however, have often met overt and/or covert resistance as they have tried to re-draw the 'political map' of the organization (Turnbull 1986;

Oliver and Wilkinson 1988; Wilkinson and Oliver 1989). Nonetheless, in both the UK and the USA, and arguably across the world, the Toyota production system and the Japanese form of industrial organization have provided the model for large sections of manufacturing industry, outside the automotive sector.

Both advocates and critics tend to agree that peer controls and heightened work intensity are characteristic of JIT regimes in the West. The impact of the work organization and practices on the employee's experience of work has, however, been given wildly different interpretations. The two extremes are represented by Dillow (1989), who claims devolved responsibility, team-work, and therefore job enrichment are the outcome of JIT and TQC practices, and Klein (1989: 61), who states that 'JIT and SPC can turn workers into extensions of a system ... they can push workers to the wall'. Referring to NUMMI, Brown and Reich (1989: 28) describe how 'the emphasis is on flexibility (rather than specialization) and on increased involvement in the production process'. Slaughter (1987), at the other extreme, is critical of NUMMI for the manner in which pressures are placed on workers to constantly increase their productivity. The experience she describes is one of work intensification and heightened management control over the labour process. At NUMMI some workers have made charges of speed-ups and during the first two and a half years of NUMMI's operation 14 per cent of employees either quit or were fired. It should be remembered, however, that at the old GM-Fremont plant before its closure, absenteeism was nearly 20 per cent, drug abuse was rife and the grievance and discipline machinery was overloaded (Kenney and Florida 1988).

Similarly divergent accounts of the experience of work have been pre-sented regarding Nissan's plant in North East England, which is the forerun-ner to Toyota's Derbyshire venture. Wickens (1987) suggests a high degree of loyalty on the part of workers and an enrichment of the job, while Garrahan and Stewart (1989) emphasize an exhausting work experience and the inability of workers to exert any control over their jobs. The latter authors further document peer monitoring of continuity and quality on the line and management's tracing of faults to specific work teams and indivi-duals who are given daily or weekly scores. Garrahan and Stewart claim many workers complained of the system of 'surveillance'.

Employee Relations

The apparently successful transplantation of the Toyota production system on foreign soil, and its acceptance by employees and often trade unions, is remarkable because it demands a very different workplace culture, a high degree of worker co-operation, and a stable system of industrial relations. In Japan the Toyota system emerged in a unique historical context with enterprise unionism, life-time employment and seniority-related pay systems as important elements. So what measures has Toyota taken to gain employee and union acceptance of its production system in the West? The answer that emerges is that Toyota has not transplanted wholesale its Japanese personnel practices, but that it has used them selectively and so far apparently successfully to create the conditions whereby the vulnerable JIT system is sufficiently protected.

First, Toyota exercises a high degree of selectivity and therefore control over workforce composition and characteristics. In Kentucky, 100,000 applications were received for the first 1,700 jobs, and selection involved between 18 and 25 hours of tests spread over three to five months. Adaptability and the abilities to learn and to work in teams were the prime criteria. Most of those selected were from the State of Kentucky, which was applauded by the authorities, and most had no record of work in the auto industry. The average age of those selected was 32 (Economist Intelligence Unit 1989). At the Ontario plant Toyota targetted senior high school graduates who had to undergo two days of testing for aptitude and teamwork and leadership skills. In addition, 25 team leaders were sent to Japan as part of a $40 million training package (*Toronto Star* 24 April 1988). Toyota will be similarly selective in Derbyshire, Nissan having provided the lead in North East England. At Nissan, adaptability and teamwork ability were central in the rigorous selection of the first 500 employees from 20,000 applicants (Wickens 1987).

In relation to employee selection, NUMMI is exceptional in that the plant was neither greenfield nor in a location without an auto industry background. In this case, 2,200 former GM-Fremont workers (from 5,000 former employees who were approached) were re-hired on new contracts with the participation of the local UAW. Brown and Reich (1989) suggest that, while the lengthy and intensive initial hiring and training processes would have been likely to encourage workers who did not like the new management style to select themselves out, far greater importance should be given to the transformation of workers' attitudes in their cooperation with the new working arrangements. The NUMMI case suggests that rigorous selection does not in itself account for employee co-operation with the Toyota production system but it undoubtedly remains an important factor.

Once selected, the importance of flexibility, attention to detail and teamworking is impressed on the recruits. Flexibility and team work are facilitated by a small number of job classification, as mentioned earlier, and constantly reinforced by group activities such as quality circles, team briefings and Kaizen sessions. Management-worker communications are direct rather than via union officials, though at NUMMI team leaders often also serve as union representatives (as they do in Japan). Toyota's western transplants are also characterized by single status facilities and conditions, such as common car parks, shared canteens, and pension funds. All these add up to a context in which flexible work practices and peer controls can be pursued, and therefore support a JIT/TQC production system.

Interestingly, in South Africa where a large plant operates under a Toyota licensing agreement, the South African managing director has expressed publicly the view that the existence of apartheid had posed problems for Toyota-style-teamwork. In particular, 1979 job reservation legislation meant that blacks were less likely to command skilled and supervisory positions. After discussions with the Minister of Labour, Toyota was allowed to go ahead with an employee development programme which meant black workers gained skilled and team leader status. The importance of this to teamwork at Toyota was described by the managing director as follows:

'You cannot produce quality in a factory if the workforce is divided and emotionally stressed ... One of the things which makes us most proud is that many of our employees refer to their place of work in the Toyota factory as 'kyalami' — the Zulu word which means home. Only this kind of attitude makes it possible for us to introduce the many management techniques we are adopting from Japan' (*City Press* (South Africa) 23 March 1986).

Elsewhere in South Africa the move towards JIT methods is reported as being hampered because of wide market fluctuations and a high incidence of labour activity (Maller 1987).

One might have expected that Western trade unions would bitterly resist a production system which depended on the firm establishment of managerial prerogatives, especially over labour deployment, on direct management-worker communications, and on a de-centralized bargaining system (disputes must not be allowed to 'spill over' from other plants). In North America, in the context of fierce Japanese competition as early as the late 1970s, the desire on the part of employers to shift from 'pattern bargaining' was being strongly expressed. Pattern bargaining was a well-established system of bargaining in the Canadian and American automotive industry which more or less assured standard industry-wide wages, conditions, and work practices. The desire was to move towards company or even plant level bargaining. In the early 1980s, with several Japanese assemblers moving into non-union plants on greenfield sites in the Mid West, the pressure grew even greater. According to Holmes (1989: 21−22):

'by 1985 the top UAW leadership ... were implicitly endorsing the team concept as a strategy to make the US auto industry competitive ... It involves a shift towards enterprise unionism where the union views itself as a partner in management.'

Since the mid 1980s the team concept and local bargaining have become widely established and are making inroads into the Canadian auto industry as well. The Toyota-UAW local agreement at NUMMI was possibly the single most important such deal, and since then NUMMI has provided a model of management-union relations as well as work practices in GM and other plants across America. Toyota Motor Corporation President, Soichiro Toyoda, was directly involved in 'efforts to communicate to the UAW our wish to introduce Japanese methods to the greatest possible degree ... in my opinion the most critical area is labour-management relations' (cited in *Productivity Digest Singapore*, 3/11, January 1985). It is not known by the authors whether the plant would have re-opened at all in the absence of the full co-operation of the union.

In Kentucky and Ontario, in common with most Japanese auto trans- plants to North America, Toyota chose the non-union option. Attempts to unionize such sites have met with remarkably little success (Holmes 1989).

In Derbyshire Toyota is yet to announce its intentions, although it is widely expected that the company will go for the single union option, following the pattern recently established by other Japanese manufacturers in the UK. In Britain, the single union deal means that one, rather than the previously typical several, union is recognized. Most of the deals are further characterized by a clear statement of managerial prerogatives over labour deployment, a unitarist preface and language and the establishment of a Company Advisory Board which has collective bargaining rights but is not necessarily made up wholly of trade unionists on the employee side. Some of the deals include a binding arbitration proviso and most have procedures which reduce the likelihood of industrial action, by employer as well as employee. Further, in most cases and to the alarm of many trade unionists, the company chooses the union in a 'beauty contest' before employees are recruited (Oliver and Wilkinson 1988).

Nissan in North England has such an agreement (without binding arbitra- tion) with the AEU. Membership at Nissan has been reported at various levels but always well below 30 per cent. According to Garrahan and Stewart (1989: 20):

'Trade unions usually articulate organized alternative positions, but at Nissan, the AEU stays clear of this, and in any event, with a membership of less than one in five it is in no position to foster an oppositional perspective. This business unionism ... fits uncomfortably with the experiences of many of our interviewees. The response of shopfloor workers tells us much about everyday concerns of health and safety and something too of the feeling of impotence generated by a union which many feel is irrelevant. It would be difficult for a union to stake a claim in anyone's concerns where it is irrelevant to their everyday fears.'

At other Japanese plants in Britain union membership levels are typically higher, often above 60 per cent but the role of the union is very much that of a 'partner' with management rather than an adversary and the relationship is frequently claimed by management and union alike to contribute towards stability in industrial relations.

Conclusion

We began this paper with the question of whether JIT production regimes could be successfully transferred outside Japan and in particular whether the economic, political and social supports which are necessary for such a highly vulnerable system could be re-created on foreign soil. In the light of our discussion our answer is a qualified yes. Toyota has so far, apparently successfully, moved strongly and quickly towards JIT production and supplies and Total Quality Control in the West. Such practices are being accepted, whether reluctantly or whole-heartedly, by suppliers, unions and employees, in the context of politically favourable environments.

With regard to supplier relations, in both the USA and Europe auto assemblers, including Toyota (in America), have placed increased demands on suppliers who have in most cases had little choice but to co-operate, particularly in the context of intense competition with a shift towards sourcing from a smaller number of companies. Suppliers to Toyota are expected to adopt total quality practices, including *kaizen*, themselves, and the industrial relations record of the supplier may be subject to scrutiny. Japanese companies have not been reluctant to attract their own suppliers from Japan where indigenous ones are found wanting.

On the employee relations front there have been few problems: JIT regimes have been accepted by employees, and in some cases embraced by unions, often in the context of high unemployment and a decline in trade union membership and power. Commenting on a strike at Toyota in 1950, in which one of the main issues was JIT reforms, Ono Taiichi commented that 'had I faced the National Railways Union or an American union I might have been murdered' (cited in Cusumano 1985: 306). The relative ease with which JIT has been introduced in some companies in Britain and North America in the 1980s is perhaps testament to the enormity of recent social and political change. Ono would not have predicted how frail a breakwater worker organizations in the USA and UK would turn out to be against the tide of Japanese corporate power.

This is not to say that Toyota, or other Japanese corporations, have re-created the wider social context of the Japanese economy, its dual labour market and close government-industry ties, for instance. Rather, in a favourable context or relative industrial decline in the host countries, Toyota and other Japanese companies have been able to introduce sufficient of their personnel, purchasing and other practices (and occasionally introduced innovative practices) to support a system of production which depends on the reliability and dedication of its suppliers, workers and other constituents.

Our 'yes' comes with qualification not because, as Domingo (1985) implies, it takes unique national-cultural attributes to be pre-disposed towards a JIT regime, but because of the continuing dependence of JIT and TQC practices on the commitment, or at least active compliance, of the company's constituent elements. We have noted expressions of varying degrees of disquiet about JIT regimes from suppliers, unions and workers. While these were limited in the 1980s during a period when suppliers and unions have had little choice but to go on the defensive, and when Japanese companies have been enjoying a 'honeymoon', there is no guarantee that such a climate will continue indefinitely. Whether the measures so far taken to support the Toyota production system would be adequate in a changed climate is a question we wish to leave open.

Giants and Dwarves: Changing Technologies and Productive Interlinkages in Australian Manufacturing Industry

Jane Marceau and Ray Jureidini

Introduction

The 'techno-economic paradigm shift' (Perez 1983) that characterises the last decades of the twentieth century has rejuvenated debates about industrial innovation and economic development. These debates in turn are implicitly reviving sociological debates about the convergence of industrial societies and the organisation designs that characterise them. Some observers see the transformation as primarily a change in core production technologies, while others are more concerned with the organisation of production and work which these technologies make possible. Thus, some see the new forms as a return to older principles in a new guise as, for instance, in the recreation of industrial districts (Piore and Sabel 1984) or the recreation of firms composed essentially of an entrepreneur and a series of subcontractors while others see them as definitive proof that the TINA (There Is No Alternative) tendency has died a ladylike death, opening the way to our understanding that 'postmodern' organisations are not driven by one structuring principle but rather are composed from a selection of available social, cultural and economic tools, logics or rationalities (Clegg 1990b).

Recent developments in core technologies and their application, notably that of microelectronics, to the productive process and to the creation of a vast range of new products coincided with a period of economic downturn in the 1970s, following the two oil crises (van Tulder and Junne 1988). The combination made both possible and desirable a fundamental restructuring of the production process in many of the world's major companies and key industries. One of the new technologies, microelectronics, developed particularly fast after the production of the microprocessor in the 1970s. By the end of the 1970s a considerable array of computer controlled machine tools as well as electronic consumer and capital goods became available.

There is now considerable agreement among analysts that physical technology alone never determines the way in which goods are produced and that much depends on the social relations of production or, put differently, on the managerial strategies adopted. In particular, much depends on the relative weight accorded by management to control of workers. If desire for control is high, the new technology adopted is likely to be labour saving, as in Italy or the USA in the automotive industry (Watanabe 1987a) rather that being used principally to increase flexibility or reduce absenteeism or accidents as Watanabe (1987b) has suggested is the case in Japan. Despite formal recognition of the great variety of possible organisational outcomes associated with the introduction of microelectronic process equipment, even within the same industry, however, much recent writing on the spread of particular production methods originating in Japan has tended to take a more mechanistic view. In particular, there has been much discussion of Japanese management techniques and organisational principles, notably the Just-in-Time system of managing inventory and, through that, client-supplier relationships and the emphasis on quality assurance and zero-defect production of components as well as final products. These two elements of the production system are, of course, particularly associated with the automotive industry worldwide, although they are now spreading to other sectors. Some of these sectors are those more usually considered hi-tech, such as the aereospace industry in France (Gorgeu and Mathieu 1988b), but they are also spreading to the low-tech end of the spectrum as in clothing and footwear in the USA and Australia, where JIT becomes QR or Quick Response, or in Italy as in the famous Benetton example.

Much of the empirical evidence brought forward seems to suggest that the most important aspect of the changes being made is the managerial strategy rather than the physical technologies themselves. Thus, the 'logic' of the new methods means that the organisational mode becomes the transforming principle rather than a logic involved in the microelectronics themselves. In this way, in the automobile industry, for example, the combination of new process equipment, new material and product design and new managerial strategies in core firms seems to be the catalyst that 'inevitably' brings fundamental changes to the whole *filière* (chain of production, from raw materials to point of sale). These changes include those in client-supplier relations and the management of what may be termed an external labour force as well as the internal organisation of the client and supplier firms from the tasks allocated to workers on the shop floor to those of managers and Boards of Directors. Like a house of cards, when the key card changes position, all the others are thought to fall in behind.

This paper uses a study of the automotive industry in Australia to examine the extent to which such convergence in techno-industrial organisation is taking place world-wide in that industry. If it is the case that the management methods developed in Japan have overwhelming advantages in the current techno-economic paradigm then announcements of TINA's demise may be premature, at least as far as dominant economies are concerned. It may, however, be that the social, economic and political characteristics of different follower countries mean that a compromise or middle techno-logical ground is developed in key industries through a particular mix of public policies and private investment decisions. If this is the case, and each country can modify its production strategies to fit local conditions while still remaining profitable, which is the game Australia is currently betting on, then we should not judge particular industries by how far they have 'advanced' in any given direction and we may expect to find considerable variety in organisational types. Whether these types are simply 'transitional' or really represent a shift to another paradigm in which many players will drop out of the game would seem at present to remain very much an open question. It is, however, an important one, both in analytical terms and in policy terms since much current government policy in Australia as elsewhere is pushing towards a national paradigm shift in the organisational modes of production.

International Developments: A Game of Follow-My-Leader

The two industrial organisation technologies which form the focus of this paper are Just-in-Time systems of production and Quality Assurance. In certain of its aspects the latter is not new since there have always been systems of quality control but quality assurance, the production of zero-defect goods (defects are sometimes now measured as in parts per million rather than the percentages common to an earlier era), is much more far-reaching in organisational terms, both within and between firms.

The Leader: Japan

Both of the systems concerned originated as full operating systems in Japan, notably with the car maker Toyota, although there too there have been developments over time and Fujitsu's system has led at least some observers to refer not only to 'Toyotism' but also to 'Fujitsuism' (Kenney and Florida 1988).

The Just-in-Time (JIT) system of management as developed by Toyota is, as the name implies, one in which goods are produced just in time for them to be used. Inside the final manufacturing or assembly plant JIT means that sub-assemblies are made just in time to be assembled into finished goods and fabricated parts just in time to go into subassemblies. In relationships between firms it means that raw materials will be purchased just in time to be made into parts and components or subcontracted work will be brought in or carried out immediately before they are needed in the final production while at the other end of the chain it may mean that particular products are made just in time to respond to consumer demand. Thus, in the most developed systems in the automotive industry, final assemblers are the leaders of a chain extending from the steel and plastic raw materials producers at one end, to car dealers at the retail end. In between lie the suppliers of components and specialist sub-contractors. This system at its most developed stands in sharp contrast to the organisation of production more typical of mass production systems in the west, systems often characterised as 'Fordist'.

Just-in-Time is a system designed to eliminate 'waste' or non-value-added elements of the production process. In particular, inventory, whether as materials, parts or part-finished goods, is reduced, thus reducing the amount of capital tied up in production and storage space needed. Eliminating materials and parts inventories, however, means that a way must be found of achieving totally reliable supply so that expensive plant and labour do not stand idle. This in turn means that quality must be perfect because if there are no stores of materials or parts production will cease if a batch received turns out to be faulty. The need for high quality is also found equally inside an assembling or fabricating plant as it is in relationships with suppliers since poor quality workmanship somewhere along the line will mean stoppages further along. For the Just-in-Time system to work, as Wilkinson and Oliver (1989) point out, tight control of the production process is necessary, both inside and outside the central manufacturing plants in the chain. The power of the final assembler, both internally over the activities of management and labour and 'externally' over suppliers, becomes critical. It is thus a system of which the logic extends the span of control outwards.

In Japan this span of control in the automotive industry has been extended outwards through the development of production 'complexes' which include, in close proximity to a core firm, a group of suppliers and subcontractors. Some of these may be subsidiaries of the major firms, as Nippon Denso is of Toyota, or they may share inter-locking directorates under the *keiretsu* system (Shimokawa 1985). As the system at Toyota at least has developed, major suppliers, notably of components, are physically grouped closely around the assembly plant and their own suppliers and subcontractors around them.

The system is to a large extend dependent on a few core relationships and the stability of demand and supply. In the core firms, production schedules are 'smoothed' for each month and these form the basis on which supply needs are calculated. Just-in-Time delivery means that suppliers of components or subcontractors must be prepared to deliver regularly and at short intervals, sometimes even several times a day. In order to facilitate this, two important organisational strategies have been developed. The first is to reduce the number of suppliers that the core firms is in direct contact with since a large number of suppliers is impossible to handle and co-ordinate. To facilitate this in the automotive industry parts and components have become more standard across models, the number of components has been reduced overall, and the number of parts required separately has been reduced by a move to the purchase of sub-assemblies. The second is to shift outwards total responsibility for the quality of supplies purchased onto the supplier firms concerned. This means that the core firm can eliminate not only stocks of parts and part finished products but also quality control at entry to the firm. In exchange for these extra duties of frequent deliveries and total quality control, selected manufactures, and, to a lesser extent, certain subcontractors, become preferred suppliers and are offered contracts of up to 3−5 years. The pattern that has built up, therefore, is a series of localised producer-supplier-assembler complexes; the selection by core firms of a chosen group of preferred direct suppliers with whom it is expected to have long-term relationships; and the creation of a major group of indirect suppliers which are usually smaller and have lesser technological capabilities, notably in the field of design.

The Followers

Major changes in the competitive circumstances faced by European and American car producers from the late 1970s and the experience of the Japanese suggested to major players in the automotive industry in these countries that they had much to learn from Japan. The growth of availability of robots and numerically controlled (NC) and computer numerically controlled (CNC) machinery suggested that technological change could and should be coupled to major reorganisation of their productive systems.

Many of the elements of the Toyotist system were taken over. Thus, for example, in France, Renault and PSA (the Peugeot group) began to introduce robots into paintshops and some assembly lines from 1983 onwards

(Watanabe 1987b) and to accelerate the introduction of NC equipment. At the same time, they began the process of development of the 'partnership' system described by Gorgeu and Mathieu (1988b and 1989) and Chanaron and de Banville (1985). This system involves both the central concerns of Just-in-Time management and the demands of quality assurance. The development of the 'partnership' (*partenariat*) since 1985 in particular has meant the selection of key component suppliers (*équipementiers*), such as Valeo and Magneti Marelli (now both subsidiaries of Fiat), and their transformation into 'partners' while it has also meant the elimination or downgrading of a large number of, usually smaller, subcontractors and parts suppliers. The *équipementier* suppliers selected have been, as in the Japanese case, those firms showing technological sophistication and design capability while those relegated to indirect supplier (supplier to supplier) or subcontractor status or eliminated altogether have been the traditional firms operating mostly in the mechanical engineering and foundry sectors. In France, as elsewhere, the process of remodelling of the automobile *filière* has now been stimulated by the increasing importance of non-metal materials, such as plastics and ceramics, which are usually produced by firms not previously significant in the *filière* such as chemical companies. Similarly, and this is *unlike* Japan, the remodelling has been used principally to make significant reductions in the labour used in cars. In Japan the automobile 'revolution' has often involved *more* labour per vehicle, robots and flexible automation being used essentially to eliminate dangerous or dirty jobs, to reduce absenteeism and increase flexibility (Watanabe 1987a). In Europe and the United States, however, the emphasis has remained on control of the labour process and hence on the reduction of numbers involved. In most cases, it seems, NC machines and robots have been used as fixed rather than as flexible automation systems.

The situation in Italy has progressed further along the control mode of rationalisation and the elimination of all but key players, whether they are to be found in the internal labour market of the car assemblers or the external labour market of their suppliers. Thus, in 1981 Fiat, for example, closed one of its major plants in Turin which had employed 8000 workers and in 1980 it put on indefinite zero-hour leave around 23,000, losing overall more than 33,500 workers over the period 1986 to 1987 (Silva, Ferri and Enrietti 1987: 142). At the same time, the company radically reorganised its supply and quality control system, losing suppliers over the same period (van Tulder and Junne 1988). These changes were accompanied by rapid automation and, particularly, rapid robotisation.

In the United States the same trends have been apparent. While it seems that the greater geographical distances have prevented full-scale implementations of JIT, most of the major assemblers have introduced modified versions. Indeed, GM with its Vanguard plant, has attempted to go further and use the technology of EDI (Electronic Data Interchange) to integrate operations both between the plant and suppliers. The success of the Vanguard operation seems to be in doubt for the moment but it seems likely that further attempts will be made (Garnett, *Financial Times* 14. 10. 89). Moreover, as Mair and Kenney (1988) show, Japanese car firms implanting themselves in the United States bring with them most of the organisational features of their parents in Japan. The eleven Japanese assembly plants and two hundred or so component factories operating in the USA by the late 1980s were expressly located so as to facilitate the use of JIT, sites chosen being close to indigenous suppliers or with room for the 'transplant' supplier companies to follow and in rural areas with access to an amenable labour force (Mair, Florida and Kenney 1988).

The Automotive Industry in Australia

Unlike the countries discussed above, Australia no longer has an indigenous automotive assembly industry, its only local company, Holden, having been absorbed in the 1930s into General Motors. It is, however, an industry which is important to Australia in the same way as elsewhere. In 1988 the assembly firms employed 30,476 people, while the sector as a whole, including supplier firms, employed a further 24 – 30,000 people (Automotive Industry Authority 1989). The industry supplied in 1988, for instance, around 70 % of local vehicle demand and exported both parts and vehicles, mostly to New Zealand.

Encouraged by the latest Federal government industry plan, the 'Button Plan' (named after the Minister concerned), the industry is going through a period of significant rationalisation. Peripheral car firms such as Volvo have either ceased or are about to cease production in Australia and the big five assemblers reduced to four by 1990 – Mitsubishi, Toyota-Holden, Nissan and Ford. The number of models made in Australia is being reduced from 13 current at the start of the Button Plan in 1984 to the six or fewer intended by 1992. The Plan provided initially for local content of 85 %, with a lower limit possible if compensated by exports and the reduction of tariffs, but local content requirements were dropped in 1989. It further provides for increased standardisation of parts and components between models, a position which is intended to be a catalyst for change in the components and subcontracting areas of the industry.

The rationalisation process in the Australia automotive industry, for instance, as elsewhere, involves the introduction by the major assemblers of new management technologies and the introduction of sophisticated computer-related equipment. It similarly seems to involve rationalisation of company structures and relationships with suppliers in a way very similar to that evident elsewhere in similar circumstances. In this way, the push for organisational change in the core assembler firms may be expected to serve as the spearhead for change down the whole automotive *filière* in Australia as it does elsewhere in the same industry and as is beginning to occur in other sectors.

This chapter suggests that the industrial structure in Australia is beginning to be radically transformed by the introduction of the combination of computer-related equipment and managerial strategies focussing on JIT and zero-defect quality. This transformation is involving the restructuring of relationships between core firms and their suppliers, much as in happening elsewhere in the industrialised countries. The peculiarities of the Australian situation mean, however, that the emerging pattern will be different and that a peculiarly Australian compromise is emerging. This is one in which the chains of production very often lead out of the country at crucial points while inside the country new networks are developing in which key firms in a *filière* intersect with another *filière*. The dynamics of the new situation in the automotive industry are explored below. The analysis is based on the results of interviews carried out in 1988 with the (then) five vehicle assemblers and a random sample of 108 supplier companies, approximately one third of local manufacturing automotive sector components suppliers in Australia. (In a second phase of the same project, ten core firms and 40 suppliers in different sectors of the electronics industry were interviewed in 1989. The third phase of the project, analysing similar changes in the clothing industry, was also carried out in 1989−90). The data presented below are those indicating changes in the industry in the key areas of equipment change, restructuring of company boundaries and changing relations with suppliers.

Giants and Dwarves: The Population of the Automotive Industry

A few statistics indicate the nature of the population concerned. First, information from core firms shows very considerable concentration in purchases made. Giants essentially serve the giants. Thus, in 1987 only three companies provided one quarter of the dollar value of component purchases made by the five assemblers. Ten companies provided half the business and twenty enterprises two thirds. In all, 50 companies out of 507 suppliers provide 86 % of all components purchased. Of the top twenty supplier companies only a small handful are of Australian origin.

In contrast, in our study, the great majority of supplier firms were dwarves. Of the 108 for which we have information only two thirds employed more than 50 people with only 35 more than 100 and only 9 more than 500. Two thirds of the sample were private companies, usually family concerns, and almost two thirds were started either by the current managing director (24 %) or a relative of the present owner (38 %). Half had never changed ownership while a further third had changed hands only once. Only half were subsidiaries of other companies and more than half of the parents were Australian owned. This sample suggests that in terms of numbers the component and subcontracting sector of the automotive industry is comprised of foreign giants and Australian dwarves.

This complexion is being encouraged by technological change in the industry and the restructuring of the sector's organisation, led by the head firms. These companies have introduced many elements of the Japanese system, especially as these affect their suppliers. They have all introduced vendor audit (though not all have chosen the same grading system and their systems are not always congruent); more frequent deliveries, sometimes daily, more usually weekly ('to take account of Australian conditions'); increased transfer to vendors for quality assurance (reduced inward sampling); and greater vendor participation in design (notably by Ford). They have all introduced JIT in conjunction with the use of computer-related equipment, including robots. Perhaps most important of all, they have greatly reduced the number of supplier firms and are still doing so (several suppliers went out of business or merged in the year following our study although this drop-out rate may have declined since). One assembler, for example, reduced its supplier numbers by between half and two thirds between 1978 and 1987 (interview 1988). While another core firm still has more than 600 component suppliers this number is declining too and the others are dropping numbers of local component vendors to between 144 and 204 companies from many more. In conjunction with this policy the number of sole suppliers (to both industrial firms and/or the industry) has grown, a move facilitated in Australia by the dearth of competition among key vendors. There were around seventeen sole industry suppliers in 1987, comprising just under half (44%) of all firms which were common suppliers to each of the vehicle assemblers. Most of these are Australian subsidiaries of multinational firms and include Bosch, Borg Warner (now part of BTR-Nylex), Nippon Denso and Brake and Clutch. One or two others, such as Kirby's and Henderson's, are Australian.

In addition the introduction of JIT and quality management by client firms and the associated demands are gradually pushing many supplier firms to reorganise and hold stocks, while others are gradually going out of business or have ceased supplying the automotive industry since they could not or would not introduce JIT or accede to more stringent quality and delivery requirements.

The outcome of these changes on the ground is the result of strategic compromises and a bargaining process both within and between the firms concerned. The outcome of this strategic bargaining process depends on several variables and cannot simply be 'read off' from knowledge of the introduction and operation of JIT or Quality Assurance in core firms. It is quite clear, for example, from the work of researchers such as Baven in the Netherlands that one should not assume that assemblers are necessarily the leaders in all aspects of technological superiority, whether in manufacturing process or in products or services such as design (1988). On the other hand, the introduction of JIT seems to go hand-in-hand with a renewed emphasis by core firms on control of the external labour force constituted by suppliers (Baven 1988). The organisational outcome in any given country is the result of the relative power and the production or marketing arrangements made by the different firms concerned. The Australian data presented below illustrate this process.

First, the push to organisational innovation and changes in the productive and managerial technologies used in supplier firms comes from the relative strengths of market position. Rather more than a quarter (27 %) of firms in our study relied extremely heavily on one customer for their business, selling more than half of their most important product to that single client. Further, half of the 71 respondents giving information relied for more than half of that product business on two clients while a quarter relied for three quarters of the business on these two customers.

Among the 67 firms giving information on three clients the proportions are completely reversed. Virtually three quarters of these respondents sold more than half their produce to only three customers, including 39% who sold between 75 % and 100 % to these firms. More than four fifths of respondents relied on five clients, including more than half who sold between 75 % and 100 % of their principal products to these five customers. The organisational push from clients is thus likely to be very powerful and difficult to resist for the great majority of vendors, unless they are sole suppliers.

The picture is, however, rather a complex one. If market share of principal products is taken into consideration the bifurcation of the group of vendors is apparent. There emerges a small group of powerful suppliers (one fifth of the total sample, almost one third of responding firms) which controls 91 − 100 % of the Australian market for their top product. They are followed by a much smaller group, 10 %, which controls 71 − 90 %. In contrast, just over half the firms controlled less than half the market, including just over a fifth with less than a fifth and 13 % with less than 10 %. The proportions with a market share of less than 10 % increase markedly for their second and third products, reaching more than half for the third product. While we do not yet know the exact proportion of business accounted for by these products and hence their importance for the long term viability of the firm, the change in proportion of market share suggests the importance of the lead products.

In terms of the daily operations of the companies, major problems were often caused for vendors by fluctuations in demand by clients (two thirds reporting considerable fluctuation) despite the use of JIT by core clients which should have involved the smoothing out of monthly demands (at least one major assembler, Ford, recognised this problem) (Indeed vendors claimed in our study that they often told core firms what those firms' needs really were).

The influence of clients' demands on change in the vendor (supplier) firms can also be judged by the reasons given for the introduction of new physical (computer-related) technologies and organisational procedures. Thus, for example, two thirds of responding firms stated that they had introduced new technology because of client demands. Half had also brought in new management techniques for the same reasons. The influence of clients had also been reinforced through specific forms of assistance. Almost three quarters of firms had attended seminars on quality assurance organized by core clients while almost half had received assistance on technical matters (47 %), quality control (46 %) and with tooling (44 %). Many had thus had to invest heavily in new physical technologies in order to accede to new demands.

In exchange for introducing new practices, however, relatively few firms had gained market security. Few had been offered contracts, at least one core firm saying that these were not necessary since demand for particular components was open ended. Only 24 had been offered contracts and these were much shorter than the 3 – 5 years nominated by assembler clients, 16 being for twelve months and the rest between six and twelve months. Most order books were short, with more than half between one and three months and a further 27 % up to six months.

The push from core firms either directly or indirectly to alter methods of work and management in Australia also continued down the line to the suppliers or indirect suppliers to the giant assemblers — half the supplier firms interviewed had already changed their own purchasing policies and hence relationships with their vendors. A third of the sample recognised that these changes had caused problems for the vendors and some had offered assistance of a kind similar to that received from their own clients. Most did not offer such assistance, however, leaving the firms down the line to fend for themselves (interviews 1988). Similarly, a third of all respondents had followed the core firms' lead and reduced the numbers of vendors they dealt with. In this way, changes in core firm practices in Australia do indeed seem to herald changes right through the *filière*. Many of these will have adverse consequences for the weaker participants in the chain, as mentioned earlier, and one year after the survey when firms were recontacted for a follow up survey several had gone out of business. Most of these were small companies, with implications for the productive structure that will be raised below.

In contrast to this apparent dependence, however, it is clear that the creation of new organisation structures, new productive methods and new patterns of activity is still very much in the process of negotiation. Data from the total range of component suppliers indicated that overall dependence in terms of proportion of product bought by one or a few principal customers was low and it is as yet hard to assess the direction of change. The assessment is difficult also partly because the technological level of the population of suppliers firms remains very mixed. While more than four fifths of respondents had introduced computer-related technology, almost all had done so only since 1980 — 84 and half after 1985. More than half had no CNC machines at all while only 20 of the 108 firms had more than five. Only a few had introduced robots. Only 20 companies used CAD-CAM and 14 CAD alone. No-one at all was involved in EDI, although a number of major firms had contracts involving open account books with the assemblers and some were 'looking around'. It thus looks as though in terms of physical technology there is a good distance to go. A group of firms had radically transformed their productive organisation, many of these using computer-related equipment to link different parts of the manufacturing process and departments within the enterprise while a quarter used it to link enterprises in the corporate network, but many had developed little of the full potential. Similarly with management technologies. While three quarters had introduced new methods of quality assurance and 59 % JIT, only a third had MRP II. The overall technological level has changed since: by 1992 EDI was commonplace, for example, but still much of the organisational potential remains to be fully developed (personal communication, 1992).

In contrast again, however, changes similar to those elsewhere are becoming apparent in the Australian automotive industry. Putting new managerial and physical technologies together has led to many of the advantages familiar from the experience of other countries for both core and suppliers firms. More than half of supplier respondents in our study had reduced tool and die changeover times and two thirds had reduced lead times. Many had reduced inventory, stock and work-in-progress levels. More than half claimed to have a technology policy and almost two thirds a long-term policy for the development and acquisition of new technology. More than half the firms had seen changes in the strategic decision-making process,

It also seems that 'progress' of this kind may not be all one way. While observers have tended to assume that productive process and product innovation is a one-way transmission, from larger to smaller firms, in practice a good deal of innovation and, in particular, technology transfer moves 'upward' in the *filière*, from indirect to direct suppliers and from direct suppliers to core firms. In the pilot study for our project, supplier firms interviewed were small and considerably reliant (for up to 80 % of their business) on a very few large customers. Despite this difference in size and apparent technological capacity, all the supplier firms reported providing assistance to clients on product design, on possible and profitable ways of making items requested and on manufacturing methods. This advice was, in the interviewees' words, 'freely given', 'as part of the service'. Interpretation there is difficult: such assistance may be a means of attracting or retaining custom or simply be a part of a 'normal' and mutually advantageous relationship. It may be 'exploitation' by the large firms of the small since the former are receiving 'free' advice not available to smaller clients or it may be the beginning of a longer term relationship in which both sides gain. At present, it is very hard to tell.

A similar uncertainty exists in relation to the location of suppliers. Japanese core firm practice suggests that co-location is an important in-gredient in the proper functioning of JIT and Japanese transplants in the USA have located close to customer firms and their own suppliers (Mair, Florida and Kenney 1988). Elsewhere, however, while co-location was the dominant norm in 'traditional' automotive areas (see Marceau in Hunt, Jackson and Marceau 1981) in Europe it has not been easy to reproduce this pattern in Australia. Sole supply to geographically dispersed clients makes co-location impossible for single plant enterprises (which many are in Australia) and selection of a small number of key suppliers difficult. The supplier firms in our study had located for diverse reasons and none indicated that they must move elsewhere to accomodate client needs. Some did, however, maintain warehouses close to customers, suggesting the importance of location in some cases and the extra costs borne by companies supplying firms operating JIT. Again, this issue seems to have suggested an organisational compromise rather than a clear movement required by a particular management technology.

Similarly, raw material suppliers are a major problem to automotive companies in Australia. In Britain, client (automotive supplier) companies have reported British Steel as laughing at them when they have made JIT requests (Baven 1988) and in Australia the only major steel maker is frequently reported as having a similar response to such requests. Small players cannot get the supplies they need and may be forced to import from Japan or hold stocks, incurring costs as a result. (In the electronics industry, Australia finds itself in a similar position. Whenever there is a

shortage of new chips Australian electronic firms face major problems,
Australia being too small a customer even to merit an allocation at all, let
alone the amount requested) (interview, electronics firms, Sydney, 1989).
In this area again an organisational compromise will have to be worked
out.

Conclusion

The international literature suggests that the growth of new organisational
forms in industrial organisations is a response particularly to changing
competitive circumstances and vast increases in the cost of R & D as
well as the adoption of Japanese management systems which encourage
devolution rather than integration of production functions. Child, for
example, has remarked on the growth of co-contracting, co-makerships,
divisionalisation, joint ventures and other organisational changes which
break down conventional understandings of the boundaries of firms (1987).
This has been further discussed in relation to small firms and their changing
relationships with large ones by Marceau (1989 and 1990). Our Australian
data show that these restructuring processes and the growth of new inter-
linkages in the productive chain are also beginning here. In the automotive
industry forty companies stated that they were making arrangements to
acquire new businesses. Because of the commercially sensitive nature of the
question only eighteen gave details but of these ten involved joint ventures,
two co-contracting, two takeovers and one a merger. Three had taken
equity in a previous customer and eleven in a previous supplier. Thirteen
had begun to source from a firm created by a previous employee of the
company. (Indeed 27 % of the companies had lost managers over the
previous few years who left to set up their own enterprises). Even more
important as a step towards the organisational patterns established elsewhere, the firms in the sample were rethinking their productive strategies.
Make, buy or import decisionmakers are considering new factors. A considerable proportion (42 firms, 40 %) now produce in-house components
they had previously sourced outside while an even larger proportion
(49, 46 %) had begun to hive off activities and to devolve functions previously carried out in-house. Doing so frequently involves new relationships
under new rules with suppliers, changing the organisation of the constituents
of the industrial structure.
    The situation in Australia as apparent in the data discussed in this chapter
suggests that as the process of radical transformation proceeds a variety

of outcomes is possible and that while some effects of powerful new technologies will be universal, many others will involve compromises and individual national patterns.

On the one hand, it does seem likely that with the move to JIT, to purchase by core firms of sub-assemblies rather than components, and to the selection of small groups of technologically and design sophisticated direct suppliers by core firms, the supply 'tail' of small companies will disappear or at least greatly reduce, as is happening in all major auto-producing countries (Lamming 1987 and 1989). Their functions will either be taken over by the 'partner' firms or integrated into core companies. In Australia, this will probably mean the loss of many of the *Australian* companies in the automotive *filière*, the companies typical of most in our sample. Hence it will mean an increase in the influence of multinational component suppliers and the opening of the *filière* to global decision-making by these suppliers to an extent even greater than that now evident. This trend is likely to be encouraged further by the drop in tariff protection which significantly reduces penalties for importing parts.

As the industry moves towards a structure composed esentially of a web of large and giant contractors a new wave of acquisitions and mergers is likely. Much has already happened over the last few years and the announcement by Valeo in Europe that it intends to 'purchase one or two companies a month from now on' indicates the likely speed of the restructuring process there.

Similarly, as the major partnership suppliers in turn globalise their own operations they too may reduce the small supplier 'tail' with which they deal, pushing the restructuring process further down the line. The implications of this for many aspects of government policy, such as urban and regional development or regeneration and employment patterns, are very consider-able.

The picture is, however, still a complex one. Not only has the whole process of technological change barely begun in Australia but a number of countervailing tendencies are present. Over the next few years the major supplier firms, drawing on developments in their operation overseas, will be rapidly increasing their technological capacity and especially their design capability. This gives them increasing power in relation not only to their own suppliers but also to the assemblers, of which in principle, according to the Button Plan, there may be only three after 1992, and which in the meantime may have been devolving more and more functions to them. It has been recently suggested in an unpublished paper by Sabel, Kern and Herrigel (1989) that the end result of this will be a post-Japanese model, one of collaborative manufacturing between a few large firms. They suggest that BMW and GM are showing two possible ways towards this already. Sole supply, which may seem difficult because of conflicting interests if a firm is working for several major companies, is not seen as a problem even with multiple clients since it seems that separate laboratories and production lines can be provided to ensure the commercial confidentiality of design and manufacture undertaken.

This, however, seems a view more harmonious than the situation likely to prevail on the ground in Australia. Large firms which are technologically sophisticated seem likely to develop their own agendas. While some may be happy to rely on the automotive industry, in a small country such as Australia it seems more likely that firms will diversify and develop their own products. Such a change may clash with the interests of the automotive firms since the component makers may want more autonomy than the assemblers are willing to grant them. It is clear that core firms in Australia are still very much concerned with control, both of their internal production process and the labour force and of the external ones of the suppliers, but it is not clear how far they can exercise it. Where competitive pricing is still used to differentiate between firms and in the choice of sourcing as between imports and local manufacture, thus remaining effectively in the 'stress' period, as Lamming (1987) calls it, rather than a partnership mode, local suppliers may well also look for business elsewhere and some are already doing so, as our study shows. Core enterprise strategy in Japan has always associated integration with considerable control over suppliers and their operations. Thus much de-integration is largely in the eye of the rather naive foreign beholder since core firms retain or acquire between 10 % and 100 % of the equity in key supplier enterprises to ensure compliance and limit other options. The considerable direct control implied in this arrangements is absent in Australia where continuity between clients and suppliers has occurred for other reasons and where there is little cross equity holding, making supplier 'independence' in strategy more likely.

Despairing firms in Europe which have introduced JIT and other central elements of what is perceived as the 'Japanese system' but find that the transplants do not 'take' have begun to talk about the 'culture' factor: the Japanese 'ethos' they fear is missing since their organisational practices seem largely intact in the new arena. The question is indeed an important one if absolute ideas of 'efficiency' are linked to the translation of 'recipes' from one area of the world to others. Indeed, much has been written recently about the 'culture' factor in explaining the economic success of Japan and the 'five little dragons', the NICs of Asia (Berger and Hsiao 1988). More convincing than a cultural explanation, however, as, in diverse ways, Redding (1988), Whitley (e. g. 1989 a and b) and Clegg (above) have suggested, is a different kind of understanding of the socially embedded nature of organisation forms and reasons for success. In particular, it seems, due account should be taken of social and political factors, arising from particular historical circumstances. The balance of social power in both organisationally 'exporting' and 'receiving' countries is especially important. The overall balance involves particular balances between managers or controllers and workers, between large and small firms, between clients and suppliers, between government policies and the strategies developed by private economic actors, between levels of government and between countries.

Each set of actors has its own agenda, and the implementation of any given item may pose problems for other agendas. Organisational compromises may result which do not suggest a clear organisational direction, at least in the medium term. Workers may collaborate with management over wage restructuring (indeed in Australia management has recently been pushed to restructure wage-formation practices by an alliance of government and unions) and improved training but be much less enthusiastic about enterprise bargaining or compulsory retirement at age 55. Unions may be highly resistant to multi-skilling and added responsibility for quality control without added remuneration, an essential part of the bargain in Japan and apparently the aim of most employers in follower countries.

Most important, the role played by public policies may be critical. In Japan in the public sector the powerful MITI has provided the long-term planning stability and support for extremely expensive long-range strategic R & D while the power and success of the major corporations has encouraged both the closer cooperation between public and private sectors and the market control which make possible the stable demand and market constancy underlying the JIT system. In contrast, in Australia the State — the Federal government at least — has veered from protection behind high tariff walls to the 'short, sharp shock' treatment meted out to manufacturing in the mid 1970s, back to protection later and on to the micro-economic restructuring manifest through industry plans from 1984 onwards and now to considerably more reliance again on tariff reduction. The current policy, while offering financial assistance to the industries concerned ($ 150 million dollars to the automobile sector) is essentially concerned with *increasing* uncertainty rather than reducing it. The reduction of tariffs on imported cars and components announced in 1989, for instance, has made multiple sourcing by core firms a financially viable proposition, reducing the need for the assemblers to collaborate with local manufacturers to raise quality. Relatively little has been done to lengthen the time horizons of the principal companies concerned and hence increase their confidence in the desirability of radically new organisational arrangements. The cut in tariffs in 1989, for example, radically changed the game for the companies which had just merged or acquired new divisions to cope with the earlier years of the Button Plan. A further stroke of the industry policy pen could irreparably alter the prospects of the whole industry, making any kind of internal organisation change irrevelant. The review of the plan undertaken by the

Industries Commissions in 1990 has suggested the acceleration of change through much more rapid cuts in tariff protection, with protection falling to 15 % in the mid-1990s. Such a course could well see full globalisation of car-industry decisions in relation to Australia and the possible change to assembly of imported parts only, the manufacture only of specialist vehicles or, indeed, the closure of all or most assembly as Nissan announced in 1992, and with them major component plants in Australia. This, however, is also not certain: Toyota has recently (1991) announced a plan for a new greenfield site for car production on the outskirts of Melbourne. This relocation, too, has implications for supplier firms' strategies.

Finally, discussion of the automotive industry raises again the question of how far strategies developed there, should the industry remain in Australia, mean that that sector will serve not just as the model but also as the spearhead for the reorganisation of other industrial sectors in Australia. There are both theoretical and practical reasons for suggesting that much change will indeed move in the direction currently led by the automotive sector. The theoretical 'logics' or rationalities which push firms to adopt 'charters' of production such as those involved in JIT have been discussed above, as have some of the limitations on their adoption. In practical terms the peculiarities of the Australian industrial structure means that a cross-industry web of key components firms may become the catalyst points for changes up and down several *filières*. Multi-domestics such as Pacific Dunlop, for instance, hold important positions in all three of the sectors covered in our study, supplying not only the automotive but also the electronics and clothing industries. Half of the electronics companies in our sample had already adopted JIT while the leading clothing retailer, which controls 70 % of the Australian discount chain sector, is pushing Quick Response into the whole clothing *filière*. Once that is in place the dominant position of the head firms will make it almost impossible for all but a few companies to retain any other forms of productive structure. Other industries, both hi-tech and more traditional, are likely to follow what seems to be a successful model. Those most likely to do so are sectors where there are complex chains, with considerable value added by each link, through from the suppliers of raw materials to the retailers in organisations at the other end. In contrast not all products, of course, are produced and distributed by complex chains, and barriers to entry (and exit) are frequently low. Unstable industries with simple products and local markets are more likely to favour production close to the individual consumer than to be concerned with interlinkages with suppliers. For this reason, perhaps, it is difficult to compare French bread with microprocessors or cars.

Similarly, in *filières* which are incomplete in Australia, where the technology of both process and product is changing extremely fast in ways generated outside the country and where Australia is a product-taker rather than initiator, many firms will find it difficult to introduce new technologies because the firms on each side in the chain will not be there. Electronics is the clearest example of this but once other new core technologies develop, for example in the field of ceramics and other new materials, similar 'gaps' will occur with similar problems. Those wishing to make productive inter-linkages will find no partners. Aware of this problem in the electronic industry, the Federal government has introduced 'Partnerships for Develop-ment', which grew out of the offsets policy to encourage technology transfer and the 'thickening' of the industrial network in that field, but the success of the initiative is as yet far from clear.

Absence of 'partners' in development is a common problem in smaller and less densely 'industrialised' countries. In part, the problem arises because of Australia's socio-geographical configuration: a few large cities separated by vast tracts of only sparsely populated areas. Because of the earlier pattern of development, Australia has never had the industrial density which characterises Europe, modern Japan and much of the USA. Industrial development has been driven by large corporations investing from overseas. Each one has brought with it a demand for new products and services but many items have had always to be imported and the network of connections common elsewhere between companies has not always developed in Australia. In particular, too, Australia seems not to have developed the great mass of medium-sized industrial firms which characterise for example, the UK, the major cities of France or the Ruhr area of West Germany. Nor, despite a few promising starts, has Australia developed new industrial areas grouped around core firms as in Toyota City. The coastal location of the major cities serving as exit points for raw materials drawn from the hinterland has also encouraged a comprador vocation with little indigenous activity to encourage manufacturing, a large skilled working class, or medium size companies. The economy has turned instead on multinational corporations, a very few multi-domestics and a mass of relatively tiny firms. Frequently, foreign firms have each brought their own organisational 'recipes' and demands and these are not always congruent with those of others. In the case in point, core firms in the automotive industry have not standardised quality or scheduling (delivery) requirements. A recent study by the Automotive Industry Authority in charge of the Button Plan showed considerable disagreement over the quality of the same products produced by given specialist component suppliers (AIA 1989). The situation in the electronics industry is equally confused and confusing.

In summary, then, study of techno-industrial innovation and of the restructuring process which results in different countries underscores the view that organisational change and particularly the adoption of radically new technologies, whether computer-related equipment or managerial strategies, has to be seen as the result of a multitude of forces, some past or long established, some current, some industrial, some social. Just as Fordism took decades to crystallise, to be adopted as the 'one best way', to become an organisational form recognisably 'Fordist', so post-Fordist, and *a fortiori* post-Japanese, forms will spread only slowly and be subject to a myriad different pressures resulting in a wide range of patterns. National socio-economic and political differences as well as the elements of any given industrial structure will shape the emerging socio-economic paradigm worldwide and help both ensure and explain why apparent similarities of organisational form hide real differences or, as Susan Helper has pointed out in an unpublished paper (1989), why many companies adopt Just-in-Time delivery while few practise Just-in-Time production. While managers are always looking for 'recipes' to increase profitability or ease of control, they adapt what they find to the exigencies of individual company and local circumstances as well as attempting to change the practices of others which they see as barriers to their own progress. As a respondent in our own study said, 'We pick the eyes out of JIT'. Relationships at the heart of an enterprise result from key socio-economic relations; they are much harder to reorganise than is inventory control. The shift to the new paradigm has a long way to go and a hard road to travel.

Developing 'Partnerships': New Organisational Practices in Manufacturer-Supplier Relationships in the French Automobile and Aerospace Industries

Armelle Gorgeu and René Mathieu

Introduction

In French industry, following the Japanese example, customer-supplier relations between major manufacturers and their supplier firms have been undergoing profound changes over the last several years and the prospect of the single European market in 1993 is accelerating the process. Large companies are seeking to establish longer-term cooperation with their key suppliers, seeing this as a means to improve the overall competitiveness of their products. This new trend, called partnership (*partenariat*), is based on the creation of special relations between first-tier suppliers and the large manufacturing firms which are their customers. In the new relationship the suppliers selected become entirely responsible for the production of assemblies or subassemblies, for the whole process of design and manufacture and for the procurement of materials. In addition, the new arrangements are leading to a formal hierarchy in which certain first rank supplier firms, which are the chosen partners of the major manufacturers, have privileged relationships, including long term contracts, and where other suppliers have no direct relationship with the large assembly firms but are relegated to 'second tier' status. Accepting responsibility for product quality assurance is an indispensable prerequisite for becoming a 'partner'. The demands now being made by large companies on their suppliers entail major reorganisation of their production methods by the suppliers. The direct suppliers pass these demands along in turn to their own suppliers, whatever the nature of the business. These indirect suppliers, too, must assume new responsibilities, in particular that of product quality assurance.

The evolution of relationships between the major manufacturers and their suppliers in the automobile and aerospace industries is the subject of this chapter. The data presented here were collected in 1988 in the course of interviews with large companies in these two sectors, as well as with about thirty of their suppliers which we had also previously studied in 1983. The first part of our report, this chapter, is devoted to examining the new demands being made by the large core companies with regard to their suppliers. In the second part, which appears in a subsequent section of this book, we analyse the reorganisations carried out by suppliers to satisfy their customers and the major modifications made in the matter of personnel management.

The Evolution of Relationships Between Major Manufacturers and their Suppliers in the Automobile and Aerospace Industries

The data collected, both from the large order-placers in the automotive and aerospace industries and from their suppliers, suggest that greater change has ocurred in the former than in the latter. Until the early 1980s in the matter of cooperation with suppliers, French automobile manufacturers had been lagging behind their foreign competitors, especially the Germans and the Japanese. This lag was threatening to penalise them in international competition. For automotive manufacturers such as the French, with little vertical integration, an improvement in relationships with component makers and subcontractors can contribute markedly to an increase in the overall competitiveness of their vehicles. French auto manufacturers have therefore played a pilot role in implementing the partnership concept.

The Gradual Implementation of the 'Partnership' Concept

The French Automobile Manufacturers

Automobile manufacturing in France is essentially dominated by two large enterprises: Renault, which has been nationalised since 1945, and the PSA Group, formed in 1974 by the merger of two independent companies, Peugeot and Citroen. Virtually all French motor vehicle production is divided between these two enterprises. Ford is also interesting to study, however, in the context of organisational change in the automobile industry, especially regarding procurement, since its purchases in France are extensive and the company has played a leading role in spreading new quality assurance standards and methods in France. The quality management methods that Ford has been using for a long time in its own plants and its requirements of its suppliers have been closely copied, with slight modifications, by the two leading French auto makers, who, in turn, have prescribed them for their own suppliers.

Under the term 'suppliers', we group all the companies which supply the large automobile manufacturers, namely the furnishers of raw materials, the suppliers of major preassembled constituents, referred to as 'component makers', and subcontractors who produce parts and subassemblies, generally from plans furnished by their car assembler customer. Here we discuss relations between the manufacturers on the one hand and the component makers and subcontractors on the other.

Automobile component makers alone account for about 25 per cent of the total value of French automobile production. The components industry is currently 70 per cent under foreign control: over recent years French automobile component makers, which used to be small or medium-sized companies which were very dependent technically and economically on the automobile manufacturers, have been gradually bought up by powerful foreign companies. The major multinational companies making automobile components, including American, German and British firms, today have subsidiaries in France. The only suppliers on a international scale that remain entirely French-owned are a tyre company (Michelin) and a glass maker (Saint-Gobain). The large French auto component maker, Valeo, recently passed into Italian ownership (De Benedetti). In contrast to the component makers, the subcontractors who supply French auto manufacturers with parts and subassemblies in metal casting, forging, diecutting, stamping, precision turning, plastic elements and so on are French. These direct subcontractors, until recently, were still small or medium-sized companies. With the introduction of the partnership concept, however, the subconstractors selected by the major automobile manufacturers are generally medium-sized and the very small firms no longer have direct relationships with the auto makers.

The partnership concept is being implemented rapidly because of increased international competition and the prospect of the single European market in 1993. The search for immediate profits had led French auto makers in the past to develop relations of dominance over their suppliers, including component makers, and to focus only on control. More recently this policy has backfired against them. Unlike their German or Japanese competitors, they cannot depend on a strong national components industry but have to procure their supplies from subsidiaries of foreign companies and from small French companies which are not prepared to take initiatives. French automobile manufacturers, like their competitors, are therefore now seeking to make use of the complementarities of their suppliers, particularly of their component makers, and to take advantage of every possible innovation in the production of each component and part.

The new procedure being followed by automobile manufacturers in France is similar to that instituted first in Japan and taken up worldwide in the automotive industry as can be seen in other chapters in this book, in particular those by Marceau and Jureidini and by Wilkinson, Morris and Oliver. The procedure consists, first, in selecting direct suppliers, the future partners. These, in turn, must learn to use methods imposed on them by the auto makers in preparation for taking on new responsibilities in design, production and their own stock procurement. In return for accepting these demands, the chosen suppliers benefit from longer-term markets through the establishment of contracts. These three steps − selection of suppliers, introduction of common methods, and transfer of responsibilities, are usually closely interlinked. The selection of suppliers is based on their ability to respond to specific demands in the areas of product quality, delivery times, innovation and competitiveness. Suppliers are evaluated first on their ability to take total charge of responsibility for product quality: through quality audits that cover the entire organisation of their companies, suppliers are advised or required to use particular management methods, not only for quality control but also for stock procurement and production flow. Automobile manufacturers check whether the chosen suppliers have followed their recommendations before delegating to them entire responsibility for quality control and before allowing them greater autonomy in design and stock procurement.

First rank suppliers are charged, in turn, with passing along the makers' demands to their own suppliers. Thus, although dealing directly with a shrinking number of suppliers, the auto manufacturers nonetheless control the entire chain of production and have available a network of companies all using the same management methods. In this way, a common production model is being established and gradually being substituted for the traditional Taylorist model of mass production.

Implementation of this new procedure began in earnest in 1985, although it started earlier. As a result, since 1980, the number of direct suppliers of automobile manufacturers in France had been reduced by half by 1989 and decreased even further as the selection process was completed in 1990. The panel of suppliers is not expected to evolve much further. The elimination process has had more effect on the subcontractors than on the component makers. Most small subcontractors were always treated by the auto makers as mere executors of orders, with no capacity to take initiatives, particularly in terms of design. But now, in order to become partners of the automobile manufacturers, all (or most) companies must become designers, develop new products, and make improvements in existing products.

The demands of manufacturers on their direct suppliers are not entirely new. Already in 1983, if they wanted to work on new models of cars, suppliers had to meet assemblers' requirements in investments and product quality control. At that time, however, these demands were essentially technical. Organisational demands are now being added, demands which are particularly formal in the field of quality assurance, where they involve the introduction of a common method of defect prevention in order to obtain consistent quality in the suppliers' products. The adoption of Statistical Process Control (SPC) by component makers and subcontractors obliges them to invest not only in equipment and plant installations but also, especially, in human resources and their skills, making new demands in the field of personnel recruitment and training.

Absolute quality assurance is the key to partnership, because it conditions suppliers' ability to meet other new demands made by the car manufacturers. Of particular importance are demands for ever shorter delivery times and for direct delivery to assembly lines, which excludes *any* quality control on reception, and for the production of assemblies, subassemblies or finished components instead of individual parts. These other demands, too, require reorganisation on the part of the suppliers. They are forced to set up their plants by product lines to avoid overstocking supplies for their current needs. Such lay out is a prerequisite for the use of 'Just-in-time' management methods, such as the pull-through, immediate order system represented by the use of *kanban* cards. In order to be able to make more sophisticated products, and especially to become designers, supplier firms may be led to expand their R & D departments, or even to create them if they have none.

The Aerospace Sector

The aerospace industry is characterised by the concentration of manufacture in a very few companies, each of very large size and mostly belonging to major nationalised groups. In this sector, state intervention is omnipresent because of the successive waves of nationalisation that have taken place since 1936 and because of the scale of state purchases. Indeed, within the nation's border, the state is the only end customer for either military or civilian orders since the national airline, Air France, is totally under public control. Exports, however, represent a major portion of the sales figures in the sector.

The aerospace industry includes both companies that build civilian or military aircraft and their components makers specialising in the manufacture of particular essential elements of aerospace craft, such as motors, capsules, navigation equipment and so on. In the aerospace industry, in contrast to the automotive sector, the large assemblers, builders and component makers have always had privileged relations amongst themselves and collaborated closely.

Both aerospace assemblers and their major component makers depend heavily on subcontractors, both for highly specialised items and for operations they do not perform themselves and to introduce flexibility in capacity, provided the required specifications can be met. The network of subcontractors in aerospace is very diffuse and diversified. Numerous companies concerned, of all sizes, often including even very small firms, belong to many different activity sectors, work both directly for the large manufacturers and for the component-makers. They also often work for the armaments industry as the two sectors of arms and aerospace are closely linked, with the aerospace industry including a large military sector.

Customer-supplier relationships since 1983 have evolved less in aerospace than in the automobile industry. The major order-placers have indeed been making more demands on their suppliers but there has been neither a transfer of responsibilities nor a development of longer-term markets. A partnership between the major firms in this sector and their subcontractors does not yet seem to exist. Subcontractors remain subcontractors: they have no more autonomy than previously and have no assurance of having durable relations with their customers, whether these are the large assemblers and aircraft builders or component makers. In contrast to the practice of core firms in the automotive sector, large firms in aerospace have not chosen certain first rank subcontractors to be 'partners' and they continue to work directly with tiny companies just as they do with larger firms. While some partnership does exist within this sector between the large builders and the components makers, it is not new, cooperative relationships having always existed between these two categories of companies of more or less comparable size.

The major order-placers in the aerospace sector have very strict technical and quality requirements and these are becoming even stricter as time goes by. With the increase in air traffic and the intensification of worldwide competition, aircraft must be more and more reliable and must be capable of an ever greater number of flight hours over the course of their lifetime (the future Airbuses, for example, must withstand 80,000 hours instead of 40,000). The technical and quality requirements imposed by the major aerospace manufacturers on their suppliers are also more formalised than in previous years. In addition, the intensification of competition has led aerospace manufacturers and component makers to refuse 'costly extras' in the work by their suppliers and are taking price into account more than before, even to the point of subcontracting abroad. In this way, they are implicitly urging their suppliers to use preventive methods of quality control, although their relationships focus on the 'technical' rather than the organisational changes necessary.

In 1983, the subcontractors who worked for the aerospace sector already had to respond to very strict technical imperatives and were obliged to perform numerous testing operation, often per unit. To be able to continue to work in this sector, subcontractors had to invest in the latest equipment, for both manufacturing and testing, and had to have a well developed quality testing department. As a result, as we found in our 1983 study, the industrial sector with the most sophisticated plant equipment and technology, particularly the latest generation of computer-controlled production machinery, in France was that of suppliers to the aerospace-armaments industry. The aerospace sector is currently unquestionably playing a leading role in stimulating technical advance in small and medium-sized companies in some regions of France, especially in the South West where many aerospace companies are located. Local subcontracting in 1983 was preferred by the large order-placers since it facilitated the development of frequent contacts between customer plants and supplier plants concerning product quality control. Subcontractors were already being selected on the basis of their ability to deliver products conforming to required specifications and already then had to obtain an official quality certification in order to be able to work for this sector.

To receive quality certification now, as in 1983, firms must follow formally specified procedures for the control of the quality of their products. The application of these procedures is verified by quality audits, carried out by the military authorities if it is a question of military equipment or by the order-placers themselves for everything concerned with civil aviation. Systems of supplier firm certification by the Department of Armaments Industry Surveillance, SIAR (Service de Surveillance Industrielle de l'Armement), and by the large aerospace manufacturers have not changed much in the past five years. However, it seems that certification is now more difficult to obtain than it was in 1983. The renewal of quality certification (which occurs every three years) poses problems for many companies, with the audits being much more precise and much more formalised than they were a few years ago. Fully thirty per cent of the companies that had obtained a SIAR certification three years ago now risk failing to obtain its renewal. Quality is so important that the large aerospace companies, even though they have imposed greater demands for quality on their suppliers, still carry out random quality testing when receiving a delivery and total delegation of product quality control is rare. Aerospace manufacturers even generally test items directly supplied by their major component-makers.

In the automobile industry increased demands by manufacturers in terms of quality and delivery times have been accompanied by some improvement in relations with their direct suppliers since price is no longer the predominant factor. In the aerospace industry, in contrast, the large order-placers not only have increasingly strict standards of quality assurance but also make new demands in term of price. In 1983, they granted less importance to price than did the automobile manufacturers since quality was the principal discriminating factor but now that is reversed and the rule henceforth is highest quality at lowest possible cost. The intensification of international competition explains the current importance of the price factor in the relations between the large aerospace companies and their suppliers.

In the market for new aircraft, competition is worldwide; for example, for the contract for the production of parts for future Airbuses, the bidding is open to all aerospace component-makers in the world and to be selected, as an official told us, a supplier 'has to be good at everything — technology, quality, price, and delivery times.' In return, once selected, component-makers chosen have the advantage of sole supplier status: this is not the case for subcontractors, at least two or three of whom are always willing and able to produce the same product. Whether they work for the large manufacturers or for the component-makers, subcontractors are selected first on the basis of quality audits and next by the purchasing departments on the basis of prices and delivery times. Considerations of price may lead major core firms to prefer a foreign company, for example, in Southeast Asia.

To get the best prices, the major order-placers in this industry tend increasingly to deal with foreign subcontractors, despite the risk of giving foreign companies the benefit of their know-how. Indeed, subcontracting is no longer even a purely European affair because of the development of 'tradeoff' subcontracting: in order to ensure the increasingly costly financing of their plans and to preserve and enlarge their market shares, large aerospace companies are shifting subcontracting so as to have an industrial presence in their customer countries and are trading off other factors against this. Even the 'major' subcontractors, so called because they are considered to be the best in terms of quality and because they produce complete components (manufacture, assembly, and testing), have no guarantee of durable markets and can be subject to reconsideration for reasons of price. The large aerospace companies do not sign contracts with their subcontractors, nor do they make tacit commitments. While they do not prescribe preventive quality control methods to their suppliers, in the way that automobile manufacturers do, aerospace component-makers and subcontractors are expected to organise themselves so as to minimise price, notably through reduction in the cost of rejects, and 'costly extras'.

Organisation Changes Made by Suppliers

Most of the suppliers that we revisited in 1988 had carried out changes to their organisation since our first visit in 1983, whether they worked mainly for the automobile or for the aerospace industry and whatever the position they occupied in the hierarchy established by the automobile manufacturers. The magnitude of these changes depends on companies' behaviour and present strategy in confronting the new demands of their client firms. The companies which in 1983 already followed a strategy of specialising in high-quality products are better prepared to satisfy or anticipate their customers' expectations than are other companies starting from scratch. We have identified two current strategies for responding to customers' demands. The first is specialisation in their client industry sector so as to benefit from partnership arrangements. This mainly concerns firms that are already partners or have the capacity to become so. The other, diversification of client industry sectors and reliance on a reputation for quality, is pursued by firms which cannot hope to benefit from partnership arrangements.

Major automobile and aerospace component-makers are already effectively partners, with the firms assembling the finished products, and are expected to remain so. The new subcontractors selected by the automobile manufacturers to become their first tier suppliers also have the capacity to become partners. Firms in both these categories follow the strategy described above as specialisation in a client industry sector so as to benefit partnership arrangements. They prefer to specialise in one sector so as to increase their competitiveness, to innovate, to have a longer-term assurance of obtaining markets and to have greater autonomy. They are expanding their marketing efforts to large firms abroad, especially elsewhere in Europe. This strategy entails major reorganisations, in which human resources play a fundamental role.

Most subconstractors, however, cannot hope to become partners and they work for either the automobile or the aerospace industries without having direct relationships with either the car makers or aerospace assemblers. They must respond to new quality control requirements in order to continue to work in these industries but receive no compensating return in the form of durable, privileged relations with their customers. Most such firms seek to work for any companies, large or small, French or foreign, in any sector, which are reputed to make high demands in terms of quality. They do this because they want to have a reputation for 'quality,' attested to by recognised certificates, such as the Ford standard of Q1 or Q101, so as to be able subsequently to broaden and diversify their customer base. Their goal is to use the full capacity of the material and organisational investments they have made at the behest of their customers, who demand a systematised quality management system. Modifications in their personnel management policies are linked to these investments.

Not all companies which make such organisational changes can hope to become partners while others do not pursue this strategy. Some, the less dynamic, are not seeking to implement a quality management system but also have no other strategy. In 1983, they made no marketing efforts and undertook no technological improvement. It seems likely that they will often be obliged to leave both the automobile and aerospace sectors as a whole.

Conclusion

The evidence presented in this chapter on the changing demands on their suppliers made by core firms (order placers) in the automotive and aero-space industries in France suggests that the 'partnership' concept pioneered in Japan is increasingly influential in shaping inter-organisational relation-ships in these sectors. Of the two industries discussed that of aerospace has advanced furthest down the *partenariat* track, in parallel with the increasing importance of quality. That industry initiated the new relationships earlier than was the case in the automotive sector. It is clear, however, that gaining partnership and sole supplier status in aerospace on the basis of a worldwide search by the core firms for quality does not exempt the selected companies from making progress on the price front. In this case initial emphasis on quality rather than price has been replaced by concern with both quality *and* price. This is principally because of the highly competitive nature of the business and serves as an indication that even in high-tech industries a strategic emphasis on technological superiority and quality does not exempt a supplier firm from competition on price.

Technology Transfer and East Asian Business Recipes: The Adoption of Japanese Cotton Spinning Techniques in Shanghai and Hong Kong

Judith Nishida

Introduction

The transferability of 'business recipes' from one societal context to another is the focus of this chapter. The study examines influences on the development of the Japanese, Chinese and Hong Kong cotton spinning industries and indicates how their differing societal contexts shaped the introduction and early development of particular organisational forms and managerial techniques. In all three of these industries there were 'foreign' influences from more highly developed cotton industries. In the case of the Japanese industry the influences were mainly British and American. In the Chinese industry there was a very strong Japanese influence and this was partially transferred to Hong Kong with the Shanghai Chinese cotton spinners who emigrated to Hong Kong in anticipation of the communist revolution in China in the late 1940s.

The Shanghai Chinese cotton spinners in Hong Kong have always exhibited a distinctive business recipe, different from that of the Cantonese who predominate numerically there. The search for an explanation for this distinctive pattern leads the analyst outside the colony's borders to look at the early development of the Japanese and Chinese cotton spinning industries. Although they both began to modernise at the same time in the late nineteeth century, the Japanese were particularly skillfull in adapting British and American technologies and evolving their own unique business recipe. Singular features of the Japanese cotton textile industry were the degree of support from the cotton trading companies enjoyed by the cotton spinners, the banks and the government and their ability to develop mass production methods and to coordinate and control a large number of mills. After the First World War, the leading Japanese spinning companies set up mills in China, in particular in Shanghai, to protect their major export market. With support from Japanese cotton trading firms, banks and their government, they proceeded to gain control of the Shanghai Chinese cotton spinning industry after successfully replicating in China the institutional context which supported them in Japan.

Evidence from contemporary writers suggests the degree to which the Shanghai Chinese cotton mill owners imitated the methods of the Japanese in the period up to the Pacific War. After the War, a number of members of the elite Shanghai Chinese spinners relocated to Hong Kong where they sucessfully established and controlled the cotton textile industry which formed the basis of Hong Kong's remarkable industrial development. Both the organisational forms used and the managerial techniques employed in Hong Kong show traces of Japanese influence. The case study indicates the degree to which managerial and physical technologies can be both transferred across and modified by different societal contexts. The theoretical basis of the study is derived from work by Redding and Whitley (1990) and by Whitley (1989a; 1989b; 1990). The effect of the societal context in the adoption and absorption of new technologies leads to only partial success in the transfer of the technology and to the evolution of novel recipes to deal with the effects of this selectivity.

In a major work Maurice and his colleagues (1980: 61) identify the 'societal effect approach' for studying organisations as being concerned with 'the conditions under which different solutions to similar challenges are chosen'. The approach focusses on the ways in which actors construct organisations but also discusses how this constructive process is influenced by the societal fabric in which the actors operate and which they continuously modify. Similarly, Whitley (1990: 49) proposes that the 'dominant institutions of nation states ... are crucial influences on the kinds of entrepreneurs and managers who gain control over economic resources, and the practices and procedures they develop for dealing with business problems'.

Some features of the distinctive systems which have developed for organising and controlling economic activities 'may be translatable to other societies (but) the recipe as a whole is not because it is interdependent with particular contextual institutions.' (Whitley 1990: 49). In the translation to another context many problems arise for different elements of any business recipe (Hirschmeier and Yui 1975: 175). These concern several areas: the ability to finance the capital requirements of large scale enterprises; the creation of external business organisations which can handle joint problems such as the development of the industry itself, of trading and marketing organisations, and of financial institutions; the management of government/ industry relations; the internal organisation of the firm enabling adequate managerial control; the technical aspects of productive organisation; and, finally, the formation of an industrial labour force. In the case considered here, the period studied covers the beginning and the early stages of the development of East Asian cotton spinning industries, when the establishment of modern cotton spinning firms was dependent on the purchase of (then) modern technologies developed in more mature industries.

The physical technology of a cotton textile industry is fundamentally concerned with the spinning of raw cotton into yarn, its weaving into cloth and the dyeing and finishing of the cloth. A particular feature of cotton textile industries throughout the world is the high degree of competition in both domestic and international markets which arises from the lack of significant economies of scale, only modest product differentiation, relatively small capital requirements and no significant technological or resource-based barriers to entry. As the industry is labour intensive, developing economies, with their abundance of relatively low cost labour, reap a cost advantage in comparison with developed economies. There, high labour costs, combined with an apparent worker preferance for employment in other industries, lead to the decline of local cotton textile industries. Moreover, the developing economies, because they benefit from technology transfer, do not need to reinvent the spinning machine and thus in theory are able to benefit from the technological advances made in the more mature industries. Chin (1965: 97), for example, asserts that what ultimately determines the outcome of a given firm or country in textile competition is its management, its ability to make the best use of given resources and keep up with the latest technology and techniques of plant operation and alertness to all possible ways of optimizing procedures and avoiding inefficiency or waste.

Discussion on the transfer of cotton spinning technologies in East Asia in this chapter is based largely on empirical and historical studies of these three textile industries, especially those by Wong (1988 a), Chin (1937), Takamura (1982), Nishikawa (1987), Fong (1931), Lieu (1928 & 1933), Wang and Wang (1935), Pearse (1929) and Chao (1977). All of these concentrate on analysis at industry level with some reference to enterprise level practices. The assessment of managerial techniques at enterprise level relies on company histories, especially the one hundred year histories of the two leading Japanese spinning companies of Kanebo (1988) and Toyobo (1986), both of which companies set up mills in China. Information at enterprise level for Chinese mills has largely been obtained from the Rong Enterprise History, a 1980 Chinese language publication researched by the Shanghai Academy of Social Sciences. The Rong family's group of Shen Xin mills was not typical of Chinese mill ownership because of its size — nine mills, while most families owned a single mill — but the Rong (Yung) family subsequently had a dominant position in the Hong Kong cotton spinning industry and is therefore particularly interesting.

A Brief Review of the Development of the Japanese, Chinese and Hong Kong Cotton Spinning Industries

The modern cotton textile industries of Japan, China and Hong Kong have very close historical links. The industries of Japan both began to modernise in the last quarter of the nineteeth century and did so independently of each other until the turn of the century when Japan's greater success led to the establishment of a Japanese presence in the Chinese market for the sourcing of raw cotton and for sales of manufactured yarn and piece goods. These activities were carried out by three major Japanese cotton trading companies which also set up spinning mills in China in the period leading up to the First World War. Although the Chinese cotton spinning industry faced many political, economic and social obstacles in its modernisation push (Koh 1966: 181 – 223), it soon achieved its own considerable expansion of yarn production, an expansion which threatened Japanese yarn exports to China.

After the First World War, the 'Big Ten' Japanese cotton spinning firms, the major exporters, retaliated and all established mills in China, in particular in Shanghai, the centre of the Chinese cotton spinning industry. These mills, supported by the Japanese trading companies and banks, proceeded to gain effective control over raw cotton, yarn and cloth markets in China. The Chinese mill-owners thus found that they had in their midst powerful competitors who employed exemplary managerial and technical skills in the running of their mills.

From the late 1920's, Japanese technologies were transferred to Chinese mills as some of the leading Chinese (Shanghainese) millowners began to imitate the mill management practices of their Japanese competitors. After the Second World War, these elite Shanghainese cotton textile entrepreneurs regrouped briefly in Shanghai before migrating to Hong Kong in the face of the political unrest leading to the Communist Revolution in 1949. From 1947, these immigrant Shanghainese cotton spinners developed Hong Kong's world-renowned cotton textile industry, upon which one of the world's largest garment industries is based. The Shanghainese cotton spinners thus pioneered Hong Kong's industrialisation but used Japanese-originated techniques.

This group of cotton spinners was remarkable as its members appeared in the 1950's and 1960's to be the only group of Chinese industrialists capable of running relatively large, capital-intensive organisations. Most of Hong Kong's industrial sector at that time consisted of small, cottage-type manufacturing concerns. How the Shanghainese acquired this industrial management skill, the extent to which they were influenced by the Japanese spinners in Shanghai, and what the influences were, the reasons why some were successful and others not are the central questions of this chapter.

The earlier development of the Lancashire and North American cotton textile industries had provided initial models for both the Japanese and Chinese millowners. The Japanese were systematic in their study and subsequent acceptance or rejection of these foreign influences. Those that were accepted were adapted to the Japanese context and together with indigenous approaches formed the basis of a uniquely Japanese business recipe.

One of the central characteristics of this recipe was the degree of institutional support from Japanese trading companies, banks and government. Traditionally supportive in Japan, these three parties continued their support when Japanese cotton spinning companies set up mills in China, mitigating to a significant degree the relatively hostile institutional environment surrounding Chinese cotton spinners in China who faced difficulties arising both from the lack of stable political and economic conditions and from a powerful foreign competitor. These three sets of problems which faced the Chinese on the mainland were absent in Hong Kong and the development of Shanghainese entrepreneurial skill in Hong Kong was hindered by few such impediments. In Hong Kong, therefore, the Shanghainese cotton spinners were able to develop a uniquely Hong Kong business recipe. It is, however, one which bears the traces of Japanese influences.

In the development of both the Japanese and Hong Kong business recipes, elements of the surrounding societal contexts both inhibited and formed the foundations for the successful transfer, absorption and development of particular managerial and technical skills, as is shown below.

Japan

In examining the historical pattern in the development of textile industries Chin (1965: 156) has traced a change from managerial dependence and finally to managerial 'aiding'. Japan was managerially dependent for a short period during the early establishment of her modern textile industry while the government guided its development with the help of foreign, mainly British, advisors. These were replaced by Japanese who had been trained by foreigners in Japan or overseas and by 1890 Japan was an independent cotton textile manufacturing power.

The Japanese cotton textile industry also benefited from the transfer of technical and managerial technologies from the more mature industries of Great Britain and the United States in the late nineteenth and early twentieth centuries and was so skillful in adapting and diffusing these technologies that it was able to achieve dominance over Great Britain in the 1930's as the world's leading exporter of cotton cloth. Di Maggio and Powell (1983: 151–152) cite Japan's industrial development as offering good examples of mimetic isomorphism, the modelling of organisational forms and practices under conditions of uncertainty. Mimetic isomorphism leads also to innovations when particular features of the model prove inappropiate in the new societal context.

The pioneers of the Japanese textile industry, having evaluated organisational forms and practices in the Lancashire and North American textile industries, at first decided on the adoption of the joint stock company as the best organisational form and spinning mules as the most appropriate technologies. Later they found that joint stock company principles integrated well with the traditional framework of a degree of separation of ownership and control but that the mule was found to be an inappropriate machine for the young female workers who provided the labour force. The structure of the Japanese labour market thus led to the widespread adoption of an alternative technology, ring spinning machines. These machines were not so effective, however, in handling short staple cotton so Japanese industrialists developed a new raw cotton blending technology, which was a uniquely Japanese innovation. Through innovations such as these Japan rapidly gained managerial autonomy in her cotton textile industry. According to Chin's model, in the independent stage, the growth of a textile machinery manufacturing industry is important because it enables a country to supply its own needs and to aid less developed cotton textile industries.

Japan in China

Japan took on an 'aiding' role in respect of China between the two world wars but her real objective was not to aid but to dominate and control the Chinese cotton industry.

Over the period leading up to and during the Second World War, the Japanese cotton textile industry had two locations, Japan and China. Its main location in China was in Shanghai where there were thirty Japanese mills in 1930, compared with twenty-eight Chinese owned mills. Many of these mills (*zaikabo*) were members of large groups of mills, owned either by the 'Big Ten' spinning companies in Japan or by the large Japanese cotton trading companies.

As mentioned above, the outstanding features of the Japanese cotton spinning industry were the degree of homogeneity of best practice and the degree of institutional support from the trading companies, finance houses and the government. The insitutional framework of Japan's cotton spinning industry successful at home was replicated by the Japanese in China to a significant extent, enabling it to avoid weaknesses in the Chinese societal fabric. In contrast, the nascent Chinese cotton textile industry had to deal not only with elements of the political, social and economic enviroment which were hostile to industrial development, but also with severe competition from this more effectively organised Japanese industry situated within its own domestic market. Certain members of the Chinese cotton textile industry soon consciously imitated *zaikabo* practices. The *zaikabo* provided a model for the achievement of consistent profit, which for many Chinese mills was difficult because they lacked the same degree of financial and managerial resources and institutional support. On Mainland China the cotton textile industry as a whole was fairly widely dispersed but there was significant concentration in the Shanghai region, where in 1930 about a third of the eighty one Chinese mills were located. If the surrounding province of Kiangsu is also included the Shanghai area was the base of about 60 per cent of all Chinese mills (China Yearbook 1931/1932: 108). Wong (1988a: 14) has defined the 'Shanghainese' as those from the Wu speaking areas of Lower Kiangsu. In his study of the ethnicity of the Hong Kong cotton spinning industry, he identified twenty out of the twenty one mills set up in Hong Kong between 1947 and 1959 as being set up by Shanghainese as thus defined. Their domination of the Hong Kong industry at that stage was thus virtually complete. Less successful than the Japanese in Shanghai itself, the Shanghainese in Hong Kong far outstripped the capabilities of the local Chinese population.

The Shanghainese in Hong Kong

The success of the Shanghainese in Hong Kong was due to four key factors; first, the societal context of Hong Kong which was conducive to the development of entrepreneurial skill; second, the considerable extent to which they had absorbed the technologies of the Japanese textile operations in China; third, the circumstances of the massive migration to Hong Kong at the founding of the People's Republic of China, which created a psychological momentum enabling large groups of skilled textile workers and people from related businesses to regroup in Hong Kong and concentrate resources on building a textile industry. The fourth factor is the ability of the elite industrialists from Shanghai, who already had experience of dealing with 'colonialist' administrators in the extra-territorial districts of

Shanghai, to assume an elite position in colonial Hong Kong society. From this position they were able to gain and maintain control of the rapid development of the cotton spinning industry of Hong Kong.

The Degree of Absorption of Japanese Mill Management Practices by the Shanghainese Cotton Spinners in Hong Kong

The degree of absorption of Japanese cotton mill management practices by the Shanghainese cotton spinners in Hong Kong can be assessed at three levels — intrafirm, interfirm and societal.

Intrafirm Level

The similarities between the Japanese and Hong Kong spinners in their managerial practices at the intrafirm level were the technical efficiency of machinery and environmental control within the mills, the training of staff, the provision of staff welfare facilities such as housing and dormitory facilities, the existence of well educated management and the vertical integration of weaving, dyeing and finishing operations. Allied to a long term perspective and avoidance of speculative gains, these were crucial to the success of the Hong Kong cotton spinners. In the early stages of the development of the Chinese cotton textile industry, there was no systematic effort to fully exploit and adapt the potential benefits of foreign technologies and organisational forms. Under these conditions, indigenous approaches to industrial management developed, assisted by British and North American trading companies which provided a limited range of expertise in the commissioning of machinery and advising on technical matters. Although, despite severe handicaps, Chinese spinners did produce enough coarse yarns and cloth to become self sufficient by the end of the First World War they were unable to meet competition in the international market place. The post war dominance of their market by the *zaikabo* exposed the weaknesses of the Chinese indigenous approach. In contrast, the spinners who came to Hong Kong in the post-war period demonstrated the degree to which they had taken note of the potential benefits of foreign technologies and organisational forms.

The common desire for and the use of similar techniques to build an internal labour market in order to develop and retain a skilled labour force is a striking feature of their organisation and points to a strong Japanese influence on the Shanghainese spinners. Pye (1988: 91) suggests that in the early stages of East Asian development there is a tendency for companies and families rather than governments to bear welfare costs. For example, in Japan, Korea, Taiwan, pre-war China, and Hong Kong, welfare was primarily the province of private companies or of families themselves. The Japanese, however, in particular, have long considered fringe benefits such as housing, family allowances, and welfare benefits, such as dormitories and dispensaries, to be extremely important in facilitating the shaping of a Japanese-style internal labour market overseas. In Hong Kong, England and Rear (1981: 84−85) have identified in large Shanghainese corporations the same desire to build an international labour market and this wish has been identified again by Tomita (1985: 403) in a comparison of training and promotion practices among Japanese, Shanghainese and Cantonese firms in Hong Kong as is shown in Figure 1 below:

type of firm	in house promotion	in house training
large scale Japanese firms	very high	very high
medium scale Japanese firms	high	high
small scale Japanese firms	high	high
Japanese firms in Hong Kong	high	medium
Shanghainese firms	high	medium
large Cantonese firms	medium	low
small Cantonese firms	low	low

Source: Tomita: 1985.403

Figure 1   Extent of in-house training and promotion of middle managers: a comparison of Japanese and Chinese firms in Hong Kong

The nature of a Japanese company's internal market differs, however from that of a Shanghainese firm in Hong Kong and this for a number of reasons. Not least important is the different structure of the labour market. The Hong Kong market is characterized by high labour turnover. Many firms, especially those run by Cantonese and which are at the heart of Hong Kong's economy, view labor as a commodity to be hired at the cheapest price and laid off or dismissed as the market dictates. Employees do not find much incentive to identify with their employing companies unless these are run by their own family or kinship group. Tomita

(1985: 402) has observed that much of human relations policy in Hong Kong is based on pre-existing personal connections.

In contrast to their Cantonese colleagues, the Shanghainese spinners had been exposed to the demonstration effect of the *zaikabo* whose managers had promoted training and welfare practices as a means of improving the quality of the workforce and through this productivity and efficiency which contributed to profits in a highly price sensitive market. The *zaikabo* had also demonstrated the utility of investment in the latest spinning and weaving technologies. Vogel (1989: 266) has noted that Japanese firms are prepared to invest in technology at seemingly high prices if it might pay off later and to invest in plant modernization even when present plants meet immediate demands: Japanese firms thus show themselves less interested in short term profits and more concerned with the long run. As products become competitive, they conduct extensive preparatory work to lay a solid grounding for markets.

The Shanghainese in Hong Kong showed a similar predilection for investment in new spinning and weaving technologies and by the 1960s achieved the highest rates of machine productivity in the world. They adopted a long term view in the face of volatile international supply and demand for raw cotton, yarn and gray cloth and avoided the reliance on speculative gain which had been a tendency in pre-war Shanghai. Another factor was also important to Shanghainese success. In contrast to the Lancashire textile industry, there was a considerable degree of forward integration from spinning to weaving to dyeing and finishing in both the Japanese and Hong Kong cotton textile industries. Vertical integration facilitates technical change as the impact within the chain of production can be more readily identified, assessed, coordinated, controlled and changed in conformity with other parts of the chain than is possible through reliance on market mechanisms.

The nature of the management controlling these operations, however, was dissimilar in Hong Kong and Japan. In Hong Kong, Shanghainese businesses were controlled by family members whereas in Japan they were controlled by 'professional' managers. This difference stems fundamentally from differences in trust relations among the Overseas Chinese and the Japanese. Redding and Whitley (1990: 97–99) argue that the different nature of trust relations in Japanese and Chinese societies arises from different historical antecedents which enable trust relations between strangers to be supported in the Japanese case and not supported in the Chinese case. In the Chinese case, strong trust bonds develop and are maintained within familial and regional networks.

This emphasis on the importance of family has other implications. Redding (1989: 7) proposes that an Overseas Chinese chief executive's view of an appropriate strategy for his firm is likely to be influenced by the need to retain control in the interests of long term family prosperity, by the belief that risks should be hedged to protect family assets, by the associated belief that key decisions should remain within an inner circle and by the view that dependence on 'non-belongers' for essentials such as managerial, technical, and marketing skills should be carefully limited. The scope for the development of a professional managerial elite is thus severely limited. Despite these beliefs, the need for expertise was fully recognised and family members were not recruited into mill management solely on the basis of kinship. They were given a good preparation for their managerial roles through education, often at prestigious overseas universities, and brought into the business at relatively junior levels where they worked under the guidance of senior members (see Redding 1986: 277–279).

The reliance on family, however well-trained, and the exclusion of 'outsiders' for senior management positions have important effects on the shape and size of Chinese organisation. This reliance makes it relatively difficult for Chinese family businesses to grow large and large firms usually eventually split into smaller firms so as to follow the Chinese practice of divisible inheritance. Hamilton (1989: 28) identifies a common strategy for prosperous families to start multiple businesses but these multiple businesses are likely to draw upon kinship ties in an effort to create a network of mutually supporting firms, each of which is run by individuals linked through kinship. This practice contrasts with operations in Japan. In Hong Kong, the forward integrated operations of textile firms are managed by family members whereas in Japan they are managed by professional managers. In Hong Kong, each unit manager within a vertical set-up is given a degree of independence in the management of his operations, being able to buy from or sell to companies, but despite this in all cases the family's business interests are protected (interview with Mr T. Shaw, Hong Kong Cotton Spinners' Association 11 November 1989).

In a comparison of Japanese and Overseas Chinese entrepreneurship, Redding (1988: 109) observes that in Japan there are values and structural factors which facilitate and enhance entrepreneurship in both its initiating and coordinating features. These values contrast with those of the Overseas Chinese whose values facilitate the initiating phase but put barriers to the higher levels of coordination necessary for the growth of the individual firm to a large scale. Redding identifies the values of cooperation, trust and professionalism as being particularly pertinent for coordination; the former two are particularly crucial in relations with non-family. In the Shanghai spinning industry there were instances of firms breaking up in the early stages of growth during which 'outside' partners were recruited of their skills, connections or capital. The Rong family business survived this stage and grew to a very significant size but the quality of the coordination of the business was poor and it was subject to the conflicting ambitions of the mill managers. In Hong Kong, firm size remained small in comparison with the large Japanese combines. Thus a very significant difference between the Japanese and Hong Kong industries is the prevalence in the former and the absence in the latter of large organisations controlled and coordinated by 'professional managers'.

The Shanghainese cotton spinners in Hong Kong therefore lacked several elements which had been central to the success of the Japanese: lack of development of a 'professional' middle management; lack of motivation and ability to develop very large organisations which in particular have a considerable degree of horizontal integration; and the lack of the ability to generate high levels of labour productivity.

The ability of the Japanese spinners to ensure high levels of labour productivity reflected their attention to human factors as well as to mechanical factors as shown through their emphasis on the well-being and training of workers to improve their skill. Moser (1930: 13) also found that levels of labour productivity, measured by the number of looms/spindles per worker, were constantly being improved by the Japanese. This achievement implies a willingness by the workers to identify with the fortunes of the company. In this respect the attitudes of top management were an important influence. Japanese top management, for example, continued to dress like others and to live modestly, a promotion of egalitarianism by top executives designed to ensure the continued devotion of the worker Hasegawa suggests (1986: 8 – 10). The proximity of Japanese middle management to the mill operations also resulted in constant attention, interest and involvement in issues relating to improvements in machine and labour productivity. In contrast, the Shanghainese mill owners kept a certain distance from day-to-day production operations, which compounded the lack of identity by the workers with an organisation owned by an unrelated family. The centrifugal tendency of employees to start their own business led to 'an atrocious down-grading of standard and quality'. (See Wong 1988a: 102 and also Tam 1990 for discussion about the centrifugal tendencies of Chinese employees.) The Shanghainese mill owners had thus to find ways of dealing with the low motivations of their workers and the constant threat of desertion. They therefore attempted to build an internal labour market through in-house training and promotion, much on the Japanese model.

Another factor which reduced labour productivity in Hong Kong was the degree of skill in the labour force. Papanek (1988: 67) has observed that the colonial heritage and other political pressures in South East Asia have resulted in education systems which are poorly adapted to the needs of a modern industrial society. Such colonial systems primarily train clerks at the secondary level and lawyers, administrators and liberal arts graduates at the higher levels, rather than technicians, engineers, and businessmen. In Hong Kong, the development of technical education for the cotton textile industry was sponsored to a significant extent by the spinners themselves. Indeed it is only now, in the 1990s, that the first bachelors degree in textile technology is being introduced in Hong Kong. Until now, higher levels of education in textile technology have had to be undertaken overseas. This limitation of the supply of technically trained manpower inevitably had an impact on the quality and productivity of mill operations.

Interfirm Level

The differences and similarities between the Japanese and Hong Kong spinners at interfirm level are numerous. The similarities between Japanese and Shanghainese cotton spinners lie in some functions of the Cotton Spinners' Association, the existence of a supporting coalition of interested institutions — banks, trading companies — and the creation of a mechanism for the control of interfirm competition.

The dissimilarities between Japanese and Hong Kong cotton spinners were numerous. Most important, the Shanghainese spinners in Hong Kong exhibited tendencies to lack of sharing of cost information and intercompany support for training; lack of long term support from banks and trading companies in shouldering risks associated with the development of innovations in products and markets; inability to impose discipline (the sacrifice of individual performance for the common good) on member firms of the Cotton Spinners' Association.

Differences in interfirm relations in the industries considered here are a matter of a difference in degree rather than substance but the manner in which relations are conducted is unique to each industry. For example, both the Japanese and Hong Kong cotton spinning industries had mechanisms for controlling the degree of interfirm competition but in Hong Kong the main mechanism was the textile export quota system which was administered by the government while in Japan self-discipline was imposed through *sohtans*, voluntary production reductions.

The differences and similarities have long-term historical, cultural and organisational roots. Thus, for example, the ability to impose short term disadvantages at firm level for the longer term benefit of the industry as a whole is attributed by Moser (1930: 5) to a 'one for all for one' maxim which was a rule of action in Japan. The Japan Cotton Spinners' Association represented 97 per cent of cotton spindles and 80 per cent of power looms — there was no other organisation in the industry. The Association's

decisions had the force of law. Long term interests were also supported by
the high degree of coordination between all branches of the cotton industry
resulting from interlocking interests. According to Moser (1930: 5−6), in
1930 70 per cent of Japan's trade and industry, foreign and domestic, was
in the hands of fifteen families, including the Mitsui, Iwasaki, Yamagata,
and Susuki families so that every branch of every industry moved under
the direction of the same group of powerful heads. Nine of the fifty five
principal mill combines manufactured or controlled 80 per cent of Japan's
cotton textile exports; while three raw cotton buying companies handled
70 to 80 per cent of the total raw cotton consumed in Japan and were the
principal distribution agents. The large interests in the cotton spinning mills
were also often the ruling interests in the banks and shipping companies.
The Japanese Spinners' Association was successful in operationalising its
perception of the benefits of cooperation between millowners, financial
institutions, trading companies and shipping companies. Each of these
parties was prepared to make sacrifices for the common good of the
industry in the long run whereas the Chinese millowners were hampered
by a number of factors which are displayed in Figure 2 below and which
hinge upon the low propensity to cooperate with non-family colleagues in
a manner which requires denial of individual, short term advantage for the
longer term benefits of a larger group external to the family. Whitley argues
that:

'the historical nature of the Chinese village and lack of integration of households
in production, consumption or common defence activities have reproduced a
sharp distinction between family members and outsiders which makes the
development of social cohesion and common identities between families difficult
in Chinese societies. Rather, distrust tends to be pervasive since each person is
held responsible for his own household and [must] put its interests ahead of
broader objectives.' (1989b: 24)

The role of the Japanese Spinners and their government in blocking attempts by Chinese Millowners to strengthen their industry over the inter-
war period heightened the latter's realization that the *zaikabo* intended to
ensure the failure of the Chinese owned mills. Indeed, during the period
1924 to 1930 many Chinese mills were weakened by Japanese action while
fourteen were in some way controlled by the Japanese. By 1924, the *zaikabo*
had 30 per cent of the Chinese yarn market and 32 per cent of the cotton
cloth market. Japan was interested in the prevention of the growth of
Chinese industry, and in the political dominance of China. Utley (1938: 41)
observed that Britain's economic imperialism hold over China, while very
strong, was compatible with the political independence of China, whereas
Japan, as a weak country economically, had to practise military imperialism

Factor	Japanese association	Chinese association
membership	almost 100 percent by 'merchant' elite	factional; initially dominated by official gentry; after 1925 great disparity
degree of homogeneity of mill operations	extensive diffusion of best practice	also presence of foreign mills: British mills supportive, Japanese mills antagonistic
links with 'service industries'	strong links with banks, trading & shipping companies	links were weak or non-existent
main functions	promotion of the growth of the industry in the international market place	incremental improvements to the infrastructure of the domestic industry eg. training, surveys, raw cotton improvement, mediation of trademark disputes.
effect	control of competition; enabled large scale operations to be generated and maintained	unable to counteract the strong negative factors which restrict the development of the industry, eg. foreign domination, competition between mills

Figure 2 Comparison between the Japanese Cotton Spinners' Association and the Chinese Millowners' Association (in the 1920's and 1930's in Japan and China)

to promote its interests and political independence was incompatible with this.

For political, social and economic reasons, then, the Chinese cotton mill owners failed to develop their Association into a mechanism for limiting competition between mills. Fong (1937: 264) has identified the damaging effects of this competition; he observes that every favourable opportunity, such as the decrease in foreign imports during the First World War, had at once led to cut throat competition between the Chinese mills. All the millowners were operating with about the same major costs, including a wage cost set at or below subsistence level for the workers. Their competitiveness reduced their ability to generate the financial resources to put their operations on a much larger scale while this financial weakness was also a critical factor inhibiting growth.

The leading Japanese spinning companies in Japan and in China could rely on support from the trading companies, banks and, ultimately, the government should they face economic difficulty. Hence the risks associated with innovations could be met with a considerable degree of confidence of long term support in overcoming the inevitable short term difficulties experienced in pioneering new ventures. Moser (1930: 90) observed that the degree of exchange of intelligence between these supporting companies enabled new markets to be developed through efficient merchandising and selling, close attention to be given to market preferences and understanding of business methods in the new markets to be increased.

The Shanghainese were able to replicate a degree of this coordination and control of the Hong Kong textile industry. In Hong Kong at the time the Shanghainese arrived there were two leading banks, a handful of leading trading companies, many vital kin connections and a very strong regional collegiality among the cotton spinning firms (Wong 1988a). Hamilton (1989: 23) indeed identifies regional collegiality as among the most binding of all social relationships other than kinship and suggests that it can be considered as an extension of kin relationships. Collegial relations formed the foundation for merchant and artisan associations in preindustrial China and kinship formed the foundations of the family firms. It was regional collegiality which built trust and predictability into the market place, and formed the basis of the 'federated' organisations with which the Shanghainese textile industrialists were associated in Hong Kong — the Cotton Spinners' Association, the Weavers' Association and the Hong Kong Federation of Industries. There was also a large kinship network among the spinners which was derived from the dominance of the Rong family enterprise in Shanghai; the majority of mills set up immediately after the War in Hong Kong had owners who were connected to the Rong or Yung family (as they are known in Hong Kong), either as family members or as former employees (interview with Mr T. Shaw, Hong Kong Spinners' Association 11 November 1989).

These kinship networks enabled the Shanghainese to invest in a range of businesses and to establish an area of economic concentration in the cotton textile industry. Kin and regional networks enabled the Hong Kong spinners to find export markets in South East Asia. Hamilton (1989: 29) has observed that the Chinese have expanded their economic network into South East Asia and into large urban enclaves throughout the world and that, because these networks build on trust and on reciprocal economic advantage, they largely bypass Western market institutions which lodge trust in impersonal laws and seek economic advantage only in economies of scale and in individual entrepreneurship.

This degree of cooperation based on kin and regional ties is modified only by the high value put on entrepreneurial independence. Wong (1988b: 142 – 144) describes the system as 'entrepreneurial familism' in which the *jia* is the basic unit of economic competition and the family provides support for risk taking and the impetus for innovation. Wong suggests that such family-based enterprises are unlikely to join in long term collusion because each family's independence is jealously guarded and oligopolistic groupings which will block new entry are indeed a rarity. However, the Hong Kong spinners did manage to block new entry through the mechanism of the quota system which allocated to individual firms permits for textile exports on the basis of previous export levels. New firms, therefore, had to buy quotas from existing well established firms. The degree of independence, the limits to cooperation and trust between the spinners is illustrated by the lack of information-sharing about costs of mill operations and the lack of intercompany training.

In contrast, the Japanese spinners regularly exchanged information on operating costs; each company monitored its costs closely and embarked on investigations of identified problems. Innovations were discussed between companies and training opportunities shared. Among the Shanghainese millowners such information remained within the domain of the owner's family in order to retain control based on private subjective information. They exhibited a dislike of objective methods such as costing and delivery control because then the information necessarily becomes more public.

The way in which the Shanghainese cotton spinners financed the setting up and development of their mills has to be discussed in relation to the financial and industrial contexts of Hong Kong in the immediate post-war period and in relation to Japanese influence arising from previous experiences in Shanghai. In Figure 3, a comparison with the *zaikabo* is made. The financial status of the Hong Kong mills was influenced not only by Japanese internal managerial practices, such as the adoption of sound cost accounting, capital investment and depreciation policies, but also by the nature of the competition in the market and the degree of support from associated institutions. As Figure 3 indicates, the ways in which competition between mills was managed and the degree of risk-spreading between the spinning companies and associated organisations such as the trading companies were not the same among the *zaikabo* and among the Hong Kong cotton millowners, first in Shanghai and then in Hong Kong, because of the differences in the nature and degree of interfirm cooperation. The most critical achievement of the Shanghainese spinners in Hong Kong was sound financial management practices which were basic to withstanding the volatility of the cotton markets and to developing the technical efficiency to enable yarn and cloth to be produced at competitive price and quality levels.

Factor/Level *Enterprise Level*	*zaikabo*	Chinese Mills	
		Shanghai	Hong Kong
focus of economic allegiance	organisation	family	family
financial practices	conservative emphasis on growth, reserves accumulated	speculative short term focus, profit oriented	conservative emphasis on profit
investment in new equipment	important & consistent	inconsistent	important & consistent
depreciation policy	adopted	not adopted	adopted
use of cost accounting	adopted	not adopted	adopted
sources of capital:			
a) fixed	shareholders, retained profits, banks	family, clan, retained profits, banks, trading companies	family, clan, interested parties, banks, retained profits
b) working	retained profits, trading companies, banks	same, but with more dependence on banks	similar to *zaikabo*
location of risk	trading companies	spinning enterprise	spinning enterprise
curbing of competition	by Spinners' Association	none	through quota system
size of enterprise	unit size moderate, but financed by large parent company	smaller than Japanese, large compared with other Chinese enterprises Wide range of size	} same; all mills of moderate size
Societal Level			
attitude of government	supportive	hostile	positively non-interventionist

Figure 3   Comparison of the financial practices of the *zaikabo* and the Chinese cotton spinners in Shanghai & Hong Kong

The Shanghainese spinners in Hong Kong had less support from trading companies than did the Japanese at home. The Shanghainese millowners were therefore required to have a wider range of managerial skills, not only for mill operations but also in purchasing raw cotton and selling yarn and cloth. They did have access to the specialist expertise of trading companies but these trading companies — European, Chinese and Indian — were not as powerful or well organised as their Japanese counterparts. They were not aggressive in opening and developing new markets for the spinners and failed to provide any strategic perspective for the development of Hong Kong's cotton textile industry. The burden of the development of the industry fell to the spinners themselves, with some assistance from the government, and this resulted in penetration of only a narrow range of markets and considerable vulnerability to protectionist measures in these markets.

The similarities and differences between the *zaikabo* and Chinese spinners' cotton trading practices in Shanghai and Hong Kong are summarised in Figure 4. The similarities are found in relation to attitudes towards speculation in raw cotton and in the emphasis on quality, price competitiveness and efficiency in production.

The most striking similarities which suggest the importance of *zaikabo* influences on the Shanghainese are practices relating to the purchase of raw cotton. To compete successfully in yarn export markets the spinners had to adopt prudent practices in relation to speculation, stock levels and maintenance of quality. The difference in the roles of the Japanese and Hong Kong trading companies meant that the Hong Kong spinners had to shoulder the risk of the volatile raw cotton and yarn markets. The different role of the Hong Kong trading companies also forced the spinners to take a more active role in the development of markets for yarn and cloth; they therefore took advantage of the political status of Hong Kong as a British colony which bestowed on them advantageous access to British and Commonwealth markets under the Imperial and Commonwealth Preference systems while the United States market was to some extent buyer-led. In this way they were able to meet the post-war consumer demand for economically priced clothing. The consequence of this institutional framework was thus that the Hong Kong spinners gravitated towards a narrow range of markets, aided initially by Imperial or Commonwealth preferences and by the circumstances of the Korean War.

Factors in the international market place pushed the spinners over time towards more extensive forward integration from spinning to weaving to finishing to garment making so that the sales and marketing activities of the spinners themselves became less important. Involvement with trading activities gradually became narrower, focussing more on the sourcing of

	zaikabo	Chinese Mills	
		Shanghai	Hong Kong
raw cotton:			
reliance on Chinese raw	weak	strong	weak
stock levels	high	low	mixed
quality consciousness	high	low	medium
support from trading company	high	low	medium
location of risk	trader/spinner	spinner	spinner
speculation	low	high	low
yarn:			
sales channel	trader	trader/spinner	trader/spinner
forward integration	high	moderate	high
cloth:			
sales channel	trader	trader/spinner	trader/spinner
			buyer
overseas markets	wide	nil	narrow
importance of colonial factor	high	negative	high
governmental support	high	negative	high

Figure 4   Comparison of circumstances and practices relating to cotton trading: *zaikabo*, Chinese mills in Shanghai & in Hong Kong

raw cotton, which, assuming standardisation of yarn production, became
a routine activity, notwithstanding the importance of judicious buying to
maintain quality and competitive cost levels.

The Influence of Societal Level Factors on Chinese Spinners in Hong Kong

The role of the government in the development of the Japanese and
Hong Kong cotton spinning industries was very important. In both cases
governments were supportive but were so in different ways. Members
of the Japanese government and large company elite had similar social
backgrounds, especially as university alumni, which, alongside other factors,
facilitated a close coordination of interests in Japan. In Hong Kong, the
government provided good infrastructure, was supportive in international

trade relations and was non-interventionist in the domestic economy. Close coordination of interests between the government and the large-company elite consisted essentially in maintaining a non-interventionist stance.

The mainland Chinese government was, of course, in contrast, generally unsupportive. Dernberger (1975: 47) has found 'the Chinese government itself was the greatest and most obvious obstacle to economic development: it failed to create a favorable legal, financial, and economic environment for the support of the emerging Chinese modern sector.' There were many factors which limited the ability of the government to take positive action, some of which were imposed by the West. Although some Chinese entrepreneurs were able to escape the inhibiting limits of their tradition and reacted favourably to the forces of modernization, the government did not. Yang (1977: 321 – 322) suggests that in order to pursue industrialization it is necessary for developing countries to formulate systems of modern bureaucracy and take the lead in the field of public administration, the economy and business and to develop education. Japan met all these conditions, China met none, and Hong Kong only the former.

The lack of emphasis on education in Hong Kong has already been referred to. Levy (1985: 119) has observed that pre-Revolutionary China lacked the ability to organize and maintain a planned programme for industrialization and most of the things which Japanese leaders feared for Japan happened to China, Japan herself being an outstanding participant in the exploitation of China's weaknesses. By the nineteenth century, the Japanese probably had the most advanced and thoroughly monetized economy in Asia and were well prepared for further economic development. They had little trouble understanding and adopting the commercial and industrial patterns of the West. Freed from the constraints of the pre-Revolutionary Chinese societal context, the Shanghainese cotton spinners could follow suit, change their practices and pioneer Hong Kong's industrial growth which was based largely on the expansion and upgrading of textiles and garments.

The advantages enjoyed by Hong Kong when it began to industrialize were a good infrastructure, an effective civil sevice, an adaptable, outward-looking population and no large backward agricultural sector. The colony industrialized at a time when the developed countries were enjoying fast economic growth and world trade was expanding at an unprecedented rate. Hong Kong is nonetheless still facing problems generated by the excessive preoccupation of firms with short term profit maximisation, insufficient attention to quality and technological upgrading and inadequate public and private investments in training and capital equipment. All these are deficiencies which large organisations with their characteristic longer planning horizon could help to remedy as they do in Japan. In Hong Kong, however, Pang (1988: 225, 231) identifies the strong influence of the immigrant mentality, with its preoccupation with short term goals and reliance on extensive intra-group social networks. The elite Shanghainese cotton textile entrepreneurs relied substantially on relatively uncodified, undiffused knowledge (see Boisot 1983: 159 – 190) in the running of their enterprises and their industry. Transactions required shared values and attitudes and a climate of trust which the kinship and regional networks provided. The nature of the colonial elite administering Hong Kong was complementary to that of the spinners in its attitudes and values but did not counteract their limitations, itself making few long term public investment decisions.

The domination by the British of the top echelons of the civil service and political positions meant that the private sector was the only route to wealth, security and social status for the Shanghainese entrepreneurs. All the latter's energies are devoted to the pursuit of economic gain, in part achieved through a close relationship with government. Thus, Deyo (1987: 245) has identified in Hong Kong a strong social cohesiveness and unity between commercial, financial and industrial leaders and colonial authorities which has resulted in the existence of a small elite among whose members power, wealth and social status have converged. Economic and political concentration has been assured by the extreme concentration of financial institutions through interlocking directorates and by extensive subcontracting. Implicit development strategies have emerged as pervasive, shared assumptions among members of a closed establishment regarding the needs of the economy. The generation and implementation of these strategies have been politically insulated from the demands of other small business, organized labour and other non-establishment groups.

Conclusion

In conclusion, the impact of the *zaikabo* influence on the Shanghainese spinners in Hong Kong has been substantially demonstrated in the early development of the Hong Kong cotton spinning industry. With time this influence has weakened in response to the exigencies of the Hong Kong context and because of the weak codification of knowledge about developments in mill operations which lead to increasingly divergent methods. The strongest Japanese influences operate at *intra*-firm level and are particularly seen in operational practices relating to technical efficiency and in employee training and welfare, of which the Shanghainese could obtain direct experience. In contrast, the Shanghainese did not absorb Japanese managerial coordination and control mechanisms as the strategic levels of their enterprises because there unfavourable institutional and cultural factors intervened. These factors were also important in explaining different practices at *inter*-firm level. Although the institutional structures surrounding the Japanese, Chinese and Hong Kong cotton spinning industries were similar — for instance, the trading companies, banks and machine suppliers — the role they played in each area and their inter-relationships with the spinners varied because of the different societal contexts of their activity.

Western Technology in a Chinese Context: New Technologies and the Organisation of Work in Hong Kong

Teresa Poon

Introduction

New technology has been a major subject of concern in advanced industrialised countries for quite some time[1]. Empirically, microelectronics technology has raised issues of great interest and concern for labour and trade union organisations, as well as companies and governments. There have been big worries over the effect of new technological devices on the level of employment. While some believe that large scale job obsolescence will be the inevitable result of the widespread application of microelectronics technologies in production, others maintain that a low rate of technological innovation would be more disastrous in the long run as more people would be out of work in a bleak economy where industries had lost their competitive edge to other countries. There are also other important concerns: the impact of technological changes on pay and work conditions, on the form of managerial control, on the skill composition of jobs, on health and safety at work and on the prospects for women's employment (Robins and Webster 1982: 15–16).

Debate on new technology at a theoretical level is no less intense. Recent discussion on new technology in Western literature seems to have shifted

---

[1] The term 'new technology' has been used throughout the chapter as if its definition is clear and widely agreed upon. In fact, the term is a confusing concept requiring some clarification. Much of the confusion originates from the concept of technology which for some means just the 'technical hardware', for others includes the 'software' and for some others still (e.g. Hill (1981: 86)), 'implies the division of labour and work organisation which is built into, or required for efficient operation by productive technique'. 'New technology' is treated in this chapter as a general concept referring to an innovative device which use micro-electronics in processing information. Devices and systems such as computer numerical- controlled (CNC) machines, electronic-point-of-sale system, computerised information systems, even word-processing and electronic filing can all be subsumed under the concept.

from a deterministic view, in which new technology is treated as a neutral and independent variable with an impact on both the quantitative and qualitative aspects of employment, through a view of technology as a functional tool serving the capitalist system of domination and control and, more recently, to the view that new technology is itself a variable subject to influence from other factors.

Questions on the outcome of technological changes are thus also different relative to the variety of views on the nature of new technology. Where new technology is taken as neutral and inevitable, the salient question is how to adapt and adjust to technological innovation, no matter what the outcome is and whether the outcome is positive or not (Mansfield 1968; Bird 1980). In contrast, when technology is treated as a tool serving capitalist interests, the question is how to avoid the forecast universal degradation and deskilling of labour (Braverman 1974; Edwards 1979). Most commonly now, however, the outcome of technological innovation itself is regarded as a contested and negotiated phenomenon because technology is taken as a dependent variable contingent upon social and political choice (Wilkinson 1983: 17−21). It is this approach which is taken here in the discussion of technological change in Hong Kong.

Recent literature on new technology shifts the emphasis from 'managerial strategies' to 'social choice'. For example, Wilkinson (1983: 17−21) shows that the outcome of any technological innovation should be seen not as fixed arrangements prescribed by the technological capabilities of the innovative devices nor as the realisation of managerial intention to control labour, but rather as the outcome which has been chosen and negotiated. Organisational actors such as managers, engineers and workers must be seen as political beings with particular interests, having a particular position of power and mediating between potential and actual technology chosen (Wilkinson 1983: 82−84). These are some dissenting voices. Clark et al. (1988: 11−12), for instance, in their recent study suggest that technology should be taken as engineering systems composed of three primary elements (the system principles, an overall system configuration and a system implementation) and two secondary elements (the system dimension and system appearance). Because of the technical requirements of some elements in the engineering systems, an independent role is played by technology in the outcome of technological change. However, even for Clark et al. (1988), technology is one of the factors which defines the 'design space' within which organisational actors can shape the outcomes of technological change. The salient question then becomes: who can influence what outcome of technological change, at which stage and how?

While there is evidence indicating that Hong Kong's major industries have already adopted certain new technological devices in their production processes, new technology as such does not seem to be a major issue to either academics or to trade unionists in Hong Kong (see Hong Kong Government 1989)[2]. There is no *prima facie* evidence to indicate that Hong Kong trade unions have reacted strongly to the adoption of new technology. Nor does the issue of new technology attract much attention from academics. Thus, while Western literature on new technology has proliferated, similar literature in the context of Hong Kong is extremely scarce. There is also little information on workers' reaction to new technology in specific workplaces despite the fact that, given the existence of a weak trade union movement in Hong Kong, an examination of the reactions of workers to the adoption of new technology at the workplace level is very important. This chapter suggests that an investigation of Hong Kong's technological scene within its own economic, social and cultural contexts will help to indicate the complexity of forecasting the impact of technological change on job design in different cultural contexts and, even more, of predicting worker responses to it. This chapter takes the view of Knights and Willmott (1988: 3) that '... what is needed are studies of new technology within the context of political, socio-cultural and organisational development; its treatment not as an isolated or uniformed phenomenon, but as something that varies depending on its particular form and on the nature of the organisation, industry and society in which it is developed and used.'

Since the outcome of technological change is a negotiated and contested product, the situation in Hong Kong is analysed in the chapter using a recent study of the impact of technological innovation on work and work behaviour in a sample of six industrial/service organisations in Hong Kong. As managers and workers behave not as isolated individuals but as social beings bringing with them external influences into organisations, a brief description of Hong Kong's economic, social and cultural environment will be given first. The progress of technological development in Hong Kong indicates how far the adoption of new technology in organisations is affected by the general industrial climate and by government policies. The case study allows a thorough analysis of the effect of technological innovation on the organisations examined. The focus will be on what and why changes take place, if there are any, and on workers' reactions to the new technologies introduced into their workplaces.

A study carried out in Hong Kong in 1985 illustrates the different ways in which similar technology can be used in different organisational settings.

---

[2] Evidence can be obtained from the findings of the techno-economic studies commissioned by the Hong Kong government on major industries such as textiles and clothing, electronics and plastics in the 1980s (see the section on 'A Portrait of Hong Kong's Technological Development') and from the 1989 *Report on the Survey of Overseas Investment in Hong Kong's Manufacturing Industries* (see the same section referred above).

The study was sponsored by the Asian Productivity Organisation and, as one of the projects carried out in 16 East Asian countries for a transnational research programme, aims at ascertaining the implications of technological innovations on human behaviour in the context of work organisation and productivity (Kao, Ng and Taylor 1986: 2 – 3). Case studies were carried out on three industrial and three service enterprises of different size and owned by different capital holders. The enterprises concerned were chosen because they had all recently introduced computer-related technologies either into specific departments or enterprise-wide. Senior managers of the organisations as well as a sample of their workforce affected by computer-isation were interviewed using two different questionnaires in each of the cases examined. The questionnaire for the *management* was designed to collect information about the enterprise, its experience in technological innovation and on the impact of computer application on such aspects as work organisation and procedures, authority structure and supervision, skill requirements and personnel policies and practices. The questionnaire for *workers* was designed to test responses to computerisation in terms of attitudes towards task composition, perception of work and work organisa-tion and general work attitude before and after computerisation. Before examining the study in detail, the general economic, social, cultural and technological environment of Hong Kong is portrayed to provide a contex-tual framework for the analysis.

The Economic, Social and Cultural Environment of Hong Kong

Hong Kong is a city-state located on the southern border of China. It is still one of the United Kingdom's overseas territories but will be returned to mainland China after 1997. Until the 1950s, the economy of Hong Kong was mainly founded on entrepot trade. Since then, in contrast, the territory has seen its export-oriented manufacturing sector growing very fast. The manufacturing sector has grown considerably over the past thirty years and, despite some decline from its peak in 1970, remained the largest single contributor to Hong Kong's gross domestic product (GDP) until 1986 when it began to be edged into the second place by the wholesale, retail and import/export trades, restaurants and hotels sector. In 1986, however, it still accounted for 22 % of GDP (see Table 1) and for the largest share of the employed labour force, despite relative decline from 50 % in 1976

Table 1   Contribution to GDP by Major Economic Sectors, 1970 – 1987 (Share
in percentage terms)

Economic Sector	1970	1975	1980	1985	1986	1987
Wholesale, retail and import/export trades, restaurants and hotels	19.6	20.7	20.4	21.8	21.3	23.2
Manufacturing	30.9	26.9	23.8	21.9	22.3	22.1
Financing, insurance, real estate and business services	14.9	17.0	22.8	16.3	17.3	18.4
Community, social and personal services	18.0	18.7	12.5	17.3	16.6	14.9
Transport, storage and communication	7.6	7.2	7.5	8.1	8.1	8.7
Other	9.0	9.5	13.0	14.6	14.4	12.7
Total	100.0	100.0	100.0	100.0	100.0	100.0

Note: # Provisional estimates.
Source: Estimates of Gross Domestic Product 1966 to 1988, Census & Statistics
Department.

to 35.5 % in 1988, a period over which the share of tertiary sector employment rose from 40 % to 53 % (see Table 2).

Major local manufacturing industries include textiles, clothing, electronics, household electrical appliances, plastics and metal products. These industries together accounted for 72 % of Hong Kong's total manufacturing employment and 74 % of total domestic exports in 1988. The textiles industry started off as the largest export earner but since the 1950s its relative importance has declined and been replaced by the clothing industry. The textiles and clothing industries taken together, however, are still the largest export earner of all manufacturing industries and accounted for 38 % of total domestic exports in 1988. The next most important manufacturing industry, in terms of its relative share of Hong Kong's domestic export, is electronics, followed by watches and clocks, plastics, toys and dolls industries.

One of the major characteristics of the manufacturing sector in Hong Kong is the predominance of small establishments. Though that sector accounts for the largest share of employment as a whole, in the manufacturing sector nine out of ten establishments employed fewer than 50 persons in 1988 (see Table 3). A second central characteristic crucial to manufacturing is the widespread practice of subcontracting. A survey conducted on

Table 2   Contribution to Total Employment by Major Economic Sectors, 1976 – 1988 (Share percentage terms)

Economic Sector	1976	1980	1985	1986	1987	1988
Manufacturing	49.7	46.0	39.2	38.9	37.8	35.5
Wholesale, retail and import/export trades, restaurants and hotels	23.9	23.1	27.2	27.5	28.0	19.4
Financing, insurance, real estate & business services	4.7	6.5	8.3	8.5	9.1	9.7
Community, social and personal services	8.0	8.6	9.4	9.3	9.2	9.3
Transport, storage and communication	3.3	3.9	4.4	4.4	4.5	4.8
Other	10.4	11.9	11.5	11.4	11.4	11.3
Total	100.0	100.0	100.0	100.0	100.0	100.0

Source: Reports of Employment, Vacancies and Payroll Statistics, Census & Statistics Department.

295 small and medium-size industrial firms (SMI, below 200 employees) in Hong Kong from 1983 to 1988 found that 27 % of the sample firms sold or did business based on subcontracts received from contractor factories. These SMI firms in turn also offered subcontracts to other factories; 24.5 % of the sample firms obtained their material supply or industrial services through such an arrangement (Sit and Wong 1989: 180).

Several factors are commonly held to contribute to the fast development of Hong Kong's manufacturing industries. These include the presence of a versatile and industrious workforce and a group of innovative entrepreneurs, a simple tax structure and low taxation rate, a good communication network and infrastructure and the government's commitment to free trade. The continued fast development of Hong Kong's major manufacturing industries has, however, faced severe constraints, especially since the early 1980s. The growing pressure of protectionism in Hong Kong's major overseas markets such as the U. S. and the European Economic Community (EEC) is among the most important factors hampering the growth of the textile and clothing industries. In 1988, 60 % of Hong Kong's domestic exports of the textiles and clothing products was subject to quota restraint severely limiting expansion possibilities (Hong Kong Government 1989: 37).

This limitation is further aggravated by the increase in manufacturing costs. The shortage of labour and hence the increase in labour and produc-

Table 3   Number of Manufacturing Establishments by Employment Size,
           1975–1988

Size of Establishment (No. of Persons Engaged)	1975	1980	1985	1986	1987	1988
1–9	20 254 (65.3)	29 747 (65.5)	32 827 (68.3)	32 987 (67.8)	34 354 (68.2)	35 066 (69.3)
10–19	4 639 (14.9)	6 970 (15.3)	6 760 (14.1)	7 010 (14.4)	7 241 (14.4)	7 219 (14.3)
20–49	3 438 (11.1)	5 119 (11.3)	5 040 (10.5)	5 084 (10.5)	5 336 (10.6)	5 032 (9.9)
50–99	1 486 (4.8)	2 111 (4.6)	2 016 (4.2)	2 115 (4.3)	2 090 (4.1)	1 977 (3.9)
100–199	733 (2.4)	895 (2.0)	904 (1.9)	889 (1.8)	869 (1.7)	828 (1.6)
200–499	356 (1.1)	410 (0.9)	393 (0.8)	414 (0.9)	387 (0.8)	356 (0.7)
500–999	88 (0.3)	117 (0.3)	99 (0.2)	93 (0.2)	104 (0.2)	105 (0.2)
1 000 and above	40 (0.1)	40 (0.1)	26 (0.1)	31 (0.1)	28 (0.1)	23 (*)
Total	31 034 (100.0)	45 409 (100.0)	48 065 (100.0)	48 623 (100.0)	50 409 (100.0)	50 606 (100.0)

Note: Figure in bracket denotes the percentage share of the respective column's total.

Source: Reports of Employment, Vacancies and Payroll Statistics, Census & Statistics Department.

tion costs has led Hong Kong to find it increasingly difficult to maintain its competitive edge, especially over such newly industrialising countries as Thailand and the Phillipines, in the production of low-cost products.

In the electronics industry, moreover, Hong Kong can no longer rely solely, as it did in the nineteen sixties and seventies, on the production of low-cost consumer products, such as radios and cassette-tape recorders, and fashionable fad products such as calculators and digital watches. The rapid growth of mature consumer products has levelled off over the last decade and the fad products sector does not provide a stable base for sustained growth since such products have short product life cycles. Similarly, in the plastics industry rising production, materials, and labour costs in recent years have cut sharply into manufacturers' profit margins (Hong Kong Government 1989: 86). The domestic export value of these major

Hong Kong manufacturing industries all declined in 1985. Although partly resulting from recession on a global basis, the growth of these industries was indeed faced with constraints, either from their internal industrial structure or the external markets or both.

With the growing importance of the tertiary or services sector, there has been a relative shift in employment away from manufacturing and towards such non-industrial activities as finance, insurance, real estate, hotels and tourism and business services. According to the most recent Hong Kong census (1986), most major occupational categories grew in absolute numbers between 1976 and 1986 but the proportion of the workforce engaging in production and related occupations, which accounts for the largest share of the active working population, decreased from 52 % in 1976 to 43 % in 1986. There has, in contrast, been a rise in professional, technical and related occupations from 5.5 % in 1976 to 8 % in 1986. Engineering technicians, systems analysts and computer programmers are included in this category and are expected to be in relatively high demand in the near future. It is projected that in 1996, for example, around 40,000 engineering technicians and 10,000 system analysts and computer programmers will be needed, representing a 50 % growth in the former category and a 100 % increase in the latter one over their respective number in 1988 (Education and Manpower Branch, Hong Kong Government 1990: 36).

The role of external capital is important in industrial development in Hong Kong. Over the ten-year period between December 1971 and December 1981, the size of foreign investment grew more than eightfold, from HK $ 0.759.5 billion to HK $ 7.023 billion and led to a substantial growth in the export-oriented manufacturing sector (Ng and Sit 1989: 191). According to a survey of overseas investment in Hong Kong's manufacturing industries conducted by the Hong Kong Government in 1989, cumulative foreign investment amounted to HK $ 26.17 billion in 1988. The United States is the top overseas investor in manufacturing industries, followed by Japan and China. Most foreign investment is channelled into the electronics, textile, clothing and non-metallic mineral products industries. These overseas investors offer Hong Kong companies licensing assistance, engineering and technical support and assistance in the acquisition of machinery. This kind of assistance provides a good basis for technology transfer to Hong Kong's manufacturing industries. The availability of technical know-how arrangements through foreign-local joint ventures and the number of patents registered are taken by Hung (1984: 199) as indicators of foreign capital's contribution to the transfer of technology to Hong Kong.

Since the Second World War, Hong Kong has been experiencing steady economic growth. In 1975, its per capita GDP was US $ 1,700, advancing to US $ 4,768 in 1981. Notwithstanding a slower economic growth rate in 1984 and 1985 as a consequence of global economic recession, Hong Kong has been able to experience growing affluence and steady improvements in the standard of living. Unemployment levels have always been low, hovering around 3 − 4 % since the early 1980s, while in 1988 the unemployment rate was at a low of 1.6 % (Hong Kong Government Printer 1989: 95). A labour shortage problem indeed has recently emerged. The Joint Associations Working Group which consisted of nine Employers' Associations already reported an estimated shortfall of 200,000 workers across all sectors of business, industry and public service in late 1988. The level of skill in short supply is not the same for all sectors. In the construction sector, for example, about 80 % of the labour shortage identified can be considered as semi-skilled and skilled. Alternatively, in the retail sector, unskilled labour is in high demand. No report on the shortage of the level of skill in the manufactoring sector was made but some semi-skilled and unskilled vacancies have been absorbed by workers in mainland China as many Hong Kong manufacturers have shifted part of their operations there, taking advantage of lower labour costs and improved infrastructural support.

Economic growth in Hong Kong has been matched by a rise in the educational level of the population. The percentage of the population aged 15 and over attaining secondary school level increased from 32.2 % in 1976 to 42.9 % in 1986. The domestic population grew rapidly after the Second World War and only in the 1960s did both birth and death rates begin to settle down at low levels. At the beginning of the 1980s, a new influx of Chinese immigrants and Vietnamese refugees increased the size of the population, which amounted to 5.2 million in 1981. With a tightened immigration policy, the annual population growth rate fell to an average of 1.3 % for the period 1981 to 1984, compared to 4 % over the period 1978 to 1980. The total population stood at 5.74 million in 1988 (Hong Kong Government 1989: 328).

The culture of Hong Kong largely reflects the nature of its population. The early population was mainly composed of migrants who fled to Hong Kong from mainland China after the Chinese Revolution in 1949. For some of them, Hong Kong was not a place for permanent residence; for most others, returning to mainland China would mean a huge sacrifice, both politically and economically. For those who decided to stay in Hong Kong, the pressure to earn a living combined with their aspirations to provide their children with better education and a more prosperous future bred a great emphasis on material reward. Several studies carried out in the nineteen sixties and seventies showed that 'good pay' was regarded by workers as the most important aspect of their job and that the level of pay was the most significant factor accounting for labour turnover (cf. Chaney 1971; Ward 1972; Carr 1973; Turner 1980; Ting Chan and Ng 1983 and England 1989: 46−48). Added to this materialistic orientation is the traditional Chinese Confucian value of familism which gives high priority to family matters above wider social concerns. Workers' allegiance is given to the family and work is seen only as instrumental in furthering their familial interests (Lau 1982: 72).

Familism also manifests itself in work relationships in organisations run by Chinese families. In these Chinese business concerns, the ideal Confucian relationship among family members is reproduced in employment relationships. Confucian ideals emphasised the authority of the father within the family, the need for solidarity between brothers, and the importance of harmony and order in the household (England 1989: 39). According to a survey of 1,000 representative Hong Kong employees in 1976, most believe that their employer should behave towards them like the head of a family. Management and workers should work together like a team (Turner 1980: 142 & 198). A majority of workers hence appear to accept that the 'natural' state of industrial relations should be one of harmony and teamwork and that they should be loyal to their employers who are expected to be paternalistic and in control of absolute authority. There is, however, as yet little research on whether these traditional Chinese cultural values still prevail in the younger working population in Hong Kong. The rise in the educational level and the concomitant increase in awareness of individual legal rights may mean that such a harmonious ideal employment relationship cannot be assumed to continue.

Few workers join trade unions. The proportion of employees who were trade unionists fell from 25 % in 1976 to 16 % in 1981, a level at which it hovered throughout the 1980s. In 1987, there was a total of 415 trade unions with a declared membership of 381,685 which represented 15.7 % of the active working population (England 1989: 120 – 121). The Chinese cultural trait of preferring to express collectivism in the family and individualism at work is held to be one of the reasons for the weakness of trade unionism in Hong Kong. Protective government labour legislation, benevolent and paternalistic employers, a relatively constant shortage of labour, which is more conducive to individualised haggling than to collective bargaining in response to wage differentials, and a general cynicism about the effect of trade unions on the economy are some other reasons suggested for low membership rates (Ng 1982: 63). The fragmentation of trade unions resulting from ideological differences between pro-China left-wing and pro-Taiwan right-wing unions also retards the growth of the labour movement in Hong Kong.

The approach of 1997 and the return of Hong Kong to mainland China, however, have led to important political changes affecting the development of trade unionism. With constitutional reforms introduced by the Hong Kong government in 1985, labour, long been excluded from the representative political system, is now recognised as a functional constituency in the indirect elections to the Legislative Council. Moreover, in addition to the pro-China Federation of Trade Unions and the Taiwan-linked Trade Unions Council, the two largest federations of trade unions in Hong Kong, there recently emerged a third confederation known as the Hong Kong Congress of Trade Unions. The Congress was formally established in the summer of 1990 with a membership of 100,000. It is the first confederation set up in Hong Kong to advance the solidarity of independent trade unions. Without a particular political orientation, the major objective of the Congress is to fight for labour rights and benefits and to improve the welfare and social status of Hong Kong workers (*South China Morning Post* 15/11/1989). It is highly probable that the formation of this independent Congress of Trade Unions will fuel the development of the labour movement in Hong Kong.

The outstanding characteristic in the arena of labour-management relations in Hong Kong is the very low level of conflict as measured by disputes and work stoppages. During the ten-year period from 1978 to 1987, there was an average annual loss through disputes of only 6.4 working days per 1,000 employees, one of the lowest averages among industrialised countries (England 1989: 216). Statistics on industrial disputes and stoppages alone cannot be taken as the only indicator of the level of labour-management conflict; other indicators such as absenteeism, labour turnover, working-to-rule, sabotage, restriction of output, industrial accidents and even dismissing workers may tell one much more about the true nature of industrial relationships and hence cannot be overlooked.

A Portrait of Hong Kong's Technological Development

There are no available statistics, official or otherwise, assessing the level of technological advancement in Hong Kong. Information showing the gradual change in the occupational structure in recent decades and the increase in the share of overseas investment in Hong Kong's industrial and financial sectors (as discussed earlier) can, however, be taken as indicators of technological advancement. The growing demand for people in technical-related occupations such as computer programming suggests a wider application of microelectronics technology, be it in the manufacturing or the service industries. The tremendous growth of foreign investment in Hong Kong in recent decades suggests a high degree of technology transfer. The type of technology transferred was not only restricted to ordinary machinery; in engineering and technical systems, advanced technology applied in research and development, product design, production process, testing and calibration, quality control and management was also included. According to a survey of 605 manufacturing companies financed in part by overseas investment carried out by the Industry Department of Hong Kong Government in 1989, 97 (16 %) reported that these same overseas investors had been involved in the transfer of one or more types of advanced technology. The more common types of technology transferred were management information systems, total quality management systems, computer-aided design systems and material requirement planning software systems (Hong Kong Government, Industry Department 1989: 38 – 39). In addition, other types of advanced technologies specific to particular industries were transferred.

While Hong Kong has certainly made some technological progress in the past few decades, the pace of technological advance is not even across and within different economic sectors. Much depends on the size and the ownership of the firm, the nature of products produced and the nature of product markets.

As was indicated above, Hong Kong's industrial structure is such that each industry encompasses a large number of small local manufacturing establishments whose activities are largely responsive to buyers' orders. Many of these small firms lack the capability to find and absorb new technology and the resources to invest in product/process improvement because of the high cost of much of the equipment involved (Hong Kong Government 1979: 254). Because of the export-oriented character of the industries and the corresponding difficulty in predicting future demands, small firms, even when capable of it, are usually quite reluctant to invest in advanced technology, especially when such technology is needed to produce only specialised products. Many of these small firms, however, must still adjust to market demand to survive and are therefore prepared to change their production methods by introducing new machines or automation devices when clear market needs exist and when the equipment payback period is short. These demand-induced changes are inevitably responsive and passive. The products to be produced in some manufacturing firms are already established in the market or specifications of the products prescribed by the buyer; product development and the use of advanced technology seem hardly necessary to these firms.

The nature of ownership of the firms is a another factor to be considered. Foreign-local joint ventures might benefit from the transfer of technical know-how and skills from the parent companies. Similarly, companies wholly owned by foreign capital might have readier access to the type of new technology needed than do purely local ones.

One general factor is central in affecting the pace of technological development in Hong Kong's manufacturing industries. This is the subcontracting system. Unlike that in Japan, Hong Kong's subcontracting system does not contribute to the upgrading of technology and product design. The subcontracting relationship in Japan is relatively permanent. There, contractors, besides getting parts, components or industrial services from the subcontractors, are also actively concerned with the subcontractors' technical, management and other business developments. Contractors in Hong Kong, in contrast, normally have only a temporary relationship with their subcontractors. Few small-medium firms will be tied up with a single contractor for a long period and little technical, market and management information and assistance flows between contractors and subcontractors. The system of subcontracting in Hong Kong can therefore be characterised by the term 'mechanical market-response' in the sense that subcontractors are often used to absorb uncertainty in the market caused by fluctuating product design and demand volumes (Sit and Wong 1989: 178 – 179). This kind of subcontracting system works against long term technological development and product innovation.

The current status of technological development is not uniform across different industries in Hong Kong. In the clothing industry, for example, local garment manufacturers and machinery suppliers surveyed in 1989 took the view that their level of technology is among that of the top nations in the world. This might not be the case, however, since it was also found that management in this industry is quite reluctant to invest in advanced technology for specialised product applications because of the need for flexibility and the uncertainty about the future applicability of the technology. Factors such as the proliferation of styles, frequent style changes, and smaller production quantities are believed to limit the effective application of technology (Kurt Salmon Associates 1987). The textile industry is more capital-intensive than is clothing, however, and is characterised by the application of rapidly developing technology to improve productivity. The product capabilities and flexibilities of the textile industry are dependent on the technology in place and textile technology has advanced rapidly in Hong Kong in the last two decades.

As was indicated above, in Hong Kong as in other places, investment in technology is made when the market need exists and when the equipment payback period is short. In the textile industry, large numbers of computerised, automatic flatbed knitting machines, for instance, were installed in 1985 and 1986 because of the need to replace the import of knitted sweater panels (Kurt Salmon Associates 1987). In the electronics industry, the nature of the industry itself plays a part in hindering the development of manufacturing technology; with few exceptions, the bulk of the industry comprises small and medium-sized operations manufacturing consumer products typically assembled from imported components. Little is spent on technology development work such as product design and process improvement. The industry is becoming more and more specialised in the production of fad products such as TV games, electronic watches and telephones, products which require rapid styling and product changes in order to meet changing fashions and taste in consumer market. With these characteristics, it is not surprising that the electronics industry in Hong

Kong is not capital- and technology-intensive. According to a survey conducted by the HKPC in 1981, most electronics factories employed almost no advanced manufacturing technology. Automatic component insertion machines, for example, were used by only a handful of Hong Kong manufacturers even in the early 1980s (Hong Kong Government 1983: 27–31). In the third important industry, the plastics conversion industry, in Hong Kong, large mould-making factories generally use high precision, computer numerically controlled (CNC) machines to ensure proper quality assurance throughout the manufacturing process but in general, computer-aided design (CAD) and computer-aided manufacture (CAM) are not widely used in the industry, although some industrialists in the field may be aware of these technologies (SRI International 1986: 71–72).

The Push to Innovate

While the extent and the degree of technological advancement in Hong Kong may not be very clear, it *is* clear that both sections of industry and the government of Hong Kong have been keen to increase the rate of technological innovation, the latter especially in the context of industrial development policies since the late 1970s. The recommendations of the Advisory Committee on Diversification (ACD) were important in fostering this forward-looking government stance. The Committee was appointed in October 1977 by the Governor to investigate the factors facilitating or hindering diversification of industries and to advise the government on suitable policies, given increasing restrictions imposed by the importers on some of Hong Kong's major manufacturing industries. It was found that at that stage diversification had hardly gone beyond existing major product groups such as textiles and clothing, electronics products, toys and plastic products. It was also found that the speed with which Hong Kong manufacturers could diversify and manufacture high-tech, upmarket products was greatly hindered by the inadequate provision of industrial support facilities, such as those relating to research and development, the acquisition of technical information and the transfer of new technology and technical back-up services including the testing of materials, components and products, the quality certification of finished products and the calibration of the firms' measuring instruments and systems. As Hong Kong's manufacturing industries comprise predominantly small firms which lack the resources to invest in industrial support and technical back-up services, the Committee recommended that the government should strengthen its role in the provision of these services and facilities to industries.

The government accepted these recommendations and made a number of moves. The first major governmental initiative was the establishment of the Industrial Development Board (later renamed Industry Development Board) in August 1980 to plan, monitor and advise on various programmes leading to the provision of industrial support and technical back-up facilities for industries. The Industrial Promotion Division of the Industry Department has also sought to attract to Hong Kong new industries or more sophisticated processes for existing industries and continued to contribute indirectly to advances in technology. In addition, a number of applied research projects on electronics and CAD/CAM technology have been funded by the government and infrastructural support to industries has also been gradually improved.

A key infrastructural component for industrial and technological development is the availability of a pool of qualified and adaptable manpower. Following the recommendation of ACD in 1979, the government established in 1982 a Vocational Training Council to link technical and industrial training and in the early 1980s adopted a policy to rationalise the system of technical education in Hong Kong to promote export-quality products. The polytechnics were restructured to allow greater concentration on technological, professional and degree-level courses while the lower-level courses were transferred to the technical institutes (Ng 1987: 41 – 43 and 57 – 58). In May 1986, a plan to build a third University, the Hong Kong University of Science and Technology, was approved.

Technology is thus seen by the government as an important contributor to the upgrading of Hong Kong's industries and hence enhancing the general economic efficiency and competitiveness of the city. As was recognized by Mr. A. G. Eason, Assistant Director of Industry:

'Hong Kong has hitherto been engaged less in exploring the frontiers of science in such fields than in applying established technology for commercial purposes. The importance of technology to the manufacturing sector in Hong Kong lies mainly in the contribution it can make towards improving the quality of products and the efficiency of the production processes, hence achieving higher "value-added" '. (Eason 1986: 90)

In March 1988, the government went further and the Governor appointed a Committee on Science and Technology the aim of which is to 'seek out and develop new scientific ideas which might be of use to Hong Kong and to advise the government on how these might best be applied'. Never before has the role played by the government in the development of science and technology been so obvious.

That Hong Kong had to move up the technological ladder in order to maintain its competitiveness in the world market has been recognised not only by the Government but also by academics, industrialists and trade unionists. Constant calls have been made by academics for Government to increase funds for research and development. Businessmen are also keen to raise Hong Kong's general level of technology. One of Hong Kong's leading entrepreneurs, David Kwok-po Li, Chief Executive of the Bank of East Asia, in 1988 called on public policy makers to:

'... encourage increased competitiveness in the manufacturing sector ... by providing higher technology and assisting companies to move up-market.' (*South China Morning Post* Dec.)

Besides attempting to influence policy makers, entrepreneurs themselves also contribute to the upgrading of Hong Kong's industries.

Most relevant groups in Hong Kong thus perceive the need for Hong Kong to innovate so as to survive in an increasingly turbulent local and international business environment. The government, especially since the early 1980s, has conspicuously been pushing towards that end and whether they innovate or not, firms themselves are well aware of the need to introduce new technology to increase their market competitiveness. A survey carried out in 1989 jointly by the Industrial Centre of the Hong Kong Polytechnic and the Hong Kong Productivity Council on the training needs of eighteen companies (twelve of which were product manufacturers and six were tool making manufacturers) found that over two-thirds were aware of advanced technologies such as CAD, CAM, computer numerical-controlled (CNC) milling and CNC tuning while almost half of them knew of such processes as flexible manufacturing systems (FMS) and computer integrated manufacture (CIM). Although fewer manufacturers said that they were capable of adopting the new technologies mentioned, there were still twelve who planned to adopt these technologies, in one form or another, in their companies within two years of the study in order to upgrade the level of technology, to improve product quality, to reduce cost and to maintain their competitive edge in the market (Hong Kong Productivity Council and Hong Kong Polytechnic 1989).

A Study of the Impact of New Technology on Work and Work Behaviour in Hong Kong

The study which forms the centre of the discussion in the remainder of this chapter was carried out by a group of Hong Kong researchers in 1985 on three industrial and three service organisations, all of which had recently introduced different forms of computerised operations. The three industrial enterprises were small (10 – 49 persons) or small-medium (50 – 199) sized organisations (Sit and Wong 1989: 6 – 7). The two larger enterprises were both printing presses. Both were similar in size (employing around 150 and 180 employees respectively) but one was owned and managed by Chinese and another used British capital and management. The Chinese printing press was engaged in the printing of books and was to a large extent export-oriented with about 85 % of its products going into export sales. The British printing press, on the other hand, was engaged in security printing of items such as cheques, bonds and certificates. It was owned by a British newspaper consortium and was less export-oriented than the Chinese press with about 70 % of its output consumed locally. The third industrial entreprise studied was a garment-making factory and was smaller. The plant was Chinese owned and managed and was a typical Chinese family business, started off from a modest beginning and gradually growing to have a workforce of about forty. The plant specialised in pleating and was a subcontracting workshop that served a network of principal garment factories.

In contrast to the industrial enterprises studied, the three service organisations investigated were large bureaucratic establishments, each of which employed a workforce exceeding 3,000. They were the University of Hong Kong, established in 1911 as a non-profit making academic institution, the Hong Kong and Shanghai Banking Corporation, founded in 1864 with British capital and management, and the Hong Kong Telephone Company, incorporated in 1925 as a monopoly public utility enterprise. All three organisations had a relatively long history but computerisation was only a recent phenomenon. The study focussed specifically on the effect of computerisation on the library of the University and on the Directory Enquiry Service of the telephone company which is staffed by operators who answer telephone enquiries from members of the public.

All six establishments underwent computerisation in one form or another in the late 1960s or 1970s. Numerically-controlled machines were introduced into the press rooms of both the Chinese and the British printing shops in 1979. Although 'computer' printing was introduced, both printing presses still retained the more traditional type of printing technology such as 'sheet-fed' and 'rotary' printing. About 30 % to 35 % of the printing work of the Chinese press and 12 % of that of the British press was computerised under the automation process. The British printing press was especially technology-conscious and its printing technology had always been quite advanced. Automated technology was also introduced into the pleating process of the garment-making factory in 1979, coinciding with an expansion of the volume of business. As in the case of the printing shops, the old 'hand pleating' section in the garment factory remained intact in spite of the adoption of new technology. The University library was first subject to the process of computerisation much earlier, in 1969. Computers were initially used essentially in the retrieval of information but were gradually applied in cataloguing the service of almost the whole library. The bank commenced its programme of computerisation in the early 1970s. The key functions of teller operation, customers' account register and transaction records had already been fully computerised. The Telephone Company first introduced electronically controlled exchange into its cable network from the beginning of the 1970s and automation of the exchange network was more or less completed by 1980. In the Directory Enquiry Service examined, the public telephone enquiries which used to be processed by manual methods using a paper directory could, upon computerisation, be stored up and distributed in sequential order to be answered by the operators.

Rationale for Computerisation

The reasons given by the management for introducing new technology were similar for all six establishments studied. For the three industrial cases, computerised operation was brought in to increase productivity, to improve quality of products and to enhance the company's capability to compete on both the product and the skill markets. Though not given in the same order of importance, these were the three reasons named by the industrial companies concerned. For the University library, computerisation upgraded the quality of service to users and enlarged capacity for handling a larger volume of data and information. In the bank, computerised operation served to improve the quality of customer service and to enhance staff productivity. For the telephone company, the reasons for the adoption of modern technology were, first, to enhance productivity and, secondly, to improve the quality of services rendered to subscribers. Labour saving was thus not a reason given by the management of any single organisation investigated for introducing new technology. In actual fact, however, computerisation brought with it in all cases a reduction in the level of labour required but the level of reduction was more than offset by the growth of business or the expansion of services in the companies examined.

Innovation Approaches Adopted

While the rationale behind the introduction of automated technology into the cases studied might be more or less the same, the approaches adopted by some of the organisations in introducing and subsequently managing new technology were quite different from those of the others. None of the three industrial establishments had a co-ordinated and systematic approach to introducing new technology, whether numerical-controlled printing machines or automated pleating devices. There were no specific departments responsible for research and development and meeting the need for technological innovation. The decision to invest in new technology was largely made on an *ad hoc* basis, being driven by the exigencies of market needs. Technological change, as in the case of the Chinese printing press, was thus very often 'limited to the hardware considerations of commissioning without corresponding exercises in work study, job redesign and the specification of new work process' (Kao, Ng and Taylor 1986: 12). New measures associated with the changes were usually communicated to the affected employees orally. Even where research and work study for technological innovation were carried out by a specific department as in the British press, the managerial approach adopted to manage the human aspects related to technological change was still informal and fragmented. The company did not, for example, prescribe any policy guidelines or written set of procedures upon the introduction of new techniques of production. Employees affected by the change were briefed only informally by their supervisors. The approach adopted by these industrial establishments to the introduction of new technology was usually 'piecemeal, ad-hoc and fragmented' (Kao, Ng and Taylor 1986: 57). Probably because of such a fragmented approach, no one industrial organisation studied wiped out the traditional skills and conventional operations completely with the introduction of new technology, even after a certain period of time.

Automated technology was introduced into the bureaucratic non-industrial organisations in a more coherent fashion and with a longer term perspective. In the case of the library, the Computer Centre of the University acted as an internal consultant to advise on and give support to the computer programmes and systems developed for the library. The Technical Service Department and the Group Method and Research Department of the bank were responsible for initiating research into innovative ideas and conducting organisation and method studies respectively. These studies resulted in work rationalisation, office automation and the simplification of clerical tasks. In the telephone company, technological innovation was well-planned. The introduction of electronically controlled exchange into the cable network had begun in the 1970s and was more or less completed by 1980. Given the nature of the industry, the corporation had long been technology conscious in formulating its corporate and marketing strategy and the adoption of electronics technology enabled the company to diversify into an array of new business activities in the information industry.

The Impact on Work Organisation

As has been noted earlier, in no case studied did the adoption of new technology lead to a reduction of manpower; on the contrary, more labour was needed because of an expansion of business or service, made possible largely by computerisation. The impact of technological innovation on work structuring did, however, vary greatly in the enterprises investigated. In the Chinese printing press, computerisation of part of the printing process did not bring with it any fundamental change in the formal structure of work organisation. No new departments or units were created. The manning ratio for the press had been slightly reduced. Its British counterpart had a new computer section added to the Production Department with the introduction of numerically-controlled printing technology while the 'composing' section for letterpress became largely obsolete. There was also a widening of the span of control on the shopfloor. Conspicuous changes to work organisation were also recorded in the garment-making factory. With computerisation, three automated pleating sections had been created and added to the old 'hand pleating' section. Under the automated arrangement, the work group was reduced in size from ten to about six to eight workers led by a section head. The style of supervision remained informal, traditional and paternalistic, although work procedures were rationalised and the requirement of technical knowledge intensified. Though decision making power was still very much centralised in the hands of the Managing Director (typical of the Chinese family type of business), the complex character of automated technology and the growing size of the firm made it necessary to adopt a more decentralised arrangement. As part of this, for instance, the authority to hire and discharge manual workers was devolved down to the level of the Production Superintendent.

In the service sector organisations the organisational effects also varied. In the case of the library, computerisation did not bring any major changes to work organisation. The size of the work units and their composition persisted more or less under the same work arrangement. Staff size was stable and the span of control within the supervisory structure did not change conspicuously. Computerisation enabled the bank to collect, collate and retrieve a much augmented amount of information at strategic points for managerial decision making. This enhanced flow of data contributed to more centralised control at the head office but at the same time a devolution of the lower-level decisions to the branch offices. Greater managerial control was also facilitated by the standardisation of work procedures made possible by the computerised information system and the increasingly programmed nature of decisions implied some reduction in the scope of human discretion at work. While vertical control was clearly enhanced, lateral communication was also improved with a better data base. In support of the computerised and automated process, the span of control in the operational divisions expanded and new departments and functions were created. In the telephone company studied, computerisation led to major job restructuring. The telephone operators on the shopfloor were grouped into 'T-shape' work stations, each of which was made up of two work units of eight workers. Supervisors' span of control over operators increased while the style of supervision also changed from the previous pattern of floor patrol to a centralised check based on distant electronic monitoring devices.

Manpower policies in the different enterprises studied were also not affected or altered by technological change in the same way. In the Chinese printing press, the manpower and skill structure did suffer great pressure for drastic modification and rationalisation with the adoption of new technology. Although more semi-skilled workers were demanded for the automated printing process, the design, photo and plate-making work still required highly skilled technicians and craftsmen. Major personnel policies such as recruitment, selection, training and lay-off were not greatly affected and the press did not introduce long-term manpower planning. Manpower provision continued to be largely situation-responsive, tailored to meet the numerical and technical requirements for production.

Unlike in its Chinese counterpart, computerisation in the British press did bring with it a change in manpower policy, especially in the areas of training and the acquisition and retention of skills. The company's recruitment policy increasingly emphasised formal educational standards but instead of recruiting qualified and skilled personnel direct from the wider labour market outside the enterprise, the company preferred to train up its own workers and staff. Such a strategy suggested some rudimentary changes to the internal labour market. Gradual changes also occurred in the manpower and skill structure of the garment factory. Younger workers became preferred as they could generally adapt better to technological changes. Training became more important. The factory did not, however, have an explicit strategy for manpower and skill development, even with the introduction of new technology. This was more like the Chinese printing press.

In the University library, computerisation as such did not entail many changes to its manpower policy but brought with it a plan to strengthen the technical component of library manpower. The task nature and skill requirements for certain jobs changed but they were largely confined to the substitution for clerical work of computerised operation. The job content of the professional library staff, for example, was not saliently affected. Whether computerised or not, the primary concern of the library, as part of a large, bureaucratic and non profit-making organisation, was to maintain a stable labour force within a given budget. Any shortage of manpower was to be alleviated first by recruiting from the external labour market or, as a second option, by training up and promoting in-service staff. Computerisation brought no change in staff training policy, which was still haphazard and unstructured in manner.

In the case of the bank's tellers some shift in skill requirements did occur on computerisation. There was a shift of emphasis from technical accuracy to human relations skills in handling customer transactions and more emphasis was laid on the staff's sociability, demeanour and hospitality in dealing with clients. Along with technological growth, the bank had evolved over time a relatively well established structure of manpower planning, control and development. With computerisation, the function of manpower forecasting was largely devolved to individual departments, regulated and coordinated by a set of guidelines prescribed by central management. Any deficiency in skills was as far as possible alleviated by staff training which was a strategy typical of large bureaucracies wishing to consolidate their internal labour markets.

Computerisation in the telephone company led to a rationalisation of operator manpower programmes. The functions of recruitment and training were devolved to the Directory Enquiry Service and the criteria for selecting operators were increasingly oriented towards communication skills, voice quality and social manner while criteria for promotion to supervisory position became weighted towards the possession of a better technical knowledge of computer application.

It is important to emphasise here that in none of the six establishments did computerisation meet noticeable resistance from workers. Apart from a high labour turnover rate which marked the time when computerisation was initially introduced into the British printing press and the Telephone Directory Service of the telephone company, there was no violent or intensely hostile reaction of the workforce towards computerisation, despite the diversity of the nature of the industries and the size and ownership of the firms sampled. Though a qualification was made by the authors that workers' responses might be only adapted opinions, since they were asked to recapitulate past impressions, it was nevertheless found that all the workers surveyed in all the enterprises studied felt that there were no significant differences to the dimensions of work as tested before and after computerisation.

Four work dimensions were tested. The first one was task composition. Workers' feelings about the nature of their work tasks after computerisation were tested to see whether they felt that work had become more simplified, standardised and monotonous. The second dimension was perception of work, using such indicators as powerlessness, normlessness, social isolation and self-estrangement while the third dimension was workers' attitudes to work in terms of personal development, colleague relationships, workload and working environment. Finally, workers' perceptions of the work organisation with regards to such variables as authority, division of labour, programmed instruction and regulation were analysed. On the whole, no significant differences in workers' attitudes towards the job dimensions tested, both with or without computerisation, were found in any of the six cases studied.

New Technology in Hong Kong: What Kind of Managerial Strategies Were in Action?

How can the findings of this Hong Kong study on new technology be interpreted within the framework derived from Western literature in the field? Do we, for example, have enough evidence to say, as suggested by Braverman (1974) and his supporters, that management uses new technology to control and degrade labour in Hong Kong? As we have seen, the managers of the organisations examined stated that the reasons for introducing various forms of new technological devices into the firms were to enhance productivity, improve the quality of products or services and, in the cases of the profit making companies, to enhance their competitive edge in the market. None of the firms mentioned as a reason the desire to tighten control over labour. Nor was labour saving given as a reason by management for the technological changes undertaken. Instead of focussing on the labour process, the decision on the part of management to introduce new technological devices into their companies seems to have been very much framed within their more general corporate strategy designed to enhance productivity and improve product/service quality so as to remain competitive in the market. For those small and small to medium industrial firms which did not have long-term strategic plans the introduction of new technology nonetheless represented a decision made by management after similar consideration of the pros and cons of such a move.

While the rationale given by management for the adoption of new technology in the organisations studied has nothing to do with the control of labour, one might argue that even though management intended to do so, they would refuse to admit it overtly. One therefore needs to ascertain whether there was in fact no tightening of control and degradation of labour by examining the work organisation, control structure and skill composition of the companies before and after computerisation.

No such signs occurred in the Chinese printing press and the University library examined. The size and composition of the work units, the span of control and the style of supervision before and after computerisation remained more or less unchanged. Where changes did occur in the rest of the organisations examined, they were not the kind of universal changes leading towards more intense control and the deskilling of work. Computerisation undoubtedly facilitated greater centralisation in decision making in the bank and a closer and more centralised supervision in the telephone company studied but similar arrangements in the garment factory on the contrary led to a devolution of the power to hire and fire manual workers, previously held by central management, to the Production Superintendent. Given the limited size of the factory, such an arrangement can be taken as a considerable degree of liberalisation of the control structure. Even in the bank, where computerisation facilitated a higher degree of centralisation, the same process also contributed to a devolution to branch offices of power to make certain decisions. On the skill side, there was undeniably a higher demand for more semi-skilled workers for the numerically-controlled printing machines in the printing presses examined but in the cases of the bank and the telephone company, the need for technical accuracy and capability of the bank tellers and the telephone operators gave way to greater emphasis on human relations skills, which is a qualitatively different kind of skill. The Bravermanian view of new technology as being essentially a device used by management to control, deskill and degrade labour seems not to be borne out by evidence in this particular Hong Kong study.

The analysis of managerial strategies suggested by Child is more appropriate in accounting for the introduction of new technology into the organisations examined in Hong Kong. As Child (1985: 118) clearly puts it:

'New technology is being introduced to advance managerial strategic objectives, ... these (technological) changes are regarded as being in the nature of managerial strategies towards the labour process in so far as they are initiatives which stem originally from corporate objectives and decisions, whether directly and explicitly or not.'

Changes to work organisation, skill composition and control structure occur not as a direct outcome of managerial intention to control labour but rather as secondary consequences of the strategic decision made by managers to survive in an increasing competitive environment. As can be seen from the study examined, all six organisations underwent different forms of computerisation in the 1970s. The three industrial establishments, in particular, introduced computerised operation in 1979. This coincided more or less with the time when the government began to realise that the future growth of Hong Kong's major industries depended very much on their ability to diversify into producing higher quality and higher value-added products. As we saw above in the section on the 'the Push to Innovate', the government has since then played an active role in assisting manufacturers to upgrade their technology so as to move up-market. While size and ownership of the firm and the nature of the products produced in the firms affect managerial decisions to invest in new technology, the general ideological climate of the inevitability of technological innovation coupled with governmental support to that end have clearly their part to play in fostering the faster introduction of new technologies in Hong Kong.

No matter whether the Bravermanian or the Childian type of management strategies in relation to labour govern the adoption of new technology, what is important to the workers is the kind of changes brought about by technological innovation and whether these changes are beneficial to them or not. Two important questions emerged from the study examined. The first question is why there occurred changes in the work organisation, skill composition and control structure in some organisations in the cases examined but not the others. Secondly, in those cases where changes did occur, why did they change in that way? No definite answers can be derived from the cases examined as reported by their authors. That the University library's work organisation remained more or less intact even after computerisation can perhaps be accounted for by its non-profit making nature and hence general orientation towards maintaining organisational stability rather than change to survive. The reason why there was also little change to work organisation after the adoption of the numerically-controlled printing machines in the case of the Chinese printing press, however, is less clear.

At first sight, it seems that the reason lies in the nature of the capital and management concerned. Computerisation brought changes to the British press examined which is similar to the Chinese press in all fundamental aspects except that the former press is owned and managed by the British instead of the Chinese. But a closer examination revealed that this is not a convincing reason as the adoption of automated pleating machines brought changes to the garment factory which is also founded and managed by the Chinese. Similarly, it is difficult to account for the tightening of control on labour in the bank and the telephone company while a liberalisation of control structure in the garment factory occurred. One can hypothesise that it is the informal, fragmented and low-key approach adopted by the managers in introducing new technology into the garment factory that made such a difference but the same approach was also adopted by the Chinese press where little change to the control and skill structure of the organisation occurred. While the number of samples in the study is too small to identify strong patterns, the diversity of responses to the introduction of new technologies alerts us to the need for greater sophistication in our analyses, especially where the technologies conderned are 'Western' and introduced into a 'Chinese' environment. The diversity also alerts us to the need to recognise that 'culture', and the organisational forms surrounding it, has many aspects; some of these reflect 'traditional' Chinese attitudes while others reflect particular management approaches (for example, in the Chinese garment factory) which do not derive directly from 'traditional' cultural elements at all. The findings suggest that no one dimension − size, technology, culture or form of organisation can supply answers to the questions posed above. They refer us back once again to particular aspects of each workplace and the importance of a detailed workplace analysis.

New Technology in Hong Kong:
An Uncontested Terrain?

While the impact of technological innovation on work organisation, skill and manpower structure was quite different in the organisations examined, workers' reaction to the adoption of new technological devices in these firms was very much the same. As was stated above, in the six cases examined, there were no violent and intense reactions from the workforce to the introduction of new technology, no matter whether the organisation was large or small, Chinese or British owned and managed and in the manufacturing or the service sector. The workers studied did not, on the whole, have significantly different attitudes towards their work and work organisation before and after computerisation. Some might argue that those workers who could not adapt to technological innovation had already quit, leaving those who could accept the changes behind so that the lack of strong worker reaction to new technology was therefore simply a self-fulfilling phenomenon. This argument, according to the authors of the study cited here, was, however, not borne out by labour turnover statistics in the organisations examined. Thus, even though the number of firms examined in the case study is small, a pattern of workers' reaction to technological innovation, which seems to be in direct contrast to the reaction of their counterparts in the more advanced industrial countries, can be discerned. What are the reasons for such an acquiescent response by workers to the introduction of new technology in Hong Kong?

One of the major reasons suggested by the authors of the study is the commitment by employers to retain the workforce at all skill levels without any large-scale skill obsolescence (Kao, Ng and Taylor 1986: 585). The retention of the whole workforce in spite of technological advance was made possible by organisational expansion and activity growth. Very often, flexible manpower deployment was sustained by the structurally versatile way in which new technology was introduced. In both of the printing press cases, for example, the adoption of modern numerical-controlled printing machines was supplemented by the conventional printing method such that workmen with traditional skills could be continuously employed. A similar situation occurred in the garment factory where the old 'hand-pleating' section remained alongside the newly created automated pleating section. In these cases, few workers possessing traditional skills needed to be transferred involuntarily to new jobs which would entail an intense process of re-training and adjustment to new machines.

The second reason given by the authors of the study was the specific mentality of the 'mild degree of acquiescent cynicism vis-a-vis authority and changes issued from above' characterising the Confucian cultural tradition inherited by the workers of Hong Kong (Kao, Ng and Taylor 1986: 585). The technological changes introduced were very much seen as inevitable and legitimately within managerial prerogative to decide. As long as these changes did not challenge the basic tenet of the contractual relationship in employment by, say, endangering workers' job or income security, the Chinese Confucian values which upheld respect for paternalistic employers and the importance of harmonious work relationships reign in the organisations investigated, whether they are in manufacturing or services, are British or Chinese-owned, are large or small.

While trade unions and workers seek active participation in negotiating changes brought about by new technology in the more advanced industrial countries, no report has been made in the study quoted on whether the workforce affected by computerisation participated in the formulation and implementation of the decisions to introduce new technological devices. One might, however, gather from the study that the methods of initiation and installation of the new technology are very much management prerogatives. Variations in work organisation and job arrangements in the enterprises studied cannot be attributed to differences in the negotiating power of various organisational actors and their ability to advance their own interests. Unlike their counterparts in the more advanced countries, workers in Hong Kong thus seem to have played a rather insignificant role in shaping the outcome of technological changes. Nonetheless, managers are conscious of the risk involved in forcing through any technological innovation and so, as far as practicable, they adopt an informal and a low-key approach in introducing new technology. This approach may be part of the answer to the puzzle.

Despite acquiescence by workers in technological innovation in all the cases examined, a high rate of labour turnover *was* recorded when new technological devices were initially introduced into both the telephone company and the garment factory. This may be interpreted as encompassing an element of passive worker resistance towards certain policies or practices in organisations since in Hong Kong, where collective worker unrest in the industrial context is the exception rather than the rule, workers who are highly dissatisfied with their work environment may well 'vote with their feet'. As we saw, labour force growth, complemented by the retention of traditional technologies and re-training, is crucial to the acceptance of new productive methods: were these to change, worker attitudes could also change and in some cases the new technologies are clearly breeding long-term changes.

Passive resistance, moreover, might turn into active opposition if the ingredients needed to maintain stability were to disappear. The adoption of new technological devices in the companies studied, for instance, fostered a gradual change in the skill composition and the manpower structure of the firms, as we saw above, and in manpower policy areas such as recruitment and training. In the British printing press and the garment factory, younger applicants with better formal educational standards were preferred as they could in general better adapt to technological changes. Training also became a much more important function in the British printing press, the garment factory, the bank and the telephone company after computerisation as most of them wanted to alleviate any shortage of skill by training up their own staff. An emphasis on training and development was in fact a common strategy for large, bureaucratic organisations to consolidate their internal labour market. This manpower strategy could, however, generate problems. Upgrading the skill of a portion of the workforce as a result of the adoption of new technology may dichotomise labour into two classes in Hong Kong as elsewhere and lead to the development of a core layer of skilled employees with secure employment and good employment packages, complemented by a periphery layer of workers who may be easily taken on or shed depending on the performance of the firm. This trend may well become an important issue for trade unions in Hong Kong in the future. Unless labour displaced by new technologies can be successfully retrenched or retrained and technological innovation does not impinge on the area of skill and dichotomise labour into core and periphery classes, workers' acquiescence in Hong Kong cannot be taken as given.

Conclusion

The impact of the introduction of new technologies has generated much discussion and debate in the field of industrial relations, particularly in the more advanced countries. A review of Western literature indicates a shift in emphasis. First a move occurs in attitudes, from treating new technology as neutral and inevitable to seeing it as a managerial tool to deskill, degrade and control labour and then, more recently, to the view that new technology is itself a product being contested and negotiated. Despite these various themes, the Bravermanian thesis that new technology is one of the tools being used by capitalists to control labour has been and is still influential, especially among labour process writers. Nor is the influence felt only among theorists: trade unionists are not slow in including issues such as form of managerial control and skill composition of jobs into the agenda when negotiating new technology agreements with their employers. While new technology is viewed as a great potential hazard to workers in advanced industrial societies, the same technology does not seem to generate serious problems in Hong Kong. Not that new technology is irrelevant to the Hong Kong context; studies indicate that advanced microelectronics technology is being transferred by overseas investors to Hong Kong companies and that major local manufacturing industries have already adopted relevant new technology, albeit to an extent which varies according to the structural characteristics and the market constraints of these industries. No strong reactions from trade unions towards technological innovation can, however, be detected at a territory-wide level. Nor does there seem to be much resistance from workers towards new technology in specific work places. A study carried out in 1985 to examine the effect of computerisation on a sample of industrial and service organisations in Hong Kong found general acquiescence by workers in the introduction and implementation of new technology in these organisations. No signs of active worker resistance were detected: only the passive resistance seen in a relatively high level of labour turnover recorded in two and only two of the organisations at the time when new technology was initially introduced into them.

Two main reasons were given by the authors of the study for workers' acceptance of new technology in Hong Kong. The first is the way in which new technology is introduced into the organisations. In implementing new technological devices, management was careful not to disturb the fundamental content of the employment contracts. No worker was made redundant and there was seldom a need for existing workers to shift to jobs requiring new skills. Not only did the basic contractual relationship remain unchanged but there was also no universal degradation of skills and tightening of controls on worker activity following the adoption of new technology in the organisations examined in the study. In computerising production processes or customer services in the sample organisations, management's focus was not on the labour process and the issue of labour control but rather on the means to increase the organisation's competitive edge in an increasingly competitive market situation. Such an organisational decision can be seen as framed within a general climate pushing for innova-

234   Teresa Poon

tion in Hong Kong and one where the Hong Kong government is taking
the lead in assisting organisations to move up the technological ladder.
Thus this study, far from illustrating the Bravermanian view that new
technology is used by capitalists to control, degrade and deskill labour,
suggests that the pattern of technological change in Hong Kong seems to
be more in line with the Childian thesis that the adoption of new technology
is itself part of a strategic decision made by managers to increase the
competitiveness of the organisations. More important, no matter what the
managerial intention is, it is the *outcome* of technological changes which is
important in determining workers' response to the adoption of new technology, not the fact of the new technology alone.

The second reason given by the authors of the study for workers'
acquiescence towards new technology is the influence of the specific Chinese
Confucian culture. Workers in Hong Kong pay much respect to those in
authority who are expected to be paternalistic and benevolent to them in
return. Technological changes which originate from above and are seen as
inevitable and not as challenging the basic contractual elements such as
job or income security are likely to be accepted by workers. A difference
in culture is therefore held to account for different reactions to technological
change on the part of Hong Kong workers and their counterparts in the
more advanced western societies. It is in fact now commonplace to attribute
the difference in behaviour between western and oriental people to that
of a difference in culture (Berger 1987). Workers' response to technological
change is no exception. Although few can argue against the role played by
culture in shaping human behaviour, it is, however, teleological to say
that people in different cultures behave differently because of cultural
differences. More important is the analysis of how culture interacts with
other social, economic, technological and organisational variables to produce specific types of behaviour. In the present case of technological change,
an examination of the place of culture amidst other factors, such as the
nature of organisations, the state of labour market, the state of union
development and the level of social and technological development, is
imperative for a better understanding of workers' response towards technological advance. As has been gathered from the findings of the study
quoted, the same acquiescent response from workers to the introduction and
implementation of new technology was recorded in all the organisations
examined, be they British or Chinese owned, large or small, profit-making
or not and in the manufacturing or the service sector. It seems therefore
that organisational characteristics alone play a rather minimal role in
influencing workers' response to new technology. Nor can one attribute
workers' reaction to the influence of trade unions. Although there is no
indication as to whether workers surveyed in the particular study examined
belong to any trade unions, a general lack of concern from trade unions

over the impact of technological advance on both the quantitative and qualitative aspects of employment in Hong Kong means that even the existence of a strong trade union organisation does not necessarily have a significant impact on workers' reaction to new technology in specific workplaces. New technology was introduced into the organisations examined in the late 1970s when the unemployment rate was low and when the government of Hong Kong had just initiated actions to boost up the general level of technology. Workers' acquiescent reaction to technological innovation may be interpreted best as the result of a combination of specific Chinese Confucian cultural influences with a tight labour market in a period when the effect of technological development in Hong Kong had not been fully felt.

New technology has not generated any problems so far in Hong Kong but one cannot assume that this situation will continue. It is highly probable that the pace of technological advance will be speeded up in the coming years. Hong Kong is now facing a rather acute labour shortage problem and manufacturers generally agree that industry should increase investment in automation and computer-related technological devices (*South China Morning Post* 21/6/1990). Workers also welcome this move as a higher degree of automation seems better for them than a relaxation of labour importation policy, the economic implications of which are more easily seen. As more industries are introducing new technology and more organisations are adopting more new technological devices, there will come a point where labour displaced by new technology cannot be fully absorbed by a growth in business, even assuming that that growth occurs. A change in the skill elements of jobs and the concomitant changes in recruitment and training policies will also be unavoidable. New workers possessing the required skills seem likely to be recruited while only some existing workers will be given the opportunity to acquire new skills. Those who are deprived of what they see as their opportunities might not be at all acquiescent.

Technological change in Hong Kong cannot be seen as isolated from changes in the political, economical and social spheres. A rise in the educational level and an increase in the general awareness of workers' rights, the possible weakening of specific Chinese cultural traits among the younger generation of workers in Hong Kong, the emergence of a neutral trade union confederation focussing on protecting workers' benefits and interests and the increasing role played by trade unionists in the legislature with the introduction of recent political changes in Hong Kong are all but just a few factors which must be considered in assessing considering the impact of new technology on Hong Kong in the immediate future.

Section Three
Technological Innovation:
The Search for Control

Introduction

Jane Marceau

The rapid and far-reaching transformations of the major forms of organisation of industrial production indicated and illustrated by the contributions in the preceding section raise crucial questions about the *direction* of organisational change and about the mechanisms for *control* which will be chosen in the new order.

The three papers presented below, and the long excerpt from a fourth included in this introduction, address particularly the question of control in current restructurings of the productive system. They focus both on issues of control of the technology introduced and on the conflicts over outcomes which occur in a period of technological watershed when the technologies selected have major competitive (market) implications. These conflicts occur both over the physical equipment (hardware and software) and the managerial strategies selected. Thus, van Tulder and Dankbaar's chapter on the struggles between major producers and users of electronic data interchange systems, notably in the area of Computer Integrated Manufacturing (CIM), illustrates clearly how large companies in larger countries attempt to seize the technological and organisational lead in the design of the factory of the future. They show how taking that lead provokes a complex series of responses and counter-organisations from actors whose existing interests are threatened or who see their future market opportunities shrinking. We take for granted the existence of a common (open) standard for telephone communications, where a supranational interest has clearly prevailed, but, van Tulder and Dankbaar remind us, the struggles behind the creation of open standards of this kind involve a wide range of interests — public and private — crossing countries and sectors (services and manufacturing) and extending both across companies and across users and producers. The outcome of such struggles for a common standard is by no means a foregone conclusion, as the CIM case demonstrates.

The chapter by van Tulder and Dankbaar also illustrates the limitations faced by companies introducing and using a far-reaching technology and the perils of neglecting the organisational and 'political' dimensions of this kind of reworking of the manufacturing world. While a powerful company may decide that it is 'rational' to introduce a new system, its capacity both to do so and to use the technology's full potential is severely limited by other players in the field with whom negotiations must be conducted. This is especially the case where, in order for a producer to use a technology, other players (notably suppliers) must change their own established business practices. Where the players must interact across national boundaries there is every chance that governments (and international bodies) will intervene, bringing yet another set of concerns to the arena.

The common standard for electronic data interchange in manufacturing is one aspect of the attempt by large assemblers, whether of cars, domestic appliances, aircraft or other sophisticated and complex products, to use a particular physical technology as part of a new managerial strategy, itself a response to new competitive challenges. Thus the search for *quality* as the new basis of competition in the car industry and the possibility of greatly reducing costs through eliminating stocks using a JIT system, allied with the urgent need to standardise the dozens of incompatible computing systems used both inside the company and by its suppliers, led General Motors in the 1980s to seek to develop a whole new productive system. A key element in the strategy was to be control of the JIT-led production process through control of suppliers by using computer-integrated production decision-making. A 'technological fix' was to be applied to what was essentially an organisational issue. The enormously slow progress of this project (centred on the Saturn plant) during the late 1980s and into the 1990s and the still uncertain outcome of the initiative led van Tulder and Dankbaar to ask broader questions about the way in which the new technologies were being introduced. Answering these questions involves working through an investigation of leading actors' (companies) decisions about compliance with and attitudes to the new possibilities.

The paper resulting from their work illustrates the various strategies developed for interorganisation control over what became a much broader international issue than the original concept of the Saturn plant suggested. The issue of open systems became so important in the USA and in Europe that there rapidly grew up a whole range of specialist 'expert' committees whose proliferation indicates both the significance of the issue and the enormous conflicts of interest generated. These committees were intended to oversee research and development decisions in the field of Computer Integrated Manufacturing and other EDI areas so as to foster the emergence of a common interest, a standard transcending national frontiers, and to ensure that the interests of users would be met as well as those of the producers of the technology. The project began well, with the creation of a seven-layer OSI (Open Systems Integration) model and agreed base layers. Decisions about products for the higher levels, however, led to worldwide dissension. As a result, the authors of the chapter sadly conclude that in this arena, as in others, the search for a common supranational interest (and not just a standard) may prove to be the search for an illusion since progress in cooperation is very slow and patchy while corporate power seems to be tending to ensure that the interests of equipment vendors are taking priority over those of users while workers who will operate the system are not consulted at all. The issue of *control* of the emerging standard, because of its long term importance and enormous markets, takes precedence over all other interests in this reworking of the relations between the corporations, and, indeed, between corporations and governments, who will be prime users of the system selected. 'Democratic' decision-making, taking into account the interests of smaller players, has not occurred.

From a different perspective, Muetzelfeldt's paper takes up the theme of organisational control again. He focusses on corporate efforts to maintain control of enterprise operations in a period where accepted management wisdoms (recipes) are rapidly changing and 'devolution' rather than centralisation is becoming the objective of fundamental organisation restructuring. Devolutionism as a doctrine advocates the centralisation of strategic control but also the simultaneous decentralisation of tactical responsibility within the context, as Muetzelfeldt describes it, of management controlled incentive structures and an altered corporate culture. Van Tulder and Dankbaar pose the question of whether the search for a supranational interest in the formation of a common standard 'democratised' decision-making about technological change in an area of prime concern to both many nations and many businesses. Their answer is that it did not. Muetzelfeldt asks a similar question in the context of relationships between managers and workers and responds with the same answer: the new organisation forms, he says, *mimic* decentralised decision-making but in practice are controlled at least as much as before by the powerholders in the (public or private) enterprise. The only difference in power relations in the new kind of organisation which distinguishes it from its predecessors is that the power structure is more heavily disguised. Instead of a pyramidal, hierarchical structure, which makes the unequal relationships immediately clear, the devolved organisation is presented as a web, in which the powerholders are centrally located rather than being clearly placed at the top of the pyramid. In this new form of organisation, responsibility is devolved to operating units and individuals but power, notably power to take the strategic decisions which determine both the organisation's directions and the resources to be allocated to its constituent parts, is retained by a small group of the most senior managers.

Acceptance by lower-level managers and workers of a restructuring which in practice gives them responsibility (and hence visibility) for their actions without compensating power is achieved, suggests Muetzelfeldt, through the creation of a new corporate culture which enables the values and practice favoured by managers to be internalised by workers as if they were their own ideas. Thus, 'people-centred' management, quality circles, and emphasis on 'communication' serve to create a culture which promotes individual initiative, entrepreneurship, and effort while still ensuring organisational cohesion in the directions set by top executives. The resulting 'structured chaos', Muetzelfeldt believes, does not give employees more control of their working lives but is a 'soft' management tool made possible by the conjunction of computer-related systems building and the widely accepted definitions of 'efficiency' and 'effectiveness' promoted by the 'rationalist' economists who have dominated both public policy and private sector reorganisation strategies for the last decade. These definitions act as crucial legitimating 'rationales' (see also Pusey 1991).

The thrust of Muetzelfeldt's paper is that such restructurings are simply a new form of the age-old search for control and for control at the lowest cost. He believes that the devolutionist vogue is one further example of a management ideology, or indeed management fad, of a kind which has always been used but which has proliferated recently in the face of a new technology which greatly increases both the range of organisational forms open to enterprises (whether public or private) and the possibilities for their control.

An important element in obtaining acceptance of new organisational structures lies in the development of a corporate ethos emphasising entrepreneurship as an internal motivating and operational value. The corporate culture which results from the creation of small, semi-independent operating groups, headed by 'intrapreneurs', as Pinchot (1985) calls them, is one of competition for results. The discourse is not one of competition for *inputs*, for resources, as in the more traditional hierarchical model but one which emphasises the *outputs* of the production process, using the fewest possible resources to achieve results, in the most 'efficient' manner. 'Doing best with less' might be the catch cry, eliminating 'waste', whether in human labour or production materials. This approach culminates in some cases in the 'hollow corporation', to use Lambooy's (1986) phrase, where the group at the centre of the web provides only design and marketing advice, all the production risks being taken by the operators who are franchisees. In public service departments the same approach may involve the change to fee-for-service to other such departments, whether the service is the provision of statistical information or legal advice, both of which are now operated in this way in Australia, for instance. The notion of 'public good' is frequently thus lost in the effort to 'make managers manage' with the frequent consequence that the public purpose of public services is neglected in the interest of accounting and economic 'rationality'. Such rationality is not the panacea claimed but only another form of legitimating discourse as can be seen in the private sector where, for instance, the competition between units, notably franchisees, causes many to cease operation or even the company as a whole to go under, as Muetzelfeldt's examples show.

If devolution is not the panacea for industries seeking to rework their operations and structures in the emerging international economy what other recipes are being tried? Palmer and Allan in their chapter in this section of the book discuss another development, that of the rise of the 'Quality Manager'. From the management technologies imported from Japan to the West comes the emphasis on the importance of *quality*. Quality assurance, perfect products every time, is an essential prerequisite for the success of a supplier providing goods to clients operating a JIT system and to the companies themselves operating JIT production methods. Quality rather than price has also become the new basis for competition in many areas of the consumer goods market.

One outcome of this change of emphasis has been the emergence of a new kind of quality manager in charge not of quality *control* but of quality *assurance*. The new system has involved changes in management hierarchies with high status being bestowed on those in charge of the crucial 'quality' area.Such changes in the relative position of different kinds of management personnel seem always to accompany major changes in productive organisations. Thus, just as the introduction of an industrial system using Fordist production lines to produce relatively simple products for a mass market heralded the rise to pre-eminence of the marketing director and his department and the simultaneous demotion and loss of power and prestige of production engineers in the late 1960s and early 1970s (Bourdieu, Boltanski and de Saint Martin 1973; Marceau 1981) and the creation of divisionalised or matrix business, organisations, coupled with the development of multinational conglomerates, signalled the rise to power of the finance experts in the later 1970s and early 1980s so the change to a new industrial system has heralded the rise to prominence of yet another group of new professionals.

With the emergence of the new professionals has come a new managerial movement, the Quality Management movement. As Palmer and Allan point out, this movement has to be seen as the latest in a series of attempts to promote significant changes in managerial practices. As they say, all such movements advocate a set of policies and techniques for operations control and promote their value with a legitimating rationale. This is important because the rationale used has real effects on policies towards wide areas of corporate activity, notably in the field of human resource management. The broad impact made makes the movement particularly significant when great public (government and trade union) emphasis is being put on the restructuring of the labour force, both in the training available and the awards covering labour relations, with a view to improving quality and hence efficiency.

In understanding all corporate restructurings it is important to keep an historical perspective and to analyse changes at a level deeper than that of the rhetoric of new management fads, each of which is usually presented as the ultimate panacea. Palmer and Allan show how the Quality Management movement has direct roots in the Scientific Management school which spread in the USA in the first decades of the twentieth century and became widespread internationally in the middle part of the century.

The Scientific Management movement is, of course, renowned for its emphasis on the *control* of the labour process. Similarly, the later Human Relations Management approach, while assisting with 'humanising' work in the companies which adopted it and contributing greatly to the introduction of specialist personnel departments, did little to alter power relations in the factory. In the light of the experience generated by these earlier movements, Palmer and Allan pose a question about the organisation and labour relations impact of Quality Management: will it involve devolution or greater central control? In an interesting twist, they suggest, since Quality Management uses a marketing approach which encourages all employees to treat all persons using their output as customers, the movement reduces work to a single market relation in which the activities of the producer are subordinated entirely to the demands of the customers. Because of this subordination the movement's results can be either devolutionist or lead to greater control. Much, as with other movements for change, will depend on the particular organisational circumstances and the way in which the inevitable conflicts are resolved. Just as JIT when introduced to countries and companies outside Japan is seldom if ever introduced as a total system and provides a new arena for older conflicts to take place so the installation of Quality Management as a system will involve as much focus on control as on individual responsibility. After all, as Palmer and Allan remind us, F. W. Taylor 'sold' his ideas in America as the way to eliminate conflicts between managers and workers! This ambiguity and duality at management level will, as we shall see in the next section and is already clear in the multitude of debates internationally on the demise of Fordism and its replacement by 'post-' or 'neo-Fordism', inevitably be seen in the labour relations outcomes on the ground.

Many of the aspects of the Quality Management movement which enable greater control do so, of course, just as do the 'devolutionist' organisations discussed by Muetzelfeldt, because of their inherent inter-dependence with information technology. As a neutral set of machines and software, information technology can be used in an almost infinite variety of ways. As Stephen Hill has said, behind the meaning of *any* modern technological artifact lie *shadow systems* which provide a grammar of meaning within which action is played out, shaping meaning according to total industrial system values and shaping the social relations which allow the technology to be used and integrated with collective productive action (1989a: 6). This shaping of present usage of technologies by past practices and their associated social relations is described and explained by Hill in his paper presented to the Third APROS International Colloquium. As he says in that paper,

'Technology embodies knowledge, encripted from past practices and ingenuity, and assumes knowledge of how to use it. Technology embodies values, also encripted from past values and social practices — such as those concerning *power* and systematic order — and assumes these same values will be brought to life in the *use* of the technology. Behind the facia plates, dials, push-buttons, levers that connect our action with a particular technology, there is therefore not only a mechanical or electronic system and circuitry but, more fundamentally, a *cultural text* that makes sense of what goes on inside in terms of *linking* the technology with social and productive action.

As with a written text, the cultural text of technology therefore assumes literacy — the ability to *read* what the technology is for and to use it, and, at a more active level, the ability to *write* the text, to fashion technological invention to one's own uses. As with the use of a written text, literacy concerning technology is unequally distributed, particularly the level of literacy that is required to move beyond the rather more passive 'reading' (or copying) stage to the more active 'writing' (or innovating) stage. Along with increasingly specialised domains of knowledge and its control within contemporary industrial society, technological literacy (particularly to 'write') is therefore in the hands of small numbers of elites. Equally, the technology text, like a written text, is accessible to those who have the purchasing power to have access to it. The technologies are not lying in wait within a technological 'library' or 'museum' for members of the public to take them home, as the source of power to *do* within industrial society is also the source of power to *profit* within an industrial economy and society where order subscribes to the serial of competitive advantage. Contemporary technology's meanings therefore mirror the meanings of industrial society, and along with these, the elite advantages that the values of an industrial order imply.'

As Hill goes on to say, actions in the present are the product of

'the historical revolution of an increasingly complex and inter-related fabric of technological systems, a progression that was unleashed onto modern social order along with assertion of the superordinancy of technological systems *over* social relations of production that accompanied the first modern textiles factories. Within the text to be read in the present are the institutionalised accretions of the past. Deeply buried in the grammar of the modern technology text is therefore the progressive encoding of just the 'useful', 'powerful', instrumental edge of the whole range of *social forces of production* that have characterised industrial history. Where technological systems can therefore incorporate human craft, knowledge and communicative skills that comprise the larger fabric of the social forces, they have done so. So there is no difference in kind between the encoding of mule-spinner skills into textile machinery, the encoding of spray-painter skills into a Puma robot arm, the encoding of information processing skills into computer systems, and the encoding of professional knowledge into "expert systems". What is brought to life in the present is the whole of industrial history, as well as the assertion of all other contemporary systems, for action in the present lies at the intersection of historical and contemporary interlinking of systematisation. Meanings are constituted *within* this context, *not against* it.

It is within the historical progression that we therefore find the core values of the text itself, or the "grammar" that has guided each new writing of the text within innovations that are taken on by the industrial world. The core property is *order*, an order that derives its power from the systematised and repetitive relationship between specialised parts, an order that draws a boundary around the inside system world and the outside "unordered" environment. Linkage between system and environment requires "standardising" inputs so that they fit ... and producing outputs that carry the system's own order back into the outside world. The successful "ordering" of technological systems therefore implies *expansion* of the order into the system's environment. As Marx observed back in the early days of industrialisation,

"spinning by machinery made weaving by machinery a necessity, and both together made the mechanical and chemical revolution that took place in bleaching, printing and dyeing, imperative ... (which led to) ... the revolution in the general conditions of the social process of production, ie. in the means of communication and of transport".

... as James Beniger observes, each progressive wave of systematisation of the technology text brought with it a core organisational problem of *control* – of increasingly complex and ubiquitous systems of productive action. For example, the evolution of railways systems during the 19th Century was accompanied by a series of crises of control that had to be solved before the system could progress: a crisis of "safety" in the 1840s where train wrecks and loss of shipments were significant costs; a crisis of "distribution" in the 1850s before the potential commercial advantages of commission trading and wholesaling could be actualised; a crisis of "production" in the 1860s where further expansion of the rail networks depended on expansion of rail mills and metalworking industries; and a crisis of "marketing" in the 1880s when the vast outputs of continuous processing industries (flour, soap, cigarettes, matches, canned goods, photographic film, etc.) could be shipped by rail only if the market accepted the avalanche of products that was now possible. To jump forward to the mid-20th Century, computerisation marched, without needing to make an appointment, into managing directors' offices because it offered the level of information control that had by now become essential in the management of the immensely complex and inter-related technological *systems* of the international post World War II economy.' (Hill 1989a) [emphases in original]

This reminder of the historical experiences which have shaped both present-day technological usage and industrial relations in the West and the corporate cultures within which industrial relations issues are decided is the background to the discussion of reworking the world of work which is the theme of the section which follows this one. First, however, the question of *control* is addressed in the chapters below.

The Illusion of a Common Supranational Interest: Democratising the Standardisation Process in Factory Automation

Rob van Tulder and Ben Dankbaar

Introduction

The process of international restructuring (reworking the world) centres around a number of crucial developments. On the one hand, there is the process of technological change itself. On the other hand, lie the circumstances under which major technologies are implemented and diffused. Microelectronics is clearly the most pervasive technology of the past two decades. It will continue to be so for a few decades more. Perez (1983) has described microelectronics as a 'meta-paradigm' because it is so pervasive that all aspects of society, including the international division of labour, are affected (see also Castells 1989: 8). This new paradigm creates possibilities for what some observers call a 'post-modernist' society. The diffusion of microelectronics includes also major problems for any design of society because the micro-electronics revolution potentially also raises the level of control. Revolution and 'counter-revolution' in this respect are but two sides of the same coin. The 'post-industrial' era as a whole, however, is still far distant and growing numbers of scholars, politicians and industrialists have again become aware of the crucial strategic role of manufacturing. Manufacturing, it seems, does indeed continue to matter (cf. Cohen and Zysman 1987; Destouroz, Lester and Solow 1989).

Because of the continued importance of manufacturing, one of the most important arenas of struggle in the international restructuring battle will be in the design of the factory of the future and conflicts over this design will be intense, especially in the area of factory automation. A crucial strategic element in the design search is the determination of standards and the whole standardisation process. The technological, economic and political history of the industrial revolution has always been closely related to the development of standards. With the developing micro-electronics revolution, standardisation, particularly in different areas of communica-

tions, has become even more important and the standardisation process
has become part of an intensified worldwide battle of interest, a battle
rarely fought out in the open but no less bitter for that.

The official impression given of the process of creating the new electronics
communications standard is one of consensus and rational decision-making
by a group of key actors drawn from both public and private sectors. The
official image stresses the process of consensus building and the provision
of 'optimal' benefits for the international community; it is the view of
standardisation as a common supranational interest. In practice, however,
the arena is dominated by conflict. The image obscures the fact that
powerful groups with strong conservative interests operate in the arena and
plays down the *effects* of standardisation and the standards chosen on
other players (such as small companies, workers and their trade unions)
who are often not included in the 'consensus-building' process. Observing
the process and the conflicts indeed suggests that standardisation is the
area where a technical fix is not simply a dangerous byproduct of the
efforts of specialists but is in fact the *intention* of the whole process.

To indicate whether international standardisation, affecting the core of
international restructuring, represents only the illusion rather than the
reality of a common supranational interest, this chapter will examine two
interrelated phenomena. First, we consider the move towards completely
integrated manufacturing systems aided by computers. This move represents
not only a physical technological change but also an ideological quest for
a 'factory with a future'. The supposed end-result of this movement is often
captured under the heading of 'CIM', Computer Integrated Manufacturing.
CIM is one of the great current buzz-words in management circles. It refers
to a new level of automation that goes beyond the mechanization and
computerization of separate operations and process. The demand for CIM
arises from the considerable savings promised by this integration of hitherto
unconnected 'islands of automation'. Such integration can be achieved
basically by two different means: either by connecting every piece of computerized equipment or every island of automation through separate cables
('point to point') or by installing a network for communiucation into which
every individual machine can be plugged. The difference is like having a
separate telephone cable to every person you want to call or having a single
cable connecting your home with the public telephone network.

Second, we look more in detail at the efforts to create *open* standards in
factory communication systems, standards which would enable the integration of products from different vendors. In seeking a standard for open
systems only an international approach seems to make sense. The international telephone system is an example of successful international
standardisation which has facilitated communication so that people all over
the world can phone each other without having to know the details of the

different steps being made in the system in order to make the connections. By dialing a specific set of numbers the whole apparatus of switching centres, transmission media and the like is activated and a meaningful dialogue can be achieved as long as both parties at the end of the line speak the same language and do not speak at the same time. In 1977, the International Standardisation Organization created a subcommittee with the mandate to develop an architecture for open systems interconnection (OSI). They developed a seven-layer OSI reference model which did not depart from existing standards and more or less laid down a future 'agenda' for the orderly development of protocols at each of the seven layers of any conceivable communication network. This made it possible for users and producers to develop their own specifications within the framework of a supranational model. It made it possible to turn around or 'democratise' the whole process of standardisation which has hitherto usually been based simply on the *de facto* standard of a strong actor. It therefore also nurtured the idea of a common interest among companies and nations involved. We shall see, however, that this 'democratisation' of decision-making in the crucial area of standards was strongly resisted and a variety of much less open standards emerged.

A considerable number of initiatives developed over the years following the initial announcement of the OSI model. Some large vendors (such as IBM) developed a whole gamut of specifications within their own layer-model while other firms specified only one or two of the layers. The most important initiative, however, with regard to communication networks in a *factory* setting of the 1980s clearly has been the Manufacturing Automation Protocol (MAP) propagated by General Motors.

Over the past decade, several vendors of computerized equipment and computers have developed 'local area networks' (LANs) to enable integration between their various products. These 'proprietary networks' are intended to help integrate the products a single vendor is offering to the network. Seldom do they allow for the easy integration of products from different vendors. In contrast, most producers use equipment from different suppliers, using products which best fit the specific requirements of their manufacturing operations and their organization. It is very difficult and expensive, although not impossible, to integrate all these in one system because of the different ways of organizing data and programming each piece of equipment. It is therefore not surprising that General Motors, as a giant user of computerized equipment and of products from many different vendors, ultimately took the initiative to promote a common standard for factory communication systems. GM announced that all vendors of equipment would have to adhere to this standard, at least if they wanted to remain suppliers to GM.

The initiative promoting this Manufacturing Automation Protocol immediately met with great interest all over the world. The GM Task Force promoting the protocol decided to link to the OSI standard and tried to internationalise the whole project. This chapter analyses the extent to which such initiatives have led to greater acceptance of supranational and open standards and thus to a 'common' interest, not only between different regions but also between the different actors involved, or whether the 'common supranational interest' has proved to be an illusion. In particular, we wonder whether the history of MAP can figure as a model for the democratisation of standardisation because it has been user initiated and user guided. We try to answer these questions by analysing the way the MAP initiative developed throughout the 1980s, and the actions of the different groups involved at each stage of what became a long, complicated and highly contested process, involving the proliferation of many groups with inherently diverse aims.

A simple 'consensual' and apolitical vision of standardisation with regard to production automation is quite inadequate. At a minimum there are multiple interest groups: large and small user-companies, large and small producers, so called user-producers, governments, trade unions and consultants. Each of these groups has a particular interest in the process of standardisation and the design of the factory of the future. For some the factory of the future might indeed become a factory without a future because of the marginalisation of their interests. Some have stressed the importance of adding a letter to the CIM acronym and suggested that one should try to develop Computer Human Integrated Manufacturing (CHIM). The more the interests of smaller users and trade unions predominate, the more the human aspects of production automation may perhaps gain ground in the design process. In contrast, the more large producers and vendors of computers dominate, the more CIM in its most technical (fixed) form will develop. Differences of interest can also appear as between different regions of the world. Three regions (the EC, Japan and the US) form the most dynamic breeding ground for factory automation and are therefore those considered in this study.

The information on which this chapter is based is derived from a questionnaire sent to 175 persons in 110 firms and institutions. The rate of response was quite high — almost 40 %, totalling 67 respondents from 63 different firms and institutions. The answers, especially those of the larger European and American firms, are statistically representative since a large proportion of the major players in the MAP game are included. Only four Japanese firms responded but they are all major players on the Japanese standardisation scene. The results of the questionnaire are presented anonymously in the figures. In presenting them, the *totals* are used and a distinction is made between different *actors*. Governments institutions, standardisation bodies and consultants together form a fifth category ('others'). Within the latter category, consultants are best represented. The answers are organised according to *region*.

The Construction of an Open Standard in Factory Communication

The push towards acceptance of the Manufacturing Automation Protocol represents one of the clearest and most broadly based examples of a user-oriented movement in the process of spreading technological change. The World Federation of MAP/TOP user groups now represents the world's largest user organisation with over 2000 actors participating while MAP version 3.0 has been considered by some to be the first OSI network operational on all seven layers. These outcomes are major achievements of the group organised around the original MAP initiative of General Motors from its inception in 1980.

The decade-long history of MAP reads like a 'who's who' of leaders of international production automation. MAP has been a focal point for developing basic building blocks of communication networking for Computer Integrated Manufacturing (CIM) and thus forced many important players (willingly or not) to state their position. The history of MAP can also be seen in the growth of groups and organisations created to support the move towards open and multi-vendor standards. The growth of such groups can be seen to be closely related to presentations of MAP made at international exhibitions such as Autofact and the Enterprise Network Event '88. At these exhibitions the most open and clear 'coalitions of consent' to the protocol appeared while the dates of the exhibitions also set deadlines for some of the development work and so speeded up progress. The counterpart of such signposts of progress, however, was over-hasty announcements of success and in premature coalitions.

This chapter analyses the history of the MAP project as an international socio-political phenomenon. In our view, it is these socio-political circumstances which crucially influence the feasibility of the whole trajectory towards a specific open network architecture in manufacturing and thus influence the way in which CIM will or will not be achieved.

In the section following we show the initial factors behind such a relatively successful user-oriented standardisation initiative. We also show how, in reaction to this user-orientation, the dominant vendors developed their own strategy and explore whether they wholeheartedly supported the idea of user-selected specifications or not. We also consider the effectiveness of the strategy chosen, including specific problems of timing, and, finally, ask whether recent developments in the organisation of the standardisation process in the area of production automation balance out the interests of large and small firms, of vendors and users and of different world regions. This will provide us with an indication of whether the supposed common supranational interest in an open international production network between manufacturers of end products and the suppliers of equipment and components is an illusion or not.

User-initiated Standardisation

In 1980, General Motors, the largest industrial firm in the world, organised an internal MAP Task-Force. More than fifteen divisions were represented in the Task Force which, after much consideration, decided to move away from the OSI reference model. After two years of internal deliberation MAP 1.0 was adopted and GM issued an ultimatum: any vendor wishing to do business with GM in the future must adhere to the specified protocol. There are two reasons for this. First, a large and increasing part of GM's budget on automation was spent on solving communication difficulties between the more than 40,000 devices with data-processing capabilities, such as NC-machine tools, robots, etc. which it used and had bought from different vendors. By the end of the 1970s, over half of GM's automation budget was going into customising the interfaces between incompatible machines. By then the price of computer equipment had begun to drop but the cost of networking had increased. In one plant, for instance, GM has seventeen different computer-based systems in use, each with its own cabling. These systems could not communicate unless special bridging software was written at great expense (*Financial Times*, June 24, 1986).

The second reason for the development of MAP was that GM was then experiencing fierce competition from Japanese producers of small and medium sized cars. Japanese companies were able to make a car for $2000 less than GM could for a comparable model. GM decided to use its enormous financial and R & D might to technologically leapfrog Japanese firms in order to raise productivity, thereby producing a price-competitive car and regaining its lost share of the American market. The SATURN project has been the most published example of this shift in general strategy towards integrated and automated plants. GM's aim, we believe, was basically to find a *technological* solution for an *organisational* problem. SATURN, therefore, in its initial design came as close to the concept of

CIM as was possible given the technological state-of-the-art. SATURN also represented an altered concept of management and of the organisation of labour. To achieve this change, the company management struck a deal with the Union of Auto Workers (UAW), thereby substituting a plant-specific deal for its traditional practice of company-wide bargaining. By the end of the 1980s, GM had already invested huge amounts of money, more than $40 billion, in this strategy. Pressing for open and multi-vendor standards by means of a manufacturing automation protocol fits exactly into this more or less technology-driven strategy.

In 1983, the internal GM Task Force initiated the idea of organising worldwide a broader group of users. This was very successful for a number of reasons. First, GM was very active in 'externalising' the initiative and made use of its subsidiaries and partners in the EC and Japan, which also became active supporters of the initiative. Then, within a few years, another large user of computerized equipment, aircraft producer Boeing, also became active in the search for a multi-vendor solution to its automation needs. This means that coalitions could be struck with government organisations such as the Pentagon and other large users with the same problems, such as Eastman Kodak and McDonnell Douglas. Finally, the extensive and successful public relations campaign undertaken attracted a number of user-firms who may have thought that MAP would immediately lead to CIM.

The members of the Task Force and the American MAP user-group travelled around the world spreading the MAP gospel. They intended to obtain the support of other major vendors so as to increase the likelihood of successful international standardisation and harmonisation since GM, as a worldwide operating and purchasing company, would be adversely affected by different regional specifications. Moreover, because GM is also a (medium sized) vendor of automation equipment itself, the MAP experiment could make it possible to cash in on its own internal expenses. General Motors' subsidiary for networking, Electronic Data Systems (EDS), would become the communication network specialist providing other large firms with multi-vendor solutions.

The early and rapid spread of the MAP initiative to Europe and Japan is understandable once it is considered who GM's most obvious coalition partners have been. All were closely linked to GM operations. In Europe, EDS-Germany was a member of the first Steering Committee of the European Map User Group (EMUG). The Italian firm COMAU (a subsidiary of FIAT) was also on the first board of EMUG and one of the first developers of a MAP product. COMAU and GM have a joint US factory. In Japan, Fanuc was the first Japanese firm to adhere to the MAP idea: Fanuc has joint ventures both with GM in robotics and with General Electric, the latter also a leading user of automation equipment and a user who in January 1985, together with Ungermann-Bass, formed Industrial Networking Incorporated (INI), the first firm exclusively committed to providing MAP solutions to all segments of the manufacturing and automation industry.

Many other large users were also at the same time experiencing the same problems as GM. By 1980, Boeing, for instance had 45 mainframes, 400 minicomputers and nearly 20,000 workstations and terminals from more than 85 different vendors (Jones 1988: 71). Both firms almost immediately recognised the similarity of their situations, the only main difference being that GM's problems related more to the sphere of the factory, whereas Boeing's problems had more of a technical office background. The close cooperation between both initiatives spurred awareness among vendors that these two large users were serious in their demands.

Large industrial computer-equipment users and departments of governments both have a similar interest in user-oriented multi-vendor standardisation. Governments are often the largest users of data processing equipment in any country. Some government departments, such as the Pentagon in the United States and the Department of Trade and Industry in the UK, have also explicitly supported local developments in production automation. User-oriented standardisation by both is considered to be vital for national industrial competitiveness. A quote from a Boeing senior executive illustrates the search for publicly supported coalitions among both users and suppliers:

'If American industry is going to maintain its worldwide leadership position it must do as General Motors is doing with Manufacturing Automation Protocol and Boeing with TOP. That is, industry must promote international architecture standards. American industry must also continue to receive strong support from the user community. We cannot overlook the efforts of the National Bureau of Standards, which has done a remarkable job of promoting this activity under severe political and budgetary restrictions' (Robert L. Dryden, President Boeing Computer Services, MAP Users' group meeting, September 10–11, 1985, Anaheim, California)

The power of GM's public relations campaign in obtaining supporters and pushing its case forward should not be underestimated either. GM more or less promised that CIM would be obtainable in the nearby future. The European Map User group mirrors this statement in its brochures in which OSI and MAP are presented as 'Your Route to the Factory with a Future', drawing a one-way (EMUG) road. The alternative cross-road is drawn with four question marks added. MAP, therefore, has been promoted as the direct and only road to CIM.

The actors participating in the MAP user-groups worldwide, however, seem often to share more passive reasons for joining the groups according to the results of our questionnaire. Many actors participate simply to be able to monitor developments while only a more limited number of firms participate in order to develop their own applications as soon as possible. In contrast, the European firms as a group take less of a wait-and-see stance: in order to influence standards for CIM, they participate actively in the user group.

Progress in the development and spread of MAP, however, has been considerably slower than expected by many actors. It soon became clear, for example, that MAP is only *one* of the steps towards CIM rather than being almost coterminous with CIM and original optimism about quickly achieving full CIM has been withering away slightly, as was acknowledged by many of our respondents. The slow progress indicates the limitations of even GM's appeal. In the 1988 and 1989, partly as a result of this slowdown of progress, membership of the European Map User group started declining.

The Vendors' Response

As we have seen, GM took the initiative in attempting to develop a common standard and managed to attract considerable numbers of participants to conferences and observers of user groups. It was less successful, however, in mobilising major vendors behind the idea, as Jones (1988: 71) reports:

'The response by computer vendors was underwhelming. GM wanted generally available, competitively priced multivendor networking. What they got instead was high-priced, custom-implemented specials developed just for bidding on GM contracts. Even the world's largest corporation did not have the clout to move mainstream vendors from business as usual with proprietary networks.'

Over the period since the early days of MAP, different response strategies have been adopted by vendors. Some vendors have indeed developed MAP products on their own while a strategy of interfirm cooperation has been used by some in order to spur the development of MAP products. In addition, vendors (as well as users) have used different introduction strategies in different markets. Finally, vendors have even openly opposed the choice of MAP specifications by GM and the user groups.

The early in-house development of MAP products has especially been taken up by more or less specialised network providers. Major players have been Concord Data Systems (CDS), which became one of the first MAP-compatible product developers, Ungermann Bass, a leading supplier of general purpose Local Area Networks (LANs), and Allen Bradley. Ungermann Bass (in its joint venture, INI) was the first company to pass full

MAP 2.1 conformance testing at the MAP test facility at the Industrial Technology Institute in May 1986 and had 70 % of worldwide MAP sales in 1988.

Very often, the announcement of a joint-venture or an Original Equipment Manufacturing (OEM) agreement in which one of the major vendors was engaged has been used by companies to announce the full adherence to MAP of a vendor and therefore the success of the MAP initiative. The OEM agreement made with Siemens in August 1986 on a specific family of MAP-compatible products, for instance, prompted the chairman of the supplying firm (CDS) to announce MAP as the worldwide *de facto* standard. This was clearly an overstatement and an example of wishful thinking.

In considering the general pattern of cooperation agreements it seems likely that the large computer and communications firms used alliances with specialised network providers to be able to bet on more than one horse, their own proprietary products as well as MAP-compatible products basically developed by their smaller partners. Such cooperation thus can be interpreted as a *substitute* for companies' own MAP product development and hardly as a complementary strategy. This pattern comes in many shapes and centres around the already mentioned specialised firms. Thus, for example, Ungermann Bass has been in the centre of attention with General Electric (joint venture, INI, January 1985) and IBM (jointly developed MAP products, starting 1986). During 1986 alone, Concord Data Systems has been a most attractive cooperation partner for large vendor firms such as Digital Equipment Corporation (interfaces), Honeywell and Fairchild (OEM for Map 2.1 products), Omron Tateisi Electronics (jointly developing MAP products), Siemens and Philips (both OEM agreements). Furthermore, Concord, together with SISCO (Systems Integration Specialists Company) and Eastman Kodak have been cooperating since the fall of 1988 in support of MMS. Others have followed suit. Data General allied with Allen Bradley in January 1987, DEC asked Simpacts Associates Inc. to supply interfaces for MAP, AT & T sought a joint prototype development agreement with Concord Communications in November 1986 and Toyo Corp of Japan agreed on the development of MAP test equipment with Vance Systems Inc. Finally, Tandem Computer Inc. took over Ungermann-Bass in June 1988.

Given their very cautious strategies towards the development of MAP products, large vendor firms find it easier to supply MAP products on markets where they are *not* well established. They have many more problems in supplying markets where they already have a strong interest in existing production processes. As a result, spokespersons confirmed to us that, for instance, Siemens has been far more active in supporting MAP on the US market than in Europe. An American-owned firm like EDS also seems to be more eager to implement MAP in Europe than the European firms themselves are. The same can be seen at the user end, with large multinationals such as Ford which looks far more cautious in the US than in Europe. According to Ford Europe's Chairman: 'by 1990, we expect to have MAP-compatible networks in all of our manufacturing plants' (*Ward's Auto World* July 1988: 65). Progress in the diffusion of MAP, therefore, may depend on the successful coalitions of user firms with large vendors not yet established in any given market. In trying to compete with established vendors in new markets these firms may be more willing to provide MAP-compatible products.

There have been both open and less direct criticisms of MAP by many companies, particularly by players with much to lose. Thus, for example, the most open criticisms over MAP specifications were linked to the refusal in 1985 by GM to use the Ethernet standard developed by Digital Equipment, whose product provides a particular choice of specifications at the basic layers of the OSI model, and to the early announcement of MAP Version 3.0. Digital, as a firm already active and successful in factory networks, found itself threatened by GM's choice of a version incompatible with DEC's Ethernet. GM also rejected the token ring standard of IBM but, unlike DEC, IBM played no major role in factory automation and, therefore, had an incentive to keep criticising both the choice and, indirectly, MAP itself. Under such circumstances, counter arguments are easily found. In February 1987, DEC's Chief Executive Officer, Ken Olson, for instance, stated that MAP was too expensive to implement because of its complexity. Large computer vendors, such as DEC, face the dilemma that they feel compelled to support MAP in view of GM's influence 'but at the same time must recoup money spent on developing their own systems by winning orders for them'. (*Financial Times*, February 2, 1987)

At the end of 1988, with the change-over from MAP 2.1 to 3.0, it became clear that the most successful supplier of MAP products, Ungermann Bass, was refusing to support MAP 3.0 because it also considered the choices made to be less than optimal. Because of the incompatibility between MAP 2.1 and 3.0, it is hardly surprising that the most successful firm in the previous generation of MAP products was not really enthusiastic about the early introduction of new and competing products.

Other criticism is less explicit and is seen in actions rather than words. Most computer and communication vendors, most notably IBM, continue to use proprietary networks in their own factories, thus effectively rejecting open standards.

The question of whether the official commitment of large vendors to MAP is real thus remains open. DEC, for instance, has been at great pains to state and restate its adherence to the principle of MAP and of open communications over the past years while at the same time continually disputing the specific choices made in the process. The former is an indication of the power of General Motors, the latter of DEC's determination, as a large vendor, not to write down earlier investments. This has kept pressure alive in MAP user groups to consider Ethernet as a possible alternative every time a new major choice has to be made and is an important incentive for DEC to remain active in the user groups.

The divergent strategies of larger and smaller vendors in the development of MAP products make it unsurprising that a major group of respondents to the questionnaire made clear that they believe MAP will only become a dominant feature of CIM provided the large supplier firms really support it, something which they do not consider very likely at the moment.

The Effectiveness of Present Attempts at Standardisation

In recent years, MAP has clearly been one of the most publicised large-scale attempts at user-oriented standardisation. Although the initiative is still developing, we will try to assess its effectiveness both for GM itself and with regard to the spread of MAP as a multi-vendor standard. The latter depends on the particular developmental path chosen, on the motives and the nature of the participants and on the timing of each step undertaken.

For GM itself all has not gone smoothly on the MAP path. In trying to assess the internal effectiveness of MAP, General Motors organised an 'Advanced Manufacturing Engineering Staff' of 30 people to assess the whole initiative for the company's internal reorganisations and for its external effects, spending approximately $ 30 million on managing this staff who also represent the firm at ISO level. No other user-company has matched this effort which suggests very considerable commitment on the part of GM. Paradoxically, however, the MAP project seems to have been a mixed blessing for GM itself since the company is now bearing the burden of pioneering a complex process technology, the introduction and spread of an undertaking much more difficult than expected. It is widely agreed that GM *overestimated* what could be done through *technology* and *under-estimated* what had to be done with *people*, including the training of the operators. Recent far-reaching modifications to the SATURN project, for instance, point to the same lack of effectiveness in the 'wishful thinking' approach of both management and unions.

The reaction of GM-suppliers has also been mixed. Most suppliers have indeed developed MAP products, but not at the speed which GM would have liked, as we saw above. GM was so far ahead of even its own suppliers that the suppliers did not know how to integrate their components into the system. The other users in the car industry did not follow wholeheartedly either. Ford and Chrysler, for instance, while they have said that they back MAP to the full, have only installed limited MAP networks.

The MAP Task Force and other MAP user groups have opted to choose between existing standards at the different OSI layers and consider MAP to be a specification or a 'standard-fed standard'. This set of choices was well received by almost ninety percent of respondents. Significantly, all the smaller companies responding agreed with the approach, whereas large users, and especially large suppliers, presented some opposition. One of the respondents with a negative assessment of MAP as a standard-fed standard indicated that MAP seems to solve the wrong problem.

Moreover, GM's behaviour itself did not encourage adoption by users and vendors. Rather strangely, GM decided to make MAP versions 2.1 and 3.0 (its successor) incompatible. This means that MAP 3.X products are only interoperational with other MAP 3.X products and not with MAP 2.X products. Because of rapid developments in the specification of new MAP generations, users as well as suppliers quickly adopted a wait-and-see strategy in determining their response. For many, the 1985 Autofact show was a very painful experience since at that show 'prototype systems built around MAP/TOP version 2.1 went on display but then production versions bogged down in conformance testing and later were shunned by potential users − they saw Version 3.0 on the horizon and baulked at installing a soon-to-be-obsolete system' (*Electronics* 26 May 1988). MAP Version 3.0 was announced very early but only released very late. Waiting for the required standards to stabilize meant that it took more than a year before the 3.0 version was released. This hampered the effectiveness of marketing version 2.1 considerably. At the MAP exhibition, SYSTEC'88, sponsored by the European Map Users Group, MAP 2.1 was still demon-strated in addition to MAP 3.0 because of the lack of available MAP 3.0 products. GM in 1988 also still used 2.1 for investments in major new internal networks.

In order to mitigate the major uncertainties arising from past experience, GM announced in 1988 that MAP 3.0 would be 'frozen' for six years. This was to help stabilize MAP specifications and give vendors time to develop many new products and sell them on the market, thereby creating sufficient product diversity for users. Conformance testing was also expected to help convince vendors and users that 3.0 is a stable option. It was expected that 3.0 products would really become available in the second half of 1989. This expectation was in practice only marginally fulfilled. According to 16 vendors studied in the United States, four factors were likely to influence the availability of MAP 3.0 products (*Gateway* Sept/Oct 1988): these were, the release of the 'final' 3.0 specification, the size of vendor companies offering 3.0 products, user demand and the availability of conformance tests.

The last factor is considered by the vendors to be the biggest stumbling block. The first two factors mentioned, the appearance of the final version and the size of supporting vendors, however, should not be underestimated as factors limiting the effectiveness of the six year freeze. New products not compatible with MAP 3.0 are still being developed by major vendors. A major impediment to the full implementation of MAP 3.0 in the next few years may also be the issue of the 'Inactive Network Protocol Subset' (INPS) which has been eliminated in GM's MAP 3.0 version. The INPS creates faster networks but is functionally more limited. The elimination of INPS raises questions about whether MAP really conforms to the OSI model. The Europeans think that an OSI standard (no. 8473) defines support of INPS as obligatory, whereas the Workshop for Implementors of OSI (Special Interest Group for Lower Layers) in the United States in August 1988 opposed this view. GM's answer to the European criticism was been that INPS was announced 'too late' and could not be integrated into MAP 3.0 (*Telecommagazine*, February 1989). It is not very likely that the large European vendor firms which support the Inactive Network Protocol, such as Siemens and Bull, will change their position because of the non-cooperative stance of GM.

The effectiveness of a developmental path in the introduction of new technologies can be hampered if errors slip into the specifications and this is true of MAP as of other systems. The error problem may be solved by the World Federation of MAP/TOP User groups which has developed a reference specification, providing a technical overview and a list of inter-national documents to which it refers. According to a spokesperson, this slim document (20 pages) is approaching the status of an international profile. Error resolution in the past was tackled by the US MAP/TOP Task Force managed by GM people; since there is no similar European Task Force error resolution has been provided only by the Americans. Since GM ended its financial support of the User Group's secretariat and Task Force in 1988 the latter group now only consists of volunteers, which makes effective error resolution far more difficult. Only when conformance testing is properly developed in coming years will errors be dealt with effectively again.

The analysis presented above suggests strongly that the effectiveness of the MAP user-induced trajectory has been far more limited than might be expected considering the original publicity campaign. This impression is confirmed by the small size of the market for MAP products (hardware and software): in 1988 Advanced Manufacturing Research estimated sales of only $ 24 million, only a minute part of the total market for LANs, then estimated at $ 1.5 billion (*Telecommagazine*, February 1989), and the world market for MAP products is not likely to grow very fast in the coming years.

Despite its many problems, the international MAP movement has achieved considerable momentum in institutionalising a number of interest groups. The future success of 'user-oriented' standardisation and thus of open and multi-vendor standards will depend on the specific organisational shape chosen by these groups. Their importance in determining the outcome of this area of technological advance is thus considerable.

Balancing Different Interests in the Search for the Common Standard?

The emergence of a supranational standard implies that different interests are more or less balanced in the outcome of the standardisation process. In assessing the nature of this balance it is important to consider how far smaller or larger firms, users or vendors have influenced developments and whether recent changes have altered the position of either group of actors. The 'balances' obtained can be seen in the institutionalisation of the MAP project and the standardisation initiatives related to it.

Whose interests then seem to prevail in the MAP initiative? This question can be answered partly by looking at the way the relevant user groups are organised and the way they cooperate. Within the groups, not all members are equal. The size of the membership fee, for instance, indicates the power of certain interests: the higher the costs of membership, the lower are the chances of smaller actors participating in, let alone, influencing standardisation. The influence of small actors has indeed varied and changed, both over time and between groups, as is shown below.

After its March 1984 meeting, the US MAP user group grew rapidly. As membership was relatively cheap ($ 100), many smaller firms joined and the professional MAP Task Force and other financial support by GM (for instance, for the Industrial Technology Institute) assisted the user group's growth. The original participants in the 1986 TOP technical and test committee had been large users (Boeing, McDonnell Douglas, Lockheed, Motorola) but after the formation of a joint MAP/TOP steering committee at the end of 1985, both types of users were well represented on the United States standardisation landscape.

In the US, MAP users and producers have been more separate than in Europe or Japan but gradually larger firms have come to dominate the deliberating organisations. In 1988, after GM had dropped its financial support, a major restructuring of the user group took place with the creation of an Information Technology Requirements Council (ITRC) over the top of the user group (see below). Two vendors, Hewlett-Packard and Apple, joined the initial board. A new type of membership fee structure was arranged: individual membership ($ 100), corporate affiliate ($ 1,500), corporate managing affilitate ($ 20,000) and ITRC membership ($ 100,000). Corporate managing affiliates were to be on the Steering Committee and 'highly influential in guiding the organization' whereas ITRC corporate members were to 'provide companies with the opportunity to impact the organization's longterm direction and policy through representation on the Board of Directors (*Gateway* 4(5):8). Other vendors are bound to participate in ITRC also. These changes have meant stronger presence and influence by vendors on MAP and financial discrimination against smaller participants.

The European user group was initiated in 1985 after GM's MAP Task Force had visited Europe. The EMUG Steering Committee is supposed to defend the user profile of the organisation so a fixed 3:1 representation ratio between users and vendors was chosen. The distinction between users and vendors was not, however, an easy one to make and the question very soon arose of which firms to count as users and which as vendors. Philips, for instance, is represented as a user but could equally be considered a producer. At the first Steering Committee election in 1986 COMAU became one of the five official vendor representatives whereas FIAT was elected as a user representative, despite the fact that COMAU is a subsidiary of FIAT. Similarly, Volkswagen and Renault were also among the first elected user representatives although both firms are large robot producers and thus should count as user-producers rather than as mere users! Indeed, Renault Automaton was one of the first European firms to present a MAP product.

Despite such obvious difficulties and ambiguities, present EMUG membership, according to official statistics, is equally divided between users and vendors. At the first annual general meeting held in Paris in April 1986, more vendor members than users were present (68 versus 44) but since then major changes have become apparent in formal representation in the policy-making body of EMUG. In its June 1988 meeting almost no pure users were represented at the Steering Committee. All vendor and systems integrators of the Steering Committee were present but only one real user, Peugeot, (Minutes, Paris, June 30th 1988). Some of the original user-firm supporters like Jaguar, Unilever or BP, who were among the founders of EMUG, had become busy with the implementation of their own automation projects and withdrew. Representatives of the first two firms have occupied the chair, which for a considerable part of 1988 had remained vacant.

What about the representation of large and small actors in EMUG? The membership fee is £ 1,500 for ordinary members and £ 500 for observing members. This perhaps does not present a big barrier to smaller companies subscribing but to participate actively and exercise voting rights additional costs have to be met. Only those firms (or their designated alternates) which have attended at least 50 % of the previous four meetings are allowed to vote. A glance at the attendance lists of major meetings shows that it is mainly large and multinational firms which are represented. Smaller companies find it very hard to invest in much travelling and therefore have rarely attended and exercised their voting rights.

Each year since its creation the Steering Committee had changed members and in 1988 overall membership dropped. Rapid changes of membership of the Steering Committee and the difficulties encountered in getting a chairperson in 1988 do not suggest a stable environment in which vendors can be influenced to comply with a European users' point of view. The limited financial capabilities of the European group also do not facilitate a strong coordination effort between all members (large *and* small, users as well as vendors). It is not surprising, therefore, that, according to the chairman of EMUG, the organisation has had major difficulties in spurring even its own vendor members to adhere to the user interests:

'... Some of our vendor members, who just happen to be among the top handful of established computer suppliers, incredibly still have not fully understood their industrial customers' multi-vendor requirements. Because they are very wealthy they are jogging with MAP/TOP whilst running with their alternative unique proprietary developments. Their customer requirements in industry, governments, banks, airlines, etc. who require multivendor formats in worldwide operations plus those thousands of firms of all sizes who require flexible highly responsive CIM multivendor installations will not change. So if these few major suppliers do not stop their selfish private developments and unreservedly work with the MAP/TOP user-vendor effort establishing a universal solution, they will not be major suppliers in CIM and TOP areas in the 1990's.' (*EMUG preview for 1987*, February 1987, Annual General Meeting, Zurich)

Since 1987, however, there have been no indications that this situation has changed very radically, suggesting the continuing power of the major vendors.

Since the mid-1980s, a variety of other players have entered the scene, complicating the story of the search for a common supranational standard considerably. First came the Standards Promotion and Application Groups (SPAG). The twelve large European computer vendors who were also active in creating the European ESPRIT programme founded SPAG in January 1984. SPAG was officially requested by the European Commission on the basis of the ESPRIT success story. Importance was attached to multi-vendor solutions for integrated systems to enable users to optimise the components of their system and to create homogeneous markets, especially in Europe (SPAG brochure, *Guide to the Use of Standards*). SPAG promotes the application of standards relating to the Basic OSI Reference Model. SPAG does not want to define new standards and does not take a position on the major international issues, according to its own guide. With regard to MAP, SPAG considers itself a follower. The organisation recognises the importance of compatibility with public data networks, telematic and message services, which means that it intends to cooperate closely with the European standardisation institutions of the telecommunication authorities (PTTs).

SPAG itself is undoubtedly dominated by large vendors. It assisted in formulating the goals of European standardisation as one of the major issues of the ESPRIT project and has influenced the initiatives of the EC Commission considerably. At the end of 1987, because of the arrival of three newcomers (IBM, Digital, Hewlett Packard, as well as British Telecom), SPAG lost its exclusive European focus but remained largely vendor oriented (*Computable* 11/12/87).

Second came the Corporation for Open Systems (COS). The long range objective of COS is to achieve multi-vendor products (under OSI, ISDN) and establish a single consistent set of test methods. Since the end of 1986, large vendors (Amdahl, Honeywell, NCR, Burroughs, Hewlett Packard, CDC, IBM) and users (CCIA, NBS, Boeing, Kodak, Citicorp, GM, Carter Hawley & Hale, Northern Telecom, AT & T, Bechtel) have been cooperating in COS. There is a high fee, $ 25,000, for becoming a member, which makes the participation of smaller firms difficult and if firms engage in research contracts, as do large communication and computer firms, the contribution rises to $ 200,000 per year, which effectively eliminates smaller company participation. A distinction is also made between ordinary members and research members: the former have lesser access to the results of COS so that, although large users participate, vendors pay the most and have the most influence.

Third came the World Federation of MAP/TOP user groups, which organises all MAP user groups around the world: in Europe, the US, Canada, Japan and, more recently, in Australia.

The creation of organisations such as SPAG, COS and POSI (in Japan, organised around six major computer vendors) has raised questions as to whether the international balance in standardisation can be turned in favour of users. According to a statement by Mr. Hoptroff, chairman of EMUG, speaking in 1987 at the annual meeting of EMUG, the World Federation has an important function in this respect:

'With the strong emergence of COS, POSI and SPAG Services as basically the three regional world vendor groups furthering the MAP/TOP objective the MAP World Federation is the sole *balancing user voice at international level*' (Minutes, Zurich, 1987: 2; emphasis added).

The World Federation, however, has so far been a rather lightweight organisation with few staff and domination by the USA. The secretariat is based in the US which, according to EMUG, is not appropriate since the Federation should not be tied to any national organisation. Comparable problems have arisen in connection with the chairpersonship. The first two chairpersons were not only American (Kaminski and Gardner) but also chairpersons of the American MAP/TOP user group. From time to time this gives a confusing mix of interests. In 1988, it was envisaged that the Japanese member organisation should take over the chair but this was refused. The Japanese are very interested in MAP but do not want to become too actively involved in international political struggles since it is clear that the role of the chairperson of the World Federation will be, as one respondent called it, 'techno-political'. The Europeans at the same time were struggling with their own chairperson problems and could not find a candidate either. As a result, in 1988 Gardner still headed the World Federation. With the major changes taking place in the US, the World Federation many no longer be able to mediate between vendors and users on a world scale.

Finally, in 1988 a European Workshop on Open Standards (EWOS) evolved, after five years of negotiations, which can potentially integrate and balance the interests of users, vendors and standardisation bodies as well as the PTTs. The SPAG consortium was behind the creation of EWOS, intending it to be comparable to the Workshop with the American National Bureau of Standards (NBS). EWOS is intended to influence the *de jure* international standardisation process in advance and to balance the interests of user groups, vendors and standardisation bodies, which all participate. The arguments for this move are of a remarkable political-strategic nature. The United States National Bureau of Standards is also dominating standards development in establishing effective user-vendor exchanges in MAP/TOP. Europeans have to attend NBS workshops to influence their pre-standards.

'The result from the above and other similar activities means that when we get draft International Standards (DIS) they get stuck in endless and time consuming international revision loops whilst the views of experts previously not involved are assessed. European experts are currently frequently raising significant points at DIS stages due to a lack of opportunity for their active involvement within Europe'. (C. D. Hoptroff, Jaguar Cars Ltd, Elected Steering Committee Chairman from 1986, in letter to EMUG, January 1988).

Hoptroff urged EMUG to go along with the initiative:

'The other groups are expected late 1988 early 1989, so Europe could be first. This should overcome our difficulties in speed of standards formulation, co-ordinate effectively Europe's greater technical capability and within a decade *balance out the current North American lead role*'. (emphasis added).

In the European MAP user group, however, a discussion arose about whether one should become a member of the EWOS Steering Committee ('Is EMUG getting value for money?') and in the EMUG Technical Committee the vote on approving this step in June 1988 typified the reservations of the group: although two members voted for and more against, eleven abstained. Since the vendors in EMUG also work on behalf of EMUG users, concern soon led to a protest to EWOS whose official policy seemed to discriminate against users' influence. In June 1988 EMUG resigned from EWOS because it had not been able to get direct technical work onto the EWOS agenda. If EMUG's fears are valid, the potential of EWOS as an instrument to balance the interests of vendors and users must be limited.

In parallel with the proliferation and bifurcation of user and producer groups trying to make decisions about standards to be adopted, a new group emerged in 1985, which was much more closely concerned with on-the-ground development of MAP projects. This was the Communication Network for Manufacturing Applications (CNMA) located within the CIM part of ESPRIT in the European Commission. It brought together four users, where pilot projects were planned, six vendors which offered the equipment and one institute (IITB). CNMA is thus one of the few organisations where users and vendors are actively cooperating in developing MAP pilot projects. Most of the participants are, of course, still large firms. Although the European Commission pays half the project's expenses the firms concerned still bear a considerable financial burden, which makes it highly unlikely that smaller vendors and/or users will effectively participate in CNMA. However, since the EC Commission will try to diffuse the project's results, the chances of smaller companies in Europe benefiting seem larger.

CNMA has also encountered difficulties. When the group tried to gain a seat on the World Federation of MAP/TOP user groups it was not accepted. CNMA also performed a specific European-oriented function in the relationship with the Corporation for Open Systems (COS). COS intended to found its own OSI test center in Europe but the Europeans quickly made clear that 'cultural' differences between American and European companies may cause problems. COS therefore chose to provide its test-equipment through the distribution channel of CCT, the conformance testing part of CNMA (and SPAG) instead of marketing it itself. It thus bypassed its British partner, the National Computing Centre in Manchester, which does not participate in CCT (*Computable* 12/2/88).

The Players in the Standardisation Arena

Who then are the players in the search for the common standard and a supranational interest? In considering this question it is important to remember that it is not easy to distinguish clearly between users and vendors. User-initiated standardisation is, therefore, not always what it seems or is stated to be in public. Some trends are clear, however.

First, it is clear that *individuals* are very important in international standardisation, particularly in finding a way through the maze of competing, conflicting and only rarely cooperating organisations, companies and institutions. Very often coordination between different organisations depends solely on the persons occupying a seat in both. In the United States, the relationship between the MAP/TOP group and COS is maintained by a Joint Advisory Council. The First Council in February 1987 consisted of Kodak, GM, Boeing (MAP/TOP) and Tandem, Data General, Northern Telecom and Boeing (for COS), with Boeing Computers represented at both sides of the table. A firm like Tandem has also a major interest in MAP through its Ungerman Bass subsidiary. General Motor's Kaminski and Kodak's Gardner are also member of COS. In Europe, Dr. Donner of Siemens is chairman of SPAG as well as of the Steering Committee of EWOS. Members of EMUG believe that coordination between EMUG, SPAG and CNMA is essential to avoid diverging proposals on MAP and this coordination should be achieved informally through the common members of these organisations rather than through more formal links. If we consider the firms which are represented in all three organisations, however, only vendors can be counted on to build these linkages. If this approach is adopted, only Bull, Olivetti, Siemens, Nixdorf and GEC will coordinate MAP in Europe. The influence of the large user-producers on the different user and vendor organisations related to MAP thus seems to be greater in the USA than in Europe. Where relations between Europe and the US are concerned, COS and SPAG have opted for a form of association but without any voting rights. The joining of the SPAG initiative by three US vendors (IBM, DEC and HP) also represented in COS has reinforced the personal links and has facilitated cooperation with COS, at least at the vendor side, but it is not very likely that these individuals will actively search for a common supranational interest.

The search for a supranational interest thus seems to rely heavily on informal cooperation by major firms, with relatively little input by smaller vendors (or users) and little by public authorities. The maze of organisations making decisions, the competing interests of many, with less openly declared overlapping concerns by some, make it extremely difficult to suggest that this essential step in the design of the factory of the future will have any input from other partners, such as small companies or trade unions. In this area, as in others, the interests of large companies will predominate and in the organisational and institutional confusion it is key individuals who will effectively ensure that decisions are made and made with the interests of the companies they represent at heart. Moreover, our questionnaire shows that a number of key members of user groups are in fact suppliers, thus confusing the process further.

Second, over the years some actors may change position, enter or leave the coordinating organisations according to their own interests and activities. Thus, for instance, representatives from companies active in the user-organisations (such as BMW, British Aerospace and Jaguar in the European organisation) *withdrew* once they started installing their own pilot projects. Clear cycles in which actors participate and then withdraw are evident and these militate further against the creation of a common supranational interest since this creation requires *constant* representation.

Third, the story of the quest for a supranational standard raises questions about the dominance of actors from particular regions. At first sight, MAP seems to be an 'American' standard because of GM's leading role in it. On this the opinions of our respondents are divided by location. The majority of both large European users and small European suppliers see MAP as indeed predominantly American, aimed at American problem definitions, whereas the large users and small suppliers of American origin think the opposite. Japanese respondents are particularly aware of the 'American' nature of MAP.

A *regional* orientation has certainly been emerging in Europe. In 1985, rumours went through the computer press that European firms, with the support of the EEC, were going to develop their own MAP (*Computable* August 30, 1985). This particular proposal did not materialise, and was never seriously considered by anyone (except perhaps by the French) because by that time the US MAP trajectory had already gained considerable support, but that does not mean that nothing has happened. On the contrary, the CNMA project, which was undertaken within the framework of the ESPRIT program (and formed the basis of the rumours), has both made an important contribution to the development of MAP and clearly introduced some European perpectives to it. It is clear from the responses to our questionnaire that it is not lack of know-how which has caused the Europeans' failure to establish their own MAP.

In explaining the failure, conflict between interests again comes to the fore. Almost a third of respondents (19) point to conflicting interests between European multinationals as a possible cause, although most would probably agree that it would have been in any case a foolish initiative because of the clear need for a world standard.

Others suggest that the CNMA is in practice a European MAP. The CNMA initiators found several weaknesses in the (American) MAP approach, at least from the European point of view, and CNMA therefore came about as a major project of cooperation between users and vendors with support from the European Commission. The aim of the project was to carry out development work in those areas where MAP had not yet been fully specified. By doing so, one could hope to have an impact on the standardisation process, to incorporate European user needs into the standards adopted and to strengthen the position of European vendors. The development work was to be driven by the requirements of a number of manufacturing installations (pilot projects) in the user companies. From its start on January 2 1986 the project progressed rapidly and has become highly successful. It began by defining a complete profile of unambiguous communication standards and specifications, detailed in an Implementation Guide. The next stage was the implementation of this profile by the participating vendor companies into their respective computers and controllers. This implementation exercise culminated in a CIM demonstration at the Hannover Fair of 1987 and the construction of real production cells at British Aerospace and BMW. A great deal of effort was spent on maintaining compatibility with MAP as it was being developed in the USA and through the Technical Committee of EMUG and with developments in other standards-promoting organisations such as CEN/CENELEC and SPAG. No effort was made to conform to the then current MAP version 2.1 but the aim was to 'intercept' MAP 3.0 by anticipating the choices to be made. An agreement was reached in the summer of 1986 between the Europeans and the Industrial Technology Institute (ITI) in Ann Arbor (USA), which at that time was the only recognized test centre for MAP 2.1 and a developer of test tools on behalf of the NBS, covering the development of conformance test tools for the new protocols for the application layer.

In the second phase of the project, effort was directed to showing CNMA at the major international Enterprise Networking Event '88 (ENE '88) in Baltimore, Maryland, USA, 6 – 8 June 1988. At the same time, a second pilot implementation project was carried out at Aeritalia, Italy while a third phase of the CNMA project which focused on conformance testing, increasingly recognized as crucial for a breakthrough in OSI standards, got under way. The project was managed by Siemens and a subset of the initial CNMA partners, BMW, Bull, ICL, Nixdorf, Olivetti and Siemens, joined by two additional funding partners, ACERLI (a French consortium) and SPAG, Phase 3 came to be known as CNMA Conformance Testing (CCT) and was primarily set up to develop MAP/TOP conformance testing tools (which of course would also be testing CNMA conformance) for the Enterprise Networking Event. The testing tools for the upper layers were developed by the IITB and for the lower layers by the Networking Centre (TNC) in Hemel Hempstead (UK). 'The aim was to retain the influence which CNMA Phases 1 and 2 had on MAP stipulations by virtue of its contribution towards the definition and establishment of test systems for MAP/TOP 3.0.' (Siemens 1988: 3).

The participation of SPAG in this period of testing 'on the ground' suggests that important commercial interests are involved here. The conformance test tools developed within CCT are called the SPAG-CCT Tool Set CCT-Platform. These test tools are complementary to the COS-

Platform, a tool set produced by the North American combination of ITI, Vance Systems and COS, the explicit American counterpart to SPAG. An important strategic and commercial aim of the whole exercise was to have the CCT-Platform recognized by MAP/TOP as the official conformance tool set in the US and in European test centres for certification of MAP/TOP 3.0 products, breaking the monopoly of ITI.

The CNMA Phase 3 project has been very successful. The contribution of the SPAG-CCT Tool Set to the success of ENE '88 was widely recognized and there was immediate interest in the commercial availability of the tools. An agreement was reached between SPAG and COS, by which COS will distribute the SPAG-CCT Tool Set in the Americas, while SPAG will take care of the distribution of the COS-Platform in Europe. The Siemens report mentioned above proudly quotes the business press acclaiming the European contribution and concludes that 'through the foresight of the European Commission and the CCT industrial partners a major competitive edge for Europe has been secured in this market' (Siemens 1988: 56). Not mentioned by Siemens is the startling headline provided by *Computer Weekly* (June 16 1988): 'Europe beats US on MAP, says GM.' The article quotes Mike Kaminski of GM as saying that Europe is ahead of the US in MAP conformance testing and in the implementation of the latest manufacturing standards. This certainly seems to be a major success for the CNMA project and the ESPRIT program. Several of our respondents were similarly positive about the position of Europe in this respect: 'The technology they use in the USA is often much older than the technology we use here. In networking, Europe (including the Netherlands) is ahead of the USA in several areas. We are certainly not behind in the field of communication in automated systems,' and, with regard to the position of the Japanese: 'I doubt that the Japanese will overtake us: we are three years ahead.'

This European success led to the next round of counter-moves in the United States. Notable among these was the creation of the Information Technology Requirement Council (ITRC). By the mid-1980s, the US MAP/TOP user group was making a loss and could only continue its work with the financial support of GM. The foundation of ITRC in 1988 was to change this. Although ITRC is 'incorporated', it is intended to be a non-profit organisation, according to one spokesperson, and the objective is to bring together the information technology requirements of business and industry and to try to fulfil them.

In practice, however, it has proved extremely difficult to get the support of major firms and their chief executive officers, an indication of the slim base of support within American industry for initiatives supporting an open standard (*Datamation* November 15 1989: 33). The firms which constitute ITRC can decide who else can enter the corporation. The problem for some actors is now the $100,000 a year required to become a member of ITRC.

At the end of 1989, participating firms were all large, being GM, Boeing, Eastman Kodak, Bechtel, while potential members were DEC, IBM, HP, Apple, Alcoa and John Deer. Firms with an interest in previous MAP generations, such as Ungerman Bass, will not take part. The $100,000 fee has already proved too high for some actors initially active: for example, the Canadian Standards Organisation and the Information Technology Institute have backed out.

International Intellectual Copyright Issues

A great part of the work involved in the creation of MAP and a common international standard in the field involves the writing of specifications, instructions, revisions, corrections and other information. This published work is of considerable commercial value and the question of ownership is of great importance. Conflicts between the Europeans and American groups similar to those over standards are evident in this sphere too. EMUG and the US-MAP/TOP user group in 1987/88 established a joint agreement on the publication of specifications in Europe and the publication right for EMUG. It was never clear, however, exactly who *owned* the copyright. The agreement implied that the American secretariat, in the hands of the Society of Manufacturing Engineers (SME), owned the rights. These rights were then reassigned to the regions, with the regional groups having sole publication rights as long as they guaranteed that the technical contents were *identical*. According to one of our informants, however, GM and Boeing have given their copyright to ITRC which now owns the copyright and can sell specifications at specific prices. The latest MAP and TOP specifications constitute a document of 2500 pages. Copyright in this regard is a sort of 'authors' copyright. There are two price tags: approximately $300 for non-ITRC members in the US and $400 for actors outside the United States: ITRC, however, claims that US MAP/TOP is not an incorporated body while ITRC itself at the moment remains a somewhat shadowy organisation.

Regional or Universal Standards?

In discussing actors in the field of the search for an open standard, this paper has so far focussed on the standards-creation story in terms of developments in the EC and the US but the Japanese are clearly also

important players. The Japanese MAP User group has been very active in
the World Federation, despite its refusal to take the chair in 1988. Most
respondents to our study (including the Japanese firms) note, however, that
because of the different approach of Japanese firms to CIM they have
adopted a very pragmatic, cautious wait-and-see strategy with regard to
MAP.

If MAP becomes an accepted standard, Japanese firms will, of course,
be able to make MAP products. If not they will supply other products.
Some consider the Japanese stance to be the most realistic view on MAP,
a view which sees MAP as only a small part of CIM and much less
important than many in Europe and the USA think. Only a small minority
of European firms think that Japanese firms are generally not interested in
international standardisation. Hardly any of our respondents doubted that
the Japanese firms have evaluated the best advantages of MAP and implemented the products in some pilot sites so as to increase further the
competitiveness of Japanese industry. Some note, for instance, that 30 %
of the attendees at the ENE '88 exhibition were Japanese, that they organised their own exhibition in 1988 where they showed a high level of
knowledge of MAP and that they have already invested considerable
amounts of money in the standard within the framework of the government-
sponsored FAIS project.

This set of activities indicates also a broader point: Japanese firms
seem to take a path to innovation in industrial production which is
different from that of the West. They *start* by changing their organisational structure and only afterwards seek technological progress, whereas
American firms such as General Motors have usually adopted a technolo-
gy-induced strategy, emphasizing the complexity of the system. The
incremental approach of the Japanese, using simpler integration, as
one respondent notes, is fundamentally different from the top-down
approach of MAP as elaborated by GM. There are also different technical preferences. For example, Japanese firms consider optical fibre media
(at the cell level according to some) as more important than the American
option for coaxial cables. The Japanese also have a different software
culture and are the only user group actively interested in an adapted
version of MAP for simpler ways of communication (the so called 'Mini-
MAP' version). These divergences in practice and focus do not seem to
worry American actors but a large number of European actors responding to our questionnaire anticipate a growing polarisation in the international standardisation process related to CIM between Japan on the
one hand and the EC and the USA on the other hand because of
differences in strategy adopted by Japanese users and producers.

Conclusion

This chapter has discussed the impact of user-initiated standardisation in the area of communication networks of production automation (CIM) in order to find out whether the claim of 'democratisation' in the search for a 'common' and 'supranational' interest has materialised in the past decade. To analyse the issue we described the socio-political history of the Manufacturing Automation Protocol (MAP) initiated by General Motors and looked at the supportive coalitions and the way the whole initiative developed both in terms of the spread of the idea of CIM and with regard to its 'effectiveness' in taking care of the interests of users (both large and small) and smaller producer firms.

In answering the 'democratisation' question as it concerns the role of users, the paper indicates a complex situation. First, the user-orientation of the 'user' groups is not always identical. In the United States the realms of users and producers in the past have been rather separate whereas in Europe, it is more difficult to speak of user-oriented standardisation because of the mix of activities of participants in the 'user' groups. In Japan, this is even more difficult. The influence of EMUG and the American group on technical specifications has been limited, not least for financial reasons, and has shown a degree of organisational instability. It is clear, however, that a general shift from user-domination to vendor orientation has been witnessed. This is largely because the specification of standards is closely tied to development work and to implementation efforts to fill in all the details and clear up possible ambiguities. After some early decisions, for instance, to use the ISO-OSI model, the further specification of a complete standard is dependent on development efforts that only vendors are normally able and willing to undertake. In these later stages, the danger is clearly present that elements of proprietary standards return in the equipment and networks offered. CIM in the end is a very important and strategic constellation of products: the more you reach the final point of production, the more the interests of producers seem to prevail. This is corroborated by the impression of the recent 'colonisation' by vendors of the user groups.

In principle, the ISO reference model, and MAP as such, opens up real possibilities of developing and implementing a common interest. If MAP were established as an open standard, with a large number of products available at a competitive price, it would serve the interests of many (smaller) firms not present in the standardisation process because it would limit their dependence on single vendors offering proprietary standards. Larger firms, however, have been very dominant in the process of MAP specifications and are likely to remain even more influential in the future.

This does not give much hope that the MAP will come out as the only standard. The international standardisation process has not changed fundamentally towards more democratic practices. Moreover, there are also clear tendencies towards regional differentiations in a number of areas of the MAP initiative. The effectiveness of international coordination yet has been limited.

The history of MAP shows once again that when the creation of an initiative such as MAP develops through formal organisations, fragmentation and the establishment of special interest groups is bound to take place. This can only be overcome by strong coordination and the large overhead costs required by a more or less bureaucratic organisation. Since international standardisation is very much a process led by 'volunteers' from specific interest groups and because many firms are not willing to pay much for strong organisations, fragmentation is very likely. Differences of interest arise between regions (the biggest difficulty in overall coordination), but also between different actors, such as companies in process industries and batch industries. The large number of users and vendors organised in the US does not present a homogeneous group. In the USA the first interest group was founded for special research and education activities aimed at the process industry. That group was intended to dissolve itself but continued operations because of the clear needs of its members. A major concern of the group is real-time applications (*Gateway* March/April 1987) which led to a separate exhibition booth at ENE '88i. In 1986/87 four other groups were added, representing broad alignments of special topics of interest such as aerospace, fibre optics and government. The effectiveness of the user groups thus more and more becomes also a problem of coordination between special interest groups, nationally as well as internationally.

Finally, it should be noted that the whole MAP move represents an interesting paradox. Standardisation in search of a multi-vendor environment results in a declining number of vendors per large user. The large users such as GM and Boeing use the MAP initiative to limit the number of prime suppliers. General Motors now not only boycotts Ungermann Bass but has also cut the number of first tier subcontractors considerably in the last years. Similarly, Boeing once dealt with several dozen office equipment manufacturers but since has cut the number to six.

'Committed to the adoption of common communications standards, each understands that we will not buy stand-alone systems or devices not strategic to that vendor's product line. We insist on vendor adaptation of international, rather than proprietary, communications standards'. (...) We have achieved this rather extraordinary understanding with our vendors through president-to-president communication and a consistently applied procurement policy'. (User Group Summary 10/11/1985)

Thus, while MAP is supposed to be an initiative leading to integration of *many* vendors, the final result might be more appropriately described as a 'limited-vendor' approach. Indeed, the case for the need for *open* standards (vertical disintegration, for instance, as part of a common/general interest of all societies) as a major reason for public support for MAP might be considerably overstated in present circumstances. The history of MAP, one of the most advanced experiments in open and multi-vendor oriented standardisation, shows that the search for a supranational interest as part of a 'democratising' process for the factory of the future might be simply an illusion.

Yet Another Panacea? The Quality Management Movement in Australia

Gill Palmer and Cameron Allan

Introduction

Management education and the study of management everywhere have long been bedevilled by a focus on prescription rather than analysis. The origins of this focus are not hard to understand, given the financially-backed cries for help that can be heard from many who are responsible for running private and public organisations. Prescriptions are in demand and are richly rewarded. This chapter considers one particular fashion, that of the Quality Management movement, often considered in Australia as a cure for many ills.

If we turn to current issues within Australian management debates there are two areas that can be usefully addressed. The first is Quality Management, which is currently strongly advocated in Australia by private consultancy firms, by several well organised management groups and by Federal and State governments. The second area concerns the causes and effects of different policies towards human resource management. The social, political and economic causes and effects of these policies have a significance that extends well beyond the strictly managerial sphere. The interrelationships between Quality Management and Human Resource Management are particularly worthy of study at a time when Quality Management is a concept used to impart a sense of value or 'parenthood' to policies as varied as the Australian Council of Trade Unions-supported initiatives to incorporate unions through to New Right policies designed to exclude unions and individualise the relationship between employer and employee. Quality Management seems to many to be a panacea. The movement, however, deserves further analysis.

While the Quality Management movement has attracted considerable attention in Australia in the last few years, precise, easy to operationalise definitions are not readily available and the term is used differently even within the quality movement itself. Many speakers at forums on quality management have grappled with the problem of finding a simple, clear definition of the management system that they are concerned to promote. A focus on efficient, flexible production systems and on matching production more closely to customer needs is caught by definitions such as: 'good quality does not necessarily mean high quality. It means a predictable degree of uniformity and dependability at low cost with a quality suited to the market'. (Deming, quoted in Sprouster 1987); 'Quality is continually satisfying customer requirements' (PA 1986); and Total Quality is 'The empowerment and development of people in order to meet or exceed customer standards' (Lacey 1990).

Such definitions usefully emphasise managerial concern with performance indicators that are carefully linked with customer or client needs but are not easily operationalised. The question of 'which customer and whose requirements' can cause difficulties. For example, if we were concerned to judge the quality of the management of tertiary educational institutions, would we measure the educational expectations or requirements of fee-paying current students? Or the existing professional careers the current students might be expected to follow? Or the requirements of the wider society as expressed through surveys or the outcome of the political process? This problem does not only relate to complex products with a wider social impact. Even if customer requirements can be assessed in terms of specific product, reliability, durability and environmental impact measures, the question of relating these measures to particular management techniques and practices still needs to be addressed. Definitions like those above do not give guidance on the managerial processes associated with quality management.

If we define quality management in terms of particular managerial techniques, the impact of statistical modelling and the influence of Japanese systems of management appear to be the most significant identifiers.

Computer-based statistical analysis, control systems and experiments are the techniques most easily associated with 'Quality Management' and the theories of Deming and Taguchi lie behind many of the practices used. Deming was an American who recommended the development of statistical models of production processes in order to identify and eliminate problems in the flow of work and the supply of inventory. In order to tie statistical techniques into a general approach to management he developed fourteen points which focus on the need to create consistency of purpose for improving product and service. His ideas were influenced by Japanese management practices (indeed four of the famous fourteen points were added after a trip to Japan). His recommendations were more readily adopted in Japan than in the USA and his influence within Japanese management circles can be traced from the early post-war period (Deming 1982).

The other major theorist, Taguchi (1988), popularised the use of statistical experimental techniques to focus on *acceptable degrees of variability*, rather than absolute standards of quality in production processes. His status within the quality movement can now be gauged by the audiences attracted worldwide to his speaking tours (500 senior Australian managers attended an obscure rendering of his thoughts in Sydney in August 1989).

The early acceptance of these methods in Japan, and the interest they now attract from western audiences, highlights the extent to which Japan has replaced the USA in providing the models of good management practice which others emulate. When the contrast between Japanese and Western management practices was first the subject of comment in the post-war period, Japanese practices tended to be characterised by American authors as irrational hanagovers from a feudal past (e. g. Abegglen 1958). It is symptomatic of Japan's economic miracle in the post-war years and of concerns surrounding the stagnation of the giant American economy that Japanese management practices are now the focus of much study and debate.

Within Australia, the beginning of the 'Quality Movement' can be traced to the 1950s when some industrial engineers became aware of Deming's ideas. Slowly Quality Assurance groups were established by such practitioners at State level. They acted as lobby organisations to promote and provide training and support to the industrial engineers who practised these techniques. In 1965 a national organisation was formed to act as an umbrella to the State-based quality organisations. The Australian Organisation for Quality acts as a loose federation of State-based organisations and accepts individual, largely practitioner, membership.

Over the last five years the Quality Management movement has widened its scope and heightened its profile within Australia. In the process, advocates of quality management have moved beyond concern with specific statistical techniques and quality assurance systems in order to embrace several of the management techniques that are seen to have wide application in Japan, in particular what is seen as the Japanese managerial focus on continuous improvement. This widening scope has been reflected in the changing names used to describe quality management.

Quality Assurance (QA) was the term first popularised to describe a focus on measurement processes verifying conformity to specifications combined with a Japanese-inspired concern to involve employees in the monitoring and implementation of the measured standards of product quality during the production process, thereby eliminating the need to rely on final inspection (Ishikawa 1985). The extension of a role in quality management to unskilled and semi-skilled operators, through voluntary participation in Quality circles, was part of this process. The operation of Just-In-Time (JIT) inventory control systems also found acceptability early. By tightening supply, production and delivery schedules JIT systems also seek to lower the water until the rocks appear so that bottlenecks in the production process can be identified and removed. The introduction of computerised

JIT inventory control systems was often combined as a package with Quality Circles and statistical problem solving tools in the early quality management days.

Critics of the original QA put the view that the adoption of one or two Japanese paractices did not represent the total commitment to continuous quality improvement that was thought to be necessary and that the Japanese were thought to demonstrate. *Total Quality Management* (TQM) was the name given to distinguish this wider view of the range of practices required. Within Australia, the lobby and consultancy group 'Enterprise Australia', run by Bruce Erwin, was particularly important in promoting a wider view of quality management and aiming the message to the highest point in the organisation, going above the quality practitioners directly to Chief Executive Officers. In line with the desire to promote this broader view, a new organisation was established, initially with some opposition from the Australian Organisation for Quality. The Total Quality Management Institute was founded in 1986. It takes corporate not individual members and seeks to promote awareness of the general need for quality improvement at the most senior levels of management and govenment. Any breaches that may have existed between the old and new quality organisations are now being overcome by a proposal to establish a unifying *Australian Quality Council*, which will have the resources to overview the various promotional groups that have developed to spread the message of quality management within Australia. This attempt to unify and strengthen the organisations promoting Quality Management within Australia is being fostered and sponsored by the National Industry Extension Service, run from the Department of Industry, Technology and Commerce. With Federal and State government support it sponsors the promotion of Quality Management and was instrumental in establishing the Quality Forum to help coordinate the various groups involved in the Quality movement.

Because TQM is deliberately wider than the old Quality Assurance and because the advocates of TQM have been concerned to promote general consciousness at senior levels of the need for change rather than focus on specific techniques, it is difficult to identify precisely which management practices are being promoted. The emphasis seems to be upon an attempt to create employee commitment to organisational success and on an overall concern with the total eradication of error. Left at the level of such generalities, such a focus is in danger of being dismissed as the managerial equivalent of a messianic call for repentance and reform. Clearly TQM needs to be associated with an identifiable set of management practices and appropriate evidence of the impact of their application. The practices discussed at the First National Conference of the Australian TQM Institute in June 1989 were JIT inventory, task analysis, quality improvement teams, use of statistical tools, and incentive payment systems. It can, however, be difficult to draw a clear line around the 'quality' elements of some of the prescriptions offered. Many look very like practices that have been promoted by earlier managerial movements and some prescribe practices developed overseas without too much thought about the particular differences likely to affect their implementation within Australia.

The Quality Management Movement in Context

In order to sort out the different elements of Quality Management and reach a clearer analysis of what it involves, the recipe needs to be placed in context. The Quality Management movement can be seen as the latest of a series of attempts to promote significant changes in managerial practices. All such attempts advocate a set of policies and techniques and promote their value with a legitimating rationale (the sales pitch or 'bullshit' factor. See Palmer 1987). This is hardly surprising, given the mixed history of different movements for change and the need for the advocates of managerial reform to adopt the ideological baggage of change agents. To sort out passing fad from significant change and to distinguish marketing hype from valid claim all the movements for managerial reform need to be given serious analysis.

If the Quality Management movement is compared with previous movements for reform that have swept the western managerial world, it becomes clear that there are both interesting areas of similarity and significant differences. It will also become apparent later in this chapter that evidence about the real impact of previous movements can also be used to point to the likely effects of Quality Management.

'Scientific Management'

The first and probably most significant movement to promote particular managerial policies was the Scientific Management movement which spread in the USA in the first decades of this century. Fathered by F. W. Taylor, this movement promulgated the rationalisation and bureaucratisation of work processes that became a distinguishing element of the mass production techniques adopted by the growing American steel, engineering (especially automobile) and transport industries.

Taylor was not the only influence behind the movement but he became the main progenitor of scientific management theories (Braverman 1974; Littler 1982; Rose 1985). He advocated a central planning department to study work and pre-plan all work processes, the adoption of a detailed specialisation of labour, including functional foremen and the separation of skilled from unskilled, direct from indirect and managerial from operational labour. The rationale behind this was that all the information necessaary to control work processes could be centrally assembled. Centralised decision-making that could then be built upon this centralised information and managerial control would be more rational and efficient. The social and organisational impact of the techniques advocated by Taylor has been analysed as the bureaucratisation of task performance (Littler 1982: 58).

It is important to recognise that the package which Taylor advocated was never implemented in its entirety. Existing senior and middle levels of management did not relinquish power to central planning departments staffed by industrial engineers; instead they established the first of the specialist 'staff' departments to be latched onto the side of the line management hierarchy. In practice, what had been promoted as a total revolution at work became primarily associated with work study and the spread of individual incentive payments schemes in which bonuses above a basic rate were related to the achievement of targeted work times set by the work study engineers. In these areas Taylorism spread fast and its impact across the growing secondary industries of the USA and Europe was considerable.

The impact of Scientific Management and the timing, coverage and nature of its spread across North America and Europe have been the subject of considerable research in recent years (Braverman 1974; Littler 1982; Edwards 1979; Friedman 1977). This has stimulated a similar interest among Australian scholars and the work of Nyland (1987), Patmore (1988) and Wright (1989) all throw valuable light on the spread and impact of Taylorist ideas within Australia.

The growing literature on Scientific Management in Australia tends to oscillate around the key issues of the timing of the introduction of managerial practices, the relative significance of their impact and the primary agents responsible for their promotion and dissemination. Nyland, for example, points to the important role played by the state in the introduction of systematic managerial notions in the inter-war years. This, he argues, can be seen most readily in the activities of key state functionaries. The most notable example is Justice Higgins who had a powerful role in the establishment of the Arbitration Court in 1904. He was personally acquainted with some of the American systematic rationalisers and sought in his arbitral judgements to promote industrial efficiency through the rational and scientific analysis of work methods and work processes. The enthusiasm of Higgins for Taylorist ideas in the Federal arbitral sphere was matched with equal vigour by G. S. Beeby in the New South Wales Commission. Both believed that by international standards Australian management was poor and in vital need of upgrading and systematisation (Nyland 1987).

Patmore puts forward a similar thesis, arguing that the state, as a significant employer, played an important role in the application and promotion of Tayloristic conceptions. The New South Wales (NSW) Railway, for example, began as early as 1915 to introduce systematic scientific management techniques to work study and payment systems. As a very large employer with a bureaucratic organisational structure, the NSW Railway sought to increase labour productivity and lessen labour unrest by the application of the new management techniques. This course of action, Patmore contends, was met with union hostility, arbitral interference and pre-existing customary practices that modified and altered the form of the management devices employed (Patmore 1988).

Discussing a rather later period, that of post-1945 reconstruction, Wright (1989) argues that it is necessary to distinguish between the rhetoric of systematic management theorising and concrete practices. This means that the key question is how 'management techniques have been transmitted from the world of ideas into practice' (1989: 1). In Australia, Wright argues, the most important factor in the spread of new labour practices has been the activity of management consultants in the period after the Second World War whose work was accepted in part because of the increased productive capacity of the post-war Australian economy and companies' desire to increase production and productivity and to reduce labour turn-over. The spread of scientific management techniques at that time was primarily the work of two major management consultancy firms, W. D. Scott & Co. and Personnel Administration Pty Ltd (now known as PA). The new practices were introduced initially into the textile industries, then spread widely into the metal industry and by the late 1950s had reached clerical and office work. In common with other writers, Wright notes that resistance from workers was encountered to time study techniques and incentive payment systems and that the forms of systematic management which were implemented were diverse (Wright 1989).

The introduction of Taylorist ideas thus began as early as the period preceding the First World War as local capitalists and arbitrators travelled to the USA to learn management technologies personally from Taylor and other rationalisers (Nyland 1987: 189—190). The real emergence of these kinds of ideas into management and industrial discourse, however, must be dated to the inter-war years, with their more wide-spread promotion taking place in the post-war Second World War years.

The Human Relations School

In the standard historical review of managerial prescriptions it is said that
the bureaucratic specialisation of Taylorism was overlaid by the humanising
force of the Human Relations management ideas in practice. Whether these
ideas replaced Taylorism or simply added a new gloss to a basically Taylorist
work structure has been the subject of much debate and it is certain that
many Taylorist structures were not altered. The Human Relations School
can, however, be identified as the second major movement advocating
particular managerial practices. If we analyse the distinctive features of the
Human Relations School prescriptions, we find their antecedents in the
'welfare capitalism' of 1920's America and in the development of industrial
psychology. A paternalistic assumption of responsibility for employees'
personal welfare was combined with a new interest in the subjective side
of personal and interpersonal life. Human Relations advocates saw management as responsible for the motivation of employees and provided industrial
psychology as the tool to be used to this end.

The managerial prescriptions related to the Human Relations approach
emerged in the industrially dominant USA at a time when the growth of
unskilled, mass unionism was a serious source of managerial concern.
The analyses of worker behaviour and attitudes that emerged from the
Roethlisberger and Dickson (1934) study of the Western Electric Hawthorne
Plant and from the writings of the Australian observer based at Harvard,
Elton Mayo (e. g. 1966), were all influential in affecting American consultants' promotion of the new ideas. Indeed Mayo can be regarded as the
most enthusiastic publicist for this school of thought in its early stages
(Hodgetts and Kuratko 1986). The onset of the Great Depression removed
the threat of rising mass unionism and the more hysterical of Mayo's
visions of a future, conflict-free utopia lost their appeal.

Industrial psychology, however, continued to be used to provide a critique
of existing management practices. More sophisticated studies of socio-
technical systems and their implications for job design emerged from London's Tavistock Institute and from Scandinavia. As Miller and Rose (1988)
explain, the subjective features of individual and social life became a new
theoretical object, the study of which gave rise to ideas on how to manipulate and regulate this new realm.

'The minutiae of the relations of group life within the enterprise were opened
up to systematic analysis and intervention in the name of a psychological
principle of health which was at the same time a managerial principle of
efficiency'. (Miller and Rose 1988: 186)

In support of group relations that would support 'mature' personal behaviours and promote group morale, and therefore efficiency, this school of thought produced a range of new managerial prescriptions. In the industrial sphere they studied poor group functioning in terms of absenteeism, accident-proneness, intergroup conflict and low productivity. The focus of their early prescriptions was on selection, training and leadership. Trist and Bamforth's study of the problems associated with longwall coalmining and Indian cotton mills led to the development of the concept of 'socio-technical systems' and concern to ensure that workgroup functioning was not adversely affected by technological change. The Glacier project added the proposal that 'an industrial relations model of "bargaining" be replaced by a psychotherapeutic one of "working through" and a form of industrial democracy aimed at the level of workgroups rather than Boards'. (Miller and Rose 1988: 185–186).

A paternalistic concern for the 'whole man' and a psychological commitment to organisational membership were features of this neo-Human Realions approach. If we ask what results the new humanism had on everyday management practices, however, there is room to debate the extent to which management as a whole was affected by the newer ideas. Despite the spread of concern about job design after the work of the Tavistock Institute was published in the 1950s, job specialisation remained largely untouched. Organisational structures, however, changed almost everywhere and new staff departments of specialists in psychology were created, the new concerns of recruitment and selection were added to managerial structures and personnel departments began to spread.

The new humanisation of work can be associated with the encouragement of forms of joint consultation and the careful recruitment, training and succession planning required if a relatively permanent labour force is to become committed to a single organisation whereas, in contrast, earlier welfarism was associated simply with the introduction of canteens and holiday pay. Within the development of business organisational structures, Taylorism was responsible for the emergence of industrial engineering departments, while Human Relations helped promote the growth of the personnel manager and personnel departments.

The impact of the Human Relations school upon Australian industry has not received the same degree of research attention as has that of Scientific Management. There is some evidence that the creation of certain personnel departments can be traced back to as early a period as the 1930s (Cochrane 1985) but it was not until the post-war period that strong industrial growth and high labour turnover prompted their widespread development. By 1947 the Institute of Industrial Management in Melbourne reported that of 70 firms in Melbourne which were interviewed, 65 % reported that they possessed an organised personnel department (*Manufacturing and Management* 1947: 82).

The point at which the Human Relations school began to make a major impact is more difficult to ascertain. Dunford (1991), following Cochrane (1985), suggests that whilst these ideas were filtering through management discourse in the 1940s, it was not until the 1950s that they became an essential part of the management ethos. Some evidence would appear to support this hypothesis, as in the example of the speech made in the mid-1940s to the Australian Institute of Management by Dr K. S. Cunningham who quotes the work of Roethlisberger and Dickson and points to the importance of these findings for personnel management in Australia. On the other hand, Dunphy (1987) argues that the era of the Human Relations school was rather later, covering the 1960s and the early 1970s.

Australia thus was in the forefront of the changes promoted by American management experts. Scientific Management spread to Australia as soon as the ideas were developed in America. Moreover, it seems likely that their introduction in Australia was in some respects faster and smoother than in the UK. Work study was being implemented in the New South Wales Railways between the wars and was spread by the growing body of management consultants just after the second world war. The nature of the spread of Taylorist ideas was heavily affected by trade union policy and was influenced by the position taken by arbitration commissioners. These ensured that incentive payments systems did not proliferate in Australia as they did in the U.K. and the U.S.A. Personnel departments began to spread in the 1930s.

The next major and distinctive movement for managerial reform, the new panacea, is associated with the growing dominance of Japan as an ideal model and can be identified with Quality Management.

Quality Management: Devolution or Control?

Narrowly speaking, Quality Management focuses upon the way in which commodities are produced to conform to user requirements. As such, Quality Management is concerned with the reorganisation, manipulation and control of material and social aspects of the production process. The theoretical object of Quality Management, then, is work process adaptations such that the results of production match customer needs at least cost. This narrow theoretical orientation must be seen in contrast to the more recent, more general and less clearly defined 'soft' focus of Quality Management as an overarching managerial philosophy and ideological imperative for organisational commitment. (It is at this level that Quality Management acquires the connotations of moral rearmament.)

Quality Management focuses upon the way in which production occurs and therefore needs to be studied at the level of concrete practices and techniques but it is quite difficult to isolate practices which are specific to a 'Quality' approach. The most important are as follows. First, statistical techniques are used to analyse, identify and eliminate waste and problems of work flow. Such techniques focus on the acceptability of product quality variations and indicate areas in which quality can be enhanced. Second, TQM implies the use of the JIT inventory system. Third, it suggests the need for company work processes to reunite the quality inspection function with actual task performance. Fourth, and associated with the last point, TQM involves the use of Quality Circles as a mechanism of locating responsibility for quality performance within the workgroup rather than an individual. Other types of participative decision-making arrangements could be included in this category as representing an attempt to use employee decision-making skills to improve management. Finally, a general ideological commitment from the CEO downwards is necessary to an acceptance of constant improvement and change.

As a collection of practices and techniques, Quality Management has consequences for production processes and employment relationships, some of which will be intended, others not. Subject to a later detailed workplace analysis, a number of initial propositions could be entertained.

Quality Management appears to focus upon an overall concern with the eradication of error and the production of 'quality' at least cost. The focus upon the eradication of error and built-in quality may intensify worker concentration and attention to detail and thus work effort. Further, where JIT inventory systems are used, work may also be intensified as the lack of buffer stocks means that production must proceed smoothly. However, it also heightens inter-dependency and implies that workers may achieve a new and strategic bargaining advantage because of the nature of the production process.

Quality Management advocates propose increased worker or workgroup responsibility, a proposal which raises a range of issues concerning new forms of work relations. Where the capacities of workers as knowledgeable subjects in the work process are recognised, the question of how to ensure the full utilisation of these capabilities arises.

Quality circles are one way in which the creative capacities of workers may be harnessed but it is not clear to what extent this type of mechanism, divorced from the other primary conditions of work that are enjoyed by the core Japanese worker, will be effective in soliciting worker commitment. Other strategies may have to be developed to allow workers greater input into the way in which work is organised and performed since the Quality Movement places such emphasis upon the contribution each employee can make to the overall performance of the organisation. Participative decision making is a prime Quality focus here. Flatter, less bureaucratic organisational structures are advocated to 'empower' workers and elicit commitment. The mechanisms for achieving such changes in the division of labour, however, are less clear. In the case where participative forums do not substantially affect how work is organised, they may be considered to be vehicles for discourse constituted at a different level from the formal range of productive activities and as dependent for their effectiveness on managerial goodwill and not their location within the productive process. These structures of communication can be decomposed as readily as they are established because they are suspended above productive processes rather than being integral to them.

In contrast to Human Relations Management (HRM), Quality Management does not appear to have developed a clearly defined set of techniques and expertise to marry individual satisfaction with increased productivity. HRM has as its theoretical object the relation of people to task and to other employees. It constitutes a body of knowledge, a methodology, a set of practices and a basis of information accumulation and analysis (Miller and Rose 1988). Quality Management, on the other hand, extolls an ethos of quality and commitment but lacks directions on the mechanisms to be instituted to achieve them. Leadership, for instance, is touted as a decisive means of achieving the corporate culture for success but without more concrete prescriptions it is difficult to imagine that this is little more than an ideological assertion about the indispensability of top management, especially the CEO, to the success of companies.

Quality Management uses a marketing approach, focussing on the importance of customer requirements as a key motivator for employees. Employees are encouraged to conceive of all persons that use their output as customers, whether they be outside end-users or the next person or group in the construction stage. Production is to be Just-In-Time to meet all requirements. This type of prescription is reductionist. In the attempt to enlarge the realm of work relations and experiences to harness employee enthusiasm, the approach reduces work to a single market relation, a relation in which the activities of the individual producer have significance only to the extent that they are effectively subordinated to the requirements of the superordinate customer. Quality Management, in this respect, obscures rather than clarifies the implications it will have for work relations.

If the employment implications of fully implemented quality management are to be assessed, issues concerning training, education, pay, career structures, skill recognition, multiskilling, broadbanding, flexibility, decision-making forums, worker motivation and commitment, access to information and a host of other matters need to be raised. The impact of changing practices on the organisation structure and especially on workforce jobs both at shopfloor levels and in certain managerial departments is considerable, most obviously those of personnel and human resources, where the specialisation and forms of professionalism are affected.

If Quality Management as a management movement is placed in the context of the earlier movements to promote changed managerial practices, then some elements of it can be seen as extensions of Scientific Management while some elements represent a reversal or change in direction.

Aspects of Quality Management clearly continue the efforts of earlier movements to promote rationalisation and central control. The use of computer technology to enable management to produce statistical models of work flow and product variability and to increase control of complex inventories can all be seen as the application of software technology to traditional problems of information control. As such these can be analysed in terms of Max Weber's classic thesis on bureaucratic organisational control. The development of sophisticated Management Information Systems does not represent new directions for management, but only provides a greater capacity to collect and digest information for the benefit of more centralised decision-making.

In contrast, although computer technology is being used to empower centralised decision-making on financial control, inventory and the elimination of work process problems, other aspects of the Quality Movement can be seen as promoting decentralisation and greater flexibility in bureaucratic business organisations. In this regard the emphasis is upon more participative forms of work organisation as opposed to autocratic hierarchies. Quality Management's emphasis on customer requirements reflects the rise of marketing and the increased concern of corporate executives to manage demand at a time when competitions is fierce. If earlier managerial movements focused on saving dollars on the supply side, Quality Management directs attention to the need to satisfy more discriminating demands. The exact policies that emerge from these concerns are more difficult to specify and some have little to do with a specifically 'Quality' approach. TQM, for example, appears to promote a number of practices which are thought to promote flexibility and they do not necessarily form a neat package with computer techniques.

The policy which is most clearly associated with the Quality movement is the attempt to de-specialise the inspection function. Whereas Taylor advocated the separation of direct production from indirect servicing, inspection and maintenance tasks, Quality Management advocates the reabsorption of the task of monitoring output back into the operator's job description. Quality Circles are a method of promoting this change and of developing group, rather than individual, responsibilities for standards of output.

It is difficult to know whether other attempts to devolve authority can be claimed by the Quality movement. For example, many economists and business policy analysts have described recent changes in corporate structure towards M-form organisations (Goold and Campbell 1987) which operate with tightly centralised financial controls but with all other 'operational' management decisions devolved to become the responsibility of 'business unit managers'. This form of organisational structure is made possible because of management's ability to use computerised information systems to greatly increase the sophistication of budgetary controls but it does not seem to us to be a specifically 'quality' phenomenon. The M-form does not derive from Japan but from an analysis of the development of Western conglomerates and multi-national enterprises.

Another aspect of the devolution of operational management has been an attack on central staff departments, which once devised policy or gave advice in such areas as human resource management and legal issues. Where such staff departments have been eliminated and their activities absorbed back into the line management function or subcontracted to external organisations, it could be argued that western organisations are following Japan and this might be seen as part of the 'quality' prescription − a return to Japanese generalism, or what has been described as 'de-differentiation' (Lash 1988, quoted in Clegg 1990a). We find it difficult, however, to relate this change to the specifically 'quality' rationale. In several cases the elimination or weakening of central staff departments has taken a less radical form and the staff functions are preserved in decentralised, but still specialised, departments.

To summarise, if we are to understand the nature of the 'Quality Management' movement then it needs to be seen in the context of other movements to promote managerial reforms. Contrasting it with the two major reform movements which were associated with the spread of American managerial ideas earlier in the century shows that some components of 'Quality Management' increase central control of information and act to centralise strategic planning, merely using new technology to further policies that have been advocated since 1911. It is only those elements that seek to devolve responsibility for monitoring standards of output which represent a trend away from classic Taylorist principles. This de-differentiation could be associated with the neo-Human Relations school's attempts to enrich job design but we see little evidence of any direct input by this school or any focus on the industrial psychology that underlies human relations ideas. To the extent that de-differentiation is influenced by Japanese management systems, it could be claimed as part of TQM. Within Japan the diffusion of managerial skills across a 'generalist' management cadre and the lack of a labour market for occupationally or professionally based 'staff' expertise is a function of the Japanese preference for internal labour markets within large-scale organisations. The TQM movement, however, does not appear to adopt a clear stance on such central issues as internal labour markets, the use of direct versus contract labour or the elimination of professional staff management roles. Indeed, within Australia, a recent proposal to establish a new Australian Society for Quality to act as a professional group to promote the occupational training and accreditation of specialist quality practitioners and consultants would seem to run counter to the generalist preference for the integration of quality skills throughout the workforce and suggests some confusion on the issue of the elimination of old occupational and job boundaries.

Total Quality Management: The New Panacea?

As a managerial 'recipe', TQM, like Scientific Management, draws its main expertise from engineering or systems science but, like the Human Relations school, recognises the value of employee motivation and group morale, the power of subjective experiences and the managerial value of a committed workforce. TQM, like Scientific Management and Human Relations before it, makes major claims about the social and economic impact of its prescriptions. It is argued, for instance, that TQM entails 'the removal of all barriers: between the shop-floor and engineering; between sales and engineering; between accounts and sales; and between the shop-floor and the CEO!' (Sandland 1989). It is said that it changes the role of supervisors so that they 'approach their jobs, not as policemen or referees, but as coaches involved in a team activity (Irwin 1989). Indeed, TQM is said to engender 'excellent cooperation across the total organisation' (Spong 1989).

In order to sort out the possible interface between TQM and the organisation of the labour process, it is important to understand the nature of the claims that are likely to be made. All reform movements come complete with their persuasive baggage, for no change agent can afford to miss an opportunity for sales talk. F. W. Taylor may have believed the claims he put so enthusiastically to the US Senate investigating committee when he argued that his system would involve 'linking the worker to the scientific manager in "willing, hearty collaboration", [and] ... would create an authentic industrial partnership; ... [such that] ... one could hardly imagine a more equitable, more harmonious, more reciprocally beneficial relationship, except perhaps in the case of the team spirit of a baseball side and their coach' (Rose 1985: 34, 40, 51).

If Taylor did believe that all distributional conflict would cease he stands convicted of considerable naivety. If he understood that resistance to his system could be based on perceived self interest, then his claims need to be seen as a form of public relations and sales pressure and should not taken at face value as an indication of the actual consequences that were expected.

In the case of the value of the Human Relations movement the writings of Elton Mayo provide the most extravagant claims. Mayo believed that people's 'desire to be continuously associated in work with [their] fellows is a strong, if not the strongest, human characteristic' (Mayo 1966: 99). He suggested that 'industrial unrest is ... caused by the fact that a conscious dissatisfaction serves to "light up" as it were the hidden fires of mental uncontrol' (Quoted in Bourke 1982: 226). For management what

'could be more appealing than to be told that one's subordinates are non-logical; that their unco-operativeness is a frustrated urge to collaborate; that their demands for cash mask a need for your approval and that you have an historic destiny as a broker of social harmony'. (Rose 1985: 51)

TQM similarly also has adherents who make extravagant claims. Research is needed to separate real outcomes from the extravagant claims that go with each attempt by management consultants to promote new forms of managerial control.

As a significant, and growing, managerial movement, Quality Management in Australia as elsewhere in the world provides us with an important case study about the ways in which a wave of ideas and associated practices about work processes are disseminated. First, we need to understand the nature of the ideas that are promoted, thir origins, consistency and purpose and, second, to distinguish the social actors who act to promote, to subvert or to adapt and alter the nature of these ideas. Although the principal agents in the dissemination of managerial prescriptions may be assumed to be managers, or agents of management, this assumption needs to be checked. Management as a whole is not unitary; both within organisations and between different sectors of the economy there are many differences. The roles of management consultants, of government and of unionists also need assessment. Within Australia at the present time, for example, some trade unionists and certain industrial commissioners are promoting quality management ideas in many regards, while management consultants are eagerly transferring similar ideas. This conjunction of interested parties is important since Australian managers have to act within the constraints imposed by the national wage arbitration system and the actions of unions and workers while often the state and the union movement together act as major change agents in the reform process.

In addition to mapping the flow of ideas and the principal transferring actors, we need to assess the power resources available to those actors and the mechanisms through which they act. The growth of the various lobby and promotional organisations that have developed surrounding quality within Australia in recent years provides a fertile ground for such study. Finally, the practical results of all this social mobilisation of resources, and of the resistance and constraints which the promotion of new managerial ideas will meet, need to be investigated since strategic management endeavours will entail a series of consequences, some of which will be planned whilst others will be unintended. The potential 'downside' to the Quality Management push also needs to be understood.

The emergence and apparent rapid spread of Quality Management ideas in Australia poses a number of significant questions as to why the movement should have developed in the way and form that it has. Important in the explanation is the development of Quality Management as a response to the broader economic imperatives for restructuring of the Australian economy. The rise of Japan as the premier manufacturing producer, the growing industrialisation of South East Asia and the international success of some European and Scandinavian nations have highlighted the current and long-standing inability of Australian producers to effectively compete, both domestically and internationally. Without wishing to appear overtly economistic, it would seem that these overarching structural conditions have provided the context for and the imperative towards a quest for solutions. Quality Management has emerged as one type of solution amongst many. In analysing its spread in Australia where the quality management movement has gained considerable attention and probably more government support than in the USA or Europe, we need to ask which human agents have been most influential in pushing the movement into prominence. Which sectors of business or management are most enthusiastic and supportive? Has the role of the arbitration system or of trade unions, for instance, been irrelevant, negative or supportive? What of the role of government and why was it more important than in other countries?

Conclusion

Quality Management is an important new area of managerial, state and union concern. As a more or less coherent body of thought it exhibits significant similarities and differences with other management movements of this century, such as Taylorism and the Human Relations School. In Australia, as elsewhere where it has been enthusiastically espoused, at least in principle, it comprises a range of techniques, practices and notions that will have important connotations, not only for the way in which work is organised but also for employment relations. Quality Management borrows some Japanese production techniques (making use, for instance, of statistical analysis for work flow assessment), emphasises flatter and more participative organisational structures and stresses the importance of individual motivation to organisational success. The implications of Quality Management thus need to be understood in terms of the impact that such practices will have on material processes of production and the social relations of work. The question remains, however, of whether this panacea will work any more effectively than those which went before.

Organisational Restructuring and Devolutionist Doctrine: Organisation as Strategic Control

Michael Muetzelfeldt

Introduction

The 1980s saw the restructuring of a wide range of organizations in both the private and public sectors of industrial societies worldwide. Despite their diversity in form and context, these restructurings were all based on the new doctrine of devolutionism, which advocates the centralization of strategic control and the simultaneous decentralization of tactical responsibility within a context of management-controlled incentive structures and corporate culture.

Devolutionism is usually said to increase organizational effectiveness and to democratize the workplace. This chapter argues that the first of these propositions is unproven and the second is false. Despite its apparently democratic thrust, devolutionism is politically partisan, mobilising not only the skills but the initiative and motivation of workers for the organization's ends. The devolved mode of organization has become desirable and possible not because of instrumental motivations but because of the conjuncture during the 1980s of economic rationalist ideology, systems theory and information technology. As devolutionism is embedded within these new discourses and practices, traditional concepts of organizational politics and power are inadequate in assessing critically this new organizational form.

Despite the considerable diversity among these various private and public sector organizations and the changes implemented within them, their devolutionist restructuring shares a common basis: a move away from the conventional organizational form of centralized hierarchies of task-oriented operatives controlled by bureaucratic rules, and towards distributing operational decision-making widely through the organization. The new organizations tend towards being decentralized networks of output-oriented entrepreneurs, regulated by systems of incentives and information feedback within suitable corporate culture contexts.

Under devolutionism the traditional visual metaphor of the organization as a pyramid is replaced with the image of a net. Hence it becomes inappropriate to speak of organizational politics in the traditional terms of conflicts between the organization's top or head and its bottom or base. Indeed, the doctrine of devolutionism denies that there is any organizational politics, and the loosely woven net imagery supports this, because it is difficult to identify or name the power centre. In contrast, devolutionism in practice depends on the powerful but indirect regulatory mechanism of corporate culture, incentive structures and management information systems. Through these mechanisms, strategic control is centralized at the same time as operational decision-making is decentralized, and this leads to practices that are usually no more than pseudo-devolutionist. Organizational politics continues but follows new and less visible trajectories. To make the politics more visible, I use the image of the organization as a web rather than a net. In the web image, power can be identified as being concentrated at the centre and exercised over the periphery so that traditional top-down organizational politics are replaced by centre-periphery politics, which are less easily recognised by both participants and analysts and so tend not to offend established interests and constituencies.

The discussion first traces the emergence of devolutionism and argues that its claim to deliver increased effectiveness is not well substantiated and that its current popularity is based as much on the way it apparently dissolves, but actually contains, organizational politics. The chapter then addresses the question of why devolutionism is so widely supported despite its unproven efficacy and its insidious political partisanship. I argue that the answer lies in the conjuncture and interlinking during the 1980s of economic rationalist ideology, systems theory and information technology, each of which contributes to the discourse and practices through which devolutionism is produced and reproduced. The relationship between these three factors is symbiotic and together they have a pervasive hegemonic influence over current organizational consulting and practice. Many writers fail to recognise that devolutionism involves centre-periphery power relations and so view it as democratic and work-enhacing. They are able to take this view because there is no discourse within which centre-periphery politics in devolved organizations can be readily identified and portrayed. The discussion concludes by arguing that conventional notions of organizational power (and here strategic contingency theory is taken as the example) are inadequate to the task of critically analysing this new organizational form.

The Emergence of Organisational Devolutionism

It was Chandler (1962) who first identified and publicised the multi-divisional 'M-form' pattern of organization, which was designed around quasi-autonomous operating devisions based on products, brands, or geography.

He distinguished the M-form from the traditional unitary 'U-form' organization, which was designed around functional divisions. M-form organizations set up their divisions as quasi-firms which are made to serve the overall organizations's strategic aims through an 'extensive internal control apparatus' based on 'manipulation of the incentive machinery, internal audits, and cash flow allocation' (Williamson 1975: 145). The thrust of the M-form design was towards establishing an enviroment in which central office executives were provided with 'the psychological commitment to be concerned with the overall performance of the organization rather than become absorbed in the affairs of the functional parts' (1975: 137). Given this thrust, there was no need to replicate within the operating divisions the pattern of relationships between them and head office, because establishing quasi-firms was all that was necessary to free central office executives from functional details. Consequently within M-form organizations the internal organizations of the quasi-firms were often based on the old U-form pattern.

The M-form model started being widely used in the USA in the early 1970s (Williamson 1975: 140−41) and at the end of that decade Byrt found that in Australia it had been widely adopted among the large non-monopolistic Australian organizations he studied (Byrt 1981), laying the foundations for acceptance of the still more devolved model. The restructuring of the 1980s involved combining the central concept of the M-form organization with notions of corporate culture and entrepreneurialism.

During the 1980s management concern broadened from establishing suitable psychological commitments in head office executives to motivating all workers in the organization. This concern harked back to the work of the Human Relations school but was now seen as a management-directed project to both mobilize and shape workers' values. 'Corporate culture' was adopted as a management tool, a set of techniques initially put forward by Maccoby (1981) and by Peters and Waterman (1982) and intended to achieve a 'crafting of the corporate self' (Howard 1985). According to Maccoby and to Peters and Waterman, this crafting was to be achieved by deliberately using techniques which formalise and bring under management control the organization's industrial subculture (Turner 1971; Deal and Kennedy 1982) and acting on workers' sense of self as if it were a 'fine-tuned instrument' (Maccoby in Howard 1985: 124). These techniques communicate the values of the corporation through stories, rituals and myths (Howard 1985: 124). The resulting corporate culture is supposed to produce a re-enchantment that transcends the spiritual barrenness which Weber identified as characteristic of instrumental bureaucratic rationality.

'It is almost as if he [Maccoby] is inadvertently suggesting [that re-enchantment is] not the transcendence of instrumental rationality but its extension into the realm of the human personality. ... But this opens the door to a dangerous phenomenon that truly deserves to be called cynical – the systematic manipulation by corporate managers of peoples' desire for meaningful work.' (Howard 1985: 123)

The development of corporate culture as a management tool articulates within the organization the marketing objectives and techniques which were originally developed to deal with external needs, such as product advertising, and then extended as corporate image building. The organization and its pursuits are projected onto the members of the organization, and onto its client suppliers and agents, much as its products and image were previously projected into the target market. In both cases, the intent is to build values, attitudes, identity-giving affiliations and habitual attachments so that people will choose to act in ways that further the organization's interests.

If a suitable corporate culture can be established, the values, attitudes and practices instilled by management can be activated in workers as if they came from the organizational grass roots.[1] 'People centred' management, quality control circles, and the organization-wide pursuit of excellence become feasible management tools. A recent trade journal article by a marketing executive with a PhD in physical chemistry (Hoernschemeyer 1989) summarises these strategies as the four cornerstones of excellence:

- A quality context. 'Context is the soul of an organization and is expressed in the company's style and culture. It is moulded by the attitudes, beliefs and prejudices of the top executives.' (1989: 37);
- Empowering people. 'At a minimum, empowerment means giving people the power to do the job demanded by their position. At a higher level, people are empowered to a degree that permits them to exhibit their best abilities. ... People must know and understand quality goals and how to get there. They also need the power and motivation to produce the results.' (1989: 38);

---

[1] Whether or not in any particular case an all-inclusive corporate culture has in fact been established is another matter. There is some evidence that, at least in some contexts, what appear to be successfully imposed corporate cultures do not produce the deep attachments that they aim for, but rather produce workers' instrumental compliance with required behaviours (Ogbonna and Wilkinson 1990). These behaviours may be misread by management to substantiate their belief in the success of their corporate culture programs. More generally, there is growing argument that it is not possible to effectively manage occupational or corporate cultures (Ackroyd and Crowdy 1990; Anthony 1990). However the important point here is that the devolutionist strategy is available to a management that *believes* that its corporate culture is in place.

- Quality communication. 'Communication is the medium for establishing teamwork and moving people to enthusiastic and effective action.' (1989: 39);
- Removing barriers to performance. 'Unmotivated people are unlikely to produce quality results. People become unmotivated by the thoughtless, irritating, unconcerned way they are treated; by conventional operating practices; and by old attitudes, myths, and prejudices.' (1989: 39).

To the extent that management believes that the corporate culture project is successful in establishing managerial definitions of context, empowerment, communication and performance, the culture provides an overarching management-oriented framework within which the entrepreneurial motivation, initiative and effort of individuals can be encouraged at all levels in the organization while still being harnessed to organizational goals. The ideas underlying the framework draw on the trend during the 1980s, in the wider culture as well as within organizations, of uncritically celebrating entrepreneuralism. In the mass media and in the management literature small and large entrepreneurs were hailed as heroes, despite the strong arguments that small businesses were not the motor of productivity that their supporters claimed them to be (Muetzelfeldt 1986) and despite the always visible but until recently ignored debt-building and tax-minimising activities on which corporate entrepreneurs inflated their empires.

Increasingly, the corporate culture project is linked to internal entrepreneurialism or 'intrapreneurialism' in the management jargon of the day (Pinchot 1985; Cornwall and Perlman 1990). The linkage is created by extending Chandler's devolved mechanism, replicating down through all levels of the organization the incentive structures, audit controls and resource allocation mechanism originally developed to control the M-form organization. The result has been characterised as structured chaos:

'The function of the genuine entrepreneur ... appears to work best when decentralized throughout the enterprise. ... Successful workplaces seem to be organized as 'structured chaos' — chaos from dynamic experimentation and autonomy at the grass roots, 'structured' by personal understanding of, and sharing in, the values and purposes of the enterprise. ... This is particularly important now as people seek expression for post-industrial values, for 'counting as a person', in the workplace.' (Blandy et al. 1985: 93—4)

For Blandy and his colleagues structured chaos is a 'chaos' to which everyone in the organisation should be subject and which is generated by and is intended to serve the interests of those who control the organisation. This is different from the externally generated and uncontrolled 'chaos' experienced by the organisation which Peters (1988) urges managers to proactively thrive on rather than reactively thrive within. Structured chaos encapsulates the doctrine that operational decision-making should be widely distributed throughout the organization, and that, given an appropriate corporate culture, this will serve the interests of those who control the organization, taken here to be the managers. The same doctrine underlines other related prescriptions for organizational restructuring, such as Benveniste's (1987) profession-oriented organization and Cornwall and Perlman's (1990) entrepreneurial organization.

I use the term devolutionism to refer to this broad doctrine. Devolutionism, however, does not involve the authentic dispersal of autonomy and power throughout the organization. Rather, it is a management technique for mobilising the skills, ideas and energy of people at all levels in the organization, shaping and harnessing these for organizational purposes that are determined by management alone.

During the 1980s, organizational restructuring was widely based on devolutionist principles. In the private sector, such restructuring ocurred in both industrial production and service industries. Industrial production lines were replaced by nodal work groups, retail chains became franchised networks and within corporations operational divisions were reorganised as profit centres. There are many examples, such as the particularly thoroughgoing implementation of devolutionism by the transport conglomerate Mayne Nickless in Australia. As well as setting up its various divisions as distinct firms, which might compete with one another as well as with others in the industry, in one regional branch of its freight forwarding firm, Skyroad-Express, the entrepreneurial work of cultivating customers was devolved to the drivers, who, as sub-contractors, got (some of) the rewards of their effort (Kriegler et al. 1988).

Devolutionism shifts the focus from rule-bound conduct within formal *organizations* to purpose-oriented conduct within *systems*. As a result, the conventional and intuitive notion of an organization with formal boundaries gives way to a sense of organization as the capacity of those with strategic control to impose organising effects across as well as within formal organizations. This aspect of devolutionism in particular can be seen in the restructuring of industrial production. In this volume, Wilkinson and his colleagues discuss such control by a major producer of its suppliers in Britain, Marceau and Jureidini consider the 'logic' of inter- as well as intra-organizational firms in an Australian case and Gorgeu and Mathieu similarly describe the 'partnership' relationship between a French producer and its suppliers. Some of the control mechanism used, including those that appear in the guise of technical standards, are discussed in the chapters by van Tulder and by Palmer and Allan.

Devolutionism now also operates in the public sector. Over the last decade public bureaucracies have adopted corporate management, regionalised their previously centralized offices, devolved decision making to budget centres, sub-contracted out part of their work and come to control their clients in new ways. Following the end of the long boom in 1974–75 in Australia, the Fraser Liberal National government in the late 1970s and early 1980s adopted at least the rhetoric of deregulation and the Hawke Labor government subsequently moved to implement deregulatory policies with an accompanying restructuring of public sector organizations. During the 1980s, particularly under the Hawke governments,

'the broader environment of economic recession, budgetary pressures, and economic rationalist ideologies has stimulated public sector reform at state and federal level in the direction of a new managerialism, performance measurement, program budgeting, cost-recovery mechanisms, reducing regulation, and encouraging economies of scale.' (Head 1988: 3-4).

An example will illustrate how these reforms express the devolutionist doctrine. The Victorian State Electricity Commission initially implemented government equal employment opportunity (EO) policy requirements by appointing three equal opportunity officers. They were located in head office and had the task of implementing EO principles and practices throughout the SEC's dispersed and diverse organizations and plants. After two years, the EO program was restructured. Implementation of EO objectives is now written into the performance criteria of all branch managers or their equivalents and just two head office EO officers maintain these criteria and evaluate branches' progress in implementing them. As a result, managers are made to manage, regulation is reduced, performance is measured, and the identifiable costs of the EO program are reduced.

As well as controlling the organization of public agencies, devolutionism is also being used to control the agencies' clients in new ways by forcing clients to monitor their own behaviour. For example, following a cost blowout in Victoria's Workcare, a workers' compensation program, a revision of the scheme was proposed early in 1989. One of the objectives was to reduce the number of long term beneficiaries, a high proportion of whom had suffered stress or soft tissue injuries that cannot be unambiguously diagnosed by physical examination. It was proposed to reduce the compensation paid to beneficiaries after twelve months off work, thus modifying the incentive structure under which clients were placed so as to give them incentive to recover from their disability within twelve months. Clients themselves were to be incorporated into the Workcare decision-making structure, shifting from the Workers' Compensation Commission to the clients themselves some of the regulatory/bureaucratic task of making decisions about their recovery, with the expectation that this would lead to a substantial cost reduction.

Devolutionism and Effectiveness

Devolutionist restructuring of public and private sector organizations is often claimed to make them both more productive or effective (for example, Paterson 1988; Kriegler et al. 1988; Mathews 1989b) and more democratic. In this section I examine the first claim, and conclude that it is not definitely substantiated. In the next section I argue that devolutionism does not have the democratic impact on organizational politics which is claimed by its proponents and in the final section I examine why devolutionism is so widely supported despite its uncertain effectiveness.

In the public sector in Australia the efficacy of corporate management restructuring remains debatable. While it may increase short-term productivity as measured by easily quantified performance indicators, it can also have counter-productive effects. Performance targets that are easily quantified are not necessarily representative of the organization's full purpose, an issue of considerable importance in the public sector which can not choose clients and must operate under the terms of particular Acts of Parliament. The emphasis on achieving easily quantified targets, and these targets alone, can skew short-term effort towards clients and projects that fit cost-performance profiles, with other clients and projects being off-loaded to other budget centres regardless of how effectively those centres can respond. Moreover, in the long term, the emphasis on achieving given targets can produce inflexibility and lack of innovation (see Considine 1988 and 1990; Head 1988; Paterson 1988).

The core issue here concerns what is to count as 'effectiveness'. Public sector corporate management aims to pre-empt this issue by measuring effectiveness solely in terms of variously defined performance indicators, which, as Considine (1988 and 1990) argues, is unsatisfactory. In the private sector the effectiveness issue remains open, despite the availability of apparently self-evident and easily qualified measures such as profitability and market share. Effectiveness is a multi-dimensional notion, expressing the achievement of possibly conflicting ends (Benveniste 1987: 135 – 7) and involving both short and long term outcomes. Despite these difficulties, a range of studies aims to link devolutionism to productivity and effectiveness.

One such study is that by Kriegler and his colleagues (1988) who make an enthusiastic case for the productivity and effectiveness of devolutionism in two private sector and one public sector organizations in Australia. However, in a review of the available literature (1988 ch. 1), they show that the evidence concerning the effect of structure on organizational effectiveness and productivity is mixed, so organizational planners can not be confident that organizations based on the new 'structured chaos' principles will be more effective than the old and, in particular, can have few grounds for thinking that structural reorganization by itself will lead to greater effectiveness. The overall thrust of this international literature review tends to support Kriegler and colleagues' own findings about the importance of management capacity and employee enthusiasm and commitment (1988: 122). This echoes Byrt's conclusion, based on an earlier study of Australian organizations, that:

'... the extent to which strategies are likely to be pursued successfully will depend more on the quality of an organization's management than on the nature of its structural arrangements. An appropiate organization structure is desirable, but efficient management can make almost any organization work, and the best-designed organization is unlikely to function effectively given inefficient management.' (1981: 142)

Despite the celebration of devolutionism by authors such as Kriegler, organizations based on 'structured chaos' do not necessarily do well when subjected to the test of the commercial world. For example, two of Australia's once most successful companies, Budget Rent A Car Systems and Budget Transport Industries, were decentralized some years ago, when branches were franchised to the previous branch managers. For some years this group had the type of growth and profitability that is so easily taken to indicate organizational effectiveness but in 1989 both companies were put into provisional liquidation with debts of over $ 70 million and the group's charismatic managing director, who advocated and seemed to epitomise the leadership style advocated by many managements recipes, was sacked from that position (Sevior 1989). The euphoric pen picture that Kriegler and colleagues painted of the now radically devalued Skyroad in New South Wales (NSW) (1988: 172), and the correspondingly bleak depiction of unsuccessful centralized organizational units (1988: 122 – 123) have given us no indication that such undesirable outcomes are possible.

   There are many instances of management and organization studies in which authors draw conclusions with more or less overt devolutionist agendas from case studies with weak theoretical and empirical foundations. For example, Stewart (1989: 52 – 57) advocates non-unionism to achieve a 'running hot' organization such as the Canadian low-technology auto parts factory which so impressed him and Cornwell and Perlman (1990) use qualitative open-ended notions of effectiveness together with a series of anecdotal American case studies to support their advocacy of entrepreneurial organizations which embody devolutionist principles.

   In part, the problems of assessing the advantages of devolution as an operating strategy reflect the difficulty of defining the notion of 'effectiveness'. When it (or its short-term correlate, 'sharpbending') is carefully defined and operationalised to reflect its multi-dimensional quality, analysts find that it is associated with many organizational features in complex and non-determinate ways (Denison 1990; Grinyer, Mayes and McKieman

1988). These features cannot be reduced to simple formulae or images and even if they could there is no certainty that the cause-effect relationships are direct enough for management to be able to achieve effectiveness by implementing such strategies alone.

The conceptual and methodological indeterminacy apparent in these studies raises the question of why devolutionism has such appeal as to lead these authors, as well as the practitioners who implement organizational restructuring, towards uncritical acceptance of devolutionist doctrine. The answer seems to lie in the extent to which devolutionism has become a new management orthodoxy. The new orthodoxy includes the view that management and employees are so much partners in the organization that the differences between them can pass unnoticed, that it is possible for all 'corporate players' to 'work and win together' (Keidel 1988). In effect, it denies power to workers by asserting that they and management have common interests. This political partisanship can be seen in the choice of case studies by authors such as Kriegler and his colleagues (1988), Denison (1990) and Grinyer, Mayes and McKieman (1988). In contrast, Cable and Fitzroy (1980a and b) found, for instance, that:

'... it is participation [by employees] in the strategic decision-making areas of investment, prices and product policy which is of most significance for performance − areas of decision-making where employees are usually given little say in the more common consultative structures.' (Kriegler et al. 1988: 30)

Despite such findings, most analysts seeking ways of improving effectiveness are silent on the question of the effectiveness of real employee involvement in strategic decision-making. This silence follows from their failure to include in their research any organization that comes close to being a labour-managed cooperative, as the Cable and Fitzroy findings suggest would be appropiate. In short, the advocates of devolutionism make the instrumental claim that following the path of devolution is the best way to enhance organizational effectiveness but their arguments lack clear definitions of the key concepts, their analysis confuses supposed causes and supposed effects and they do not follow available research leads that the literature suggests may prove more critical.

In their description of the 'tight-loose' property of organization, Peters and Waterman (1982) distinguish between tight centralized control and the looseness which frees subunits to respond to local situations. Similarly, Kriegler and colleagues recognise that there are tensions between decentralization and centralization and between structure and chaos (1988: 83, 113) and that 'structured chaos' involves simultaneous centralization and decentralization, with qualitative differences between what is being centralized and what is being decentralized. Functions which they consider should be centralized are:

'... imposing financial controls, defining business performance feedback criteria, developing management information systems, strategic planning, developing an appropriate corporate structure and maintaining a corporate image to provide a sense of integration and unity to the many and varied activities.' (1988: 84)

Within this overarching framework and control system,

'... managers of small units are expected to develop a wide range of professional managerial skills — technical, financial and human. There is a very real sense of 'managing your own little business', which requires commitment and dedication from managers at all levels, and this sense of purpose frequently gravitates down to the shop floor. [Decentralisation also] establishes closer and more effective relations between the business and its customers.' (1988: 88)

Despite their recognition of the qualitative differences between the types of decisions that are centralized and the types that are decentralized, they have no trouble in talking about 'decentralization of the locus of *control* and, on the same page, describing this as 'pushing *responsibility* for service delivery closer to the customers ... pushing operational and budgetary *responsibility* closer to the action' (1988: 111, my emphasis). Indeed, they see these notions as linked, with power and responsibility being delegated together through decentralization and profit centres (1988: 83).

This claimed conjunction of control and power with responsibility does not fit with earlier texts in which organizational devolution was advocated through the M-form model of organization which make it clear that the split between what is centralized and what is decentralized does not involve a sharing out of power. For example, Williamson identifies the M-form organization as having strategic decision-making centralized and operational decision-making decentralized, with control being exercised by 'the elite staff' through a 'requisite control apparatus' which is 'systematically employed', 'securing greater control over operating division behaviour' (1975: 137, 152).

As well as the declared intent of the original devolutionists to centralize strategic control, there is empirical evidence to challenge the optimistic assertions of devolutionism's current advocates that control of power is devolved together with responsibility. In a study of a regional board of education in Victoria, for example, Watkins, Rizvi and Angus (1987) found considerable frustration among elected representatives over the lack of collaborative and participative decision making and tension between the central Ministry and the regional board as these board members sought to contest the Ministry's budgetary guide-lines that limited the board's ability to pursue its aims. Watkins has further argued that these boards are caught in 'an essential tension between corporate management and the rhetoric which advocates administration of a democratic, participative kind.' Their institutional location 'encourages participation but at the same time restricts and limits the effectiveness of that participation' (1988: 454).

In the private sector, there is also anecdotal evidence that at least some Budget Rent A Car branch managers who took up the offer to become franchisees became very discontented because their increased independence had been bought at the price of longer hours, increased uncertainty and reduced financial security. Clearly, there is a need for a more thorough examination of the responses of operational managers to devolution.

The responses of workers, as well as managers, also needs closer scrunity. In the New South Wales branch of Skyroad, drivers were given the task of cultivating and competing for customers. This set Skyroad apart from all the other freight forwarding companies in that state, which were more conventionally structured. The reported enthusiasm amongst the drivers for this devolution (Kriegler et al. 1988: 76) needs closer examination. Did some drivers leave because they did not want to work under the new structure? What would happen if all freight forwarding companies provided incentives for their drivers to act like 'small entrepreneurs' so that in a saturated market each driver's extra initiative, effort and time were not rewarded with extra payment? Considering the chaotic state of the local tow truck industry before it was regulated and the current exploitatively competitive conditions under which nominally independent Australian interstate freight truckers currently work, it seems reasonable to hypothesise that drivers would find themselves locked into cutting rates against one another and in real conflict rather than economic competition for clients. Under such conditions, driver enthusiasm for structured chaos would soon evaporate.

These examples suggest two major limitations on the universal applicability of this new management recipe. First, a competitive strategy which is successful for a market leader does not necessarily work when taken up across a whole industry. And second, structured chaos ultimately means structure for the powerful centre and chaos for the weaker periphery.

Devolution provides an opportunity and a resource for powerful actors in central organizations to use rhetoric to impose responsibility on to weaker subordinates in peripheral organization units. This is most visible in the public sector where discursive contests between centre and periphery are understood to be 'news' or 'current affairs' and so are (at least in part) conducted in the media. It is likely that in private sector organizations there is a comparable centre-periphery politics, even though it may be conducted through private discussion between head office executives and branch managers. There, too, a similar rhetoric is used to impose on branch managers the responsibility for impositions which the central organization makes on branch staff or on branch managers themselves.

As with all rhetorics that serve political interests, the rhetoric of responsibility is most powerful when it is internalised by those against whom it is used. When this occurs, groups and individuals in the organizational periphery take it upon themselves to 'bite the bullet' and 'make the hard decisions', without perceiving that their practices are being shaped by the requirements or interests of the powerful centre. This is, after all, no more than an extension into organizational life of the ideology of the free market that is inscribed in and structures our self-imposed acceptance of economic restraints in our financial and domestic lives.

The mechanism for such an internalization is provided through both the discourse within which the devolutionist rhetoric speaks and the practices which devolutionism enables. The discourse, as well as the perceptions and valuations which it calls forth in people, is evoked in contexts which express the structural interests which underlie practices. In particular, the rhetoric of devolution is evoked in contexts where managerial authority is dominant and where the language of managerialism — excellence, effectiveness, productivity, involvement and pride in one's work, for instance — prevails.

An indication of the strength and pervasiveness of this internalized rhetoric is given by the way in which devolutionism has become identified with industrial democracy, even by those associated with the political left. For example, Mathews (1989b) is an enthusiast supporter of devolutionism, not only on productivity grounds, but also because:

'Worker involvement in the design of technology, of jobs, of work organization, of patterns of skill formation and industrial relation systems, amount to the *democratisation of work*. It is seen as a *direct form of industrial democracy*. (1989b: 172). Original emphasis)

All of these things are desirable and may indeed make the experience of work more congenial but, with the arguable exception of the last mentioned (the design of industrial relations), they hardly come to grips with the major issues of industrial democracy: namely, real employee involvement in strategic decision-making and/or labour-managed cooperatives. Within a strong corporate culture framework, the worker involvements which Mathews advocates are more likely to be effective mechanisms for co-option than mechanisms for democratization.

Discourse, Practice, and Devolutionism

Devolutionism is regularly advocated in the context of the perceived national need to become more productive (see, for example, Mathews 1989b). It is not necessarily a rational response to the problem of how to increase organizational efficiency and productivity, because there is no conclusive evidence that it will achieve that result, but it can be an effective political strategy for those who wish to centralise organizational power and simultaneously incorporate workers and their political organizations into those power relations. This is because it *appears* to decentralise and disperse power throughout the organization, giving the impression that it contributes to industrial democracy.

I have argued above that, despite appearances, devolutionism does not in fact decentralise and disperse power. Rather, it delegates *responsibility* to workers and other employees within a managerial context which mobilizes the distributed initiative and energy of people throughout the organization for purposes and projects determined by a powerful central management. The claim that this empowers people is based on an undemocratic rhetoric: 'empowerment means giving people the power to do the job demanded by their position' (Hoernschemeyer 1989: 38). This rhetoric is itself part of the corporate culture project of winning the consent that devolutionism requires. The resulting hegemonic effect is so pervasive that commentators normally thought of as being on the Left vie with the managerialists to be in the front line of the devolutionist campaign.

The rest of this paper addresses the question of why devolutionism as a managerial strategy is so widely supported despite its unproven efficacy and its insidious political partisanship. I argue that devolutionism has become desirable and possible because of the conjuncture and linking together of three factors, each of which contributes to the discourse and practices through which it is produced and reproduced. The three factors are economic rationalism, systems theory and cybernetics, and information technology.

Economic Rationalism

After the 1980s, economic rationalism needs little introduction or comment. Based on a celebration of the market, it advocates minimal regulation of all forms of capitalist activity. Like other ideologies, is a combination of discourse and practices. The discourse provides meanings which enable the practices to be developed and the practices provide a 'real world' which generates experiences that becomes topics in the discourse and serve to validate it.

In Australia the deregulation of the labour market and the privatization of public sector activity have been the issues central to the main battle fronts. Proponents of labour market deregulation wish to replace centralized industrial relations mechanisms with labour contracts based on enterprise, small group or individual bargaining. In Australia as elsewhere New Right activists argue that workers should be as independent from the encumbrances of formal organization as possible and that this independence should be achieved through subcontracting, franchising and payment based on piece work and/or incentive payments. These proposals are put forward as being democratic because they give each individual more 'freedom'. However, they also have the effect of dividing workers, setting them in competition with one another rather than in conflict with the organization's managers. Devolutionism captures the thrust of these proposals and their rationale as it aims to replace institutionalized relations between management and organised labour with fluid relations between management and small groups or individuals.

Similarly, from its election in 1983, the Hawke government adopted strategies of change in the public sector which include 'enhancing Cabinet solidarity, introducing performance contracts, centralising budgets and detaching managers from their departments' (Yeatman 1990: 37). From the Cabinet down, there has been a new devolutionist emphasis on economic rationalism and on corporate management. This form of organization replaces bureaucracy with the quasi-market mechanism of incentive structures and rewards based on product (performance) rather than process (Considine 1988). As Head (1988) argues, corporate management was introduced into the Australian public sector in concert with the rise of economic rationalist ideology which also served to legitimize the new management principles.

Devolutionism's links to economic rationalism can be seen in the former's antecedents as well as in the current discourse: for example, some time ago Williamson (1975: 145) advocated that the M-form organization ought to be regarded as a miniature capital market, while more recently Blandy and his co-authors have linked 'structured chaos' to the market, writing that:

'Deregulation induces apparently chaotic, but highly innovative, services in place of lumbering moribund monoliths. Policies that work through market mechanisms are more likely to sort winning from losing innovations than [are] government attempts to 'pick winners'.' (1985: 92)

Systems Theory and Cybernetics

The overt application of cybernetics[2] to the study and design of organization started with Beer (1959), although two years earlier Kaplan (1957) had already advocated applying systems theory[3] to problems in international politics. From 1961 to 1968, US Secretary for Defense McNamara attempted to apply a systems approach to the organizational and military problems of his department and during the same period a noted organization analyst, Simon, also gave qualified support to the use of cybernetics and system theory, writing that:

'Metaphor and analogy can be helpful, or they can be misleading. All depends on whether the similarities the metaphor captures are significant or not. ... The ideas of feedback and information provide a frame of reference for viewing a wide range of situations, just as do the ideas of evolution, of relativism, of axiomatic method, and of operationalism.' (1962: 467)

These theories continue to be relevant to the study of organizations, even when discussed critically (see, for example, Baker 1973; Magnusen 1977;

---

[2] Cybernetics is the study of control mechanisms in systems, and is said to be as basic a science as physics. As Beer (1959) puts it, physics and its related sciences are interested in how an embryo uses energy to grow, while cybernetics is interested in how it uses information to control its growth to become a rabbit rather than something else.

'Cybernetics has to do with feed back and control in all kinds of systems. Its purpose is to maintain system stability in the face of change. Cybernetics can not be studied without considering communication networks, information flows, and some kind of balancing process aimed at preserving the integrity of the system.'

[3] General systems theory is concerned with understanding how the properties which systems exhibit arise from the relationships between their component parts (their subsystems). For example, the noise of an internal combustion engine is an emergent property of the dynamic interaction between its components: the noise can only be understood in this way and not found by dismantling the engine into its components. The analytical focus is on the relationships between subsystems, rather than on the subsystems themselves. Hence it is methodologically appropriate to consider each subsystem as an internally closed 'black box' provided that all its relevant functions (its output or response for each possible input or stimulus) are known. The axioms and theorems of general systems theory are held to apply to all classes of systems, be they living or non-living, physical or social, mechanical or cybernetic.

Burrell and Morgan 1979; Morgan 1986). More recently, however, initial claims that these are global theories which could be applied to any, including organizational, problems have been modified and at present these theories are usually seen as metaphors which may inform, or add discursive legitimacy to, organizational descriptions and prescriptions.

There is a strong functionalist tendency in cybernetics and the well developed parts of classical systems theory (that relating to relatively simple systems). Although this tendency has led many organizational sociologists to reject these theories, it seems to have made their conclusions and prescriptions (if not their theoretical complexities) attractive to managerial organization practitioners and their ideologues.

Observations derived from cybernetics and systems theory are frequently imported into organization and management literature and into consultants' reports as self-evident propositions, with their intellectual antecedents not made explicit. For example, Williamson says that in M-form organizations 'the whole is greater (more effective, more efficient) than the sum of the parts' (1975: 137) without identifying this as a characteristic of systems and notions such as the desirability of feedback, information and adaptability are bandied about with little recognition of their cybernetic bases.

Yet at least some organizational professionals have formal training in these fields. Starting in the early 1970s, tertiary education institutions sought to establish degree status for computing studies (or, as it was often called, computer science). Systems theory and cybernetics were introduced into the curriculum as an academic buttress for practically oriented training in the craft of programming and system design, resulting in a steady flow of systems-knowledgeable computing professionals into the practical world of middle management.

As a result of these influences, the conventional wisdom of senior organizational practitioners has come to include the broad outlines of cybernetics and systems theory, even though many of these practitioners may not be aware of the theoretical bases of their practical reasoning. The process started in some (mostly large) organizations in the 1960s and has since become widespread, following the proliferation in the 1980s of computing professionals and 'cook book' management advice in popular management books, journals and even radio programs.

Cybernetics and systems theories have contributed to the discourse and practice of managerialism primarily through their functionalism, the associated denial of the importance of power to organizational form and their emphasis on the regulation of discrete system components through the control of the stimulus/response environments within which they operate.

These characteristics of systems theories have led to an emphasis in systems design on the construction of incentive structures which will elicit from discrete system components the required behaviour and an associated minimization of overt regulation. Early examples of this approach are the USA Health Maintenance Organizations (HMOs). In HMOs clients make annual contracts with a medical clinic for all necessary medical treatment in the next year. The clinic thus has an incentive to encourage clients to adopt health-maintaining life styles and to avoid over-servicing — the opposite incentive structure to that supposedly produced by fee for service for medical practitioners plus health insurance for clients. In the organizational context, this emphasis on appropriate incentive structures supports and provides a rationale for devolutionism.

Information Technology

It is now well recognised that technologies do not necessarily determine social practices, social organization or social structure. This recognition has led diverse scholars to respond to Braverman's pessimistic analysis (1974) by insisting that information technology has the potential not only to enhance the experience of work but to be an instrument in its democratization, although this will not be easily achieved (Child 1985; Muetzelfeldt 1986; Greif 1988). The enthusiastic adoption of IT technology over the last decade, however, has been explicitly stated by managerial strategists implementing it to have been motivated by expectations of productivity increases and cost savings. In practice, many expected benefits have not materialized in administrative work (cf. Bowen 1989; Warner 1989; Franke 1989). That they had previously failed to materialize in the 1970s did not inhibit further computerization in the 1980s and current experience may well still not lead to critical re-evaluation. The reason for this uncritical acceptance of lower than expected 'pay offs' from the introduction of IT is that this technology carries with it a powerful cultural load which has the capacity to involve organizational workers as well as decision-makers in its use (Hill 1988; Muetzelfeldt 1988; Webster and Robins 1986).

Information technology is inserted into organizational life in both material and discursive ways. Materially, it provides the potential for a wide range of data to be gathered, stored and processed, so much so indeed that 'data overload' can become part of the explanation for the lack of productivity benefits. When this technology is used judiciously, however, it makes possible the production of highly selected and processed key information from the data. The crucial point of systems design is that it provides the ability to confidently identify which selection and processing of the data will generate the pertinent information and to whom and in what form that information should be made available. It is here that principles from systems theory and cybernetics, as selected and applied by those in control of organizational structures, come into play. The synergy between devolutionism and the three conceptual fields of systems theory, cybernetics and economic rationalism, and the status of each as a major and legitimate part of the conventional wisdom of the dominant culture, tend to mean that management information systems are designed in support of devolutionism, even in cases where there is no overt intent to use them in this way (see Dunford and McGraw 1988 on the need to avoid simplistic voluntaristic or structuralist explanations in situations like this). The result is that a devolved organization form appears, giving 'devolutionism' as a doctrine a material reality through the use of information technology, which then confronts people in the organization as an objective fact.

IT technology also has a strong discursive presence in contemporary culture, particularly in discussions about the future of work and organizations (see Forester 1985 and 1989), and for a critical review, Roszak 1986 and Webster and Robins 1986). The debate over whether information technology will centralize or decentralize social life and whether it will work for or against democratization, is the debate most relevant to this paper. Its most notable discursive feature is the unrestrained optimism of the post-industrialists. For example, Dizard confidently forecasts 'a viable technology-powered democratic society' (1982: 15), a claim that finds an echo in the supposed democratic thrust of economic rationalism.

In contrast, Webster and Robins (1986) convincingly argue that although this debate is cast in terms of the technology providing choice between centralization or decentralization, the proffered choice is no more than a rhetoric behind which centralization is proceeding. They suggest that:

'... current discussions of I.T. which emphasise a freedom to choose in fact positively delimit genuine choices being exercised, since they so obscure realities.' (1986: 80)

The combination of the centralizing material reality embedded in information technology with the discourse of democratic decentralization which surrounds it is a powerful force behind widespread acceptance of devolution as the 'best' organizational form for the 1990s. However, as Howard (1985) demonstrates, despite the outward form of 'user participation' in the introduction of 'user-friendly' computers into the white-collar workplace, computerization brings no fundamental change to the underlying relations between workers and the organization. Workers still have no effective control over the details of their work or the hierarchies within which they work, let alone over the wider purposes which their work is designed to further. Indeed, computerization provides a technology for detailed performance monitoring which can extend the organization's surveillance of work patterns, giving it a new tool for control (see also Shaiken 1985).

Howard goes on to argue that computers can be used to mask this maintenance and extension of control, giving the appearance of autonomy and responsibility to workers. Similarly, Webster and Robins (1986) argue that information technology provides centralizing reach and control to corporate capital and the means for pseudo-decentralizing of work within a framework of centralized surveillance and control (1986: ch. 11). Quoting Barnet and Müller (1975), they say that 'it is a deceit, a cruel mystification', where a 'decentralizing ideology masks a centralizing reality' (1986: 153).

Howard (1985) argues that in the large corporations he studied this masking is achieved through 'corporate culture' strategies. White collar workers can, however, be persuaded to accept a pseudo autonomy and responsibility, even in organizations where there is no corporate culture program. I have argued that this acceptance relies on the broader cultural force of this technology, especially its ability to import into the workplace the ideology of consumerism and the sense of identity which goes with it (Muetzelfeldt 1988).

Conclusion

The symbiotic relationship between the discourse and practices of economic rationalism, of cybernetics and systems theory and of information technology have provided motive and means for the rise of the doctrine and practice of devolutionism. The motive comes from the conjuncture of the prevailing ideological force of economic rationalism which suggests a particular path for organizational and societal reform with the appeal of the instrumental rationality promised by systems theory and cybernetics and the discourse of democratic decentralization associated with computerisation. The means are provided by the techniques of incentive structures and systemic control which again derive from the tenets of economic rationalism and cybernetics, together with the technologies of the information systems and computers which are used in implementing these techniques. The compound effect is to generate a constellation of discourses and practices which appeals powerfully to many and diverse groups and interests. Consequently the devolutionists, like the post-industrialists before them, count among their number analysts normally thought of as being from the political left as well as those from the political right, and are surrounded by a large force of pragmatically oriented troops.

Part of the reason for this hegemonic consensus lies in the difficulties which devolutionism throws up for established analyses of power; yet it is precisely the analysis of power that should provide analytical purchase for democratic critics. To illustrate these analytical difficulties, consider the matter from the perspective of strategic contingency theory. Hickson and his colleagues (1971) argue that 'organizations do not necessarily aim to avoid uncertainty nor to reduce its absolute level, ... but to cope with it' (1971: 220). The assumption that organizations are made up of interlinked subunits, and that the necessary coping will be done within these subunits underlies this theory. Power is seen as being exercised by those subunits that can best cope with uncertainty and best control contingencies.

Within the devolved form of organization this strategic contingency conceptualization is turned on its head in a two-fold way. First, uncertainty – or, at least, certain types of uncertainty – is no longer seen and treated as just a problem to be coped with, to be effectively dealt with (Hinings et al. 1974: 29). Rather, it is seen and treated as also being a resource to be mobilised. It certainly remains the case that within devolved organizations the subunits are expected to prevent, forewarn about and absorb uncertainty but it is equally the case that this work is seen as providing motivation, challenge and satisfaction for people in the subunits. The task of coping with uncertainty has been replaced by the mission of working at its management. In the cliche of the times, the creators of the new organizational form aim to change uncertainty from a problem (for the organization as a whole) into a challenge (for the subunit).

Secondly, and in a structural sense more importantly, instead of the control of uncertainty being viewed as solely a function of subunits of the organization, it is now also viewed as a function of the interfaces between them. Indeed, the very practice of designing devolved organizations consists precisely in constructing those interfaces in such a way that particular types of uncertainties become the focal concern of subunits. Power thus no longer resides in the subunits which can best cope with uncertainty and control contingencies but rather in the design of the interfaces and with those who control that design. The organization is no longer conceptualized mechanistically as a set of components and the exchange relationships mediating between them. It is now conceptualized systemically as a set of interfaces that constitute and structure the practices of the components. In other words, an organization is seen as primarily constituted by the interface relationships, rather than by the component subunits. As a result, power also has to be conceptualised in terms of the interfaces.

Organizational interfaces are primarily channels for the regulated flow of data. The primary explicit task of many organizational subunits is to receive, process and transmit data but all subunits, including those where data processing is not their primary task, are monitored through these data flows. Foucault's notion of power as panoptic surveillance is appropriate here (cf. Webster and Robins 1986: 343-347). Devolutionism combines a mechanism for surveillance with incentive structures designed to win compliance. Clegg may well have had devolutionism in mind when he wrote:

'[Disciplinary] practices are not simply constraining: they do punish and forbid, but more especially they also endorse and enable obedient wills and constitute organizationally approved forms of creativity and productivity through a process both transitive (via authoritative externalities such as rules, superiors, etc.) and intransitive (via the acquisition of organizationally proper conduct by the member).' (1990a: 192)

If democratic critique is to keep up with contemporary changes in organization, it will need new analytical tools such as these concepts of power to regain a purchase on the new organizational forms that now surround us. Established concepts of power are inadequate for the task: they merely ensure that analysts, together with workers, are co-opted by devolutionism.

Section Four
Innovation and Disillusion:
Firms at the Leading Edge

Introduction

Jane Marceau

In the previous section of this book, three chapters focussed on the search for control in the emerging productive system. One traced the conflicts between large firms, users and vendors of the new technology, arising in the search for an open standard or supranational interest in the developing 'factory of the future' in which computer-integrated manufacturing is expected to play a central part. The second pointed to the rise to prominence in firms focussing on quality in their manufacturing process and products of a new professional, the Quality Manager, but also traced that development from longer-standing policies for control of process and workers. The third discussed 'devolutionism' as a new form of organisational control.

The present section is in part a continuation of the theme of control while also emphasising the importance of culture and organisational form for successful innovation. The first chapter emphasises *conflict*, the clash of cultures which sours relatonships, stifles creativity and encourages employees to move elsewhere in the aftermath of mergers and takeovers. The second, in contrast, tells the story of an organizational success. There, problems of balancing control and creativity, financial prudence in a high risk area and leading edge R & D by persons of world-class scientific reputation have been solved through the creation of a new, cell-like, organisation structure. Potential conflicts are contained through the considerable attention and resources devoted to devising, maintaining and continuously improving organisation practices which inculcate respect for individuals and their ideas, which foster excellent communication flows and fast learning and which integrate human resources management with technology strategies. All these strategies aim to keep the firm operating at maximum capacity, in the forefront of its new and fast moving field, that of biotechnology. The philosophy and practices combined to give the company concerned the foremost place for a time among dedicated biotechnology firms in Europe. It must be added here that the company has recently faced problems. The story of its organisation, however, loses none of its interest as a story of innovation in organisational design.

The fields in which the companies described in both chapters operate are leading edge, fast moving, hi-tech, covering computer hardware, software and technical documentation in the chapter by Garnsey and Roberts and biotechnology in the paper by Dodgson. Small firms in these fields are the prototypes of the hi-tech companies run by scientific whizz kids which often dominate business media headlines and journal stories and which have also been the subject of considerable attention by both academic analysts and the public policy community. It is this sector which has been seen as both the heartland of sunrise industries and the location of the regeneration of entrepreneurship through the creation of new businesses by young scientists with bright ideas who find the hierarchical structures of their seedbed universities or large companies too constricting. It is these companies, in short, which have often been thought to be the wave of the future, creating products and processes which will mean that in future industries may never 'mature' but can constantly be renewed through scientific and technological advance. Such companies in such areas have thus been given a key role in re-working the productive world, both in terms of products devised and the renewal of the industrial structure through the birth of new firms created by a new breed of scientific entrepreneurs.

It is becoming increasingly clear, however, that this population of new firms is one which is highly unstable. As I have written elsewhere (Marceau 1990), they are subject to forces in the market place which make it likely that many will be taken over or will merge, while a few will become large firms and themselves spin-off new firms or create sub-contracting relationships with their smaller *confrères*. These larger firms in the same area may, of course, suffer the same fate as their smaller neighbours and themselves be taken over. Even those which remain independent, or apparently so, will find themselves operating within considerable constraints generated by the large firms which dominate the manufacturing sector as a whole in all industrialised countries. The products of new technologies are too important for large firms to leave their development and manufacture to 'chance' and large enterprises are too powerful and too acquisitive to leave lucrative market untapped. Moreover, large firms, using the very technologies created in part by the small ones, are now in a position to invent new productive structures and to create more flexible organisational forms while still retaining control. Already major firms are developing a variety of 'intrapreneurship' (Pinchot 1985) schemes to encourage innovative managers to remain in post while the firms themselves are reorganising to create new structures. These new structures span traditional firm boundaries and, amoeba-like, reach out and absorb, albeit in many cases temporarily, or join forces with others more innovative or specialised in new fields. Thus, as Child in a 1987 paper suggested, they are creating new forms of hierarchy, semi-hierarchy, coordinated contracting, coordinated revenue links, joint ventures, co-making and spot-networking as interorganisational responses to new market challenges.

In other words, the hi-tech sector is a very active and volatile one, one in which firms, operating in an environment of constant change, sometimes of quantum leaps, must continuously seek out new opportunities, promising avenues of research, new development directions. Scanning the environment, detecting changes and sifting masses of information, becomes a top priority for successful enterprises.

The whole field, however, is too big and diverse for any individual firm to master, or even to scan adequately. Moreover, it is also too expensive to follow up every good idea. Established firms, therefore, frequently seek out firms which have already made important advances in areas significant to the scanning firms' business or complementary to it. Where they find such enterprises, especially smaller ones, they often buy out and merge in the smaller entities. In this way, the purchasing firms acquire expertise (people) as well as products and processes.

Such buy-outs may be hostile take-overs or may be desired or even volunteered by the smaller companies. For their part, staff in the smaller companies, especially the founders, soon discover that a good scientific idea may demand more entrepreneurial, commercial and managerial time and skills than they either possess or wish to devote to work not directly concerned with research and development. They may also feel the need for considerable investments of capital if their work is to go ahead satisfactorily and the company is to expand to take advantage of new opportunities. In such cases the small company believes that it will find some security as well as new skills and complementary activities and welcomes the takeover or merger.

Neither side, however, in such cases seems always to be aware of the organisational issues involved in the merged ventures. Often they do not take sufficient account of the very different motives for the acquisition and sale which dominate the expectations of post-merger activity on each side. The small company's R & D focus, need for capital and relief at finding extra managerial resources often mesh poorly with the acquirer's desire to integrate product development, reduce overheads and rationalise plant and laboratory locations. As Garnsey and Roberts show, even where the advantages to each side look obvious initially, the clash of organisational cultures is often deep-seated and impossible to overcome, not least because neither understands the other's viewpoint. Line managers of larger corporations, accustomed to hierarchically organised and regular reporting and accountability and to decision-making from the top down, often fail to understand completely that what the scientist entrepreneurs whom they have taken over felt they wanted was precisely the reverse: freedom to pursue their scientific and product development tasks supported but untrammelled by managers concerned more with financial control, marketing or product rationalisation. These contrasting expectations are, of course, only magnified when the two parties to the merger are from different national cultures, speak both different tongues and different corporate languages and view the world from geographically as well as commercially different perspectives.

Thus, in a very stimulating chapter, Garnsey and Roberts carefully document the processes and problems of three different mergers. All the cases involved small, hi-tech or ancillary (technical documents) product-making companies being merged with larger, more complex, although in most cases equally hi-tech, firms. They trace out the genesis, development and outcome of the ensuing cultural clashes which ultimately left each side feeling that it had gained little from the partnership or merger ventures and which in some cases seriously depleted the scientific personnel of the merged company. Each case demonstrates how difficult it is to reconcile divergent interests and expectations and, especially important, to maintain the flow of ideas and production which made take-over of the smaller companies initially so attractive to the larger. Equally, the cases show how little additional commercial and financial support in fact became available to the managers of the acquired firms who tended to focus only on what they saw as the constraints imposed by the bureaucratic management of a company whose range of interests and both geographical and managerial horizons were much broader than those of the small firms. What was rationalisation of activities to some managers was simply seen as reduction in resources, power and job interest by personnel closer to the operating face. The first chapter in this section is thus a cautionary tale.

The second chapter, in contrast, is an exemplary tale. It tells the story of the strategy of a science-based firm to ensure that it is ahead in a highly competitive field, a strategy so successful that the company has become a world leader, not only in its products, but also in both strategic and organisational terms. Using, as seems obviously appropriate for a biotechnology firm, a 'cell' structure, the company concerned, Celltech, has devised an organisation which links resource management, project management and ideas teams in a matrix structure to ensure that proposals which pass each carefully designed decision gate are both well thought out and properly supported. In stark contrast to the larger firms discussed by Garnsey and Roberts, Celltech's organisation grew out of the felt needs of the scientists working on R & D and was foreshadowed, guided and implemented rather than dictated by senior management. Again in considerable contrast to the practices in the companies described by Garnsey and Roberts, Celltech takes care to recruit scientific personnel on the basis of their long-term, fundamental scientific skills rather than their immediate usefulness for particular projects, thus engendering security and commitment to re-invest-ment in those skills by the persons concerned. In the case described by Garnsey and Roberts, the attrition of the research and development scien-

tists crucial to the long-term success of the enterprises was directly attributable to the fear that the staff would have no security once given projects
were finished. Similarly, Celltech provides proper long-term career structures in the R & D field, thus discouraging scientific personnel from feeling
they must transform themselves into managers to rise in the hierarchy, a
problem faced by many organisations, including schools and hospitals,
which employ highly-skilled technical staff but reward them less highly
than their line managers.

Finally, Celltech engaged actively in boundary spanning, developing
collaborative relationships with the big players in its field (in this case
multinational pharmaceutical firms), providing services to them while also
improving its own scientific base. In this way, the company, equipped both
with its own innovative, supportive and successful management structure
and high class technical staff, was able to maintain its independence and
financial viability in a fast-moving and highly competitive field.

From his analysis based on involvement extending over a two year
period, Dodgson is able to conclude that the company illustrates good
organisational practice in circumstances of rapid change. He also concludes,
however, on a note which emphasises the importance for the development
of similar hi-tech companies of a supportive surrounding institutional
(financial) structure with a culture which values long-term investments
rather than short-term returns. The success of the hi-tech entrepreneurial
business recipe, especially as it resides in smaller companies, will greatly
depend on the provision of such institutional support. This, at least in most
Anglo-Saxon industrial countries, will involve a considerable change in the
culture and ethos of controlling financial institutions.

Perhaps the lesson from both chapters is, in other words, that the
production of advanced technologies will not be able to proceed smoothly
without a major change in organisational cultures both within the majority
of larger and more predatory enterprises and their smaller firm *confrères* —
since the small ones will in the end have to be financially viable as well as
scientific powerhouses — and in the other institutions which play an
important role in all productive structures. Just as the Chinese mainland's
cotton spinners seeking to transfer Japanese technology to a society which
offered no institutional support and no cultural sympathy found that the
technology failed, so a similar technological failure may take place in the
West without proper institutional support and sympathetic understanding
of both the risks involved and the rewards to be reaped in the longer term.

Clashes of Technology and Culture: Enterprise Acquisition and the Integration of New Ventures

Elizabeth Garnsey and John Roberts

Introduction

This chapter examines the acquisition of small firms by large corporations concerned to buy their innovative products and capabilities. Small firms in volatile advanced technology markets are quick to seize opportunities and adept at innovation; they are also highly vulnerable to competition and chronically short of resources. Often independence cannot be substained and entry into a corporate group through acquisition may appear to be the only viable option. We use evidence from three recently acquired UK firms to examine the difficulties entailed by the clash of cultures to which an acquisition typically gives rise.

As the market for a new product or service matures, the small firm finds itself increasingly disadvantaged in relation to its better resourced competitors (Schumpeter 1939). In principle, potential reciprocal benefits from liaisons between the large and small firm are considerable, offering wealth to the founder-owners, access to international markets and the resources necessary for R & D. For the larger firm, acquisition may appear to be a way of gaining for itself a leading edge product or service and an R & D facility with further innovative potential.

In practice, however, a number of serious problems arise in integrating the new venture, no matter whether integration is attempted through loose or tight coupling. We focus on cultural clashes generated in three areas, which can be isolated for purposes of analysis, though in practice they are closely interrelated. The first concerns the compatibility of products or services between the two companies. We find that the internal market of the large corporation creates pressures which may overwhelm the small unit and reduce responsiveness to external market needs. This is more likely to occur when respective 'technological cultures', the climate and ways in which technology is developed and applied, differ significantly between the two companies. Technological development may differ, for example, with respect to adherence to industry standards, and R & D may be more or less open to user-input. Differences in technological culture, including the autonomy and perceptions of members of R & D teams created serious difficulties for the integration of our case study firms within larger corporations.

The second, and related, area of difficulty for integration involves the procedures and style of the large and small companies concerned, which in its simplest terms can be seen as a clash of entrepreneurial and corporate culture. The introduction of inappropriate controls, cumbersome reporting procedures, formal accountability and tedious routines can stifle the innovative capacity which the new parent company set out to buy and drive out technical staff with irreplaceable skills.

Finally, because many take-overs are by foreign or multi-national corporations, there is a confrontation of national cultures which can make for confusion and distrust in day-to-day interaction. Moreover, the institutional differences between countries can result in serious differences in strategy and style between corporate parent and acquired venture.

Inevitably these difficulties frustrate expectations and affect the gains actually realised on both sides from an acquisition. Although these is no simple formula for resolving such problems it is important for those involved in an acquisition to be alert to the issues and to recognise the importance of the cultural aspects of the process of integration, which are more subtle and intangible than the quantifiable dimensions of integration planning.

Methodological Approach

We illustrate our analysis with material from studies of three recently acquired UK companies which we call Micro-Computers, Techno-Documents and ISD (later Dynamic Computers), a CAD company which pioneered the industry standard software. In all three cases what we term anti-synergy (a coming together to mutual disadvantage) was the initial outcome of the investment: the performance of the acquired unit was impaired and the large company expended a disproportionate amount of time on the problems of integration without improving its capacity for innovation. In each case this outcome was not to be anticipated when we began our study. The case study methodology which we used involved relatively close contact with members of the small venture before and after the take-over. The evidence presented here is based on at least 30 hours of interviews, talks and meetings with members of the companies over a period of two or more years. The aim of the research was to obtain interpretations of their own and the collective experience of the take-overs from participants, who played a variety of parts in the companies' acquisition. Each case is unique but each illustrates critical dimensions of the problems with which we are concerned and issues of general importance can be identified from a comparison between the cases. It goes without saying that not all acquisitions give rise to negative synergy but to explore cases of this kind is to uncover important aspects of an increasingly common phenomenon.

Three Chronicles of our Time

The theme of cultural incompatibility emerges from the accounts participants gave us of the events leading up to and following the acquisitions. Problems of product or technology integration, of organisational incongruence and of clashes of national culture were described by participants, and confirmed from much other evidence. The acquisitions cannot be understood without reference to the entrepreneurial history of the firms in question. In presenting the case studies we reveal the impact of constraints on outcomes in such a way as to show how subjective experience both shapes and responds to objective circumstance. Subjective experience provides the motivation for action, and in this respect a cultural analysis has considerable strength in making sense of action from within, from the perspective of the actor, rather than viewing action from without as a set of behavioural trajectories. Our cases, however, also explore other constraints on action, which did not derive merely from the perceptions of actors but shaped the outcomes. This approach allows our analysis to escape from 'the dualism associated with objectivism and subjectivism' (Giddens 1984: xxvii).

Case I: Micro-Computers

The Start-up

Micro-computers Company Ltd., founded in 1978, was one of the first of the entrepreneurial high technology firms to reach the attention of the public. Developments in microelectronics made it possible to produce a

computer without the capital costs of large mainframe production. Rudimentary products had already been launched on the market; the British
consumer was innovative and tolerant and prospects were promising. Two
computer specialists, Schmidt and Dunn, the one with academic research
experience, the other with some commercial experience, joined forces with
the aim of setting up their own company. They were convinced that it
should be possible to produce a powerful personal computer, to professional
standards but available at a reasonable price to the ordinary consumer.
They worked with staff in a Computing Department so, although not a
direct academic spin-out, the company was closely associated with a leading
university.

Micro-Computers started as a 'hole-in-the-wall concern', described as
'shambolic' by the first professional manager to be taken on. All the
company had initially by way of financial controls was a drawer full of
cheque stubs. The founders kept the figures in their heads. The focus was
on the technical challenge: moving on the development work was what
counted.

Micro-Computers might have been just another small computer company
had it not been for Dunn's eye for market opportunity. He heard in time
that the BBC was planning a computer literacy course and that an inexpen-
sive computer was to be commissioned to be available for purchase on the
market. The course would demonstrate computing on this product. The
designs for Micro-Computers' latest model could be adapted to meet the
BBC's specifications, which were demanding ones at that time. Dunn
succeeded in having Micro-Computers invited to tender for the contract.
Schmidt recalled: 'The BBC asked to see the prototype on Monday. We
worked through three nights ... I fed the team tea and biscuits ... after a
final panic over the internal clock we had it up and running on Friday'.
The authorities at the BBC were sufficiently impressed to award Micro-
Computers the contract, an unusual one which consisted of the right to
bear the BBC emblem and to function as the demonstration model on the
BBC computer programmes. Effectively, the BBC provided a new market
in return for royalties. This was an enormous coup for a small venture but
it also required that members of the group transform themselves overnight
into a serious company and themselves into serious managers of it. The
market expanded twice as fast as initially predicted when in 1982 the
Department of Education and Science announced the 'Micros in Schools'
scheme and the BBC model became the top runner among the models
approved for schools' use. Micro-Computers' market was increased not
only by the expanding educational market but by purchase by private
consumers, often parents buying for their children.

Micro-Computers recruited four professional managers between September 1981 and January 1982 to take charge of manufacture, sales and

technical functions. This formalised the authority structure of the company but in practice Micro-Computers remained a company without many middle management positions. This seemed desirable to retain the impetus and creativity of the place. The unintended consequence was a lack of experienced management and lack of on-the-job management training in the company.

Consolidation?

By April 1982, Micro-Computers had firm orders for 25,000 machines, more than double the volume forecast by the original market research, and demand was increasing rapidly. From the start Micro-Computers had contracted out production work to specialist electronic assembly firms. The subcontractors initially chosen proved unable to manufacture the required volume of machines to an acceptable standard and quality problems were only resolved by employing a new subcontractor.

Micro-Computers formed its own subsidiary to handle the distribution of the BBC microcomputer and to deal with the backlog of orders which had built up. The BBC model continued to sell well throughout 1983 both to educational establishments and consumers; a new product was due to be launched in August 1983 as a cheaper version of the BBC micro for home use. Things seemed to be going well.

In September 1983, 10 % of Micro-Computers' equity was placed on the Unlisted Securities Market (USM). This enabled the company to set up subsidiaries in the US and West Germany and finance further development work. Problems with the new chip, however, delayed the launch of the new model which failed to achieve the important Christmas sales in 1983. Production of the BBC model could not be speeded up beyond the availability of component supplies. Demand for microcomputers was so high that rumour had it that customers were buying machines off the delivery vans before they reached the shelves. Competitors benefitted from demand deflected from unavailable Micro-Computers' products and the press abounded with stories of disappointed customers.

Further expansion of the market seemed certain since, for example, early in 1984 the high street retailers were showing interest in placing large orders for Christmas. Thus encouraged, the Board of Micro-Computers decided to bring forward production and build up stocks throughout the summer. In order to finance production, Micro-Computer negotiated credit arrangements with the subcontractors and deferred payment to them until the autumn.

Looking back on the summer of 1984, Schmidt commented 'We were congratulating ourselves. We'd got it right: quality, delivery: one success after another. We were really flying high. You really think you can do anything after that ... We saw the need for a professional M.D. at some stage, but there was no urgency'.

Declining Demand

By the autumn it was clear that demand was considerably lower than had been anticipated. Orders from the multiple retail chains in August and September did not meet the sales forecast. The finance director pointed to disquieting figures but he was viewed as a pessimist whose reports were 'too boring to read'. Soon, however, Micro-Computers' machines were being returned by the giant retailers. The company instructed the subcontractors to slow down production but, as Schmidt put it, 'Production just kept on pouring out. There was no way of stopping it'. Micro-Computers was committed to orders placed with the components suppliers by their subcontractors. Ominously, some big retailers began to discount prices.

Sale or Collapse

Late in 1984, the four executive directors, realising that action was required to save the company, made an attempt to reorganise the company into four market-oriented divisions. 'But we were too busy chasing our tails to develop anything like a strategic plan', the finance director later reflected. Each function was carried out without adequate coordination from the centre. Schmidt and Dunn had to acknowledge the crisis and by the end of the year they announced that they were the wrong people to be in charge. A new non-executive director became acting Managing Director early in 1985 and assumed responsibility both for this reorganisation and for cutting staff from 450 to around 300. By January 1985, sales were 35 % below the April 1984 forecast. Early in 1985 Micro-Computers' weak financial position and high levels of unsold stock were made the subject of a series of articles in the national press and these alerted creditors to the company's precarious postition.

Earlier in the year attempts to arrange a refinancing deal with a major British electronics company had failed, to the relief of the founders who did not welcome that particular alliance. The Thatcher government pursued a hands-off industrial policy, despite the fact that public sector demand had set in motion the hectic pace of growth at Micro-Computers. In February, the threat of receivership was looming and shares on the USM had been suspended. Micro-Computers' new merchant bankers began to search for a large partner.

Informatico had at the time a corporate policy of investing in small companies with promising technologies. After a period of intense negotiation Micro-Computers signed an agreement with Informatico, which took a 49 % share in the company. At the time Informatico did not wish to become closely involved in the management of Micro-Computers but by September 1985 it became clear that sales targets agreed between the two companies had been missed. 'By this time there were excuses to paw all over Micro-Computers. There were ten, sometimes it seemed a hundred, Italians in every week', Chris Angle recalled from his early days as M. D. A second round of refinancing was eventually implemented. By September 1985 Informatico had acquired 79 % of Micro-Computer's shares, having paid a total of £ 14.4 million.

The Reckoning

The account of the winning of the BBC contract at the beginning of this case reflects the ethos of technical achievement and the excitement which characterised Micro-Computers as a group to work with. Early success against considerable odds had created an atmosphere of pride, achievement and collective commitment. Even when crisis loomed in the autumn of 1984 the founders were confident that their record of success could be kept up. The founders still owned 85 % of the company and were able to override the advice of their divided managers.

When disaster finally struck early in 1985, members of the company were thus unprepared for the struggle ahead. The founders left; Dunn to another venture, Schmidt to take on responsibilities for technical development at Informatico. Before leaving they had at last appointed an experienced Managing Director in the Canadian, Chris Angle, who replaced the previous M. D. Angle faced an uphill struggle in effecting the transition from independent company to subsidiary of Informatico and his two years spanned the most difficult adjustment period for Micro-Computers. In coming to the company from outside the computing sector he had both to win the confidence of his staff at Micro-Computers while at the same time forging links with Informatico which would enable Micro-Computers to benefit from the world-wide resources of the Italian-based company.

Informatico and the Micro-Computers Investment

'Informatico saw the potential for taking the technological skills and speed of movement of a smaller company with high-technological capability (and Micros UK was seen as being a source of that), as being something that would be advantageous to the group; the group had already got to the point of being somewhat large and relatively dinosaurian in its approach to things. And secondly the experience of IT in education was seen as being a very strong plus and something which was potentially reproduceable on a European-wide basis'.

This account by a senior Informatico manager is supported by other versions of events. Thus it appears that Informatico had two major reasons for the acquisition. Micro-Computers had 80 % of the UK educational market and, with other European governments funding information technology in education, it was hoped that this market share could be achieved elsewhere. These market expectations proved unfounded.

'Informatico were being over-optimistic about the possibility of the educationalists in Europe seeing the implications of Micro-Computers' tremendous success story, ... of using Information Technology within schools and assuming that it could just be picked up and reproduced, albeit in foreign languages, across the board throughout Europe ... They found the educationalists just did not want to know'.

In retrospect this was entirely predictable: Micro-Computers had been successful only in educational markets in countries which had some cultural affinities with Britain, notably Australia and Canada. There had been no success in the German educational market. (Here there was a marked contrast with the CAD industry where the INTERACT software from Cambridge proved successful in gaining from the German government subsidies to its engineering industry to introduce Computer Aided Design, before the Germans had produced a product competitive with INTERACT.)

The other major incentive leading Informatico to acquire Micro-Computer was, in principle, sounder. In the eyes of some at Informatico, Micro-Computers was worth the price simply as an R & D team. There were over a hundred development projects underway at Micro-Computers, where producing for the future had from the start been a major priority and a way of attracting leading technical staff to the company. Micro-Computers' R & D offices were located in a Californian high-rise building overlooked Palo Alto, the information centre of Silicon Valley. Their head commuted alternate months between California and the UK. Thus Informatico had acquired an R & D team which was at the forefront of developments in operating systems, microchip developments and user-interface. Major projects underway included development work on the still revolutionary RISC chip technology, a new micro-computer operating system with wide applications and interactive video development.

Early Integration Problems

Like any major corporation Informatico was not a unified entity. 'Basically, Informatico is no more than particles in Brownian motion', one technical manager reflected. 'I had to tell myself every day: 'There is no such thing as Informatico', Angle recalled after he left the company. Beyond this apparent randomness, it appeared to some that there were identifiable forces in Informatico. In the UK branch of Informatico there was support for Micro-Computers' new developments. There were two major Italian camps; those committed to new technical developments, mainly in the small strategy group of Informatico, and the more cautious operational groups in the company, which favoured standard, well-proven technology. This division within Informatico shaped the diverse reactions to Micro-Computers in the new parent corporation. The main structural problem facing Micro-Computers was the absence of processes for integrating their innovative products into the main operating branches at Informatico.

Angle was remarkably effective in gaining the confidence of staff at Micro-Computers and in introducing professional management procedures. He introduced a matrix structure of the kind he knew worked in large engineering companies. During 1986, sales to the educational market continued to grow and there was an operating profit of £1.4 m on a turnover of £46.7 m. In the dark days of 1985 the rapid and powerful RISC chip had been made functional, a success which in Schmidt's words 'restored our souls'. Later IBM was to go for RISC technology and this endorsement raised interest at Informatico in Micro-Computers' development work. As Micro-Computers' financial position improved there were renewed hopes for product development and morale among staff rose again. But persistance was needed in the struggle to gain acceptance and support at Informatico. In the course of this struggle not only Angle, but also the four technical managers who had sucessfully led the team throughout Micro-Computers' eventful early years, departed.

Angle was as unsuccessful in building links with Informatico as he was successful in gaining his staff's confidence at Micro-Computers. Indeed, his style of open democratic meetings and his insistence on sticking to what he viewed as firm commitments were interpreted as inflexibility and a lack of subtlety by some of the Italians, 'They could never believe when I said

ABC that I meant ABC'. It did not occur to Angle to post an agent by
the coffee machine in Italy and set up lines of contacts within the operating
branches of Informatico. Micro-Computers managers encountered warring
camps in Italy and both the style of interaction among Italians when
disputes came into the open and the abuse of subordinates struck the
British team at times as an Italian tragi-comedy which they could not
interpret. Angle relied on the Informatico representatives who sat on the
Micro-Computers' Board and it was some time before he realised the
implications of their failure to promote Micro-Computers's products within
the operating branches of Informatico.

Informatico's own financial performance in 1987 was disappointing and
pressures on Micro-Computers to keep out of the red increased. The timing
was bad: capital investment was urgently required for the launch of the
new personal computer and for development of a UNIX workstation
designed as competition for the highly successful Sun Microsystems product. The support from Informatico was not forthcoming. Collaborative
work on interactive video development had to be dropped for lack of
support from Informatico. 'Micro-Computers had paid the bills while the
BBC and Philips got the credits,' reflected one of the dismissed managers.
It was felt that Schmidt did not help to generate support for Micro-
Computers within Informatico, 'He'll go round an Italian lab and say 'Oh,
yes, we had people doing much better work than this at Micro-Computers'.'

Angle found that the Informatico men from the strategy group with
whom he was dealing had failed to liaise with product planning branches
and that he was being accused of failing to inform Informatico of developments at Micro-Computers. Angle felt he had to take a stand as performance figures at Micro-Computers deteriorated again in 1987. With the
limited funding Informatico was offering he maintained that it was impossible to develop both the 'Sun-beater' workstation and the new personal
computer simultaneously. He was dismissed 'for insubordination' in December 1987.

Integration: The Long Haul

Informatico has been unique as a major international electronics corporation in the extent to which it has acquired shares in or otherwise undertaken joint ventures with small high technology companies, which were
'incubated' by the strategy group. Micro-Computers was unique in many
ways but not least in that Informatico owned 80 % of its shares. Micro-
Computers took up an enormous, indeed a disproportionate, amount of

top management time at Informatico and the question of a successor to Angle was a serious matter. It was decided that a senior Informatico manager who was also an Englishman should take charge of Micro-Computers in place of Angle in 1987. Despite these advantages, the new man, Humphries, also met with difficulties in gaining acceptance for Micro-Computers' new product development. Some managers in the Informatico operational branches clearly resented an upstart British company jumping over them with new products.

Humphries, the new M.D., felt that the structure of Informatico was the main factor militating against the integration of Micro-Computers' development work. Micro-Computers had to struggle on its own to promote its powerful new micro-computer and develop the next model. Humphries believed that Informatico's operating branches had no incentive to introduce new products based on Micro-Computers' work. Fortunately, as Humphries saw it, a change in Informatico's structure was carried out in 1988. As a result of this change,

'the strategic company disappeared and a series of operational companies was set up which embraced the investments made by the strategic company. We therefore became part of an operational company. And the operational company set out very pragmatically to find the synergy between it and the investments.'

Humphries was optimistic that under the new Informatico structure, in which each operating company has senior managers charged with introducing innovative products, Micro-Computers would receive much more support. In the event, however, he himself was moved to another international branch of Informatico in 1990.

Opportunity Costs

Whatever ultimately transpires in relationships between parent and subsidiary, the wasted potential represented by the failure of integration between the companies over the first years of life together represents a heavy opportunity cost. The lack of effort devoted to software development at Micro-Computers was the most serious failure but it was not perceived in the struggle for recognition and resources in which Micro-Computers managers were engaged.

'It should have been possible for Micro-Computers to develop software applications but this required the commitment of significant resources. Angle did not realise that software development was critical and Informatico was not interested in providing the necessary resources',

one of the technical managers reflected after his own dismissal from his post late in 1987.

For a variety of reasons, the market opportunities provided by the BBC model were not followed up. 'The British have no sense of loyalty to their own products, unlike customers in other countries, and especially public sector customers elsewhere,' a Micro-Computer sales manager remarked, 'Hewlett Packard is currently developing the British market in university workstation equipment which under another scenario might have been Micro-Computers'. Meanwhile the British balance of payments deficit indirectly but inexorably reduced resources available for educational spending.

Some of those who were at Micro-Computers in the early days have argued that it would have been preferable to allow the company to go to the wall rather than to sell out to Informatico. If Micro-Computers had died, these opponents of the acquisition hold, there would have been rebirth through local start-ups developing ideas from Micro-Computers' advanced R & D projects, including interactive video, which instead were slowly stifled within the corporate grasp of Informatico. The rejoinder to this argument centres on the resource problems of new companies, not on the undeniable propensity of Cambridge to engender new ventures. Throughout the difficult period, staff turnover at Micro-Computers was remarkably low. New concerns have spun out from the company, though fewer than might have occurred without the take-over.

Scepticism on the gains from the take-over is found on both sides. 'What has Informatico gained from acquiring Micro-Computers?' 'Nothing. Nothing. I don't think Informatico has got anything out of it,' was the wry response of an Informatico manager four years after the acquisition. He went on to reflect that

'The easiest thing would have been to divest ... But Micro-Computers is a unique company in Europe. In the end it may have been worth the effort for European industry. But it's been a long haul!'

Case II: Techno-Documents Ltd.

Techno-Documents Limited was founded in 1982 by James and Helen Andrews. The company specialises in providing technical documentation, computer manuals and allied computer services to clients. During the first five years, the company created value of over £ 3.1 m, having started with zero capitalization. This case study traces developments over this period, focussing on the acquisition in 1988 by CSC (which itself merged with the French company Ordinex in 1989 to form the second largest computer services company in Europe, Ordinex Group plc). We present the perspective of Helen Andrews in particular from Techno-Documents Ltd. and MS, formerly Managing Director of the CSC Group, who was instrumental in acquiring Techno-Documents.

The Techno-Documents case illustrates the realisation of an opportunity for pure enterprise initially free of the need for outside capital or expertise. The Andrews started up on a freelance basis doing consultancy work and avoided the pitfalls of early dependence on outside capital. The achievement of the founders was to draw strength from weakness.

'We made a virtue of our ignorance. I said to my clients: the less I know the better. Your people can explain to me how your client can get the most out of the equipment and we can produce really clear documentation for you.'

This disingenuousness, coupled with a flair for design and presentation and careful attention to detail, paid off. The market proved buoyant. Contracts with clients big and small enabled the Andrews to take on more technical writers and designers and the company expanded to 20 employees in four years.

An Unexpected Opportunity for Realizing Value

A lawyer representing CSC knew that the Group was on the look-out for promising acquisitions to extend the range of services provided by CSC. Helen Andrews was approached to see if she would consider selling to a corporate group. Entry into the CSC Group appeared to be too good an opportunity to forego. The firm needed capital but she knew that the problems of other small companies had not been solved, and in many respects had even been exacerbated, by flotation on the USM. Moreover, it would cost a minimum of £ 250,000 to float their company. It was clear that the CSC group favoured decentralisation and the members of the group were given considerable autonomy. The price CSC were prepared to offer was very good, amounting all told to over £ 3 million. After years of intense effort negotiating short-term contracts under conditions of extreme uncertainty the prospect of financial security was like being let off a tightrope. To be allowed autonomy and to keep her staff together, to retain the integrity of her venture and yet benefit from the experience and market capacity of a larger group seemed an ideal solution to the company's problems. The CSC Group had recently embarked on a set of edge-out acquisitions and had shown itself highly successful both in its own activities (profits were up 40 % in the last year) and in integrating new acquisitions. The alternative was to look for a corporate parent in PR or advertising or a computer company but it was clear that the company's strength was in combining the technical and the creative and not in pursuing one line at the expense of the other. CSC provided a range of computer services for which Techno-Documents' activities appeared to represent both extension and complementarity. The CSC corporate style and culture, decentralisation and encouragement of innovation appeared highly congruent with Techno-Documents' company style. To the founders the prospect of financial security on the terms offered was highly attractive and the proposal they could offer to their staff meant that share options and the prospect of career advancement in a larger corporate group could be used to improve motivations. Moreover, they saw the prospect of new markets opening up via CSC's extensive client base.

CSC and the Acquisition of Techno-Documents

We can now consider the reasons leading the chief executive of CSC to acquire this small company, Techno-Documents. For Daniel Brown, the CSC Managing Director, as for Helen Andrews, there was an element of chance in the encounter of large group and small firm. Daniel Brown had been at CSC since 1963 and seen it grow from seven people to several thousand. The company ran into difficulties, however, in the late 1970s. By 1980 most of its reserves had been wiped out and the managers had to turn to venture capital to refinance the company. The financial backers required the resignation of the founder and placed Daniel Brown in charge as M. D. He found it necessary to divest the firm of all loss-making activities and to return to the core business. By 1981 the company was out of the red and by 1985 the track record was good enough to allow flotation on the stock market, which was required to refinance the venture capital obtained prior to 1980. Market capitalisation of £25 m enabled Brown to embark on development through edge-out acquisition into growth areas in computer service activities. There was, it appeared to Brown and like-minded colleagues, no option but to grow through acquisition. The computer services industry was becoming more complex and concentrated and it was necessary to grow and to acquire if only to avoid becoming a target for acquisition. Moreover, the industry was becoming international and to obtain access to offshore markets it was necessary to pursue a policy of coordinated diversification through acquisition. Brown's first success came in 1986 when he acquired a Glasgow engineering consultancy firm, which had a subsidiary (400 employees) with a large market share in computer systems' provision to the Royal Navy and maritime market. In 1987 Brown succeeded in acquiring the Systems Development department of a privatised public authority, which had 150 staff, skilled in managing data networks.

In comparison, Techno-Documents with 35 or so employees was a tiny concern. Nevertheless, Daniel Brown sensed the importance of its activities.

'As soon as that introduction was made I could see that it fitted very well with our philosophy. What I perceived Techno-Documents as doing was building a friendly interface between computer systems and their users. One of the huge problems with computer systems is that they are often not user-friendly and that the manuals are uselessly written and the user never puts enough money into training people ... It was clear that what Helen had started was something that really attacked this particular problem. It seemed to me that if Techno-Documents joined the group we would offer our clients a much broader service, we could offer them this back-end service which would bring in more revenue to us and would make the system more serviceable, more acceptable to the client. It was a service which would hopefully differentiate us from our competitors because they weren't doing this.'

Thus Daniel Brown saw Techno-Documents as performing a function of vital importance despite its small size. It had a good track record, having doubled its turnover every year, reaching £360,000 in 1985, and had high price to earnings ratios. For this reason Brown was prepared to pay as much as £3.1 million upfront for the company, with £1.9m promised as an 'Earn-Out' incentive for meeting future profit targets. The earn-out clause was designed to defer some of the payment and to retain the management team in place. From the Techno-Documents perpective it had the advantage of ensuring that for at least an initial period unwelcome interference from the centre would be minimised and that incentives to staff could be provided. The deal was settled late in 1986.

In April 1987, Techno-Documents' profits for the previous year stood at £260,000, turnover had increased and, with new market opportunities opened up by entry into CSC, profits looked set to rise further.

Integration: Hopes and Outcomes

'We were still at it at five o'clock on Saturday morning, signing the deal. Nine o'clock Monday morning it was back at the coal-face. There was no holiday period.'

For the founders of Techno-Documents, the euphoria of pulling off the sale was soon dissipated by awareness that efforts could not let up if the new targets were to be met, if Techno-Documents was to prove its worth and justify CSC's latest investment in its expertise. The Andrews aimed to include their staff in the benefits of membership of the Group through share options and the earn-out agreement, phased over three years, offered the incentive of another £1.9 m to be shared with staff as and when profit targets were met. This, however, required Techno-Documents to increase profits by a fairly substantial percentage each year. Not only would the firm have to continue to expand the volume of business with existing clients but there was also an enormous amount of work to do if CSC's contacts and client base were to be used to expand Techno-Documents' activities. First, it seemed necessary to explain to managers in the other parts of the Group what Techno-Documents could do for them. Daniel Brown's awareness of the importance of high quality technical documentation had to be spread around the Group so that Techno-Documents could become involved in the many activities where there was scope for improving user-interface. This was 'missionary work', as Daniel Brown put it, and here Helen was an evangelist. Helen's efforts at selling Techno-Documents' expertise took her to meetings of senior managers in every part of the CSC group. Her presentations were received with interest at this level. In her first year as a member of CSC she received a great deal of attention at a major conference of the entire group where she was the only woman manager among over seventy senior executives.

Helen Andrews had not reckoned, however, with the difficulties and slowness of persuading middle management, the project managers, the men who put through the orders for documentation and ensured the cheques were signed, of Techno-Documents' utility. This group proved difficult, as Daniel Brown came to realise:

'People dont't see why they should do extra work, as it seems, for Techno-Documents and risk losing a contract by raising costs. There was also some resentment inside CSC at the price we paid for the company. It's not easy to grow that kind of expertise. You probably have to acquire it and you have to pay for it ... But people don't see it the way. People internally who have been working hard for years without that kind of pay-off can get resentful. 'Why should we put ourselves out for you: You've already made a million. Now get on with it'.'

This type of reaction among some CSC staff in other parts of the group did not lend speed to the message of user-friendly documentation. 'CSC itself is a really difficult market because traditionally computer systems people did not care about users' Helen Andrews remarked wryly in 1988 after a year of intense effort and little success at converting other parts of the Group.

Integration Problems at Techno-Documents

These efforts were at the expense of Helen Andrews' usual work drawing in new and repeat business. This and other integration problem took its toll on performance and on custom generated. Even under the changed financial year and reporting procedures it was becoming clear in 1988 that performance figures were suffering. New staff had been taken on in anticipation of new work for CSC; recruitment had built numbers up to over fifty. Techno-Documents was making the difficult transition from small firm where face-to-face interaction was possible among 30 or so people to medium sized firm, where more formal procedures and communication were required, under distinctly unfavourable conditions. The effort of screening, interviewing and training while adjusting to changes in reporting procedures required by the new corporate structure was considerable.

Looking back on the period after the acquisition, Helen Andrews felt that many of their problems were attributable to the earn-out clause.

'There was no way we could reach the targets, they were set too high. To achieve 50 % growth on top of a 50 % growth year just was not possible. Internally people knew things were not going well and it affected morale.'

Helen herself did not enjoy the amount of paper work she was now required to handle. 'I was doing things I hated and don't do well. There was so much figure work, reports, forecasts, order book analysis ... at Executive Group meetings the figures would go up on the screen and I was called on to defend my figures. It was being very exposed to the gaze of the rest of the Company.'

CSC's Merger with Ordinex

From CSC's perspective, the acquisition of Techno-Documents was judged 'only very moderately successful', producing only half the initial results Daniel Brown had expected. In retrospect, he maintained that 'We undoubtedly paid too much for the company.' But he had little time to concern himself with the reasons for this situation or to attempt to remedy it. From March 1988 to March 1989 he was deeply involved in negotiations designed to expand the international dimension of CSC. Contact was made with Ordinex at a conference in France at which companies were presenting themselves to potential investors and, in practice, to each other. Managers from both companies were struck by the match between the two Groups. They were at a similar stage of development, each approaching 3,000 employees, and had a comparable spread of business limited to the computer services industry. The decision was reached to bring the two companies together fully in a merger. Technically CSC acquired Ordinex; it remained a British quoted company, with a flotation on the Paris Bourse. This technical take-over by CSC to set up the new Ordinex Group was preceded by a raid on the group's shares by the large rival computer services group, CSC-Gemini-Sogetti, which gained 15% and later 25% of the new Group's shares. This shifted the balance of share-holding to Paris. The bank which had founded Ordinex increased its shares in the new Ordinex Group to 41% to ward off further raids and by 1989 80% of shares were held in France.

Daniel Brown was struck by the way in which the French management team had built a close and long-term relationship with the bank, typical apparently of companies set up by French banks. This was to strengthen the hand of the French management when the performance of CSC UK, now Ordinex Group, in Britain in the first year of the merger proved disappointing. In the course of deliberations over the membership of the Board and top management teams, Daniel Brown resigned in December 1988, after 25 years with this group, and moved shortly thereafter to Thorn EMI Software. Brown's policy of decentralisation was criticised by the new French management, who claimed that the units of the UK group were out of control, and a policy of central control was advocated by the new French MD, on the model of the American corporation where he had formerly worked.

Consequences for Techno-Documents of the Change in Corporate Structure

Techno-Documents thus found itself caught up in the great forces of concentration and internationalisation sweeping the maturing computer services industry. Changes in UK defence procurement policies hit CSC's performance in 1988 and the slow-down in the financial services market affected demand from this sector. Even in relation to these global developments, changes at Techno-Documents have significance in revealing the contrasting nature of the corporate versus the immediate market enviroment. Instead of gearing themselves to customer needs in the world outside, as they had successfully done in the company's first years of life, members of Techno-Documents became caught up in the organisational world of the expanding Group, with its elaborate reporting procedures and internal markets. The apparent need to sell Techno-Documents' image and pursuade existing members of the Group of the new unit's potential took precedence over raising revenue for independent survival and expansion.

Past and Future

If CSC failed to make the investment in technical documentation services pay off in the short term, it was not for want of effort on Techno-Documents' side. Integration of a new unit, providing new services with a distinctive culture and style of its own, requires effort from both sides but top managers at CSC were too taken up with other matters, and especially with the merger, to involve themselves in the problems of integrating this small concern with the Group at large. Ironically, efforts by Helen Andrews proved counter-productive in the short term because of the absence of effort from the CSC side. Her attempts could only have succeeded as part of a genuine joint venture to make the most of the entry of Techno-Documents into the Group. There is now a growing recognition of the need for activities requiring Techno-Documents' expertise, including consultancy work in user support and training. Though initial results were disappointing, the importance of Techno-Documents' activities had not been misjudged and some successful joint work with other branches of Ordinex has now been carried out. In retrospect, it is possible to see how an approach which had the character of a joint venture in integration would have had immediate benefits for both sides.

Case III: The Acquisition of Interactive Design Co. Ltd.

Introduction

'This is the story of an American Company coming into a British Company and destroying it' was one participant's view of the story told here. The Interactive Design Company Ltd. (IDC) was founded in 1977 but enjoyed only six years of independence before being voluntarily taken over in 1983

by an American CAD company, Newdesign. This acquisition was in part
a defence against an eventually unwelcome bid from Dynamic for ICD. In
December 1987 Dynamic launched a contested but successful bid for
Newdesign Ltd and by this route IDC was finally embraced by Dynamic.
The case is the product of fourteen interviews with existing and former
members of IDC/Dynamic over a two year period. It is intended not so
much as an objective or exhaustive account of events in this period, but
rather as a vehicle for exploring the depth of the cultural divide that can
stand in the say of successful acquisition.

Early Contacts

Dynamic's first contact with IDC was in 1979 when IDC used Dynamic
hardware to develop and run the early version of its 3-D software modelling
system INTERACT. For IDC the link with Dynamic in these early years
meant a lenient attitude towards payment and favourable discounts of up
to 40 % on Dynamic hardware. Dynamic had made the strategic decision
to enter the CAD/CAM market and an internal evaluation of CAD/CAM
software by Dynamic identified the INTERACT product as potentially
world beating. IDC has separate sales companies in the U.K. and Europe
but no access to the U.S. market. In 1981 Dynamic sought and gained the
licence to market INTERACT outside Europe. Although the relationship
took some time to become effective it provided IDC with the source of the
revenues judged vital to its survival as an independent company during
1981 and 1982. Dynamic at this stage made it clear that it would be
interested in investing in or even buying IDC. Although IDC was then
financially viable, there was growing awareness of the need to seek additional finance to support further product development. Dynamic's offer,
however, had the effect of opening up deep divisions amongst the IDC
directors. Initially, various possible alternatives were explored by different
factions amongst the directors. Finally, John Dino, in the role of Chief
Executive, assumed personal responsibility for the negotiations with Dynamic. At the eleventh hour of these negotiations Dino received an entirely
unexpected phone call from Newdesign's Chairman. Dynamic had offered
£ 10 m. for IDC alone and there was the fear that on acquisition the
company would be broken up. Newdesign offered £ 25 m. for IDC and its
sales companies combined and gave a promise of continuing independence
within the corporation. Newdesign Ltd was, however, IDC's main competitor, especially in West Germany, and there was the suspicion that IDC
were being bought out of the market. The IDC Board voted on the rival

bids and split 3-2 in favour of Newdesign. The deal was completed in March 1983: IDC had escaped the hands of Dynamic but now had to find its way in the corporate world of Newdesign.

IDC/Newdesign

For IDC the relationship with Newdesign promised access to the American market and funding for product development. It quickly became clear, however, that Newdesign, having kept IDC out of the hands of Dynamic, had no clear strategy for integrating the enterprise into the parent firm. Perceiving both the dangers and possibilities of this vacuum, John Dino and Dominic Jones (who joined the company and Board in 1982) began a fierce battle to secure and preserve the independence of IDC within the corporation. For both men, their direct and close relationships with the most senior executives of Newdesign Ltd gave them the ability to influence corporate policy where it affected IDC. For Dino, the battle was to prove exhausting and he resigned in 1985 but Jones, as M. D, established himself as a very effective umbrella, shielding IDC from some of the more destructive aspects of the larger corporation.

On the sales side, the IDC sales companies in the UK and Europe were quickly merged with the Newdesign operations. On the sales side the merger caused great disruption in the short term and little obvious benefit over the long term; at the time of the acquisition by Dynamic in 1988 INTER-ACT's pattern of market strength in the UK and Europe was virtually unchanged from 1983. Hopes for the penetration of the US market with INTERACT were similarly disappointed. Attempts to get Newdesign salesmen to sell INTERACT alongside their own CAD product failed completely and only after much struggle did Jones win permission to set up his own independent marketing operation in the USA for INTERACT although by 1988 this was beginning to work very effectively.

On the development side, the relationship with Newdesign was more immediately successful. Despite attempts by Newdesign's middle management to incorporate it, the decision was taken to leave development at IDC alone, subject only to budget constraints. A vital technique for securing this independence was the creation and presentation of IDC as a separate profit centre within Newdesign. IDC's continuing profitability within the corporation allowed Jones to secure generous finance for hardware and new facilities at Newstone. As a result of this independence, the technical creativity of the group continued even after the loss of Dino. The INTER-ACT software was increasingly perceived to be approaching the end of its development life but alongside this a whole new group of products began to be developed.

This continued creativity was not just the product of increased resources; effective independence meant that the unique culture which had developed within IDC could continue to develop and prosper. In the light of subsequent events, several key features emerge. From the earliest days all the development staff had as an integral part of their work very close relationship with their customers. This ensured that development never lost sight of the necessity for commercial relevance. At the same time there was a deep pride in, and concern with, the quality of the product that could and should be released to customers. An attitude of openness was encouraged with customers and built considerable loyalty in the user group. Within IDC the atmosphere at the time was most commonly described as that of a family group, whose members were aware but accepting and tolerant of each others' strengths and weaknesses, with strong professional and social ties. As the company grew towards 100 employees a greater division of labour and a more formal hierarchy became necessary. There was, however, little conventional management but rather inspirational technical leadership. A newly recruited member described the company as 'working like an ant hill' by which he meant that instructions were not required because needs were anticipated through close partnership and shared understandings. Status concerns were apparently almost entirely absent in a group which conceived of itself as being made up of intellectual equals. Problems were resolved through the force of technical argument rather than through hierarchical imposition. Into this open and energetic culture came the news on the 28 th December 1987 of Dynamic's bid for Newdesign.

Dynamic/Newdesign

In 1983, Dynamic, its bid rejected, had been left with the licence to sell a product which was now owned by its major American competitor. In June 1984 a deal was concluded with Newdesign Ltd in which Dynamic purchased for £5m. the source code to its own version of INTERACT. Dynamic then set up its own development group for the product in Baldock in the offices of a company which it had bought in 1983 from a government agency. This group had no experience of INTERACT and attempts to entice staff from IDC were almost entirely unsuccessful. Within Dynamic, the expectation was that Newdesign Ltd, armed with INTERACT and its original development team, would be able to attack Dynamic's market base in the U.S. As we have described above, the Newdesign salesforce would not accept INTERACT and the expected assault on Dynamic never materialised. Although the independent IDC sales force began to have some success from 1986 onwards, by this time Newdesign as a whole was in some difficulty, having reported large trading losses in both 1985 and 1986. During the early 1980's, Dynamic had focussed on the engineering CAD/CAM market as a key strategic area for growth and the acquisition of Newdesign presented itself as an obvious vehicle for gaining customer base and market share. Early overtures were strongly rebuffed but Newdesign's poor trading results depressed its share price, which was knocked even further down by the October 1987 stock market crash. When Dynamic made its final bid in December 1987 Newdesign Ltd was powerless to resist. Dynamic acquired Newdesign Ltd early in 1988. What it perceived as Newdesign's failure to incorporate IDC and thereby exploit the market potential of INTERACT was to be crucial in its own approach to the management of IDC.

IDC/Dynamic

The IDC directors' prior experience of Dynamic meant that the news of the bid was particularly unwelcome. In the initial period of inactivity and uncertainty after the acquisition, Dominic Jones briefly contemplated mounting another battle to secure the independence of IDC within its new corporate environment. As contacts with America developed, however, the impossibility of such a strategy quickly became apparent. Dynamic, convinced of Newdesign's error in leaving IDC independent, made clear its own intentions to integrate it fully within its own strongly functional structure. As a symbol of this integration, the IDC sign at the entrance to the Newstone site was changed in 1988 to read 'Dynamic'. Since it was no longer to be treated as a profit centre, what was seen as the unnecessarily weighty IDC Board was dissolved and the Directors offered roles in the functional structure remote from the corporate centres of power. Few had the taste for, or much hope for the outcome of, another battle to make themselves understood within another major corporation. The financial independence that the Newdesign takeover had given most of them, coupled with the severance packages negotiated for senior Newdesign staff at the time of the acquisition, meant that there was no necessity to keep them with IDC. Most of the directors had left by August 1988. Only one, Nathan Riley, remained as Technical Director, reporting to a newly appointed Site Director and, more importantly, to the Vice President of Dynamic's CAD/CAM R & D in the U.S.

The subsequent history can best be described in terms of a fundamental clash of cultures. The superficial signs of this clash were to be found in the respective unflattering characterisations of the other by each party. For IDC staff, Dynamic was a 'technically dead' company full of conformists. In return IDC staff were variously characterised as 'a bunch of Communists', 'immature', 'arrogant' and 'unworldly' by Dynamic. More soberly, the difference was described to us as being between the mentality of a successful small company and a corporation playing in a global market. Dynamic, by virtue of the acquisitions, was now the number two player in the CAD/ CAM market and saw itself as a marketing-led company playing for global market share. IDC, in contrast, saw itself as market-led development company, relying on close continual contact with individual customers. These competing self-conceptions came into direct conflict when an instruction came down from management at Dynamic in the USA that there was to be no unauthorised contact with customers since this was a marketing rather than technical function. Predictably, the IDC staff reacted with outrage to the severance of this vital contact.

The problems of the merger, however, went beyond mere cultural incompatibilities. Having acquired its own version of INTERACT in 1983, Dynamic now found itself in the position of owning two versions of the product and two INTERACT development centres at Newstone and Baldock. This was seen by Dynamic as a duplication of products, potentially confusing for customers and inevitably doubling overheads and costs. Soon after the acquisition, a task force dominated by marketing was formed and quickly announced its intention of merging the two products, closing Baldock and relocating the staff to Newstone. The effect of this was to bring together two previously rival development groups to work on one project. The Baldock group saw the Newstone group as suffering from an extreme technical arrogance; the Baldock people were seen as routine technicians. The move to the larger Newstone group and the appointment of IDC people to the senior technical management roles left the local Dynamic victors from Baldock feeling as if they had become victims. The merging of the two products threatened at least 18 months of boring technical work for all concerned. Staff were diverted from interesting development work to deal with the priority work of the software merger. There was also a background fear that once this work was completed the future of the Newstone site would itself be a risk since it was now only one development group within one product division of the corporation. At best, so the fears went, it had the prospect of becoming a contract R & D centre for the rest of Dynamic and deprived of interesting work or any local initiative.

Within months of the acquisition, then, IDC staff had seen the departure of all the senior technical gurus and the loss of interesting work and the valued contact and open relationship with customers and faced an uncertain future beyond the completion of the merged product. Staff began to look for work elsewhere and the attrition began. Dynamic managers could not understand the desertion of the team by the senior IDC managers and their unresponsiveness to financial incentives. It was virtually impossible to break into the tight web of loyalties between the IDC staff, past and present, who continued to meet in the pub just beyond the site entrance.

A vicious circle began to develop. As staff left so more people would be diverted from genuine development work to the software merger project, feeding further discontent and departures. Dynamic was itself beginning to suffer financial difficulties and was the target of a leveraged takeover by an American venture capital group, Venture-C. Recruitment of additional development staff at Newstone was prohibited. The timetable for the completion of the merged product began to slip, straining the already difficult relationship between the Dynamic manager in control of the Newstone site and Nathan Riley at Newstone. After six months Riley resigned; his successor was dismissed after just two months. By the time Newstone was given permission to recruit more staff, word was out in the local labour market that it was an unhappy place to be and no-one could be recruited. In the ten years from its founding to the acquisition by Dynamic, IDC had lost no more than a dozen staff. In the fifteen months following acquisition it lost 43 of the combined technical group of 110. Amongst those who left were a group of nine working on a promising new project which was cancelled by Dynamic and who have now set up on their own again. For those who remained at the Newstone site the prospect of the Venture-C bid for Dynamic raised the hope that they might be sold off as a separate unit into more appropriate hands. Dynamic was acquired by another Venture Capital group, J. H. Houston, in the summer of 1989.

The Lessons

In all three cases the acquisition was caught up, at least in the short term, by unintended consequences which resulted in a kind of negative synergy affecting both parties adversely. It is evident that not all acquisitions have this outcome and the question may be raised as to the representativeness of our findings. We must point out, then, that we did not set out to choose cases for their representativeness but selected companies where the products or services were particularly innovative and commercial success had been achieved. Outcomes were not predictable at the time we started on our studies; contingent circumstances inevitably affected developments. The sequence of events was not purely random, however, but rather resembles the kind of unpredictability studied in chaos theory where 'The simplest systems are now seen to create extraordinarily difficult problems of predictability.' (Gleick 1987: 7). In the case of merging of two social systems, outcomes reflect the 'double contingency' of social interaction: as Giddens says: '... the reactions of each party to a process of interaction depend upon the contingent responses of the other(s) ...' (1979: 86). From these cases we aim to gain a better understanding of processes at work which will also be relevant to the analysis of other cases. Detailed qualitative work revealing such processes has not been reported in the literature (Napier 1989).

In the cases studied we set out to describe the real consequences of three attempts to merge social systems through acquisition of companies. Some degree of merger after acquisition is clearly necessary: if the acquired firm is left wholly independent after acquisition then there can be no reciprocal benefits. The requirements for integration depend on circumstances in particular cases. The three new ventures discussed here all required resources but their needs took differing forms: IDC required facilities and autonomy for development work; Techno-Documents' performance under new conditions depended on integration of its activities with those of the new parent; while Micro-Computers needed development funding and adoption of its products by the operating branches at Informatico. Moreover, the appropriateness of tight or loose coupling between acquired unit and parent corporation differs for various parts of the two organisations. In general, however, the greater the degree of integration sought, the greater is the likehood that the distinctiveness of the small firm will be obliterated in the process. If what is being acquired is purely an existing technology then, from the corporate perspective at least, such obliteration may not seem too disastrous. If it is a capability that is being acquired, however, this outcome is considerably more damaging. The assets of the small company are often individual skills and the intangible and precarious group climate that has allowed particular individuals to work creatively. If the effect of integration is to weaken or destroy this climate then individuals' capacity or willingness to work is likewise impaired and in extreme circumstances the 'acquired capital' can simply walk out the door, one of the unintended outcomes of acquisition illustrated to different degrees in the three cases.

The Clash of Cultures

In the introduction we suggested that the encounters brought about by acquisition could be characterised in terms of three related forms of cultural clash; technological, organisational and national. In practice these three aspects of cultural divisions are closely interrelated but they can be separated for purposes of analysis. In the following sections we present an analysis in these terms, drawing on evidence from our three cases. We go on to point out the limitations of a 'voluntarist' cultural approach and the need to address the issue of constraints and power relations in the acquisition process.

Technology as a Source of Culture

Ways of Working

By the term 'technological culture' we mean established ways of working in relation to developing and applying technologies and the outlook which promotes and follows from these ways. Members of development teams create and routinise procedures which from past experience they know to be effective when put to the test. To the extent that routines can be relied on, they create a sense of security in conditions of uncertainty. Technical staff also develop beliefs in certain ways of doing things 'as a matter of faith, not for reasons that can be objectively defended, though they will put up a defence as if they had good rational grounds instead of a hunch to go on ...' (Chris Angle, M. D. of Micro-Computers, Jan. 1987) People have an emotional investment in technologies they have developed: 'taking your technology to people in the corporation and having it rejected is like having your child's head bashed in.' (M. D. of Micro-Computers, Aug. 1989) The beliefs of technical staff may be well founded; they may also have an element of pride and exclusion, as experienced by the technical immigrants moved to IDC by Dynamic Computers.

Considerable attachment is felt towards approaches which have generated innovative work, as with the RISC chip at Micro-Computers and modular computer architecture at IDC. Such attachments are not easily relinquished with acquisition but instead become the basis of opposing group identities. Similarly, in both Micro-Computers and IDC there was a clear commitment by those concerned to their own style of working. Both groups took pride in the diversity of their work, seeing the company as a seedbed of new ideas. In both companies this diversity was eventually restricted by the corporate parents and in this respect the apparent resource richness of the parent turned out to be illusory. Much of the pride and interest of the staff seemed to come from a sense of working at the forefront of technology. The technical staff at IDC and Micro-Computers were depressed at the prospect of becoming merely another development arm of the parent company, restricted perhaps to contract research that was generated by remote instructions elsewhere in the corporation, or doing merely routine support work on existing products. As a manager at Micro-Computers said in 1989, 'It is anathema to a good development team to have to work on someone else's technology that they don't really have confidence in ...'

There can be a lack of affinity between research and development work carried out with care and energy in an atmosphere of trust, such as occurred in the early days at Micro-Computers and IDC, and a corporate setting in which development groups compete with each other for work and where, in the corporate mind, it is believed that innovation can always be 'bought in'. Pride and interest in customer contact, which would constantly feed and inform development work within the firm, was part of the climate at both Techno-Documents and IDC. Such contact was clearly felt to be vital to survival by members of the young independent companies. When they became part of a larger group the internal world of the corporation seemed to become more vital to survival and closeness to customer needs less important than awareness of internal politics.

The Problems of Industry Standards for New Technology

The contrasting requirements of leading edge work and conformity to industry standards can be a major source of tension within organisations concerned with research and development. In part this may be an outcome of the very maturation of the market which stimulated the acquisition. Micro-Computers, for instance, had to abandon development work on a new operating system in favour of the UNIX system since creating a new non-standard operating system had become unrealistic as the market matured. This provides an example of a constraint which shaped outcomes despite a strong preference by the development team for the in-house operating system, viewed as technically superior to UNIX. Staff at IDC had to accept routine work on INTERACT when they wished to move to new development work; in this case the development team viewed the constraint not simply as the outcome of market requirements but of corporate policy.

If the acquiring company only favours technology based on current industry standards, leading edge work may not be tolerated. As a consequence, whether anticipated or not, the company will fail to be the source of industry standards of the future. The effects of this intolerance may have serious consequences for the retention of staff who need professionally exciting work to motivate them. This is especially so when alternative ventures provide new openings which can lure technically competent staff away from the acquired venture. Both Micro-Computers and IDC lost staff to new spin-out ventures after the acquisition. Significantly, this did not occur during the period of maximum uncertainty and confusion which followed the acquisitions when the solidarity and common commitment which had developed in the early lives of the new ventures kept staff turnover low at both Micro-Computers and IDC. Staff loss became a problem after the consolidation period had begun and the acquiring corporations were attempting to enforce new forms of integration.

Organisational Problems

Cultural problems reflect and reinforce more clear-cut differences such as product incompatibility and divergent marketing requirements. These affect ways of working in innumerable respects. We start by examining differences in outlook which are characteristic of entrepreneurial and corporate cultures and go on to organisational clashes which result from attempts to integrate products and markets.

The Demise of the Early Enterprise Culture

The clash of technological cultures is in some respects an aspect of the clash between entrepreneurial and corporate cultures. In part this is the product of size and functional differentiation. The vulnerability of the small innovative firm is both real and exhausting; acquisition seems to hold out the promise of security. With the achievement of this security, however, some of the excitement of working in the company vanishes and many of the integrative forces of common external threat to survival are lost.

At the same time, the participants' sense that each can make a difference in and to the company also tends to vanish. Action is now caught up in much longer chains of interdependence which are less open to influence and where care is less certain to produce results. A sense of powerlessness and insignificance can begin to infect individual action. The connection between individual effort and group results is increasingly weakened; there is either a loss of motivation or a retreat to a more individualistic orientation to career. As a project manager at IDC/Dynamic put it, 'after the acquisition it was suddenly each man for himself'. In this kind of setting, individual and company success are no longer synonymous. Competition which was previously a force uniting employees in the quest for survival now becomes an internal process, which threatens the openness of communications between groups and functions. The corporate acquisition is seen to have been generated on the basis of the vision of a few key senior individuals, who are themselves vulnerable in the byzantine politics of corporate life. The success of the integration runs up against the entrenched interests of middle managers, who had no part in the decision to acquire and who may well feel criticised, envious or adversely judged by the decision.

Changes in Corporate Structure

Finally, the parent is itself vulnerable to intercorporate competition. Rapid changes in corporate structures reflect wider changes in industrial structure. The founder-owners of Techno-Documents Ltd and IDC, who did not seek acquisition from sheer necessity but as deliberate strategy, were unaware how vulnerable the potential parent was to take-over (or merger) which would put negotiated arrangements seriously at risk. Members of both small companies were to some extent misled by the apparent impregnability of their corporate parent. In general, the acquired company finds that its fortunes are now tied to overall corporate performance in which profit and return on capital are dominant concerns. Both Techno-Documents and IDC found themselves in new and unchosen hands whose views of their desirability did not match those of their predecessors. In Informatico, divisions between the strategic and operational groups and the caution of the operational branches in making new product choices left Micro-Computers exposed. The interorganisational struggles within Informatico, which resulted finally in a major restructuring of the Italian company, were not initially understood at Micro-Computers.

New Products, Marketing and Organisation

In the area of new product development there is considerable overlap between organisational procedures and technological culture. A company like IDC was very much geared to user-input and to frequent iterations between technological development and user-response so there was no predetermined development route. Indeed, some would see in this the secret of their innovative success (von Hippell 1989). The technological culture of user contact and attention to users' current requirements is quite different from that found in a corporation aiming at a mass market with a standard industry product where a launch date is set which dictates the development route. Thus new pressures are brought to bear on the development team, from within the corporation rather than from user demand.

Techno-Documents tried to move from an approach dominated by cus-tomer needs to one where they would be less hard-pressed and have more control over the terms on which they produced their products. These hoped-for results of entry into a corporate group were not achieved, however. Instead, it was agreed by staff at Techno-Documents and at corporate headquarters that '... they are now working much much harder and to less effect because they are less tied-in with outside customers.' (Ordinex man-ager, Nov. 1989) Once a small company loses touch with the outside market during the adjustment period when it can become fully absorbed by the organisational world of the new corporate parent, there can be serious difficulties in re-establishing ties with outside customers. There are very rapid changes in the wider market and increasing competition as the product matures. Improving performance after this has occurred can be difficult to achieve even with the threat of divestment hanging over the management team.

Integration: Mechanisms and Procedures

To overcome objectively identifiable integration issues such as product incompatibilities and disparate marketing objectives, which affect the organisation of work in innumerable ways, demands considerable reciprocal efforts at integration. In these three cases there was no vision of how synergy could in practice be achieved. Though the acquired unit had ambassadors to speak for them in high places, the word did not appear to reach the appropriate operational levels. Even when it did so, overt hostility was encountered. No mechanisms for easing the integration were set up and there was a marked absence of open dialogue on ways of achieving synergy and overcoming the negative impact of cultural differences.

Procedures which were standard in the large corporations concerned were imposed at an operational level in the acquired company and required administrative efforts directed towards forecasting, monitoring and reporting in the smaller unit. These changes in accountability and procedure are no mere formalities: they entail the disruption of unwritten as well as formal rules guiding procedure and bring about important changes in the allocation and use of resources. In other works, they bring about changes in social structure (Giddens 1984: 16). In the case-study firms, these structural changes detracted from the capacity to get on with meeting user needs. As we have seen, the acquired unit became caught up in the organisational world of the large corporation to an extent which reduced capacity to anticipate and meet user needs in the market.

National Differences

Style and Institution

There are number of ways in which national differences seem to affect the success of integration. National differences in style and institution add a further level of potential confusion and misunderstanding to an already difficult situation. Differences in style, often mentioned by members of the acquired venture, are especially difficult to pin down but they include the ways in which networks of support are built and meetings conducted. Chris Angle's alleged failure to 'post an agent at the coffee machine' to gain support for Micro-Computers within Informatico is symptomatic of wider differences between Italian and Anglo-Saxon cultures in the creation of personal networks. British managers at CSC were struck by the way in which networks were used in France:

'French managers at Ordinex wear the emblem of their Grande Ecole on their lapel. They pick up the phones and the deal is done. They are not used to having to fight for custom the way we have to ... They are so high-powered; in comparison the British old boy network is just a gin-and-tonic brigade.' (Ex-CSC manager 1989).

The conduct of meetings also shows marked differences across national cultures. Chris Angle ran meetings at Micro-Computers in Quaker-style, eliciting support for major decisions on a consensus basis, a lengthy process but effective for maintaining solidarity within Micro-Computers. He did not attempt to build personal support within Informatico and 'anyway, without knowing how Italian meetings are run, he would have been completely lost in Informatico', as an Informatico manager reflected in 1989.

Some difficulties which were attributed by participants to national differences in style appear to have arisen rather from the clash between corporate and entrepreneurial cultures. Some of the complaints by members of IDC about the ways in which Americans conducted business were generalisations about procedures in a corporate environment, viewed as American by British former academies working at IDC who had little exposure to the ways of large corporations, whether in the UK or the US.

Differences in institutions which were relevant in these cases included the contrasts in educational institutions which made it unrealistic to expect Micro-Computers' success in the British educational market to be achieved in other European countries. The US capital market made Newdesign and Dynamic more vulnerable to take-over than equivalent Italian or French corporations would have been. Managers at CSC did not initially know the strength which the French management team could gain from their close links with financial institutions; the British management team had no support from their bank equivalent to that provided by Paribas. When conflicts arose between Ordinex and CSC managers over the constitution of the top management team in the newly merged corporation, French institutional arrangements worked in favour of the Paris team and the British manager who had acquired Techno-Documents was forced to bow out.

Distance

Difficulties which members of the acquired venture attributed to take-over by a foreign concern were also in part the results of the effects of physical distance. Distance has both benefits and costs to the acquired unit. One implication of distance, as we have seen, is the imposition of new impersonal forms of accountability through routines and corporate reporting procedures. There is no longer the ready availability of easy face-to-face contact with decision makers. The trust that proximity allows is replaced by the distrust of distance and difference. But distance can also provide welcome degrees of autonomy; the corporate centre simply does not have the knowledge to impose a detailed control upon day-to-day activities within the acquired firm. IDC clearly benefitted from the distance of Newdesign in this respect. The other side of this distance, however, is the difficulty of building up personal contacts and the lack of control or influence within the Corporate group. Corporate ignorance can make the acquired unit prey to damaging and insensitive decisions made on purely financial grounds for lack of detailed strategic knowledge.

Distance can also make it easier for inaccurate reciprocal stereotypes to gain currency and momentum in place of any serious attempts to recognise and reconcile real differences. It requires staff with a good knowledge of both cultures to overcome national stereotypes.

'I'm fairly sure that initially you could have divided people down the middle inside Micro-Computers — those who saw Informatico's entrance as being the saving of the company and other people who resented it because it was a foreign company. Also ... we do have images of people and I believe that the British image of the Italians was one which didn't actually work very success-fully — it didn't work towards making that a successful marriage. One of the things I've regularly had to try and get over to people is that Italy is actually more than just the South which is where most of the images come from.'

Experience, Action and Outcome

We reflect briefly here on the uses of the analysis based on the notion of a clash of technological culture, organisational culture and national culture in exploring acquisition and integration. There are some dangers in conduct-ing this form of analysis. We recognise the implications of Bateson's re-minder that such categories are 'merely abstractions which we make for our own convenience when we set out to describe cultures in words. They are not phenomena present in culture but labels for various points of view which we adopt in our studies.' (Bateson 1935). Indeed, because the various aspects of culture are so closely interrelated, the convenience of our categories is itself in question. For example, we found the culture of technology indistinguishable from organisational culture in some respects. We found confusion between national and organisational sources of difference: corporate procedures were equated with national characteristics of management in the parent company even where this was questionable.

In addition to the problem of interpenetration of categories, an analysis focussed solely on culture could give undue prominence to subjective experience; a voluntarist approach can neglect objective constraints on action which are an unmistakeable feature of organisational life. We have attempted to avoid a one-sided emphasis. Thus our aim has been to present the case studies as a basis for a dynamic perspective which explores ways in which objective conditions shape subjective experience and action stimulated by this subjectivity becomes embodied in forms of organisation and production. Thus, for example, the shortage of resources in the new venture focusses the efforts of the team and their perceptions of the need to make common cause for survival; this can enhance the creativity of the group and here constraints prove enabling (Garnsey and Roberts 1989a). The perception that many resources are available to buy in further innovative capacity may give rise to cavalier treatment of the acquired team by managers in the large corporation. These are examples of objective conditions shaping subjective interpretations and giving rise to further action. The case studies also show how decisions based on subjective experience have objective outcomes; for example, managers from the corporate centre tended to view uncooperative behaviour by members of an 'upstart' acquired unit as 'insubordination' rather than as adherence to a different set of values to which their sense of professional integrity had committed them. These differences of outlook resulted in the dismissal and resignation of managers at IDC and Micro-Computers and the shelving of new development work. On the other hand, the sense that the acquired unit has unique qualities, albeit of unquantifiable future value, explains in part the amount of time certain corporate managers were prepared to spend on the new acquisitions.

Relations of Power

We hope that we have been able to offer some illustration of the value of a cultural analysis of the process of acquisition and integration. In our experience, the implications of the cultural nature of differences encountered are seldom acknowledged by participants. Even where some participants do understand that cultural differences are part of the problem, relations of power encourage those in the acquiring corporation who propose to deal with differences by imposing terms rather than working towards reciprocal understanding through dialogue and experiment. This is particularly the case where the takeover is hostile and subsequent events carry overtones of success and failure or victory and defeat.

Sources of legitimate authority and the symbolism of power are very different in the large and the small company. The external vulnerability of the small firm often serves to generate a sense of interdependence as a source of power within the company, while the power of the large corporation in relation to the external world allows the internal proliferation of different and often antagonistic functional and hierarchical interest groups. These differences then work through into the process of acquisition. Staff in the large company, believing in its power, expect that ownership should be followed by conformity to its ways and are accustomed to the imposed resolution of difference through hierarchical authority. In contrast, although the corporate parent has legal ownership of the new venture, it does not necessarily have legitimacy in terms of the norms and values of its members. Staff in the small company see recourse to hierarchy and the use of sanctions to impose terms as 'playing politics' and as the cause of the ultimate weakness of the large firm. They locate the source of this weakness in the large corporation's use of promises, threats and sanctions to advance or hold back individual careers in order to impose conformity on its members, practices which destroy members' capacity to innovate. The corporation thus has to buy in innovation but perversely sets about stifling the creativity of the acquired group. Our analysis indicates that the integration of the large and small firm, the finding of appropriate forms of interdependence and autonomy, cannot be realised merely through imposed terms. Cultural differences reveal that each brings different sources of power, different capabilities to the relationship. If these are not recognised the ensuing relationship is likely to be mutually destructive.

Conclusion

There are, as Bateson showed fifty years ago, a limited set of possible modes of interaction when two cultures come into contact with each other, which range between complete autonomy and complete assimilation

(Bateson 1935). When a knowledge-based unit enters a larger corporation, the autonomy may work in the short run but in the longer term is unlikely to meet the requirements of the acquiror. Complete assimilation on the other hand is accompanied by the disappearance of the innovative characteristics which provided the rationale for the acquisition. A new culture for the acquired unit, compatible with the needs of both parties, takes time to develop and can only be realised when both parties are committed to working effectively together.

In the introduction we stated that under certain conditions instead of reciprocal benefits, acquisition could bring about mutual impairment. We did not set out to provide a categorical statement of conditions required for successful acquisition. Instead our evidence provides further demonstration of the unpredictability of outcomes in social systems (cf. Gleick 1987 p. 7/8). The conclusions we draw are in the nature of general provisos, identifying factors which can affect the potential for synergy. 1. Acquisitions of knowledge-based ventures by foreign corporations are susceptible to cultural conflict of various identifiable forms. 2. These conflicts can become increasingly serious if interaction sets in motion a cycle of misunderstanding, leading to action on both sides which increases distrust. 3. The disparity in resources encourages attempts by members of the larger corporation to impose terms, but this closes channels of communication and can exacerbate distrust. 4. Open communication, on-going dialogue and experiment with new forms and procedures are necessary to improve mutual understanding of values and conventions. 5. If the innovative culture of the new unit is allowed to remain intact the acquired asset is preserved, but this may not be compatible with close integration. 6. Whether close integration is needed depends on contingencies of market and function. 7. Close integration calls for the emergence of a new culture in which certain central values and objectives are shared, a process which takes time and commitment from both parties.

Notes and Acknowledgements

We are grateful for time and assistance offered to us by members of acquired and acquiring firms. This research was supported by Barclay's Bank and The European Foundation for Entrepreneurial Research. The interviews at the micro-computer company were carried out with the collaboration of Vivien Fleck. A version of this paper has appeared in the volume of proceedings of the conference on Emerging Growth Companies, Paris December 1989, edited by S. Birley and published by Elsevier in 1991.

Strategies for Technological Learning: New Forms of Organisational Structure

Mark Dodgson

Introduction

Many industrial companies are currently confronted by a period of turbulence and uncertainty engendered by the rapid changes taking place in their competitive and technological environments. We are in what Klein (1977) might call a period of 'fast history'. New and pervasive technologies, such as information and communications technology, have already profoundly influenced industrial structures and emerging technologies, such as biotechnology and new materials, have the potential to do the same. Many firms have found that in order to comprehend the nature of these changes, and to retain and improve their competitive position as a result of them, they have to consider technology strategically (Horwitch 1986; Link and Tassey 1987; Dodgson 1989). The strategies adopted to deal with rapidly changing environments often have profound impacts on the organisational structures of firms.

This chapter[1] reports on a year-long intensive study of a company at the forefront of biotechnology, one of the most rapidly changing core technologies. As an example of a company which has successfully manoeuvred itself into a position to take advantage of the emerging possibilities of biotechnology, it provides a number of interesting insights into the development of strategies and organisational structures appropriate for dealing with rapid change.

---

[1] This chapter is based on Dodgson, M. (1989) *Celltech: The First Ten Years of a Biotechnology Company*, Special Report, Science Policy Research Unit, University of Sussex. The chapter, and the larger report, have benefited considerably from the comments and suggestions of Gerard Fairtlough, Margaret Sharp, Roy Rothwell and Keith Pavitt.

Strategy in Science and Technology-Based Companies

Figure 1 conceptualises the role that strategy plays in linking companies' organisational structures with the environment in the specific circumstances of a science-based company. In this model (based on Chandler 1962 and Snow and Miles 1983), strategy is an analytical tool which can be considered as a filter mediating the complex interrelationships between a company's environment and its internal organisation. Thus strategy is a means by which the links between an organisation's strengths and weaknesses and its environmental opportunities and threats (competitive, scientific, regulatory and so on) can be conceptualised.

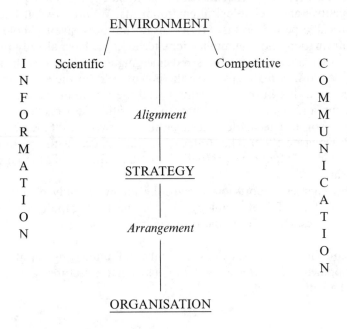

Figure 1   Conceptualising Strategy

The model which sees strategy in this way is also a descriptive model. It describes how, in order to be effective, strategy should be aligned with the competitive and scientific environment. This is a two-way relationship: strategy generally responds to the environment but also can be formulated in order to alter it. Similarly, the relationship between strategy and organisation is two-way. Although a company's structures, capabilities and organisation should be arranged in line with strategy, the model also emphasises that for strategy to be effective in linking organisations with their environment, it is essential that there be suitable information flows into and about the various activities of the company and that these be communicated fully throughout the organisation.

The Technological Environment

Very simply, biotechnology can be separated into two elements: recombinant DNA and hybridoma technology. Recombinant DNA (rDNA) involves recombining fragments of the genetic structure to produce a desired product; this is also known as genetic engineering. Hybridoma technology involves fusing together cells with specific properties such that a desirable protein is produced in large and identical batches; this is often called monoclonal antibody (MAb) technology. Biotechnology is potentially useful in the discovery of new products and processes in the healthcare (therapeutics and diagnostics), agricultural, metal recovery and waste disposal industries. At present it is healthcare applications which have provoked the greatest corporate interest.

Biotechnology as a technology possesses a number of novel and distinctive features. Although the 'new' biotechnology — focused on the engineering of changes to the genetic structures of micro-organisms — incorporates a number of more traditional technologies (Sharp 1985), much of it is new. This novelty means that many of the techniques used in research and application are experimental. It is also a technology which is so qualitatively different from what went before that if cannot easily augment previous know-how and practices. Another important feature of biotechnology is its interdisciplinarity. It integrates a wide range of skills and knowledge, including, for example, in healthcare, molecular biology, microbial and cellular physiology, enzymology, biochemical engineering, separations science, downstream processing and pharmacology.

A recent OECD report examining the economic and wider impacts of biotechnology considered that, although the technology has the potential for inducing very radical change, such change was still some way from occurring (OECD 1989). The report goes on to say, however, that biotechnology would probably become a major basis for new investment and the growth of the economy in the second and third decade of the next century and that in healthcare this would occur much faster. The report's authors considered that biotechnology '... will be at the heart of a rapidly growing cluster of new industries and an essential element of competitive survival in an increasing number of established industries' (OECD 1989: 54).

The Competitive Environment

Firms based upon developments in biotechnology — so called dedicated biotechnology firms (DBFs) — began to emerge in the United States in the early to mid-1970s. It is estimated that there are over 400 such firms in the US (OTA 1988) and over 80 in Europe (Orsenigo 1989). The largest DBF, Genentech, by 1989 was a $1.5 billion company. DBFs are significant contributors to the growth of biotechnology; in the US, DBFs conduct the majority of industrial R & D in this area (OTA 1988).

Large multinational pharmaceutical companies are also rapidly developing their own biotechnology interests, either by acquisition or by establishing their own specific R & D departments (OTA 1988). Given their financial strengths — it is estimated that the cost of the regulatory process to gain approval for drugs is around $100 million — and their marketing strengths — a US salesforce can number over 2000 — then it would appear that these firms potentially possess significant advantages over DBFs.

The competitive advantage of DBFs has changed over time (Pisano 1989; Pisano, Shan and Teece 1988). DBFs emerged primarily as R & D organisations, a strategy developed in line with a number of organisational and environmental factors. Scientific discoveries with significant potential for commercial development were emerging in research institutes. These discoveries provided opportunities which were generally not being pursued by large companies, whose managers perceived the novelty of the science and technology as incongruent with their existing competences and highly risky. In contrast, small start-up firms could seize the opportunity to pursue the science of biotechnology as they were inherently flexible and unburdened by existing scientific structures and routines and because they often had the advantage of exceptionally good personal links with leading research institutes. They also benefited initially from the enthusiastic support provided by venture capitalists.

As time progressed, however, the competitive environment began to alter, first with the formation of increasing numbers of DBFs and secondly, and very importantly, with increased interest in biotechnology on the part of large multinational companies. The scientific environment also began to change, with greater clarity in the regulatory and patenting situation and clearer identification of target products. The DBFs, which had originally relied on technological expertise supplied from research institutes, began to develop their own. Their organisational strengths began to include manufacturing capabilities as well as R & D. Just as DBFs were beginning to integrate their business activities downstream, large pharmaceutical companies, whose strengths in biotechnology lay in marketing and often in manufacturing, began to integrate more upstream. In response to the converging interests in biotechnology of large companies, which did not possess the scientific capacities of DBFs, and the increased need by DBFs for financial and marketing support from large firms, a variety of forms of collaborative arrangements were negotiated between the two. This collaborative organisational strategy included a range of contract R & D and contract manufacturing collaborative deals (Hagedoorn and Schot 1988; Chesnais 1989).

The same strategy continues amongst DBFs, although a number of environmental and organisational changes are beginning to affect it. To meet the threat of large pharmaceutical companies' biotechnology skills in R & D and manufacturing and to attempt to realise the full value from the new products that are emerging, DBFs are beginning to identify products which they will themselves develop, manufacture and market. They are thus beginning to complement their existing R & D and manufacturing skills with marketing skills. As though following Teece's analysis (1987), DBFs are accessing 'complementary assets' in order to maximise returns from innovations.

Strategies developed in line with these new environmental circumstances are now determining new organisational arrangements. How effective DBFs will be in targeting those products most able to compete with large firm efforts is something of an open question. It is, however, worth highlighting here the value in biotechnology of possessing a protectable lead through patent position, manufacturing know-how and market presence and this value underlines the importance of quick responses. If being first is the key to competitive advantage, then organisational efficiency and interfunctional cohesiveness are at a premium. Both efficiency and cohesiveness are facilitated by good information flows and communication within the firm. In essence, considerable value can accrue to the firm most capable of aligning its strategy with its environment and arranging its organisation in line with its strategy.

Strategy in an Exemplar DBF

Celltech Ltd. is a ten-year old British, 400 employee, biotechnology company. It is one of the top ten independent biotechnology firms in the world and is, by some distance, the leading biotechnology firm in Europe. In some of its major activities, such as the bulk manufacture of biotechnology products, it is the most advanced company in the world. It is one of the few independent biotechnology companies to have adopted a strategy of attempting to become a fully integrated biopharmaceutical company, developing, manufacturing and marketing its own drugs.

The company has pursued an adaptive commercial strategy to deal with the rapid changes in technology and competition which it faces and to utilise the organisational strengths it has created. Initially, it was intended to become an MAb company but it took an opportunity provided by the recruitment of a leading rDNA team to pursue both technologies. In its early years its managers examined commercial possibilities in agriculture, food, chemicals, metal recovery and pharmaceuticals before deciding to target the last named. The company pursued a drug discovery programme based on the fusion of rDNA and MAb technology in 'antibody engineering' and without obviously identifiable product targets. Potential products are presently beginning to emerge. The company is a prime exemplar of the development of DBFs described above: an original R & D company gradually integrating downstream.

To operate an adaptive commercial strategy effectively the company has also pursued long-term constant technology and human resource development strategies. These strategies have focused on the fast generation and acquisition of technology through organisational structures, employment practices and incentive structures conducive to learning. A key feature of these strategies is their interdependence.

Celltech is highly knowledge intensive, with just under 50 per cent of company turnover spent on R & D and 38 % on labour costs. Over half of Celltech's employees are graduates and one quarter hold PhDs. Three quarters of all employees are under 35 years of age. Developing what Georghiou et al. (1986) call a 'knowledge-base' has been a basic tenet of company strategy. The firm has placed great emphasis on organising its R & D functions to stimulate creativity, on encouraging the acquisition of external technological knowledge and on maintaining scientific excellence. The Research and Development functions are organised on a matrix basis and projects are established and controlled using a systems approach. Scientific excellence is assured through a variety of mechanisms including intensive academic liaisons, a Science Council of leading academics and the provision of distinctive career paths for scientists. External knowledge is brought into the company by these mechanisms and by a strategy of gaining additional benefits from the company's many strategic alliances.

The emphasis placed by senior managers on technology strategy is matched by that which they place on the promotion of good employee relations. The Personnel function is highly active in its training policies and spends a great deal of time assisting managers and heads of department in undertaking the personnel evaluations for each Celltech employee which inform the payment system based on individual assessment. Personnel staff also help to establish quarterly objectives and to assist the formulation of training programmes and the development of career paths. Human resource development strategy and technology strategy are necessarily interdependent (Gattiker and Larwood 1988; Senker and Brady 1989) and in Celltech they are in many ways indistinct. This fusion is apparent everywhere, from internal organisational issues to methods of obtaining the best from strategic alliances (Pucik 1988).

The basis of this company's strategy and competitiveness is fast response to market and technological opportunities. The company has achieved a number of benefits from its 'fast learning' as shown by a number of indicators, including rapid growth in patents and manufacturing capacities. The latter is considered an indicator of technological performance since Celltech is the world leader in the field and is creating technologies which previously did not exist. The company's learning processes apply also to attempts to learn from experience and from failures. Reviews are undertaken of past failures in order to learn from them.

Organisation is an Exemplar DBF

In line with the strategy of fast learning, Celltech has in place an organisational structure designed to facilitate excellent communications and information flow patterns. Much of the theory and practice of these structures derives from the views and efforts of the company's chief executive (Fairtlough 1984, 1985, 1986a, 1986b, 1989). The company organises its creative activities using features of cell structures, essentially the biological activity of compartmentalisation, the partial closure from the environment which allows multiorder feedback to develop between the components of a system. Fairtlough describes a number of features of cells attractive to designers of organisational structures in firms:

— cells are largely self-contained and are densely organised for intensive internal communication;
— at the same time, they constantly communicate with other cells in a complex networking system;
— despite their diversity, all cells live by rigid rules of competition and cooperation set by the larger cellular framework;
— cells are continually evolving. New molecules emerge, new reactions are attempted, new relationships are assessed and either adopted or

discarded. In such trial and error, however, only those relationships that promote the well-being of both the cell and the host organism are permanently integrated into the cellular life.

Using the analogy of cells to describe organisational structures, Fairtlough considers three areas to be important when considering the best mechanism for inducing good internal communications within a compartment. The first is architecture; the physical environment of buildings and layout, which can be structured to assist communication. The second is climate; the ethos and morale of an organisation. A climate conducive to innovation can be attained by openness and respect for individuals (these aspects are considered to require the greatest effort to inaugurate and maintain). The third is systems; methods for consultation and direction of effort. These are more readily designed effectively, and accepted, if the organisation's architecture and climate are correct.

Cells do not exist in isolation and do communicate intensively. Fairtlough believes that organisational compartments should be the same and designed so that compartments should put great effort into spanning their boundaries, actively seeking knowledge from outside. Also important for organisations, as well as for cells, is awareness of the contribution of compartments to the greater whole. Compartments' contributions have to be validated and, if found lacking, may be discontinued. A full description of the many ways by which Fairtlough's cell structure simile accords with practices within Celltech requires more space than this chapter allows. The chapter will instead focus on two features of the company's organisation structures — its systems approach and boundary spanning mechanism.

The R & D Function and the Systems Approach

Systems thinking has underlain much of Celltech's development. Four key systems ideas have been used in particular. These are Checkland's (1981) Soft Systems Methodology; the establishment of coherent systems for managing strategic and operational matters and the development of people; a project management system using a matrix approach; and an approach to external relations influenced by Ashby's Law of Requisite Variety (Ashby 1956; Fairtlough 1989). The project management system is an example of the use of systems in Celltech.

The systems thinking which influenced the development of project management at Celltech was intended to assist the company with three key tasks: the generation of ideas for new products and technologies, the selection of the most promising of these and their organisation for further development. Two typologies emerged within the company and were used to deal with these tasks. The first classified the stages of evolution from ideas to products, the second classified the people responsible for organising each new stage. See Table 1.

Table 1   Project Management

Stage	Person Responsible
Idea	(Self Appointed) Idea Champion*
Candidate	Candidate Champion*
Research Project	Research Project Manager
Development Project	Development Project Manager
Product	Product Manager

* Part-time responsibilities

These typologies proved to be less effective than initially expected and were soon amended. First, the idea of 'Decision Gates' operated by decision makers was introduced. Ideas had to pass through these gates in order to become candidates for action; candidates for action had to pass through in order to become research projects, and so on. Second, to help decision makers reach the right decisions, two systems were introduced: a resource management system, which appraises resources and priorities between projects; and a project management system, which ensures that trained and experienced management is available for all stages. The early stage is to provide professional backing to these idea champions to make the best possible case to present at the next decision gate. This system is shown in Figure 2. (Fairtlough 1989).

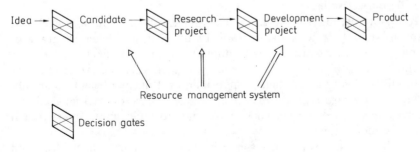

Figure 2   Decision Gates

Such systems thinking has resulted in practice in the Research and Development function being organised on a matrix basis with project managers coordinating resources drawn from the scientific departments. Project managers are responsible for budget approval, planning and control, establishing objectives and ensuring that these are met. This enables the Heads of Departments in R & D to concentrate on keeping the resources of their departments (people, equipment and facilities) up to the required level and to maintain high standards of work practice and the scientific development of their group. Each Head of Department is responsible for the costs and revenues of projects. In Celltech nine project managers run around 20 projects, the largest of which employs 17 people. These managers currently report to the Directors of Research and Development. Project planning for the larger projects is computerised.

The matrix organisation evolved within the company as awareness grew amongst department heads of the problems they were having in combining the functions of both line managers and project heads. Rather than being formally imposed by top management, the present project management system grew organically from the needs of the R & D function, although it was foreseen and supported by top management. The transition to matrix management progressed without too many problems caused by conflicting authority structures. The system is believed to be working well, although it is known that this depends on the project managers working well with individual line managers and being committed to the matrix principle.

The general principle used in organising the R & D function has been that of recruiting people with the requisite skills and then pulling them together in project teams. This has been used since the start of the company and is preferred to the alternative of recruiting people for specific projects. The reasons for adopting this skills-based approach are, according to Celltech's Director of Science, that it improves scientists' feelings of security since they feel that they are needed for their skills and not just for a short-term project and it encourages cohesive, problem-solving and creative activities, with people improving their long-term scientific skills as well as specific project skills.

A major method for ensuring scientific excellence within R & D was introduced in 1988 with the creation of the Principal Scientist grade of employee. This innovation was to allow appropriate financial reward for people wishing to concentrate on developing their scientific expertise rather than undertaking management responsibilities. Principal Scientists are appointed following an assessment which includes the use of external academic referees and they are expected to have, and to build upon, international scientific reputations.

Another mechanism which Celltech uses to stimulate new ideas and creativity is the sanctioning of scientists spending up to 10 per cent of their time on their own projects. In its earlier years this was an explicit policy, whereas currently the practice is less formally constructed. It has always been necessary for those wishing to undertake these so-called 'preliminary studies' to have the approval of the Head of Department. It is still possible for scientists to undertake these studies, which may on occasion exceed 10 per cent of their time. The intention underlying the arrangement is to allow scientists flexibility to use their knowledge in a direction unconstrained by project requirements. It is believed that it is important for the company to protect enough time in the face of immediate commercial demands to allow scientists to develop the know-how useful for a number of projects wider than their immediate one.

Having described the theory and practice of the organisational structure of Research and Development, it is worth emphasising another salient feature of the system at Celltech. That is, the system continues to evolve, the present system is not assumed to be the perfect mechanism and the company continues its efforts to learn about the problems of the existing system and the advantages of alternatives.

Boundary Spanning

The development of biotechnology worldwide has been characterised by extensive collaboration between firms. Such collaboration has been a particular feature of biopharmaceutical development and has tended especially to concern R & D. Celltech has engaged in a range of contract collaborations with many of the world's largest pharmaceutical companies. The company has clearly benefited financially from such collaborative ventures and has also done so in the building up of skills and competences necessary to undertake the contracts. In addition, the company has also always attempted to derive benefits additional to those related to the specific project.

Within Celltech, three generic types of technology are conceptualised: background, enabling and project specific. These are schematically portrayed in Figure 3. The classification relates to the interactions between research which can be done for contract clients and the company's own products and technological development. Background technology is all the technology existing in the company at any point in time which is not contractually allocated in some way. In contract terms, it is preexisting technology belonging to Celltech before the start date of a new contract. When undertaking any contract, both project specific and enabling technologies are generated. Project specific technology is directed towards, and is applicable only to, the objective of the project. It must be very tightly

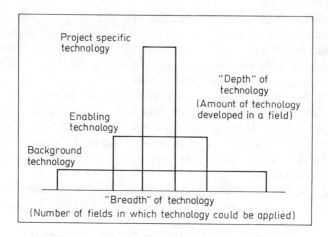

Figure 3   Conceptualisation of Technology

defined and will belong, or be licensed exclusively, to the project sponsor. Enabling technology is developed during the contract but is applicable in fields wider than that project. Celltech retains this technology but may license it non-exclusively to the project sponsors where necessary to practice the project-specific technology. Enabling technology involves learning and it is a cardinal purpose of contract research to build up enabling technology so that in subsequent projects it becomes background technology.

Perhaps the clearest practical example of this strategy at work is provided by a contract for a major US company. In this programme, designed to develop MAb-based aids to cancer diagnosis and treatment, Celltech has retained all rights to non-cancer discoveries, thus formalising its expectations regarding the development of enabling technology. In the past, however, building up enabling technology has often been a problem. A balance has had to be attained between meeting short-term (project) objectives in order to earn income and fulfilling the long-term objective of building the company's science-base. In practice, managers have had to be extremely flexible in conflating these long and short-term demands. Potentially the tensions between long- and short-term needs could manifest itself in disputes between line managers and project managers. To prevent such disputes and to ensure that enabling technology is given high priority, project managers are not asked to deal with the allocation of resources between project and enabling technology. These decisions are referred upwards in the organisation; the bigger the decision, the higher it is referred.

Links with academia have been very important for Celltech. Arrangements with the UK's Medical Research Council were crucial to the formation of the company and remained central to both its past and present scientific development. Another important mechanism for linking the company with academia is a Science Council, an academic consultative body developed to provide strong academic input. Many US DBFs have similar scientific advisory bodies.

Celltech also has an executive director responsible for academic liaison. In 1988 it spent 7.5 per cent of turnover on external academic collaborations. Most of these collaborations tend to be longer term than simple licensing agreements. Typically they involve Celltech funding a laboratory or individual researchers (usually for three-year projects) in return for the assignment of exclusive rights in any discovery to Celltech. The company must, however, be flexible in its negotiations as it is impossible to control all intellectual property rights in scientific networks. Some of these collaborations are complex and require considerable management skills, as shown in Figure 3 which reveals one such network of coordinated research collaboration.

Celltech is involved in a variety of forms of academic liaison, including a number of government and research council research initiatives. As a proportion of Celltech's total academic collaborations, however, such initiatives are small, accounting for less than 12 per cent of expenditure. As a proportion of Celltech's entire R & D expenditure, its involvement in these public sector schemes accounts for only around 2 per cent.

An additional mechanism used for 'technology watching' by the company is via the efforts of the company's Information and Library Service (ILS). This service provides an extensive range of information to company employees, from scientific papers and patents to information about competitors. It has constructed numerous databases; including those specific to important projects. One such project has over 1000 papers stored. The project databases include information on patents, science and commercial information and academic liaisons.

In addition to requests on patents from scientists, the company also acts proactively in its information search through its patent department. This department of four staff oversees the company's patenting interests and has one member who has a permanent brief to watch the patenting of competing organisations and spends a great deal of his time in national patent offices. Scientific information is also brought into the company by the 50-odd seminars given each year by external speakers. This complements the weekly internal seminar programme by Celltech staff.

Boundary spanning is also encouraged by extensive intra-and-inter-functional meeting. In the Manufacturing function, for example, there is a weekly managers' meeting and a monthly meeting for all Manufacturing staff. The latter is frequently well-attended and may on occasion include a presentation from someone from another function, for example, speaking on a new R & D project. Additionally, there are monthly liaison meetings between Manufacturing and Development, and Manufacturing and Sales and Marketing.

Conclusion

In this chapter we have examined the notion that strategy can be considered as a filter between a company's environment and its organisation. New, rapidly changing technologies place priority on firms' strategies and abilities to respond flexibly and quickly to competitive opportunities. A central role in such strategies is played by good information and communication flows. By examining a company skilled at reacting to rapid environmental changes we have seen some of the features of its strategy related to technological generation and acquisition and to human resource development. Strategy has been particularly directed towards 'fast learning'. The company's structure has been arranged according to its strategy. Particular features of the structure, its systems approach in Research and Development and its boundary spanning, have also been considered.

Celltech is, of course, an exceptional company with exceptionally good management. The lessons it provides for the majority of industrial companies may be limited, except in the sense that it illustrates good practice in circumstances of rapid change. Few industrial companies can remain unaffected by changing technology or competition and none can afford to ignore good practice when dealing with these changes. There are also lessons for academics concerning the strategic management of technology and its operational organisational form.

To conclude, it is perhaps worth highlighting a major problem that Celltech has faced in its history to date. An adaptive strategy is a risky strategy and commercial uncertainty is not favoured by UK investors. Similarly, Celltech's technology and human resource development strategies are long-term strategies: UK financial markets are more geared towards the short-term. An essential element in the environment-strategy-organisational model is the financial investment environment. A culture which favours short-term financial returns, as much of contemporary British industry does, is not conducive to the development of growth oriented, strategically-led firms such as Celltech.

Section Five
Reworking the World of Work

Introduction

Jane Marceau

In this final empirical section of the volume the focus is on that other essential aspect of restructuring the productive system, that of reworking the world of work. The two themes are *practice* and *politics*.

The first follows immediately from the chapters in the section on the introduction of 'Japanese' management methods to the automotive industry in France, the UK and Australia and to the aerospace industry in France. The papers in that section focussed on changing management technologies and notably on the introduction of Just-in-Time methods of inventory control and, with much more radical consequences, of the whole system of production. Attention was drawn in these papers, as it has been elsewhere, to the importance to the success of JIT and related managerial technologies of reworking the ways in which labour is organised. As part of the logic of the JIT system, emphasis is placed on total quality, not only of the entire assembled product but also of the parts which make it up. Where no back-up inventory of components is maintained and, especially, where modules from suppliers' factories are placed in position literally as the frame goes past on the line, there is no room for error at any stage of the production chain. Firms must therefore ensure that both their internal and external (suppliers') workforces are well-trained, motivated and capable of taking considerable responsibility for their output. In theory, and as the system works at Toyota and other Japanese assemblers, this means a wholesale change in work practices. People performing closely related tasks are divided into teams; 'broadbanding' of skills to break up the narrow traditional job divisions is introduced; employees are encouraged both to take responsibility for their output and to acquire the new skills necessary to allow them to monitor quality and diagnose reasons for defects occurring.

At least since Kern and Schumann (1984) published their work on such practices, which could be construed as they say in their title as the *End of the Division of Labour* but which they pose as a question, debate has raged among observers over the implications of the logic (or theory) of the new system and the degree to which, in practice, a new organisation of labour is emerging. In the debate over the development of the new techno-economic paradigm many shifts have been discerned (see e. g. Dohse, Jurgens and Malsch 1985). In particular, the demise of 'Fordism' has been announced as imminent because it is essentially incompatible with the managerial strategies dominating the leading edge of the new industrial order. As observers tried to come to grips with the new system, the many complex and patchy changes involved caused some to talk of the new system not as 'post-Fordism' but rather as 'neo-Fordism'. These debates have been well summarised in several places (see, e. g. Badham and Mathews 1989; Greig 1990) and empirical studies have begun to appear.

In many descriptions, a rather mechanistic conception of the relationship between technologies available and their translation into the organisation of labour soon became apparent. Much as Braverman's (1974) work suggested the 'inevitability' of deskilling in the modern industrial world, so a similar 'inevitability' sometimes seems to dominate thinking about the new order. Those views have needed modification and the case for recognising the importance of power relations in particular in determinating the labour organisation outcomes obtained has been powerfully made by observers such as Noble (1979) and Shaiken (1985).

In the process of the discussion of these labour organisation outcomes, however, much labelling has gone awry and short-hand nameplate terms such as the 'Japanese model' or the 'Swedish model' have been bandied about. As with other areas of the new order, it has become increasingly clear that local conditions, local traditions and local political and social frameworks − the institutional rationalities discussed by Clegg and Biggart earlier in this volume, for example − continue to play a vital role in shaping outcomes, especially in the organisation of the labour process but also in the general role played by labour in the restructuring of the whole productive system in any nation.

It is thus clearly important to look past the rhetoric at the *practice*, to indicate the leading actors and the reasons for which they are able to lead. In turn, the reasons why some actors are able to lead return the observer to an analysis of the political structure and environment within which the changes are being made, to the political and institutional cultures which inform, constrain and encourage particular decisions amid the choice of paths to take. In turn again, the political culture and socio-political institutions concerned influence the developments which make certain choices 'successful' or 'unsuccessful' for the economy as a whole. Particular policy options not only have to be formed and come onto the agenda; they also have to be implemented and, once initially implemented, sustained in operation. In the second section of this book, for instance, Poon makes clear that some of the reactions by workers to technological change in Hong Kong do indeed derive from Chinese cultures and practices but she also indicates how important are contingent social and economic factors, notably the situation of an expanding demand for labour which generates job security. One may hypothesise that this economic basis for security is likely to be especially important where public social security systems and other public support infrastructure are not well developed.

Consideration of influences such as these on outcomes mean that the *politics* of the changes to forms of labour organisation have to be at the centre of analysis. These politics obtain at many levels. They may be *organisational*, using a particular rhetoric of change such as 'devolutionism', as in the cases discussed by Muetzelfeldt earlier in this volume, to organise and frame acceptance of work redesign. They may be *institutional*, where a particular set of institutional arrangements provides a support and framework for organised social groups to take the lead. Or, and this is the aspect most often ignored in the literature at present, they may be much more broadly *political*, involving public policy decisions and governmental encouragement or even intervention.

These broader politics have to become part of the analysis of the direction of change *even inside companies*, as well as in public sector bodies, themselves undergoing considerable change in labour organisation. It is this linking of the reworking of work and its outcomes to national and institutional politics which is especially valuable in John Mathews' chapter in this section of the book.

Mathews makes the centrally important point that there are many different models of industrial restructuring. He presents the current Australian model as one of the most successful in bringing together public and private sector interests through collaboration with organised labour and the transformation of the productive culture through a social partner — trade unions — with an enormous interest in the process and outcome of such transformation but to whom little credit for *change* is usually given. In most studies of industrial restructuring, unions (organised labour) either have a low or non-existent profile or are viewed as retarding not advancing the process. In strong contrast, in Australia the union movement, organised through the Australian Council of Trade Unions (ACTU), remained at centre stage for most of the 1980s.

In Mathews' presentation of the role of the ACTU in industrial restructuring in Australia not only is organised labour the force managing and steering the process of change but it is the process of wage formation which is driving the restructuring. This is only possible because of the way in which the ACTU has managed to join with the Federal Labor Government in a series of *Accords* using, paradoxically, the centralised wage fixing arrangements through the Australian Conciliation and Arbitration Commission (AC & AC), now the Australian Industrial Relations Commission (AIRC), to link industry policy (industry restructuring) to wage agreements. The *Accords*, in place since 1983, are dependent on the Labor Government sustaining an agreement to manage economic change at the macro level in conjunction with the ACTU, through the AIRC, introducing restructuring at shopfloor level. Thus, the agreement has introduced flexibility at work-place (enterprise) level while persuading workers to trade off reduced real wages for maintained or increased social benefits, such as health, social security, and superannuation.

Mathews contrasts the current Australian model with earlier models: first, Federation Australia, the era covering the first decades of the twentieth century, those following the creation of the Commonwealth of Australia, in which industry agreed to establish itself in Australia if it were protected by high tariff walls; second, 'quarry-Australia' and subsequently 'quarry-resort' Australia associated with the late 1970s resources and the early 1980s tourist booms. As Mathews points out, moreover, the new model contrasts both with simple 'prices and incomes' agreements which came badly unstuck under social-democratic governments in Europe in the 1970s and with the free-market models of industrial change championed in the 1980s by conservative governments in the UK and the USA. In the latter countries, the same objective − the restructuring of work practices in industry − led to running down public sector activities while in Australia the *Accord* approach has supported public provision of crucial services such as education and other infrastructure. In addition, the *Accord* agreements ended the widespread industrial conflicts of the pre-Labor Government years and have ensured overall industrial stability, an essential pre-requisite for orderly change. At the same time, each variant of the original *Accord* has delivered many benefits to workers, including both improved immediate working conditions and a career structure developed through the provisions of the industrial award system. A totally deregulated system, with its inevitable attendant disruptions, has been avoided, despite persistent lobbying by employers and the Federal Parliamentary Opposition.

The success of the Australian model thus depends on a pre-existing institutional framework and the alignment and convergence of views between union leaders and the central political authorities. The ACTU's activities are both part of a traditional labour-oriented politics and an important element of the transformation of these politics on the ground. The restructuring of the world of work in Australia thus has a crucially important political dimension and the eventual shape of labour organisation in the productive system as a whole is not intelligible without considering the broader politics.

The importance of both the political dimension and the organisational structure itself has recently come sharply back into focus. In 1991 the *Accord* came under considerable pressure. The ACTU, in a bid to add extra wage flexibility to the system, pushed towards enterprise bargaining in key industries, a move generally supported by at least the largest employers and by the federal government. The proposed deal for the sixth variant of the *Accord*, to run 1991−92, and which included a move to enterprise bargaining in appropriate cases, was rejected in April 1991 by the Industrial Relations Commission on the grounds of the 'immaturity' of both unions and employers. This decision, reversed in October of the same year after lengthy negotiations, set back the cause of economic restructuring for some months and prejudiced for a time the development of the 'Australian model'. The conflict shows the fragility of cross-'partner' agreements arbitrated by an independent authority and emphasises once again how the decisions of a very few key people can greatly influence a whole organisational system, especially perhaps in a small industrial country. It reminds us again that the path to major organisational change is always paved with power, authority and politics.

At the level of the company, the outcome of moves towards restructuring work will depend greatly on much more local conditions. Even in a highly centralised system, such as that long obtaining in Australia, it is at company level that the nationally arbitrated awards, which determine minimum wages and conditions, are implemented. Union power and a company's management capacity, as well as its ability to pay, together build the work structure. Outcomes of the national bargaining system thus vary greatly. In countries where the reworking of work is being conducted without such a national political supporting structure and centralised wage-fixing institutions it is thus not surprising that empirical studies find enormous variation. For one thing, it is clear that the new technologies do contain some of the seeds encouraging particular forms of labour organisation. In other words, the 'logic' of new management systems such as JIT does suggest certain priorities (see Section Two above and the Conclusion Section of this volume below). Prominent among these is the greater need for training, recognised everywhere by firms introducing JIT in their search for improving quality. The outcomes of the new system, however, may differ. The desire for more highly skilled people may cause companies to shed their less-skilled workers and re-recruit, relying heavily on public training facilities, or it may lead to the development of internal upgrading and retraining schemes.

Much again will depend on the surrounding political climate, perceptions of the competence of the public education system and the degree to which such systems can be persuaded to provide, for example, 'customised' training courses now usually part of local development packages proferred in many countries by local authorities trying to encourage industry to relocate to their territory. Much of this is itself, of course, also a political process, with incentives such as low taxes and rural, non-unionised 'fresh' labour being important elements in, for instance, the location of Japanese transplant companies on greenfields sites in the USA (Mair, Florida and Kenney 1988). In Britain, too, similar inducements have been part of the industrial location battle, as Wilkinson, Oliver and Morris show in their chapter of this volume, and unions overall in the UK have not been so much involved in the restructuring of labour processes through their central organisation, the TUC, as in Australia. In Britain, the crucial elements of the centralised wage-bargaining institutions and a labour-oriented government have been missing, opening the way to ever greater variations in factory organisation. Many of the disagreements among observers about 'post-Fordism' and 'neo-Fordism' stem from failure to recognise the political dimensions of the processes determining work outcomes.

Diversity in *practice* is thus the second theme of the papers in this section of the book. The theme runs through the two chapters on the automobile industry in Sweden and France. The French paper follows on from the description presented above in Section Two and focusses on the implications of 'partnership' in the core firms in the car and aerospace industries for the organisation of work and the demand for particular skills, both new and old, in France. Changes to skill levels are particularly important following the introduction of technologies which eliminate the need to control quality in the work of unskilled workers (since that part of their jobs is incorporated into the machine) while final quality check is carried out by skilled workers but no longer as a specialised function. Sections of the supervisory hierarchy have contracted — notably at foreman level — while, as Palmer and Allan reported above, new managerial tasks, such as those of Quality Assurance, open up opportunities at the higher level in France as elsewhere. In France, too, training has become a central concern, transforming blue collar work, while broadbanding is breaking down barriers between job functions. These two changes are the basic elements or reworking manufacturing work everywhere. Their particular configurations in any one country and indeed within industries and companies *within* countries, however, depend, as Mathews suggests, on the broader political climate and the power of industrial unions at the negotiating table. The power of the technology in *beginning* the process of change, not only in the core firms but also in their selected first tier suppliers, however, is clear.

This importance of the broader political climate is especially evident in the chapter by Sandkull on the evolution of production organisation at Volvo. The Volvo story shows clearly the importance of local traditions, political pressures and particular social orientations in the design of even 'Fordist' production systems. Not only did the company include elements of a strong 'pre-industrial' or craft metal work in Sweden but it also very early on modified American practices so as to increase worker participation in the system. Equally important and perhaps much less well-known, Volvo pioneered a method of overcoming its small production output and spreading its market risks with its suppliers which developed in paralled to the now much copied Japanese system. Working together with its suppliers, Volvo very early introduced a system of annual component delivery scheduling and the technological rationalisation and upgrading of vendor capacity through inspection of supplier plants by Volvo engineers. The cost savings thus obtained were shared between the contracting parties while the high quality achieved became the hallmark of Swedish products.

The third paper on 'practice' has been included because it illustrates the process of work organisation change in an organisation which is very large indeed — the Commonwealth Government in Australia, a set of institutions employing around 170,000 people. Rapid technological change, notably in the data processing field, led to a perception by the Hawke Labor Government in the mid-1980s that job classifications in the Australian Public Service needed updating. A small group in the then central public service industrial relations body, the Public Service Board, was charged with the reclassification. Progress was astonishing: 93 job categories were rapidly reduced to eight and educational credentials for entry to different grades eliminated. As Selby-Smith notes, the public sector in Australia was then well ahead of the private sector in job restructuring. It is important to emphasise the politics in the practice here. While the reform was 'technology led', or, more exactly, technological change was the element which brought work restructuring to the public service controllers' attention, the outcome owed a great deal to the government's broader political agenda, including public commitment to equal opportunity, to lack of discrimination in employment, to social justice and, to a lesser extent, to industrial democracy. In other words, job reclassifications were used as a major instrument in the push to restructure work with the achievement of particular *social* as well as efficiency objectives in mind and the major beneficiaries were indeed the lower paid, especially women, the two categories often being coterminous. Unfortunately for the survival of the Public Service Board, the more apparently 'efficient' ideas encapsulated in the notion of 'managerialism' later came to dominate reform of the public service and were perceived by decision-makers as obstructed by a commitment to equity while at the same time the tensions — inevitable in such a large organisation, with employees spread over many functions and across a huge geographical area — between centre and periphery ultimately led to the Board's demise. The reform of the Australian Public Service through such radical reform of its job classification system must nevertheless rate as one of the largest reorganisations ever undertaken using a single mechanism and undertaken with such a complex mix of social and technological objectives. For that reason alone the tale is worth telling but it also illustrates once again the political dimensions of the outcomes of work restructuring. Had the Federal government, as might a non-Labor Government, *not* been committed to broad equal opportunity and social justice goals, the outcome could well have been different. When other ideas gained greater support in the political system, these ideals were lost and the Board was abolished.

The final paper in this section returns to Sweden. Using Swedish experience as his exemplar, Winton Higgins poses the question as to why in such
a fast-changing technological world and, in countries such as Sweden at
least, a world in which quite remarkable social progress has been made in
some areas, there has been so little progress towards more fundamental
economic democracy. He asks, for instance, why unsafe working conditions
and poor wages are concentrated still in blue collar jobs, despite more than
a century of industrial change and political and social reform. Higgins'
answer suggests that neither the political culture nor the social structure of
Sweden have been significantly altered over past decades: while the distribution of social rewards, such as retirement income, has been altered, the
distribution of opportunities to determine the redistribution of working
conditions, the heartland of capitalist society, has continued essentially
unchanged. Whatever the technologies concerned, in Sweden as elsewhere,
capital continues to hire labour and not labour capital. Control of the
productive process has thus not shifted. The story he tells of the failure of
workers' funds to shift that control through taking control of the capital
market reminds us yet again of the close relationships between politics,
power and economic dominance, returning us, from another perspective,
to the questions of control of the design and functioning of economic life
under the emerging techno-economic paradigm which were discussed earlier
in the book.

Reworking the world of work thus remains a highly complex process
with a highly political, moral and cultural core. While technologies undoubtedly open the way and suggest to managers the need for change and even
the direction of change, it is essentially non-technological factors but rather
political frameworks which determine outcomes observed on the ground.
Whether the emerging structures are indeed 'post-Fordist' or merely 'neo-
Fordist' thus depends on relationships of power and politics as much as
did the Fordist model.

An Australian Model of Industrial Restructuring

John Mathews

Introduction

All the OECD economies have been swept up over the past decade in a process of fundamental structural change, whose watchwords have been 'flexibility', 'responsiveness', 'privatisation' and 'deregulation'. At the end of the decade, the Soviet Union and Eastern Europe have added their weight to this movement, as they have thrown off the shackles and dead hand of a State-bureaucratic 'socialism'. The traditional political philosophies have had a hard time keeping up with these changes, which have largely run ahead of ideology. Liberal-individualist governments such as those of the UK and USA have had to accommodate to strong economic pressures forcing them to abandon monetarist adventures, while governments of the centre-left, such as those of France and Spain, have had to accommodate to market forces and international financial pressures, forcing them to abandon traditional platforms of nationalisation and state control. In the midst of this pell-mell change, the Australian version of social democracy not only maintained itself in power through the whole of the 1980s, acquiring a responsibility and credibility that Labor had never previously enjoyed, but it stood its ground in the face of constant calls for wholesale deregulation. What emerged by the 1990s is a form of adjustment that uniquely blends the elements of regulation at the macro level and flexibility at the micro level; it amounts to the emergence of a characteristic 'Australian model' of structural adjustment.

In this chapter, arguing in historical and comparative mode, I identify the elements of this 'Australian model' of adjustment. I claim that the current system has emerged out of the 'Federation Australia' model, first put in place at the turn of the century. In this system, Australia's wealth derived from raw material exports, enabling a domestic trade-off to occur between workers who wanted wages kept high through arbitration, and industrial employers who wanted to be able to pay these wages through being protected from foreign competition. This model has proved to be remarkably resilient but is now seen to be quite inadequate for current global conditions where the emphasis is on high value-added, elaborately transformed manufactures and services. Out of the fiasco of the 'quarry Australia' model, promoted in the 1970s through the ill-fated resources boom, new efforts to create a 'smart Australia' model are being developed.

The key to the successful transition to any such model is the flexibility of the labour market, both in terms of short term responsiveness to change and in terms of long-term adjustment to changing technologies and skill levels (OECD 1986a; Meulders and Wilkin 1987). There are, however, several ways of achieving this. In spite of repeated calls for deregulation, the major industrial parties in Australia have maintained a regulated labour market as the core, not just of a social strategy of equity and justice but of an industrial restructuring strategy placing primary emphasis on productivity and efficiency. It is this feature of the 'Australian model' which is worthy of considerable international attention.

The following discussion traces the evolution of the Australian industrial system, placing the current debates on strategic direction into an historical context. Focusing then on labour market adjustment mechanisms, the chapter reviews the outlines of the major changes in the Australian labour market and industrial relations system in the 1980s, setting them in the context of international debates. Particular focus in placed on the enhancement of enterprise flexibility and strategic responsiveness achieved in many Australian firms and public sector organizations as a result of these changes. The analysis concludes by identifying the major elements of the emergent 'Australian model', tracing out in detail how the model links macro-level regulation with micro-level flexibility and in this way avoids the heavy social costs associated with purely market-driven processes of restructuring.

The 'Federation Australia' Model

At the turn of the century, Australia led the western world in the advanced nature of its democracy. It was first with female suffrage; first with independent Labor governments; first with industrial arbitration to remove the full force of employers' powers over employees; and amongst the first with substantial numbers of agricultural cooperatives and regulated commodities trading. At the time of Federation of the previously separate colonies, in 1901, the basic elements of the current 'Australian model' were established. These were:

- the backbone of the economy was production of primary resources (wool, wheat, minerals), which were supplied to world markets and generated substantial export earnings;

- on the strength of these earnings, wages were kept high through industrial arbitration, across the whole economy ('comparative wage justice');
- industry was protected by high tariff barriers from overseas competition to allow it to pay these high wages;
- the labour market remained regulated, not just in terms of wages but also in terms of immigrant labour, a provision aimed in particular at plantation owners who wished to cut wages by importing coolie labour (the 'White Australia' policy).

This is what this chapter describes as the 'Federation Australia' model. It has been described by other authors as an early case of the welfare state (before it was known generally in Europe) but of a peculiarly 'workerist' kind — what Castles calls 'working class welfare' delivered through the industrial arbitration system (Castles 1985). The notion of the 'breadwinner wage', formulated in the famous judgment of Justice Higgins in the Harvester case of 1906, remained the cornerstone of this system, seriously retarding Australia's move towards a more universally based welfare system in the post-war years.

The 'Federation Australia' model served the country well, underpinned as it was by Australia's wealth in primary resources. In the postwar years it was enhanced by the immigration program, which brought abundant quantities of skilled labour to Australia (but in the process allowed the country's domestic skills formation processes to atrophy). Industry developed in its own way, seeking to replace imports and relying on overseas firms for technological developments.

By the 1970s, as other OECD countries began the painful processes of 'structural adjustment', Australia went in precisely the opposite direction, seeking to maintain its standard of living through a further push in the raw materials area. This was the ill-fated 'resources boom', unsuccessfully engineered by the Fraser government and lambasted by its opponents in the unions as the 'quarry Australia' model. Industry development was debated and implemented in Australia at this time largely in terms of public sector research, following the 'linear model' hypothesis that development and commercialisation would naturally follow technical research breakthroughs. The few breakthroughs that did come out of this policy, in CSIRO and other government agencies, were largely ignored by Australian industry and taken up by overseas interests.

Out of this fiasco new restructuring efforts in Australia were developed from the election of the Labor Government in 1983. These efforts intensified through the 1980s, based on two widely agreed premises. The first is that there is no future for Australia as a producer solely of primary materials. The terms of trade in primary commodities have turned down in a secular trend throughout the decade, with a big drop in 1986 which prompted the remark from the Treasurer that Australia could become a 'banana republic'. The second premise follows from this and suggests that Australia must develop a manufacturing base which will enable it to compete in the fastest growing area of world trade, namely in elaborately transformed manufactures and advanced services.

Unfortunately, Australia starts from a low base in this key area of trade-exposed manufactures, because of the years of inefficiences and insular perspectives fostered by the high levels of protection enjoyed by domestic industry. The dismantling of these protective barriers is now seen by all parties as a necessary prelude to Australia's developing an advanced industrial structure.

The crucial question which follows from the two premises — what should take the place of ineffective tariff barriers — is currently the subject of major debate. Many influential advisors in Treasury and Australian financial circles believe in the need to do away with all forms of intervention and let market forces determine the industrial structure of Australia. The trouble with this argument is that it could well mean Australia ending up with no industrial structure at all, offering nothing other than raw materials and tourist services to the rest of the world. This is the 'quarry-resort Australia' model. The polar opposite of this approach, involving wholesale government intervention to direct industrial investment and nationalise key sectors, is seen as equally unattractive.

In the light of such problems and policy dilemmas, from the mid-1980s the Australian Council of Trade Unions (ACTU) orchestrated a coalition with export-oriented manufacturing business, through the tripartite Australian Manufacturing Council (AMC), to push for a new form of creative intervention. This novel approach recognises the enormous obstacles that export-oriented firms in Australia have to overcome if they are to succeed in world markets and seeks to facilitate the efforts that firms make themselves. The key statement from the AMC, *The Global Challenge* report prepared by consultants Pappas Carter, Evans Koop/Telesis (1990), spells out these difficulties in extended and discomforting detail and adumbrates a strategy directed at building a manufacturing base around adding value to our raw materials. This is in line with national business strategies as formulated by such commentators as Harvard's Michael Porter in *The Competitive Advantage of Nations* (1990).

The 'smart Australia' model (or what the Prime Minister has dubbed the 'clever country' concept, as opposed to the years when we were called, ironically, the 'lucky country') is one in which Australia continues to operate in world primary materials markets but simultaneously systematically seeks to build a manufacturing base around clusters of firms oriented to serving these industries and adding value to the raw materials. This means, on the one hand, abandoning notions that Australia can compete on an equal basis with Japanese and European giants in the core technologies of electronics, computing, and biotechnologies. On the other hand, it means forming clusters of producers in key areas of strategic significance to Australia, such as in agricultural and mining equipment, for example, as well as establishing downstream processing of minerals (such as the rare earth-containing mineral sands) and primary commodities such as wood pulp and timber (Marceau 1990; Mathews 1990). Such a strategy is seen as drawing on the current thinking regarding the success of cooperative cluster- and network-based industrial districts (Sabel 1989; Weiss 1988).

Behind this debates lie the realities of the struggles between firms, sectors and nations seeking to develop the enhanced productivity and efficiency of the 'new production systems'. Led by an advance guard of firms in Japan, Germany, Italy and Scandinavia, the new production systems, which dispense with the Taylorist work organization approaches introduced earlier this century along with mass production, have proven themselves in terms of flexibility, productivity and profitability (Dertouzos, Lester and Solow 1989). These systems have created a new 'common sense' in the design and organization of work, integrating it with new technologies, skills formation and industrial relations systems (Mathews 1989b; Badham and Mathews 1989). The obstacles to the implementation of these new industrial strategies and production concepts faced by Australia are formidable. The first and most intransigent is the role of the primary producers themselves, particularly the mining companies. They form what amounts to a separate economy in Australia, one which is totally integrated into the world economy (or rather, in many cases, into the Japanese economy as, for example, the markets for our coking coal and iron ore exports show). It is this economy which drives the Australian exchange rate but the interests of participants in that area diverge sharply from those of manufacturing (Curtain and Mathews 1990).

The second obstacle derives from geographical size and patterns of population distribution. Australia may be a small economy but it is a very large country with population centres scattered along the East coast. This situation creates very large infrastructure cost problems, particularly in the area of transport. Infrastructural questions, such as power generation, telecommunications, road and sea transport, are currently being tackled by State and federal governments under the rubric 'microeconomic reform' but their direction will be crucially affected by views on the kind of future Australia is likely to have.

The third set of obstacles arise from the outdated labour market regulation system inherited from the cosy arrangements of the Federation Australia model. While such matters as microeconomic reform, industry shifts towards value-adding activities and the promotion of export performance in place of multidomestic activity dominated the debate over how we can reach the 'smart Australia' model, it is the more down-to-earth labour market questions which really drive the processes of change. Whereas up to the early 1980s, Australia was cursed with a wages system that actively impeded change, by the 1990s Australia could boast that it is now the wage formation process that drives and facilitates the process of change towards a more open and innovative industry.

The Transformation of Australian Industrial Relations

The 1980s witnessed fundamental changes in the Australian system of industrial relations and above all in wage formation processes. At the beginning of the decade, Australia was locked into a system that had barely changed from the 'Federation Australia' model. By the end of the decade, the industrial relations system had become a key factor in facilitating structural adjustment.

The key to the series of changes was a peculiarly Australian invention. This was the Prices and Incomes *Accord*, an agreement between the ACTU and the Australian Labor Party cemented just before the 1983 federal election win by Labor. Indeed, the Accord was widely credited as providing Labor with its election-winning card, ending seven years of turbulent Coalition rule by the Liberal and National Parties under the prime ministership of Malcolm Fraser. In particular, the Accord gave Labor an argument that it could control wages, against the chaos of the Fraser years, ending with the 1982–83 wage freeze and serious recession.

The Accord has been widely known internationally but has been much misunderstood. Often seen as a rerun of the failed 'wage freeze' social contracts of the 1970s, of which the most ignominious was that under the Callaghan Labour government in the UK in 1976–79, the Accord, on the contrary, defined itself as a broad-based prices and incomes agreement. In the Accord, unions committed themselves to wage restraint in return for commitments on the part of the ALP in government to foster prices and other incomes restraint and, especially significant, to make up for the money wage sacrifices with enhanced social wage expenditure (e.g. on social security, health and housing). Most far-reaching of all, the Accord laid the foundations and provided the framework for union participation in economic regulation at both macro and micro levels. Thus, from the outset the Accord was modelled much more on the corporatist 'social pacts' familiar from Scandinavian or Austrian experience than on any narrowly conceived wage control policies inherited from Anglo-Saxon traditions (Mathews 1989c).

The Accord ushered in the first shift in the Australian industrial relations framework in the 1980s. In September 1983, a decision of the Australian Conciliation and Arbitration Commission (AC & AC), the central wage-bargaining institution, acknowledged the existence of the Accord wage agreement and laid down a set of rules (including 'no extra claims' commit-ments) under which unions and employers could participate in the national system and receive uniform national wage outcomes linked to the Consumer Price Index. This took the heat out of wage confrontation and took the unions off the treadmill of endless wages campaigns, allowing both unions and employers to set their sights on longer-term goals.

The next shift occurred in 1985 under the impact of a downturn in the terms of trade. Again the shift was triggered by an agreement between the ACTU and the Labor government. This agreement provided that the CPI-indexed wage increase would be discounted by two per cent and a four per cent general productivity claim would be taken in the form of an employer contribution to bipartite industry superannuation funds. This agreement was upheld by the Commission, against the wishes of employers, and the important precedent was established that the superannuation negotiations would be conducted at sector level, between the parties, with the Commis-sion playing a monitoring role.

The third shift occurred with the March 1987 decision of the Commission, at the specific request of the employers, to end automatic wage indexation and move instead to a 'two tier' system in which a first element of a wage increase was awarded in line with cost of living while the second instalment was made conditional on unions and employers reaching agreements relat-ing to 'restructuring and efficiency' matters (AC & AC 1987). Protection was accorded to lower-paid workers through the Supplementary Payments Principle.

Thus, by 1987, the Australian wage fixation system had moved a consider-able distance from its traditional highly centralised and regulated character. Unions accommodated wage restraint in return for trade-offs made outside the industrial relations system proper (delivered by government). Wage fixation was linked for the first time, albeit in a very tentative fashion to 'productivity and efficiency' through the second tier agreements and an impetus towards enterprise bargaining was set in motion. Further, the Commission explicitly set itself a monitoring rather than an arbitral role, with the important precedent of the superannuation decision establishing a model that has become central to award restructuring. Through the Accord the industrial relations system became linked with a series of sector-specific industry policy initiatives, covering the car industry, textiles, clothing and footwear, heavy engineering, and so on.

In August 1988, the Australian Industrial Relations Commission (AIRC, successor of the AC & AC) launched the fourth phase of the transformation, with its Structural Efficiency Principle (AIRC 1988) which now forms the heart of the emergent Australian model. The Commission put its own interpretation on the Structural Efficiency Principle (SEP), in these words:

'Any new wage system introduced should build on the steps already taken to encourage greater productivity and efficiency. Attention must now be directed toward the more fundamental, institutionalised elements that operate to reduce the potential for increased productivity and efficiency ... To sustain real improvement in productivity and efficiency, we must take steps to ensure that work classifications and functions and the basic work patterns and arrangements in an industry meet the competitive requirements of that industry. It is accepted, at least by some, that a more highly skilled and flexible labour force is required not only to assist in structural adjustment but also to provide workers with access to more varied, fulfilling and better paid jobs.' (AIRC 1988)

The gist of the SEP is its emphasis on tying wage increases to increments in skill, providing for internal labour markets and career paths where none had existed before. Its radical break with the traditions of wage fixation in Australia was underscored by its insistence that while overall shifts and frameworks would be established within restructured awards, the details of adjustment could only be negotiated at enterprise level. *Thus the move towards enterprise flexibility has been institutionalised within this Australian IR system but within a framework laid down centrally.* This is what McDonald and Rimmer (1989) have called 'managed decentralism'.

Despite the halting nature of negotiations, achievements under the SEP have been considerable. In the metals industry, traditionally the pace-setter for Australian awards, the previous Fordist and Taylorist job classification systems, skills formation structures and wages system have been transformed. In their place has been established a streamlined series of fourteen general job categories, succeeding each other in terms of skill and responsibility and linked by wage premiums that reward skills enhancement. The final shape of the new metals award was ratified by Justice Keogh in the Commission in March 1990 (AIRC 1990). The next step is up to employers and unions at enterprise level. The new award sets a wages, skills and job classification framework which facilitates plant-level restructuring but this will be implemented only if the will to restructure is there.

Similarly in other sectors such as textiles, clothing and footwear (TCF), award restructuring is well advanced, along lines similar to those established in the metals sector. Restructuring in the TCF sector is under the further pressure of intense low-cost import competition, driving Australian firms to close down, move off-shore or grasp the challenge and innovate with high quality products (Mathews and Weiss 1991).

In the public sector, restructuring has accompanied moves to make public sector agencies and government business enterprises (such as airlines) more accountable. In the public sector case, award restructuring has been caught up in privatisation debates but nonetheless, in some agencies, such as the Australian Tax Office, formerly rigid and authoritarian clerical and data-processing work systems have been transformed, by enlarging jobs and linking them to the introduction of computerised systems that enable operators to manipulate files in a coherent manner (Carmody 1989. See also Selby-Smith in this volume).

In some industry sectors international competition has led to enterprise restructuring in advance of general award restructuring. One example has taken place in the insurance sector, where giant firms, exposed to inter-national competition through financial deregulation (such as AMP or National Mutual), have restructured their job classification systems and salary structures along lines remarkably similar to those proposed for the Tax Office in advance of general industry-wide negotiations (Rimmer and Verevis 1990).

The AIRC itself reviewed the progress of restructuring under the SEP in hearings in 1989 and in individual cases in 1990 (AIRC 1989). By the end of 1990, after 30 months of restructuring, it was becoming clear that a new phase of the industrial relations system was imminent. It meant either evolving further towards productivity bargaining or relapsing back to a wages free-for-all reminiscent of the early 1980s.

Elements of the 'Australian Model'

We are now ready to identify the key features which may be taken as characterising the emergent 'Australian model' of restructuring. Six features are crucial. First, the model is wages-led, linking wages directly to productiv-ity enhancement and restructuring. Secondly, a central, national institution provides a neutral forum in which unions, employers and governments determine the overall framework of wages and IR policy. Despite the 1991 decision to move further towards enterprise bargaining, the IRC will still retain a role, both as a central discussion forum and as the place where agreements made can be given legal status as awards should employers and unions desire it. Third, positive-sum outcomes are achieved through 'cooperative accommodation' between unions and employers over shared objectives. This meant that the fourth element, micro flexibility, is possible and is achieved through sector and enterprise negotiations conducted within the national regulated framework. Fifth, macro stabilisation is achieved through the national negotiation of measures designed to inhibit polarisation (such as national skills standards). While, sixth, a national productive culture is evolving, formed out of multiculturalism, a greater respect for the environment, better awareness of the contribution of 40,000 years of Aboriginal settlement and increased openness to the world of the Pacific and East Asia.

The 'Australian model', then, is wages-led, with the overall structure and movements of wages determined centrally. The effect of award restructuring has been to put national wages policy in the driving seat of structural adjustment at the macro level. This achievement is unique to Australia amongst OECD countries. In all the advanced nations, such as Japan, Germany or the Scandinavian countries, wages in the 1980s have been determined company by company, sector by sector, but never nationally. Wages have always been a residual variable in national budgets. In Australia, because of the Accord wage agreements, the overall wage level can be set with some accuracy in budgets. Even more important, employers and unions can agree on a national framework for their sector-level and enterprise-level bargaining. The Accord, in its various guises (up to Mark VI by 1990) was therefore central to macroeconomic management in Australia throughout the 1980s.

The record of the Accord over its first seven years (despite constant attacks from both the political right and the left) was very impressive. Econometric evaluation has demonstrated positive results, not just in restraining money wage outcomes, but in enhancing employment growth, reducing the level of strike activity and in fostering real maintenance of social wage levels (Chapman and Gruen 1990).

In the Australian model, wages are determined centrally, through the auspices of the AIRC which is a neutral national forum, lacking in all other OECD countries. In Australia, the AIRC (or rather its predecessor, the AC & AC) was reviled as an industrial dinosaur, imposing the dead hand of regulation on a labour market which could thus not let wages reflect 'equilibrium' levels. Now the debate has shifted. The AIRC now serves the extremely useful function of setting a national wages policy in terms of the three key variables of growth in macro wage levels; developments in macro structure (e. g. skill-based sector-level classifications) and a focus on social justice outcomes (e. g. equal pay, supplementary payments in low-paid occupations).

The strength of the AIRC is that it is a neutral and independent social institution, which commands the respect of both employers, unions and governments. This respect, however, has constantly to be fought for and the pros and cons of the institution are endlessly debated in Australian IR circles. Many questions are asked: does it protect unions too much, or alternatively does it make life too easy for employers? does it institutionalise demarcations? does it inhibit real wage adjustment to real economic changes, such as productivity growth, or alternatively does it institutionalise wage inflation?

Focussing on these issues largely misses the point. These are all dangers in *any* regulated system; they are unavoidable. It is up to the parties who use the institution to ensure, insofar as they are able, that the negative outcomes are avoided while the positive ones are pursued. This is what has happened over the past seven and a half years; the parties have cooperated to the extent required to achieve a positive sum outcome. They may not continue to do so; indeed towards the end of 1990 it looked as though there could be a serious breakdown in the painfully established industrial relations procedures.

The parties, however, have learnt to cooperate where it is in their interests to do so. This cooperation is clearly seen in the maintenance of the regulated labour market. Here the hallmark of enterprise agreements and of award restructuring has been the element of cooperation around strategic object- ives achieved by unions and employers. This is the basis of the 'production coalition' that was so successfully put in place in the 1980s by the ACTU and its partners.

Through the 1980s there was endless pressure on the federal government to deregulate the labour market since the regulated labour market was seen by many, including the opposition Liberal and National parties (in coali- tion) and many major employer groups, as *the* major obstacle to opening up Australia to the full force of international competition. Strikingly enough, however, this pressure did not come from *mainstream* employer bodies. The ACTU stood its ground on this question and its Accord-partner, the federal government, had to follow suit even if there were individual finance ministers who would have liked to go the deregulation route. In standing its ground the ACTU did not take a dull, 'nyet'-saying stance. On the contrary, the ACTU has led the employers through a series of breathtaking manoeuvres and strategic policy switches, always keeping the initiative and always maintaining the momentum of change. The mainstream employer groups have largely cooperated with this strategy.

Meanwhile, at enterprise level, this cooperative framework has facilitated the negotiation of a series of enterprise agreements and awards, such as at Southern Aluminium, at ICI Botany, at Tubemakers, and at BHP Steel. These agreements establish novel IR frameworks and procedures such as annual wages, abolition of overtime, expanded job responsibilities, and self-managing teamwork arrangements. It is such agreements and their implementation that provides unheard of micro-flexibility for firms, allow- ing them to shift strategic direction by negotiation and agreement (Eco- nomic Planning Advisory Council 1991).

At the level of companies this micro-flexibility is achieved through controlled enterprise bargaining and through the firm-level implementation of award restructuring. Once the macro-framework is set, the parties must interpret its specificities at company level, through negotiation and consultation. A learning process is involved here and there are frequent examples of backsliding by both unions and employers, the former by reverting to across-the-board wage demands and the latter by seeking to restructure unilaterally. This learning process is taking firms towards models of adjustment based on internal rather than external labour markets and towards the non-market adjustment mechanisms identified by Dore and his colleagues as central to the success of Japan (Dore, Bounine-Cabale and Tapiola 1989).

In Australian debates, the question of micro-flexibility has been tackled through the issue of 'enterprise bargaining' (Business Council of Australia 1989). In the latter half of the 1980s, the Business Council of Australia (BCA) successfully forced such bargaining onto the IR agenda, although it did so only after the ACTU had already come round to this position in different terms, those of award restructuring. The BCA has found it hard to distinguish the benefits of its 'enterprise bargaining' position (with an implied drift away from the centralised system and even fainter drift towards enterprise unions) from the tangible enterprise focus delivered in practice by the ACTU's push for award restructuring. The recent Pappas Carter report to the tripartite Australian Manufacturing Council in effect put paid to the BCA position by arguing for an 'achievable' union restructuring position, one carried out along industry lines. This effectively put the BCA's (unstated) goal of enterprise unions off the political agenda for at least the next decade. Enterprise bargaining, however, has now (1991) been incorporated into the wage-fixing system for all who wish. The negotiations are to be conducted by unions and management, not by individuals, however, although New South Wales, so far alone of the States, has passed such framework legislation.

In general terms, the key feature of such job and wages restructuring is macro-stability. This clearly distinguishes the emergent Australian approach from that favoured in Anglo-Saxon countries. In the USA and UK, micro-flexibility achieved by the free rein given to market forces is bought at a heavy social cost. Firms and industries become polarised between those with high skills, high wages and high profits and those who struggle on the margin (Atkinson 1987). At the same time, in these countries social and public infrastructures have been run down in the name of privatisation. Such polarisation leads to alienation and ultimately threatens the foundations of democracy.

In contrast, in the Australian model, the central determination of overall wage levels, skills paths and classification systems provides both the opportunity to check these polarisation tendencies and the stimulus to modernise the public infrastructure that industry shares, such as an innovative and responsive public training system. National standards of skills or competence recognition, assessment and portability can be set, bypassing the problem of standards set wholly at the enterprise level which inhibit worker inter-firm mobility.

The benefits obtained from the Australian model are not achievable through a totally market-oriented industrial relations system. Significantly, they also represent advantages of the kind described by Perez and Freeman in their discussion of social and institutional adjustment by a country to the new techno-economic paradigm (Freeman and Perez 1988) and emphasized by the OECD in numerous recent publications (e. g. OECD 1989). Thus, we can argue that the 'Australian model' is well suited to the making of a *paradigm shift*; whether it is so suitable for facilitating the process of adjustment within a given paradigm would be another matter. To effect the paradigm shift at all, however, is seen as an outstanding problem in Australia, given the country's heritage as a wealthy raw materials producer cosseting an inefficient, neo-colonialist industry behind high tariff walls.

Australia has one further feature which it is important to mention here. Australia has an industrial formation which is unique in its multiculturalism. Waves of post-war immigration have made the Australian workforce a source of great cultural heterogeneity. While such heterogeneity has obvious disadvantages, such as problems with English language literacy, it has a deeper strength that is becoming clear in Australian debates. The successful productive nations of the future, I suggest, will be those which can respond flexibly to emergent market trends and needs; productive cultures which are nationally homogeneous and less sensitive to foreign cultures (the arch-example being the Japanese) may fare badly under these conditions.

Conclusion

The elaboration here of an 'Australian model' is necessarily general and tentative in nature. It is advanced as an 'ideal type' to distinguish it from its free-market ideological rivals, and from its more corporatist or more centrally interventionist variants. The model is offered as a way of making sense of the interesting series of social experiments which have been conducted in the social democratic laboratory of Australia in the 1980s.

There is nothing particularly novel in any individual part of the model — its originality lies in the synthesis of separate streams of thought and practice coming from industrial relations, organizational innovation, industry strategy, and the formation of a new productive culture. It is precisely this power to synthesise, however, that will determine the success or failure of nations in the 1990s.

Reorganising Labour: The Volvo Experience

Bengt Sandkull

Introduction

Sweden is a small country but Swedish cars have become well-known trade names all over the world and Swedish car makers are frequently held up as the model for countries concerned with 'democratising' or at least 'enriching' production workers' jobs. This chapter outlines Swedish experience in the car industry using Volvo as an example in order to demonstrate the complexity of the picture. While 'post-Fordism' may be on the way out, as Mathews (1989a and b) and others have suggested, in practice even within the same company, there are many variations. Much depends on management attitudes on the dates of plant construction, on regional or national plant location and on the ability of the company's different plants to attract suitable labour. In such a complex industry, change is not smooth and uniform, it is both piecemeal and patchy.

The Production System Model

The theoretical basis for the analysis of work design is a model of a production system. This model describes how input material is transformed in a production process into products by using labour and equipment. A production system is a set of people and equipment which has been organized under some form of leadership for the purpose of making input material into products. A production system can be defined on the level of the shopfloor, the factory, or the industry.

A production system embodies the production which is simultaneously a process of manufacturing (a concrete transformation), a process of creating a surplus (value added through the labour process), and a social process (reproduction of labour) (Sandkull 1984. See also Littler 1982). The design of a production system has its origin in the product and is based on an analysis of which steps or operations would be necessary to complete the transformation from inputs to a finished product. The sequence of the steps or operations specifies the machine work and as a consequence the flow of additional materials and the need for direct labour. The physical flow in the production process follows from the layout of machinery and other kinds of equipment in the plant. In the model, the outcomes of all these decisions are called the *technical relations of production* (cf. Burawoy 1979).

The production system comprises an additional number of operations which usually are not incorporated into the physical flow, such as maintenance and repairs of tools and machinery, quality control and adjustments, cleaning, or keeping of records. Very often activities like maintenance are carried out in company workshops; these workshops can be regarded as production systems in their own right, although dependent on the main system.

Before the general use of the methods of 'scientific management' (in particular, time measurement) in the 1960s, it was not uncommon in Sweden for a skilled worker in a small plant to complete a number of different work tasks on a unit or make the whole assembly himself (as in the case described in Sandkull 1980). In contrast, in a plant where the principles of mass production reign, the division of labour is strict and any one worker has only a very limited range of tasks. This limitation excludes most workers from responsibility for the product or the equipment. Instead, that responsibility has been allocated to special workers in departments of quality control and maintenance.

The core of the conditions and rules that regulate the work of employees (the social relations of production in the model. cf. Burawoy 1979) concerns the horizontal and the vertical division of labour. Any modern production system reflects two different forms of logic. First is the techno-economic logic which dominates the second, human logic, which is based on the actions of and communication between human beings (Habermas 1971 and Israel 1979). The situation in any particular plant is modified by the attitudes and actions of production managers broadly considered and the factory regime and the ways in which workers cope with it. In the model used here, this dialectic is expressed by the relations between the technical and social relationships of production (see figure 1).

This model enables us to distinguish between different forms of production systems and to clarify the ideas of 'post-Fordism' which have been aired recently (see, for example, Kern and Schumann 1984 and Mathews 1989a and b).

Taylor's basic contribution to the theory of production system design was to separate work from the worker. In this way, not only the components

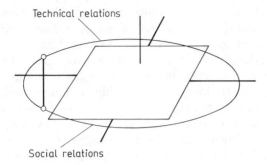

Technical relations

Social relations

Figure 1   Technical and social relations

of a good became standardized but also the work operations necessary to manufacture it. As a consequence, workers became largely interchangeable for many types of work. In such cases, a worker's familiarity with a particular job which had become an obstacle to standardization was removed from the 'commodification' process which had started much earlier on the labour market (Polanyi 1944). To put it another way, the skills of the workers became visible to the employer and could thus be an object of rationalization and mechanization, as Braverman has suggested (1974).

In pre-industrial or non-industrial work the technical and social relations of production are still united but when new methods of industrial production which employed standardized methods and produced standardized outcome were introduced, managers and engineers could develop the technical relations of production without paying much regard to the social relations. The mass-production system of Ford thus became the blueprint for organizing most industrial activities.

Even in modern industrial production, however, all work cannot be standardized, for example, tool making, machine repair and product design. The irregular nature of these tasks has not prevented production engineers from trying to bring them under their control but despite these efforts workers retain a degree of discretion in their work because their knowledge is not easily standardized. The same is true for most work in industries making products on order, which are 'one off' and not carried out on a production line of the 'Fordist' kind.

In industries with batch production the situation is intermediate between mass and one-off production. Some tasks are more easily standardized and controlled than others (Burawoy 1979). The intention of management, however, has so far been to establish as much standardization as possible since standardisation is one of the conditions for control. Advances in computerization, such as CAD-CAM, are often used just for that purpose

(Wilkinson 1983 and Shaiken 1985), although there is nothing inherent in computerization to encourage such control as has been demonstrated in the UTOPIA project (Bjerknes, Ehn and Kyng 1987 and Ehn 1988).

Although ideas of 'Scientific Management' are still very much the norm and rhetoric in industry, in practice Taylorist or Fordist solutions coexist with craftmanship and, indeed, loss of craftmanship in modern production could be attributed to the poor state of American or British manufacturing, compared with Japanese or German (Melman 1983 and Lawrence 1984) industry, rather than to particular theories of management.

In Germany, Sweden, and Japan the process of reproducing industrial labour is no longer the same as it was during the nineteen fifties and sixties. Traditional factory regimes based on rigid rules and regulations have almost ceased to work and instead participation by workers in the production process has increased in one way or another (Sandkull, Fricke and Thurley forthcoming).

In Figure 2 imputed shifts in the exchange relations between participation and efficiency are illustrated. The uppermost line (I) represents the peak of 'Scientific Management' or the situation in most American or British firms, the second one (II) corresponds to common solutions found in the other three countries mentioned above, and finally the lowest line (III) represents what could be regarded as necessary today.

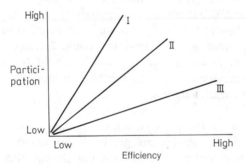

Figure 2   Participation-efficiency ratios

In the new plants built in the 1970s technical relations and logic still dominated despite an intention to include a 'social' element. The solutions adopted by car manufacturers such as Volvo were basically Taylorist production lines. Instead of maximizing utilization of machinery, the production flow was put into focus. As a consequence, the social relations of work had to be modified to persuade workers to participate more fully in the labour process. Car assembly at Volvo became organized in team work and work cycles were expanded (in Kalmar 16−20 minutes). According to the philosophy governing the design of the new plants, the worker should no longer simply sell his labour power but participate more fully through 'enriched' job design. The new social relations meant some relaxation of the traditional prerogatives of management, less direct control and more autonomy. In particular the role of the foremen had to be changed. The new socio-technical systems approach was based on an attempt to put technical and social relations on an equal footing. No satisfactory theoretical solution to that issue has been found yet and in practice technical relations have had to be taken as given, only allowing marginal changes, despite further scope for improving the social relations which appeared in some Norwegian experiments (see Bolweg 1976 and Sandberg 1982). In Sweden, the socio-technical ideas were assimilated by many organizational consultants, including the technical department of the Swedish Employers' Association. These ideas, which suited socio-economic conditions in Sweden at that time, were diffused to many employers. The resulting changes in the workplace, however, were rather modest, as in the example of the modified line production in the Kalmar plant of Volvo from 1974.

During the 1980s other changes in plant design and production philosophy were made. In particular, union representatives participated in the planning which introduced more advanced ideas to the design of Volvo's new plant in Uddevalla (Ellegård, Engström and Nilsson 1989). This plant is based on the principle of work integration: the line has been abandoned and replaced by teams, each assembling a whole car. We do not know yet whether this may represent a successful case of balanced socio-technical sytem.

Current practices in the car industry adopted by Volvo, Toyota and German manufacturers (Agurén, Hansson and Karlsson 1976; Kamata 1983; Kern and Schumann 1984) illustrate the evolution of the labour process. All represent modernizations, not rejections, of the basic Ford philosophy and are 'neo-Fordist' rather than 'post-Fordist'. Far from representing a break with established methods of mass production, they are more sophisticated versions of it, having simply incorporated a predetermined range of variation into the work and production practice.

'Fordist' solutions to production needs, even in their most advanced form, are based on the supremacy of capital and management. A true 'post-Fordist' production system would mean that social relations would dominate over the technical ones (Cooley 1980). To achieve such solutions would require a thorough democratization of enterprises, to the point even where labour hires capital, according to Vanek (1977). In Sweden as elsewhere such change is far from being achieved. The current situation is illustrated below by the case of Volvo.

The Evolution of Work Design in the Car Industry: The Case of Volvo

The car industry is the principal symbol of modern industry and modern productive relations but a symbol with many problematic aspects. The highest degree of worker alienation has long been found in that industry, because the level of mechanization was high and work operations were broken down into their simplest elements by the Fordist system (Goonatilake 1982). The assembly line enforces a uniform pace that most workers find distressing and everywhere have responded to with high turnover, absenteeism, negligence and even sabotage. Social relations in the car industry worldwide long clearly articulated a basic antagonism between management and labour.

General acceptance of the principles of mass production in the car industry, however, did not completely over-rule the maintenance of some conditions specific to each country of production. This can be clearly seen in the case of Volvo which developed a very specific system over the years. In Sweden, for instance, a strong tradition of metalwork, based on respect for trade and craft skills, was common in all small metal-working firms well into the 1950s and 1960s and survived in the departments of tool-making even in the larger firms. Volvo started in 1926–27 in this tradition (Ellegård 1983) and maintained much of it in its work relations, although it was also in the forefront of the adoption of some 'modern' mass manufacturing methods.

Thus, although Swedish industry in general was late in following the practices of American industry, during the 1930s Volvo pioneered the organization of manufacturing operations in machine groups and introduced the conveyor belt into its assembly work. During the 1950s time-measurement methods were introduced, although only after lengthy labour disputes (Giertz 1982; Hermele 1982).

Much more important, Volvo managed to become internationally competitive despite its small scale of operations. During the 1960s, Volvo's production was far smaller than that regarded by industrial economists internationally as the viable minimum and even the Swedish Treasury refused to support financially Volvo's attempt to launch its cars on the US market. From the start, however, Volvo led the world and anticipated much more recent developments in Japan in certain of its production organisation decisions. In particular, Volvo increased its competitive strength by creating a system embracing the operations of all its major suppliers so as to offset its competitors' economies of scale (see figure 3) and made it competitive with much larger American and European car makers. Volvo' s management succeeded in running the whole supply system in a way that combined efficiency with flexibility. The company operated its supply system (including wholly owned component factories) by agreeing on annual delivery schedules specifying the expected quantities to be delivered at a negotiated price. The contracts contained clauses for revisions of volumes because of changes in demand and for rationalization of production by letting Volvo engineers inspect the plants in order to find ways of simplifying the process. Cost reductions thus achieved were shared between Volvo and the suppliers. In this way Volvo could distribute the inherent market uncertainty to all its suppliers and at the same time keep tight rein on production costs. With few exceptions, two sources for all components were used. Most suppliers are found in Sweden or in Germany.

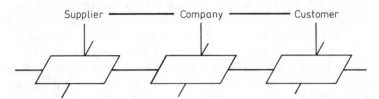

Figure 3   The supply system

Volvo's overall success in its field can be seen in its impact on the whole Swedish economy. Together with its suppliers, Volvo became a prominent local employer in many towns and other communities: in 1976 Volvo and the other Swedish car manufacturer, Saab-Scania, together employed about 67,000 people, directly and indirectly, in Sweden (Hermele 1982). In addition, after its decision to enter the North American market in the 1960s, Volvo became one of the country's major earners of foreign currency with Saab-Scania and Volvo together generating about 12 per cent of total Swedish exports. Given the success of the Volvo group there was every reason to transfer the famous slogan 'What is good for General Motors is good for America' to the Swedish scene: 'What is good for Volvo is good for Sweden'. (Indeed, the impact of Volvo's operations on the Swedish economy is about twice the magnitude of GM's impact on the U.S. economy, as Volvo's own calculations suggest). Volvo also became the symbol of Swedish quality, which for many years was the hallmark of Sweden's export goods. Volvo's top executives were also skillful in their dealings with the Swedish government, heeding the principles of the welfare state and complying with the local rules of the political game. In short, Volvo became a model Swedish national company.

On the 'social' side of work Volvo was also in the forefront of Swedish industry. Already in 1946 an agreement on the creation of an advisory corporate Works Council was signed between the unions and Volvo's management. When Pehr G. Gyllenhammar took over as head of the corporation in 1971, he signalled a new era of collaboration with the unions and started to nurture them as junior partners in management. The Group's Work Council was transformed into a forum for information and discussion with eight management and fourteen union representatives. The Council established a Working Committee (two management and four union representatives), which later was assigned the responsibility of dealing with all issues related to the new act of joint regulation (MBL in Swedish, which is often misleadingly called the Codetermination Act). In addition, Volvo corporation offered each of its unions a place on the Board two years ahead of the legislation on Board representatives.

Although Volvo had over time become firmly entrenched in the Scientific Management tradition, Mr. Gyllenhammar, who came from an insurance company, introduced views that differed radically from established thinking in the car industry. The deterioration of quality, the high labour turnover in the old plants and later the large stocks of unsold cars highlighted the need for cooperation on the part of the workforce. The previous concentration on maximizing production capacity utilization was no longer paramount and production *flow* came into focus instead. The importance of workers' consent to the production process was thus recognized in a new way and a good deal of experimentation with new forms of organization followed.

During the late 1960s, Volvo car sales increased greatly. When the company's operations in Ghent, Belgium, were expanded into a complete factory, the body plant in Gothenburg was left with a surplus of bodies. In 1971 a decision was made to build an assembly plant at Kalmar, where there was a surplus of labour from agriculture. Volvo planned an assembly plant capable of building 30,000 cars annually on a one shift system and with the capacity to double that volume if required. The first blueprints showed a fairly conventional, albeit modern, auto plant. But Mr. Gyllenhammar wanted a more far-sighted layout. He believed that the focus should be on the people working in the plant, with humans running the machines and not the other way round. Studies using his ideas called for a production layout based on work in production teams so as to recreate the climate of the small workshop. The studies suggested that each assembly team should have its own area of the factory where it carried out its part of the assembly operation. The apparent autonomy of the teams was emphasized through the shape of the building and each team's access to its own personnel facilities. The stores of components supplied to all the teams are located in the center of the building. The six workshops are spread out along the outer walls of the building and have separate entrances.

Given the team working framework desired, the major innovation required was to find a substitute for the traditional assembly line. The solution proved to be a mobile assembly carrier which could serve both as a transport device and assembly platform. Assembly work under the vehicle body was facilitated by a device that could tilt the body to 90 degrees. The carriers are steered by electrical impulses from loops in the floor. Between each workshop there are buffer zones which make it possible for the team to work ahead and accumulate time for extra breaks (maximum 15 minutes). The work is paced by MTM 110 and the work cycle is about 20 minutes, compared with one to two minutes at a traditional assembly line. As a result total assembly time is less than in a conventional plant. Much time and care were put into recruiting and training the workforce for the new plant and absenteeism there has always been lower than in most other Volvo plants.

Although it is the best known experiment, the Kalmar plant does not in fact constitute the most advanced solution in the Volvo group. In retrospect we can see that the Kalmar plant and the other new plants in the Volvo Group primarily represented a great achievement in production technology and much improved physical working conditions rather than a fundamental change in approach. Time measurement methods still reigned, for instance, and opportunities for good work and worker participation have remained meagre, despite the eagerness of Volvo's management to foster more involvement, or at least a sense of involvement, by workers (Agurén, Hansson and Karlsson 1984).

'Technical' considerations are also still paramount. The engine division of the Volvo Components Corporation has always been extremely technically oriented. During the late 1960s however, the division suffered from high personnel turnover and difficulties in recruitment. At the beginning of the 1970s, 'advisory groups', joint working groups with the labour unions, were established to seek new ideas and directions. An early lesson from the Volvo components example was that it is very hard to develop a new organization in traditional technical systems. In the new engine factory that started operations in 1974 the latest technology was utilized to create machining and assembly routines that would meet demands for socio-technical solutions. The design of the assembly line even incorporated some of the features of the Kalmar plant but the machining section resulted in a fully automated transfer line except for a few manual and very narrow operations that were difficult to mechanize. The personnel manager of the engine division once said to me during a visit:

'We changed the situation on the shop floor, but we did not change anywhere else. We thus created a setting for worker participation in shopfloor management but our administrative routines which are based on scientific management are

formidable obstacles to a new philosophy. In that language, worker participation does not exist. To achieve the expected results on the shop floor, it is
neccessary to change the entire organization.'

The Kalmar plant, then, did not bring the expected breakthrough in worker-
management relations and ten years later even one of the main innovations,
dock assembly, was abandoned in favour of a modified assembly using an
invisible conveyor belt. At Kalmar, it was always still the workers who had
to adapt to the technology. The new thinking and the rhetoric involved,
however, have had repercussions both on production technology and on
labour relations in the whole Volvo Group. In continuing to refine its labour
processes, Volvo's management has favoured increased mechanization of
production in combination with schemes for inculating greater loyalty and
more responsability for production into the workforce. In the press shop, for
example, Volvo has retrained its workers into becoming skilled 'mechanical
engineers', working in teams with a much higher degree of responsibility.
The developments at Kalmar, however, suggest that an overall strategy for
transforming assembly work into craftmanship still seems to belong the
realm of rhetoric (Jönsson 1981).

Despite this false start, today Volvo's management is in principle even
more convinced that efficiency must be combined with human concerns.
This view is exemplified in the most recent engine plant in the Volvo
Components Corporation and the new Uddevalla car assembly unit. The
solution chosen there was to form a team of ten to assemble a whole car
and have full responsibility for ordering materials, planning the work and
assuring quality: the approach was thus extremely ambitious (see Ellegård,
Engström and Nilsson 1989), although it failed to break away from the old
tradition of worker submission, or even to recognize it. Whatever its
shortcomings may be, Volvo's approach to the question of consent nevertheless stands in sharp constrast to the mainstream mode which still resembles
a 'war on labour' (Goldman and van Houten 1980).

The present chief executive of the Volvo Group has initiated a process
of change in labour relations which, if successful, may indeed have the
potential to liberate workers from their 'commodity' status and set off the
kind of 'good circles' of participation (situations of participation that breed
further participation) that were long ago envisaged by Carole Pateman
(1970: 43). If this happens, Volvo workers may then feel encouraged to
take part in open communication in the company and become creative
participants in the labour process rather than passive operators or mere
observers. This would fit in with the view that 'Industry of the future will
need the whole man', as one prominent Swedish union leader has observed
recently.

Volvo does not, however, always operate at the forefront of new ideas.
It operates different policies in different circumstances. At its plant in

Ghent, in Belgium, the production system is a conventional continuous line with cycles averaging two minutes. Wages are hourly, without any piece rates, although pay is better than in other companies in the region and industrial relations are good despite the existence of three competing unions. Volvo has even so far succeeded in getting the best male workers in the region, who adhere fully to the Fordist system. Presumably, the visions formulated below do not yet apply to Belgium.

'The modern working man needs a sense of purpose and satisfaction in his daily work. He feels the need of belonging to a team, of being able to feel at home in his surroundings, of being able to identify himself with the goods he produces and − not the least − of feeling that he is appreciated for the work he performs. Factory work must be adapted to people, and not people to machines. This calls for innovation both in the field of human relations and as regards technical aspects. I believe that humanization of work and efficiency can be compatible. Indeed, I believe that, in today's society, they are insepar-able.' (Pehr G. Gyllenhammar)

In determining the likelihood of implementation of the ideals expressed by Gyllenhammar in a real work situation and of the transition to a 'post-Fordist' system of production organisation in major 'mature' industries, the state of the worldwide market for the products made will doubtless play an important role. In the automobile industry this future seems problematic, at least as far as traditional vehicles are concerned, and much restructuring will take place internationally (see Altshuler et al. 1986). Over recent years the costs of designing new models have increased dramatically and put great burdens on small firms in particular. In addition, there is overproduction in the world. Sales are stagnant in the U.S., a calamity which recently has hurt Saab severely and forced the company to enter into a joint venture with General Motors. Several other mergers have occurred and Volvo, too, has recently announced an 'alliance' with Renault. Further, the market segment in which Volvo and Saab have specialized is threatened by Japanese competition. Other segments face competition from new car makers from Korea and perhaps Taiwan or Malaysia. These problems will be felt in all producing countries and, unless clear productivity improvements can be demonstrated, may adversely affect both the speed and direction of job design changes.

The Move to 'Partnership': Human Resources in Organisational Change

Armelle Gorgeu and René Mathieu

Introduction

The change to a Just-in-Time system of production involves fundamental reordering of almost all aspects of factory organisation, especially in large assembly industries still largely operating on a Just-in-Case basis in Europe. This reordering goes far beyond simple machine layout and particularly involves changes in the skills which workers need, especially those who work on or close to production lines. The search for perfect quality in component manufacture also ensures that such changes spread well beyond the assemblers' factory boundaries. Suppliers too must reorganise work practices and ensure that skill levels are high. Altering these levels involves changes in personnel policies, giving extra responsibilities to some employees and fewer to others. This paper illustrated these changes in the automotive and aerospace industries in France.

The changes in their organisation made by the direct suppliers of automobile manufacturers and by the aerospace component makers are quite similar. They occur for different reasons and in different ways, however Automobile component-makers' and subcontractors' organisational changes are responses to very precise directions from the automobile manufacturers while the aerospace component-makers have more freedom of choice in their methods.

The Direct Suppliers of Automobile Manufacturers

For the first tier suppliers of automobile manufacturers 'partnership' consists in applying management methods prescribed by their customer firms and in engaging the necessary material and human resources to take charge of new responsibilities. A total reorganisation is required, one in which human resources occupy an important position and one in which strong staff motivation is the prerequisite for success. Implementing the partnership concept therefore entails important changes in personnel policies. These include particularly *longer term personnel management horizons; a major expansion of training programs for all categories of personnel; a gradual transformation of the contents of blue-collar work; a breakdown of barriers between job functions; and a constant awareness of quality*, with quality management taking on strategic importance.

Longer Term Personnel Management Horizons

In general, the development of partnership in the car industry has meant a need for increased skills and some reduction in the workforce. In 1983, personnel policy in these companies consisted of attention to immediate needs and medium goals. The decline in automobile production in 1980 had already both led to accelerating staff reductions and foreshadowed the technological changes then appearing. The combined use of selective measures of staff reduction (layoffs, early retirements, departure incentives, hiring freezes) and of flexible working arrangements (fixed term contracts, temporary workers, internal reassignments) had enabled companies to modify the structures of their work forces. The investments made in advanced technology entailed changed workforce structure, increased the need for technicians and skilled workers and precipitated the disappearance of many jobs for unskilled workers.

'Partnership', the development of long-term contractual agreements between core firms and selected suppliers, facilitates longer term personnel management since the chosen suppliers have some assured demand for their products and thus information about their workload for several years to come even though they have no written contracts. In addition, taking charge of new responsibilities entails new needs for highly skilled personnel. New functions are created or expanded (Quality Management, Research & Development, Methods, Logistics, Purchasing, Marketing), both at local sites and at the head offices, since direct relationships now develop between the plant sites of the customer and the plant sites of the supplier. The partial decentralisation of the departments of Marketing, Methods and Purchasing from the company's head office to the production sites is a new organisational form linked to 'partnership'. New positions are created for senior engineers and technicians, which are largely filled by external recruiting but also by internal promotions and reassignments.

At manufacturing level, recruitment of young college graduates has already begun. These young people, who usually have a *brevet de technicien supérieur* (BTS, a secondary school vocational training certificate) are hired as all-purpose metal tradesmen (*adjusteurs* and *régleurs*), with the idea of promoting them after a few years to positions as technicians in the Production or Methods departments. Production reorganisation by product lines has also led to new jobs for automated production-line workers at the level of shop floor technician, and for automated production-line operators at the 'P3' level (skilled worker). These jobs are intended for young people who have earned a *baccalauréat* (secondary school general studies certificate) or *brevet de technicien supérieur*, who receive further training in quality management, in the control of automated machines and robots and in maintenance. The shop floor technician is taking the place of the foreman in an earlier era. He (or she) is responsible for the quality of the products manufactured on his production line and works with a small number of blue-collar workers. His (or her) role is to act as team leader and to stimulate cooperation with and among workers.

In contrast, the introduction of quality management and investment in a modern stock management system are leading to the elimination of certain skills. In manufacturing, the integration of quality control into the machines themselves has eliminated the need for quality checking formerly done by low-skilled workers at the level of 'OS' (*ouvrier spécialisé*) or 'P1' (a low grade of skilled worker) and final quality check, once the responsibility of specialised checking personnel, is tending to be replaced by systematic operator self-checking. Production line operators now do their own quality control, following strict specifications, and share in responsibility for product quality since they oversee the proper functioning of the machines while also performing checks on products selected randomly at regular intervals. The disappearance of jobs for general checkers has posed problems of personnel retraining. In planning the launch of a new system, job eliminations are scheduled to be coordinated with the installation of computer-aided production management. The reclassification of the personnel assigned to these jobs, an essential part of the process, is prepared long in advance.

The Expansion of Training Programs and the Transformation of Blue-Collar Work

All the companies studied are establishing and multiplying training programs of varying duration, some spread over several years. Current training budgets, in all the companies interviewed, greatly exceed the legal minimum of 1.2 per cent of the total payroll while many go as high as 5.0 per cent. Some, such as those connected with the installation of sophisticated equipment, are not new but require frequent updating and now must include concerns of quality, while others are specifically concerned with quality assurance. As was mentioned earlier, core client firms require their suppliers to use anticipatory methods of defect prevention such as Statistical Process Control (SPC). SPC involves the use of statistical data not only by the Quality Management department but also by shop floor workers who become assistants to the Quality Management department, which needs their information to analyse the reasons for flaws in quality.

Training in SPC ultimately concerns all personnel, even if not everyone is directly involved in it at first. Ford offers its suppliers free SPC training courses for their managers and can send instructors out to their plant sites to train other categories of workers. SPC training is always done in stages, by worker categories, and in successive phases, with refresher courses for those first trained. For shop floor personnel and foremen it comprises education in awareness of the philosophy of quality, instruction in handling simple control instruments (measurement rings, sliding calipers) and training in the SPC method itself. This method requires some understanding of statistical tools, even for machine operators, who must calculate averages and projections in order to fill out control charts and understand when a machine requires intervention or when maintenance workers must be called. In companies where shop floor personnel have little formal education, courses in literacy and basic skills have to be organised first. Temporary workers are also trained in SPC because today the hiring of temporary personnel is not used only to manage an exceptionally heavy workload but also as a screening process for possible permanent hiring and assists the certification required.

Training always precedes the implementation of SPC in the factory. The SPC method is applied first to new equipment, with priority given to machines that perform major operations. Before using SPC, workers learn to do quality control by random sampling, without having to fill out control charts but following very precise instructions. SPC training generally provides companies with the opportunity to develop multi-skilled workers who not only learn how to check their own production, use measuring instruments, and understand some notions of statistics, but also how to perform minor adjustments, make needed corrections and even do small repairs.

Giving the operator responsibility for quality control is a challenge to the long-established habits and attitudes of foremen and unskilled workers used to traditional mass production techniques. In the past, the operator's job was to produce and keep up the pace while it was the checker's job to test whether the finished pieces were any good and intervene if necessary.

In all the companies we studied, especially in those with a large unskilled labour force, the psychological shock of recent changes has been and still is very significant, meeting strong resistance among foremen who came up through the ranks. In some companies, the implementation of SPC has in fact been a failure since it removes their special area of responsibility. Often operators only fill in measurements on the control chart and do not do any calculations while some companies have begun to replace the manual control chart with an automated chart where the workers puts the pieces to be tested into a testing device and the measurements appear on a control chart on the screen.

As a general rule, in France training in self-checking or SPC does not imply either subsequent promotion or a higher salary. Promotion only occurs if the trained person moves to what is considered a higher position. The operator's taking responsibility for quality control, acquiring a broader range of skills, or learning to make minor adjustments and repairs are not considered justification for reclassifying the job. Despite the fact that the content of the work is changing and the blue-collar worker is having to take on both a bigger workload and more responsibility, the classifications are not changed.

The introduction of SPC in plants often coincides with the organisation of autonomous production islands. In this system, collective responsibility for product quality is given to a group of workers having the same level of qualification, who take turns by mutual agreement at all the jobs on an automated production line. This reorganisation frequently involves the initiation of a system of bonuses for product quality improvement (a bonus is given to the whole crew in proportion to the number of good pieces produced).

The Breakdown of Barriers between Job Functions and the Increasing Importance of the Quality Management Function

Close cooperation between the personnel of different functions within the company has become a necessity with the introduction of quality assurance systems. The idea is that the later a given defect is discovered, the more costly it becomes and that the cause of defects lies in the organisation of production; nearly 80 per cent of defects are thought to be due to causes that escape the span of control of the operator. Collaboration between various functions within the company has become frequent, giving rise to workshop quality groups, bringing together senior executives from different departments (Marketing, R & D, Methods, Quality Management and Production), who receive training in an analytical method called AMDEC (analysis of manufacturing defects). The method consists of working in groups led by the Methods or Quality Management department, with a view to eliminating, right from the design of the products, any risk of not meeting the required specifications, through rigorous analysis of potential defects based on their seriousness and the probability of their detection.

The creation of Quality Management departments took place, depending on the company, between 1983 and 1986. The Quality Manager is the person who understands the company's workings better than anyone other than the Managing Director; this person is the one who can break down the barriers between the different departments and facilitate the exchange of information. The job of Quality Manager is becoming a key position; it can be a promotion for the head of the R & D Methods departments and can even be a route to the position of Managing Director. The Quality Management department, staffed by engineers and senior technicians, positioned next to the quarters of the General Management of factory or company, is charged with analysing all data on quality, from whatever source (customer complaints, rejects, control charts). The Quality Management department, or the Quality Manager, writes or updates the Quality Manual, carries out quality audits in plants and among suppliers, is responsible for machine capability studies, and is gradually taking over from the old Checking department. The Quality Manager's responsibilities also include leading the quality workshop groups, which have been set up in many companies to reduce rejects. They bring together shop floor workers, managers and technicians from different departments but they are not true Quality Circles since the Quality Manager initiates them, chooses the participants and decides on the subject of each meeting. In the companies we studied there were no true Quality Circles; either there never had been any, or the experiment had ended in failure. These companies preferred to develop their own forms of staff participation in ways which they could control.

Aerospace Component-Makers

The changes in internal company organisation carried out by aerospace component-makers are intended to gain a competitive edge over rival firms worldwide. Operational reorganisation is often accompanied by structural changes within the corporation or in relations between companies in order to rationalise production. The organisation strategy presented below was carried out as part of a merger of two companies decided upon by the parent company which had recently bought both of them.

The new company born out of this merger was created in 1986 and proceeded with major reductions in staff inherited from the pre-existing firm, dropping employee numbers from 1900 in 1986 to 1300 in 1989. Combining the two firms' production capabilities involved organisation alterations aimed at getting better quality products at lower cost and meeting the requirements of French aerospace manufacturers and foreign customers, since exports represent 30 per cent of the new firm's total sales. The two former companies both had quality certificates from the French armaments authorities for their military products as well as specific quality certifications from each customer for civil aviation components. Each also already had a quality control system that satisfied existing customers but needed improving because clients' demands were becoming ever stricter and because manufacturing costs had risen because of the heavy cost of internal rejects and testing. The new company therefore took action to build in quality 'as far up the line as possible.' It uses the same, or similar, methods as those recommended by automobile manufacturers to their suppliers, such as AMDEC, which aims to detect potential defects right from the design of the product. It has also been trying to introduce self-checking by workers of their own production, using control charts, seeking to eliminate the old system where final checks, including testing the individual parts, the whole assembly, and trial runs were made. To avoid 'costly extras,' the company uses computer-aided design software and computarised calculations; it is striving in this way to encourage dialogue between the different categories of personnel and joint decision-making by the managers of different departments.

These organisation changes are accompanied by changes in personnel management similar to those taking place among automobile manufacturers. Major changes are occurring in the Quality Management and Checking departments, with a significant upgrading of the level of qualifications. The Quality Manager is becoming the most important associate of the Managing Director, and simultaneously heads a Quality Management department, now staffed by engineers instead of technicians, and a Checking department, which is now reduced in size and will soon only be staffed by checkers qualified at technician level. Restructuring of these departments is proceeding through internal promotions to positions as engineers, through the reassignment of technicians from the Quality department to the Checking department and through the recruitment of an engineer as Quality Manager.

The introduction of worker self-checking with control charts means a major expansion of training programs. The workers, all skilled, had already been checking their own products for several years and had already learned how to use measuring instruments. To make them aware of their responsibility for quality, they were even required to sign after checking but, since they knew that there would later be a final check, they were not very careful. Worker self-checking with control charts requires new training which is longer than that needed to use measuring instruments.

To reduce costs, the Quality Management department is interested both in product quality and in 'administrative quality', reducing problems of information circulation and of task redundancy that can greatly increase production costs. To improve information circuits, the Quality Manager is seeking to set up Progress Groups and Quality Circles and to develop dialogue with the workers during quality audits performed by the Quality engineers in the plants. In this company, as with the direct suppliers of automobile manufacturers, the traditional Taylorist model of mass production is being called into question, with overspecialisation of tasks being considered a hindrance to improved competitiveness.

The Introduction of a Quality Management System in Companies Which Do Not Have 'A Vocation to Become Partners'

Subcontractors working for the aerospace industry and their *confrères* working indirectly for the automobile manufacturers cannot, as already pointed out, hope to benefit from 'partnership' arrangements but most are still striving to introduce a quality management system so as to continue to work for these industries and diversify their clientele into other industries through a good reputation for high quality. The introduction of a quality management system means making material and other investments which are sometimes considerable. Subconstractors who have worked for many years for the aerospace or armaments industries have long had to use very strict quality assurance procedures and to modernise their equipment to meet the technical requirements of their customers. They have all had a specialised quality testing department and more or less complex testing equipment. In these companies, equipment purchases and organisational changes may actually be less important now than in other companies which did not previously have to meet such requirements. The subcontractors working for automobile component-makers generally fall into the latter case and the transformations they are undergoing to set up a quality management system can be very considerable. At present, however, all these subcontractors have the same goals, consistent quality of product, and reduction in manufacturing rejects which are leading them to change working methods. Instead of being small crafts operations, they now have to become industrialised. This implies better organisation, more formalisation and new personnel requirements. The introduction of a quality management system is thus translated into a number of changes in personnel policy. These are: a more precise definition of job descriptions and tasks, often resulting in promotions and recruitments; the introduction of operator self-checking according to strict requirements, including a minimum amount of education; the emergence of a Quality Management function different from the Checking function, even though the same person might be responsible for both; and the need for a more qualified blue-collar work force, with workers expected to have a broader range of skills.

Whether they are subcontractors for the automobile or the aerospace industry, these companies are redrawing organisation charts, so that each manager's responsibilities are clearly defined, and are creating or expanding their Quality, Marketing, and Checking departments. The high level positions are generally filled by internal promotion while young people are recruited to blue-collar jobs and technicians' posts in the Methods department. The new demands being made on blue-collar workers described earlier now mean rigorous selection in the hiring process and the expansion of training programs under the responsibility of the Quality Manager.

The salary policy of these companies has also changed. To motivate personnel to take on more responsibilities and be more involved, firms are establishing systems of individualising salaries and are instituting bonuses both for quality and for 'merit'. Changes in personnel management are accompanied by investment in production and testing equipment and in computerisation. The manufacturing equipment needs to be both multipurpose enough to satisfy a diverse clientele and reliable enough to ensure consistent quality.

Subcontractors working for the aerospace industry have often anticipated the requirements of their customers and, in the interests of diversifying their clientele and improving production, they have sought to earn quality certificates that were said to be difficult to obtain, notably from the military authorities. They have tried to improve their organisation and investment not only in production and testing equipment but also in computer software and training programs; they have recruited an engineer as Quality Manager or have filled the post of Quality Manager by promoting an experienced manager from the Methods department whose seniority gives him or her a good understanding of the firm. They implement the advice they are given by their customers during quality audits as they consider this essential to reduce costs.

Many of the subcontractors studied who work for the automobile component makers have never worked directly for the assemblers but the component-makers and the manufacturers' direct subcontractors who must put the quality philosophy of the automobile manufacturers into practice have warned their suppliers that they must follow the assemblers' quality rules. Some have assisted their suppliers to comply by asking them to send someone responsible for quality to be trained in the SPC method. Few as yet have a Quality Management department so the person who is trained may be the Managing Director of the company, a tester, a technician, or a shop floor maintenance worker. The component-makers and the manufacturers' direct subcontractors are beginning quality audits among suppliers to select those to whom they can delegate responsibility for product quality but the selection itself is not happening yet. All the subcontractors interviewed complained about the absence of partnership with the automobile component makers and about the demands of the latter, who impose stricter quality assurance procedures and methods on them while simultaneously requiring shorter and shorter delivery times.

The companies studied which work indirectly for the manufacturers fell into two categories: those which were selling even a little to technically demanding customers or aiming to specialise in high-quality products and those which were not prepared for new conditions, where everything needed to be done from scratch. Firms in the first category continue to organise themselves in the image of their customers, creating a Quality Management department or hiring a Quality Manager poached from one of their main customers with good knowledge of clients' requirements. These companies are also strengthening other departments such as Marketing and Methods. They are training their blue-collar personnel in self-checking methods, training workers to be multi-skilled, and continuing to invest in new equipment for manufacturing, testing and computerised stock management. Firms in the second category must reorganise their entire production to obtain good quality and invest heavily if they want to make up their lag. All companies must deliver products without defects, since if one piece is defective the whole lot is rejected, and must often deliver every day, sometimes several times a day. For example, one company studied had to recheck every unit in a lot of several thousand pieces because a wood shaving had found its way into one piece in the lot concerned.

The repercussion effects of the manufacturers' requirements down the chain to the subcontractors are still very recent and it is still too early to see the final effects on employment and personnel management. Nevertheless, some subcontracting firms working for the automobile component-makers have managed to anticipate their customers' requirements. In spite of the imperatives of a continuous flow of deliveries, they manage not to overstock materials since they are beginning to computerise their stock management or know how to take full advantage of the capacities of their computer-controlled machinery. These are the companies which have most increased their staff in recent years. To judge by these examples, the push of manufacturers' requirements down the production chain to the subcontractors could have positive effects in terms of employment. On their direct and indirect suppliers alike, automobile assemblers are imposing a common model of production, uniting the flexibility of a small company with the strict organisation of a big one. But perhaps it is easier for a small company to organise itself in the image of its customers than for a big one to gradually abandon the traditional model of mass production. In return for new services the 'lagging' companies are offered little. They have little autonomy, are not asked to take initiatives in design or manufacturing methods, only work according to furnished plans, and must strictly respect the specifications. Moreover, they have no assurance whatsoever of having privileged relations with their customers. 'Partnerships' arrangements seem to be limited to core assemblers and first tier suppliers. For second tier suppliers the control relationship is as before while the requirements demanded of them are harder than ever to meet.

Conclusion

The research reported here indicates the *intra*-organisational changes being introduced as a function both of technological advances and new managerial methods of regulating *inter*-organisational arrangements in the aerospace and automotive industries. The changes include the introduction and increasing importance of new departments, notably those of Quality Assurance, and of their leaders, the Quality Managers. They also include major changes at shopfloor and supervisory levels: some supervisory funtions are disappearing as a result of the shift of responsibility for checking and on-going quality control from specially qualified checking staff to production workers. The latter are now required to learn new skills, notably those associated with Statistical Process Control, which in turn require a higher minimum level of the broader skills of literacy and numeracy. Despite the need to learn these new skills, however, it is clear that workers are not compensated either for their skill acquisition or their extra responsibilities through job reclassifications leading to promotion or increased salary payments. Managerial strategies instead focus on incorporating these new elements into existing job requirements.

The evidence also suggests that while it is the core firms who are initiating such intra-organisational changes their suppliers are expected to follow suit. This is especially clear as a factor in the selection of 'partner' companies but also in the chances of subcontractors of becoming suppliers to the first tier suppliers. The same trends are evident in both automotive and aerospace sectors and are further advanced in the latter.

Workplace Strategic Change: Classification Restructuring in the Australian Public Service

Chris Selby-Smith

Introduction

This chapter describes job reclassification as a major mechanism of organisational change in the public sector. It covers the period from the establishment of the Classification Group in the Office of the Public Service Board (PSB) within the Australian Public Service (APS) in the reorganisation of mid-1984 until the abolition of the Board by Prime Minister Hawke in July 1987. Against a background of progressive decay over some years in the APS classification arrangements the period saw major change, including a move from a reactive, even disinterested, stance to a highly proactive pursuit by the government of both equity and efficiency goals. These changes both made a significant contribution to reworking this part of the world. Examining them shows links to a number of wider theoretical and practical issues.

The classification management function in both public and private enterprises is concerned with the organisation of work, determining in what structures, by what staff and under what conditions given jobs will be carried out. It is thus central to the operation of any large-scale organisation. Often considered to be boring, albeit necessary, and little referred to in the literature, the management of job classifications is in fact central to effective performance by public (and private) sector agencies everywhere and is a challenging area where significant reform can be achieved for the benefit of various stakeholders, including staff and unions, management and governments. Good management of job divisions can, for example, serve to promote efficiency in departmental operations, either directly through enabling work to be appropriately organised, or through broadbanding and multiskilling, thus providing more responsibility for workers at lower levels of the organisational hierarchy with resultant improvements in workflow, commitment and initiative. It can also serve to promote equity objectives by reducing occupational health and safety risks and improving training and career opportunities. It can even, on occasion, facilitate the achievement of both equity and efficiency objectives.

Technology is a factor in organisational change in the public sector but is far from the only factor and not always the most important. Culture, however, is always important and so are the ways in which change can occur in organisations, technology and culture together.

The activity reported on below raises issues about innovation and the processes by which new ideas develop within complex organisations and confirms that the engendering of commitment facilitates the subsequent process of implementation. The different elements do indeed interact, but change can become more endogenous, particularly at the larger system level, as a result of conscious effort, vision and leadership. Marceau and Clegg, both in this volume, claim that 'postmodern' organisations are not driven by one structuring principle, but rather are composed of a selection of available social, cultural and economic tools, topics and rationalities and this was apparent in the reforms considered here.

Over the period covered here classification reform in the APS was in advance of that in the Australian private sector. It also provides some interesting comparisons with relevant overseas development in countries such as the U.S., U.K. and Canada. In many ways, the Australian organisational mechanism chosen and the ways in which it was used led to broader results than elsewhere and to more far-reaching modifications. It also was a more 'democratic' mechanism since it involved unions and departmental offices far removed from the centre in Canberra.

The first section of the discussion here describes the political background to the change in classifications, the second focusses on the work of the 'change agents' most concerned (the classification group). The next four sections describe the mechanism used to make the changes, notably the review processes both internal and external, and their results. The chapter as a whole tells the story of job classification reform in the Australian Public Service between 1984 and 1987. It particularly illustrates the role played by a central agency, the Public Service Board, until its abolition in 1987. More broadly, it illustrates the use of a specific mechanism to achieve quite radical change in a very large scale and substantially decentralised organisation (albeit once under ultimate central control). The extent of both scale and decentralisation can be seen in a few figures. The APS at that time employed around 170,000 people scattered over a continent the size of Europe, with concentrations in half a dozen cities but with many in small towns and country areas. It is the story of how a government with the triple objectives of increasing efficiency, equity and industrial democracy used the Board's job classification powers to achieve major changes at the level of the whole system despite having as a fourth objective the devolution of powers to individual government departments. Relations between centre and periphery became crucial. The Board began as a major force and achieved many of the goals set in this area but in the end was defeated by decentralising 'managerial' forces.

In the context of rapid technological change, notably in relation to keyboarding and other areas greatly affected by advances in information technology, APS job descriptions had to change. One objective of the reform, advanced both by the government and, especially, by the Board, was to use these pressures to achieve changes which contributed greatly to equity between occupational groups and especially between women and members of minority groups in relation to their male colleagues. Another objective was to strengthen industrial democracy by giving staff and unions greater say in the new classification structure and the detailed organisation of work in the APS.

Classification Management in the Australian Public Service

When the Hawke Labor Government was elected in 1983 it was committed to substantial reform of the APS. It had devoted considerable thought to this matter while in Opposition and the Minister charged with the responsibility of finalising the reform package and then implementing it, John Dawkins, was senior and energetic. The reforms were introduced in mid-1984, following consideration by Parliament of the Government's proposals, and were much wider than classification alone. A Senior Executive Service was created to replace the former Second Division, which was seen as more focussed on the needs of individual Departments than on the APS as a whole, and the reforms provided for substantial devolution of financial authority to agency heads. In both cases, the Government wanted to devolve authority, to give greater autonomy to departmental managers and to judge them by the results they achieved. The Public Service thus began to take up the paradigm of 'managerialism' from business, drawing from experience in national and multinational firms and on advice from business schools and from consultants. Indeed, the public service environment is now in its own turn beginning to impose similar 'managerialist' requirements elsewhere on organisations with which it deals (e. g. through contractors or suppliers). The government was also intent on involving Ministers more closely in various aspects of public administration and blurring the traditional distinctions between administration and policy (for further details see Selby-Smith 1989).

In relation to classification management, responsibility prior to the APS Reforms of 1984 clearly rested with the Public Service Board (PSB), which was a central agency, located in Canberra with regional offices in the major State capitals where the bulk of Federal public servants were located. The PSB was formally the employer of Commonwealth public servants. It was concerned with the recruitment, selection, training and promotion of APS staff, had a particular concern with more senior staff and a general role in management improvement and the promotion of equal employment opportunity throughout the Service. There had been some operational devolution to Departments but this was relatively minor in comparison with subsequent changes. For some years the PSB had, however, been preoccupied with other matters, particularly the management of the staff ceilings arrangements. The classification management function had not received high priority and overall it was not in good shape. For example, most APS positions did not have written classification standards. Those standards which did exist were often out of date or becoming so; the overall approach to classification management had not been critically reviewed for a considerable period; reviews and subsequent revision of classification structures had been at a low level; and classification training had almost ceased. The general view in the Service tended to be that the area was primarily a responsibility of the PSB and most Departments had undertaken relatively little activity in it.

As part of the APS Reforms of 1984 the power to classify and reclassify positions — the Service continued with a position based system — was given to the heads of individual agencies, such as the Comptroller General of Customs, the Australian Statistician, the Auditor General or the Secretary of a Department. The PSB was given power to audit classification decisions made by Departments and the general thrust of the changes was seen as consistent with 'letting the managers manage'. As we shall see, the situation as it developed illustrates Bamber's (1989) thesis that sectors and employing organisations which face more turbulent environments will be more likely to innovate, introducing greater job flexibility, than those with relatively stable environments.

An important element of the new arrangements was that agency heads could only use those classification structures which were approved by the PSB. The head of an agency could decide whether to place a position in one classification structure rather than another, or at one level rather than another within an approved structure, but could not introduce a new structure or modify existing classification structures approved by the PSB. The arrangements implied the responsibility of the PSB to maintain up-to-date classification structures which continued to be appropriate to APS requirements. Given the historical background this was a substantial responsibility for the Board, which had no chance of discharging it adequately in the immediate future. The 1984 Reforms also transferred the function of controlling the overall number of staff in agencies from the PSB to the Department of Finance.

The new arrangements presented challenges to both individual Departments and central agencies. The new devolution brought to the surface many ambivalent attitudes. For instance, some Departments were inclined, at least on occasion, to look to the Board as the guardian of the classification management interests of the APS as a whole but most did not want interference by the Board in their own affairs. Some unions too, particularly in the initial period of the new arrangements, were inclined to argue that they should be able to deal bilaterally with agencies, untrammelled by the requirement to pass information to the PSB (and allow the PSB involvement where it wished).

The position was further complicated because the reform measures failed to spell out at all clearly the balance which was expected to be struck between Departmental autonomy and the management of the classification function for the Service as a whole. As Clegg (1989b) has commented more generally, relationships between centre and periphery have profound implications for the functioning of organisations. In the reform of the APS, centre-periphery relationships were to prove a continuing problem, particularly with respect to audit and monitoring activities. Responsibility for maintaining the integrity of the classification system in the APS was divided two ways — between Ministers and bureaucrats and between central agencies and the operating Departments. Thus the Board, with its long history of statutory independence, had the prime responsibility in relation to APS employees for overall industrial relations, adherence to the National Wage Case principles and appearances before the Conciliation and Arbitration Commission, while the Department of Finance, with its closer links to Cabinet in general and its own Minister in particular, was responsible for the financial aspects of control and staffing numbers in a period of tight expenditure restraint.

Other players were important too. First, the relevant unions were an important part of the classification process and had been promised a closer involvement in classification management matters during the negotiation with the Government on the 1984 Reforms. Second, the Board had complicated 'coordination arrangements' in industrial relation matters and had responsibility not only for APS staff but also for staff in Commonwealth authorities, which had a statutory relationship with the PSB. At the end of 1987 there were 38 bodies in statutory relationship and this arrangement could cause formidable problems. Other Commonwealth authorities did not have a statutory relationship with the PSB but were within the wider area of Australian government employment; for example, Telecom, Australia Post, Qantas, the Health Insurance Commission or the Commonwealth

Bank. These authorities had a considerable measure of autonomy, but insofar as their activities were relevant to classification management (or related matters such as pay and arbitration) were subject to the Department of Employment and Industrial Relations (DEIR).

These were the arrangements which applied over the period covered by this paper, from mid-1984 to July 1987. Following its return to power at the Federal election in July 1987 the Hawke Government initiated large scale changes in the machinery of government arrangements. These included abolition of the Public Service Board. In relation to the classification management function there was a three-way split: the new Public Service Commission became responsible for recruitment policy, qualifications and general training matters; the Department of Finance acquired responsibility for Senior Executive Service matters, the classification training further function and the overall audit and monitoring role; while the new Department of Industrial Relations assumed responsibility for structures and reviews (as well as pay, arbitration and overall industrial relations aspects).

The changes involved alteration in high-level responsibility for classification matters. In particular, through the Departments of Finance and Industrial Relations — and individual agencies — it was Ministers (rather than a PSB with statutory independence) who became responsible for particular classification management decisions, while those authorities or agencies formerly responsible to the PSB or DEIR respectively now all became subject to the Minister for Industrial Relations and his Department. Thus, while in theory the new arrangement gives greater autonomy to Departments and hence more flexibility in the organisation of work, in practice it has become more difficult to achieve radical change in that field across the APS and its associated organisations as a whole. A major tool for system-wide change was thus blunted. This reflected a trend towards greater conservatism on a wider front. The next section describes the organisation of the 'tool' in the period 1984 – 87.

The Agent of Change: The Public Service Board

The Office of the Public Service Board was reorganised during the first Hawke government in 1984. The Board itself consisted of a Chairman and two Commissioners: the Deputy Commissioner, while not formally a member of the Board, attended Board meetings regularly and participated fully in discussion. During the period which is reviewed in this paper, corporate planning was introduced into the Office of the PSB.

After considerable discussion the objectives of the classification component of the Board's corporate plan were defined as: to design, develop and define occupational structures which facilitate the achievement of organisational efficiency and effectiveness and which contribute to the attainment of the Board's personnel policies; to assist departments to maintain proper classification processes and use existing classification structures effectively; and to monitor the way in which departments and agencies used the existing classification arrangements (including audit of systems, procedures and decisions as well as broader trend monitoring activity). Five operational areas of activities were identified and it was these which were primarily used for the development, management and evaluation of classification activities in the Board's Office. These reform components, were: information and training; audit and monitoring; standards and guidelines; and structures development and review (internally and externally initiated).

Using the Board's classification powers as a tool for system-wide change meant that, although total numbers of staff available to initiate and implement change were static, there had to be considerable changes in the deployment of staff among different activities. This reflects both the pressures of the external environment and the conscious choices of management. The majority of most senior clerical staff were used on external review activity. These reviews were often difficult, sensitive and time-critical. The pressures on these staff was increased by the deliberate decision of management to give a higher priority than previously to internally initiated review activity and to adopt a much more proactive stance in relation to overall classification management in the Service for both efficiency and equity reasons. This was a policy of short term pain for long term gain.

Secondly, the distribution of staff reflects particular pressures such as the need for additional attention to be given to information and training activities following the substantial changes to classification management arrangements which were associated with the introduction of the APS Reforms in 1984. Another example concerned the need from time to time to insist on completion of classification audit tasks despite other pressing demands. Management also adhered to its decision that some resources would be devoted at all times to each reform activity, so that even when pressures elsewhere were at their greatest and staff resources for a particular activity were at their lowest progress was never completely halted. This also contributed to the maintenance of a minimum core of skill and experience in each area at all times.

Thirdly, to ensure involvement across the APS in the changes to be made and to generate commitment to them, conscious attempts were made throughout the period to involve staff in the Board's Regional Offices. Cooperative efforts were made by Regional Directors and by Central Office.

The results were variable. Overall resources for classification development work were expanded, the additional perspective was often valuable and significant experience was gained by individual staff. In general it proved to be easier to involve staff from the Board's Regional Offices in areas such as standards and guidelines, audit and monitoring, or information and training rather than in structures development and review activities where tight deadlines and the frequent need for close and continuing involvement with other areas of the Board's Office and the central offices of Departments were inhibiting factors.

Methods of Operation: The Components of the Classification

Some organisational change using the classification structures was internally generated and some developed from an external push. Changes thus followed different paths and are discussed in turn below. First, internally initiated change. As already mentioned, between 1984 and 1987 a conscious decision was made to adopt a more proactive stance in relation to the review of classification structures and there was substantial reallocation of staff resources towards this activity, including substantial SES resources. In terms of the distinction drawn by Curtain and Mathews (1990), the overall approach to organisational restructuring emphasised 'productivity maximisation', with a focus on expanding jobs tasks, enhancing the skills and capacities of workers and developing a more democratic and participative workplace rather than a 'cost minimisation' emphasis.

Internally Initiated Reviews

To begin the process of change, two kinds of review were undertaken. The *internally* initiated reviews used as the bases for change were small in number but each constituted an enormous task and dealt with key sections of the public service as a whole. Three examples are particularly important here. First, there was the review of keyboard structures, such as typing, word processing or data processing, which began in 1983. It eventually grew to encompass the Clerical Assistant structure and the lower four levels of the Clerical Administrative structure by 1985. This was the major review, the largest ever undertaken in Australia and has *major* implications for the way in which all work is undertaken throughout the whole Australian Public Service in the future. The review covered some 73,000 staff in March

1987: 13,6 % in the keyboard structures, 37,3 % in the clerical assistant structure and 49,1 % in the lower levels of the clerical administrative structure. The majority of these staff were women and a majority of the women in the service as a whole were thus included in the classification structures being reviewed: 98 % of staff in the keyboard structures were women, as were 68 % of those in the clerical assistant structure and 42 % of those in the lower levels of the clerical administrative structure. Members of other equal employment opportunity target groups were also significantly represented in these classification structures. The exercise thus had considerable equal employment opportunity potential and, indeed, the successful conclusion of the review in 1987 involved substantial improvements in equity and equal opportunity as well as in efficiency. The whole exercise was a major achievement, introduced with the support of the relevant unions, and will take some years to have its full effect in transforming the working environment of the Australian Public Service.

The old job structures presented problems both to management, creating as they did a good deal of inflexibility, inefficiency and many demarcation disputes, and to staff, providing them with limited career paths and presenting occupational health and safety risks. A major objective of the review was to remove these problems and to enable both more efficient operation by APS agencies and more equitable treatment of staff. The new structure was intended to have benefits for all the major stakeholders and this was an important reason why the very extensive changes were successfully introduced. (For a more detailed discussion of this major classification reform see Selby-Smith 1989). Tripartite agreements acceptable to unions, staff and management have many benefits but are not easily achieved, particularly given the legacy of adversarial employer-union relations which is widespread and illustrated by events in the reforms described here.

Secondly came a review of the upper levels of the then Clerical Administrative structure (Classes 6 to 11), covering some 32,500 staff, of whom one fifth were women. This began as an internally initiated review separate from the review of lower levels which has just been mentioned. It covered a large group of workers and a group very important for the effective operations of the APS. This group had never been covered by formal Position Classification Standards and there had been allegations that some unjustified classification changes had been occurring, especially at the upper levels. In addition to this link to audit and monitoring activities there was a concern that in neighbouring structures, such as the professional areas whose members were covered by a different union, there was a tendency for agencies to classify positions which the union saw as properly in the professional structure (and thus within its area of coverage) into the Clerical Administrative structure where higher rates to pay could be provided and where another union had coverage.

The reforms had the further objective of reducing the number of separate levels in the structure, creating flatter structures, ensuring the devolution of authority and responsibility, a more streamlined administration and a more modern management approach. Over time changes in attitudes had occurred, favouring, for example, program delivery rather than policy work, functional Departments rather than central agencies and regional rather than central offices and these also fed into the reform process.

The review of these structures began as one internally initiated by the Board's Office but as it developed it became closely connected with the review of lower levels and they both went to the Conciliation and Arbitration Commission as one case, with the Government and the unions in agreement. The number of persons involved was enormous. Overall 115,000 staff were covered by the agreements, representing two-thirds of all permanent Public Service staff in December 1986. The total number of classifications, counting separate levels individually, was *dramatically* reduced, falling from 93 to a mere 8 levels in the new Administrative Service Officer structure (with the number of separate pay points, excluding junior pay points, dropping from 166 to 43). Over 90 % of all women in the APS were in the areas restructured as were some two-thirds of the men. The result was a radical transformation in the career structures of people in almost all public service office-based work. The classification structures so reorganised are central to the work of APS agencies and the new simplified structures both enable substantial improvements to be achieved in productivity and efficiency and also advance equity between staff and equal employment opportunity. The provision of formal Position Classification Standards for the affected staff is a very large step forward in this area: no PCS's previously existed for the 95,000 staff in the clerical assistant and clerical administrative structures, while those for the 10,000 staff in the keyboard structures were increasingly outdated.

The reforms, moreover, had an additional intention and effected broader organisation change. The simplification of the office-based classification structures has led to clearer classification distinctions and substantially strengthened the move initiated by the Government in its 1984 reforms towards greater power for agency heads to classify and reclassify positions in their own organisations.

The changes made include the development of the so-called 'Package Approach' to the restructuring of Senior Executive Service (SES) complements in Departments. SES staff are the top level executives and managers immediately below the Secretary or head of the Department. In a large department there may be some fifty or more SES officers. The SES structure contained six distinct levels, at each of which one salary rate only was paid (plus some other benefits, such as expenses of office allowance or contribution to the cost of home telephone). There was pressure to move away from the job-by-job approach so as to give departmental Secretaries greater scope to use their SES resources in more flexible ways and to enable them to make greater use of Levels 2 and 4, rather than Levels 1 and 3. There was growing pressure, both within the APS and outside it on the government to address what were increasingly seen as inequities in top structure and classification arrangements such as the tendency to classify Division or Branch Head positions in program departments lower than those in central policy departments or in regions lower than those in central office. There were also pressures in relation to what was widely seen as inadequate remuneration for SES officers compared to public and private sector managers elsewhere with similar levels of work value and responsibility. The arrangements outlined earlier in this chapter implied that any solution to these problems would need to be agreed between the Department of Finance and the PSB and that at least two major criteria would have to be met, those of cost constraint and those deriving from National Wage Case Principles. The Board, through the Classification Group, in close cooperation with the Senior Executive Staffing Unit, developed an approach which, after very extensive discussions with the Department of Finance over many months and wider discussion with Secretaries, was finally agreed. This was communicated to Departmental Secretaries by the Board's Chairman in November 1985 and was endorsed by the Government in early 1986. The approach, which involved savings in SES numbers and costs while increasing classification levels, has been extensively used by Secretaries and has assisted considerably in achieving solutions to the problems which led to its development. It constitutes a major change in the structure and operation of the APS at the highest level and a very important move since, although SES numbers are relatively small in the context of the APS as a whole (1489 in June 1984, 1583 in June 1985, 1629 in June 1986, 1664 in June 1987 and 1517 in June 1988), they are crucial to its successful operation.

Externally Initiated Reviews

Externally initiated reviews were also important agents of work organistion change and were very large in number. Some 65 such reviews were undertaken in April 1986 and 64 in April 1987. They varied widely in size and complexity and also in the time they took to complete, although the general pattern was one of a continuing flow. All required close and continuing supervision at a senior level. Of the two Branch Heads in the Classification Group one was almost wholly devoted to this work, with assistance from other SES staff as required. The reviews involved a careful examination of the work in the area selected to see how it had changed and the effects of the change on work value, together with a knowledge of the wider classification management arrangements in the APS, appreciation of the National Wage Case Principles and their application, and appropriate personal qualities. The results could be confirmation of existing arrangements or suggestions for modification to existing structures, to boundaries between work in different structures or the levels within a particular classification structure or, occasionally, the proposal for a completely new structure altogether. The jobs concerned were extremely diverse and scrutiny varied accordingly. Sometimes single positions were under examination while at others large numbers (hundreds or even thousands) of staff were concerned, as in the review of nursing classifications and career structures, the review of the engineers' structure and other reviews of the positions of therapists, foremen, research scientists and social workers. There were also reviews of more general policy matters, covering for example, the claims of undue clericalisation of professional positions, the relevance of educational qualifications to classification processes and decisions, ways of enhancing mobility between particular classifications and structural aspects of systemic discrimination alleged by unions (e. g. between staff in classifications predominantly employing women and those in classifications predominantly employing men).

Two management decisions proved helpful in carrying out this large scale review activity. First, negotiations were held with particular unions to identify important problem areas and devise a work programme which met the union's interests as well as those of the Board. This enabled the Board's Office to deploy its limited resources more effectively in meeting the needs of agencies, unions and staff and fostered more cooperative working relationships in a wider context. Secondly, it became an accepted part of review activity that, wherever possible, existing Position Classification Standards would be revised (or new PCS's developed) as part of the particular review.

Developing Standards and Guidelines

During 1984 a substantial project was already underway to develop and provide classification guideline material to departments for positions not covered by formal classification standards (some 70 % of the APS, particularly in the clerical assistant and clerical administrative areas). As part of this program the internal classification guideline material used by departments, in particular that used by the Australian Taxation Office, the Department of Social Security, the then Department of Employment and Industrial Relations and the then Department of Industry and Commerce for their large families of positions (such as employment officers) was identified and assessed. The draft guideline material was sent to relevant departments for their comments on its accuracy and its appropriateness for wider distribution in the APS as a guide to both classification practices and documentation. The guidelines were issued throughout the APS in the second half of 1985 and covered 18,000 jobs. Another important element of the standards and guidelines program was the development of benchmark descriptions for clerical/administrative and clerical assistant positions in the common work streams across the APS (for example, finance and accounting, recruitment, security). A revised Position Analysis Form was prepared for use in this context to provide the basic data for the benchmark descriptions of positions in the various work streams. The PSB survey of departmental classification needs and practices (see below) revealed strong support for the development of such guidelines for common work streams. Over 85 % of all respondents considered that this activity would suit their needs.

The project also provided an opportunity to utilise regional office resources for national tasks. By the time the Board was abolished, the projects on the first two workstreams (accounting and registry, which each covered just over 5,000 clerical administrative and clerical assistant positions), had made substantial progress, although competing priorities, such as the review of office structures and other second tier activities, were limiting the departmental resources which could be devoted to them. In 1985 the Board sent a questionnaire to agencies seeking their views on current classification practices and future priorities. Almost all respondents claimed to use comparisons in making classification decisions but responses indicated that comparisons with other positions were inhibited by the lack of readily available information on other suitable positions. Respondents gave clear support to the development and greater availability of good benchmark descriptions, especially those which covered positions in workstreams common to a number of departments. While almost all respondents claimed to use the formal PCS when they were available, their actual use was restricted since many did not exist or were seen as in need of revision. The development of standards for certain groups where there were currently no PCS was seen as having a particularly high priority, including clerical administrative (the largest structure, affecting virtually every agency, and receiving the top priority overall from respondents), clerical assistants, technical assistants, and the science group. Revision and updating were seen as particularly important for certain groups, such as keyboard workers, librarians, technical officers, engineers or computer systems officers.

Progress on updating existing PCS, and developing them where they did not exist, was also substantially assisted by the practice, noted above, of using reviews to develop up-to-date PCS's. This resulted in a number of small advances on a continuing basis and occasionally a major step forward, as in the case of the review of office structures. Structural reviews of major groups, such as engineers, also resulted in significant improvements in coverage and appropriateness of the standards and guidelines material. By the time the Board was abolished the situation in relation to standards and guidelines had been transformed, from one where over three-quarters of position in the APS were *not* covered by formal PCS's (and many of the remainder were only covered inadequately) to one where there were up-to-date position classification standards for the great majority of APS positions.

Finally, considerable preliminary work had been undertaken in relation to possible alternatives to, or less dramatic improvements in, the position classification approach generally in use in the APS. For example, in 1985 the Board's questionnaire to agencies had found that a majority of respondents favoured no change (or very limited change). It was clear that most repondents would be satisfied if the current classification guidelines were revised and extended fairly soon and were not seeking a completely different approach to position classification in the APS. However, it appeared that respondents in agencies with significant numbers of technical, professional and scientific staff favoured investigation of the possible use of more rigorous, perhaps quantitative (e. g. points based) approaches. In 1986, Regional Directors undertook a survey for their State, of classification systems used in State Public Services, major public utilities and prominent private firms. The material was very helpful in the development of thinking about possible future classification arrangements in the APS, and was complemented by visits to New Zealand, North America and Europe in 1986 and 1987 by one of the SES officers in the Classification Group to explore their current arrangements and likely future developments. They would have been valuable inputs for future consideration of possible changes to classification management arrangements in the APS.

A conference on classification management was organised for July 1987 and senior representatives from State PSB's (or equivalent), the Commonwealth Department of Finance and the New Zealand State Services Commission attended. The conference had a number of objectives, of which the further development of our thinking on future classification management in the APS was one. It went ahead successfully, but the Board had by then been abolished: the project lapsed and the relevant staff were dispersed.

Audit and Monitoring: Issues of Control of Compliance

The auditing of individual classification decisions and the monitoring of trends in overall statistical profiles provided the most difficult problems of review because of the tendency to upward 'classification creep' in large organisations. Questions arise, for example, about whether objective of the central agency should be to ensure that 100 % of APS positions were correctly classified 100 % of the time and if not, why not. If 100 % accuracy were judged not to be a practical objective, what lesser levels of compliance might be adopted as a basis for audit activity? Also what weight should be given to resource implications of the alternatives and what degree of certainty about the level of classification performance by agencies should the Board aim for?

The issue of control of compliance in a very large and complex organisation with a clear commitment to decentralising decision-making but with continuing and important central obligations was raised: organisation, technology and culture were all involved. The tendency to upward movement in overall classification profiles was the net result of many individual decisions and could be influenced by a wide range of factors (including changes in the work to be done, interaction between classification structures and between classification and pay aspects). Nevertheless, there was a danger that individual classification decisions were being made without due regard to their cumulative effect. Agency managers were not accountable, in the sense of being effectively brought to account, for the way in which they were managing the classification system. Lack of accountability was frequently accompanied by lack of commitment. While similar problems might arise in large private sector organisations this aspect of work and salary administration has been little studied in comparable Australian firms and, in any case, the resultant effects may be more easily handled because of the simpler output measures, particularly profitability and growth, in the private sector.

The APS Reforms of 1984 involved substantial devolution of classification management powers to the heads of agencies but also provided a power for the Public Service Board to direct that the classification of an office be altered. The continuing responsibility of the PSB for classification standards involved some tension between central and departmental views in this area. Traditionally, the Conciliation and Arbitration Commission tended to look to the Board rather than to individual departments as the guardian of the integrity of the APS classification system and this continued even after the greater devolution which the Government had introduced. There were also pressures from the broader pay system within which the classification system existed and over this period these pressures were exacerbated by a tightly controlled and centralised wage-fixing system, to which the Commonwealth was firmly committed, in which APS pay rates tended to rise less rapidly than those in some other parts of the community, and from pressures to produce results comparable with community standards. The approach which the Board adopted was to develop systems for monitoring classification profile change and to undertake a series of programmed audits of agency classification decisions and management systems. The monitoring activities were intended to provide information on overall classification trends and within major classification structures, to assist in targeting the audit program and to provide indications of classification movement which might be unwarranted. The classification audit strategy had three main components: ad hoc auditing of positions coming to notice (through, for instance, complaints from unions or departments); the overall monitoring of classification trends leading to more detailed investigation of particular areas; and a programmed schedule of audits in agencies staffed under the Public Service Act. Three rounds of audits were carried out in 1985, 1986 and 1987. The most consistent finding was the inadequacy of agency documentation of classification decisions. The other consistent finding was that the rate of increase in the number of positions considerably exceeded growth in staff numbers.

The PSB audit program operated under three serious constraints. First, available resources were very limited and the necessarily small sample sizes could not be used, in a statistically valid way, to draw Servicewide conclusions: this contrasts with approaches taken elsewhere. Secondly, the correctness of the majority of sampled classification decisions could not be readily assessed, often because of the lack of adequate documentation, so that the audits could not establish beyond reasonable doubt whether or not significant misclassification was taking place. Thirdly, given the strong deregulatory thrust of the Government's 1984 Reforms, the Board did not consider it appropriate to invoke all its powers, choosing instead to rely on the persuasive powers of its classification staff. While, in many cases this approach was successful, the non-application of the available statutory sanctions removed the sense of urgency from classification management compliance. The Board's position in the last few months before it was abolished was tending to firm but the general climate at political and senior administrative levels was in favour of further reductions in regulation by central agencies. The Board stressed, at Secretary level and in a range of discussions with classification management areas in departments, that the prime responsibility for correct classification decisionmaking rested with departmental Secretaries, not the Board.

It is worth noting here that the Australian Federal service is unusual amongst other public services in Western democratic countries which have decentralised classification systems. In Australia the classification system has been decentralised through the transfer of classification powers from the central agency to departments whereas in other systems powers have generally been delegated, with the head of authority (and thus final accountability) remaining with the central agency. In the US and Canadian Federal system, experience with decentralised classification management arrangements has been similar to that of the APS. The upward movement in classification profiles, evident in the APS, has been of major concern to the respective central agencies, to the Canadian Parliament and the US Congress. Within Australia, the recent experience of the Victorian system is also similar. The North American evidence suggests that sanctions applied on the basis of individual classification decision are not necessarily effective in improving the accountability of those authorised to undertake classification decisionmaking. While North American systems make provision for delegations to be withdrawn in instances of serious or continued noncompliance, the APS system provided only a reserve power for the central agency to direct a secretary to alter the classification of an office. This was an all or nothing power, which in the prevailing climate a central agency would inevitably be loath to exercise.

Getting the New System to Work: Information and Training

Training activities were accorded a high priority, especially in the days immediately following the APS Reform legislation. Training had several objectives: to assist departments to train their staff in the skills required in establishment areas; to promote a better understanding of the principles and practices of classification in the APS amongst all staff (experience demonstrated that this was very important, even among senior SES staff); to disseminate information and foster interdepartmental contact to ensure that classification standards were maintained; and to identify and meet the training needs of staff in the Classification Group (and elsewhere in the Board's Office). Training and skill formation were also accorded a high priority by the relevant unions. The importance of training relates closely to Dodgson's observation in this volume that in the knowledge intensive, research and development-based UK firm he studied, technology strategy is closely linked to the firm's human resource strategy, and 'puts a heavy emphasis on organisational forms'. In relation to technology and organisational change Garnsey and Roberts (in this volume) also argue that 'technology can be seen as a source of culture', seen in ways of working, beliefs, attachments and contacts.

In implementing change in the APS, experience was consistent with the expectation advanced by Bamber (1989) that effective implementation of work place changes and subsequent job flexibility are positively correlated with the involvement of first-line managers (as well as staff, union representatives and senior managers) in their design and development. The process has been part of what Hill (1989a) calls 'building a social architecture' for change (including technological change). A network of classification and establishment officers was developed, who promoted consistent and equitable classification practices and helped to ensure that classification standards were maintained. Devolution was the order of the day but some agencies both needed and wanted considerably more assistance than was provided, suggesting the limits to devolution of responsibility in undertaking major organisational change.

Conclusion

The case-study reported on here demonstrates how the use of a single organisational tool, in this case job classifications, can be made the mechanism for introducing *major* changes to the working of very large and complex organisations. Over a period of two to three years, the working conditions and career prospects of many thousands of people in the Australian Public Service were transformed through the efforts of a relatively small group of people. The case study also illustrates the crucial importance of political will and commitment to particular social ideals. The very significant classification improvements in the APS made over this period substantially assisted the achievement of equal employment opportunity objectives and provided for the large-scale application of industrial democracy principles in relation to job redesign and training which are important to the work lives and career prospects of many staff. The improvements to APS classification management arrangements also supported other political goals, notably strengthening the basis for the extensive devolution of management responsibilities to departments from central agencies. Importantly, there were also improvements in the efficiency of operation of APS agencies. Even in terms of salary savings there were substantial benefits: major proposals incorporated savings of some 10 % in SES positions and 7 % in SES salaries. Clearly reclassification activities had a significant effect in reworking this part of the world.

Difficulties is sustaining the momentum built up in the latter stages of the Board's life may be attributed to the supplementation of devolution goals and the subsequent fragmentation of the central classification function in the APS (between the Public Service Commision and the Departments of Finance and Industrial Relations) as well as a judgement by many departments that the improvements to classification management had achieved their major objectives (so that there were now higher priorities elsewhere), generating a lack of recognition of, and commitment to, the further improvements required.

It is also important to note the problems the case study reveals in managing centre-periphery relations in such a large and physically scattered organisation. These adversely affected the relationship between the Board's Office in Canberra and its regional offices in the States and Territories. The bulk of Commonwealth public servants are located outside Canberra, primarily in the larger centres of population, although a significant number (in aggregate) are in small and sometimes very isolated centres. The Public Service Board had regional offices in each State (the new Public Service Commission does not) and they had a potentially very useful role to play in the improvement of APS classification management. Considerable efforts were made, for example, by both Regional Directors and Central Office, to develop a role for regional office staff but these efforts had only limited success.

In reform of the APS, the classification management function should not be seen in isolation. There remained a partnership between the Board and operating Departments, although the reforms altered the relative responsibilities of the respective parties. There remained the need for close working arrangements with unions as well as Departments and also with other areas of the Board's Office, most clearly with pay and arbitration but also with management improvement (e. g. moves to flatter structures), with the Equal Employment Opportunity Bureau, with the Senior Executive Staffing Unit, with the working environment and conditions area and with personnel management (e. g. on entry and advancement requirements, educational or other qualifications). Successful change through the classification management function tends to be longer-term in nature, not given to sudden fits and starts, and to be conscious of the need for continuity and stability. This is reflected in the management approach, usually tripartite, seeking common ground, concerned with process as well as outcome, and also its personnel, where desirable characteristics of knowledge and experience need to be complemented with a high measure of integrity, so that relationships of trust and an expectation of fair and reasonable (as well as competent) dealing can be established and maintained. The 'salami approach', of mixing staff with different experience, skills and levels of risk aversion, proved in this case to be quite successful.

There has been extensive discussion among observers about the extent to which the introduction of information technologies into office system operations results in a predetermined set of outcomes and the scope for modifying, influencing and controlling them (see many writers in the labour process debate, including Knights). The APS experience discussed above suggests that the scope for influence over outcomes is far greater than in sometimes asserted or implied. Hill (1989a) has contrasted the degree of influence in an innovative culture of performance with that of a dependent culture of rational efficiency, while Little (1989) has suggested that culture may offer a better paradigm for understanding the link between technical and institutional orientations than rationality and emphasises that there is a cultural dimension to the outcome of institutional and task conflict. The review process for office structures in the APS was an exercise in national policy-making which seems to have succeeded in creating the conditions for that innovative, performance-related culture. It has led to the successful modification of central control arrangements in an extremely large, diverse and complex organisation — the Australian Public Service is the largest 'firm' in Australia, operating in many different businesses and at hundreds of separate locations — permitting changes in organisational arrangements, revised methods of use and allocation of resources, major alteration to unwritten as well as formal rules of conduct, interaction, social and work arrangements. It has provided an entry point for change (Hill 1989), provided learning situations for democracy in the workplace (Sandkull in this volume) and acknowledged the centrality of people for the effective operation of a highly complex organisation.

Swedish Wage-Earner Funds: The Problematic Relationship Between Economic Efficiency and Popular Power

Winton Higgins

Introduction

'The ruling order gains legitimacy if utopias are dissolved and 'the other future' is forgotten about. A utopialess state preserves existing society. The End of Ideology is the battlecry of the ensconced ruler. Many rulers govern by witch-craft: oppression by reasonableness and moderation, by sapping their under-lings' imagination.'(Ehnmark in Ehnmark and Therborn 1988: 66)

Sweden-watchers whose sympathies lie with organised labour — and we account for the bulk of the profession — are often accused of merely being 'in trade', the vulgar importers of a foreign model. This view carries the implications that if the model starts to wobble visibly, as it has for a decade on the wage-earner fund issue, we should abandon it in favour of a newer entrant on the model market (Japan, say, or South Korea), reskill and relocate. While Japan- and Korea-watching can also be pursued for both fun and profit, the latter values have far from evaporated from Sweden-watching, which retains its monopoly over considerations on economic democratisation. The conventional wisdom notwithstanding, the Sweden-watchers' mission is not to market a model; it is to reconnoitre — cost-effectively at that — possible futures in comparable western societies. It is true, of course, that a long line of Swedish labour movement successes has largely accounted for the emergence of Sweden-watchers and their clientele. But, by and large, both groups know that the only models that work at home are locally designed and assembled, using mainly local content, with foreign components playing only a minor role.

To use a more fitting image, the successes of the Swedish labour move-ment have made it the whiskers on the Western labour cat. Thanks to its successive leaders' strategic astuteness and deft manoeuvring, mixed with a conventionally overestimated modicum of good fortune, the Swedish movement long since attained a unique place among other western move-ments, in terms of its level and forms of mobilisation and its institutional penetration of the usual sites of power in capitalist society (Higgins 1985a,

1988). This success has left its mark on the development of Swedish industry, social provisions and political culture. In the process, percipient labour strategists and policymakers elsewhere have had an opportunity to discern promising directions in which to take their own movements. *Australia Reconstructed* (ACTU/TDC 1987) exemplifies this use of the Swedish experience.

Now that the whiskers have wedged firmly in the space marked 'economic democracy', the more prudent, and less painful, response for the cat is not to brusquely withdraw its whiskers but rather to investigate this space and discover why it has proved initially impassable. Readers unfamiliar with the wage-earner funds conflict which raised the issue of economic democracy in Sweden will find it summarised at the beginning of the second section.

The virtual defeat of the wage-earner fund proposal represents the Swedish labour movement's first serious setback since the 'cossack election' of 1928 when the social democrats committed a rare and simple error of political judgement (Higgins 1985: 221). The current setback has more diverse causes and much deeper ramifications. Two immediately obvious causes are the ambivalence of the Social Democratic Party when LO, its affiliated blue-collar union peak council, presented the Party and the Swedish electorate with the original proposal in 1976 and the superior unity and mobilisation of the employers' federation (SAF). But the funds proposal also constituted a quantum leap in the magnitude of socio-economic change which organised capital and labour were now contesting, a leap which explains the intensity of capital's reaction. The proposal constituted such a leap by crystallising two historical turning points, one in the development of Western socialist perspectives and one in economic (particularly industrial) organisation. Whether it did so in the most appropriate form is one of the questions I will address in this chapter, but both turning points problematise macro-social and macro-economic power and its institutional embodiments, which is why they have overlain each other in the battle over the funds. In the next section I outline the wider changes that the funds may be seen to herald before explaining and criticising how they do so in the succeeding section. Finally, I want to draw out some strategic conclusions for organised labour in other Western countries.

Civic Socialism, Postmodern Organisation

If, as I have suggested, we now find ourselves at two superimposed turning points, the one political and the other organisational, it behoves us to step back from them to see them in a wider historical and tendential perspective, as well as in terms of first principles. Recent writings in these respective areas have done much to illuminate the turning points. I want briefly to explore the political issues from a Swedish perspective before using Stewart Clegg's (1990b) framework which contrasts modern and postmodern economic organisation to provide greater specification of the historical trends that the funds proposal has tapped into. In 1988, LO added another anthology, optimistically entitled *In Mid-stride*, to the now formidable Swedish literature on wage-earner funds and their objective, economic democracy. In his introduction the editor, Dan Andersson, observes:

'If those who started the union movement a hundred years ago were to visit Sweden today they would be astonished at the material welfare, the state services and social security. But despite that they would have little difficulty recognising the conditions of industrial work and the hierarchy in the hospitals. The transformation of worklife has thus barely begun' (LO 1988: 13)

The latter reaction does not diminish the importance of the former. Therborn notes how decades of labour's strenuous reform efforts have forced capitalism to retreat on issues of social equity to an extent that late nineteenth century socialists could hardly have imagined (Ehnmark and Therborn 1988: 148−9). Andersson identifies some of the ground conceded − housing standards, dental health, education, rising pensions − and emphasises that in all these areas the movement has changed social power relations by democratic means. Despite these, however, 'so far it has been amazingly difficult to even out differentials in worklife', he says and recapitulates the depressing Swedish statistics about the concentration of hazardous and unpleasant work tasks and of job insecurity in blue collar jobs, while a declining industrial accident rate goes hand in hand with an explosion in repetition strain injury (LO 1988: 8,12). Capitalism has been pressed back from some of its outlying provinces and, at least in Western countries with historically strong labour movements, Dickens' representations of social injustice find little resonance in today's society. But the heartland remains more or less intact: Chapter X of *Capital* on the working day retains a scaring immediacy. This uneven progress both focuses and revitalises the socialist project today, for it is within this project that LO located its wage-earner fund campaign. The historical trajectory of socialist theory and practice, as capitalism's permanent 'counter-culture' (Baumann 1976: 36), has predictably responded to the changing conditions of capitalism itself. But in so doing it has often succumbed to a chronic tendency of all human endeavour in which means usurp ends. As Ehnmark reminds us, socialism *comprises means*, not ends (Ehnmark and Therborn 1988: 24) and Western socialism has pursued the goal of attaining 'an egalitarian, just and free society'. In accepting this view Therborn brings the goal down to an even starker level of human rights, reminding us that 'every woman and every man in this world has the right to be able to be happy'. Unlike the framers of the US constitution, who immortalised a similar sentiment, Therborn, however, adds, 'Happiness has an existential dimension outside the ambit of political action; but poverty, illness, exploitation and oppression make it impossible for people to be happy.' (Ehnmark and Therborn 1988: 24, 42).

In fulfilling their countercultural role, socialists in the nineteenth and early twentieth centuries saw their objectives as best served by pitting the notion of a well-ordered nationalised economy, under the aegis of parliamentary sovereignty, against the anarchy and arbitrary brutality of market capitalism. In more recent times, as capitalism centralised, bureaucratised, cartelised and entrusted important functions to the state, Western socialism developed the opposite orientation, towards a decentralised and democratised market economy under the umbrella of a looser, more residual notion of indicative planning. On the way, socialists have suffered numerous identity crises (to say nothing of political importance) by fixing too firmly on given means instead of seeing these as contingent and dependent on shifting predicaments, opportunities and policy dilemmas.

Prefiguring Baumann's (1976) magisterial argument for a mobilising utopian element in any effective politics of social change, Swedish social democracy's major theoretician, Ernst Wigforss, advocated the use of 'provisional utopias' to crystallise and popularise concrete achievable futures. These rolling futures, so to speak, were to overcome whatever the present predicament happened to be; they were to be constructed out of socio-economic materials already to hand, using political skills already being learned (Wigforss 1980; Tilton 1984). Consistent with this method, Wigforss' politics developed a markedly organisational emphasis, in contrast to mainstream socialism's habitually juridical orientation (see Clegg and Higgins 1987).

As Ehnmark and Therborn's (1988) dialogue brings out, the two salient predicaments today converge into a single problem complex: the organisation of, and power over, the process and direction of production. The first predicament is the barbarity of the work place — the inequality, unfreedom, alienation, oppression, physical and psychological damage that concretise Weber's deathless phrase 'the dull compulsion to labour'. The second predicament encapsulates the present-day manifestations of the older socialist problematic that capitalist production means production for profit, not for use. We might well dub this the dull compulsion to consume, one that extends beyond the culturally dubious products we actually buy to include the toxins and radiation we ingest less voluntarily and a rapidly deteriorating local and global environment. Both predicaments raise formidable obstacles to human happiness.

As I have elaborated elsewhere (Higgins 1985b, 1988), Wigforss imbued Swedish socialism with its orientation towards economic reorganisation. To achieve equality, justice and freedom, we have to invent replacements for the capitalist organisations that generate the negations of these values. Therborn formulates the problem thus: 'how is a power to be developed that combines an economic competence with a popular will?' (Ehnmark and Therborn 1988: 15). Elements of the Swedish labour movement have shown a tendency to be distracted by apologists' untenable claims that capitalism has already found a − indeed, the only − solution to this problem. More interestingly, the undistracted elements have undertaken reorganisation at a time when the modernist constitution of capitalist organisations and power is decaying. The danger for socialists is to build the still prevalent modernist assumptions into their own organisational frameworks, thus importing not only atavistic agendas, hierarchies and interests but also inbuilt obsolescence. The challenge for socialists, in contrast, is to pre-empt capitalism's adoption of postmodern organisations and imbue the latter with 'a popular will' or, in other words, to make them bearers of economic democratisation.

Stewart Clegg's (1990b) recent work draws out the implications of the modernist/postmodernist distinction in organisation analysis while making explicit the political partisanship of the influential champions of modernist organisation. His work supplies a critical link between the aspirations discussed above − 'civic socialism' in Rothstein's (1989) felicitous phrase − and the organisational choices on which their realisation depends. I shall selectively summarise his argument to point up that link, especially as it relates to the discussion of wage-earner funds in the next section.

Clegg characterises modernist organisations in terms of their differentiation of functions and roles. These organisations are moulded by the capiltal/labour differentiation and are bureaucratised, mechanistic structures of control erected upon a fully 'rationalised' base of occupationally divided and de-skilled labour. 'Fordist' production best exemplifies organisational modernism, although the latter is equally at home in hospitals, armies and organs of public administration. This description brings us inside Max Weber's familiar 'iron cage' of bureaucracy and Clegg's argument about modernism is partly an argument with Weber. More crucially, however, it is an argument with Weber's modernist vulgarisers who attempt to attribute to him, as well as to a wider metaphysical universe, the necessity of their own notion of 'efficiency' in organisational life. Such vulgarisers forget that the operative concept in Weber's theory of bureaucracy was *rationality* which, as Weber himself indicated, was something quite different from 'efficiency'.

Efficiency is a question of technical fit between ends and means but in the event is invariably overlaid with cultural meanings. Rationally, on the other hand, is a cultural value; one that, in Weber's most famous argument, is the heritage of the Protestant Reformation (See Weber, 1976, in the last chapter of which, incidentally, the image of the iron cage makes its appearance). The 'iron cage' of modernist organisation, the characteristic embodiment of rationality, is thus itself a cultural construct.

One can hardly resist interpolating here a point from another tradition. Capital's permanent agenda of accumulation, which the culture of rationality expresses, includes equally permanently an element of (re)distribution of income to itself. Under earlier industrial-capitalist conditions, profit and capital accumulation presupposed competitive success in manufacturing, which meant that technical efficiency also had a self-evident, if historically contingent, cultural value. With the rise of finance capital to its present domination of economic calculation, capital accumulation in individual financial units no longer depends on manufacturing success as more 'rational' avenues of posting maximal profits present themselves, ones that circumvent the vagaries and complexities of industrial production. The historical link between rationality and 'efficiency' thus breaks in an era nicely summed up in the title of Seymour Melman's book, an era of 'profits without production', a syndrome that Weber himself anticipated in his distinction between formal and substantive rationality (Higgins and Clegg 1988).

Profitability today carries no necessary implication of efficiency and/or technical competence, only of formal rationality, which may in the event *negate* both of these. Modernist organisations, moreover, typically contain elaborate, technically inefficient mechanisms of control, surveillance and containment of resistance, which is why they now tend to be out-competed (a circumstance buried under the 'rational myth' that managerial control is *synonymous with* efficiency). As Clegg argues in this volume, however, orthodox theory illegitimately seeks to anchor in Weber's work a notion of efficiency as the categorical, culture-transcending imperative of modern organisations. As a pro-capitalist tendency it at once has to grapple with modernism's central contradiction: is 'efficiency' a function of markets or their opposite, large-scale hierarchical and rulebound bureaucracies. Williamson's (1975) attempt to deal with this contradiction is perhaps the most prestigious, as well as an argument serving to cover a prominent line of retreat from giving power to wage-earner funds in Sweden, as we shall see. Williamson starts with what all good economic liberals know, that markets deliver the optimality of outcome and self-regulation reserved exclusively to pure expressions of the Laws of Nature. But it is in the nature of the mytical beast that future supplies of capital, labour and commodities, time frames and prices, are ineffable, which creates awkwardness for rational calculation. Calculation becomes impossible, or has to be based on guesswork, both of which creates 'transaction costs'. Large-scale organisation internalises, and so controls and minimises, these transaction costs. Organisation takes over where markets fail. First we have the efficiency imperative, which in turn generates the existing mix of unregulated markets on the one hand and hierarchical and differentiated organisations on the other. What exists does so because it has to. There Is No Alternative is the message of what Clegg thus calls the TINA tendency in organisation theory. It is, of course, an intellectual trick that political scientists familiar with convergence theories of the 1940s will have little trouble recognising, and students of Machiavelli even less trouble interpreting.

Weber pointed up what this *soi-disant* Weberian discourse suppresses: that markets and organisations express and generate the *power* of some economic agents over others: 'a modern market economy essentially consists in a complete network of exchange contracts, that is, in deliberate, planned acquisition of powers of control and disposal' (Weber 1978: 67). Far from simply expressing a laudable pursuit of 'efficiency' (the fashion-conscious may read 'excellence' here), both markets and organisations are moulded by an overriding logic, that of the calculation and representation of the interests of the economic agents who dominate them. Organisations institutionalise this domination in the form of rules and 'rational myths' gleaned from the wider economic culture.

The plurality of dominant economic agents and economic cultures produces the wide variations in organisational forms which successful industrial enterprises in fact exhibit, TINA tendency notwithstanding, whether they be progressive Swedish carmakers or the patriarchal Taiwanese bicycle factories. TINA analysts focus exclusively on the single organisation as their object of study and ignore the economic agents and their networks which provide that organisation with its external context and its internal dynamic; they also ignore the economic culture which these agents colonise and then elaborate in both the external and internal environment. By negative example such conceptual frailties point to a better approach to organisational analysis, one that sensitises us to the presence and interests of 'dominant coalitions' and to the way organisations are 'embedded' in power networks and cultural meanings.

It is this sort of organisational imagination, Clegg suggests again in this volume, which we must bring to the analysis of postmodernist organisations. Having escaped the clutches of the modernist TINA tendency, we should now avoid the potential postmodernist ones as well. Postmodernist organisations are as multifarious as modernist ones and the ambiguities will be resolved, as is usual in these matters, by political means. In contrast to its predecessor, the hallmark of a postmodernist organisation is '*de*-differentiation', typically seen in the dissolution of occupational and skill boundaries and in the emergence of a multi-skilled, flexibly-specialised 'collective' worker in semi-autonomous work groups, flexible manufacturing systems and the like. Undoubtedly, new technologies, especially those applying micro-electronics, do facilitate the re-organisation of production along these lines but herein lies the danger of a new and equally technological-determinist TINA: either a radical one that assures us that the new technology will of itself topple the hierarchies and *necessitate* democratic organisation or a managerial one which says that it sees no alternative to appointing the tenured inner circle of workers to be their own supervisors and disciplinarians while letting the rest test their luck in the Coliseum of the peripheral post-Fordist labour market.

Postmodernist organisation is an index of human possibilities, Clegg tells us, not a prediction. But two 'extremities' within the range of possibilities are emerging and they are already establishing the battle lines in the politics of industrial organisation: Sweden's economic democracy and Japan's neo-feudal managerialism. Both countries are clearly industrial highflyers but the latter 'possibility' is well matured while the former is struggling in the birth canal. It is time now to investigate the blockage.

Funding Democracy

Antipodean legend has it that an Australian union official on a study tour of Sweden finally overcame his native scepticism as he watched a massive demonstration against wage-earner funds in Stockholm from his hotel window. The scene was typical of several in the Battle of the Funds: expensively turned-out senior executives and drably-dressed TINA militants from the academies in their tens of thousands and in high dudgeon. Yes, Sweden *is* different: here it is the ruling class that is forced out into the streets to demonstrate. Yet what they were demonstrating against in the end has been dismissed by one radical Swedish political scientist as a situation where 'some more or less clever professional finance matadors have been given the chance to speculate on the stock exchange with wage-earners' money.' (Rothstein 1989: 150). I shall very briefly sketch the course of the Swedish conflict before trying to disentangle some of the themes that underpin these widely differing perceptions of the funds.

In the Swedish debate two meanings of 'economic democracy' are often ascribed to the term. The more general meaning refers to the democratisation of economic relationships and decisionmaking *tout court*. In the seventies, this overarching ambition broke down into two 'campaigns', one for industrial or enterprise democracy (see Higgins 1986) and a second for economic democracy in the narrower sense of collective capital formation through the development of wage-earners' funds, the point of which was to partially and gradually democratise resource allocation. This ambitious project found its way onto the labour movement's agenda almost accidentally when LO's 1971 congress established a committee to explore ways to shore up its traditional egalitarian wage policy in a new situation of unstable international economic development and uneven profit rates at home.

The terms of reference were modest enough, and the result might have been equally so in political terms but for the composition of the group — Rudolf Meidner, Anna Hedborg and Gunnar Fond. The first had co-authored the postwar Rehn-Meidner Model that underpinned LO's — and to a large extent Sweden's — economic policy from the 1950s, while Anna Hedborg was a rising and radical force in LO's ideological development. The report which the group produced (often known as the Meidner proposal) and which the 1976 congress adopted (see Meidner 1978) recommended legislation to establish wage-earners' funds. In this version, excessive profits, which otherwise subverted central wage bargains and wage solidarity, would be 'sterilised' by retaining them as working capital in the firm which would issue equity shares of an equivalent value to the funds. The boards that were to manage the funds were to be composed of union delegates and to act as trustees for the wage-earner collectivity. Their capital placements and the exercise of the voting rights attached to the shareholdings were thus required to further wage-earner interests in the long term by promoting industrial renewal and employment and the enhancement of labour skills. The report also estimated that if 20 per cent of pre-tax corporate profits were funded annually the funds would hold 52 per cent of issued capital in affected firms after 20 years of operation. The proposal claimed to offer a solution not only to the vagaries of LO's wage policy but also to the declining level of industrial investment, which was universally recognised as a central problem of economic management, and the extreme concentration of industrial ownership in Sweden. The *causus belli* in the decade of political confrontation that followed, however, was that a date had now been fixed (as it were) for socialist transition as collective capital would crowd out private capital on the capital market within a foreseeable future.

LO's action could not have come at worse time for its political affiliates. After forty four years in government, Swedish social democracy's main stock-in-trade had shrunk to sound economic management and political moderation. Its electoral fortunes were at a low ebb as it faced a fateful election just after the LO congress. It had already signalled its real political response to the proposal by establishing a commission of inquiry into forms of employee shareholding in 1974 as a way of holding the issue off the immediate political agenda. But, even though the commission limped on indecisively well into the nineteen eighties, neither LO nor the now apoplectic political right were prepared to accept this evasion. In political opposition between 1976 and 1982, the social democrats were thus forced to negotiate with LO to produce a joint proposal. By 1981, the wage-earner fund concept had been severely watered down into a joint proposal, the one that the social democrats faced the electorate with in 1982 when they were returned to power.

The new social democratic treasurer, Kjell-Olof Feldt, who had represented the party in these negotiations, then framed and introduced enabling legislation to take effect from 1984 but in the process even the 1981 proposal was emasculated. There was to be no compulsory issue of shares, which now had to be acquired on the stock exchange. Initial accumulation of the funds was no longer to be done by creaming off superprofits but by way of a sort of payroll tax and was in any event to cease in 1990. Each of the five funds set up was to hold no more than eight per cent of the issued share capital in any company, was obliged to meet minimum annual profit requirements and to pay dividends into the national superannuation (ATP) funds. 'Actually existing funds' (to adapt an Eastern European phrase) are minor, if somewhat scruffy and unwelcome, institutional investors, small and handicapped players on the unchanged capital market.

This débâcle should not blind us to the 'de-differentiating' element in the original fund idea. In his discussion of the modern market economy, Weber (1978: ch. 2) describes the extreme *differentiation* of private capital and the capital-owning function which obtain under ideal economic-liberal conditions: ownership bestows unqualified prerogatives of control and disposal exercised on free markets. Included in this exclusive empowerment of capital is control of appointment over managers, free access to labour on an unregulated labour market and complete freedom of contract. Exercise of all these powers is facilitated by rational technology, rational administration, a universalistic legal system, and a complete differentiation between enterprise and household organisation.

As Weber rightly infers, this schema excludes workers from any influence over capital as well as from financial returns to its investment, and subordinates them to entrepreneurs (see Higgins and Clegg 1988: 71). Should a collective form of capital ownership, genuinely representing workers (perhaps among others), crowd out private capital, then this differentiation breaks down quite fundamentally. Its thrust would converge with the reform of Swedish worklife which, while still far from complete, has done much to compromise capital's differentiated status in the enterprise as Weber characterised it. The emergence of 'post-Fordist' industrial organisation in Sweden is one aspect of this de-differentiation process. In this context, Clegg (1990b: ch. 7) makes explicit the link between postmodern industrial organisation and postmodern capital formation.

Why, then, did LO fail in its attempt to advance its socialist project by diluting private capital and breaking its hold on resource allocation in accordance with the postmodernist *Zeitgeist*? The most obvious reason is that it depended on an affiliated party whose political horizons had long since shortened to a social-liberal acceptance of basic capitalist economic arrangements (see Higgins 1988). Indeed, Treasurer Feldt, who played such a prominent role in the emergence of actually existing funds, has recently stirred up considerable controversy by publishing an article (republished in English: Feldt 1989) in the party's theoretical journal *Tiden* making the collapse explicit. 'Socialism', he says, now refers to redistributional functions only and capitalism will continue to be the organising principle of the Swedish economy. An export-dependent economy requires capitalist 'efficiency'. TINA again.

The next question, however, is this: was the Meidner proposal the best means to clinch this postmodernist democratic future? On this point a debate that might have been of considerable interest to organisation theory has been somewhat stillborn. Walter Korpi received little thanks for trying to start it in the heat of the conflict. Now that the dust has settled for the time being, it is worth considering the succinct summary of the issue which he suggested at the time:

'The funds' starting point in union wage policy led to quite a few ideological problems. No distinction was made, for instance, between which groups should own the enterprises and who should lead and administer them. This led to some old syndicalist themes suddenly turning up in LO, when it demanded that the unions control the funds. Some old leninist flotsam floated up the surface when LO wanted only wage-earners to control the funds. These sorts of conclusions and demands naturally arise if we see the funds primarily as a complement to union wage policy but the consequence was a probably unnecess- ary contradiction between the people, who are the foundation of all democracy, and wage-earners in enterprises.

Failure to resolve this contradiction meant that the funds could never be effectively promoted as a step towards economic democracy. It meant that the labour movement could never pose the question in terms of the basic democratic principle, one person - one vote. Its opponents could link wage-earner control to unions and 'union bosses'. The battleline did not go between the people and the minority of prominent wielders of economic power, but rather between the people and the unions. The labour movement thus lost the initiative in the development of public opinion around economic democracy. The battle over the funds turned out to be one step forward and two steps back in its effect on public perceptions of economic democracy.' (Korpi 1986: 43).

In Lenin's economical terms, then, 'who are the people' in the context of economic democratisation, the electorate or organised wage-earners?

In the Korpi article quoted above, as elsewhere, economic democracy is often referred to as 'the third stage' within the Swedish labour tradition. This usage refers back to a famous speech in 1928 by the then newly-elected party leader, Per Albin Hansson, who projected social democracy's mission into three historical stages: the attainment of political democracy, social democracy and, finally, economic democracy. His audience then had fresh memories of the completion of stage one just nine years before. Attaining political democracy had meant that both wings of the social-democratic labour movement had been preoccupied in their formative decades with the battle for *universal suffrage*. The operative identity of 'the people' had, during those years, been the central issue of Swedish politics and Hansson's three-stage schema for the democratisation of society contained the strong implication that the constituency would be identical in each stage. Certainly, the suppression of *all* social differentiations underpinning privilege and lack of access to social amenities has been a *Leitmotiv* of stage two, the construction of Welfare Sweden.

At first sight, then, wage-earner funds, as opposed to citizens' funds, seem an awkward graft onto the social-democratic root stock. Yet, interestingly, in launching the fund concept within the LO membership in 1975, Meidner in an interview nominated Marx and Wigforss as its ideological godfathers. The latter is the more significant in this context, not only because of proximity in place and time but also because he problematised both democratic control and economic efficiency.

A I have argued elsewhere (Higgins 1985b and 1988), Wigforss drew a great deal of inspiration in the nineteen twenties from English collectivist liberalism, from the pre-first world war 'new liberals' to the Liberal Summer School of the 1920s. From this tradition and from a great deal of contemporary empirical data he extrapolated the basic proposition that the prevalent 'waste' in industry and macro-economic dislocation are causally linked to hierarchical work organisation and the concentration of economic power in the hands of the few. In the first instance, the workers' competence and enthusiasm were excluded from, and neglected by, the organisation of production. In the second, non-correspondence between private and social economic interests meant that calculations of the former were often ruinous for the latter. Democratic work organisation was thus the cure to industrial capitalism's inefficiency at the point of production: it both developed and empowered a far wider range of competences. Similarly, economic democracy promised to develop and empower civic competence and an aggregated economic interest. Wigforss' project contained a strong implicit critique of modernist organisation.

As a democratic theorist, Wigforss stressed two classical themes: first, the role of democratic participation in the development of competence; and second, the need to universalise the natural constituency in each social or organisational setting. In a complex economy there is, of course, a plurality of such settings and therefore of constituencies. In the workshop 'the people' are those who work there and Wigforss picked up the English collectivist-liberal catchcry that the worker must become a 'citizen' of the workshop just as he or she had become a citizen of the polity with the coming of universal suffrage. But in the macro-economy, the universalising or de-differentiating principle brings us back to the constituency that universal suffrage itself posits.

Wigforss thus emerges as a nascent postmodernist in his advocacy of economic democracy, concerned to transcend the capital/labour differentiation rather than to sustain it by championing one of the differentiated interests against the other. This, of course, hardly disqualifies the labour movement from being the champion of a universal interest − a role that progressive labour movements can and do assume (Higgins 1987) − and a necessary element in any reforming coalition. Its perspective has exposed the rational myth of profits without production in particular. Today, however, a reforming coalition has to be much broader, not only to mobilise majority support but to pick up the feminist and ecological themes to deal with other 'rational' myths of economic life. The single-minded pursuit of conventional wage-labour for all, for instance, colludes in fostering an epidemic of repetition strain injury, environmental destruction and consumerism's cultural degradation. Rational myths thrive on differentiated interests which the reforming coalition must transcend. A de-differentiating economic democracy provides us with the vantage point to interrogate 'efficiency' in terms of what goals and whose interests imbue it with its present meaning. Perhaps the environment movement's notion of sustainable economic development could be, in this democratic context, the starting point of a search for a less mythical efficiency, as it explores the social and environmental costs, benefits and opportunities of advanced industrialisation. Armed with this kind of rationality, we could begin to redefine not only the notion of economic competence but also that of economic power. But, as Therborn notes (Ehnmark and Therborn 1988: 80; see also Hindess 1982), the discussion of power in the funds debate was markedly abstract and did not address the potential *uses* of economic power and the socioeconomic development they imply. This under-specification simply leaves the door open for the continued obfuscation of power issues by opponents of economic democracy, as the following example illustrates.

The TINA Regression: Learning by Negative Example

In 1987, one of the veterans of the long-running Swedish commission of enquiry into employee share ownership, Rolf Eidem, published his 432-page rumination on the wage-earner fund issue under the title *Share Ownership and Democracy* (Eidem 1987). He adopts as his intellectual foundation Willliamson's (1975) theory of transaction costs: organisations in the form of the firm take over when markets fail. The successful taming and minimising of transaction costs calls forth the differentiated functions and competence that are represented in the firm. The shareholders exercise an essential function of competence as they pilot the firm through the shoals of uncertainty while at the same time their share-dealings contribute to the basic functions of economic coordination and capital allocation.

The demand for economic democracy, Eidem argues, forces us to choose between two models of democracy. The first model is one that calls for some readjustment to the pattern of shareholding to make it more compatible with (and perhaps even to enhance) political democracy, while the second involves a more radical democratisation of society to extend the principles of existing political democracy to economic decision-making. He advances two basic arguments as to why the latter is unviable. First, and this is a further twist to the Williamson thesis, the political realm, he says, is essentially a collectivist, residual function which takes over when market-cum-firm fails and it would be a category mistake to generalise its modus operandi (be it ever so democratic) to the economic sphere. Second, to attempt to do so would be to abolish the special function and competence of the shareholder at the expense of 'efficiency'. Here we have a classic example of what Clegg (1990b) means by the Panglossian logic and underlying normative tenet of the TINA tendency: we already inhabit the only possible world, which is therefore the best of all possible worlds.

Eidem admits, however, that this optimal world could do with some fine tuning. Concentration of shareholding in a few hands and employees' lack of shareholding mean that the latter are comparatively disadvantaged in the distribution of 'influence' (which is what power is called in more polite Swedish circles), both economically and politically. Moreover, and very importantly, non-participation in the discussions and calculations which shareholders engage in prevents wage-earners from developing a more adequate understanding of their own firm's situation and a wider civic competence in economic questions to bring to the political process. The most direct way, he suggests, to overcome these problems would be to encourage employees to acquire shares in their own firms, possibly through state-subsidised acquisitions, with the shares administered by local union organisations. The effect of this reform would be to initiate employees into the rational myths promulgated by the existing dominant coalition in the firm. Thus, far from introducing an alternative system, it would socialise and incorporate them into the existing one, bringing them into what he calls 'inescapable capitalism's old cathedral' (Eidem 1987: xvi).

Eidem's is a stereotypically modernist discourse that moves entirely within the rationality of capital accumulation in a modern market economy, begging all the issues of power, rationally and efficiency I mentioned in the preceding section. His object of study is the firm, divorced from its context

in a specific economic culture and network of power relations. In his view
the firm comprises a number of differentiated functions arranged in a
constellation which is the only workable response to the efficiency imperative. Behind this view is the ancient, fundamental differentiation that
economic liberalism introduced and has defended ever since, the distinction
between the political and economic spheres, capital's protective moat
against those who pursue socio-economic alternatives through political
means. Such starting points are today quite antithetical to both a defensible
notion of efficiency and economic competence and the empowerment of a
popular will in economic development.

In contrast, the vehicle of a viable economic democracy is likely to be a
de-differentiated productive organisation 'embedded' in a more pluralistic
network of power and democratic constituencies and in a social-democratic
economic culture (Clegg, Higgins and Spybey 1989). The central value in
that culture will be that the constituency in each organisational setting
includes all those directly affected by decisions made in it and that one
person has one vote. At the macro level, this means that the constituency
for political and economic purposes is the same. Above all, economic
democracy, like any other democracy, must rest on a real process of
mobilisation around alternative futures.

Economic Democracy in Australia?

At first sight the conflict over economic democracy in Sweden may have
no more than utopian interest to the labour movement in Australia in
the 1990s. In the preceding decade a federal Labor government radically
deregulated the capital market in such a way that the interests and antics
of a new breed of paper entrepreneurs displaced what little prudence, social
input and national priority the formerly regulated banks had allowed for.
In this new environment, the placement of the huge capital funds accumulated as a result of the union push to generalise superannuation entitlements
has been left to 'market forces'. The possibility of steering these funds in
accordance with socio-economic priorities, such as industry development,
remains a central unexploited issue for the labour movement.

It is not that the latter has been silent on the issue. Manufacturing unions
generated a rising tide of interest in a comprehensive approach to national
industrial regeneration (Ewer, Higgins and Stevens 1987), a tide that peaked
with the publication of *Australia Reconstructed* in 1987. Under the significant rubric of 'collective capital formation', this report discussed the Swedish experience of steering superannuation funds into national development

and went on to propose channelling part of Australian superannuation funds into a 'national development fund'. The latter was to be administered by the Australian Industry Development Corporation in accordance with formulated national priorities (ACTU/TDC 1987: 14–16 and 21–23). The report also highlighted the place which industrial democracy and the reform of worklife would have in industrial regeneration (ch. 5).

The federal government, however, made it clear through ignoring the report that selective interventions and institutional reform had no place on its deregulatory agenda. The union movement thereupon temporarily retreated into the narrower, relatively uncontroversial project of award restructuring to facilitate the introduction of new technologies and the emergence of new work practices and multiskilling. This necessity has sometimes been presented as a virtue by linking it to a brave new post-Fordist world that would in itself re-empower labour through the skills and work organisations that the new technologies supposedly prescribe (see for instance, Mathews 1989a). The political problem with both award restructuring and the post-Fordist project is that both are containable within dominant conceptions of efficiency and divert attention from the financial market in whose hands the fate of the new technologies and of Australian industry now rest, to say nothing of the uses to which they are to be put.

There are signs, however, that capital formation will soon be politicised again. As the current recession exposes the myths of deregulation and of the national gains from paper entrepreneurialism, the union movement through the Australian Manufacturing Council has once more unfurled a strategy for industrial regeneration which inevitably problematises capital formation (AMC 1990: ch. 5). If a new campaign for an overarching strategy of this type gathers momentum, the need for a purposive allocation of capital resources will raise wider questions of macro-economic control to which economic democracy is one answer. As my colleagues and I have suggested elsewhere (Ewer, Higgins and Stevens 1987: ch. 9) a re-industrialised Australia may have to be a more democratic society in which even capital formation serves a popular will. En route, Sweden-watching may once again prove to be a useful trade.

Conclusion

In September 1991 the Swedish social democratic government was defeated at the polls, to be replaced by a motley non-socialist coalition. One of the latter's first initiatives in office – and one of the few it could agree on –

was the symbolic step of dismantling the wage-earner funds. It is unlikely that socialist tears will flow at their passing as the funds set up were hardly adequate to making resource allocation either efficient or democratic. And in a sense the whole fund episode is subsumed into the wider phenomenon of social democracy's demise as a politically distinctive, reforming current in western politics.

But as reformists begin to regroup, they are likely to go back to first principles, jettisoning 'rational myths' in defining anew both organisational democracy and economic efficiency in the light of arguments about power, competence and ecological sustainability. Central to their reforming project will be capital formation on a capital market, the engine of the entrenched system. In learning from the past, then, an analysis of the wage-earner fund issue in Sweden is of unique importance. It challenges us to specify, in the context of an alternative capital-formation strategy, whom we are trying to empower to do what in the service of which ultimate socio-economic values.

Conclusion. Reworking the World: Lessons from Everywhere

Jane Marceau

This book has been about change. It has been about experience in different areas of the world at a time of techno-economic paradigm shift. The notion of such a paradigm shift is an abstracted idea or 'ideal type' of the possibilities being opened up through the introduction of new technologies and their adoption. It suggests the extent to which old certainties must be replaced by new questionings. The corollary is the suggestion that old explanations for observed socio-economic patterns and configurations must be replaced by new analyses.

Different chapters in the volume have investigated the changes occurring in practice in business and public sector organisations in many countries around the world. They raise three particular questions or sets of issues: how far and in which ways have elements of the new technological paradigm, whether encapsulated in physical technologies or in managerial strategies, been introduced into productive and administrative organisations? Is there, or to what extent is there, a 'logic' inherent in the new technologies which suggests that a particular trajectory has occurred and will continue to occur? Which socio-economic forces are shaping the organisational outcomes, including both the forms which the organisations as wholes take, or are likely to take, and the work practices adopted?

As Giovanni Dosi points out in his book, *Technical Change and Industrial Transformation* (1984), the notion of a technological paradigm is modelled loosely on Kuhn's delineation of a scientific paradigm. A technological paradigm is thus a 'model' and a 'pattern' of *selected* technological problems, based on *selected* principles derived from natural sciences and on *selected* material technologies. A technological paradigm contains both a positive and a negative heuristic which embody strong prescriptions as to the *directions* of technological change to pursue and those to neglect. Technological paradigms also have a powerful exclusion effect such that the efforts and the technological imagination of engineers and of the organisations they work in are focussed in certain directions while they are 'blind' with respect to other technological possibilities (1984: 15). This internal 'logic', which includes the exclusion effects, also defines some idea of 'progress'. The dimensions of a technological paradigm, Dosi says, include the generic task to which it is applied, the material technology it selects, the physical/chemical properties it exploits and the technological and economic dimensions and trade-offs it focusses upon. To those dimensions, I suggest, one should add the social and the moral or the 'values' which may be embodied in the cultural context. Once the technological and economic dimensions are given, 'progress' may be seen as the improvement of the trade-offs related to those dimensions.

As Dosi further suggests, a crucial question concerns the way in which an established technological paradigm became dominant and how (why) it was preferred to the range of others theoretically possible. The answers, says Dosi, become easier to see as one travels down the stream science-technology-production. Along that stream economic forces together with institutional choices operate as a selective or focussing device (Rosenberg 1976 quoted Dosi 1984: 17). 'The economic criteria acting as selectors define more and more precisely the *actual* paths followed inside a much bigger set of possible ones' (Dosi 1984: 17).

Very important when considering the organisational outcomes, and thus all three questions posed at the outset of this chapter, is the further proposition that once a path has been selected and established it develops a momentum of its own which helps determine the directions of further development within the paradigm. This, as Dosi says, is what Nelson and Winter (1982) define as the 'natural trajectories' of technical progress. In this way, a technological trajectory can be viewed as the movement of multi-dimensional trade-offs between the variables which the paradigm defines as relevant. A technological trajectory is thus a cluster, 'a cylinder in the multidimensional space defined by ... technological and economic variables', to use Dosi's own graphic expression (1984: 17), of possible technological directions whose outer boundaries are defined by the nature of the paradigm itself. Dosi picks out several further features as relevant here: the existence of both more general and more circumscribed trajectories; general complementarities between knowledge, skill and experience; 'competition' between technologies such that development of one may inhibit or encourage others; the cumulative nature of progress along a technological trajectory and the relation of future advance to the position already occupied by a firm or country and the fact that when a trajectory is very 'powerful' it may be difficult to switch to an alternative one (1984: 17–18).

The trajectory is determined then by the selection operated among different potential paths. The selections made seem likely to depend, Dosi suggests, on the economic interests of the organisations involved in relevant R & D and their technological history and areas of expertise but also on many institutional variables such as, and most importantly, the role of public agencies or the military, as can clearly be seen in the history of semiconductors and computers. Moreover,

'The point we want to stress ... is the general weakness of market mechanisms in the *ex ante* selection of technological directions, especially at the initial stage of the history of an industry ...' (Dosi 1984: 19)

More generally, Dosi says, existing

'patterns of industrial and social conflict are likely to operate, within the process of selection of new technological paradigms, both as negative criteria (which possible developments to exclude) and as positive criteria (which technologies to select). In this respect, one might be able to define some long run relationship between patterns of social development and actually chosen technological paradigms. One quite clear example is the relationship between industrial relations at the turn of the last century and the selection and development of 'Tayloristic' patterns of technical change in mechanical engineering' (1984: 19).

In the final stage of the stream of decisions leading from science to production — the choice of *what* to produce — market decisions operate again, determining, *ex post* rather than *ex ante*, which products will be chosen from the range made possible by earlier technology decisions. Choices are determined through the market rewarding particular choices made through the 'trial and error' mechanism by risk-taking actors, although market success is also determined by corporate strategies which define the public's 'needs' which the products will satisfy.

Ultimately, of course, feedback from the market also modifies and encourages progress along the continuum of technological decisions made earlier, 'upward', in the stream. These changes, however, Dosi suggests, are usually modifications made along the same trajectory (1984: 21). It is these modifications, emanating, it seems, from the socio-economic and socio-technical environment, which constitute the familiar changes made *within* a technological paradigm. Translating this idea into the history of work patterns, one might include the 'job enrichment' schemes introduced into 'Taylorist' or 'Fordist' organised workplaces such as in the automotive industry in the late 1960s and 1970s in response to pressure from organised labour as in the Swedish example discussed in this book. These thus might be included in what Dosi calls 'normal technological activity'.

In contrast, *extraordinary* technological attempts emerge either in relation to new opportunities opened up by scientific developments or as a result of the increasing difficulty encountered by firms trying to move forward in a given technological direction, difficulties generated either by technological or by economic factors. (Basing his analysis on Schumpeterian theories Dosi presents a more general theory of technological and productive innovation in his 1984 work. In this volume, however, we are concerned more particularly with the *organisational* issues and outcomes and I therefore do not discuss Dosi's more specific working through of his theory of productive system change).

Following Dosi's presentation of the different stages and aspects of technological trajectories and of the development of a new technological paradigm allows us to make more sense of both the diversity of the changes in the productive structures and organisations of the world detailed in different chapters of this volume and the common trends which seem in some ways to be part of the 'logic' of the emerging system. So let us return to the present book.

Looking about the world, as this book has suggested, it is clear that change is the order of the day everywhere. As Clegg indicated in Section One of the volume, the importance of such changes and the resulting diversity of organisation forms suggest the emergence of a 'post-modern' world. In this world, the 'iron cage' of bureaucracy as the paradigmatic model of the 'rational' structure of large organisations may disappear. First, it is already coming to seem 'normal' that enterprises abandon the divisions between market and hierarchy in organising their transactions which have become familiar and indeed expected, as the still evident TINA Tendency reminds us. Second, large organisations, whether in the public or private sectors, have begun to lose and will probably increasingly lose the clarity of boundary which has typified so many in the past. As the possibility of achieving economies of scope rather than of scale becomes open to enterprises in more and more industries so we may expect far greater 'stretching' of the mechanistic relationships between 'form' and 'function' characteristic of the declining paradigm. Weiss, in her chapter in this book, has already reminded us of the 'horizontal' networking by firms in the industrial districts of Italy and Japan which show us a successful alternative. In a paper published elsewhere Lambooy (1986) has discussed the emergence of the 'hollow corporation' which retains for itself only design and marketing functions, all the rest being subcontracted out while the chapter by Marceau and Jureidini above reminds the reader of the existence already of two possible 'post-Japanese' models of corporate organisation as well as the many factors constraining organisational outcomes. In this book, too, Clegg also reminds us of the coexistence of such diverse organisational forms as those of the artisans making French bread, the small firms creating Italian fashion and the large firm variants of Asian capitalisms. In other papers elsewhere also, Child (1987) has indicated the new, sometimes ephemeral, sometimes 'amoeba-like', structures being developed by large firms in the West to respond to the emergence of new competitive challenges. As mentioned earlier, in the introduction to Section Four of this book, those new forms of organisation include semi-hierarchy, coordinated contracting, coordinated revenue links and spot networking.

In contradistinction to such diversity, however, we also see a trend in the transfer of technologies, especially from East to West, which is pushing towards the widespread adoption of *one* new overall system, albeit with several variants. This new system seems to emerge from two sources. First, it derives from the paradigm shift itself which in practice has some paradoxical results. On the one hand, it permits an increase in the range of possibilities of both products and productive processes made possible by micro-electronic technologies and, to a lesser extent, the emergence of other new core technologies. These possibilities are potent in 'dematuring' existing industries once thought mature in product and in organisational form. But, on the other hand, the competitive circumstances of the introduction of these new techniques seem to be pushing many companies to focus on one aspect of production, that of quality, and to organise their production process is much the same way. Thus, second, the new system is driven by the remarkable increase in productivity, and quality, at least in the early stages of the new paradigm, made possible by the management technologies derived from a quite different technological and cultural context. These were developed in Japan and exported through Japanese transplants and simple copying to the West. This 'Japanisation' of the world, to use Barry Wilkinson's colourful phrase, is fast coming to dominate automotive production and is colonising other industries producing complex goods which emphasise quality as well as innovation as the basis of their markets. It seems increasingly likely that some more or less similar form of 'Japanese' organisation will spread widely into the productive structure. This will be partly because of its clear (initial at least) competitive advantage in some industries and markets but also partly because, as was suggested earlier in the book, the 'logic' of Just-in-Time production means that supplier firms all down the chain of production of core industries must adopt similar methods if they are to be retained as suppliers and themselves to be able to increase productivity and competitiveness.

In contrast again, however, it is clear that the outcomes in terms of organisation design worldwide will not all be the same. The shapes of productive organisations will continue to be influenced and constrained by cultural factors, by greater or lesser degrees of technological advancement, lag or superiority, by differing local, national and international interorganisation patterns in the distribution of power, including the relative power of capital and labour, and by the activities of public instances, including states, regional and local governments.

Let us unpack this suggestion a little further. Dosi's outline of a technical paradigm and technological trajectory suggests that these are defined by a multiplicity of technological and socio-economic forces which determine choices made at the most 'general' stage of the science-technology-production stream. Thus the first selection is much determined by *local* factors which affect the answer to the question 'what can we produce with this "science" and how profitable will these products be?'.

These local factors are institutional and cultural, social and economic, financial and managerial and the choices they constrain owe much to past events and practices, to the business recipes dominant and to the nature of the public-private, business-state interface. It is at this stage in the development of the new paradigm, one might argue, that the most abundant diversity of organisational form is to be found and that 'post-modern' organisations are most apparent. Individual enterprises (public or private) are at different places along the technological trajectory and much still remains to be worked out. There is still, moreover, a good deal of competition among the core technologies themselves, such that some are still developing while their very development inhibits others. The general complementarities (knowledge, skill and experience) outlined by Dosi have also not yet fully been worked out or come into play while much of the old system is still extant.

Once a technological paradigm or trajectory becomes dominant, however, it becomes increasingly difficult for organisations which do not adopt both physical technologies and the associated management strategies to survive, or to survive unchanged. Thus, even while controllers of organisations may resist taking new technologies on board — and in any real productive structure many firms will be unable to make the transition — they will nonetheless be obliged to change and reorganise many activities if they are to remain players in the new game as defined by dominant actors. Thus, once one form of organisation proves itself very successful in a much contested market place others must follow suit or devise new strategies for play. In the automotive industry, for example, major assemblers worldwide have been both obliged and pleased to take on central elements of the new technologies and to reorganise accordingly where local elements (such as lack of skilled labour or management or a small local market) constrain that path. In the latter case, the reorganisations involve generating new relationships with unions and public authorities.

For these reasons, there is visible a global pattern of reorganisation, built up like a house of cards, with more or less deliberate copying of the trajectory successful elsewhere. Analysing organisations, technologies and cultures in comparative perspective must thus take account of the relationships established in the stream of science-technology-production and the point of development of the new paradigm as well as the general direction of change.

We should not shift our analysis too far, however, I suggest, and rely too heavily on a 'stage of the paradigm' approach; not only is this view too mechanistic but we also need to specify more clearly the factors affecting local variants. It is in this investigation that the frameworks for analysis developed by Biggart and Clegg in the first section of this book are perhaps most useful. The particular cultural and institutional practices of a society help determine the forms of organisation chosen, the selection of technologies made from the range available and the directions to be taken in the further development of the systems adopted. They help determine the degree of emphasis on control or decentralisation in the workplace and organisational responses to changing competitive circumstances. Equally important, they help to determine the degree to which large productive and administrative organisations are 'democratic' in form and substance. Family structures and values, the nature and emphasis of education systems, the availability of alternative 'rationalities' for ordering social and economic relationships all contribute determining outcomes. So too does the relative power of the social partners, capital and labour, as many writers in this book have emphasised.

The *mechanisms* of change are also important in understanding both directions and outcomes. The ways in which new technologies, both physical and managerial, are transferred depends greatly on the existing organisation of the productive structure. Reconceptualising the 'atoms' of the structure and their relationship to each other helps visualise the trajectories which particular technological changes are likely to follow and hence the dynamics of the system and the factors influencing outcomes.

In this connection, it is useful to use a variety of analytical tools to help paint a series of pictures of a national productive structure (economy). The three central approaches may be summarised in the terms of the concepts of productive chains, complexes and clusters, supplemented by the analysis of 'sectors' of enterprises and the configuration and coordination decisions taken by major multinational enterprises. All of these have been mentioned earlier but deserve summarising here. The concept of 'chains of production' refers to the relationships established in organisational forms between 'core' firms and their suppliers and distributors. These chains draw together all the productive activities necessary to the creation and sale of a product, from the suppliers of raw materials, components and finished or semi-finished parts through assembly by the core firms to the products' distributors and repair services. The chains established thus cross the traditional economic divisions into primary, secondary and tertiary activities. The chains may be shorter, for example, where the products are less complex, or longer, including firms in a variety of areas of production. The chains may be conceptualised as the 'spines' or 'ribs' running through an economy and as performing an integrating function such that firms in each are affected by the decisions of others 'up' and 'down' stream, each outcome being affected by the relative power of the players, the availability of alternative markets or the degree of specialisation.

A second analysis focusses on 'complexes' which are arenas of economic activity which bring together not only firms but also bodies such as public authorities and industry-funded research organisations. The construction complex, for instance, may be conceived as a group of large firms, innovative technologically, building the large buildings which dominate city skylines and working in conjunction with planning authorities, engineering consultants, building research bodies and computing specialists. Similarly, the health complex may be conceived of as embodied in hospitals which organise an enormous variety of inputs from medical research to protheses, computing equipment and furniture and thus organise the activity of producers in many fields. In each complex the organisation and functioning of one element enormously affects the choices open to and made by others, even though the players play in apparently quite diverse arenas.

Thirdly, 'clusters', as delineated in the work of Porter (1990), are conceived of as a group of firms, geographically contiguous, which collaborate and/or compete in such a way as to make for continuous innovation in both product and process. The principal examples Porter gives are the tiles, shoes and clothing companies of Spain and Italy which, although small, dominate the international market in their fields but there are many in other countries, such as Germany and Japan. It is in clusters such as these that innovation in both technologies and organisations may be expected to be fastest.

In addition to these ways of describing or 'cutting into' the productive structure for analytical purposes, Child (1987) has suggested that one needs to focus on what he calls 'sectors', which are composed of firms which regularly transact with each other in a supplying or service role. Each firm's strategic decisions are moulded by this regular process of interaction.

Finally, of course, the particularities of enterprise structures found in a given country owe much to decisions made about coordination and configuration by multi-national companies operating multi-domestic or global strategies. One can thus see organisation structures as 'stretched out horizontally' across the world, with a varying number of activities located in any one country or across many national boundaries. Organisational change will thus depend crucially on how 'stretched out' particular firms decide to be.

These different images or conceptualisations of the productive structure can be superimposed or used separately to inform our picture of how the world is being reworked according to the purpose for which the analysis is to be used. Each set of lenses will generate different pictures of the production system and the interrelations between its segments and of the alterations occurring, especially at a time of rapid technological change. Any one organisation viewed with these different lenses may appear to take on a quite different form. In this way too, we can account both for much of the organisational diversity and change observed and for the similarity of trends discerned.

Using these different sets of lenses enables us to paint pictures of economies in terms rather different from those of the past. We may focus on an institutional analysis, especially in the early stages of technological paradigm change when a variety of new directions is open, and, as Biggart suggests in this volume, we can use these analyses to decipher initial factors shaping the development of the particular business recipes selected. But we must also renew our focus on the *structures* of the productive system itself and on the relationships between its constituent parts in our understanding both of current 'shapes' and likely directions of change. The analyses are dynamic, focussing on the relationships between different players in the arena, large and small firms, public bodies and governments, as well, of course, as the creators of the science initiating and developing the new paradigm. Such analyses suggest the existence of a creative tension or stress, as Lamming (1989) calls it in another context, which shapes the outcome at any given time and contains the potential for radical change. If the position of any of the key players changes then changes to the whole system are likely. Inter-organisational power may thus be the key to understanding the factors which shape the directions of technological change chosen and which are selected from the multiple possibilities available (Pfeffer 1987).

Some aspects of inter-organisational power, of course, extend beyond the strictly business arena and bring the analyst to consider again the role of the state and other public instances of power. Changed competitive circumstances, a major factor leading to an organisational paradigm shift are much affected by public policies which may directly change the environment which existing organisation forms were designed to meet. Current public policies include the deregulation of markets for capital (finance markets) as well as for goods and commodities, the creation, as in the EEC, and the dissolution, as of Comecon, of international trade blocs and the adherence or not to GATT rules. In particular, government decisions affect the location of productive plants and other elements of the value chain and in many cases both the technologies introduced and the speed and spread of their introduction. Private choices are influenced by public policies about the building or demolition of tariff walls, quotas and anti-dumping provisions but also, in a more positive way perhaps, by export and R & D subsidies, the provision of infrastructure (transport, communications, education etc), by public purchasing decisions and so on. Regional development incentives are used by local and national authorities, to such an extent indeed that these authorities have been called the 'last entrepreneurs' (Goodman 1977). Weiss has indicated in the present volume how important the role of the state in Italy has been in encouraging the formation, maintenance and expansion of a large population of firms with a number of employees below a specified size and a family-based ownership structure. The French government pursues much the same policies, using slightly different categories (Marceau in Hunt, Jackson and Marceau 1981), as indeed do many Western countries.

At present, the roles of governments in the industrialised world and hence in reworking that world are themselves in a state of flux. The overtly interventionist policies of national governments during the post-war era and the 'indicative plans' and merger policies which, for instance, encouraged in France the growth of 'national champions' in core technologies have largely gone or changed form or focus to become part of the portfolio of responsibilities of sub-national authorities. Deregulation and/or privatisation have become, or remained, the order of the day in many parts of the world while, in contrast, a 'New Protectionism' is also emerging, seen, for instance, in the techno-nationalism of the USA and the measures contained in the Super 301 provisions of the US Omnibus Trade Act of 1988.

The deregulation trend in ideology and practice has had many results. Notably it has left the way open for mergers and concentrations of companies at national and international level, especially the latter. In conjunction with other elements, including the rise to economic prominence of Japan and a broader north east Asian ascendancy (Garnaut 1989) and the growth of new technologies, one corollary of the deregulation approach has been the rapid deindustrialisation of the UK and some parts of the USA and Australia in particular. The take-over in July 1990 of ICL, Britain's only remaining computer company, by a Japanese firm (Fujitsu) is symptomatic. The export of Japanese management practices is increasingly accompanied by the export of Japanese capital in a series of bids for presence in strategic geographical and other areas. In Australia the break-up in 1990—1991 of some of the most successful manufacturing groups, covering a range of industries from food processing to clothing, and the sale of major local brandnames to overseas companies is an example of the effect of deregulation of the financial system coupled to poor local management practices in an era boasting paper 'entrepreneurship' as the new culture of business.

The configuration of skills and work practices mentioned by Dosi (1984) indicates another area where, at certain stages at least, the new technological trajectory seems to encourage a particular direction of change. Broadbanding and the reduction of highly differentiated jobs tasks are often an important corollary of the introduction of computer-related technologies to productive and administrative processes. This trend is important although such changes have also been thought to encourage de- rather than re-skilling and there is still much debate about the extent of broadbanding and the factors determining the boundaries of new tasks, as was indicated in my introduction to Section Five of this book. It is clear that both the speed of introduction of the new technologies and their effects in factories and offices depend greatly on the power of (organised) labour in the negotiating process, a negotiating process assisted crucially in Australia by the existence of only one confederation of labour unions and a centralised wage (and conditions) bargaining instance. Much also depends on the job divisions already existing. If, historically, there have been few divisions of task at shop floor level, as in Germany, for example, and if the development of monthly rather than hourly or piece-work wage rates has already been achieved (as in France) then the move to a 'post-Fordist' labour process will demand fewer changes and lesser negotiating strength than in countries such as the UK or Australia.

Finally, and most important here, the patterns of work organisation which eventually come to typify the new paradigm will owe much, as Selby-Smith shows in this volume, to the attitudes of management and the place of work organisation in a broader agenda for change. As we saw above, Selby-Smith, points clearly to the importance of the employer's (government) political goals and commitment to the incorporation of social objectives such as equal employment opportunity into organisation strategy. *Political* goals and political power are thus once again evident as an important ingredient in the transfer and choice of organisations, technologies and cultures.

This is clear in the final paper in the fifth section of this book which focusses on the political conflicts and power struggles which mould the progress of organisational change into social transformation. In this chapter, Higgins describes the rise, fall and redefinition of the political project attached to the idea of 'wage earner' funds' in Sweden. These funds, in the strong form of the project, were to give workers more than 50 % ownership of the companies which employed them and thus enable them to gain control of many enterprises through the compulsory redistribution of 'excessive' profits to workers in the form of equity in the companies in which they worked. This scheme would, as Higgins points out, effectively have set a date for the achievement of socialism. It is no surprise then that the proposal proved extremely controversial and soon union leaders were persuaded that such a project was 'irrational'. Whether or not Higgins is correct in assuming that 'workers' or 'the people's' (proposed in another formulation of the project) control is the best way of democratising or indeed managing industry, his story and analysis remind us forcefully that the agenda for radical organisational change is not essentially concerned with 'efficiency', however conceived, but with more fundamental transformation. In themselves, broadbanding of skills, the creation of longer career paths, even the power to 'stop the line' allocated to workers in some Japanese factories, do little to change power relationships. They do not alter the broader logic of the 'rational' western capitalist system. While organisation forms may diverge, both in terms of the overall division of functions and of the internal structure of work relationships, new technologies, whether encapsulated in computer-related technologies or in managerial strategies, are introduced with the 'rational' goal of increased efficiency and hence profitability in mind. Few, if any, changes emanate from other concerns, except perhaps 'later' in a technological trajectory. This is exemplified in the Volvo case, discussed by Sandkull in this book, where 'human relations' concerns were important in the introduction of altered ('enriched') work practices in Sweden but were not considered important in Volvo's Belgian plants where labour willing to work in 'unreconstructed' ways was in adequate supply. The balance of power deriving from labour supply and demand and labour's relations with the political process thus have to be a prime consideration in analysis of factors pushing both physical technological change and altered work organisation. Looking around the world, then, it seems clear that Higgins is right in suggesting that radical change can come only from changes in that balance of power and the adoption and implementation of a political project which would decisively shift the balance. Such a fundamental change to a central tenet of capitalist society is seldom seriously on the agenda of even Social Democratic governments, however, and, indeed, such governments are themselves currently something of a rarity.

Without such a shift, the shape of the organisation structure, the choices among available technologies adopted and the cultures developed, both within and 'between' organisations, do indeed seem likely to follow an increasingly dominant 'Japanese' model. The success of this model has recently been said to depend on close connections between the internal elements of the productive systems and the relationships generated by foreign policy between Japan and its Asian neighbours. While this aspect of the recipe may ultimately have to change, the 'Japanisation of the world', to use Wilkinson's phrase again, seems likely to continue as long as it provides a competitive edge. We have seen in this volume how an overarching techno-economic paradigm shift is represented and interpreted in a multiplicity of ways at the different levels of organisational design and practice and is driving different phases of the science-technology-production stream. We have also seen that the emphasis is likely to remain on *control*, just as it did in the past in most of the countries considered, perhaps even more so in a world of heightened competitive pressures, particularly in the international arena.

In short, despite the many changes occurring worldwide, it seems that it is important in analytical terms to view the emerging system as at least as much a continuation of past practices as a creation of new ones through other uses of the technologies now available. Many 'old' choices continue to be made. Is this because the new technologies, especially those associated with micro-electronics, have not spread so far or so fast as many observers have repeatedly predicted? or because employers have not realised (or been allowed to realise) the full potential of the technologies? Almost a decade and a half ago, for example, a French (the Nora-Minc) report on the employment implications of the widespread introduction of information technologies predicted massive job losses. On the whole these have not occurred. Even in the present world economic downturn, labour shedding still seems to be due essentially to shifts in markets rather than to the inherent labour saving effects of the new technologies or to progress along a new technological trajectory. Equally the vision of a mass return to 'home-working' in the 'electronic cottages' made possible by the technology of the 'information economy' has not yet materialised. The decision to shed labour remains an essentially social process just like the configuration of decisions about production location and organisation shape. The turmoil apparent everywhere in the reworking of the industrial world is essentially about a reordering of the social processes of production as much as it is about technology transformation.

Interestingly, however, while reordering the world of production is well underway, much less progress is being made in the world of the social distribution of the resulting profits. Current reworking of the world of work has little or nothing to say about reworking the social relationships surrounding the productive system, about social, or even economic, equality, or about social protection, except perhaps to increase the divide between those included in the world of work and those excluded from it or living on its margins. The political is linked to the economic only in the sense of creating a single market in Europe or of public encouragement of the introduction of new technologies or public subsidies to capture export markets or to train or re-train employees. This mix of organisational, technological and cultural change contains no overt political rhetoric concerning a social agenda. Lessons learned from all the countries considered in this book suggest that reworking the productive world has done little to build new visions beyond the immediate organisation and culture of factory and office. The comparative perspective adopted here in the analysis of organisations, technologies and cultures indicates the continued primacy everywhere of belief in a 'technological fix' rather than a more fundamental reordering of our organisations and culture. Indeed, the collapse of the Communist regimes of eastern Europe and the Soviet Union has made the development of new world visions even more problematic. The existence of a powerful alternative greatly encourages progress in organisational and political change as Raymond Williams' analysis of the two 'revolutions', the political in France and the economic in Britain, long ago reminded us.

About the Authors

Cameron Allan (B. Comm) is Research Officer in the Key Centre in Strategic Management, Queensland University of Technology. His research interests include Australian industrial relations, industrial sociology and critical management theory. He is currently researching and publishing with Gill Palmer on the use of new management technologies in Australia.

Nicole Biggart holds a Ph. D in sociology from the University of California, Berkeley, and is now Professor of Management and Sociology at the Graduate School of Management at the Davis campus. In 1989 she published *Charismatic Capitalism: Direct Selling Organisations in America* with the University of Chicago Press and she is the author or co-author of numerous influential articles on East Asian business and the comparative analysis of business organisations.

Stewart Clegg holds degrees from the Universities of Aston and Bradford. After 10 years at Griffith University from 1985 to 1990 he was Professor of Sociology at the University of New England, both in Australia, and is currently Professor of Organisation Studies at the University of St. Andrews in Scotland. He has published numerous books on organisation theory and power, including most recently *Frameworks of Power* (Sage 1989) and *Modern Organisations* (Sage 1990). He also edited *Organisation Theory and Class Analysis* (1989) and, jointly with Gordon Redding, *Capitalism in Contrasting Cultures (1990)*, both with de Gruyter. He has also been editor of the *Australian and New Zealand Journal of Sociology* and *Organisation Studies*.

Ben Dankbaar studied social sciences and economics and then taught economics at the University of Amsterdam before moving in 1982 to the Wissenschaftzentrum in Berlin. In 1987 he joined the Maastricht Economic Research Institute on Innovation and Technology (MERIT) where he heads the Technology and Labour area. He publishes in many technology and industrial relations areas and in 1990 co-edited a book on *Perspectives in Industrial Organisation*, published by Kluwer.

Mark Dodgson has a BSc in Society and Technology, an MA in Industrial Relations and a Ph. D from Imperial College. Previously a Fellow at the Technical Change Centre, he is presently a Fellow at the Science Policy Research Unit at the University of Sussex. He is the author of numerous articles and reports and edited the 1989 SPRU book *Technology Strategy and the Firm*. He is the author of the *Management of Technological*

Learning (de Gruyter 1991), and is presently writing books on technological collaboration and technology transfer for Routledge and editing with Roy Rothwell a handbook on industrial innovation for Edward Elgar.

Elizabeth Garnsey is University Lecturer in industrial organisation in the Department of Engineering, Cambridge University. She did her first degree at Oxford, specialising in economics and a Ph. D at the University of California, Berkeley on Soviet manpower planning. She has consulted for the EC at Brussels and other international organisations on employment issues and published on labour markets and on innovation and technology transfer.

Armelle Gorgeu has a doctorate in 'Sciences Economiques' from the University of Paris I and is *Chargée de Recherches* at the Centre d'Etudes de l'Emploi (under the joint aegis of the Ministries of Labour and Research) in Paris. She has published extensively (with René Mathieu) on changing relations between core firms and suppliers in the automotive and other major industries in France. She and René Mathieu are currently researching the way new technologies are restructuring industrial space and the impact of the creation of the Single Market in Europe in 1993 and the enhanced competition this will generate.

Winton Higgins is an Associate Professor in Politics at Macquarie University and a graduate of the Universities of Sydney, Stockholm and London. He has published widely on socialist theory, Swedish labour politics and the politics of industry policy in Australia. He is the co-author of *Unions and the Future of Australian Manufacturing,* Sydney: Allen and Unwin, 1987.

Ray Jureidini holds a BA and Ph. D from Flinders University, Adelaide. After holding a National Research Fellowship at the Australian National University where he worked on the automotive industry, he lectured at La Trobe University and is now teaching at Deakin University. His research interests centre on new technology and industrial relations and he has recently published on the automotive industry.

Jane Marceau holds a BA from the London School of Economics and a Ph. D from the University of Cambridge. She lectured at the University of Essex before moving to Paris in 1972. Between 1972 and 1980 she taught at Nanterre (University of Paris X), worked with INSEAD, and joined the OECD, and held a half time lectureship at Manchester Business School. In the 1980s she was Professor of Sociology at the University of Liverpool and since 1984 has been Professor of Public Policy at the

Australian National University. She has published in areas ranging from the structure of French society, through urban education and small business organisation to class analysis. Recent publications include *A Family Business? An International Business Elite in the Making* (Cambridge: Cambridge University Press 1989) and numerous chapters in books on technological change and organisational issues.

John Mathews is Senior Lecturer in the School of Industrial Relations and Organisational Behaviour at the University of New South Wales. He currently directs a research programme in Case Studies in Organisational Innovation. He holds a BSc (Econs) from the London School of Economics and an MEng and Ph. D in Control Systems from Imperial College. He has worked as a technology adviser to trade unions in the UK and Australia, as head of the ACTU's occupational health and safety unit and from 1985 to 1989 as a senior executive in the Victorian government. He is the author of *Tools of Change: New Technology and the Democratisation of Work* (1989), *Age of Democracy: the Politics of Post-Fordism* (1989), and 'Structure, Strategy and Public Policy: Lessons from the Italian Textile Industry for Australia' (co-author, 1991).

René Mathieu has a *Diplôme d'Etudes Approfondies* from the University of Paris I (Panthéon-Sorbonne). He is *Chargé de Recherches* at the Centre d'Etudes de l'Emploi in Paris. He has published extensively on subcontracting and employment (with Armelle Gorgeu), specialising in the automotive, areospace, electronics and computing industries. He and Armelle are currently researching the impact of new technologies and the restructuring of industrial space.

Jonathan Morris, MA and MPhil., is a Lecturer in Organisational Behaviour at Cardiff Business School. His research interests include Japanese corporate strategies, investment patterns and organisational forms. He is the co-author of *Transforming Buyer-Supplier Relations: Japanese Style Practices in a Western Context* and *Wales in the 1990s*. He edited *Japan and the Global Economy* and co-edited *A Feasible Future?*.

Michael Muetzelfeldt, BSc Ph. D, is Lecturer in Social Policy at Deakin University, Geelong, Australia. He is the editor of *Society, State and Politics in Australia,* Pluto Press, Sydney, 1991. He has researched social movements and information technology in administrative organisations and is currently working on the politics of the emerging 'information society'.

Judith Nishida holds degrees from the Universities of Birmingham and Hong Kong. Currently Senior Lecturer in the Department of Management at the Hong Kong Polytechnic, her research interests focus on forms of business organisation and managerial practice in East Asia. Her current research and most recent publication are on the cotton spinners of Japan, South Korea and Hong Kong.

Nick Oliver holds degrees of MA and Ph. D. He is a Lecturer in Organisational Behavior at Cardiff Business School. His research interests include Japanese manufacturing systems and their transfer to the West. He is co-author of *The Japanization of British Industry* (with Barry Wilkinson).

Gill Palmer holds degrees from the University of Birmingham, the London School of Economics and City University (Ph. D). Following several years in senior positions with the British Government and managing her consultancy firm, she joined City University in the early 1980s. In 1987 she became Professor of Human Resource Management and Director of the Key Centre for Strategic Management of the Queensland University of Technology and in January 1992 moved to head the Department of Management at Wollongong University. Author of a best selling text on British industrial relations and numerous articles, her recent and forthcoming books include works on Australian personnel management, industrial relations and quality management.

Teresa Shuk-ching Poon is Lecturer in the Department of Management in the Hong Kong Polytechnic. She holds an MA degree in Industrial Relations from the University of Warwick, UK. She has recently worked on industrial reform and the labour contract system in China and is now researching the impact of new technology on work organisation and industrial relations. Her most recent publication is a joint report on labour-management consultation in Hong Kong, published in *Industrial Relations and Labour Management Consultation: Asian Experiences*, 1991, Tokyo, Asian Productivity Organisation.

John Roberts is currently a University Lecturer in the Judge Institute of Management Studies at Cambridge University. He took his first degree and Ph. D in the Department of Management Sciences at the University of Manchester Institute of Science and Technology. He then held research posts at Manchester University and the London Business School, publishing in the areas of accounting, accountability and strategic change. His current research interests focus on the problems of managing growth in small high technology companies.

Bengt Sandkull is Professor of Industrial Management at the Institute of Technology at Linköping University, Sweden. A graduate of the Graduate School of Business Administration (MBA and Ph. D) at the University of Göteborg, Sweden, he held positions at the Universities of Göteborg and Lund before joining Linköping. He has also held visiting positions in the USA, China and Australia and has consulted to Swedish industry and public institutions. His research interests include new-product development, organisation design, work organisation, industrial democracy and industrialisation in developing countries and, currently, the participatory design of productive organisations as continuous learning systems under innovative management. His published works include more than ten books and research monographs, contributions to several international books and a number of articles in various professional journals.

Chris Selby-Smith holds an Economics Degree from Melbourne University and D Phil. from Oxford where he was a Rhodes Scholar. He held positions at universities in Australia and Canada before joining the Australian Public Service in 1975, serving in the Departments of Prime Minister and Cabinet and Health before joining the Public Service Board. He is currently Professor of Management at Monash University and one of the founding Directors of the National Centre for Health Programme Evaluation. He has written, solely or jointly, or edited thirteen books and published numerous articles, mainly on public sector management, health, education and training.

Rob van Tulder studied social sciences and economics at the Free University, Amsterdam and the University of Amsterdam. He is currently Senior Research Fellow at the University of Amsterdam and Associate Professor at the Erasmus University, Rotterdam and the Rotterdam School of Management. He publishes in the fields of technology development and diffusion, multinationalisation processes, European integration and the position of smaller industrial countries. In 1988 he co-authored (with Gerd Junne) *European Multinationals in Core Technologies,* in 1990 edited *Small Industrial Countries and Economic and Technological Development* and is now working on a book dealing with the global car industry.

Linda Weiss (Ph. D London School of Economics) is a Lecturer in Comparative Political Economy in the Department of Government at the University of Sydney. Her publications include *Creating Capitalism: the State and Small Business since 1945* (1988) and 'Structure, Strategy and Public Policy: Lessons from the Italian Textile Industry for Australia' (1991, co-author). She has also published in C. Crouch and D. Marquand (eds.) *The New Centralism: Britain out of Step in Europe?* and in several European journals. She is currently finishing a project on the political and social foundations of national competitiveness and is jointly writing a book for Polity Press (Cambridge) on *States and Economic Development in Comparative Historical Perspective* (co-author John Hobson, forthcoming).

Barry Wilkinson holds degrees of BSc., M. Sc and Ph. D and is Professor of Human Resource Management at Cardiff Business School. His research interests are currently the transfer and emulation of Japanese work organisation methods in Western firms and Japanese transplants. He is the author of *The Shopfloor Politics of New Technology* and co-author of *The Japanization of British Industry*.

Select Bibliography

Abegglen, J. (1958): *The Japanese Factory*. Glencoe, Ill.: Free Press.

Abercrombie N., S. Hill and B. Turner (1980): *The Dominant Ideology Thesis*. London: Allen and Unwin.

Abrams, P. (1982): *Historical Sociology*. Shepton Mallet: Open Books.

AC & AC (1987): *National Wage Case Decision*. Print G6800. Melbourne: Australian Concilation and Arbitration Commission.

Ackroyd, S. and P. Crowdy (1990): 'Can culture be managed? Working with "raw" material: the case of the English slaughtermen', *Personnel Review* 19 (5): 3 – 13.

ACTU (1989):'ACTU Blueprint for changing awards and agreements', D8-89. Melbourne: Australian Council of Trade Unions.

AFNOR (1987): *Normes internationales SSISO 9000 – 9001 – 9002 – 9003 – 9004 pour la Gestion de la Qualité et l'Assurance de la Qualité*. Paris: AFNOR.

Afriat C., E. de Banville and J.-J. Chanaron (1987): 'Rapports entre Constructeurs automobiles et Fournisseurs aux Etats-Unis'. *Centre de Prospective et d'Evaluation Etude* 90:92.

Agurén, S., R. Hansson and K. Karlsson (1976): *Volvo Kalmarverken*. Stockholm: Rationaliseringsrådet SAF-LO.

Agurén, S., R. Hansson and K. Karlsson (1984): *Volvo Kalmar revisited – Ten years of experience*. Stockholm: Utvecklingsrådet.

AIRC (1989): February 1989 *Review*, Print H8200. Melbourne: Australian Industrial Relations Commission.

AIRC (1990): *Metal Industry Award 1984, Decision* (Keogh, D. P.), Print J1935. March. Sydney: Australian Industrial Relations Commission.

Alford, R. and R. Friedland (1985): *The Power of Theory: Capitalism, the State, and Democracy*. Cambridge: Cambridge University Press.

Altshuler, A., M. Anderson, D. Jones, D. Roos and J. Womack (1986): *The Future of the Automobile. The Report of MIT's International Automobile Program*. Cambridge, Mass.: MIT Press.

Amsden, A. (1985): 'The State and Taiwan's Economic Development', in P. Evans, D. Rueschemeyer and T. Skocpol (eds.) *Bringing the State Back In*. Cambridge: Cambridge University Press. pp. 78 – 106.

Anderson, B. (1983): *Imagined Communities: Reflections on the Origins and Spread of Nationalism*. London: Verso.

Anthony, P. (1990): 'The paradox of the management of culture, or "he who leads is lost" ', *Personnel Review* 19 (4): 3 – 8.

Aoki, M. (1987): *A New Paradigm in Work Organization: the Japanese Experience*. Helsinki: World Institute for Development Economics Research.

Ashby, W. (1956): *An Introduction to Cybernetics*. London: Chapman and Hall.

Atkinson, J. (1987): 'Flexibility or fragmentation? The UK labour market in the eighties', *Labour and Society* 12 (1): 87 – 108.

Australian Council of Trade Unions/Trade Development Council (ACTU/TDC) (1987): *Australia Reconstructed, ACTU/TDC Mission to Western Europe*. Canberra: AGPS.

Australian Industrial Relations Commission (AIRC) (1988): *National Wage Case Decision.* Print H4000. Melbourne: Australian Industrial Relations Commission.

Australian Manufacturing Council (AMC) (1990): *The Global Challenge: Australian Manufacturing in the 1990s.* Melbourne: AMC.

Automotive Industry Authority (1988): *Report on the State of the Automotive Industry.* Canberra: AGPS.

Automotive Industry Authority (1989): *Report on the State of the Automotive Industry.* Canberra: AGPS.

Automotive Industry Authority (1990): *Report on the State of the Automotive Industry.* Canberra: AGPS.

Badham, R. and J. Mathews (1989): 'The new production systems debate', *Labour and Industry* 2 (2): 194 – 246.

Bagnasco, A. and Pini, R. (1981): 'Sviluppo economico e trasformazioni socio-politiche dei sistemi a economia diffusa', *Quaderni fondazioni Giangiacomo Feltrinelli* 14 (1): 43 – 60.

Bain, J. (1968): *Industrial Organization.* New York: Wiley.

Baker, F. (ed.) (1973): *Organizational Systems: General Systems Approaches to Complex Organizations.* Homewood, Ill.: Irwin.

Bamber, G. (1989): 'Flexibility and Reform of Work Organisation: International Perspectives'. Paper presented to the Third International APROS Colloquium, Australian National University, 13 – 15 December, 1989.

Barberis, C. (1980): *L'Artigianato in Italia e nella Comunita' economica europea.* Milan: F. Angeli.

Barnard, C. (1938): *The Functions of the Executive.* Cambridge, Mass: Harvard University Press.

Barnet, J. and R. Müller (1975): *Global Reach: the Power of the Multinational Corporations.* London: Jonathan Cape.

Barney, B. and G. Ouchi (eds.) (1986): *Organisational Economics.* San Francisco: Jossey-Bass.

Bateson, G. (1935): 'Culture contact and schismogenesis'. *Man* 35 (December): 178 – 183.

Bauman, Z. (1976): *Socialism: The Active Utopia.* London: Allen and Unwin.

Baumol, N. (1967): *Business Behaviour, Value and Growth.* New York: Macmillan.

Baven, G. (1988): 'Just-in-Time policies in the car and electronic industries'. Unpublished paper, University of Amsterdam, Centre for International Relations and Law.

Beck, S. and J. Child (1978): *Mastering the Art of French Cooking.* Vol. 2, Harmondsworth: Penguin.

Beer, S. (1959): *Cybernetics and Management.* New York: Wiley.

Belussi, F. (1989): 'Benetton — a case study of corporate strategy for innovation in traditional sectors', in M. Dodgson (ed.) *Technology Strategy and the Firm: Management and Public Policy.* Harlow: Longman. pp. 116 – 133.

Benedict, R. (1946): *The Chrysanthemum and the Sword.* Boston: Houghton-Mifflin.

Benveniste, G. (1987): *Professionalizing the Organization: Reducing Bureaucracy to Enhance Effectiveness.* San Francisco: Jossey-Bass.

Berger, P. (1987): *The Capitalist Revolution*. London: Wildwood.

Berger, P. and M. Hsiao (eds.) (1988): *In Search of an East Asian Development Model*. New Brunswick: Transaction Books.

Berger, S. and M. Piore (1980): *Dualism and Discontinuity in Industrial Societies*. Cambridge and New York: Cambridge University Press.

Bertaux D. and I. Bertaux-Wiame (1981): 'Artisanal bakery in France: how it lives and why it survives', in F. Bechofer and B. Elliot (eds.) *The Petite Bourgeoisie: Comparative Studies of the Uneasy Stratum*. London: Macmillan. pp. 121–154.

Bessant, B. (1988): 'Corporate management and the institutions of higher education', *Australian Universities Review* 2: 10–13.

Biggart, N. (1989): *Charismatic Capitalism: Direct Selling Organisations in America*. Chicago: Chicago University Press.

Biggart, N. (1990): 'Institutionalized Patrimonialism in Korean Business', in C. Calhoun (ed.) *Comparative Social Research* 12: 113–133.

Biggart, N. (1991): 'Explaining Asian Economic Organisation', *Theory and Society* 20: 199–232.

Biggart, N. and G. Hamilton (1984): 'The Power of Obedience', *Administrative Science Quarterly* 29: 540–549.

Biggart, N. and G. Hamilton (1987): 'An Institutional Theory of Leadership', *Journal of Applied Behavioral Science* 23: 429–441.

Biggart, N. and G. Hamilton (1990): 'The Western Bias of Neoclassical Economics: on the Limits of a Firm-Based Theory to Explain Business Networks'. Paper presented to the Networks and Organisations Conference, Harvard Business School, August.

Bird, E. (1980): *Information Technology in the Office: The Impact on Women's Jobs*. Manchester: Equal Opportunities Commission.

Bjerknes, G., P. Ehn and M. Kyng (eds.) (1987): *Computers and Democracy: The Scandinavian Challenge*. Aldershot: Avebury.

Blackburn, R. and M. Mann (1979): *The Working Class in the Labour Movement*. London Macmillan.

Blandy, R., P. Dawkins, K. Gannicot, P. Kain, W. Kasper and R. Kriegler (1985): *Structured Chaos: The Process of Productivity Advance*. Melbourne: Oxford University Press.

Blumberg, P. (1973): *Industrial Democracy: The Sociology of Participation*. New York: Schocken.

Boisot, M. (1983): 'Convergence revisited: the codification and diffusion of knowledge in a British and a Japanese firm', *Journal of Management Studies* 1: 159–190.

Bolton, J. (1971): *Report of the Committee of Inquiry on Small Firms*. London: Cmnd 4811, HMSO (The Bolton Report)

Bolweg, J. (1976): *Job Design and Industrial Democracy*. Leiden: Martinus Nijhoff.

Bonacich, E. and J. Modell (1980): *The Economic Basis of Ethnic Solidarity*. Berkeley: University of California Press.

Bottomore, T. (1985): *Theories of Modern Capitalism*. London: Allen and Unwin.

Bourdieu, P., L. Boltanski and M. de Saint Martin (1973): 'Les Stratégies de Reconversion', *Social Science Information* 12: 61−113.

Bourke, H. (1982): 'Industrial Unrest as Social Pathology: The Australian Writings of Elton Mayo', *Historical Studies* 20 (79): 217−233.

Bowen, W. (1989): 'The puny payoff from office computers', in T. Forester (ed.) *Computers in the Human Context: Information Technology, Productivity and People*. Oxford: Blackwell. pp. 267−271.

Brandon, R. (1983): *The Other Hundred Years*. London: Collins.

Braverman, H. (1974): *Labour and Monopoly Capital: The Degradation of Work in the Twentieth Century*. New York: Monthly Review Press.

Brodner, P. (ed.) (1987) 'Strategic Options for 'New Production Systems'−CHIM: Computer and Human Integrated Manufacturing'. FAST Occasional Papers No. 150, Brussels.

Brown, C. and M. Reich (1989): 'When does union-management co-operation work? A look at NUMMI and GM-Van Nuy's', *California Management Review* 31 (4): 26−44.

Brown, F. and A. Oxenfeld (1972): *Misperceptions of Economic Phenomena*. New York: Sperand Douth.

Brusco, S. (1982): 'The Emilian model: productive decentralisation and social integration', *Cambridge Journal of Economics* 6 (2): 167−184.

Bunge, F. (1982): *South Korea: A Country Study*. Washington, D. C.: United States Government Printing Office.

Burawoy, M. (1979): *Manufacturing Consent: Changes in the Labor Process under Capitalism*. Chicago: University of Chicago Press.

Burrell, G. and G. Morgan (1979): *Sociological Paradigms and Organizational Analysis*. London: Heinemann Educational Books.

Business Council of Australia (BCA) (1989): *'Enterprise-based bargaining units: a better way of working'*, Melbourne: BCA.

Byrt, W. (1981): *The Australian Company: Studies in Strategy and Structure*. London: Croom Helm.

Cabinet Office, Advisory Council for Applied Research and Development (ACARD) (1978): *Industrial Innovation*. London HMSO.

Cable, J. and F. Fitzroy (1980a): 'Productive Efficiency, Incentives and Employee Participation: Some Preliminary Results for West Germany', *Kylos* 33 (February): 100−121.

Cable, J. and F. Fitzroy (1980b): 'Cooperation and Productivity: Some Evidence from the West German Experience', *'Economic Analysis and Workers' Management* 14 (2): 163−180.

Capecchi, V. and E. Pugliese (1978): 'Due citta a confronto: Bologna e Napoli', *Inchiesta* 8: 218−235.

Carmody, M. (1989): 'Modernization: The Australian Taxation Office Approach to introducing New Technology'. Paper delivered to Australian Computer Society Conference, Melbourne.

Carr, N. (1973): 'Employee Attitude Survey in a Hong Kong Engineering Company', *Journal of Industrial Relations* 15 (1): 108−111.

Castells, M. (1989): 'High Technology and the New International Division of Labour', *Labour and Society* 14: 7−42.

Castles, F. (1985): *The Working Class and Welfare: Reflections on the Political Development of the Welfare State in Australia and New Zealand, 1890–1980.* Sydney: Allen and Unwin.

Caves, R. and P. Williamson, (1976): *Industrial Organization in Japan.* Washington, D. C.: Brookings Institution.

Center for Business and Economic Research (1988): 'Kentucky's automotive supplier industry: trends and implications'. University of Kentucky.

Centro Studi Confindustria (CSC) (1984): *Settimo Rapporto sull' Industria Italiana* (Seventh Report on Italian Industry). Rome: CSC.

Chanaron, J.-J. and E. de Banville (1985): 'Le Système automobile français: de la Sous-Traitance au Partenariat? Eléments d'une Problématique', *CPE Etude* 56: 77.

Chandler, A. (1962): *Strategy and Structure: Chapters in the History of the American Industrial Enterprise.* Cambridge, Mass.: M.I.T. Press.

Chandler, A. (1977): *The Visible Hand.* Cambridge: Harvard University Press.

Chandler, A. (1982): 'The M-Form: industrial groups, American style', *European Economic Review* 19: 3–23.

Chaney, D. (1971): 'Job stratification and unionisation: the case of shopworkers' in K. Hopkins (ed.), *Hong Kong: The Industrial Colony.* Hong Kong: Oxford University Press.

Chao, K. (1977): *The Development of Cotton Textile Production in China.* Cambridge, Mass: Harvard University Press.

Chapman, B. and F. Gruen (1990): 'An Analysis of the Australian Consensual Incomes Policy: The Prices and Incomes Accord', Centre for Economic Policy Research, Discussion Paper Number 221, Canberra: Australian National University.

Checkland, P. (1981): *Systems Thinking, Systems Practice.* Chichester: Wiley.

Chesnais, F. (1989): Technical co-operation agreements between firms', *STI-Review* 4: 51–119.

Child, J. (1964): 'Quaker employers and industrial relations', *Sociological Review* 12 (2): 293–315.

Child, J. (1972): 'Organizational structure, environment and performance: the role of strategic choice', *Sociology* 6: 1–22.

Child, J. (1984): *Organization: A Guide to Problems and Practice,* 2nd ed., New York: Harper and Row.

Child, J. (1985): 'Managerial strategies; new technology and the labour process' in D. Knights and H. Willmott (eds.) *Job Redesign: Critical Perspectives on the Labour Process.* London: Gower. pp. 107–141.

Child, J. (1987): 'Information Technology, Organisation and the Response to Strategic Challenges'. Paper presented to the Eighth EGOS Colloquium Antwerp, 22–24 July on 'Technology as the two-edged sword of organisational change'.

Child, J. and A. Kieser (1979): 'Organization and managerial roles in British and West German companies: an examination of the culture-free thesis', in C. Lammers and D. Hickson (eds.) *Organizations Alike and Unlike: International and Inter-Institutional Studies in the Sociology of Organizations.* London: Routledge and Kegan Paul. pp. 251–271.

Chin, R. (1937): 'Japanese-owned Cotton Mills In China: A Study in International Competition'. Ph. D thesis. New Haven: Yale University.

Chin, R. (1965): *Management, Industry and Trade in Cotton Textiles*. New Haven: College and University Press.

Clark, J., I. Mcloughlin, H. Rose and R. King (1988): *The Process of Technical Change: New Technology and Social Choice in the Workplace*. Cambridge: Cambridge University Press.

Clegg, S. (1975):*Power, Rule and Domination: A Critical and Empirical Understanding of Power in Sociological Theory and Organizational Life*. London: Routledge and Kegan Paul.

Clegg, S. (1989): *Frameworks of Power*. London: Sage.

Clegg, S. (1990a): 'Postmodern Organizations?', Key Centre in Strategic Management Working Paper Series, Queensland University of Technology. Brisbane: QUT.

Clegg, S. (1990b): *Modern Organizations: Organization Studies in the Postmodern World*. Los Angeles and London: Sage.

Clegg, S. and D. Dunkerley (1980): *Organization, Class and Control*. London: Routledge and Kegan Paul.

Clegg, S. and W. Higgins (1987): 'Against the current: organisational sociology and socialism', *Organization Studies* 8 (3): 201 – 221.

Clegg, S., D. Dunphy and S. Redding (eds.) (1986): *The Enterprise and Management in East Asia*. Hong Kong: Centre of Asian Studies, The University of Hong Kong.

Clegg, S., W. Higgins and T. Spybey (1990): 'Post-Confucianism', social democracy and economic culture', in S. Clegg and S. Redding (eds), with the assistance of M. Cartner, *Capitalism in Contrasting Cultures*. Berlin: de Gruyter. pp. 18 – 46.

Cochran, S. (1982): 'Enterprises Spanning Economic Time and Space in China, 1850 – 1980: The Introduction of Vertical Integration'. Paper presented to the Conference on 'Chinese Entrepreneurship at Home and Abroad, 1900-82', Cornell University, October.

Cochran, S. (1984): 'Economic Institutions in China's Interregional Trade: Tobacco Products and Cotton Textiles, 1850 – 1980'. Paper presented to the Conference on Spatial and Temporal Trends and Cycles in Chinese Economic History, Bellagio, Italy, August.

Cochrane, P. (1985): 'Company Time: Management, Ideology and the Labour Process, 1940-60', *Labour History* 48: 54 – 68.

Cohen, S. and J. Zysman (1987): *Manufacturing Matters: The Myth of the Post-Industrial Economy*. New York: Basic Books.

Cole, R. (1973): 'Functional alternatives and economic development: an empirical example of permanent employment in Japan', *American Sociological Review* 38: 424 – 438.

Collins, R. (1980): 'Weber's last theory of capitalism: a systematisation', *American Sociological Review* 45: 925 – 942.

Commission Technique de la Sous-Traitance (1986): *Livre blanc sur le Partenariat, le Point sur l'Evolution actuelle des Relations de Sous-Traitance*. Paris: AFNOR Gestion.

Committee on Science and Technology (1989): *Annual Report for 1988—89*.

Considine, M. (1988): 'The corporate management framework as administrative science: a critique', *Australian Journal of Public Administration* XLVII (1): 4—18.

Considine, M. (1990): 'Managerialism strikes out', *Australian Journal of Public Administration* XLIX (2): 166—178.

Cooley, M. (1980): *Architect or Bee? The Human/Technology Relationships*. Slough: Hand and Brain.

Cornwall, J. and B. Perlman (1990): *Organizational Entrepreneurship*. Boston and Homewood: Irwin.

Coser, L. (1956): *The Functions of Social Conflict*. London: Routledge and Kegan Paul.

Crellin, K. (1989): *Concepts of Quality*. Seminar given at Queensland University of Technology, Brisbane. September.

Crozier, M. (1964): *The Bureaucratic Phenomenon*. London: Tavistock.

Cummings, B. (1984): 'The origins and development of the Northeastern Asia political economy: industrial sectors, product cycles, and political consequences', *International Organizations* 38: 1—40.

Cunningham, K. (1946): 'The scientific approach to personnel problems', *On Personnel Management. Australian Institute of Management, Special Lecture Series. Sydney*.

Curtain, R. and J. Mathews (1990): 'Two models of award restructuring in Australia', *Labour and Industry* 3 (1): 58—75.

Cusumano, M. (1985): *The Japanese Automobile Industry: Technology and Management at Nissan and Toyota*. Cambridge, Mass.: Harvard University Press.

Cyert, R. and J. March (1963): *A Behavioural Theory of the Firm*. Englewood Cliffs, N. J.: Prentice Hall.

Daly, A., D. Hitchens and K. Wagner (1985): 'Productivity, machinery and skills in a sample of British and German manufacturing plants', *National Institute Economic Review* February (111): 48—61.

Deal, T. and A. Kennedy (1982): *Corporate Cultures: The Rites and Rituals of Corporate Life*. Reading, Mass.: Addison-Wesley.

Deming, W. (1982): *Out of the Crisis*. Boston: MIT.

Denison, D. (1990): *Corporate Culture and Organizational Effectiveness*. New York: Wiley.

Dernberger, R. (1975): 'The role of the foreigner in China's economic development, 1840—1949', in D. Perkins (ed.) *China's Modern Economy in Historical Perspective*. Stanford: Stanford University Press. pp. 19—47.

Dertouzos, M., R. Lester and R. Solow (1989): *Made in America: Regaining the Competitive Edge*. The MIT Commission on Productivity. Cambridge: The MIT Press.

Deutsches Institut für Normung e. V. (DIN) (1988): *The Standardisation of Interfaces for Computer Integrated Manufacturing (CIM), Current State of Development and Future Requirements*, Prepared by the DIN Commission for Computer Integrated Manufacturing (KCIM), Berlin/Köln: Beuth Verlag GmbH.

Deyo, F. (1987): 'Coalitions, institutions and linkage sequencing: toward a strategic capacity model of East Asian development', in F. Deyo (ed.) *The Political Economy of the New Asian Industrialism.* Ithaca: Cornell University Press. pp. 227–247.

Dillow, C. (1989): *A Return to Trade Surplus? The Impact of Japanese Investments on the UK.* London: Nomura Research Institute.

DiMaggio, P. and W. Powell (1983): 'The Iron Cage revisited: institutional isomorphism and collective rationality in organisational fields', *American Sociological Review* 48: 147–69.

Dizard, W. (1982): *The Coming Information Age: An Overview of Technology, Economics and Politics.* Harlow: Longman.

Dodgson, M. (1989): *Technology Strategy and the Firm: Management and Public Policy.* Harlow: Longman.

Dodwell Marketing Consultants (1986): *The Structure of the Japanese Auto Parts Industry.* 3rd Edition. Tokyo: Dodwell

Dohse, K., U. Jurgens and T. Malsch (1985): 'From "Fordism" to "Toyotism"? The social organization of the labour process in the Japanese automobile industry', *Politics and Society* 14 (2): 115–146.

Domingo, R. (1985): ' "Kanban": crisis management Japanese style', *Euro-Asia Business Review* 4 (3): 22–24.

Donaldson, L. (1985): *In Defence of Organization Theory: A Response to the Critics.* Cambridge University Press.

Donaldson, L. (1987:) 'Strategy, structural adjustment to regain fit and performance: in defence of contingency theory', *Journal of Management Studies* 24 (1): 1–24.

Dore, R. (1973): *British Factory-Japanese Factory: the Origins of National Diversity in Industrial Relations.* Berkeley: University of California Press.

Dore, R. (1986): *Flexible Regidities.* London: Athlone Press.

Dore, R., J. Bounine-Cabale and K. Tapiola (1989): *Japan at Work: Markets, Management and Flexibility.* Paris: OECD.

Dosi, G. (1984): *Technical Change and Industrial Transformation.* London: MacMillan.

Dosi, G., C. Freeman, R. Nelson, G. Silverberg and L. Soete (eds.) (1988): *Technical Change and Economic Theory.* London: Pinter.

Douglas, M. (1986): *How Institutions Think.* Syracuse, N. Y.: Syracuse University Press.

Douglas, M. and B. Isherwood (1978): *The World of Goods.* New York: Basic Books.

Dunford, R. (1991): *Organisational Behaviour: An Organisational Analysis Perspective.* Sydney: Addision-Wesley.

Dunford, R. and P. McGraw (1988): 'Quality circles in the manufacturing industry', in E. Willis (ed.) *Technology and the Labour Process.* Sydney: Allen and Unwin. pp. 81–95.

Dunning, J. (1986): *Japanese Participation in British Industry.* London: Croom Helm.

Dunphy, D. (1987): 'The historical development of human resource management in Australia', *Human Resource Management Australia* 25 (2): 40–47.

Eason, A. (1986): 'The role of government in the development of high technology' in The Society of Hong Kong Scholars (ed.) *The Role of High Technology in Hong Kong's Industrial Development: Proceedings of a Symposium Organised by the Society of Scholars.* Hong Kong, February 22, pp. 88–93.

Economic Planning Advisory Council (EPAC) (1991): *Improving Australia's International Competitiveness.* Council Paper no. 45. Canberra: Economic Planning Advisory Council.

Economist Intelligence Unit (1989): 'Update on Nissan', *Japanese Motor Business:* 42–61.

Education and Manpower Branch (1990): *A Statistical Projection of Manpower Requirements and Supply for Hong Kong,* Hong Kong: Government Secretariat.

Edwards, R. (1979): *Contested Terrain: The Transformation of Work in the Twentieth Century.* New York: Basic Books.

Ehn, P. (1988): *Work-oriented Design of Computer Artifacts.* Stockholm: Almquist and Wicksell.

Ehnmark, A. and G. Therborn (1988): *Samtalet om socialismen.* Stockholm: Arbetarkultur.

Eidem, R. (1987): *Aktieägandet och demokratin.* Stockholm: Arbetslivscentrum.

Ellegård, K. (1983): *Människa-produktion. Tidsbilder av ett Produktionssystem.* Gothenburg: Department of Geography Dissertation.

Ellegård, K., T. Engström and L. Nilsson (1989): *Principer och realiteter vid förnyelse av industriellt arbete. Projekteringen av Volvos bilfabrik i Uddevalla.* Stockholm: Arbetsmiljöfonden.

England, J. (1989): *Industrial Relations and Law in Hong Kong.* Second Edition. Oxford: Oxford University Press.

England, J. and J. Rear (1981): *Industrial Relations and Law in Hong Kong.* Hong Kong: Oxford University Press.

Ewer, P., W. Higgins and A. Stevens (1987): *Unions and the Future of Australian Manufacturing.* Sydney: Allen and Unwin.

Eymard-Duvernay, F. (1986): 'Qualité des Produits et Emploi', *Lettre d'Information du Centre d'Etudes de l'Emploi* numéro 1: 8.

Fairbank, J., E. Reischauer and A. Craig (1985): 'Japan's Response to the West', in S. Shirk (ed.), *The Challenge of China and Japan: Politics and Development in East Asia.* New York: Praeger. pp. 106–119.

Fairtlough, G. (1984): 'Can we plan for new technology?', *Long Range Planning,* 17 (3): 14–23.

Fairtlough, G. (1985): 'Getting Organised for the 1990s'. Society Medal Address Chemistry and Industry, 19th August. London.

Fairtlough, G. (1986a): 'Creative Compartments', *London Business School Journal,* Summer: 2–12.

Fairtlough, G. (1986b): 'Consider the Cell', *High Technology* June: 9.

Fairtlough, G. (1989): 'Systems Practice from the Start: Some Experiences in a Biotechnology Company'. Paper presented to the UK Systems Society, 26th May.

Fama, F. and C. Jensen, (1983): 'Separation of ownership and control', *Journal of Law and Economics* 26: 301–325.

Feldt, K. (1989): 'What shall we do with capitalism?', *Inside Sweden* 3: 3–5.

Fligstein, N. (1985): 'The spread of the multidivisional form among large firms, 1919–1979', *American Sociological Review,* 50 (3): 377–391.

Fong, H. (1931): *China's Industrialization: A Statistical Survey.* Shanghai: China Institute of Pacific Relations.

Fong, H. (1937): 'Industrialization and the rural industries in China', *The China Quarterly* Spring: 259–279.

Forester, T. (ed.) (1985): *The Information Technology Revolution.* Oxford: Blackwell.

Forester, T. (ed.) (1989): *Computers in the Human Context: Information Technology, Productivity and People.* Oxford: Blackwell.

Foucault, M. (1965): *Madness and Reason: A History of Insanity in the Age of Reason.* New York: Random House.

Foucault, M. (1979): *Discipline and Punishment: The Birth of the Prison.* New York: Vintage.

Fox, A. (1974): Beyond Contract: Work, Power and Trust Relations. London: Faber and Faber.

Franke, R. (1989): 'Technological revolution and productivity decline: the case of US banks', in T. Forester (ed.) *Computers in the Human Context: Information Technology, Productivity and People.* Oxford: Blackwell. pp. 281–290.

Freeman, C. (1974): *The Economics of Industrial Innovation.* Harmondsworth: Penguin.

Freeman, C. and B.-A. Lundvall (eds) (1988): *Small Countries Facing the Technological Revolution.* London: Pinter.

Freeman, C. and C. Perez (1988): 'Structural crises of adjustment, business cycles and investment behaviour', in G. Dosi, C. Freeman, R. Nelson, G. Silverberg and L. Soete (eds), *Technical Change and Economic Theory.* London: Pinter. pp. 38–66.

Friedman, A. (1977): *Industry and Labour.* London: Macmillan.

Friedman, D. (1983): 'Beyond the age of Ford: the strategic bases of the Japanese success in automobiles', in J. Zysman and L. Tyson (eds.) *American Industry in International Competition.* Ithaca, NY: Cornell University Press. pp. 350–390.

Friedman, D. (1988): *The Misunderstood Miracle.* Ithaca, NY: Cornell University Press.

Fujita, K. and R. Child-Hill (1988): 'Global Production and Regional "Hollowing Out" in Japan'. Paper presented to the 40th Annual Meeting of the Association for Asian Studies, San Francisco, 25–27 March.

Gambetta, D. (ed.) (1988): *Trust Making and Breaking Cooperative Relations.* Oxford: Blackwell.

Garnaut, R. (1989): *Australia and the North East Asian Ascendancy.* Canberra: AGPS.

Garnett, N. (1988): 'Man struggling to master the machine', *Financial Times.* 14. 10. 88: 17.

Garnsey, E. and J. Roberts (1989): 'The Experience of Growth in Small High Technology Firms'. Paper presented to the 9th EGOS Colloquium, Berlin.

Garnsey, E. and J. Roberts (1990): 'Acquisition as Joint Venture? Perspectives on Growth for Small High Technology Firms; in S. Birley (ed.) (1990) *Building European Ventures*. Amsterdam: Elsevier.

Garrahan, P. and P. Stewart (1989): 'Working for Nissan'. School of Social Studies, Sunderland Polytechnic, UK. Unpublished paper.

Gasparini, I. (1977): 'Relazione Generale', in Federlombarda (ed.) *La Piccola e media industria in Lombardia*, Vol. 1. Milan: Edizioni Industriali.

Gateway (1985−89): *The MAP Reporter*. Michigan Industrial Technology Institute, various issues.

Gattiker, U. and L. Larwood (1988): *Managing Technological Development: Strategic and Human Resources Issues,* Berlin: de Gruyter.

Geick, J. (1987): *Chaos: Making a New Science*. London: Penguin Sphere Books.

Georghiou, L., S. Metcalfe, M. Gibbons, T. Ray and J. Evans (1986): *Post Innovation Performance*. London: Macmillan

Giddens, A. (1979): *Central Problems in Social Theory: Action, Structure and Contradiction in Social Analysis*. Berkeley: University of California.

Giddens, A. (1984): *The Constitution of Society: Outline of the Theory of Structuration*. Cambridge: Polity Press.

Giddens, A. (1988): *Chaos,* London: Heinemann:

Giertz, E. (1982): *Om arbetsstudieutbildningens institutionalisering*. Stockholm: Kungliga Tekniska Högskolan (dissertation).

Giunta Regionale della Lombardia (1974): *Indagine conoscitiva sull'artigianato lombardo*. Milan: Zanolla.

Goglio, S. (ed.) (1982): *Italia: centri e periferie*. Milan: F. Angeli.

Gold, T. (1986): *State and Society in the Taiwan Miracle*. Armonk, New York: Sharpe.

Goldman, P. and D. van Houten (1980): 'Uncertainty, conflict, and labor relations in the modern firm II: the war on labor', *Economic and Industrial Democracy* 1: 263−287.

Goldthorpe, J. (1984): 'The end of convergence: corporatist and dualist tendencies in modern western societies', in J. Goldthorpe (ed.) *Order and Conflict in Western European Capitalism*. Oxford: Oxford University Press. pp. 315−343.

Goodman, R. (1979): *The Last Entrepreneurs*. Boston: South End Press.

Goold, M. and A. Campbell (1987): *Strategies and Styles*. Oxford: Blackwell.

Goonatilake, S. (1982): *Crippled Minds. An Exploration into Colonial Culture*. New Delhi: Lake House and Colombo: Vikas.

Gorgeu, A. and R. Mathieu (1988a): 'La Mise en Place progressive de l'Assurance Qualité dans les Relations Clients-Fournisseurs' in *Plan Construction et Architecture: la Qualité en Chantier: un Enjeu du Travail*. Paris: Centre d'Etudes de l'Emploi. pp. 121−136.

Gorgeu, A. and R. Mathieu (1988b): 'L'Application du Partenariat par les Constructeurs automobiles et ses Répercussions sur la Mode de Gestion de la Main-d'oeuvre des Equipementiers et Sous-traitants'. Paper presented to the Journées PIRTTEM CNRS conference on The Economy of Work, Paris, 16−18 November.

Gorgeu, A. and R. Mathieu (1989): 'New organizational practices in manufacturer-supplier relationships in the French automobile and aerospace industries'. Paper presented to the Third International APROS Colloqium, Canberra, Dec. 1989 and reproduced in an amended version as chapters 6 and 16 in this book.

Gorgeu, A. and R. Mathieu (1990): 'Le nouveau Partenariat industriel dans l'Automobile' in *L'Emploi, l'Enterprise et la Société. Débats Economie-Sociologie,* Paris: Centre d'Etudes de l'Emploi. pp. 103–114.

Gorgeu, A., R. Mathieu and B. Gomel (1986): 'Marchés, Investissements, Emploi chez les Fournisseurs de l'Industrie', *Dossier du Centre d'Etudes de l'Emploi.* 13: 99.

Gorgeu, A., R. Mathieu and B. Gomel (1987): 'Les Fournisseurs de l'Industrie: Politiques de Produit et Gestion de la Main-d'oeuvre', in *Cahier Enterprises et Produits,* Centre d'Etudes de l'Emploi. Paris: Presses Universitaires de France. pp. 31–64.

Granovetter, M. (1984): 'Small is bountifull: labour markets and establishment size', *American Sociological Review* 49: 323–334.

Granovetter, M. (1985): 'Economic action and social structure: the problem of embeddedness', *American Journal of Sociology* 91: 481–510.

Greif, I. (ed.) (1988): *Computer-Supported Cooperative Work: A Book of Readings.* San Mateo, Cal.: Kaufmann.

Greig, A. (1990): 'Rhetoric and Reality in the Clothing Industry: the Case of Post-Fordism'. *Urban Research Program Working Paper No. 26.* Canberra: Australian National University.

Griffiths Management Ltd. (1989): *Report on Hong Kong's Labour Shortage.* Unpublished report prepared for the Joint Associations Working Group, Hong Kong.

Grinyer, P., D. Mayes and P. McKiernan (1988): *Sharpbenders: The Secret of Unleashing Corporate Potential.* Oxford: Blackwell.

Guille, H., D. Sappey and M. Winter (1989): 'Can Industrial Relations Survive Without Unions?', Paper given to AIRAANZ Conference, University of Wollongong, 1–4 February.

Gunder Frank, A. (1969): *Capitalism and Underdevelopment in Latin America.* New York: Monthly Review Press.

Habermas, J. (1971): *Towards a Rational Society.* Boston: Beacon Press.

Hagedoorn, J. and J. Schot (1988): Co-operation Between Companies and Technological Development. Apledoorn: TNO.

Hakim, C. (1987): *Research Design: Strategies and Choices in the Design of Social Research.* Allen & Unwin: London.

Hall R. (1989): 'Review of L. Zucker (ed.): 'Institutional Patterns and Organizations: Culture and Environment', *Contemporary Sociology* 18 (1): 54–56.

Hall, J. (1985): *Powers and Liberties.* Oxford: Blackwell.

Hall, J. (1986): Introduction in J. Hall (ed.), *States in History.* Oxford: Blackwell. pp. 1–21.

Hamilton, G. (1978): 'Ethnicity and Regionalism: Some Factors Influencing Chinese Identities in Southeast Asia', *Ethnicity* 4: 335–351.

Hamilton, G. (1989): 'The Organizational Foundations of Western and Chinese Commerce: An Historical and Comparative Analysis'. Paper presented to the Conference on Business Groups and Economic Development in East Asia, Centre of Asian Studies, University of Hong Kong, Hong Kong.

Hamilton, G. and N. Biggart (1985): 'Why People Obey: Theoretical Observations on Power and Obedience in Complex Organizations', *Sociological Perspectives* 28: 3−28.

Hamilton, G. and N. Biggart (1988): 'Market, Culture and Authority: A Comparative Analysis of Management and Organization in the Far East' in C. Winship and S. Rosen (eds.) *Organizations and Institutions: Sociological Approaches to the Analysis of Social Structure. American Journal of Sociology* 94: Supplement: Chicago: The University of Chicago Press: pp. 52−95.

Hamilton, G. and N. Biggart (1989): 'Market, culture, and authority: a comparative analysis of management and organization in the Far East', in C. Winship and S. Rosen (eds.) *Organizations and Institutions: Sociological Approaches to the Analysis of Social Structure. American Journal of Sociology* 94: Supplement: Chicago: The University of Chicago Press: 552−95.

Hamilton, G. and C.-S. Kao (1990): 'The Institutional Foundations of Chinese Business: The Family Firm in Taiwan', in C. Calhoun (ed.) *Comparative Social Research* 12: 135−152.

Hamilton, G., W. Zeile and W. Kim (1990): 'The network structures of East Asian economies' in S. Clegg and S. (G). Redding (eds.) *Capitalism in Contrasting Cultures*. Berlin and New York: de Gruyter. pp. 105−130.

Hardach, K. (1980): *The Political Economy of Germany in the Twentieth Century*. Berkeley: University of California Press.

Hasegawa, K. (1986): *Japanese Style Management: An Insider's Analysis*. Tokyo: Kodanshe International.

Hayashi, S. (1988): *Culture and Management in Japan*. Tokyo: University of Tokyo Press.

Head, B. (1988): 'Economic Rationalism: The New Orthodoxy in Australian Public Policy?'. Paper presented to the Australasian Political Studies Association Annual Conference, August.

Helper, S. (1989): 'Changing Supplier Relationships in the United States'. Paper presented to the International Motor Vehicle Program Conference in Acapulco, May.

Hermele, K. (1982): *Den drivande kraften. Bilindustrin som exemple*. Stockholm: Liber.

Heydebrand, W. (1989): 'New Organizationsal Forms', *Work and Occupations* 16 (3): 323−357.

Hickson, D., C. Hinings, C. Lee, R. Schneck and J. Pennings (1971): 'A strategic contingencies theory of intra-organizational power', *Administrative Science Quarterly* 16: 216−229.

Higgins, W. (1985a): 'Political unionism and the corporatist thesis', *Economic and Industrial Democracy* 6/3: 349−381.

Higgins, W. (1985b): 'Ernst Wigforss: the renewal of social democratic theory and practice', *Political Power and Social Theory* 5: 207−250.

Higgins, W. (1986): 'Industrial democracy and the control issue in Sweden' in E. Davis and R. Lansbury (eds.) *Democracy and Control in the Workplace*. Melbourne: Longman Cheshire. pp. 250−275.

Higgins, W. (1987): 'Unions as bearers of industrial regeneration: reflections on the Australian case', *Economic and Industrial Democracy* 8 (2): 213 – 236.

Higgins, W. (1988): 'Swedish Social Democracy and the new Democratic Socialism' in D. Sainsbury (ed.) *Democracy, State and Justice: Critical Perspectives and New Interpretations.* Stockholm: Almquist and Wiksell. pp. 69 – 90.

Higgins, W. and S. Clegg (1988): 'Enterprise calculation and manufacturing decline', *Organization Studies* 9 (1): 69 – 89.

Hill, S. (1988): *Competition and Control at Work: The New Industrial Sociology.* Gower.

Hill, S. (1989a): 'The Technology Text and the Culture Assumption'. Paper presented to the Third International APROS Colloquium, Australian National University, Canberra, 13 – 15 December, 1989.

Hill, S. (1989b): *The Tragedy of Technology.* London: Pluto Press.

Hindess, B. (1982): 'Power, interests and the outcomes of struggles', *Sociology* 6 (4): 498 – 511.

Hinings, C., D. Hickson, J. Pennings and R. Schneck (1974): 'Structural conditions of intra-organizational power', *Administrative Science Quarterly* 19: 22 – 44.

Hippel, E. von (1989): *The Sources of Innovation,* New York: Oxford University Press.

Hirschmeier, J. and T. Yui: *The Development of Japanese Business 1600 – 1973.* London: Allen and Unwin.

Hirst, P. and J. Zeitlin (1989): 'Flexible Specialization vs. Post-Fordism: Theory, Evidence and Policy Implications', Birkbeck Public Policy Centre Working Paper, May 1990.

Hodges, P. (1989): 'Manufacturing automation's problem', *Datamation,* November 15.

Hodgetts, R. and D. Kuratko (1986): *Management.* Second Edition, San Diego.

Hoernschemeyer, D. (1989): 'The four cornerstones of excellence', *Quality Progress* 22 (8): 37 – 40.

Hollingum, J. (1986): *The MAP Report.* Bedford and Berlin: IFS Publications Ltd and Springer.

Holmes, J. (1989): 'From Uniformity to Diversity: Changing Patterns of Wages and Work Practices in the North American Automobile Industry'. Paper presented to the Employment Research Unit Conference, Cardiff Business School, UK, 19 – 20 September.

Hong Kong 1986 By-Census, Main Report Vol. 1, Hong Kong: Census and Statistics Department.

Hong Kong Cotton Spinners' Association (1989). Hong Kong.

Hong Kong Government (1979): *Report of the Advisory Committee on Diversification.* Hong Kong: Government Printer.

Hong Kong Government (1983): *Study on the Hong Kong Electronics Industry.* Hong Kong: Government Printer.

Hong Kong Government (1989): *Hong Kong 1989.* Hong Kong: Government Printer.

Hong Kong Polytechnic Bulletin, March (1990).

Hong Kong Productivity Council and Hong Kong Polytechnic (1989): *Summary of the Survey on the Training Needs of the Hong Kong Tool Making Industry.* Hong Kong: Hong Kong Polytechnic.

Hong Kong Productivity Council, 20th Anniversary, 1967–1987 (1988): Hong Kong: Hong Kong Productivity Council.

Hong Kong Textile Annual (1956): Hong Kong: Hong Kong Cotton Merchants' Association.

Horwitch, M. (1986): *Technology in the Modern Corporation: A Strategic Perspective.* New York: Pergamon.

Howard, R. (1985): *Brave New Workplace.* New York: Sifton/Penguin.

Hu, T.-L. (1984) *My Mother-in-law's Village: Rural Industrialization and Change in Taiwan.* Taipei: Institute of Ethology, Academia Sinica.

Hung, C. (1984): 'Foreign investments' in D. Lethbridge (ed.) *The Business Environment in Hong Kong.* Second edition. Oxford University Press. pp. 180–211.

Hunt, D., J. Jackson and J. Marceau (1981): *The Ownership, Operations and Employment Potential of Small Manufacturing Enterprises.* Bruxelles: Commission of the European Communities.

Igarashi, F. (1986): 'Forced to confess', in G. McCormack and Y. Sugimoto (eds) *Democracy in Contemporary Japan.* Sydney: Hale and Iremonger. pp. 195–214.

Industry Department, Hong Kong Government (1989): *Report on the Survey of Overseas Investment in Hong Kong's Manufacturing Industries.* Hong Kong: Government Printer.

Irwin, B. (1989): 'Fortress Australia and the Trojan Horse', in *Quality: the Key to Global Competitiveness,* Proceedings of the First National Conference of the Total Quality Management Institute, Sydney, August 10th and 11th, TQMI pp. 257–268.

Ishikawa, K. (1985): *What is Total Quality Control?* Prentice Hall: New Jersey.

Israel, J. (1979): *The Language of Dialectics and the Dialectics of Language.* Copenhagen: Munksgaard and London: Harvester Press and New York: Humanities Press.

Jacobs, N.(1985): *The Korean Road to Modernization and Development.* Urbana, Ill.: University of Illinois Press.

Jacoby, S. (1979): 'The origins of internal labor markets in Japan,' *Industrial Relations* 18: 184–196.

Jacques, E. (1951): *The Changing Culture of a Factory.* London: Tavistock.

James, B. (1988): *Trojan Horse: The Ultimate Japanese Challenge.* London: Edward Elgar.

Jensen, C. and H. Meckling (1976): 'Theory of the firm: managerial behavior, agency costs and ownership structure', *Journal of Financial Economics* 3: 305–360.

JETRO (1981): *Promotion of Small and Medium Enterprise in Japan.* Tokyo: JETRO.

Johnson, C. (1982): *MITI and the Japanese Miracle.* Stanford, CA.: Stanford University Press.

Jones, D. and J. Womack (1988): 'The real challenge facing the European motor industry', *Financial Times* 28 October.

Jones, G. (1983): 'Transaction Costs, Property Rights, and Organisational Culture: An Exchange Perspective', *Administrative Science Quarterly* 28: 454—467.

Jones, V. 1988, *MAP/TOP Networking. A Foundation for Computer Integrated Manufacturing.* New York: McGraw-Hill.

Jönsson, B. (1981): 'Corporate Strategy for People at Work. The Volvo Experience'. Paper presented to the International Conference on the Quality of Working Life held in Toronto. Gothenburg: Volvo.

Kahn, H. (1979): *World Economic Development: 1979 and Beyond.* London: Croom Helm.

Kamata, S. (1983): *Japan in the Passing Lane: An Insider's Account of Life in a Japanese Auto Factory.* London: Allen and Unwin.

Kane, M. (1989): 'Regional underpinnings of the US-Japan Partnership. Commonwealth of Kentucky: a Case Study'. University of Kentucky. Unpublished paper.

Kanebo Company Ltd. (1988): *Kanebo Hyukunen Shi.* (The Hundred Year History of Kanebo). Osaka: Kanebo Company Ltd.

Kao, S., S. Ng and D. Taylor (1986): *Technology and Work Organisation: The Hong Kong Experience.* A Report to the Asian Productivity Organisation on the Hong Kong Study of the APO Basic Research III-Productivity through People in the Age of Changing Technology. Unpublished report.

Kaplan, M. (1957): *System and Process in International Politics.* New York: Wiley.

Karpik, L. (1972a): 'Sociologie, Economie, Politique et Buts des Organisations de Production', *Revue Française de Sociologie* 13: 299—324.

Karpik, L. (1972b): 'Les Politiques et les Logiques d'Action de la grande Entreprise industrielle', *Sociologie du Travail* 1: 82—105.

Karpik, L. (1977): 'Technological capitalism' in S. Clegg and D. Dunkerley (eds) *Critical Issues In Organizations.* London: Routledge and Kegan Paul. pp. 41—71.

Karpik, L. (1978): 'Organizations, institutions and history', in L. Karpik (ed.) *Organization and Environment: Theory, Isues and Reality.* Beverley Hills, CA: Sage. pp. 15—68.

Keidel, R. (1988): *Corporate Players: Designs for Working and Winning Together.* New York: Wiley.

Kenney, M. and R. Florida (1988): 'Beyond mass production: production and the labour process in Japan', *Politics and Society* 16/1: 121—158.

Kern, H. and M. Schumann (1984): 'Work and social character: old and new contours', *Economic and Industrial Democracy* 5: 1—70.

Klein, B. (1977): *Dynamic Economics.* Cambridge, Mass: Harvard University Press.

Klein, J. (1989): 'The human cost of manufacturing reform', *Harvard Business Review* March-April: 60—66.

Knights, D. and H. Willmott (1988): *New Technology and the Labour Process.* London: Macmillan.

Koh, S. (1966): *Stages of Industrial Development in Asia: A Comparative History of the Cotton Industry in Japan, India, China and Korea.* Philadelphia: University of Pennsylvania Press.

Koike, K. (1983): 'Workers in small firms and women in industry', in T. Shirai (ed.) *Contemporary Industrial Relations in Japan*. Madison: University of Wisconsin Press. pp. 89 – 115.

Koo, H. (1987): 'Industrialization and Labor Politics in the East Asian NICs: A Comparison of South Korea and Taiwan'. Paper presented to the American Sociological Association Annual Meetings. Chicago: August 17 – 22.

Korpi, W. (1986): 'Den svenska arbetarrörelsens förutsattningar och strategier', *Arbetarhistoria* 10 (1 – 2): 36 – 43.

Kosai, Y. and Y. Ogino (1984): *The Contemporary Japanese Economy*. London: Macmillan.

Kriegler, R., P. Dawkins, J. Ryan and M. Wooden (1988): *Achieving Organizational Effectiveness: Case Studies in the Australian Service Sector*. Melbourne: Oxford University Press.

Kuhn, T. (1962): *The Structure of Scientific Revolutions*. Chicago: University of Chicago Press.

Kuisel, R. (1981): *Capitalism and the State in Modern France*. Cambridge: Cambridge University Press.

Kurt Salmon Associates, Inc. (1987): *Final Report on Techno-economic and Marketing Research Study on the Textiles and Clothing Industry for Hong Kong Government, Industry Department*. February.

Lacey, G. (1990): 'Success through Quality', Paper given at the Key Centre in Strategic Management, Seminar Series, QUT. February 13, 1990.

Lambooy, J. (1986): 'Information and Internationalisation: Dynamics of the Relations of Small and Medium Sized Enterprises in a Network Environment'. Paper presented to Table Ronde 'Les PME innovatrices et leur environnement local et économique'. Aix-en-Provence, 4 – 5 July.

Lamming, R. (1987): *Towards Best Practice: A Report on Components Supply in the UK Automotive Industry*. Brighton: SPRU and IMVP.

Lamming, R. (1989): 'The International Automotive Components Industry: the next "Best Practice" for Suppliers'. Paper presented in the International Motor Vehicle Program Conference in Acapulco, May.

Lash, S. (1988): 'Postmodernism as a regime of signification', *Theory, Culture and Society* 5 (2 – 3): 311 – 336.

Lau, S. (1982): *Society and Politics in Hong Kong*. Hong Kong: The Chinese University Press.

Lawrence, P. (1984): *Management in Action*. London: Routledge and Kegan Paul.

Lazerson, M. (1988): 'Organisational growth of small firms: an outcome of markets and hierarchies?', *American Sociological Review* 53 (3): 330 – 342.

Le Duff, R., A. Maisseu and D. Soulie (1989): 'Industrie automobile: les difficiles Relations entre Constructeurs et Equipementiers' in *Problèmes Economiques* 2108, 18 janvier 1989: 14 – 19.

Lee, M. (1989): 'Management Styles of Korean Chaebol', in K. Chung and H. Lee (eds) *Korean Managerial Dynamics*. New Yorker: Praeger. pp. 147 – 162.

Levy, M. (1985): 'Contrasting factors in the modernization of China and Japan', in S. Shirk (ed.), *The Challenge of China and Japan: Politics and Development in East Asia*. New York: Praeger. pp. 114 – 119.

Lévy-Leboyer, M. (1976): 'Innovation and business strategies in nineteenth-
and twentieth-century France', in E. Carter II, R. Foster and J. Moody (eds.)
Enterprise and Entrepreneurs in Nineteenth- and Twentieth-Century France.
Baltimore/London: John Hopkins University. pp. 87–135.

Lieu, D. (1928): 'China's industrial development' in *Problems of the Pacific,*
Institute of Pacific Relations. Second Conference. Chicago: University of
Chicago Press.

Lieu, D. (1933): 'A Preliminary Report on Shanghai Industrialization'. Institute
of Pacific Relations Conference, XII (August): 1–63.

Link, A. and G. Tassey (1987): *Strategies for Technology-Based Competition.*
Lexington, Mass: Lexington Books.

Little, I. (1979): 'An economic reconnaissance', in W. Galenson (ed.) *Economic
Growth and Structural Change in Taiwan.* Ithaca, N. Y.: Cornell University
Press. pp. 448–507.

Little, S. (1989): 'Organisational Cultures & Technological Failures: Reconciling
Institutional and Task Environments'. Paper presented to the Third International APROS Colloquium, Australian National University, 13–15 December, 1989.

Littler, C. (1982): *The Development of the Labour Process in Capitalist Societies.*
London: Heinemann.

LO (Landsorganisationen i Sverige) (1988): *Mitt i steget. Om ägande och
inflytande inför 1990-talet.* Stockholm: LO.

Lockwood, W. (1954): *The Economic Development of Japan.* Princeton: Princeton University Press.

Lorenz, E. (1988): 'Neither friends nor strangers: informal networks of subcontracting in French industry', in D. Gambetta (ed.) *Trust: Making and Breaking
Cooperative Relations.* Oxford: Blackwell. pp. 194–210.

Maccoby, M. (1981): *The Leader: A New Face for American Management.* New
York: Simon and Schuster.

Magnusen, K. (1977): *Organizational Design, Development, and Behavior.* Glen-
view, Ill.: Scott, Forseman and Co.

Mair, A., R. Florida and M. Kenney (1988): 'The New Geography of Automobile Production: Japanese Transplants in North America'. *Economic Geography* 64 (4): 352–373.

Maller, J. (1987): 'Perspectives on productivity in South Africa', in G. Moss
and I. Obery (eds.) *South Africa Review* 4: 317–331.

Mann, M. (1986): *The Sources of Social Power.* Vol. 1: *From the Beginning to
1760 AD.* Cambridge: Cambridge University Press.

Mann, M. (1988): *States, War and Capitalism.* Oxford: Blackwell.

Mann, M. (1990): *The Sources of Social Power.* Vol. 2: *A History of Power in
Industrial Societies.* Cambridge: Cambridge University Press.

Mansfield, E. (1968): *The Economics of Technological Change.* New York:
Norton.

Manufacturing and Management (1947): *Survey of Australian Personnel Practices.* September 15, pp. 85–84.

Manwaring, T. (1981): 'The trade union response to new technology', *Industrial
Relations Journal* 12 (2): 7–26.

Marceau, J. (1981): 'Plus ça change, plus c'est la même chose: access to elite careers in French business' in J. Howorth and P. Cerny (eds) *Elites in France*. London and New York: Pinter. pp. 104–133.

Marceau, J. (1989): 'The dwarves of capitalism: the structure of production and the economic culture of the small manufacturing firm', in S. Clegg and S. Redding, with the assistance of M. Cartner (eds) *Capitalism in Contrasting Cultures*. Berlin: de Gruyter. pp. 198–212.

Marceau, J. (1990): 'Neither fish nor fowl: theorising emerging organisational forms in a small open industrial economy (Australia).' Paper presented to the World Congress of the International Sociological Association, Madrid, July. Published as CIRCIT Working Paper 90/2, Melbourne.

Marceau, J. (1991): Technological change and industrial location: the automative industry in Australia'. in J. Stewart and ASTEC. *Science, Technology and Australian Federalism: Getting the Best from the System. Canberra: AGPS. pp. 97–120.*

Marcuse, H. (1964): One Dimensional Man. London: Routlege and Kegan Paul.

Marris, R. (1964): *The Economic Theory of 'Managerial' Capitalism*. Chicago: Free Press of Glencoe.

Mason, E. (1960): *The Corporation in Modern Society*. Cambridge: Harvard University Press.

Mason, E., M. Kim, D. Perkins, K. Kim and D. Cole (1980): *The Economic and Social Modernization of the Republic of Korea*. Cambridge, Mass.: Council of East Asian Studies, Harvard University.

Mathews, J. (1989a): *The Age of Democracy. The Politics of Post-Fordism*. Melbourne: Oxford University Press.

Mathews, J. (1989b): *The Tools of Change: New Technology and the Democratisation of Work*. Sydney: Pluto Press.

Mathews, J. (1989c): *Towards an 'Australian Model' of Wages-linked Regulated Structural Adjustment*. Stockholm: Swedish Centre for Working Life.

Mathews, J. (1989d): 'New production concepts', *Prometheus* 7 (1): 129–148.

Mathews, J. (1990): 'Towards a New Model of Industry Development in Australia', Working Paper no. 78. Syndey: School of Industrial Relations and Organizational Behaviour, University of New South Wales.

Mathews, J. and L. Weiss (1991): 'A Tale of Two Industries: Textiles in Italy and Australia', Working Paper no. 86. Sydney: School of Industrial Relations and Organisational Behaviour, University of New South Wales.

Maurice, M., A. Sorge and M. Warner (1980): 'Societal differences in organizing manufacturing units: a comparison of France, West Germany, and Great Britain', *Organization Studies* 1 (1): 59–86..

Mayo, E. (1966): *The Social Problems of an Industrial Civilization*. London: Routledge and Kegan Paul.

McCormack, G. (1986): 'Crime, confession and control', in G. McCormack and Y. Sugimoto (eds.) *Democracy in Contemporary Japan*. Sydney: Hale and Iremonger. pp. 186–194.

McDonald, T. and M. Rimmer (1989): 'Award Restructuring and Wages Policy', in J. Nevile (ed.) *Wage Determination in Australia*. pp. 111–134.

McMillan, C. (1984): *The Japanese Industrial System*. Berlin: de Gruyter.

McNeill, W. (1983): *The Pursuit of Power*. Oxford: Blackwell.

Meidner, R. (1978): *Collective Capital Formation through Wage-Earner Funds*. London: Allen and Unwin.

Melman, S. (1983): *Profits without Production*. New York: Knopf.

Meulders, D. amd L. Wilkin (1987): 'Labour market flexibility: critical introduction to the analysis of a concept', *Labour and Society* 12 (1): 2–17.

Meyer, J. and B. Rowan (1983): The structure of educational organisations', in J. Meyer and W. Scott (eds.) *Organisational Environments: Ritual and Rationality*. Beverly Hills, CA: Sage. pp. 71–97.

Miller, P. and N. Rose (1988): 'The Tavistock Programme: the government of subjectivity and social life', *Sociology* 22 (2): 171–192.

Mills, C. (1940): 'Situated actions and vocabularies of motive', *American Sociological Review* V: 904–913.

Mills, C. (1959): *The Sociological Imagination*. New York: Oxford University Press.

Mitchell, R. (1972): *Level of Emotional Strain in South-East Asian Cities*. Taipei: Orient Culture Service.

Moore, B. (1968): *The Social Origins of Dictatorship and Democracy*. Harmondsworth: Penguin.

Morgan, G. (1986): *Images of Organization*. Beverly Hills: Sage.

Morris, J. (1988): The Changing Industrial Structure of Canada in the 1980s: The Role of Japanese Foreign Direct Investment. Report to the Canadian High Commission. London.

Moser, C. (1930): *The Cotton Textile Industry of Far Eastern Countries*. Boston: Pepperell Manufacturing Company.

Muetzelfeldt, M. (1986): 'Small business and ideological practices', *Arena* 76: 163–171.

Muetzelfeldt, M. (1988): 'The Ideology of Consumption within the Mode of Production'. Paper presented to the Sociological Association of Australia and New Zealand Annual Conference, Canberra.

Myer, B. (1986): 'General Motors' Saturn Plant, a quantum leap in technology and its implications for labour and community organisations', *Capital and Class* 30: 73–96.

Myers, H. (1984): 'The economic transformation of the Republic of China on Taiwan', *The China Quarterly* 99: 500–528.

Nakane, C. (1970): *Japanese Society*. Berkeley: University of California Press.

Napier, N. (1989): 'Mergers and acquisitions, human resource issues and outcomes: a review and suggested typology', *Journal of Management Studies* 26 (3): 271–289.

Nelson, R. and S. Winter (1982): *An Evolutionary Theory of Economic Change*. Harvard, Mass: Belknap Press.

Ng, S. (1982): 'Are Trade Unions obsolete in Hong Kong?', *Industrial Relations Journal* 13 (3): 63–67.

Ng, S. (1987): *Technological Advances and Training – A Case Study of Hong Kong*. Hong Kong: New City Cultural Service Ltd.

Ng, S. and F. Sit (1989): *Labour Relations and Labour Conditions in Hong Kong: A Study Prepared for the International Labour Office*. London Macmillan.

Nishida, J. (1990): 'The Japanese Influence on the Shanghainese Textile Industry and Implications for Hong Kong'. M. Phil Dissertation, University of Hong Kong, Hong Kong.

Nishikawa, H. (1987): *Nihon Teikokushugi To Mengyo*. (Japanese Imperialism and the Cotton Industry). Kyoto: Minerubia Shobo.

Noble, D. (1979): 'Social choice in Machine Design: the Case of Automatically Controlled Machine Tools', in A. Zimbalist (ed.) *Case Studies of the Labour Process*. New York: Monthly Review Press. pp. 18–50.

North, D. (1981): *Structure and Change in Economic History*. New York: Norton.

Nyland, C. (1987): 'Higgins, Scientific Management and the 44-Hour Week', in K. and A. Williams (eds) *Industrial Relations: Research Themes:* Proceedings of the Biennial Conference of the Association of Industrial Relations Academics of Australia and New Zealand, Hince, Melbourne, AIRAANZ. pp. 187–232.

Nyland, C. (1989): *Reduced Worktime and the Management of Production*. Cambridge University Press.

OECD (1986a): *Labour Market Flexibility*. (Report of Committee chaired by R. Dahrendorf). Paris OECD.

OECD (1986b): *Economic Survey, Italy*. (Industrial Committee) Paris: OECD.

OECD (1988): *New Technologies in the 1990s: A Socio-Economic Strategy*. (Report of Committee chaired by U. Sundqvist). Paris: OECD.

OECD (1989): *Biotechnology: Economic and Wider Impacts*. Paris: OECD.

Office of Technology Assessment (OTA) (1988): *New Developments in Biotechnology: 4: US Investment in Biotechnology*. Washington: OTA, US Congress.

Ogbonna, E. and B. Wilkinson (1990): 'Corporate strategy and corporate culture: the view from the check-out', *Personnel Review* 19 (4): 9–15.

Oliver, N. and B. Wilkinson (1988): *The Japanization of British Industry,* Oxford: Blackwell.

Orrú, M., N. Biggart and G. Hamilton (1988): 'Organisational isomorphism in East Asia: broadening the New Institutionalism', in W. Powell and P. Dimaggio (eds.) *The New Institutionalism in Organisational Analysis*. Chicago: University of Chicago Press. pp. 361–389.

Orsenigo, L. (1989): *The Emergence of Biotechnology*. London: Pinter.

Ouchi, W. (1980): 'Markets, bureaucracies and clans,' *Administrative Science Quarterly*. 25: 129–142.

Ouchi, W. (1982): *Theory Z*. Reading, Mass.: Addison-Wesley.

P-A Consulting Services (1988): *Techno-Economic Study of Hong Kong's Metals and Light Engineering Industries*. Paper prepared for Industry Development Board, Hong Kong.

PA (1986): *SEQEB Total Quality Management: Action Book*. Sydney: in-house publication of PA Consulting Group.

Palmer, G. (1987): 'Management, Industrial Relations and Organisation Theory'. *QIT School of Management Working Paper Series*. No. 7.

Palmer, G., K. Donohue and B. Thompson (1988): 'Australian Human Resource Management. The Causes and Effects of Different Policies. A Discussion of Progress on the Initial Queensland Transport Study'. Paper presented to the ANZAME conference, Perth, November 29.

Palmer, G., K. Donohue and B. Thompson (1989): 'Personnel and Employee Relations, Current Trends and Prospects for the 1990's.' Unpublished paper.

Pang, E. (1988): 'The distinctive features of two city states' development: Hong Kong and Singapore', in P. Berger and M. Hsiao (eds). *In Search of an East Asian Development Model.* New Brunswick: Transaction Books. pp. 220–238.

Papanek, G. (1988): 'The new Asian capitalism: an economic portrait', in P. Berger and M. Hsiao (eds) *In Search of an East Asian Development Model.* New Brunswick: Transaction Books. pp. 27–80.

Pappas Carter, Evans & Koop/Telesis (1990): *The Global Challenge: Australian Manufacturing in the 1990s.* Melbourne: Australian Manufacturing Council.

Parnaby, J. (1987): 'Competitiveness via total quality of performance', *Progress in Rubber and Plastics Technology* 3 (1): 42–50.

Pateman, C. (1970): *Participation and Democratic Theory.* Cambridge University Press.

Paterson, J. (1988): 'A managerialist strikes back', *Australian Journal of Public Administration* XL VII (4): 287–295.

Patmore, G. (1988): 'Systematic management and bureaucracy:the NSW Railways prior to 1932', *Labour and Industry* (2): 306–321.

Pearse, A. (1929): *The Cotton Industry of Japan and China.* Manchester: International Federation of Master Cotton Spinners' and Manufacturers' Associations.

Pearse, A. (1955): *Japan's Cotton Industry.* Cyprus: private publication.

Pelzel, J. (1979): 'Factory Life in Japan and China Today', in A. Craig (ed.) *Japan: A Comparative View.* Berkeley: University of California Press. pp. 371–432.

Pempel, T. (1978): 'Japanese foreign policy', in P. Katzenstein (ed.) *Between Power and Plenty.* Madison: University of Wisconsin Press. pp. 139–190.

Penner, R. (1990): *Sourcing Strategies and Spatial Patterns of Production in the Automotive Industry: A Dutch Survey.* Amsterdam: Department of Economics, University of Amsterdam, Research Memorandum No. 9026.

Perez, C. (1983): 'Structural change and the assimilation of new technologies in the economic and social system', *Futures* 15 (4): 357–375.

Perez, C. (1985): 'Microelectronics, long waves and world structural change: new perspectives for developing countries', *World Development* 13 (3): 441–463.

Perrow, C. (1981): 'Markets, hierarchy, and hegemony', in A. Van de Ven and W. Joyce (eds) *Perspectives on Organization Design and Behavior.* New York: Wiley. pp. 371–381.

Peters, T. (1988): *Thriving on Chaos: Handbook for a Management Revolution.* New York: Knopf.

Peters, T. and R. Waterman Jr. (1982): *In Search of Excellence.* New York: Harper & Row.

Pfeffer, J. (1987): 'Bringing the environment back in: the social context of business strategy' in D. Teece (ed.) *The Competitive Challenge.* Cambridge, Mass.: Ballinger. pp. 119–135.

Pinchot III, G. (1985): *Intrapreneuring.* New York: Harper and Row.

Piore, M. and C. Sabel (1983): 'Italian small business development: lessons for
    U. S. industrial policy', in J. Zysman and L. Tyson (eds) *American Industry
    in International Competition*. Ithaca. NY: Cornell University Press. pp. 391 –
    421.
Piore, M. and C. Sabel (1984): *The Second Industrial Divide*. New York: Basic
    Books.
Pisano, G. (1989): 'The Governance of Innovation: Vertical Integration, Joint
    Ventures, and Licensing in the Biotechnology Industry'. Mimeo, March.
    Cambridge, Mass.: Harvard University.
Pisano, G., W. Shan and D. Teece (1988): 'Joint ventures and collaboration in
    the biotechnology industry', in D. Mowery (ed.) *International Collaborative
    Ventures in US Manufacturing*. Cambridge, Mass: Ballinger. pp. 23 – 70.
Polanyi, K. (1944): *The Great Transformation*. Boston: Beacon Press.
Porter, M. (1985): *Competitive Strategy: Techniques for Analysing Industries and
    Competitors*. New York: Free Press.
Porter, M. (1987): 'Changing patterns of international competition', in D. Teece
    (ed.) *The Competitive Challenge*. Cambridge, Mass: Ballinger. pp. 27 – 57.
Porter, M. (1990): *The Competitive Advantage of Nations*. New York: Macmillan
    and The Free Press.
Prais, S. and K. Wagner (1988): 'Productivity and management: the training of
    foremen in Britain and Germany', *National Institute Economic Review* Febru-
    ary (123): 34 – 47.
Prais, S. (1976): *The Evolution of Giant Firms in Britain*. Cambridge: Cambridge
    University Press.
Prestowitz, C. Jr. (1988): *Trading Places: How We Allowed Japan to Take the
    Lead*. New York: Basic Books.
Pucik, V. (1988): 'Strategic alliances, organizational learning, and competitive
    advantage: the HRM agenda', *Human Resource Management* 27 (1): 77 – 93.
Pusey, M. (1991): *Economic Rationalism in Canberra*. Sydney: Cambridge Uni-
    versity Press.
Pye, L. (1988): 'The new Asian capitalism: a political portrait', in P. Berger and
    M. Hsiao (eds) *In Search of an East Asian Development Model*. New Bruns-
    wick: Transaction Books. pp. 81 – 98.
Ragin, C. and D. Zaret (1983): 'Theory and method in comparative research:
    two strategies', *Social Forces* 61: 731 – 754.
Redding, S. (G) (1980): 'Cognition as an aspect of culture and its relationship
    to management process: an exploratory view of the Chinese case', *Journal of
    Management Studies* 17: 127 – 148.
Redding, S. (G) (1986): 'Developing managers without "management develop-
    ment": the overseas Chinese solution', *Management Education and Develop-
    ment* 17 part 3: 271 – 281.
Redding, S. (G) (1988): 'The role of the entrepreneur in the new Asian capital-
    ism' in P. Berger and M. Hsaio (eds) *In Search of an East Asian Development
    Model*. New Brunswick: Transaction Books. pp. 99 – 111.
Redding, S. (G) (1989): 'Managerial Ideology and its Impact on Strategy in the
    Chinese Family Business'. A paper presented to the Conference on Business
    Groups and Economic Development in East Asia. Centre of Asian Studies,
    University of Hong Kong, Hong Kong.

Redding,S. (G) (1990): *The Spirit of Chinese Capitalism*. Berlin: de Gruyter.

Redding, S. (G) and R. Whitley (1990): 'Beyond bureaucracy: towards a comparative analysis of forms of economic resource coordination and control.' in S. Clegg and S. Redding (eds) *Capitalism in Contrasting Cultures*. Berlin: de Gruyter. pp. 79 – 104.

Rimmer, M. and C. Verevis (eds) (1990): 'Award Restructuring: Progress at the Workplace'. Monograph number 28. Industrial Relations Research Centre, UNSW and National Key Centre in Industrial Relations, Monash Univerisity IRRC.

Robertson, I. (1988): Japan's Motor Industry: En Route to 2000, *Economist Intelligence Unit,* Automotive Special Report No. 13, EIU, London.

Robins, K. and F. Webster (1982): 'A Survey of Trade Union Response in Britain', *Industrial Relations Journal* 13 (1).

Roethlisberger, F. and W. Dickson, (1934): *The Management and the Worker.* Cambridge, Mass: Harvard Business School.

Rose, M. (1985): *Industrial Behaviour.* Harmondsworth: Penguin.

Rosenberg, N. (1976): *Perspectives on Technology.* Cambridge: Cambridge University Press.

Roszak, T. (1986): *The Cult of Information.* Cambridge: Lutterworth.

Rothstein, B. (1989): 'Argument för en civil socialism', in *Omdaningen.* Kalmar: Sveriges Socialdemokratiska Ungdomsforbund. pp. 147 – 159.

Rothwell, R. and M. Beesley (1988): 'Patterns of external linkages of innovative small and medium-sized firms in the United Kingdom', *Piccola Impresa/ Small Business* 2: 15 – 32.

Roy, D. (1958): "Banana time': job satisfaction and informal interaction', *Human Organization* 18: 158 – 168.

Roy, G. (1987): 'Functional and historical logics in explaining the rise of the American industrial corporation'. Paper presented to the meetings of the American Sociological Association, August, Chicago.

Sabel, C. (1989): 'Flexible specialization and the re-emergence of regional economies', in P. Hirst and J. Zeitlin (eds) *Reversing Industrial Decline? Industrial Structure and Policy in Britain and her Competitors.* Berg: Oxford. pp. 17 – 70.

Sabel, C. and J. Zeitlin (1985): 'Historical alternatives to mass production: politics, markets and technology in nineteenth-century industrialization', *Past and Present* 108 (August): 133 – 176.

Sabel, C., H. Kern and G. Herrigel (1989): 'Collaborative Manufacturing: New Supplier Relations in the Automobile Industry and the Redefinition of the Industrial Corporation'. Paper presented to the International Motor Vehicle Program Conference in Acapulco, May.

Sandberg, T. (1982): *Work Organization and Autonomous Groups.* Lund: Liber.

Sandkull, B. (1980): 'Practice of industry – mismanagement of people', *Human Systems Management* 1: 159 – 167.

Sandkull, B. (1984): 'Managing the democratization process in work cooperatives', *Economic and Industrial Democracy* 4: 359 – 389.

Sandkull, B., W. Fricke and K. Thurley (forthcoming): 'The effect of technical change', in Keith Thurley (ed.) *The End of Class Struggle? A Question of Identity.* Oxford: Oxford University Press.

Sandland, R. (1989). 'Variation and Statistical Thinking in Quality Management: Opportunities and Pitfalls', in *Quality: The Key to Global Competitiveness*. Proceedings of the First National Conference of the Total Quality Management Institute, Sydney, August 10th and 11th, pp. 77–90.

Sauer, W. (1984): 'Small firms and the German economic miracle', in C. Levicki (ed.) *Small Business Theory and Policy*. London: Croom Helm. pp. 78–88.

Sayer, A. (1986): 'New developments in manufacturing: the Just-In-Time systems', *Capital and Class* 30: 43–72.

Schiattarella, R. (1984): *Mercato del lavoro e struttura produttiva*. Milan: F. Angeli.

Schonberger, R. (1982): *Japanese Manufacturing Techniques*. New York: Free Press.

Schumpeter, J. (1939): *Business Cycles*. London and New York: McGraw Hill.

Scott, W. (1987): 'The adolescence of institutional theory', *Administrative Science Quarterly* 32: 493–511.

Selby-Smith, C. (1989): 'Restructuring office work in the Australian public service', in D. Corbett, C. Selby-Smith and R. Smith (eds) *Public Sector Personnel Policies for the 1990's*. Melbourne: Public Sector Management Institute, Monash University.

Selznick, P. (1957): *Leadership in Administration*. New York: Harper and Row.

Senker, P. and T. Brady (1989): 'Corporate strategy: skills, education and training' in M. Dodgson (ed.) *Technology Strategy and the Firm*. Harlow: Longman. pp. 155–169.

Sevior, J. (1989): 'Ansett's Budget ties end with the sack', *The Age*. 6. 12. 1989: 21 & 23.

Shaiken, H. (1985): *Work Transformed: Automation and Labor in the Computer Age*. New York: Holt, Rinehard and Winston:

Shanghai Academy of Social Sciences, Institute of Economic Research (ed.) (1980): *Rongjia Qiye Shiliao* (Source Material on the Rong Family Enterprises.) Shanghai: Peoples' Press.

Sharp, M. (1985): *The New Biotechnology*. European Sussex Papers No. 15, University of Sussex.

Shimokawa, K. (1985): 'Japan's *Keiretsu* system: the case of the automobile industry', *Japanese Economic Studies* Summer: 3–31.

Siemens AG (1988): *CNMA Conformance Testing,* Phase 3 of the ESPRIT project 955. Brussels.

Silin, H. (1976): *Leadership and Values: The Organization of Large-scale Taiwanese Enterprises*. Cambridge, Mass: East Asian Research Center, Harvard University.

Silvia, F., P. Ferri and A. Enrietti (1987): 'Robots, employment and industrial relations in the Italian automobile industry', in S. Watanabe (ed.) *Microelectronics, Automation and Employment in the Automobile Industry*. Chichester: Wiley. pp. 131–153.

Simon, H. (1962): 'The architecture of complexity'. *Proceedings of the American Philosophical Society* 106: 467.

Sit, F., V. and S. Wong (1989): *Small and Medium Industries in an Export-Oriented Economy: The Case of Hong Kong*. Hong Kong: Centre of Asian Studies, University of Hong Kong.

Skocpol, T. (1985): 'Bringing the state back in: strategies of analysis in current research', in P. Evans, D. Rueschemeyer, and T. Skocpol (eds) *Bringing the State Back In*. Cambridge and New York: Cambridge University Press. pp. 3–37.

Slaughter, J. (1987): 'The Team Concept in the US Auto Industry'. Paper presented to the Conference on the Japanization of British Industry, Cardiff Business School, UK, 17–18 September.

Smircich, L. (1983): 'Concepts of culture and organisational analysis', *Administrative Science Quarterly* 28: 339–358.

Snow, C. and R. Miles (1983): The role of strategy in the development of a general theory of organizations', in R. Lamb (ed.) *Advances in Strategic Management*. New York: JAI Press.

Solinas, G. (1982): 'Labour market segmentation and workers' careers: the case of the Italian knitwear industry', *Cambridge Journal of Economics* 6 (4): 331–352.

Spong, G. (1989): 'Information systems role in managing for improvement and control', in *Quality: The Key to Global Competitiveness*. Proceedings of the First National Conference of the Total Quality Management Institute, Sydney, 10 and 11 August. Sydney: TQML. pp. 77–90.

Sprouster, J. (1987): *TQC Total Quality Control: The Australian Experience*. Maryborough, Vic: Horwitz Grahame.

SRI International and Hong Kong Productivity Council for Industry Development Board (1986): *Hong Kong's Plastics Conversion Industry: Status, Opportunities, and Recommendations for its Future Development*. March. Hong Kong: SRI.

Steedman, H. and K. Wagner (1987): 'A second look at productivity, machinery and skills in Britain and Germany', *National Institute Economic Review* November (122): 84–95.

Steven, R. (1988): 'The high yen crisis in Japan'. *Capital and Class* 34: 76–118.

Stewart, A. (1989): *Team Entrepreneurship*. Newbry Park: Sage.

Stigler, G. (1968): *The Organization of Industry,* Chicago: Chicago University Press.

Stinchcombe, A. (1965): 'Social Structure and Organizations', in J. March (ed.) *Handbook of Organizations*. Chicago: Rand McNally. pp. 142–193.

Sugimoto, Y. (1986): 'The Manipulative Basis of "Consensus" in Japan', in G. McCormack and Y. Sugimoto (eds) *Democracy in Contemporary Japan*. Sydney: Hale and Iremonger. pp. 65–75.

Taguchi, G., E. Elsayeda and T. Hsiang (1988): *Quality Engineering in Production Systems*. New York: McGraw Hill.

Takamura, N. (1982): *Kindai Nihon Mengyo to Chugoku* (The Modern Japanese Cotton Industry in China). Tokyo: University of Tokyo Press.

Tam, S. (1990): 'Centrifugal versus centripetal processes: contrasting ideal types for conceptualising the development patterns of Chinese and Japanese Firms', in S. Clegg and S. Redding (eds) *Capitalism in Contrasting Cultures*. Berlin: de Gruyter. pp. 153–183.

Tannenbaum, A., B. Kavcic, M. Rosner, M. Vianello and G. Weiser (1974): *Hierarchy in Organisations*. San Francisco: Jossey-Bass.

Taylor, F. (1911): *The Principles of Scientific Management*. New York: Harper.

Taylor, J. (1983): *Shadows of the Rising Sun*. New York: William Morrow.

Teece, D. (1984): 'Economic analysis and strategic management', *California Management Review* 26: 91−92.

Teece, D. (1987): 'Profiting from technological innovation: implications for integration, colloboration, licensing and public policy', *Research Policy* 15: 285−305.

The China Year Book 1931/32.

The Hong Kong University of Science and Technology Newsletter. Oct., 1989.

The MIT Commission on Productivity (Michael Destouroz, Richard Lester and Robert Solow) (1989): *Made in America, Regaining the Productive Edge*. Cambridge: MIT Press.

Therborn, G. (1977): 'The rule of capital and the rise of democracy', *New Left Review* 103: 3−41.

Tilton, T. (1984): 'Utopia, incrementalism and Ernst Wigforss 'conception of a provisional Utopia', *Scandinavian Studies* 56: 36−54.

Ting, W. (1986): 'International product life cycle myths and high technology developments in newly industrializing Asia', in S. Clegg, D. Dunphy and S. Redding (eds.) *The Enterprise and Management in East Asia*. Hong Kong: Centre of Asian Studies, The University of Hong Kong. pp. 229−246.

Ting-Chaun, T. and S. Ng (1983): 'Labour mobility: a study of garment-making and electronics workers' in S. Ng, and D. Levin (eds) *Contemporary Issues in Hong Kong Labour Relations*. Hong Kong: Centre of Asian Studies, University of Hong Kong. pp. 177−206.

Tomita, T. (1985): 'Japanese management in Kong Kong', *Southeast Asian Studies* 22 (4): 391−405.

Toyo Boseki Company Ltd. (1986): *Toyobo Hyakunen Shi (Jo)* (The Hundred Year History of Toyobo: Vol. 1). Osaka: Toyo Boseki Company Ltd.

Trade and Industry Committee (1987): *The UK Motor Components Industry*. London: HMSO:

Trevor, M. and I. Christie (1988): *Manufacturers and Suppliers in Britain and Japan*. London: Policy Studies Institute.

Trigilia, C. (1986): 'Small firm development and political subcultures in Italy', *European Sociological Review* 2 (3): 161−175.

Tulder, R. van (ed.) (1990): *Small Industrial Countries and Economic and Technological Development*. Amsterdam: University of Amsterdam, SICRA and NOTA.

Tulder, R. van and G. Junne (1988): *European Multinationals in Core Technologies*. Chichester/London: John Wiley.

Turnbull, P. (1986): 'The "Japanization" of production and industrial relations at Lucas Electrical', *Industrial Relations Journal* 17 (3): 193−206.

Turnbull, P. (1989): 'Buyer-Supplier Relations in the UK Automotive Industry'. Paper presented to the Employment Research Unit Annual Conference, Cardiff Business School, UK, 19−20 September.

Turner, A. (1980): *The Last Colony: But Whose? A Study of the Labour Movement. Labour Market and Labour Relations in Hong Kong*. Cambridge: Cambridge University Press.

Turner, B. (1971): *Exploring the Industrial Sub-Culture*. London: Macmillan.

Tversky, A. and D. Kahneman (1974): 'Judgement under uncertainty, heuristics and biases', *Science* 185: 1124—1131.

Useem, M. (1979): 'The social organization of the American business elites and participation of corporate directors in the government of American institutions', *American Sociological Review* 44: 553—572.

Utley, F. (1938): *Japan's Gamble in China*. London: Secker and Warburg.

Vanek, J. (1977): *Through Participation and Dialogue to a World of Justice*. Ithaca: Cornell University, NY (unpublished manuscript).

Vepa, R. (1971): *Small Industry in the Seventies*. London: Vikas Publications.

Vogel, E. (1979): *Japan as Number One*. Cambridge, Mass.: Harvard University Press.

Wang, T. and C. Wang (1935): *Ch'i-sheng hua-shang shach'ang tiao-ch'a pao-kao* (Report of the survey on Chinese cotton mills in seven provinces) Shanghai: Commercial Press.

Ward, B. (1972): 'A small factory in Hong Kong: some aspects of its internal organisation', in W. Willmott (ed.) *Economic Organisation in Chinese Society*. Stanford: Stanford University Press.

Warner, T. (1989): 'Information technology as a competitive burden'. In T. Forester (ed.) *Computers in the Human Context: Information Technology, Productivity and People*. Oxford: Blackwell. pp. 272—280.

Watanabe, S. (1987a): 'Flexible automation and labour productivity in the Japanese automobile industry', in S. Watanabe (ed.) *Microelectronics, Automation and Employment in the Automobile Industry*. Chichester: Wiley. pp. 41—77.

Watanabe, S. (1987b): 'Microelectronics and rationalisation of the French automobile industry' in S. Watanabe (ed.) *Microelectronics, Automation and Employment in the Automobile Industry*. Chichester: Wiley. pp. 107—129.

Watkins, P. (1988): 'Regional Boards of Education: mediating links between social investment and social consumption', *British Journal of Sociology of Education* 9 (4): 453—472.

Watkins, P., F. Rizvi and L. Angus (1987): 'The formation of regional boards and the devolution of Victorian state education', *The Australian Journal of Education* 31: 252—271.

Weber, F. and K. Robins (1982): 'New technology: a survey of trade union response in Britain', *Industrial Relations Journal* 13 (1): 7—26.

Weber, M. (1976): *The Protestant Ethic and the Spirit of Capitalism*. London: Allen and Unwin.

Weber, M. (1978): *Economy and Society: An Outline of Interpretive Sociology* (2 Vols), G. Roth and C. Wittich (eds) Berkeley: University of California Press.

Webster, F. and K. Robins (1986): *Information Technology: A Luddite Aanalysis*. Norwood: Ablex.

Weiss, L. (1984): 'The Italian State and small business', *European Journal of Sociology* 25 (2): 214—241.

Weiss, L. (1988): *Creating Capitalism: The State and Small Business since 1945*. Oxford: Blackwell.

Weiss, L. (1989): 'Regional economic policy in Italy', *Political Quarterly* 60 (2): 167 – 186.

Westney, D. (1987): *Initiation and Innovation: The Transfer of Western Organizational Patterns to Meiji Japan.* Cambridge, Mass.: Harvard University Press.

Westphal, L., Y. Rhee, L. Kim and A. Amsden (1984): 'Republic of Korea', *World Development* 12: 505 – 533.

White, H. (1981): 'Where Do Markets Come From?', *American Journal of Sociology* 87: 517 – 547.

Whitley, R. (1989a): 'Enterprise Structures in their Societal Contexts: The Comparative Analysis of Forms of Business Organisation'. Working Paper no. 175. Manchester: Manchester Business School.

Whitley, R. (1989b): 'The Social Structuring of East Asian Business Recipes: Towards a Comparative Analysis of Dominant Enterprise Structures'. Working Paper no. 179. Manchester: Manchester Business School.

Whitley, R. (1990): 'East Asian enterprise structures and the comparative analysis of forms of business organisation', *Organization Studies* 11 (1): 47 – 74.

Whyte, W. Jr. (1956): *The Organization Man.* New York: Simon and Schuster.

Wickens, P. (1987): *The Road to Nissan.* London: MacMillan.

Wigforss, E. (1980): 'Om provisoriska utopier' in *Skrifter i urval* 1: 274 – 313.

Wilkinson, B. (1983): *The Shopfloor Politics of New Technology.* London: Heinemann Educational Books.

Wilkinson, B. (1986): 'Emergence of an industrial community? The human relations movement in Singapore', in S. Clegg, D. Dunphy and S. Redding (eds) *The Enterprise and Management in East Asia.* Hong Kong: Centre of Asian Studies, The University of Hong Kong: pp. 111 – 128.

Wilkinson, B. and N. Oliver (1989): 'Power, control and the Kanban', *Journal of Management Studies* 26 (1): 47 – 58.

Wilkinson, B. and N. Oliver (1990): 'Obstacles to "Japanization": the case of Ford UK', *Employee Relations,* forthcoming.

Williamson, O. (1963): 'A model of rational managerial behavior', in R. Cyert and J. March (eds.) *A Behavioural Theory of the Firm.* Englewood Cliffs, N. J.: Prentice Hall. pp. 237 – 252.

Williamson, O. (1975): *Markets and Hierarchies: Analysis and Antitrust Implications.* New York: Fress Press.

Willis, P. (1977): *Learning to Labour: How Working Class Kids Get Working Class Jobs.* London: Heinemann Educational Books.

Wilson, D. (1988): *The Governor's Address at the Opening of the 1988/89 Session of the Legislative Council on 12 October 1988,* Hong Kong: Government Printer.

Wilson, D. (1989): The Governor's Address at the Operning of the 1989/1990 Session of the Legislative Council on 11 October 1989, Hong Kong. Hong Kong: Government Printer.

Wobbe, W. (1987): *Flexible Manufacturing in Europe: State of Art Approaches and Diffusion Patterns.* FAST Occasional Papers, no. 155, Brussels.

Wolf, M. (1983): *The Japanese Conspiracy.* New York: Empire Books.

Wolferen, K. van (1989): *The Enigma of Japanese Power.* New York: Knopf.

Wong, S. (1985): 'The Chinese Family Firm', *British Journal of Sociology* 36 (1): 58–72.

Wong, S. (1988a): *Emigrant Entrepreneurs: Shanghai Industrialists in Hong Kong*. Hong Kong: Oxford University Press.

Wong, S. (1988b): 'The applicability of Asian family values to other sociocultural settings' in P. Berger and H. Hsiao (eds.) *In Search of an East Asian Development Model*. New Brunswick, NJ: Transaction Books. pp. 134–152.

Wright, C. (1989): 'The Management Consultant and the Introduction of Scientific Management in Australian Industry'. Paper presented to *AIRAANZ* Conference, University of Wollongong, 1–4 February, 1989.

Woodhead, H. (ed.): *China Year Book 1931/2*. Shanghai: North China Daily Nens and Herald.

Wrong, D. (1961): 'The Oversocialized Conception of Man in Modern Sociology', *American Sociological Review* 26: 183–193.

Wurthnow, R., J. Hunter, A. Bergesen and E. Kurzweil (1984): *Cultural Analysis*. Boston: Routledge and Kegan Paul.

Yang, T. (1977): 'Entrepreneurship and social order in Southeast Asian countries', in K. Nakagawa (ed.) *Social Order and Entrepreneurship*. Proceedings of the Second Fuji Conference. Tokyo: University of Tokyo Press. pp. 293–318.

Yeatman, A. (1990): *Bureaucrats, Technocrats, Femocrats*. Sydney: Allen and Unwin.

Zelizer, V. (1985): *Pricing the Priceless Child: The Changing Social Value of Children*. New York: Basic Books.

Zelizer, V. (1988): 'Beyond the Polemics on the Market: Establishing a Theoretical and Empirical Agenda', *Sociological Forum* 3: 614–634.

Zo, K. (1970): 'Developments and behavioural patterns of Korean entrepreneurs', *Korea Journal* 10: 9–14.

Zucker, L. (1987): 'Introduction' to L. Zucker (ed.) *Institutional Patterns and Organisations: Culture and Environment*. Cambridge, Mass.: Ballinger. pp. xiii-xix.

Index

Walter de Gruyter
Berlin · New York

de Gruyter Studies in Organization
(International Management, Organization and Policy Analysis)

Editor: Stewart R. Clegg

An international and interdisciplinary book series from de Gruyter presenting comprehensive research on aspects of international management, organization studies and comparative public policy.

Bill Ryan
Making Capital from Culture
The Corporate Form of Capitalist Cultural Production

1992. 15.5 x 23.0 cm. XII, 290 pages with 11 figures. Cloth. ISBN 3-11-012548-X
(Volume 35)

György Széll (Editor)
Concise Encyclopaedia of Participation and Co-Management

1992. 17 x 24 cm. XIV, 1047 pages. Cloth. ISBN 3-11-012173-5
(Volume 38)

Toyohiro Kono
Long-Range Planning of Japanese Corporations

1992. 15.5 x 23.0 cm. XIV, 390 pages. Paper. ISBN 3-11-013793-3, Cloth. ISBN 3-11-012914-0.
(Volume 37)

Walter de Gruyter
Berlin · New York

de Gruyter Studies in Organization
(International Management, Organization and Policy Analysis)

Finn Borum/Andrew Lloyd Friedmann/Mette Mønsted/Jesper Strandgaard Pedersen/ Marianne Risberg
Social Dynamics of the IT Field
The Case of Denmark
1992. 15.5 x 23.0 cm. XVI, 328 pages. With 28 figures and 19 tables. Cloth.   ISBN 3-11-012981-7.
(Volume 39)

Peter Blunt/Merrick L. Jones
Managing Organizations in Africa
1992. 15.5 x 23.0 cm. XIV, 356 pages. With 18 figures and 26 tables. Cloth.   ISBN 3-11-012646-X.
(Volume 40)

Sukhan Jackson
Chinese Enterprise Management
Reforms in Economic Perspective
1992. 15.5 x 23.0 cm. XVIII, 324 pages. With 46 tables and 6 figures. Cloth.   ISBN 3-11-013480-2.
(Volume 41)

Walter de Gruyter & Co. Berlin · New York
Genthiner Strasse 13, D-1000 Berlin 30 (FRG), Tel.: (30) 2 60 05-0
Fax: (30) 2 60 05-2 51
200 Saw Mill River Road, Hawthorne, N.Y. 10532, Tel.: (914) 7 47-01 10
Fax: (914) 7 47-13 26